MARCO POLO'S ASIA

the book first presented as "l'asia di marco polo," translated from the italian by john a. scott, m. a. (oxon.) and revised by the author ~ ~ ~ ~ ~ ~ the university of california press berkeley and los angeles   1960

marco polo's asia

an introduction to his
"description of the world"
called "il milione"

by leonardo olschki

UNIVERSITY OF CALIFORNIA PRESS · BERKELEY AND
LOS ANGELES, CALIFORNIA · CAMBRIDGE UNIVERSITY
PRESS, LONDON, ENGLAND · © 1960 BY THE REGENTS
OF THE UNIVERSITY OF CALIFORNIA · LIBRARY OF
CONGRESS CATALOG CARD NO. 60-8316 · PRINTED IN THE
UNITED STATES OF AMERICA · DESIGNED BY WARD RITCHIE

PREFATORY NOTE

The present work is the outcome both of the author's monographic studies listed at the end of this volume and of two series of lectures given at the Fondazione Giorgio Cini in Venice by invitation of the municipality, and in Rome at the Istituto Italiano per il Medio ed Estremo Oriente, from September to December, 1954, on the occasion of the seventh centenary of Marco Polo's birth. The Italian edition was published by G. C. Sansoni, Florence, 1957, under the auspices of both these institutions. I wish to thank the Bollingen Foundation of New York for its generous subvention of the present translation. My appreciation goes to Mr. John A. Scott, M.A. (Oxon.), Assistant Professor in the Department of Italian of the University of California, Berkeley, for having faithfully rendered the Italian text. I want also to express my gratitude to Mr. Harold A. Small of the University of California Press for his painstaking editing and his countless suggestions for the formal and substantial improvement of the book.

L.O.

CONTENTS

ILLUSTRATIONS

one

INTRODUCTION

I. MARCO POLO'S TEXT AND ITS EDITIONS

The aim and character of the present work are already defined by its title. It does not pretend to offer something new on every page, but proposes more modestly to contribute toward a closer and withal an ampler understanding of Marco Polo's book and its author by outlining certain essential aspects of his surroundings and by coördinating the facts and problems presented by his famous "Description of the World." [1]

Our volume represents the first attempt to group in systematic order the huge mass of heterogeneous data and clues contained in Marco's account and in the vast monographic and exegetic literature related to it; in this respect, *Marco Polo's Asia* differs from all other works that so far have been concerned with exegesis of the text. The following chapters, with their bibliographical and explanatory notes, are intended to make possible a better comprehension and evaluation of the whole. And it is hoped that they will help to evoke medieval Asia as Marco saw and described it and as it appears, both in its typical actualities and its arcane aspects, to the modern student of its civilization.

This, as it were, stereoscopic view of Marco Polo's Asia should

---

[1] This is the authentic title of Marco's book, which is called by the Italians *Il Milione*. The latter is the form we shall generally use in the present volume. On this form and its meaning see A. C. Moule and Paul Pelliot, *Marco Polo: The Description of the World,* London, 1938 (hereafter cited as M.P.), Vol. I, pp. 31 ff. This excellent edition, equipped with an introduction, notes, and appendix, is especially useful to anyone who wishes to take into account at each step the various readings of Marco's text in English, including those not considered in the critical edition by Benedetto (see the following note). A reprint, with a third volume of notes and a fourth volume of indexes, is announced for 1960.

make its various features stand out more clearly, and give added relief to the historical figure of the famous Venetian by revealing the extent and limits of his experiences, his attitude toward the manifestations of the civilization of his times, and the universal value of his book, the first text of an Italian author written in the vernacular to pass, in various languages, beyond the confines of its native land. The "Description," known in Italy as *Il Milione,* told bewildered rather than incredulous contemporaries about the immensely varied life of man and nature in those vast Eastern regions of which he offered the first empirical description to a West long desirous of knowing its secrets and wonders.

If both the contents of Marco's book and the contributions to Polo scholarship be subjected to a sweeping yet attentive scrutiny, various pointers can be made out that suggest ways toward a systematic ordering and comprehensive appraisal. Our first avenue of approach—the least obtrusive, but so much the more valuable and commendable—is to be found in the attempts undertaken over the centuries to reconstruct Marco Polo's authentic text, which has been handed down in manuscripts renowned for their incongruity. These attempts culminated in 1928 in the first complete critical edition, published by Luigi Foscolo Benedetto in a monumental volume that sets forth the history of the research and discusses its criteria and results.[2] Ten years later there appeared the variorum edition by Moule and Pelliot of Polo's text in English translation, containing all the principal versions, with the addition of the first unabridged critical reprint of the valuable manuscript (Z) of the Chapter Library of Toledo,[3] a version known to Benedetto only in the faithful XVIIIth-century transcription found in the Ambrosian Library at Milan.[4]

Although the philological and exegetical problems presented by the various versions of the text are still far from being wholly or definitely resolved, these two editions—the Benedetto and the Moule-Pelliot—nevertheless give us a sure footing for our ex-

[2] Marco Polo, *Il Milione,* prima edizione integrale, a cura di Luigi Foscolo Benedetto, Florence, 1928 (Comitato Geografico Nazionale Italiano, Pubbl. no. 3). This work is hereafter cited as *Il Milione,* cr. ed.

[3] Cf. Vol. II of the edition by Moule and Pelliot mentioned above.

[4] Cf. the Introd. to the cr. ed., pp. clxiii ff.

ploration of its secrets and commentary upon its contents, which at times are no less obscure than the words used to convey them to the reader. No other edition of the *Milione* can at present be accepted as equaling or substituting for these sound, honest publications; least of all, those brought out with a fanfare of publicity, but without sufficient care, on the occasion of the recently celebrated seventh centenary of Marco Polo's birth.[5] The student can safely ignore these commemorative or commercial presentations, which represent neither a contribution to clarification of the text nor its conscientious restoration. Moreover, even if the proposed publication of a new critical edition, which has been entrusted to Professor Benedetto himself by UNESCO,[6] is found to be an improvement on that of 1928, the discriminating reader may still feel that with the editions named above he is close to our author and has trustworthy guides in his venture at following Marco's travels and reviewing his judgments.

Since, then, these exhaustive editions have at last supplied a sound textual basis for a revision of Polo studies, it follows that all the commentaries to the *Milione* hitherto available are either obsolescent or deficient. Without taking into account the most recent, which were compiled for the indulgent mass of a large public, only three of them cast light upon the text by making use of scientific criteria and direct reference to the Western and Oriental sources, which are exceedingly varied in origin and substance. In this sense, the French sinologist M. G. Pauthier[7] was a true pioneer, after Count Baldelli-Boni and the Englishman William Marsden. Pauthier's work is all the more praiseworthy since at the time of its publication in 1865 the scholarly discipline

---

[5] *Il Libro di Marco Polo detto Milione,* with a preface by Sergio Solmi, twenty-five illustrations in color, etc., Turin, 1954. Also *Il Milione,* ed. R. Allulli, in the "Classici Mondadori" series, 1954 (designated as the "first complete edition, rigorously based on the original text," which, by the way, is not extant). The Venetian committee for the celebration of the seventh centenary of Marco Polo's birth has reprinted the version of the *Milione* published by G. B. Ramusio in the *Secondo Volume delle Navigationi & Viaggi,* Venice, 1559. For other editions cf. R. Almagià, "A proposito di recenti studi su Marco Polo e i suoi viaggi," *Rivista Geografica Italiana,* Vol. LXII, 1955, pp. 81–100, and, by the same author, "Marco Polo," in the commemorative volume of the Istituto Veneto di Scienze, Lettere ed Arti, *Nel VII centenario della nascita di Marco Polo,* Venice, 1955, pp. 9 f., and especially the notes on pp. 37 ff.

[6] Cf. the anouncement of this new critical edition in *L'Italia che scrive,* Vol. XXXVII, No. 10, October, 1954, pp. 112 ff.

[7] *Le Livre de Marco Polo, citoyen de Venise,* 2 vols., Paris, 1865.

we have just mentioned was only beginning to develop and a large part of central and eastern Asia had barely been explored. Ten years later, Colonel Henry Yule followed with his famous commentary,[8] a monument of XIXth-century erudition that is still fundamental for every kind of critical and exegetical study of the *Milione*.

Although Yule's third and last edition, of 1903, was supplemented in 1920 by Henri Cordier's volume of *Addenda* and the notes of this French orientalist and bibliographer, nevertheless the British scholar's classic commentary could not take into account the wonderful efflorescence of Oriental studies that has burst forth in our own times, when numerous expeditions, far-reaching research, and numberless archaeological finds have much reduced the mystery that had obscured the geography and history of the Asiatic continent from time immemorial. After the successful expeditions of Sir Aurel Stein, the undertakings of Sven Hedin, the geo-topographical studies of Owen Lattimore, and the findings of numerous explorers in even the most remote parts of the continent; after the fresh impulse given to Polo studies by the masterly contributions of Paul Pelliot, by the untiring work of the Rev. A. C. Moule, and, indirectly, by the greatest orientalists of every country in the past fifty years, Colonel Yule's commentary cannot continue to satisfy our curiosity as historians and scholars or to offer a basis adequate for the task of further coördinating and developing these studies and ideas. Nor can A. J. H. Charignon's edition, in which the editor follows the limited though authentic text previously chosen by Pauthier, annotating it with notes that are in large measure inspired by preceding commentaries and adding material not always taken with sufficient critical sense from Chinese sources of dubious worth.[9]

---

[8] *The Book of Ser Marco Polo the Venetian concerning the Kingdoms and Marvels of the East*, 2 vols., first edition, London, John Murray, 1871; second edition, 1875; latest edition, with additions by H. Cordier, 1903 (hereafter cited as Yule-Cordier), reprinted 1921, with a volume of *Notes and Addenda* by H. Cordier, 1920.

[9] *Le Livre de Marco Polo, citoyen de Venise*, traduit en français moderne et annoté d'après les sources chinoises, 3 vols., Peking, 1924–1928. The reader is referred to the review by P. Pelliot in *T'oung Pao*, Vol. XXV, 1928, pp. 156 ff. The "notes explicatives" added by L. Hambis to his edition of *Marco Polo: La Description du Monde*, première édition en français moderne, Paris, 1955, are especially useful for

The present systematic study of the *Milione* proposes, among
other things, to compile a new and up-to-date commentary by
coördinating the most recent findings concerning the various
subjects treated by Marco, and to suggest such new avenues of
approach as his book may yet inspire. It is also our purpose,
throughout, to encourage a resumption of Oriental studies in the
vast field offered by the medieval Asia explored by the Venetian.

In evoking his world and illustrating his experiences we shall
for the most part draw our material from the versions of his
text which preserve a character of indisputable authenticity and
which, although elaborated by Rustichello of Pisa or altered here
and there by other medieval editors or copyists, correspond in
the main to the author's intentions. He seems to have returned
to the text on a number of occasions, adding and correcting—
probably with the help, or according to the interests, of others
—whatever he could or would reveal of the secrets of the Asia of
his times.[10] For the complex history of these various versions we
refer our readers to Benedetto's masterly Introduction to his critical edition of the *Milione*. We can accept the following texts as
of equal authenticity: the Franco-Italian text, MS Fr. 1116 of the
Bibliothèque Nationale of Paris; a large part of the Ramusian
version, compiled from various sources about the middle of the
XVI century; the adaptation into literary French carried out at
Venice in 1307 for Thibault de Chépoy, a knight in the service
of Philip the Fair and then of his brother Charles de Valois;
and the text of the manuscript in the Chapter Library at Toledo,
written in Italy in the XVth century, formerly in the possession
of Cardinal Francisco Saverio de Zelada, which was wholly trans-

---

the toponymy of the Far East and brief historical information about medieval Mongolia. Cf. also the review by Mario Roques in *Romania*, Vol. LXXVI, 1955, pp. 399 ff.

[10] It still remains an intricate and in many respects an obscure problem, since the
direct collaboration of the author and his scribe Rustichello (or Rusticiano) of Pisa
is, with few exceptions, doubtful or impossible to ascertain (cf. Benedetto, cr. ed.,
Introd., pp. xiii ff.). A biographical essay by Giorgio del Guerra, *Rustichello da Pisa*,
Pisa, 1955, considers mainly the local cultural environment of the professional writer
Rustichello. He may have followed Marco from Genoa to Venice after the comple-
tion of the book, if we can apply to him the mention of a "frate Rustegello" in a
contemporary document of the Venetian State Archives which has been briefly discussed by Count Raimondo Morozzo della Rocca, director of the Archives, in *L'Italia
che scrive*, Vol. XXXVII, 1954, p. 120.

cribed in the XVIIIth century.[11] All these fundamental versions
can be integrated with the various others to be found in the
separate codices and their groups, so far as they contain well-
founded conclusions and information not to be found elsewhere.[12]

The references to Marco's text in this volume are in large part
taken from Benedetto's critical edition; and on several occasions
we have made use of his excellent Italian translation of the
critically reconstructed version of the whole text.[13] We are aware
that, since both of our principal sources have for some time been
out of print, the lack of them must entail inconvenience; aware,
too, that the critical edition itself has always been difficult of
access for the layman interested in Marco and his book;[14] but,
taking into account the inaccuracy or fragmentary form of most
of the current editions of Polo's text, no other choice of reference
is left to the present author, who assumes that the interested
reader can always find the relevant episodes and passages from
the *Milione* by consulting the indexes usually added to the current editions.

Discriminating readers will find less instructive and at times
even misleading the numerous books intended to beckon a larger
public to a reading of the *Milione,* or to be a substitute for the
text by offering brief summaries or extensive paraphrases, with
stress upon the adventurous, exotic, and picturesque elements.
We may mention that works of this type are represented in
France by the elegant account written by the famous geographer
Paul Vidal de Lablache;[15] in Italy, by Giotto Dainelli's sober

[11] For a description of the manuscript and an unabridged transcription of its text
cf. Moule-Pelliot, Vol. II (with a description of the Toledo MS in a note by Moule).

[12] Especially the oldest Tuscan version, published by D. Olivieri in *Il Milione di
Marco Polo,* second edition, Bari, 1928 (in the series "Scrittori d'Italia"), and the
various ramifications of the Venetian version and Latin translation of Fra Francesco
Pipino, O.P., composed while Marco was still living. For all these and other versions
cf. Benedetto's Introd. to the cr. ed., and the preface to Moule-Pelliot, Vol. I, pp. 40 ff.

[13] Marco Polo, *Il Libro di Messer Marco Polo, cittadino di Venezia, detto Milione,*
Milan and Rome, 1932 (with excellent indexes and well-considered critical and
exegetical notes); English translation by Aldo Ricci, *Travels of Marco Polo,* with introduction and index by Sir E. Denison Ross, New York, 1931.

[14] This luxurious edition, now out of print, has always commanded a high price,
and the Franco-Italian text makes difficult reading for the unpracticed reader, to
whom the critical apparatus is of little help.

[15] *Marco Polo,* Paris, 1880.

little volume; [16] in England, by Maurice Collis's book; [17] in the United States, by the summary of H. H. Hart.[18] To these may be added works, various in format, published rather as commercial ventures than as critical contributions, and designed for the undiscriminating or hasty reader and the youth of all ages and countries. These works of popular appeal have nevertheless helped to keep alive the fame of the great Venetian and interest in his book, although they have generally distorted both the man and the content of his work by a more or less arbitrary emphasis on one or another aspect of himself and his experiences; for they suppress episodes or passages that are seemingly dull or difficult to understand, alter the historical picture of the author and his background, ignore technical or erudite details, and avoid any searching discussion of the numerous problems that the *Milione* presents to inquiring minds.

This category of books dealing with Marco Polo has a common characteristic: a tendency toward eulogy, fantasy, and romance. This has been instrumental in creating a conventional type and a historically elusive figure, set against an indeterminate background in which a vague reality is combined with certain clichés and is finally swallowed up in the colorful, traditional picture of an Asia that is romantic, picturesque, and quite fanciful. With its gaps and omissions, its laconic, allusive statements, its apparent exaggerations and exciting narrative, Marco's book lent itself from the very beginning to such alteration and abridgment, designed to please the public taste or serve commercial intentions or the interests of specialized readers; so much so, indeed, that this process began immediately after the first compilation of the *Milione*. This was the work of Rustichello of Pisa in the prison at Genoa—"en la chartre de Jene," as the text informs us—and was later continued in Venice or near by under Marco's direction, according to the French version written for Thibault de Chépoy, as appears from the unreliable though widely accepted Latin translation of the book produced by a

[16] *Marco Polo*, Turin, 1941.
[17] *Marco Polo*, London, 1950.
[18] *Venetian Adventurer*, Stanford Univ. Press, 1941, and subsequent editions.

learned Dominican, Francesco Pipino, who is celebrated in the annals of his order.[19]

The present volume does not intend to replace either the antiquated analytical and eclectic commentaries to the *Milione* or these introductory, illustrative writings of a popular sort. It wishes rather to place Polo studies on a new basis, in order to pave the way for a renewal of contributions to a direct understanding and evaluation of the text as a source of historical information. Even in this form our book is only a first attempt in the necessary reform of Polo studies. The vastness of the undertaking and the multiplicity of subjects to be dealt with in a systematic analysis of the *Milione* oblige us to present a fragment limited to certain essential aspects of the medieval Asian civilization observed by Marco, who depicted them with the open mind of a young explorer and in his simple language, which was often inadequate to the immensity and variety of his all-embracing task.

Although this book proposes to coördinate critically all that is contained in the *Milione* and to follow up every theme in this intricate and often disconcerting Asian symphony, nevertheless the subjects chosen here for detailed consideration are few, and even these constitute only a starting point for further investigation and study, rather than an exhaustive treatment of a particular aspect of Oriental civilization portrayed or recalled by our author. Hence, after a brief study of his literary and geographical predecessors, and an attempt to portray his personality so far as we may see and grasp it, we shall turn our attention to those aspects of nature and mankind which struck him in the course of his wanderings through regions that until then had remained hidden from the curiosity of Westerners.

However, if Marco was the first explorer of Asia from one end of the continent to the other, there had been earlier discoverers, half a century before him—missionaries who while penetrating

[19] For the French version and the circumstances of its diffusion, as well as for the person mentioned earlier who in 1307 obtained a copy of the text in Venice, cf. Benedetto, cr. ed., Introd., pp. lvi f. Francesco Pipino compiled in Bologna, about the year 1320, his successful Latin version of the *Milione,* which was printed for the first time at Antwerp in 1485 (reproduced in facsimile with notes by Shinobu Iwamura; Tokyo, National Diet Library, 1949).

as far as Mongolia had already heard rumors of lands, peoples, and customs that were beyond the limits of their own geographical knowledge and political, religious, and cultural experience. In scanning what our traveler has to tell it is therefore essential to remember those authors who preceded him as pioneers and narrators and who offered to their contemporaries in the Western world the first tidings of a vast region as yet unknown, which shortly afterward Marco was to reveal in its entirety. It is therefore with an account of these authors that the next chapter of our book deals, and it is complemented by an account of the journey undertaken by Niccolò Polo, Marco's father, and Maffeo, his uncle, who were the first to cross the entire continent and who directly prepared the way for their young companion's great adventure.

The unification of continental Asia under the dynasty of Chinghiz Khan in the XIIIth century made possible these undertakings, which formerly were inconceivable, by offering to a weak and divided Europe the vision of a vast empire supported by invincible armies imbued with a spirit of subordination and loyalty, however nominal, which was unknown in the West in Marco's times. This forms the historical background to the Venetian's great adventure, which with its lasting and more varied experiences completes the Asiatic vision of his predecessors and replaces the traditional or imaginary conceptions that had preceded it from the very beginnings of antiquity.

In spite of the objectivity and the positive quality in description that characterize Marco's style, and although he rarely mentions himself when telling of this distant world, nevertheless his was an experience so personal that it left the stamp of the man on every datum seized upon and described by him. The very choice of themes, the general picture of the contemporary world, are so bound up with his own impressions, his recollections of things seen or heard, as to make him everywhere present in his book, even in its most arid and impersonal sections. Indeed, if we are rightly to judge, interpret, and use it as a source of geographical and cultural information, a sense of familiarity with the presence and character of the author seems as indispensable to us as it is difficult to acquire. His elusive yet real personality, which is at the same time both universal and limited, will not permit itself to be reduced to a type; yet neither does it allow a precise distinction of his uniqueness or, consequently, a clear-cut historical portrait. Hence, we too often find before us a fictional figure, deriving from unhappy attempts to portray him in epic adventures and dramatic situations against a background that is both historical and imaginary.[20] The paucity of documentary information, the high coloring of certain episodes in his book, the traditional clichés, and ancient legends of local or literary origin—all have played their part in altering this figure, which nevertheless reveals itself to us in its historical and human reality if we consider how Marco observed and portrayed the world about him.

A methodical examination of this relationship between the man and his surroundings, which has not so far been undertaken, offers the best means of discovering the extent of his experiences, the breadth of his curiosity, the intellectual and practical results of his adventures, and, consequently, the very format of his singularity. In this way one may discover, too, Marco Polo's Asia in its most varied manifestations—cultural and individual, anthropological and political, religious and practical, spiritual and conventional, in sum, a well-nigh complete list of all the themes that form the subject matter of the *Milione*.

These can only be indicated and enumerated, in our treatment of them. But a survey thus undertaken may eventually make it possible for students of Marco—orientalists, medievalists, anthropologists, and historians of every discipline—to make a systematic study and analysis of the main features and expressions of contemporary Asian life and civilization recorded by him: the flora and fauna of the continent; its geographical and ethnographical structure; its varieties of climate; the customs of its peoples, and their languages; their monetary and commercial systems; the trades characteristic of the various regions, and their products; woods and metals, hides and textiles, their treatment and decora-

---

[20] A study of these fictional, theatrical, and cinematographic evocations of our traveler would constitute a separate theme, designed to exhibit the success of the book and the taste of the general public, and the aberrations and clichés that have transformed Marco's personality. The best-known example is Eugene O'Neill's drama, *Marco Millions*, New York, 1927.

tion; architecture and the fine arts; cloths and precious stones; cereals and wines; and so forth, in the immense variety of Oriental life portrayed by our author. There is no exhaustive study of Asiatic anthropology as documented in his volume. We have a work on Marco Polo's Persia,[21] but it is now inadequate; and it is only very recently that brief, though competent, studies have appeared on China and India as described by him in their multiform manifestations, both essential and marginal, problematic and characteristic, stable and ephemeral, intimate and spectacular.[22]

A large part of the present work is concerned in detail with the two richest fields of Polo's experiences, namely, the religions and the political history of the Orient. The attitude of Marco as a man of straightforward, devout Catholic faith who belonged to an age of fierce religious controversy and intense religious propaganda has not yet been studied in sufficient detail; yet there is nothing more fascinating within the scope of this material than his reactions to the no less spirited manifestations of the various Asiatic cults, which were then enduring the effects not only of doctrinal but also of political agitation. This affords an opportunity to bring back to life that exotic world which was dramatically divided and yet centralized in the various courts of the Chinghizide empire—a suzerainty apparently tolerant toward all cults, yet always watchful and ready to exploit their supernatural powers and the political and material advantages they might afford. The importance we attribute to this phenomenon corresponds on the one hand to its decisive role in medieval Asian civilization and on the other to the interest shown by Marco in all its most diverse manifestations without his ever denying his own faith but usually respecting that of others.

An eyewitness to many political events, a hardly secondary instrument of the imperialistic expansion of his Asiatic sovereign the great Kublai, and on various occasions a guest at Kublai's court, Marco Polo possessed to a high degree a sense of history, which none of his biographers has ever examined and which re-

[21] S. Franchi, *L'itinerario di Marco Polo in Persia,* Turin, 1941.
[22] Several essays by various authors treat of this subject in the volume *Oriente Poliano* published on the occasion of the Polo centenary by the Istituto Italiano per il Medio ed Estremo Oriente, Rome, 1957.

veals itself in his book in his reactions as a man of the Middle
Ages and a faithful subject of the Chinghizide dynasty. Thus
there appears in the *Milione* a unique combination of realism
and romance, of military interests and fictional phraseology,
which, while it can be attributed to Rustichello of Pisa, a professional writer of chivalric romances, nevertheless represents
Marco's way of understanding history and his method of narrating it, and special emphasis has therefore been placed upon
it among the principal themes treated in this book, which thereby
intends to fill a gap in the studies destined to evoke Marco and
his world.[23]

2. MARCO POLO'S ITINERARIES

The perspicacious reader will already have noted the absence of
the subject generally considered the most important in Polo
criticism, namely, the examination of the geographical value of
the *Milione,* and the reconstruction of the various itineraries of
the Polos both in their transcontinental journeys and in their
regional, local expeditions into the Asian interior. Our reticence
on this subject requires some explanation. First of all, it should
be remembered that, owing to the collaboration of geographers,
explorers, and orientalists, the itineraries have already been reconstructed, some in part and some in their broad outline, in
spite of persisting doubts about this or that locality mentioned in
the *Milione,* and about the routes or distances insufficiently or
erroneously indicated. The map included in this volume and the
most recent literature on the subject allow us to follow the travels
of the three Venetians with approximate accuracy, although they
leave unsolved an important problem, namely, the determination
of which among the places mentioned or described by Marco
were actually seen by him, and of those which were known to
him only at second hand.[1]

Although he honestly stated at the beginning of his book that

[23] Cf. chaps. viii and ix.

[1] The best and most recent critical description of Polo's itineraries is that of N. M.
Penzer in his introduction to *The Most Noble and Famous Travels of Marco Polo
. . .* edited from the Elizabethan translation of John Frampton (with a number of
excellent maps, topographical sketches, critical notes, and bibliography), London, 1929,
reprinted 1935.

he wished to recount "all the great wonders seen, or heard of as true," he usually makes no distinction between the two categories in the course of his narrative, and thereby makes it extremely difficult—sometimes impossible—for the reader to decide one way or the other. For example, it is only indirectly, and by a knowledge of the means of communication in medieval Persia, that one can establish with any certainty that Marco never visited the two great centers of Mesopotamia, Baghdad and Mosul, which were described by him from apparently personal experience in that laconic but concrete and at times vivacious style which is so completely his own and which fashions the objective yet personal uniformity of the whole account.[2] Likewise, it is not possible for us to decide whether he ever visited Karakorum, the first capital of the Mongol empire, in the heart of Mongolia, though its principal monuments are mentioned by him, as well as its importance as a historical and national center of Chinghiz Khan's Asia.[3] It is doubtful, too, whether he saw the splendid and fabulous city of Pagan, the ancient capital of Burma, which is recalled by him with so much enthusiasm for its fine towers of silver and gold, glistening in the glare of the tropical sun and visible from afar.[4] Furthermore, the conventionality of expression, the unusual toponymy, and the paucity of topographical data do not always permit us to establish with certainty what towns in China were actually visited by him, and the indeterminate information and fragmentary references cause us to doubt whether he ever proceeded into the interior of the Indian peninsula, beyond the coastal region, which he must have seen in part.

On the other hand, he offers strange yet correct information about the island of Socotra in the Arabian Sea, and the tropical regions of Africa, Arabia, and Abyssinia, where he never set foot, though in these parts of his narrative there is little difference in his style from that found in passages dealing with regions repeatedly traversed by him and more or less correctly described. It would be a mistake to think the selfsameness of manner a literary artifice designed to deceive the reader, so far as the re-

[2] *Il Milione*, cr. ed., pp. 17 f. (Mosul), 18 f. (Baudac); M.P., pp. 100 and 101.
[3] *Il Milione*, cr. ed., pp. 49 f.; M.P., p. 161.
[4] *Il Milione*, cr. ed., p. 124 ("la cité de Mien," from the contemporary Chinese name for northern Burma); M.P., p. 293.

liability of his information is concerned. Critics have not been
lacking who have laid this specific charge against Marco, making him out to be a braggart. But no; the parity set up between
the things the author heard and those he saw results from the
very character of the *Milione,* which is not, as is commonly supposed, a book of travel and adventure, but a treatise of empirical
geography; that is to say, it is both a guidebook and a doctrinal
work, fused into a literary combination so successful that it is
impossible to tell the one from the other.

The accurate specification of the individual localities and
itineraries that are still uncertain is both a philological and a
geographical task. Yet one should not look to the acumen of
critics or to indirect documentation for a solution to the problem
mentioned above, namely, that of distinguishing in Polo's account the things he saw from those he recorded from hearsay;
nor, therefore, what is the result of personal experience from
what is a reference to more or less correct information. The
very fact that the information was sought after shows us that
Marco did not wish to limit himself to an enumeration of things
he happened to see by chance, but that his curiosity continually
went beyond the contingencies of his travels, with obvious doctrinal tendencies which link him to the civilization of his times
and make his book a part of the vernacular didactic literature of
the late Middle Ages.

While leaving to other studies the enumeration of yet other
localities and the problem of the various itineraries, it is nevertheless possible here to retrace in their broad outline the routes
covered by Marco in the course of his wanderings through Asia.
At the same time, we may assume that he regularly collected geo-
ethnographical information in the political and commercial centers along the caravan routes, from which the roads along which
he did not have occasion to travel branched out in various directions. We shall limit ourselves to what has recently been ascertained, and we shall assign to the next chapter the account of the
first journey through the Asian continent undertaken in both
directions by Niccolò and Maffeo Polo between the years 1260
and 1269. Thus, we can divide his numerous itineraries into
various sections in accordance with their main stages and hence

with the geographical structure of his description of the world.

The first of these—at the end of the year 1271—took our three travelers from Acre to Ayas (Laiazzo). This latter Mediterranean port was the point of departure for the caravans that journeyed across the Cilicia of the ancients (called Armenia Minor by our author) and, proceeding via the towns of Conia (Iconium), Kaisaria, and Sivas (Sebaste), reached Greater Armenia, which for some time past had been a tributary of the Chinghizide empire and, more especially, of the Tartars of the Levant.[5] In this vast and rugged land of eastern Anatolia the three Venetians must have halted at Arzingan (Erzinjan), the seat of an archbishopric, and at Erzerum, the capital and an important crossroads, in order to reach—via ancient Arsissa (called Arzizi by Marco) and Tabriz—one of the temporary capitals of the Persia of the Ilkhans.[6]

In that year of 1272, this town, rich in history and trade, and still inhabited by a population of prevalently Turkish and Tartar descent, already sheltered an Italian colony, probably of Genoese, who were soon followed by a crowd of Venetian merchants, known alike for their success in trade and for their contentions and quarrels that swelled at times into destructive riots.[7] But Marco does not mention this in his description. From Erzerum the Polos set out on the way to Hormuz, an ancient port at the mouth of the Persian Gulf, crossing eastern Persia by forced marches and with numerous adventures.[8] Along the way they must have come upon Sultaniyeh, which, as another seat of the Mongol dynasty of Persia, was to become a flourishing town and

[5] *Il Milione*, cr. ed., pp. 13–16; M.P., p. 95 ff. Anatolia, traversed in the course of this journey, is called Turcomania by Marco, and the "Tartars of the Levant" are, in the terms generally used at that time, the Mongols of Persia.

[6] *Il Milione*, pp. 22 f.; M.P., p. 104 ("la noble cité de Toris"). The Ilkhans are the Chinghizide sovereigns of Persia, which was conquered and made a part of the empire by Hulagu, the grandson of Chinghiz, in 1256 *et seqq*.

[7] Cf. R. Morozzo della Rocca, "Sulle orme di Marco Polo," *L'Italia che scrive*, Vol. XXXVII, 1954, p. 120. As is well known, the first mention of the Italian mercantile colony at Tabriz is found in the will of Pietro Viglioni, a Venetian, which dates from 1264. We find traces of his descendants in the funerary inscription for the tomb of his granddaughter Caterina, who died at Yangchow in China, in 1340; cf. n. 83 to chap. vi, below.

[8] The most recent description of this Persian itinerary, with information supplied by explorers of all periods, and bibliographical references, is to be found in A. Gabriel, *Die Erforschung Persiens*, Vienna, 1952, pp. 32–42.

an important center for Catholic expansion in the East.[9] Marco does not mention it, probably because at the time of his first journey through Persia it had not yet acquired the importance that was to make it famous in the next century.[10]

On the other hand, Marco does name the village of Saba (Saveh) with the supposed tombs of the Magi and the cult perpetuated there in forms, rites, and legends of a curious local tradition.[11] The other places mentioned in this wide region, which is chiefly desert, are the great caravan centers of Yezd, Kerman, and "Camandi," which allow us to reconstruct the route followed across the highland plateau of Sardu to the province of "Reobarles," which corresponds to the torrid region of Rudbar, rich in archaeological records but now almost completely uninhabited.[12]

The port of Hormuz, reached by exhausting marches across the "great slope" and under constant menace of attack by brigands, was then still situated inland, on the banks of a river now silted up.[13] Here our travelers were to board ship in order to go by sea to the court of the Great Kaan, at his winter abode in Peking, then called Taidu or, in Turkish, Khanbaliq, which means "the King's city"; or else, as the time of year would require, at his summer residence in Shangtu, where Niccolò and Maffeo had already been received in 1265.[14] However, the

[9] Sultaniyeh, now an Iranian town, became after 1306 the second capital of Chinghiz' Persia and the seat of a succession of Catholic archbishops, the best known being John of Cori, whose report on the "state and government of the Great Khan of Cathay" to Pope John XXII is known only in a French translation. Cf. Henry Yule, *Cathay and the Way Thither,* second edition, Vol. III, London, Hakluyt Society, 1914, pp. 36 ff., 89 ff.

[10] For the various capitals and residences of the Ilkhans of Persia cf. B. Spuler, *Die Mongolen in Iran,* Leipzig, 1939 (reprinted with appendix, Berlin, Akademie Verlag, 1955), pp. 332 and 449 ff.

[11] Discussed at length by Ugo Monneret de Villard, *Le leggende orientali sui Magi evangelici,* Città del Vaticano, 1952 (Studi e Testi, no. 163), pp. 78 f.

[12] This is not to be confused with the other Persian province of the same name in the mountains of Elbruz and to the south of the Caspian Sea, for which see Gabriel, *op. cit.,* pp. 29 f., etc.

[13] *Ibid.,* p. 37, n. 9. For further data, especially on the political situation in that region, cf. J. Aubin, "Les Princes d'Ormuz du XIIIe au XIVe siècle," *Journal Asiatique,* Vol. CCXLI, 1953, pp. 77 ff.

[14] Cf. *Il Milione,* cr. ed., p. 9, chap. xiv, where the celebrated residence of Kublai is mentioned by the name of Clemeinfu; for the corrected reading, Chemenfu, see Yule-Cordier, Vol. I, p. 25, note. It is known also under the name of Kaipingfu, the capital of his empire from 1257 to 1264, before Kublai transferred his seat of sovereignty to Taidu.

Venetians, who were expert seafarers, were justified in their distrust of Persian, Arabian, and Chinese ships, which according to
Marco were ill-equipped and unsafe for the long journey and
the frequent squalls that harass sailors in the Indian Ocean.[15]
This was most probably the reason that led them to resume their
journey toward the East by land, trusting not only in the holy
oil from the lamp of the Holy Sepulcher, destined for the Great
Kaan at his explicit request, but also in the power of their imperial "golden tablets of command," which made their persons
inviolable, as Marco himself asserts, under pain of severe punishment and threat of death to any who should disregard them.[16]
Moreover, the protection generally accorded to merchants by the
regional authorities was effective enough to protect all travelers.
The Polos could also put their trust in the credentials given them
by the Roman Pontiff, since at this time he was respected and
politically feared throughout the kingdom of Persia and the rest
of the Chinghizide empire.[17]

Having, therefore, chosen to travel by land toward their distant
goal, they crossed central Persia, to the north of Kerman,
"through a most wild and barren country," visiting Cobinan
(Kuhbanan), in the metal-producing region on the edge of the
desert that separates it from the vast province which Marco calls
Tunocain, from the names of the two cities of Tûn and Qâin on
its western borders. To the north, it borders on the legendary
region of the Arbre Sec, corresponding to the historic province
of Khorasan, which Marco probably did not cross on that occasion. Instead, he advanced resolutely toward the northeast,

[15] For Chinese ships in the Persian Gulf cf. the note by P. Paris in *Bulletin de
l'École Française d'Extrême-Orient*, Vol. XLVI, 1954, p. 655; also Jung-pang Lo,
"The Emergence of China as a Sea Power during the Late Sung and Early Yüan
Periods," *Far Eastern Quarterly*, Vol. XIV, 1955, pp. 488 ff. Valuable information is
given also by J. J. L. Duyvendak, *China's Discovery of Africa*, London, 1949, pp.
17 ff.

[16] These golden tablets are described with their privileges in the *Milione*, cr. ed.,
pp. 12–13, and were preserved in the Polo family treasury in Venice, as we learn
from the will of Maffeo, Marco's uncle (reprinted in Moule-Pelliot, Vol. I, p. 531),
as well as from the list of objects found in Marco's house at his death, which probably occurred in February, 1324 (*ibid.*, pp. 555 ff.). A description of these golden
safe-conduct passes, which conferred on their bearer princely rank and well-nigh
absolute safety throughout the empire, is given by Yule-Cordier, *The Book of Ser
Marco Polo*, Vol. I, p. 352.

[17] P. Pelliot, "Les Mongols et la Papauté," *Revue de l'Orient Chrétien*, Vols. XXIII
and XXIV, 1923–1924.

"through beautiful hills and valleys, rich in grasses, good pasture, and fruit," reaching Sapurgan (i.e., Shibarghan) after long marches, in what is now the territory of northern Afghanistan.[18]

Marco's bare style and the paucity of geographical data offered by him hardly give us any idea of the immense extent of the distances covered, the unevenness of the terrain, or of traveling conditions in isolated deserts, fertile plateaus, and well-nigh impassable mountain ranges. Few explorers since his day have followed the same path, which we can indicate only approximately and of which, very occasionally, the various stages can be specified.[19] In the course of this journey the travelers visited the historic town of Balkh, the ancient capital of Bactriana and for many centuries a great center of Hellenistic, Buddhistic, and Islamic culture, until its destruction in 1220 by the armies of Chinghiz Khan.[20] In Marco's time this was the limit of the dominion of the Tartars of the Levant, namely, the Ilkhans of Persia. It bordered on Central Asia, which was then dominated by another branch of the dynasty, in the person of the warlike rebel, Caidu, whose exploits are often mentioned by our author.[21]

The journey proceeded in a direction "between east and northeast," following the present frontier of northern Afghanistan on the borders of Turkestan, which is now a part of the Soviet Union. This beautiful countryside in the heart of Asia, which evoked words of enthusiastic admiration from Marco's lips, is the region that extends from Talikan (his "Taican") to "Scasem" (present-day Kishm), through which he reached the highland plateaus of picturesque, benign Badakhshan, where he remained for one whole year. This region has kept its name until the

[18] We learn from the Ramusian version of the prologue to the *Milione*, cr. ed., pp. 12 f., M.P., p. 91, that the Polos accompanied the Princess "Cocachin" from the court of "Chiacatu" (Gaikhatu), lord of Persia and temporary successor to Arghun Khan, in Khorasan, to this remote province. The princess was destined for Casan (or Ghazan) Khan, who married her at the end of 1293, after the death of Arghun, or at the beginning of the following year. After this the Polos probably returned to Tabriz, where they stayed for a further nine months before setting out on the return to Venice. The historical and topographical information on the so-called region of the Arbre Sec was gathered by Marco on that occasion and not at the time of his first journey through Persia, which followed, as we shall see, a quite different itinerary.

[19] Cf. Gabriel, *op. cit.*, pp. 35 ff., as well as Penzer, *op. cit.*, who offers in his Introduction a good account of the route.

[20] *Il Milione*, cr. ed., p. 35; M.P., p. 134.

[21] Cf. chap. viii of the present work.

present day, although it is now applied to an area less extensive than that of Marco's "Balascian." [22]

However, it is not always clear which regional or local itinerary the three Venetians followed in the course of this long march from the deserts of Persia to the plateaus of the Pamir. Marco does not mention every stage of this stupendous journey, and the information given of the number of miles covered and of the days spent in traveling are often approximate, incorrect, or have been altered by the copyists of the various versions. Moreover, the narrative is often interrupted, to give Marco an opportunity to complement his own experiences with information concerning regions and localities not visited by him. These are examined from one central geographical point in a vision which is both swift and comprehensive, but which often follows personal interests and impressions rather than a clear topographical scheme or precise itinerary. Thus, he inserts into the account of his journey the episode of the Old Man of the Mountain and a description of his fictitious Paradise in the mountains of Elbruz, which lay far from the traveler's path, yet were present to his imagination.[23] His stay in Badakhshan therefore made him recount whatever he learned of the near-by regions: the "great province" of "Pasciai," roughly corresponding to the mountainous district of present-day Kafiristan and adjoining Chitral in the extreme north of Pakistan; then, Kashmir and the region of the upper Amu Darya (the Oxus of ancient times), which Marco calls "Vocan" and which corresponds to Wakhan on the eastern borders of Afghanistan.[24]

[22] *Il Milione*, cr. ed., p. 36; M.P., p. 136. The borders of this northeastern region of present-day Afghanistan appear to have fluctuated in the course of history. They now include the town and district of Talikan, mentioned by Marco as a "very beautiful region," rich in salt among other things. For the history of the region cf. W. Barthold, *Turkestan Down to the Mongol Invasion*, London ("Gibb Memorial" series, n.s., V), 1928, pp. 180 ff.

[23] This episode is inserted between the description of the Arbre Sec region, which corresponds to the Persian province of Khorasan, and the account of the town of "Sapurgan" (Shibarghan), far to the east of the so-called land of "Muleete," the seat of the Old Man of the Mountain, or Grand Master of the Assassins. Cf. chap. ix, § 1, of the present work.

[24] Marco, moreover, mentions a country which he calls "Dogana" (cr. ed., p. 35, chap. xlv; M.P., p. 134) without adding any data that would help to identify it. The latest hypothesis concerning it is to be found in Penzer, *op. cit.*, Introd., pp. xxxix f.

In a few words Marco has given us a dramatic and celebrated sketch of the Pamir region. Though it is inferior to the well-known description by the Chinese pilgrim Hsüan Tsang of the VIIth century A.D., in wealth of detail and exactness of information, it nevertheless portrays vividly the immense stretch of seemingly impassable mountains that lay athwart the descent to Kashgar ("Cascar") in Chinese Turkestan.[25] The path he chose to follow, however, which probably was known to his older companions from their first journey, has long been a subject of discussion and conjecture. The major commentaries treat of it in detail, and a mass of literature gathered in Cordier's *Addenda,* to which may be added the observations and conclusions of various explorers, further helps us to define the trail of this memorable journey and to decide whether the Polos did in fact cross the "roof of the world" or passed round it, on their way down to Kashgar, through the great valley of the Alai.[26] This is a matter that cannot be discussed, let alone resolved, in a few lines. A monographic study of the argument is needed, which would retrace its history, taking advantage of the wealth of ancient and modern literature on the subject.[27] However, both in this and in

[25] Hsüan Tsang's description, reproduced in part in the major commentaries to the *Milione,* can be read in its entirety in the English translation by S. Beal, *Si-yu-ki: Buddhist Records of the Western World,* London, 1884, pp. 297 ff., and in the French of Stanislas Julien, Paris, 1857.

[26] H. Cordier, *Notes and Addenda,* pp. 39 f., reports, *inter alia,* the observations of Sir Aurel Stein, who while studying the region had Marco's data with him and checked them so as to reconstruct the Venetian's itinerary. Independently of his conclusions, one may assume that the Polo brothers, who had set out from Bokhara toward China in their first crossing of the continent in or about the year 1264, crossed the fertile and historic region of Fergana, reaching the highland plateaus and passes of the Pamir to the north of the Alai range; whereas on the second journey, Marco being with them, coming from Badakhshan and the adjoining region of "Vocan" (i.e., Wakhan), they must have followed the difficult paths that lead to the watershed to the south of the Alai (the so-called Lesser Pamir), to cross the Muztagh Ata range in the extreme west of Chinese Turkestan.

[27] The weightiest study of the subject is that by Wolfgang Lentz, "War Marco Polo auf dem Pamir?" *Zeitschrift der deutschen morgenländischen Gesellschaft,* Vol. LXXXVI, 1933, pp. 1 ff., with bibliography and critical analysis of the routes given by A. Herrmann and other geographers and explorers, among them Sven Hedin (*Southern Tibet,* Vol. VIII, Stockholm, 1922) and Aurel Stein (*Innermost Asia,* Vol. II, London, 1928, p. 860). According to Lentz, Marco Polo reached Kashgar by the valley of the Alai without passing through Wakhan, but his conclusions do not seem convincing. A good brief description of the Pamir region, useful to the reader of Marco's account, is to be found in N. T. Mirov, *Geography of Russia,* London, 1951, pp. 163 ff.; the most detailed work is that by the Russian scholar A. N. Bernstam,

other passages of the *Milione,* it must be remembered that the information given about the time spent on the various stages of a journey and the distances from the places mentioned, cannot be taken as a basis for a true evaluation. Marco certainly did not suffer from amnesia, nor were his copyists always remiss or ignorant; what both he and they lacked was a sense of precision, which, as we may see in other circumstances, matured in modern culture only in the age of Galileo and was reflected in geographical literature and cartography from the XVIIth century onward. To convince ourselves of this we need only see how vaguely the distances of the Asiatic journeys are measured in the well-known "Avvisamento del viaggio del Gattaio," composed about half a century after the *Milione* by Francesco Balducci Pegolotti, who is, on the other hand, most precise in his information about commerce, banking, customs dues, and taxes.[28]

The description of Eastern Turkestan, present-day Sinkiang, which had now been reached by our caravan after so many hardships, is one of the poorest in the book and thus a disappointment to those who are aware of the importance of this region at all times in the political and cultural history of Asia. However, if Marco turns his gaze from Kashgar toward Samarkand, known to his elders only from their three-year stay in ancient Sogdiana, he thereby implies an understanding of the linguistic, ethnographic, religious, and political unity of Turkestan, which is geographically divided by the spurs of the Pamir and by the huge T'ien Shan range, but belonged to the Chagatai branch of the Chinghizide dynasty, which then ruled over the whole of Central Asia from the borders of Persia to those of Mongolia and Cathay.[29]

---

in Vol. XXVIII of the *Materiali i issledovania po archeologii SSSR,* Moscow and Leningrad, Akad. Nauk SSSR, 1952, with relief maps, topographical sketches, and bibliographical notes. The most recent scaling of the Lesser Pamir in the steps of Marco Polo is vividly described, without scientific pretensions, by Jean Bowie Shor, *After You, Marco Polo,* New York, 1955. Still of interest is Aurel Stein's classic description, *On Ancient Central-Asian Tracks,* London, 1933, chap. xix, esp. pp. 306 ff.

[28] *La Pratica della Mercatura,* ed. Allan Evans, Cambridge, Mass. (Mediaeval Academy of America), 1936, pp. 21 ff. Neither Marco nor Pegolotti, in his calculation of the duration of the stages, mentions the seasons, which affect these measurements essentially but are lacking in the hypothetical reconstruction of Marco's itineraries.

[29] For the history of this region cf. Barthold's *Turkestan,* cited in note 22 above, and, for the period of Mongol domination, René Grousset, *L'Empire des steppes,* Paris,

The path followed by him, and designated by the names of its principal centers, Yarcan (Yarkand), Cotan (Khotan), Pem (?), Ciarcian (Charchan), and Lop, is the ancient caravan trail known as the "Silk Route," the southern branch of which linked the urban oases and their busy markets in the order correctly indicated by Marco.[30] By this path, which skirted and crossed the desert basin of the Tarim and the arid sands of Taklamakan, the travelers came to the edge of the terrible desert, the crossing of which, after a month of difficulties and dangers, brought them to "Saciu" (Shachow), the first Chinese village, famous in archaeological history under the name of Tun-huang, called also "the place of the thousand Buddhas," which formerly decorated its temples.[31]

Here, in the immense Chinese province of Kansu, which Marco calls "Tangut" from the Mongolian name of an ancient Tibeto-Burmese tribe that used to inhabit it, together with other peoples from Upper Asia, he came into contact for the first time with the most diverse manifestations of pagan civilization, of which every trace had disappeared in the great centers of western and central Asia through which he had traveled hitherto.[32]

1939 (and subsequent editions), pp. 397 ff. The kingdom of Chagatai, the son of Chinghiz, who gave his name to the whole of this vast region and to its predominant Turkish language, extended, from the year 1230 onward, from Bokhara (in Transoxiana to the east of Turfan) toward Mongolia (in the northeast) and China (in the east), and in a north–south direction from Lake Balkhash to the Kunlun chain of mountains along the Tibetan border. This immense territory corresponded to that of the ancient empire of Karakhitai, of Sino-Turkish civilization, which had become a part of the Chinghizide empire in 1218, after various complex events, for which see Grousset, *op. cit.*, pp. 293 ff.

[30] Cr. ed., pp. 40–43; M.P., pp. 146 ff. Cf. A. Herrmann, *Die alten Seidenstrassen zwischen China und Syrien*, Berlin, 1900, and Sven Hedin, *The Silk Road*, trans. H. Lyon, New York, 1938, esp. chap. xviii; also L. Hambis in *Oriente Poliano*, Rome, 1957, pp. 173 ff., and the principal commentaries.

[31] This Chinese village on the edge of the Gobi Desert is now famous on account of the archaeological and bibliographical discoveries made there some fifty years ago, especially by Sir Aurel Stein and Paul Pelliot, and since visited by explorers from various lands. Cf. Stein, *On Ancient Central-Asian Tracks*, chap. xii, pp. 193 ff., and, for a bibliography of the subject, H. Franke, *Sinologie*, Bern, 1953, pp. 30 f. and *passim*. Of all these treasures, already hidden for centuries, Marco saw and learned nothing at the time of his stop there.

[32] *Il Milione*, cr. ed., pp. 44 f.; M.P., pp. 151 f. This ancient northwestern province of China, the geographical and historical limits of which are difficult to establish, was an independent kingdom from the Xth century until its conquest by Chinghiz Khan in 1227.

Here, as elsewhere, before proceeding with his itinerary, he halts awhile to glance at the surrounding regions. These included the province of Camul (Qomul), corresponding to the oasis of Hami; farther north, toward the Mongolian border, on the edge of barren western Zungaria, the territory he calls Chingintalas (a term not used elsewhere), which was situated in the scarcely explored vicinity of present-day Lake Barkol.[33] Then, more to the west, in the neighborhood of the ancient city of Turfan, the region designated as Icoguristan, i.e., the territory of the Uigur Turks, on the northern borders of Central Asia, of which Marco mentions the town of "Carachoço," or Karakhodja, a center for important and successful archaeological expeditions in the first decade of the present century.[34]

Only after this geographical survey does the itinerary proceed with a ten-day episode, as far as Suchow and Kanchow, the Chinese administrative center of Kansu, to which the Polos must have made repeated and prolonged visits. From this latter important crossroads Marco again turns his gaze, rather than his steps, northward toward distant regions. He thus includes in his account the town of Etzina, formerly Karakhoto, which had lain in ruins for many centuries, and directs his glance as far as Karakorum, then the provincial capital of Mongolia and formerly a dynastic, administrative, and military center of the Chinghizide empire.[35]

This digression, which includes a mythic account of its origins and its founder, Chinghiz Khan, is likewise couched in such a style that it is impossible to tell whether Marco actually visited the regions and towns named, which are described with his usual measured terms and judgments. Yet the geographical

[33] For these regions cf., besides Aurel Stein, *On Ancient Central-Asian Tracks,* the explorations and research of Owen Lattimore, *Inner Asian Frontiers,* second edition, New York (American Geographical Society), 1951, with full bibliography. The lake and village of Barkol (in Chinese, Chensi) are on the caravan route from Hami (now Qomul) to present-day Urumchi, an important commercial and administrative center at the southern limits of Zungaria.

[34] This historic region, several times described in masterly fashion by Aurel Stein, is mentioned by Marco only in the Z version (cr. ed., p. 46 n., where the reading Carachoto should be corrected to Carachoço; M.P., p. 156). Cf. also Penzer, *op. cit.,* Introd., p. xliii (with maps of the region).

[35] *Il Milione,* cr. ed., pp. 49 f. One cannot, however, exclude the possibility that Marco may have visited this ancient capital of the empire, in the heart of Mongolia.

vision is so clear and harmonious as to make us assume at least some direct experience of these territories, which for so many centuries had never been visited by Western travelers.[36] However, this alternation of itineraries interwoven with rapid geographical sketches in the whole of this part of the book, which deals with central Asia from Badakhshan to the Yellow River, is eminently characteristic and is worked out in harmony with a clear conception of the character and situation of the various lands.[37] The result is that the account follows a well-defined preliminary geographical concept which is the result not only of personal experience but also of a plan composed with the intention of offering systematically a maximum of material with a minimum of particular and personal data.

Taking up once more the itinerary of the three Venetians, Marco leads us, by way of Kanchow (Campiciu, or similar forms, in his book), into the vast province of Tangut, the fluctuating, ill-defined limits of which it is impossible to retrace. Suffice it to say that for the traveler coming from the west its approaches are marked by imposing segments of the Great Wall—one of the wonders of Asia that our author failed explicitly to mention.[38] Still in this immense province, where his interest was engaged by its natural rather than its geographical aspects, he leads us on toward the wide bend of the Yellow River, to which he applies the Mongolian term "Caramoran," or Black River.[39] In these regions he mentions first of all the "great kingdom of Erginul,"

---

[36] Cf. the evocation of Marco's experiences in the region in Aurel Stein, *On Ancient Central-Asian Tracks,* esp. pp. 246 ff.; also, L. Hambis, "Le Voyage de Marco Polo en Haute Asie," in *Oriente Poliano,* pp. 173 ff.

[37] In both cases, Marco's gaze sweeps round from a central point actually reached by him and returns to the halting place, thereby indicating the beginning of a new itinerary. The same procedure is repeated elsewhere in the book and determines its fundamental structure. It is helpful to remember this when one attempts to make one's way out of the labyrinth of our traveler's real and imaginary itineraries.

[38] The approximate extent of Tangut, the ancient Chinese kingdom of Si-hsia (or Hsi-hsia), can be estimated with the help of A. Herrmann's *Historical and Commercial Atlas of China,* Cambridge, Mass., 1935, maps 47 and 49, which also include the adjacent regions mentioned by Marco; but cf. H. Franke, *Sinologie,* p. 140, n. 8. Other maps and topographical sketches, more precise and extensive, can be found in the works of Aurel Stein and Owen Lattimore mentioned in note 33 above. For this territory and its peoples cf. also Pavel Poucha, "Mongolische Miszellen," *Central Asiatic Journal,* Vol. I, 1955, pp. 284 ff., and Peter Olbricht, "Die Tanguten und ihre Geschichte," *ibid.,* Vol. II, 1956, pp. 142 ff.

[39] Cr. ed., pp. 106 and 136; M.P., pp. 262 and 314.

or Erguiul, which may possibly be identified with the present Wuwei (Liangchow), and then "Silingiu," in which we may justifiably recognize the important religious and caravan center of Sining near Kokonor, toward the northern borders of Tibet.[40]

Only the province of Egrigaia is mentioned in all this vast region of steppes and deserts, designated by Marco with the name of Tangut. This, it would seem, corresponds to the zone of Ning-hsia on the same river, with its main town, "Calacian," which recently has been hypothetically identified with the village of Ting-yüan-ying, at the foot of the Alashan chain of mountains.[41] To the east of this, Marco penetrated into the huge province of Tenduc, likewise of doubtful geographical delimitation, and identified by him as the dominion of Prester John, that is to say, a Christian king of eastern Asia, lord of a Christian people, whose deeds he recounts farther on, and who was extolled by ancient legends as the sovereign of the whole Orient.[42]

This information is more useful than any topographical data for the recognition of this kingdom as the territory of the Öngüt, a Christian tribe of Mongols, dispersed here and there in the great bend of the Yellow River, and especially in the region of the Ordos, where innumerable metallic crosses have been found —witnesses to the faith and numbers of these Western Nestorians in the Far East.[43] According to Marco's account, they

[40] From time immemorial, Sining has been the junction point of two of the most important caravan routes that connect western China with southern Mongolia toward the northeast and with eastern Tibet toward the southwest. The celebrated ancient Buddhist monastery and sanctuary of Kumbum, in the vicinity of Sining, has made this region one of capital importance for the religious and artistic history of medieval Buddhism.

[41] The hypothetical identification of "Calacian" (*Il Milione,* cr. ed., p. 60; M.P., p. 181) has been made by Penzer (*op. cit.*) and would correspond to the ancient Wang-yeh in the region of Ning-hsia. For other identifications of this locality cf., apart from the major commentaries, Benedetto's short note in his translation, *Il Libro di Messer Marco Polo,* p. 439.

[42] See chap. ix, § 2, of the present volume. Marco Polo's Tenduc may well correspond to the present frontier region between China and Mongolia, to the north of the great bend of the Yellow River—a region which formed the ancient territory of the Öngüt extending in the same direction as far as the land of the Keraits in the heart of Mongolia. Prester John, as he is called, is supposed to have been both the historical and the legendary ruler of this region. In both of these tribes the Nestorian Christian element was predominant at court as well as among the ruling classes.

[43] Cf. P. Y. Saeki, *The Nestorian Documents and Relics in China,* second edition, Tokyo, 1951, pp. 423 ff.; also, a bibliography by the same author in *Catalogue of*

called this expanse of territory, made up of vast steppe-land and interspersed with oases and deserts, by the names of Ung and Mungul, which later became the Gog and Magog found in the Bible and the Koran.[44] This information, however, is too little definite to permit us satisfactorily to identify the places visited by Marco, who must nevertheless have traversed this region in both its length and breadth on his way eastward toward Cathay, northern China—that is to say, noting the town of Sindufu as the center of an important military industry, and the many silver caves in the "Idifu" region.[45]

The steps of our travelers are lost in the immensity of these territories, which are briefly mentioned in vague terms without leaving any trace of their route. Here again, the author's geographical vision asserts itself and is superimposed upon the recollections of his travels, so that any attempt to reconstruct the path followed by them turns out to be either hypothetical in its results or vain in its conclusions. The wisdom of so many learned interpreters is powerless before the will of Marco himself, who

---

the Nestorian Literature and Relics, Tokyo, 1950. For the present situation of the region cf. A. Mostaert, "Matériaux ethnographiques . . . ," *Central Asiatic Journal,* Vol. II, 1956, pp. 241 ff.

[44] *Il Milione,* cr. ed., p. 61; M.P., p. 183. As is well known, Gog and Magog are the fabulous peoples that, according to the Book of Revelation (20: 7 ff.), Satan will set free from their segregation in order to bring about through them the destruction of Jerusalem. They are first mentioned in Ezekiel's prophecy (38: 1 ff.), together with other Eastern peoples (Persians, Ethiopians, and Libyans) who had come together to destroy Israel. Until the XIIIth century they were assigned to the Caucasus and identified with the peoples enclosed by Alexander the Great behind his legendary Iron Gate near Derbend on the western shores of the Caspian Sea. The Koran takes up the Biblical tradition and the legend of the Macedonian, while fusing them in prophetic allusions to the end of the world (suras XVIII and XXI). Cf. A. R. Anderson, *Alexander's Gate, Gog and Magog, and the Inclosed Nations,* Cambridge, Mass. (Mediaeval Academy of America), 1932, with a bibliography of the subject. The phonetic affinity between Magog and Mongol, and between Tartar—the name of a people in eastern Mongolia—and the infernal Tartarus, have determined the placing of Gog and Magog beyond the Gobi Desert, where, north of the Great Wall of China, we must look for the peoples mentioned by Marco with these Biblical names.

[45] *Il Milione,* cr. ed., p. 61. The identification of these localities is still debated by the authors mentioned above, but it must be situated in the vicinity of Kalgan, now in Chahar but formerly in Chihli and not far from the border of that Chinese province with eastern Mongolia and on the way to the imperial summer residence at Shangtu (Chandu) in the Dolon-nor district, perhaps reached by the Polo brothers at the end of their first journey, about the year 1265, and then by them and Marco at the beginning of their long stay in China. For the topography of this region and the plan of the town cf. Herrmann's *Atlas of China,* p. 51, and L. Impei's article cited in note 46, below.

here as elsewhere intentionally sacrificed his actual memories to his doctrinal ambitions. Hence, we shall never know if the three Venetians journeyed from this point to "Ciandu" (Shangtu, in the Dolon-nor district), which is described by him in detail in the famous chapters in which he depicts the summer residence of Kublai Kaan.[46]

However this may be, he has led us, after various diversions, as far as the frontiers of China, of which he now begins his description. This, too, keeps step with the itineraries of his missions, and his accounts are interspersed with information concerning regions and peoples indirectly known to him and not explored from that time until the late XIXth century.

Marco orders his description of China and the adjoining countries as following two main itineraries, which are ideally made to include lands and peoples of which he received only second-hand information or intermittent, occasional experience. The difficulties in geographical specification and topographical orientation are therefore the same as those posed by the first part of his book, which are due as much to the vagueness of data and names given as to the mixture of things seen with things heard and to patent errors of observation, memory, or simply transcription.

This is the most difficult part of the book to interpret as geographical information; and commentators who are experts in medieval history, philology, archaeology, and topography are seldom equally competent in all these branches of knowledge of the Far East. The surest guide in following our author's wanderings in these regions is still Yule, who illustrated them with a series of maps and sketches that are fundamental for an accurate study of the travels.[47] Apart from this, there is the more

---

[46] Cr. ed., pp. 62 f.; M.P., p. 185. It seems probable that this was the goal of the first journey undertaken by the Polo brothers, and it is possible that they, with Marco, made their way directly to Peking (Taidu and Khanbaliq in contemporary Mongolian and Turkish, respectively). Since Marco did not indicate with any precision the time of his arrival at the court of Kublai, it is not possible for us to establish whether he saw his new lord in the summer capital of Shangtu or at Peking, the winter residence. For a description of Shangtu (the fabulous Xanadu) and its ruins cf. the illustrated article by L. Impei, "Shangtu," *Geographical Review,* Vol. XV, 1925, pp. 584 ff.

[47] *Op. cit.,* Vol. II, with Cordier's addenda.

recent work by N. M. Penzer, who, to his own specifications of
the real and imaginary itineraries found in the *Milione,* adds a
critical summary of the hypotheses and conclusions of other
students and the observations of explorers of the various regions
mentioned by Marco.[48] We need therefore only point out that our
traveler grouped his Chinese reminiscences about two main sorts
of data and information, which reveal a didactic, literary plan
without representing an actual, truly personal itinerary of his
travels and experiences. The first of these itineraries, partly real
and partly imaginary, corresponds in the main to his first mission as Kublai's personal informant, which, probably in 1276—
hence shortly after his arrival,—led him from the imperial residence, in a southwesterly direction, beyond Cathay into southern
China, which had recently been subjugated to the Chinghizide
empire, through the modern provinces of Shansi, Shensi, and
Szechwan, as far as Yunnan, which had already been conquered
by Kublai in 1253 while his brother Mangu (Möngke) Kaan was
still reigning at Karakorum.[49]

Marco's observations on the border region that includes—as he
names them—Tebet (Tibet), Gaindu, Carajan, Zardandan, and
Mien (Burma), as far as Bengal, are closely connected with this
personal exploration of central and western China. The border
countries are identifiable in spite of, or perhaps because of, the
Persian, archaic, and popular names whereby they are designated
in his book. By ingeniously fusing into one single account his
mention of places he then actually visited, information he had
gathered from other persons, and his recollections of his own
previous excursions, he makes us hear in the language he uses
an echo of the report he made to his sovereign on these indomitable peoples, and we make out a reflection of the notes he took in
the course of his long and difficult journey.[50]

---

[48] Penzer, as cited in the first note to this section, Introd., with notes and maps.

[49] For a rapid outline of the events that led to the unification of China under the
scepter of Chinghiz cf. Grousset, *L'Empire des steppes,* pp. 352 ff.; and for a more
fully documented treatment, O. Franke, *Geschichte des chinesischen Reiches,* Vol. IV,
Berlin, 1948, esp. pp. 424 ff., with notes in Vol. V, 1952.

[50] For Marco's mission cf. *Il Milione,* cr. ed., p. 10, chaps. xvi and xvii; M.P., pp.
86 ff. So far as the notes that Marco may have taken are concerned, it can be supposed that the report of his first journey as informant to Kublai may have been
compiled in writing by some court official, like the report immediately preceding

This is even more obvious in the second itinerary, which forms, as it were, the axis of his topo-geographical reminiscences of eastern China, which he undoubtedly visited on various occasions and under differing circumstances. This immense stretch of territory south of the Yellow River extends from its banks to the regions of the ancient empire of the Sung dynasty (960–1278), as far as the southern ports of Foochow and Zaiton (Chüanchow) in the modern province of Fukien, reached by the Grand Canal, which was completed by Kublai.[51] Marco describes it with its succession of provinces, towns, and villages as formerly a part of the ancient empire designated by him with the name "Mangi," which had recently been conquered by the Mongols from Cathay and annexed after the capitulation of the reigning dynasty.[52]

This itinerary, reconstructed by Colonel Yule in a series of maps and topographical sketches, represents a synthesis of Marco's experiences along a route that corresponds to the busiest and most important line of communication between the two great regions of the new Chinese empire, then reduced to a khanate of the Chinghizide empire. In 1292, with his older companions, Marco set sail for Venice from its southern port of Zaiton, accompanying Princess "Cocachin" and the daughter of the King of "Mangi," who were destined for the harem of Arghun Khan, the lord of the Tartars of the Levant.[53] In his description of in-

---

Marco's, which was that of the Chinese general Ch'ang Te written down by Liu Yu for the same Kublai,—a report which had dealt with a mission of exploration to Persia in 1259 by Mangu, Kublai's brother. Cf. E. Bretschneider, *Mediaeval Researches from Eastern Asiatic Sources,* 2 vols., London, 1910 (reprint), Vol. I, pp. 112 ff. It must, however, be noted that no trace has been left of Marco's notes except for the mention of them made by G. B. Ramusio, who refers explicitly to his memoirs (cf. cr. ed., p. 144 n.). For this see Benedetto's Introd. to the cr. ed., p. xxvi.

[51] The description of this "great province" of Mangi, corresponding to the last national Chinese empire of the Sung, is found in the *Milione,* cr. ed., pp. 134–160; M.P., pp. 309–354.

[52] The name Mangi gives an approximate rendering of the Chinese *Man-tzŭ,* a term of contempt, which was used to designate the southern peoples of the empire. Cf. O. Franke, *op. cit.,* Vol. IV, p. 475. The surrender took place in 1276, soon after Marco's arrival in China, but the resistance put up by several groups continued for some years afterward.

[53] *Il Milione,* cr. ed., p. 12; M.P., p. 88. The name Cocachin is made up of *köke* (in other Altaic dialects *kök* = 'heaven') and the suffix *jin,* so that it means 'sky-like,' referring both to the color (sky blue) and to the epithet 'celestial.' For the suffix (-*čin*) cf. N. Poppe, *Grammar of Written Mongolian,* Wiesbaden, 1954, §§ 120 and 125.

sular and tropical Asia in this section of the book, which is so
rich in adventure, the background changes from landscape to
seascape, while the descriptive and narrative process adheres
faithfully to the method previously followed.

Indeed, this section opens with the famous, fanciful evocation of Cipango, or Japan, which Marco never visited, but which
was a favorite topic of conversation with the Tartars, who were
intent on conquering the land and admiring its wonders, in the
sense described by our author.[54] Thus, too, he goes on to enumer-
ate the islands in the China Sea, so "out of the way," as he tells
us, that he never visited them and the power of the Great Kaan,
his lord, never held sway there.[55] His personal recollections, on
the other hand, begin with his description of Indochina; more
precisely, with the kingdom of "Cianba" (Champa), which corresponds in part to present-day Viet Nam, visited by Marco in
1285.[56] His stay on the island of Java, however, which is next
recorded, is more than doubtful, even as his reminiscences of
other islands, which he calls Sondur, Condur, and Malaiur, cannot correspond to a real and actual itinerary since they are too
vague and geographically incongruous to be the result of a direct
acquaintance with these well-nigh inaccessible regions.[57]

Nevertheless, with these, and the other islands mentioned
thereafter, we find ourselves somewhere between Malaya and Indonesia; that is to say, in the region of the Strait of Singapore,
on the course which the Polos must have followed, sailing from
Zaiton to Sumatra, without necessarily touching land at the
various points mentioned in the *Milione*. These would therefore
constitute the various stages of a voyage of exploration from
the China Sea to the Indian Ocean. The insoluble doubts concerning the various centers mentioned at this point arise not only
from the usual arbitrary and fragmentary measurement of time
and space but also from the toponymy learned from peoples

---

[54] *Il Milione*, cr. ed., pp. 162–166; M.P., p. 357. Cf. K. Enoki, "Marco Polo and
Japan," in *Oriente Poliano*, pp. 23 ff.

[55] *Il Milione*, cr. ed., p. 167; M.P., p. 366.

[56] *Il Milione*, cr. ed., pp. 167 f.; M.P., pp. 366 f.

[57] For a discussion of the itinerary and the hypothetical identification of these localities in Indochina, Malaya, and Indonesia cf. Penzer, *op. cit.*, Introd. For more
details cf. P. Pelliot, "Deux itinéraires de Chine en Inde," *Bulletin de l'École Française d'Extrême-Orient*, Vol. IV (1904).

who spoke different languages, then altered in the hybrid phonetics which were characteristic of foreigners in the East, and finally reproduced in the jargon certainly spoken by Marco, which later produced the ambiguous Franco-Italian style of his book. The Polos and their company of princesses and others, amounting to some six hundred persons in all, without including the sailors, had a store of food for two years, and were equipped with fourteen four-masted ships, some with as many as twelve sails. The vessels were large enough to remain at sea for long periods without touching land; hence it is quite possible that the localities vaguely described on this route were mentioned according to information received on board.

On the other hand, it is certain that the whole squadron halted for five months on the northern coast of Sumatra, giving Marco an opportunity, while remaining in a somewhat restricted sphere of personal observation, to gather strange, precise information about the regions at the western limits of the large island.[58] After this, it is possible to reconstruct the course they followed on their departure from this locality, coasting along the Nicobar Islands and leaving the Andaman Islands well to the north, touching first at the island of Ceylon, certainly visited in part by Marco, and then at places along the Indian coast as far as the mouth of the Persian Gulf and the port of Hormuz, where he landed with the few travelers still alive at this stage of the journey.[59]

In his varied and fascinating description of India and its customs his recollections of this long sea voyage are presumably fused with those of other visits, of which, however, we find no explicit confirmation in his book.[60] Hence, this vast section deal-

[58] In this large island Marco distinguished various kingdoms, all of them situated in the eastern section: namely, from east to west, the kingdoms of Ferlec, Basman, Samatra, Dagroian, and Lambri, all nominal feudatories to the Great Kaan, but safe from armed invasion on his part. Moreover, Marco mentions the kingdom of Fansur, famous for its camphor, situated on the southern shore of the island; but he does not seem to have visited it.

[59] Ceylon is described by Marco on two occasions (cr. ed., pp. 176 f. and 192 f.; M.P., pp. 379 f. and 407 f.). Of the six hundred persons who set out with the Polos to accompany the two princesses, only eighteen arrived at Hormuz (cr. ed., p. 12; M.P., p. 90).

[60] Marco, in the *Milione* (cr. ed., p. 11; M.P., p. 89), clearly refers to a sojourn in India antecedent to this voyage, adding that he returned to the court of Kublai

ing with the various "kingdoms" of Greater India loses its geographical interest as an itinerary—a prevalent interest hitherto—
and becomes a systematic description of peoples and customs,
religions and civilizations, riches and wonders, treasures and extravaganzas, in a succession of accounts which are at times credible, at others fictitious, and which are always more or less obviously inspired by the traditional conception of India as a land
of limitless wealth and wonders.[61]

During this voyage Marco was able to consult the charts, which
he calls "mapemondi," that were used by sailors in the course
of their difficult navigation among so many lands and islands
washed by the Indian Ocean.[62] Apart from these he was able

"by way of unknown seas," immediately before his departure for Venice; hence we
may assign this voyage to India to somewhere near the year 1290, without, however,
establishing its itinerary, duration, or purpose. Any speculation about the matter is
therefore superfluous; but it is permissible to suppose that, since Marco told the
imperial court "many tales about those lands," he had journeyed there in his capacity
as informant to the sovereign—as he did on previous occasions—and then, in his
book, fused the reminiscences of this stay with those of his voyage to the Persian
Gulf and homeward. Hence it is impossible to distinguish in his extensive description
of India the information gained from other visits to this land from that which he
gathered in ports of call while on his homeward journey. At most, we can believe
that the extensive description of the "great province of Maabar" (cr. ed., pp. 177 ff.;
M.P., pp. 389 ff.), especially offered by the Ramusian version and codex Z, makes use of
material gathered in the course of a mission rather than indirectly on his return
voyage. Nevertheless, it is difficult to trace the limits of the "great province," which
is commonly identified with the Coromandel Coast but which stretched much farther
northward, if Marco includes in it not only the region of Madras with its supposed
tomb of St. Thomas the Apostle but also, as he says (*loc. cit.*), "Greater India," that
is to say, "the best of all the Indies," of which he gives one of the most varied and
extensive accounts in the whole book. For the geographical concept of India in the
Milione cf. the cr. ed., p. 209, where Maabar as far as Kesmacoran (present-day
Mekran) is called Greater India, while Lesser India includes Indochina as far as
"Mutfili," and Middle India corresponds to Ethiopia ("Abasce") and adjoining regions (M.P., pp. 434 f.), the European confusion of India and Ethiopia being as old
as Virgil and, later, Servius (cf. Yule-Cordier, *The Book of Ser Marco Polo*, Vol. II,
pp. 431 f.).

[61] Such it appears, not only in classical tradition, but also in medieval geographical
literature and the various texts of the legend of Alexander the Great, in *L'Image du
Monde* by Gossouin de Metz, and in Brunetto Latini's *Trésor*, for which see Ch. V.
Langlois, *La Vie en France au moyen âge*, Vol. III: *La Connaissance de la Nature et
du Monde d'après les Écrits français à l'usage des laïcs*, Paris, 1927, pp. 167 ff., 361 ff.
Cf. K. A. Nilakanta Sastri, "Marco Polo in India," in *Oriente Poliano*, pp. 111 ff.; but
the subject deserves a more ample and correct elucidation. In Marco's times, navigation in that part of the world by Chinese ships was worked out with the help of
the stars, the sun, and the magnetic needle; cf. Jitzusô Kuwabara, "On P'u Shou-kêng,"
Memoirs of the Research Department of the Tōyō Bunko, ser. B, No. 2, 1928, pp. 67 ff.
(from Chinese sources).

[62] *Il Milione*, cr. ed., p. 176, chap. clxxiv (where we find mention of "la ma-

to find his bearings by following the course of the stars; it is thus that he gives us the only astronomical data contained in his book.[63] Whereas the charts, undoubtedly of Arabic origin, enabled him to estimate the size of Ceylon and the approximate number of the Maldive Islands, his celestial observations, although quite rudimentary, helped him—the first among Westerners—to undergo and to report an experience important for the cosmography of his times.

In the course of his lengthy stay on the island of Sumatra he did in fact observe "a wonderful thing: namely, that this island is situated so far south of the North Star that this is never seen there at all." [64] The stars which he calls "Meistre," meaning by this the Great Bear, likewise remained hidden from his gaze during all this period. [65] He caught sight of them again, with obvious joy, just off the southern tip of the Indian peninsula while following a course some thirty miles north of Cape Comorin.[66]

---

pemondi des mariner" of the Indian Ocean), and p. 209 (mention of "le conpas et la scriture de sajes mariner" of the same ocean); M.P., pp. 379, 434. These are obviously track charts and navigation manuals used by Arab and Persian sailors for this route. Cf. G. Ferrand, *Introduction à l'astronomie nautique arabe*, Paris, 1928, and L. Bagrow, *Die Geschichte der Kartographie*, Berlin, 1951. In the "Dichiarazione" which precedes his edition of Marco Polo's book, Ramusio (*Navigationi & Viaggi*, Vol. II, p. 17) mentions a "map and marine chart preserved at San Michele di Murano, which had been brought back from Cathay by Marco Polo and on which he added and marked down the towns and places he had come upon." But no trace has remained of this map or "marine chart." The maps attributed to Polo's hand have turned out to be more or less clever forgeries. For medieval cartography connected with Marco's discoveries cf. Tullia Gasparrini Leporace, ed., *Mostra: L'Asia nella cartografia degli occidentali*, Venice, 1954 (with bibliography, thirty-one plates, and an introduction by R. Almagià); also the remarks of the same scholars accompanying *Il Mappamondo di Fra Mauro*, ed. T. Gasparrini Leporace, Rome, 1956.

[63] Cf. the present author's "Dante Alighieri, Marco Polo e la cosmografia medievale," in *Oriente Poliano*, pp. 45 ff.

[64] *Il Milione*, cr. ed., p. 171; M.P., p. 371.

[65] *Il Milione*, cr. ed., p. 172; M.P., p. 372. This observation of Marco's is incorrect, since the stars of the Bear are still visible in the region where he asserts that they never appear, namely, at approximately 5° N. lat. But their position on the horizon and the unusual prospect made Marco sight them without recognizing them. The same thing happened two centuries later to Christopher Columbus, a far more expert navigator, who in the equatorial seas lost sight of the Pole Star and the northern constellations. This led him to invent a new and utterly fantastic cosmography (for which see Cesare de Lollis, *Cristoforo Colombo nella leggenda e nella storia*, third edition, Rome, 1923, chap. xxviii, and Samuel Eliot Morison, *Admiral of the Ocean Sea*, Boston, 1942, Vol. II, chap. xli).

[66] *Il Milione*, cr. ed., p. 198, chap. clxxxii; M. P., p. 416.

Thereafter, the North Star—which he calls "Tramontane," according to the custom of his times—measures the great stages of his return home. First of all, at a latitude of about 15 degrees north of the equator, he estimates its height as being approximately a cubit above the surface of the Indian Ocean. Then, he sees it grow brighter and brighter, and informs his readers that they would see it gain in altitude as they proceeded toward the west.[67] With his gaze fixed on this star, he did not bother to describe the southern constellations in his book. But he did reveal some information about them to Petrus de Abano, the famous physician and astrologer from the University of Padua, in the memorable conversations that took place between the two before 1303, the year in which the latter's famous *Conciliator* was published, where we find recorded Marco's celestial observations not mentioned in the *Milione*.[68]

He told the great Paduan scholar that "in regionibus Zingorum," which are difficult to identify but are certainly situated in the tropics, a great "star" was to be seen beyond the equator. This, according to the meaning of the term at this period, was a constellation, which was "like a sack" in appearance and with a tail "shaped in this way"—and here Marco drew the shape for his listener, perhaps the same shape as appears in ancient editions of the *Conciliator* and is reproduced here.[69] He told him,

---

[67] *Ibid.*, p. 200 (at the height of "Gozurat" in India, he measures six cubits, *goves*), and p. 201, chap. clxxxvii; M.P., pp. 419 ff. For the term *goves* cf. the article mentioned above in note 63.

[68] Cf. the text reproduced by Benedetto in the Introd. to his cr. ed., pp. ccxii–ccxiii and our first illustration.

[69] A study of the manuscripts of the *Conciliator* (recorded in part by Lynn Thorndike, *A History of Magic and Experimental Science*, Vol. II, New York, 1923, pp. 919 f.) could help to establish whether the design that adorns various XVIth-century editions of the treatise can be said to proceed from Marco's original sketch. As for the term "regiones Zingorum," it is possible that it refers to the lands of the "Zandjs" or "Zindjs," a Persian name whereby the Arab geographers of the Middle Ages designate the eastern coast of Africa (Zanzibar), sometimes in connection with Malaya and Indonesia; as, in particular, Idrisi in 1154 (cf. G. Ferrand, *Relations de Voyages et textes géographiques arabes, persans et turcs relatifs à l'Extrême-Orient*, 2 vols., Paris, 1913–1914, Vol. I, p. 193), and Yakut in 1224 (*ibid.*, pp. 205 f.), thereby emphasizing the frequent maritime, ethnic, and commercial relations between the two opposite regions of the Indian Ocean, considered as a single geographical unit. In fact, according to some old Arabic geographers, as for instance Idrisi, the southernmost African coast joined somewhere with India (cf. L. M. Devic, *Les Merveilles de l'Inde*, Paris, 1878, p. 178 and p. 172 n. 23). The Persian, Buzurg ibn Shariyār (Xth century), always uses the term *Zindjs* instead of *Zandjs* (*ibid.*, pp. 12, 31, 32, and *passim*). In a medieval

ioz circuitoz z diligens indagatoz:qᵖ eandem vidit stellam
sub polo antarctico:z ē magnā babens caudaz:cuius pin,
ᵵit talem foze figur am.
℄ Retulit ēt qᵖ vidit po
lū antarcticū a terra ele
uatū qᷓtitate lācee mili,
tis lóge in apparentia z
arcticū occultatū. Jnde
etiā nobis cāpbozam:lí
gnū aloes z verᵵi expoz
tari nūtiauit. Testat il,
lic calozé intésuᵳ z babí
tationes paucas.Iᵬ qdeᵳ
vidit in quadā isula ad
quā p mare adiuit. Dic

etiaᵳ illic boies foze z arietes qᷓmagnos valde babētes la,
nas grossas z ouras vt sete sūt pozcoᵱ nᵳozuᵳ.Et qᵖ ad bᵍ

FIG. I. *Part of a page from the Venetian edition, 1521, of the* Conciliator
differentiarum philosophorum precipueque medicorum, *1303, of Petrus
de Abano. The passage reproduced says that Marco "saw beneath the southern pole [of the heavens] a great star with a tail, of which he drew the
shape as thus [i.e., as shown on the same page with the text]. He also told
me that he saw the southern pole seemingly at an altitude above the earth
equal to the length of a soldier's long spear, and that the northern pole
was hidden. He said, moreover, that camphor, lignum aloes, and brazil
[wood] are exported thence to us. He affirms that the heat there is intense,
and the dwellings few. These things he saw on a certain island at which
he arrived by sea. He also says that there are men there, and some very
large rams that have coarse and stiff wool just like the bristles of a pig."*

moreover, that he had seen the "southern pole" (of the heavens) at a height apparently equal to the length of a "soldier's long spear," a term that is hardly appropriate to astronomical measurements and is an example of the purely empirical way in which our traveler observed the sights of nature. It is obvious that although he was able to make use of navigational charts he was unacquainted with the celestial spheres of Arabian design which were then well known in Italy and Asia, and on which the guiding constellations were marked with greater or lesser precision and described in terms then current in nautical treatises used in those regions.[70]

These celestial observations of Marco's deserve to be reëxamined, even if his strange terminology and astrognostic errors hardly seem to encourage the undertaking. Certainly the Persian or Chinese sailors who piloted the imperial ships through those waters were far more expert than he, and they would not have lost sight of the northern constellations while sailing along or near the equator, as Marco did. However, it should be noted that the astronomical information mentioned both in the *Milione* and by Petrus de Abano is the first to be offered by a Western observer, and that far more learned and expert navigators, like Christopher Columbus and Amerigo Vespucci, made no less serious mistakes, which are quite incomprehensible to us, while observing the same stars and using a terminology no less inadequate and ambiguous than that of our Venetian explorer.[71]

---

translation of Idrisi (cf. Ferrand, *Relations de Voyages,* Vol. I, p. 193) the expression "cum oris maritimis Zengitarum" corresponds with Marco Polo's "in regionibus Zingorum"; but since the Venetian never traveled along the African coast, his remarks about the southern heavens must refer to his stay in western Sumatra.

[70] For the medieval celestial globes of Arab origin and preserved in Italy cf. Edward Luther Stevenson, *Terrestrial and Celestial Globes,* 2 vols., Yale Univ. Press, 1921. Almost forty years before these conversations took place in Venice between Marco Polo and Petrus de Abano, Brunetto Latini had taught the laymen of his time (*ca.* 1260) that "the people of Europe navigate in those [equatorial] regions looking at the North Star, while others navigate looking at the South Star," using also the magnetic needle, which Marco never mentioned. Cf. *Li Livres dou Trésor,* critical edition by F. J. Carmody, Univ. of California Press, 1948, p. 107. Brunetto teaches also (*ibid.,* p. 114) that in the zones described by Marco "the stars are of no use," and mentions among the southern constellations Canopus, already known to ancient astronomers and described in the medieval treatises of Albumazar and Alfraganus. For Brunetto as an astronomer cf. H. Wieruszowski, "Brunetto Latini als Lehrer Dantes und der Florentiner," *Archivio Italiano per la Storia della Pietà,* Vol. II, 1958, pp. 171 ff.

[71] It now seems certain that the famous *Lettera a Lorenzo di Pierfrancesco de'*

In order to appreciate his understanding we need only mention that in the same year, 1293, in which he made these observations, the future first Bishop of Peking, Friar John of Montecorvino, noted that in southern India the star "which is called Tramontane is so near or low that it can hardly be seen," ingenuously adding that, if he had been in a higher position, he "would have been able to see the other Tramontane, which is placed in the opposite direction." [72] This brings into relief Marco's more coherent if not exactly correct observations.

Taken all in all, his geographical, topographical, and astrognostic information makes it possible for us to reconstruct in broad outline the comprehensive vision that he possessed of the structure of the world described by him in his book. Even in the variety and originality of his experiences it preserves the traditional picture of the great Euro-Afro-Asian continental mass, entirely surrounded by the Ocean Sea, in which appeared the more or less mysterious islands that begirt it.[73] We have no direct or indirect evidence to tell us whether he saw the earth as a globe or whether he imagined it to be flat, in the Chinese manner. But this "Oikoumene" of his extends from Zanzibar and Mada-

---

Medici of 1503, attributed to Vespucci and containing the most absurd astronomical errors, is spurious. Cf. also A. Magnaghi, "Per i presunti errori di Colombo," *Bollettino della R. Società Geografica Italiana*, sixth series, 1928–1933, Vol. V, pp. 459 ff., and Vol. VII, pp. 497 ff., and F. J. Pohl, *Amerigo Vespucci*, second edition, New York, 1945, pp. 147 ff.

[72] Epistola I in *Sinica Franciscana*, ed. A. van den Wyngaert, Quaracchi, 1929, p. 341. It should, however, be noted that the astronomical and climatic observations of the tropics recorded by Friar John are more extensive and systematic than Marco's. For example, he sees "the other Tramontane" as well as "several signs that encircled it," perhaps, indeed, the "exceedingly bright stars" of the Southern Cross, seen by Pigafetta when on his circumnavigation of the globe with Magellan between 1519 and 1521 (cf. Ramusio, *Navigationi & Viaggi*, Vol. I, p. 392 ᵛ). This constellation was described by Marco Polo to Petrus de Abano as having "lumen modicum," almost as though it were "a fragment of cloud," alluding thereby to what was later called "Magellan's cloud," which was already known to Arab astronomers and sailors. In his well-known compendium (cf. Vol. 87–90 of the series entitled "Collezione di opuscoli danteschi inediti o rari," Città di Castello, 1910, p. 139) Alfraganus uses the term "nebulous" when speaking of the austral constellations; namely, as "stellae parvae aggregatae similes nubibus," probably alluding to the same "cloud." Friar John also notes, *loc. cit.*, the "smokiness" that prevented him from seeing clearly these heavenly regions, then unknown to the "northern widowed clime," as Dante calls it (*Purgatorio*, Canto I).

[73] For these images that are reflected in medieval maps after having dominated ancient geography cf. John Kirtland Wright, *The Geographical Lore of the Time of the Crusades*, New York, 1925.

gascar, at its southern limit, to the Land of Darkness in the
north, of which the Ramusian version is perhaps the only one
to offer a correct and perhaps authentic explanation.[74]

In the extreme west, Marco hurriedly mentions the North
Sea (mer d'Angleterre) and the Bay of Biscay (mer de Rocelle)
whereas his Far East extends in an uninterrupted chain of numberless islands, both large and small, from Japan to Sumatra—
a resplendent, aromatic crown around the last continental stretch
of the earth.[75]

Within this geographical framework Marco delineates his
world, from icy Russia to torrid Ethiopia, from the Atlantic
Ocean to the China Sea, in its variety of climates, peoples, and
natural aspects, which will be set before us in systematic order
in the course of this book.

❖   ❖   ❖

The Oriental names of places and peoples appear in the present
volume mostly in the form in which they appear in the *Milione* or
in the medieval texts of the West, with here and there the addition
in parentheses of an approximate phonetic transcription of the

[74] Filled out, in its turn, by the more detailed description of Russia contained in the
Z version of the *Milione*. Cf. cr. ed., pp. 232 ff. The various versions of these chapters
are fused in the text of the English edition by Moule and Pelliot, Vol. I, pp. 472 ff.,
and in the Italian translation by Benedetto, *Il Libro di Messer Marco Polo*, pp. 405 ff.
Marco attributes the supposedly continuous darkness of the North Polar regions to
the fact that there the sun, moon, and stars do not appear. This is another obvious
error, which is, however, corrected in the Ramusian version, in which the darkness
of those northern regions is justly limited to the winter season, when indeed the
sun does not appear. It is difficult to establish which of the two opinions is to be
attributed to Marco, since either may be authentic. Indeed, Brunetto Latini, when
treating of the North Polar regions (*Li Livres dou Trésor*, ed. Carmody, p. 119),
probably follows Pliny when he notes that, whereas in the regions of Thule darkness
is a winter phenomenon, on the frozen seas beyond this point "il n'a nul devisement
ne conjungement de levee ne de couchee."

[75] Marco was the first Westerner to demonstrate by personal experience the habit-
ability of the Southern Hemisphere, which was generally denied by the scientific and
theological authorities of his times, although affirmed by Petrus de Abano in his
Conciliator (Differentia LXXII) on the basis of Marco's observations. Among the few
who at that time upheld the contrary opinion we find Albertus Magnus in his *Liber
Cosmographicus de Natura Locorum*, Part I ª, chaps. vi ff. and chap. xii; whereas
Alfraganus, *op. cit.*, esp. chaps. vi ff., insists on the distinction between the habitable
and uninhabitable zones of the earth, a notion which was also accepted by Dante in
his conception of the "unpeopled world" (*Inferno*, XXVI). For the concept of the
antipodes in popular cosmography of the Middle Ages cf. the work of Langlois cited
in note 61 above; also, Alexander H. Krappe, "Antipodes," *Modern Language Notes*,
Vol. LIX, 1944, pp. 441 ff.

original pronunciation; this permits us to do without the use of diacritical marks which are an obstacle to the reader who is not a specialist in Oriental languages, and which, as is attested by illustrious examples, may be foregone by orientalists in a work designed for a wider public. In the bibliographical notes preference is given to the most recent works, which themselves refer to the preceding literature that is still, in large part, valid; thus we avoid the inconvenience of loading down this work with bibliographical data which are of little use to the ordinary reader and which the student can easily collect to suit his own purposes.

There exists no up-to-date bibliography of Marco Polo. The works of bibliographical reference concerning medieval Asia are indicated in our notes. For works published prior to 1903 cf. Appendix H in Yule-Cordier, *The Book of Ser Marco Polo,* Vol. II, pp. 553 ff.; the list is extended to 1914 in H. Cordier's *Addenda,* pp. 137 ff. For brief information and bibliography on many topics mentioned in this book cf. Joseph Needham, *Science and Civilisation in China,* 3 vols., Cambridge, 1954–1959, plus three or more volumes to come.

The author apologizes for having treated the same argument at various places in the course of this work. He has done so because some aspects of Marco Polo's Asia lend themselves to consideration from several points of view which it is not always possible to gather together in a systematic treatment of diverse themes. Moreover, the author has wished to spare the reader annoying references to other parts of the book and has attempted to exhaust the treatment of the various subjects in the appropriate chapters, each one of which can be considered and read as an independent essay.

References to Marco Polo's text are made in accordance with Benedetto's critical edition and the Moule-Pelliot translation. The English translations by Yule (see note 8 above) and by Ricci (note 13), and William Marsden's *The Travels of Marco Polo* (Everyman's Library edition), are provided with copious indexes. The most recent English translation is that by Ronald Latham, *The Travels of Marco Polo,* London, 1958 (Penguin Classics).

two

MARCO POLO'S PRECURSORS

I. LITERARY PRECURSORS

Little was known in Europe about Asia until the XIIIth century, when missionaries and merchants made their way into the interior of the continent. At that time the scant information about the Orient was limited to what had been handed down in the treatises and accounts of late antiquity, which retained some vague ideas and many fables about the men and things to be found in those distant lands.[1] The wonders of India are a commonplace in classical texts. In the verses of Virgil and Claudian there lived the memory of the East, the mythical Seres, from which came the silk that was so precious, and about which Pliny, Ammianus Marcellinus, and other late Latin authors, repeated what Ptolemy had known about it before them.[2]

But all this sparse, indeterminate information preserved for centuries its erudite, literary character without being changed or renewed by any direct mercantile, military, maritime, political, or religious experience. The Byzantines had learned more about

The subject of this chapter has also been treated by the author in a little book now long out of print, *Marco Polo's Precursors*, Baltimore, Johns Hopkins Press, 1943.

[1] Texts and information on the subject have been collected by Henry Yule, *Cathay and the Way Thither*, second edition, revised by Henri Cordier, Vol. I, London, Hakluyt Society, 1915 (hereafter cited as Yule-Cordier, *Cathay*). Cf. also John Kirtland Wright, *The Geographical Lore of the Times of the Crusades*, New York, 1925, and the geographical anthology of R. Hennig, *Terrae Incognitae*, second edition, 4 vols., Leiden, 1944–1956. For vernacular literature cf. Ch. V. Langlois, *La Connaissance de la Nature et du Monde au moyen âge*, Paris, 1927. For geographical information see Sir R. Beazley's still fundamental work, *The Dawn of Modern Geography*, 3 vols., London, 1897–1906; also G. H. T. Kimble, *Geography in the Middle Ages*, London, 1938.

[2] Cf. George Coedès, *Textes d'auteurs grecs et latins relatifs à l'Extrême-Orient*, Paris, 1910. The name Seres for the Chinese (as also Sinae) was applied to the peoples of Central Asia as well; cf. Pliny, *Historia Naturalis*, Lib. VI, 88.

40

it, through their political and commercial contacts with the Persians and Turks of western Asia; and the account of China given by Theophylact Simocatta, a Greek chronicler of the VIIth century, the last Western author before Marco to describe the land and its customs, is famous.[3]

The Mohammedan expansion that followed soon afterward, with the conquest of the Middle East as far as the borders of India and Eastern Turkestan, placed a compact barrier between East and West, preventing the exchange of information and goods that would have allowed some reports—however vague and infrequent—about the various nations and civilizations to pass in both directions.[4] It is of course true that this same Mohammedan invasion of the first half of the VIIth century drove Nestorian missions and communities from Syria to China, where they settled in various centers of the empire;[5] but the result was an even more decisive separation between Asian and Western Christianity, and an increase in mutual ignorance, rather than common contacts and heightened curiosity.

The Crusades, which led large numbers from every quarter of Europe to the western edge of Asia, did not change the situation. Their great chroniclers do not seem to have directed their geographical, ethnographical, or historical curiosity beyond the lands won back to Christianity; indeed for the intelligent and learned Fulcher of Chartres, a historian of the First Crusade, the world of the fabulous wonders of Asia begins immediately after those fragments of the Holy Land and the Levant that had been liberated by the Christian armies, and he gives not one single hint of even the most superficial experience of the lands and peoples of the Middle East.[6]

[3] Yule-Cordier, *Cathay,* Vol. I, pp. 29 ff., reproduce the entire passage from the chronicle concerning eastern Asia; likewise, H. W. Haussig, "Theophylaktus' Excurs," with doubtful interpretations, in *Byzantion,* Vol. XXIII, 1953–54, pp. 280 ff., and G. Coedès, *op. cit.,* pp. 138 ff. Cf., too, P. A. Boodberg, "Marginalia to the History of the Northern Dynasties," *Harvard Journal of Asiatic Studies,* Vol. III, 1938, pp. 223 ff.; and, for bibliographical data, G. Moravczik, *Byzantino-Turcica,* second edition, Berlin, 1958, Vol. I, at this article.

[4] Cf. for all this subject B. Spuler, *Iran in früh-islamischer Zeit,* Wiesbaden, 1952, pp. 400 ff. (with full bibliography).

[5] Cf. A. C. Moule, *Christians in China,* London, 1930, and P. Y. Saeki, *The Nestorian Documents and Relics in China,* second edition, Tokyo, 1951.

[6] Cf. *Historia Hierosolymitana, ed.* Hagenmeyer, Heidelberg, 1913, especially Bk. III, chaps. 49, 59, and 60.

This indifference toward all aspects of exotic nature and life, at this time and for a long time to come, embraced the whole of the Mohammedan world, from the Atlantic to the China Sea, of whose peoples, customs, and ideas the Christian community remained ignorant almost throughout the Middle Ages.[7] The scanty data offered by the numerous itineraries of the Holy Land reveal the limits of the geographical curiosity of the medieval mind, which never extended beyond the Biblical and hagiographical interest of the travelers or beyond the regions visited by them.[8]

The exchange of goods between East and West contributed very little to the expansion of these geographical horizons, restricted by both experience and tradition. Textiles, gems, pearls, and spices were for centuries imported into Europe, but little was known about their lands or origin. Indeed, these limited commercial relations remained indirect, until Marco Polo's time, without there ever having remained any record of a personal exchange of goods between the two great areas of production and consumption into which the Euro-Asian world was then divided: the one, dominated by a Mohammedan monopoly of commerce, extending from Alexandria in Egypt to the China Sea, from the banks of the Volga to the northern boundaries of India; the other, Mediterranean and Christian, increasingly activated by the competition in arms and commerce that existed between the Italian maritime republics.

These two areas into which the Old World was divided during the Middle Ages were so tenaciously separated and autonomous that nothing seems to have been known in the West about the great Asian experiences of the Mohammedan peoples. Their flourishing medieval geographical literature, which had begun in the IXth century in Mesopotamia and Persia and had extended to Sicily and Spain in an uninterrupted succession of scientific and popular treatises, dealt with all the lands and areas then known to them and included works of lasting historical and

[7] Cf. Ugo Monneret de Villard, *Lo studio dell'Islām in Europa nel XII e nel XIII secolo*, Città del Vaticano, 1944 (Studi e Testi, no. 110).

[8] Cf. the texts indicated by G. Golubovich in *Biblioteca bio-bibliografica della Terrasanta e dell'Oriente Francescano*, 5 vols., Quaracchi, 1906–1927; also H. Michelant and G. Raynaud, *Itinéraires à Jérusalem et descriptions de la Terre Sainte rédigés en français au XIᵉ, XIIᵉ et XIIIᵉ siècle*, Geneva, 1882.

practical value.[9] It would be fruitless to search for a reflection of this in Western literature, which had, however, from the XIIth century onward, gathered much scientific and philosophical knowledge from the translators at Toledo and Palermo.[10]

Geography evidently did not form part of the interests of those centuries, in which other fields of human knowledge and activity, for example medicine and astrology, were preëminent in the intellectual activity of the West. Hence, all that existed beyond the limits of the Christian world entered the kingdom of fancy; even the goods that came from these inaccessible lands were from regions beyond belief. It would therefore be a mistake to think that the exchange of commercial goods also implied an exchange of culture and ideas. Thus, whereas Arab geographical treatises abound in information, both true and false, about India, Central Asia, and the Far East, the whole of medieval didactic literature, until halfway through the XIIIth century, does not offer any empirical contribution to the mass of traditional, erudite, and literary information in which it abounded.

Brunetto Latini's *Trésor* affords ample proof. This work was compiled about the year 1260, at the time when Niccolò and Maffeo Polo, Marco's father and uncle, began their first transcontinental journey, which was to lead them from the Venetian emporium at Soldaia (modern Sudak) in the Crimea to the court of the Great Kaan Kublai on the borders of Cathay.[11] When he treats of that distant land's inhabitants and its best-known product, silk, Ser Brunetto repeats what Pliny and other ancient writers, who were unaware of the nature and origin of this precious cloth, have to say about it. In fact, we read in this famous

[9] Collected and edited by M. J. de Goeje, *Bibliotheca Geographorum Arabicorum*, 8 vols., Leiden, 1870–1939. The most important Arabic geographical works have been translated into various languages. For our subject cf. especially G. Ferrand, *Relations de Voyages et textes géographiques arabes, persans et turcs relatifs à l'Extrême-Orient*, 2 vols., Paris, 1913–1914, and V. Minorsky, *Ḥudūd al-'Ālam*, London, 1937 "Gibb Memorial" series, n.s., XI), translation and commentary, with appendices. For bibliography of travelers, especially in English-language editions, although incomplete, cf. Edward G. Cox, *A Reference Guide to the Literature of Travel*, 3 vols., Univ. of Washington, 1935–1949.

[10] For the influence of Arab geographers on Western cosmographical concepts cf. Beazley, *op. cit.*, Vol. II, pp. 465 ff.

[11] Still fundamental for the sources of the *Trésor*: S. Sundby, *Vita e scritti di Brunetto Latini*, Italian translation by R. Renier, Florence, 1884, and Paget Toynbee, "Brunetto Latini's Obligations to Solinus," *Romania*, Vol. XXIII, 1894, pp. 62 ff.

work that "beyond all inhabited places we find men called Scir,
or Seres, who by a water process make a woolen cloth from the
leaves and barks of trees, wherewith they clothe their bodies.
And they are mild and peaceful with one another, and they
refuse the company of others. Our merchants, however, cross one
of their rivers, and find on the banks of this river all manner of
goods that can be found there; and, without any parleying, they
look at one another, and with their eyes give the price of each
thing. And, when they have seen it, they take away what they
want of it and leave payment for it in that same spot. In this way
do they sell their merchandise; nor will they have anything to
do with ours." [12]

Thus wrote Brunetto at a time when the silkworm had already
been introduced in the West for some centuries past, and silken
cloths were made up in the Levant, in Sicily, the Aegean Islands,
and Spain, a country visited by him. The Italian silk-goods trade
had already become concentrated in the north, especially at
Lucca, Venice, and in Lombardy. No other document expresses
more eloquently the contrast that still existed between popular,
didactic information and practical life. Nor would it be possible to find a clearer expression of the mystery which then surrounded the origin of the most valuable Oriental merchandise,
although this trade extended uninterruptedly from one end of
the Old World to the other.

The ancient fable of silent merchants symbolizes a truth not
generally recognized, namely, that an exchange of goods does not
necessarily imply an exchange of culture. The tradesmen of
Imperial Rome imported from the Far East silken cloths that
were worth their weight in gold, but they had no exact idea
either of their origin or of the methods of production. Hence-
forth, and throughout the Middle Ages, it was possible, as in
the text quoted, to describe silk as a vegetable product taken from
trees and then processed like flax or hemp.[13] Evidently, until

[12] The story is reported by Pomponius Mela, Pliny, and Ammianus Marcellinus
(cf. Coedès, *op. cit.,* pp. 11, 16, 97). For other forms of mute trade in the East cf.
Ferrand, *op. cit.,* Vol. I, pp. 146 and 166; Vol. II, pp. 304 and 423. The Chinese
knew the same story of dumb trading, attributed to several peoples, and called it
kuei[3] *shih*[4] or 'ghostly market' (better than 'Devil's or Spirit market,' the translation
given by Hirth and Rockhill in *Chau Ju-kua: His Work on the Chinese and Arab
Trade in the XIIth and XIIIth Centuries,* St. Petersburg, 1911, p. 104 and n. 15).

[13] This was, in fact, the so-called vegetable silk, which was confused with the

Marco Polo's times the commercial activity between the various regions of the earth was not accompanied by a comparable desire to know their peoples and products, apart from what was to be found in the most authoritative sources of ancient knowledge and experience—which was little enough.

In fact, it may be supposed that it was the Western merchants themselves who kept alive the fables about the distant lands from which their goods originated, thus surrounding their offerings with an air of mystery that made them still more precious and desirable; so much so, that pearls, spices, and precious stones, apart from their intrinsic worth, had not only the quality of rarity, but seemed also to possess the therapeutic and magical qualities attributed to them by Latin and vernacular texts of venerable tradition and renewed by the authority of famous contemporary authors.[14] These treatises represent the stationary basis of medieval culture, both learned and popular, in which we still find information and doctrines that date from the Hellenistic period and which no direct experience of Oriental life had ever succeeded in altering. The fact is that all this didactic literature, which comes down from Pliny, Solinus, Pomponius Mela, Isidore of Seville, and their Greek and Asian sources, did not offer to medieval culture one single statement that corresponded to the reality of Oriental life and its geo-ethnographic environment.

In the same way, these Mediterranean shores marked, at that time and for some centuries to come, the western limits of the experiences of peoples at the other end of the earth. For the Chinese and their noteworthy geographical literature the world of fables began on the borders of the Christian world, of which, in spite of the Nestorian colonies which flourished at various times in their territory, there is no definite trace in any of their books. For these Orientals the West is a mythical or eschatological world, beyond the confines of human experience and the range of common curiosity, which, as in Europe, was satisfied with fables

---

variety produced from worms, introduced into Europe in the VIth century, according to the anecdote related by Procopius (*De Bello Gothico*, IV, 17), but unknown in the West during the Middle Ages. Cf. R. S. Lopez, "Silk Industry in the Byzantine Empire," *Speculum*, Vol. XX, 1945, pp. 1 ff., and R. Hennig, *Terrae Incognitae*, second edition, Vol. II, pp. 56 ff.

[14] For these authors and their sources see Lynn Thorndike, *A History of Magic and Experimental Science*, Vol. II, New York, 1923.

as far as these distant regions were concerned. The peoples of
the Far East were also unable to penetrate the Mohammedan
continental barrier, in spite of the fact that trade and contacts by
land and sea formed a part of normal medieval Asian life.[15]

Hence, before missionaries and merchants assumed the twofold
function of informants to both the West and the East, that is to
say, before the middle of the XIIIth century, when the making
of an Asiatic empire that extended from Korea to Poland broke
the cultural supremacy and commercial monopoly of the Mohammedans, the little that remained of reciprocal intellectual curiosity
was kept alive mainly by fables that were consecrated by literary
tradition and clichés and by age-old habits of thought and teaching. Thus, all that was commonly known in Europe about the
lands of Islam and the pagans living beyond the narrow limits
of geographical experience was for the most part taken from the
exploits of Alexander the Great, which from the XIth century
onward dominated in various poetic and fictional forms the
Western accounts of the Orient.[16]

The legend of the Macedonian, relating his conquest of Asia
and describing its wonders, did in fact throughout the Middle
Ages enjoy an ecumenical diffusion greater than that of any
other literary or artistic subject of universal import.[17] Consecrated

[15] For this subject cf. the authoritative *Histoire du commerce du Levant au moyen
âge* of W. von Heyd (French translation by Raynaud), 2 vols., Leipzig, 1885 (reprinted in 1923); and, for the Mediterranean world, A. Schaube, *Handelsgeschichte
der romanischen Völker*, Munich and Berlin, 1906, and a selection of published and
unpublished documents translated into English, with bibliography, by R. S. Lopez
and I. W. Raymond, *Medieval Trade in the Mediterranean World*, Columbia Univ.
Press, 1955. For Venetian trade cf. R. Morozzo della Rocca and A. Lombardo, *Documenti del commercio veneziano nei secoli XI–XIII*, 2 vols., Turin, 1940; cf. also R. S.
Lopez, "Venezia e le grandi linee dell'espansione commerciale nel secolo XIII," in
La civiltà veneziana del secolo di Marco Polo (commemorative volume of the Fondazione
Giorgio Cini, of Venice), Florence, Sansoni, 1955. For Chinese trade in the Middle
Ages cf. Chau Ju-kua, *ed. cit.* in n. 12 above. (The author's name is generally spelled
Chao, but is listed in library catalogues as it appears on the title page of the edition
used here. For the sake of consistency the form Chau has been adopted in the present
volume.)

[16] Paul Meyer, *Alexandre le Grand dans la littérature française du moyen âge*, 2 vols.,
Paris, 1886; J. Storost, *Studien zur Alexandersage in der alten italienischen Literatur*,
Halle a. S., 1935; Emilio García Gómez, *Un texte árabe occidental de la leyenda de
Alejandro*, Madrid, 1929. Cf. also a comprehensive work on the subject, with full
bibliography, by George Cary, *The Medieval Alexander*, Cambridge, 1956.

[17] For this subject the most recent work—rhapsodic in parts—is that by Franz
Altheim, *Alexander und Asien*, Tübingen, 1953. A more sober exposition of facts

by the Biblical record of his actions [18] and by allusions found in the Koran,[19] it attained a vast measure of popularity in the Christian and Mohammedan world, while it was kept alive for many centuries in the regions of Asia conquered by him, and its echoes reached as far as Ethiopia and Indonesia, where it has survived down to our own times. Marco Polo had only to look up at the image of Alexander, held aloft by gryphons, which was to be seen on the northern façade of the basilica of St. Mark in Venice, for the various other fables of this cycle—a favorite with the minstrels—to come to his mind, as to any other of his contemporaries; for example, "the wonders of the desert," the fountain of youth, the Arbre Sec (also called Arbre Seul, or Sol), the legendary palaces of Persia and India, the stories of Brahmans and Gymnosophists, of strange and monstrous peoples at the ends of the earth, magic forests and fantastic animals—all the extraordinary aspects of that distant world which figured in the adventures of the great conqueror, and which Marco was later to recall and portray with greater or less precision in his descriptions of the lands of the East.[20]

---

and problems is offered by F. Hampl, "Alexander der Grosse," *La Nouvelle Clio,* Vol. VI, 1954, pp. 91 ff. For the historical background cf. W. W. Tarn, *Alexander the Great,* 2 vols., Cambridge, 1951. For the diffusion of the legend in the East cf. E. A. Wallis Budge, *The Alexander Book in Ethiopia,* London, 1933; P. Y. Leeuwen, *Maleische Alexanderroman,* Utrecht, 1937; also the short survey by F. Pfister, *Alexander der Grosse in den Offenbarungen der Griechen, Juden, Mohammedaner und Christen,* Berlin, Akademie Verlag, 1956. For the diffusion of the saga of Alexander the Great in Persia cf. Edward G. Browne, *A Literary History of Persia,* 4 vols., 1902–1928, esp. Vols. I and II. Since Marco Polo drew most of his information on Alexander from oral sources in Persia, it is important to know that the Pahlavi version of the romance has been handed down only in a Syrian translation (cf. C. Hunnius, "Das syrische Alexanderlied," *Zeitschrift der deutschen morgenländischen Gesellschaft,* Vol. LX, pp. 169 ff., and K. Czeglédy, "The Syriac Legend concerning Alexander the Great," *Acta Orientalia* [Budapest], Vol. VII, 1957, pp. 231 ff.), and that the various episodes are inserted into Persian chronicles and poems of different periods, particularly the famous *Shāh Nāma* of Firdausi, the *Iskandar Nāma* of Nizami, and in other texts in prose and verse. For the diffusion of the Macedonian's legends in Mongolia in Marco's times cf. N. Poppe, "Eine mongolische Fassung der Alexandersage," *Zeitschrift der deutschen morgenländischen Gesellschaft,* Vol. CVII, 1957, pp. 105 ff.

[18] Lib. I Machabaeorum, Introd.

[19] Sura LXIX (under the name of Zulkarnain).

[20] As is known, all these fables go back in large part to the Hellenistic romance attributed to the Alexandrine Pseudo-Callisthenes of the IVth century A.D., which was renewed at Naples by the Archpriest Leo in the Xth century (ed. by F. Pfister, Heidelberg, 1913) and confirmed by the apocryphal *Letter of Aristotle on the Wonders of India,* widely known in the Middle Ages. For erudite teratology which is inde-

Indeed, while journeying through those regions he heard the Mohammedan inhabitants of continental and tropical Asia repeat the same wonders, drawn from the poetical history of Alexander the Great, and likewise associated with the exotic spells chanted by the bards or simple ministrels in Venetian palaces and squares. The Alexander saga extended to all the mysterious lands from which originated the spices, pearls, diamonds and other precious stones, with their suggestive power and secret medicinal or moral qualities which connected these rare and beautiful things with the traditional picture of Asia.

Such was Marco's cultural background until his father and uncle introduced him to quite different aspects of the land and life of Asia; so much so, that his *Milione,* while intended to be an empirical description of the world, made up of reminiscences of things seen or heard, refers more than once to Alexander's deeds, as also to popular writings about the wonders of the Orient, with its highly prized products, exotic peoples, and legendary teratology.[21] In fact, his book is not dedicated to scholars or professional men of science, but, as we read in the exordium, "to emperors and kings, dukes and marquises, counts, knights, and burgesses, and to all who desire to know the various generations of men and the diversity of regions in the world," as well as "the very great marvels" the author had seen with his own eyes; for, even if this presentation almost textually repeats a formula used on other occasions by Rustichello of Pisa, Marco's scribe in the prison at Genoa, the public to whom Rustichello had addressed

---

pendent of the romance of Alexander and which passed into medieval literature from Pliny and Solinus cf. the full study by R. Wittkower, "Marvels of the East," *Journal of the Warburg and Courtauld Institutes,* Vol. V, 1942, pp. 159–197, which treats exhaustively of its origins and fortunes, with a comprehensive bibliography and iconography of the subject. See also the recent article by the same author on "Marco Polo and the Pictorial Tradition of the Marvels of the East," in the volume *Oriente Poliano* published by the Istituto per il Medio Estremo Oriente, Rome, 1957, pp. 155 ff. For Chinese teratology supposed to be of Indian or Hellenistic origin cf. B. Laufer, "Ethnographische Sagen der Chinesen," in *Aufsätze zur Kultur- und Sprachgeschichte . . . Ernst Kuhn gewidmet,* Breslau, 1916, pp. 198–210, and Otto Maenchen-Helfen, "The Later Books of the Shan-hai-king," *Asia Major,* Vol. I, 1924, pp. 550–586.

[21] The poetical history of Alexander, linked to the scene in his Asiatic venture, is mentioned in chaps. xxiii, pp. 16 f.; xl, p. 32; xlv, p. 35; xlvii, p. 36; cciii, p. 222, of the cr. ed. by Luigi Foscolo Benedetto, Florence, 1928. (M.P., pp. 98, 128, 134, 136, 456.)

his chivalric romances was the same as the one whose attention our author wished to attract.[22] He thereby limited his audience to those who, for delight and instruction, read or listened to those same stories of Alexander the Great in Asia, and similar material contained in vernacular literature. This also explains the scant esteem in which his book was held, with few exceptions, by the learned of many centuries to come, while it inspired the adventures of the French romance *Baudouin de Sébourg,* or helped the cartographers to fill in with more substantial data the gaps in the traditional geography of the Eastern world.[23]

The author's intention to delight, instruct, and edify is obvious wherever in the book demonstrable actualities are associated with devout stories—as of saints and miracles,—or with pious legends, echoes from the Bible, or mythical happenings, in such a way as to satisfy the reader's curiosity and captivate his imagination.[24] This tendency was certainly accentuated by Rustichello, a professional author who specialized in the very same task of amusing and educating the same public to whom the *Milione* was dedicated. The collaboration between the two men must have been intimate and without friction since they shared this event which accorded with both the intellectual personality and the elementary education of Marco, who had set out for the East when he was seventeen years of age. The epic finery and literary phraseology with which the Pisan scribe bedecked Marco's account not only did not alter its substance, but definitely corresponded to the taste and cultural tendencies of its author, who made no pretense of being a man of learning, but wished to be the truthful and authentic narrator of an extraordinary adventure.

The result of the book's twofold character appears somewhat paradoxical, inasmuch as, while it wishes to be an objective narration and description of the facts and aspects of an unknown world, the account does not substitute an entirely new picture for the traditional one. On the other hand, as a Book of Marvels it adds new and unheard-of wonders to ancient fables, indirectly

---

[22] For this see the observations of Benedetto, cr. ed., Introd., p. xix.

[23] For the fortunes of the *Milione* in the XIVth century cf. Sir Henry Yule, *The Book of Ser Marco Polo,* London and New York, 1921, Vol. I, Introd., pp. 104 ff. For the poem cf. E. R. Labande, *Étude sur Baudouin de Sebourc,* Paris, 1940.

[24] For the hagiography of the *Milione* see chap. vii, § 1, of the present work.

lending countenance to those stories and interweaving with them still more wonderful manifestations of the remotest civilizations. Marco therefore neither wished nor was always able to dissociate his experiences from the old geographical fables, and he proceeds into the heart of the Asian continent with tales of Alexander and of the mythical Prester John in his head—a memory which accompanies him to the very borders of China—transforming, as he goes, these and other literary reminiscences into a new reality no less wonderful and at times no less fantastic than the mirages long perpetuated in popular literature, and combining with it his realistic vision of the world.

Thus the romance of Alexander can be numbered among the literary predecessors of the *Milione,* just as much as *Prester John's Letter on the Wonders of India,* in its various popular versions, which from 1164 onward gave to the same public a fanciful, often preposterous, but always attractive picture of the fabulous lands of the East, and of an ideal empire that comprised them all.[25] Those regions were later described in didactic vernacular literature with which the *Milione* has certain links.[26] We may mention the famous *Image du Monde* of the Lorrainer Gossouin, the title of which alone bears an obvious affinity to the original one of "Divisament dou Monde" given to their book by Marco and Rustichello. The two works, separated by half a century, have in common the serious purpose of instructing the ignorant concerning the various regions of the earth and particularly those of the Orient, which until then had been known only through literary tradition.[27] As the *Milione* is in part doctrinal and in part practical, so also is Brunetto Latini's *Trésor;* the bond of kinship is

[25] For the legend and relevant texts see chap. ix, § 2.

[26] Cf. Langlois, *op. cit.,* pp. 135 ff. For the original title of the *Milione* cf. Benedetto, cr. ed., pp. 245 f., and Moule-Pelliot, *Marco Polo: The Description of the World,* 2 vols., London, 1938, Vol. I, pp. 31 ff. The title *Milione,* popularly attributed to the book and still without a definite explanation, already appears in Giovanni Villani's chronicle, and the name is given to Marco himself by the contemporary chronicler Jacopo da Acqui. See the note by Benedetto in his translation, *Il Libro di Messer Marco Polo,* Milan and Rome, 1932, p. 429. Jacopo da Acqui's chronicle also bears the title *Imago Mundi,* which was applied to various historical and geographical texts of the Middle Ages, for which cf. Langlois, *op. cit.,* pp. 135 ff.

[27] The most extensive geographical section in the French poem and its various prose versions is that which deals with Asia (cf. Langlois, *op. cit.,* pp. 167 ff., and, for the complete text, O. H. Prior, *L'Image du Monde de Maître Gossouin,* Lausanne, 1913).

symptomatic, because in both works the cosmographic interests are wide, and exemplary, because a like systematic and constructive spirit prevails throughout.

When examined against this literary, sociological, and cultural background, the *Milione* turns out to be a work inspired by the two tendencies that dominated the secular society of the times: the spirit of adventure, which was both romantic and realistic, and the characteristic didacticism of that great age of compilers, encyclopedists, and preceptors which they directed particularly toward the world of reality about them. And if we may believe what we read in the Ramusian version of the *Milione* concerning the notes Marco is supposed to have taken in the course of his wanderings, we see that his intention of making his readers share as much in his adventures as in his sober experiences greatly preceded Rustichello's idea of compiling a book by mutual agreement. This gives us an enlightening glimpse of the young traveler already marked by the spiritual imprint of his age at the time of his departure from Venice in 1271, as he continued to be while on his travels in every part of Asia.

It is possible that he was unacquainted with all this doctrinal literature, but it is not possible to doubt that its historical and practical substance represented the basis of his culture, however rudimentary, without which he could not have traveled in the steps of the Macedonian, have recognized the legendary Prester John in the chief of a powerful Mongolian tribe of Christians, or have distinguished between fable and reality, as he does at various points in the *Milione*. From this twofold background the book took on its double character, which is at the same time systematic and adventurous, doctrinal and romantic, objective and fanciful, and which reflects the intellectual tendencies of his age; the background determined, indeed, both the form and the success of the work.

2. THE DISCOVERY OF ASIA

THE MISSIONARIES

Marco Polo's generation, however, was no longer satisfied with traditional ideas and picturesque fables, since Asia had now temporarily extended its limits to the shores of the Adriatic and had made harsh contacts with the Christian world. Events of incalculable importance had transformed the mythical picture of the Orient into a concrete and terrible reality. In a little more than two decades, 1206 to 1227, Chinghiz, the Mongolian leader and founder of the Chinghizide dynasty, had increased his dominion as head of a few Mongolian tribes to that as sovereign of the whole Asian continent from the China Sea to the Black Sea, creating with his conquests the largest empire recorded in history. After him his sons, grandsons, and famous captains extended its boundaries as far as Udine in northeastern Italy, and Dalmatia, retiring in 1241 from these extreme western boundaries to the banks of the Volga but making felt throughout Europe the shock of their power, the threat of further invasions, and the consequences of their régime, which was economically disastrous and politically brutal.[1]

When, in 1260, Niccolò and Maffeo Polo set forth from their emporium at Soldaia in the Crimea toward the Asian interior, that farther region formed a political and administrative block opposed to a Europe that was weak and divided in its internal structure. Two years before, Hulagu, a grandson of Chinghiz Khan, had established his imperial sway over the "Tartars of the Levant" and had consolidated Tartar rule in Persia, Mesopotamia, and Anatolia, after having destroyed, in the person of the last Abbasid caliph, the Mohammedan religious, cultural, and economic supremacy in these same regions and the rest of the continent.[2]

The age-old Mohammedan monopoly of commerce disappeared with all this, at least officially, while the mysterious continent of Asia was opened to whomsoever had the courage, the means, and the appropriate credentials to venture there, without limits of time or space. Missionaries and merchants took advantage of this cir-

---

[1] An over-all view of these events, which will be mentioned several times later in this book, is given in R. Grousset, *L'Empire des steppes,* Paris, 1939 (with various reprints), chap. ii.

[2] Marco himself makes several allusions to these events. Cf. the *Milione,* cr. ed., esp. pp. 19 ff. Also, B. Spuler, *Die Mongolen in Iran,* Leipzig, 1939 (reprinted in 1955), esp. pp. 22 ff., and, by the same author, "Geschichte der islamischen Länder," Pt. II: "Die Mongolenzeit," in *Handbuch der Orientalistik,* Vol. VI, Leiden and Cologne, 1953, esp. pp. 34 ff., as well as "La Situation de l'Iran à l'époque de Marco Polo," in *Oriente Poliano,* pp. 121 ff.

cumstance, and were the first to bring back to Europe news of those lands and peoples which from time immemorial had remained closed to any direct Western experience. Interest in this unknown world, which had been reawakened by such portentous events, must have been universal from the first appearance of the Tartar hordes on the boundaries of the West, increasing with their further advances from 1237 onward, through Russia, Poland, and finally Hungary and other countries of eastern and central Europe.[3]

The extension of an Asian empire that was politically active and organized on a military basis, as well as the presence of the Tartars in the West, created new and critical problems for all the European powers, which had to find an empirical solution to them without aid from history or experience except for the ancient though still present memory of Attila. The problem of the defense of Europe against a new enemy, more powerful than the Arabs and more cruel than the Huns, succeeded to the now waning tradition of the Crusades. After the failure of Louis IX's expeditions to Egypt, Syria, and finally Tunisia, and at the same time that Mohammedan power tended to be consolidated in the eastern Mediterranean under the leadership of the Mamelukes of Egypt, the problem of defense against the common peril took the form of a dilemma: should the West unite with the undefeated Tartars against the Mohammedans of the Levant, in order to destroy their renascent power; or should all the Christian forces concentrate in a common effort to drive back into Asia the Tartar invaders who were apparently stronger and at that moment even more dangerous than the Mohammedans?

In order to make suitable decisions either way, the interested powers had to base their judgments on sound, authentic information about the Asian situation. And since this grave problem presented itself with both political and religious aspects, it is understandable that it preoccupied more than any other power the Papacy, which was then the arbiter of the European situation in the person of Gregory IX (1227–1241) and his successor Innocent IV (1243–1254). At this time, too, the Emperor Frederick

---

[3] Serbia, for example, then in part a feudal tributary of Hungary, and Danubian Bulgaria, which remained a tributary of the Tartar empire when the Mongols retired from Europe in 1241 as far as the Dnieper, then to the Volga, in Russian territory.

II was also directly interested; but the initiative of opposing Christian Europe to pagan Asia escaped him because his empire, which was itself in danger, no longer had either the strength or the prestige necessary to so vast and perplexing an enterprise.

The first explorers of Asia were therefore either missionaries entrusted with political missions or merchants who like the Polos ventured on their own account, with chiefly commercial and then religious aims, among the pagans. Nor is it pure chance that these lay pioneers were from Venice, since, having established themselves with increasing success in the Crimea during the second half of this century, the Venetians found themselves on the edge of the Tartar world with the twofold task of exploiting its products and purchasing power and of overcoming the competition of the Genoese, who were no less enterprising in their conquest of Eastern markets.

The first of the missionaries to bring back to the West direct news of the Tartars of Asia had been the Hungarian Dominican, Julian, who, together with a few companions, in the fourth decade of the XIIIth century, ventured beyond the banks of the Volga in search of peoples like their own but still enveloped in the mists of paganism.[4] However, when he arrived in so-called Greater Hungary—more precisely, in the region of present-day Orenburg on the western limits of Siberia—he found his way to the interior barred by the Tartars who had invaded and conquered this territory.[5] This was in 1236, when Friar Julian returned to his native land and made his way to Rome with the first authentic news about these peoples and the danger they represented for the Christian West. That same year, indeed, the diet of the Tartar empire had entrusted to the great Batu Khan, a grandson of Chinghiz Khan and lord of western Asia, the conquest of the Russian steppes inhabited by Bulgars, Comans, and other Altaic and Sarmatic tribes. He then proceeded in a cataclysmic advance to occupy eastern Europe, destroying Hungary and making sporadic incursions into Dalmatia and the Friulan plain.[6]

---

[4] For the story and documents of this mission cf. László Benfedy's article, "Fontes Authentici Itinera (1236–1238) Fr. Juliani Illustrantes," in *Archivum Europae Centro-Orientalis*, Vol. II, pp. 1 ff. (with bibliography of the subject).

[5] For events in this region cf. B. Spuler, *Die Goldene Horde*, Leipzig, 1943, pp. 10 ff.

[6] For these episodes cf. Grousset, *op. cit.*, pp. 328 ff.

The intrepid Dominican had foreseen these events, after having learned of the first successes of the Tartar advance in those border regions; and the presentiment of imminent peril for the whole of Europe was so great that King Bela IV of Hungary sent the friar's report to the Patriarch of Aquileia, on the borders of the Venetian dominions, as well as to the Bishop of Brixen and the Count of Tyrol, who protected the Alpine passes against possible invasions from the east and north.[7] It was thereby finally known who these Tartars were, of whom trustworthy information had just been received in the West. And what the friar had to say about them is symptomatic of all subsequent reports of travels to Asia, including Marco Polo's *Milione,* inasmuch as he relates, though in reduced proportions, the same mixture of fable and truth as in the picture of Asia which had been gradually formed in Europe down through the ages.

Friar Julian's brief report is a result of indirect information which he had gathered from local sources on the borders of the two continents without personal observations of men or things; hence its worth, for us, is much reduced by comparison with the accounts of later explorations, in spite of what is to be learned from it of the reports, some true, some false, that circulated between the Volga and the Urals concerning the customs and history of those mysterious peoples. The friar offers precise data about the Tartars' military organization and methods of war, pointing out, among other things, their superiority in open warfare and their custom, which they had followed on several occasions in Russia, of taking fortified towns not by force of arms in direct assault, but by laying waste the surrounding regions. He also gives a vague account of their origins and the first exploits of Chinghiz; but in this we cannot find the slightest trace of historical characters or real events.[8]

[7] Cf. Benfedy, *op. cit.,* p. 39.

[8] Friar Julian would have the Tartar conquests spring from a supposed contest between one of their leaders and a neighboring chieftain's sister, who was seized by him, ravished, and then decapitated. It is not practicable for us to go into the origins and circumstances of these obviously legendary happenings recounted by the friar, and we shall merely mention that Marco Polo also attributed fictitious episodes to the career of Chinghiz, who according to his account asked in vain for the hand of the daughter of a powerful Mongol chieftain: this was the origin of the conqueror's wrath and the war he waged against the offender. Cf. the *Milione,* cr. ed., pp. 51 ff., and M.P., pp. 164 ff. (for the war against the so-called Prester John, in reality Togrul,

He describes fancifully the palaces of the Great Kaan, with their columns and gates of gold and the other fabulous requisites common to the literary tradition of an imaginary Orient; but he draws at the same time a vividly realistic picture of Tartar expansion in Persia and Russia, and insists that the Tartars plan to become lords of the earth.[9] Eloquent proof of their intentions is the order of submission sent by their leader to the King of Hungary, the first document of this kind among those that have come down to us in the original text, already making plain, in Friar Julian's version, the arrogance and violence of the conquerors on the eve of their further victorious advance in the West.[10] Only a few years later, this same King Bela, fleeing from his country's smoking ruins, was forced, as were all the sovereigns and peoples of Europe, to realize that the Tartar threats were not vain words and that the political and military organization of the whole of Christendom against the invader had in the meantime become a necessity that would brook no delay.

Hereafter Europe lived with the nightmare of this menace even though, after the death of Ogudai Kaan in 1240, the Mongolian armies that had arrived at the gates of Italy retired beyond the Volga, leaving everywhere behind them the memory of their cruelty and traces of their might. The only comfort amid defeat and subsequent humiliations at the hands of these barbarians was the vague but insistent opinion that some of their sovereigns were Christians and therefore almost predestined, in spite of their Nestorian heresy, to return to the bosom of the Roman Church.

There is no hint of this to be found in the reports of Friar Julian, who found only Mohammedans and pagans among the

---

leader of the Keraits). These were probably common motifs in the poetical history diffused by Mongol and Turkish rhapsodists, which became elaborated in the various centers of Tartar expansion in Asia. We shall come across further examples later.

[9] The conquest of Rome as the aim of their next invasion is especially revealed by the friar (cf. Benfedy, *loc. cit.*). The palaces he mentions are similar to those described in various medieval texts that recount the wonders of Asia. For the palaces in Japan see the *Milione,* cr. ed., p. 163; M.P., p. 357. For the subject cf. the present author's *Storia letteraria delle scoperte geografiche,* Florence, 1937, pp. 73 ff.

[10] The letter to King Bela IV, reproduced by Friar Julian (*op. cit.,* p. 38), is certainly authentic, though it cannot be considered to conform absolutely to the original. Cf. E. Voegelin, "The Mongol Orders of Submission to European Powers," *Byzantion,* Vol. XV, 1940–41, pp. 378 ff.

Hungarians and Bulgars of the Volga and the Comans of south-east Russia.[11] But the idea of the existence of a powerful Christian sovereign in the remotest parts of Asia had already become traditional in Europe, having as its basis the spurious *Letter of Prester John,* which describes him, in various forms, from the year 1164.[12] This vague literary image had become consolidated into a concrete reality with the first direct contacts between Tartars and Europeans, until the first missionaries who penetrated into the heart of Asia, and finally Marco Polo himself, were able to confirm the existence of an organized Christianity that was recognized and adhered to more or less actively by influential members of the Chinghizide dynasty, important personages at court and in the army, and by entire tribes that were superficially but traditionally attached to rites and beliefs of the Nestorian heresy.[13]

The search for this legendary Christian diaspora in the unexplored regions of Asia was one of the strongest stimuli for the institutions of the missions "ad Tartaros," which among other things had the religious aim of enlightening the heretics, apart from the political one of claiming for the Christian cause, against the common Mohammedan enemy, those sovereigns and dignitaries of the Tartar world who had adhered to it because of dynastic or national tradition.

All the merit for this great initiative goes to the Genoese Sinibaldo Fieschi, who was elected Pope in June, 1243, when the Tartar peril with all its terror still hung over the Christian West.

---

[11] The evangelization of these peoples living on the borders of eastern Europe was personally entrusted by St. Dominic in 1220 to the Hungarian friars of his Order, which thereafter considered these territories to be its special province. Cf., too, the article by Benfedy already cited, and the well-informed work by B. Altaner, *Die Dominikanermissionen des 13. Jahrhunderts,* Habelschwerdt, 1924, esp. pp. 141 ff. For the region and customs of the Comans cf. J. Marquart's fundamental and searching study, "Über das Volkstum der Komanen," in Bang-Marquart, *Osttürkische Dialekt-Studien* (*Abhandl. d. k. Gesellschaft der Wissenschaften zu Göttingen,* phil.-hist. Klasse, N.F., Vol. XIII, No. I, 1914), as well as P. Pelliot, "A propos des Comans," *Journal Asiatique,* eleventh series, Vol. XV, 1920, pp. 115 ff. For the Coman language cf. Johannes Benzing, *Einführung in das Studium der altaischen Philologie und der Turkologie,* Wiesbaden, 1953, pp. 80 ff.

[12] For this famous letter turn to chap. ix, § 2, below.

[13] For Christianity in medieval Asia cf. P. Pelliot, "Chrétiens d'Asie Centrale et d'Extrême-Orient," *T'oung Pao,* Vol. XV, 1914, pp. 623 ff.; for China, the works of A. C. Moule and P. Y. Saeki cited in note 5 to § 1, above.

Soon afterward Christendom lost Jerusalem and the Holy Land, which was invaded by Turkish Mohammedans while the Emperor Frederick II marched on Rome to take up his seat there as temporal lord of the universe.[14] It was beneath this political constellation that Innocent IV organized the historic Council of Lyons, at which Frederick II was excommunicated and deposed with ecumenical approval.[15] Such was the main purpose of this great meeting; but already, before the Pontiff urged those present to defend by common action their frontiers and the whole of Europe against the Tartar menace, he had himself inaugurated the missions "ad Tartaros" in the person of the Franciscan Friar John of Pian del Càrpine, near Perugia, who was to be his personal ambassador at the court of their still fabulous sovereign.

Much has been written about this Papal initiative, which opened the way to the systematic exploration of the Asian continent. It will suffice here, therefore, to mention briefly the progress of its first phase, which came to an end in that century with Marco Polo's book. Friar John was truly his first effective predecessor. No one before him, not even Friar Julian of Hungary, had ventured beyond the confines of the ancient world and penetrated into the interior of the Asian continent. As a result, his famous report, destined for the Pope and "omnibus Christi fidelibus," with its title *Historia Mongalorum,* is written in a style that is completely new in medieval literature, and inaugurates the series of travel books of which the *Milione* is the masterpiece.[16]

It is an empirical and historical description of the countries and customs of Asia and at the same time a personal intinerary. But whereas Marco Polo's work extends this task to include the whole

[14] A recent brief description of the political and ecclesiastical situation of those years is given by A. Fliche in his *Histoire de l'Église depuis les origines jusqu'à nos jours,* Vol. X, Paris, 1950, esp. pp. 238 ff., with bibliography and notes. Cf. also G. Soranzo, *Il Papato, l'Europa cristiana e i Tartari,* Milan, 1930.

[15] For a detailed description of the Council cf. Hefele-Leclercq, *Histoire des Conciles,* Vol. V, Pt. II, Paris, 1906.

[16] Critical text in *Sinica Franciscana: Itinera et Relationes Fratrum minorum saec. XIII et XIV,* collected and annotated by P. A. van den Wyngaert, Vol. I, Quaracchi, 1929 (with historical introduction, bibliography, and mention of previous editions, translations, etc.); English translation in Christopher Dawson, ed., *The Mongol Mission: Narratives and Letters of the Franciscan Missionaries in Mongolia and China in the XIIIth and XIVth Centuries, Translated by a Nun of Stanbrook Abbey,* London, 1955.

Tartar empire at its zenith, Friar John only reached the heart of Mongolia when the dynasty was still in full expansion and its civilization had not yet been subjected to decisive Chinese, Tibetan, Persian, Indian, and Byzantine influences. Moreover, this detailed, conscientious report brings before us for the first time the Asian continent without the usual fables, traditional legends, and clichés. It is an outstanding document of that doctrinal and literary realism which, having matured in Italy toward the middle of the century, became a characteristic and decisive aspect of a new civilization.

A few years after the friar's return, his *Historia Mongalorum* became a part of Vincent of Beauvais's *Speculum Historiale,* thereby including contemporary Asia in the treasury of contemporary encyclopedic knowledge.[17] Friar John, having set out from Lyons on Easter Sunday of the year 1245, had crossed the vast continent with his companion Benedictus Polonus, undergoing innumerable hardships and humiliating experiences, after having observed the wreckage and desolation of the towns destroyed in Russia and Poland in the wake of the Mongolian armies that had descended into Europe only a few years previously to spread death and ruin in those lands. He arrived at the Chinghizide imperial court, a short distance from the capital, Karakorum, in the center of Mongolia, on July 22, 1246, to find there an immense throng of princes, dignitaries, ambassadors, and lesser folk from all over Asia, who were awaiting the consecration of the newly elected sovereign, Küyük, to the dignity of Great Kaan, or *Khagan,* of the Tartars.[18]

[17] This famous *Speculum* was compiled and published between 1256 and 1259 (latest edition, Douai, 1624); but Friar John's *Historia Mongalorum* had already been in circulation in separate manuscripts, according to Salimbene of Parma's assertion in his *Cronaca,* ed. F. Bernini, Bari, 1942, Vol. I, pp. 295 ff. Apparently, Friar John gave it to read to all those (and there were many of them) who asked him for news about the Orient that he had visited, while he would illustrate the contents by a spoken commentary.

[18] Küyük, the son of Juji and grandson of Chinghiz Khan, succeeded Ogudai in 1246 and reigned for only two years, after which the imperial throne remained vacant for a further long period of time. Chinghiz contented himself, even at the height of his power, with the title of "khan" (*han*). His imperial successors called themselves "kaan" (*khagan* or *qaan* and other phonetic transcriptions), which Marco Polo renders by the simple term *Can.* Cf. K. Shiratori, "A Study on the Titles Kaghan and Katun," *Memoirs of the Research Department of the Tōyō Bunko,* ser. B, No. 1, Tokyo, 1926, pp. 1 ff.

In this huge, swarming, imperial encampment—a veritable city of tents and pavilions, vividly described by the friar—he was able to see and observe in characteristic and worthy representatives all those various aspects of Asian life which were later set forth with exemplary fidelity and concision in the report completed at Lyons in the latter part of 1247, immediately after his return to the Papal curia, then established in that city.[19] While admiring the tenacity, the powers of endurance, and the patience which enabled him to accomplish such labors and compass such great distances, under conditions of inconceivable hardship, we find his intellectual vigor and powers of observation no less commendable, since they made it possible for him to overcome the prejudices and illusions commonly associated with the portrayal of those peoples and regions.

It is of course true that here again the old teratology of Asia makes an appearance, with the mention of Cynocephali and Monopodes; but they are relegated with other monsters to the arctic regions that lie beyond the reach of any personal or human experience.[20] Similarly, the imaginary kingdom of Prester John, the fabulous Christian sovereign of Asia, is transported by the narrator to unexplored regions beyond the Indus. However, he does draw a somewhat fanciful picture of the Chinese, with whom he must have mingled, or at least have seen, in great numbers at the court of Küyük. This picture recalls the "just Ethiopians" of Homer, the perfect Brahmans of the Alexander legend, the Seres of Pliny and of medieval tradition; and he mentions, among other things, their sacred books as though they were the Holy Scriptures and Lives of the Fathers, dedicated to the worship of Christ in their sanctuaries and monasteries.[21]

[19] Friar John had already begun the composition of his work while on his return journey. For the *Historia* see the "Prolegomena" by P. van den Wyngaert in *Sinica Franciscana*, Vol. I, pp. 11 ff.

[20] *Sinica Franciscana*, pp. 60, 74 f., 111, 138. It should be remembered that these stories of monsters recounted by the friar were told him by some Ruthenian clerks at the court of Küyük Kaan.

[21] It was commonly believed among ancient writers that there existed at the eastern ends of the earth some peoples endowed with happiness and every virtue (cf. the passages collected by Yule-Cordier, *Cathay*, Vol. I, pp. 185 f., 196 f., and 203 f.). The Chinese located similar Utopian lands in the westernmost regions of the world. Cf. K. Shiratori in *Memoirs of the Research Department of the Tōyō Bunko*, ser. B, No. 15, Tokyo, 1956.

As is obvious, China was still to be discovered in its totality, and it is impossible to know by what misunderstanding the friar had formed his idea of this land. Since he was, in the words of the chronicler Salimbene of Parma, "literatus et magnus pro-locutor et in multis expertus," he only once obeyed the dictates of the Orient's literary fascination, and, disillusioned by what he saw and experienced when among the Mongols, transported to beyond their frontiers the ancient utopias of happy, pious peoples living at the eastern limits of the earth. The good friar was un-acquainted with any form of piety apart from the Christian kind; nor can he have extended to all the Chinese the virtues of the first Christians among them, who had established themselves in China in the VIIth century, and of whom nothing was then known in the West, and scarcely more in the country that had then harbored them for two centuries.[22] Friar John presented these peoples as a new spiritual harvest for further missionary undertakings, so much the more promising inasmuch as he knew by direct experience that many Asiatic Christians lived at court in continuous contact with the sovereign, so that a chapel of theirs was always open in the vicinity of the imperial pavilion in the hope that the Great Kaan might one day receive baptism;[23] this idea was never forgotten by those who established contacts of all kinds between the West and the Orient, and it formed a dom-inant theme in all the resulting literature, including, as we shall see, Messer Marco's *Milione*.[24]

The rest of Friar John's report is concerned with things seen by him or with information obtained on the spot though not al-ways from a sure source. However, this vast collection of personal observations and data is set forth in systematic order. Beginning with a geographical survey of central and eastern Asia, it first of all offers a description of the Tartar peoples, their customs and forms of worship, and then proceeds to a minute analysis of their

[22] It is possible that the legendary Christianization of Cathay goes back to exag-gerated reports of Oriental Christianity which were later confirmed by the authority of the spurious *Letter of Prester John,* in which these legends are fantastically elabo-rated. Cf. A. C. Moule, *Christians in China,* pp. 11 ff.

[23] For Christianity at the court of Küyük and his successor Mangu (or Möngke) Kaan cf. the present author's work, *Guillaume Boucher: A French Artist at the Court of the Khans,* Baltimore, 1946.

[24] See chap. iv of the present work.

political and military organization. This latter is undoubtedly the most important part of the book; with its precision in factual matters and its breadth of information it enables us to understand in what circumstances a people of uncultured nomads, without laws or offices, was able to create, extend, and administer the largest empire recorded in history. The conclusion of the analysis follows in the seventh chapter, which is in the form of a diplomatic report, designed to teach the peoples of Europe how to defend themselves from the perils with which the expansion of the Mongolian empire threatened Western civilization. It is only at the end, almost as in an appendix, that the friar describes his itinerary, writing in the first person and recounting his adventures and travel notes, and going on to describe by ancedote all that he had learned of court gossip, ceremonial, and customs at the encampment of the Great Kaan.

This is, in fact, the first direct authentic description of Asia, in which, however, the geographical data are obviously secondary and dependent rather on historical events and personal reminiscenses than on systematic and reliable information. Our friar is not interested in the natural aspects of the continent, since he is so taken up with the idea of discovering and revealing to others its political structure and military power, its recent history and future development. He seems completely indifferent to the Asian fauna and flora that Marco Polo surveyed with so much, though brief, information. It is characteristic of the times that the only exotic plant described by Benedict the Pole, Friar John's companion, in his short but important report of the same journey, is the "sad wormwood" of the steppe, already mentioned by Ovid (*Epistulae ex Ponto,* III, i, 23). Although he includes the Cynocephali among the peoples of Russia, he says not a word about the animals, either wild or domestic, that were common to those vast regions.[25] Hence it is obvious that these travelers were not yet won over by the naturalistic tendencies of their age, as Marco was to be, and that they restricted their interest to human phenomena, historical data, and the political and religious problems of their times and missions.

[25] Cf. *Sinica Franciscana,* Vol. I, p. 137. The *Artemisia absinthium* mentioned by Friar Benedict is the characteristic plant of the steppes, and, according to Friar William of Rubruck (*Sin. Franc.,* Vol. I, p. 214), it is especially abundant in Mongolia, where it was used together with ox dung to heat the imperial pavilions.

Friar John's attitude toward the exotic world is, in outward seeming, one of serene detachment; yet at heart he is critical and hostile. Whereas he seems to appreciate the civic and family virtues of the Tartars, his inward aversion extends even to the country itself, which is "more wretched than it is possible to describe," and to the barbaric customs of that irascible, faithless people, bloodthirsty liars and drunkards all, overweening and cruel in their exploitation of the conquered.[26] In his portrayal of them, however, he leans toward a conscientious objectivity which is all the more praiseworthy when one remembers that his book is the first systematic, empirical description in medieval geographical literature, which in this respect had neither traditions to follow nor examples to offer. Indeed, in spite of his intended candor and honest procedure, he fears that he may be considered an impostor, and thus he anticipates by half a century the skepticism of certain contemporaries of Marco Polo, who, according to a famous anecdote recounted by the chronicler Jacopo da Acqui, had to defend himself on his deathbed against the accusation of falsehood.[27]

No one at the time, however, doubted the trustworthiness of Friar John's report, which certainly opened up a great part of Asia to European curiosity, but also confirmed the claims of the Great Kaan of the Tartars to bringing under his sway all the peoples of the earth, proclaiming it to be his dominion in haughty and peremptory terms in the letter destined for the Pope and entrusted to his legate the Minorite.[28] The interest in these little-known peoples and the necessity of discovering their movements and inventions in political and religious matters led to the setting up of missions which were entrusted to members of the mendicant orders, both on account of the apostolic fervor that animated them at this time and because of their diffusion in the Christian East.[29] Innocent IV sent various Dominicans to Asia, including

[26] *Sinica Franciscana,* Vol. I, pp. 32 and 45 f., respectively.

[27] The original text of this oft-repeated anecdote is to be found in the Introd. to the cr. ed. of the *Milione,* p. cxciv. Friar John mentions as guarantors of his good faith several Italian merchants he met at Kiev who were experts on Tartary and its peoples. Cf. *Sinica Franciscana,* Vol. I, pp. 159 f.

[28] For this letter, still preserved in the Vatican Archives, cf. the fundamental article by P. Pelliot, "Les Mongols et la Papauté," *Revue de l'Orient Chrétien,* third series, Vol. III (XXIII), 1923–24, pp. 35 ff., and Vol. IV, 1924, p. 225 ff.

[29] For a general survey of these missions cf. the Introd. by P. van den Wyngaert to *Sinica Franciscana,* Vol. I, with exhaustive bibliographical information. For a fuller

Friar Ezzelino, a Lombard, known also as Anselm of Ascelin, who was followed by Simon of Saint-Quentin; and André de Longjumeau, another French Dominican, arrived at the imperial court in Mongolia in the regency of Oghul Gaimish, the widow of Küyük Kaan.

All that is known of their travel reports is the part saved by Vincent of Beauvais, who inserted them fragmentarily in his famous encyclopedia. This is sufficient, however, to disclose their interests and attitudes.[30] It is in fact possible to deduce from their circumstances and judgments the manner in which they differ in character and culture from the Franciscans assigned to similar political, religious, and doctrinal tasks. A few examples will suffice to show the Dominicans' tendency to believe and recount all that they learned in the course of their missions among the Tartars. In accordance with ancient geography, André places the Tartars' origin in the vast deserts at the end of the earth, behind which, enclosed by impassable mountains, lived the peoples of Gog and Magog;[31] on another occasion he narrates the legend of a great Mongolian chieftain who was miraculously converted to Christianity and inspired by God to conquer the legendary dominions of the no less famous Prester John.[32]

It was as a result of these false reports that Louis IX of France charged another Friar Minor, William of Rubruck, with the duty of making contact with the Tartar leaders in order to strengthen their supposed Christianity and convert them, if possible, to the Church of Rome. The Dominicans who had preceded

---

and more comprehensive treatment see G. Soranzo, *op. cit.*, in note 14 above, as well as B. Altaner, *Die Dominikanermissionen,* esp. chap. vi, pp. 116 ff. Contributions to the history of the missions are mentioned annually in the *Bibliografia Missionaria* issued by the Pontificia Biblioteca Missionaria di Propaganda Fide, at Rome.

[30] Cf. the Douai edition cited, 1624, Vol. VI, chaps. xxxi ff.

[31] This remark can in fact refer to the Gobi and other deserts, extending from Central Asia to China, which separate Mongolia from China proper and isolate it from the rest of the world. Marco Polo likewise designated with this Biblical name the border regions near the Great Wall, interpreting it by "Ung e Mungul"—Tartar tribes of that region and thus named by him. Cf. the *Milione,* cr. ed., p. 61, M.P., pp. 181 ff., and the commentary in Yule-Cordier, *The Book of Ser Marco Polo,* Vol. I, pp. 292 ff.

[32] This could refer to the leader of the Keraits, a Mongolian tribe which in large part had been Christianized from the XIth century onward. Marco Polo here recognizes "Prester John," first the ally and then the enemy of Chinghiz Khan, who destroyed his kingdom and power.

him had met with no success. After they had arrived in 1247 at the camp of "Baachu," the head of the Mongols in Persia, their attitude toward this Chinghizide prince was deemed arrogant and provocative, since they appeared at his court without the customary gifts and refused to genuflex when coming into his presence, according to the usage of Oriental courts.[33] It was only with great difficulty that they avoided the wrath of the offended Tartars, and they made a miraculous escape without contributing to Christian prestige in Asia or causing the sovereigns and peoples of the West to be better known there.

The Franciscans who journeyed or lived among the Tartars and Chinese until 1368 generally adapted themselves with greater humility and patience to these exigencies and did not have to suffer injury or violence to the extent of compromising their mission, as had the Dominicans just mentioned.[34] The Franciscans' more realistic and conciliatory attitude in their dealings with the proud sovereigns of Asia and their arrogant officials was certainly a necessary condition for their own greater success, both as missionaries and as informants. In these experiences of the friars it is possible to see an expression of the differing tendencies prevalent in the respective orders, which followed the imprint and example of their founders; the one, who "in the proud presence of the Sultan" overcame the latter's anger and pride with his serene meekness and humble courage;[35] the other, who taught his followers to be "benignant to his own and cruel to his foes."[36] The Dominicans do, in fact, seem to have pro-

[33] For the name and power of this Chinghizide prince cf. *Sinica Franciscana*, Vol. I, p. 320, n. 1. For the events mentioned cf. Altaner, *op. cit.*, pp. 128 ff., and Soranzo, *op. cit.*, chap. vi.

[34] This was, on the other hand, what happened to the first Franciscan mission of 1227, which suffered martyrdom at Ceuta in that year, and to the one described at length by Odoric of Pordenone (*Sin. Franc.*, Vol. I, pp. 424 ff.), which ended in the slaughter of Tana (or Salsette, near Bombay). Cf. L. Wadding, *Annales Minorum*, third edition, Quaracchi, 1931, Vol. II, pp. 29 ff., and Vol. VI, pp. 399 ff.; also, G. Golubovich, *op. cit.* in note 8 to § 1 above, Vol. III, pp. 211 ff. All the sources present the martyrdoms as a consequence of the supposedly provocative attitude of the Franciscan missionaries and the violence of their language concerning the Prophet and local Mohammedan authorities. The two events recorded, however, appear to be exceptional in the history of the Franciscan missions, although they are represented in paintings executed by Ambrogio Lorenzetti in the Church of St. Francis, in Siena, in 1337.

[35] Cf. Dante, *Paradiso*, XI, 110 ff.

[36] *Ibid.*, XII, 57.

ceeded with greater impetus and passion in their work of Christian propaganda, whereas the Franciscans apparently practiced
greater patience and adaptability to the more or less justified
demands of the Orientals and thereby succeeded in finding a
modus vivendi with these peoples, to whom any manifestation
of religious fanaticism was both alien and repugnant.

These virtues were most evident in the person of Friar William,
who, because of his native abilities, the variety of his experiences,
and the geographical extent of his journey, became the best-
informed and wisest of Marco Polo's predecessors. His task, although inspired by a king, was more modest than that entrusted
by Innocent IV to Friar John of Pian del Càrpine. Friar William
left Cyprus in March, 1253, accompanied by Friar Bartholomew
of Cremona, another Friar Minor, with the assignment of instructing the Tartar leaders who were reputed Christians and of
converting them to Catholicism, in the secret hope that their conversion might be followed by common action against the renascent Mohammedan power in the Levant.

This was on the eve of the Mongolian armies' triumphant advance under the command of Hulagu Khan. Between 1254 and
1258 they would invade the whole of Mohammedan Asia, destroy
the Abbasid caliphate, and extend the power of the Chinghizide
Tartars as far as Syria, whence King Louis, robbed of victory and
his illusions, had to return to his native land in the same year
that marked the return of Friar William and the birth of Marco
Polo.

This royal and religious mission, with its political background,
was supposed to confine itself to the person and court of the
nearest of the Tartar princes: Sartach, the son of Batu Khan,
Lord of the Golden Horde, whose encampment was situated at
Sarai, a place not far from the mouth of the Volga and temporarily the residence of this branch of the reigning dynasty.[37]
However, according to Friar William, Sartach was not a Christian, nor was he directly interested in religious questions. He
obviously divined the political aims of the mission, and made

[37] For this capital, composed in large part of pavilions and tents, cf. B. Spuler, Die
Goldene Horde, pp. 264 ff. Sartach, the son of Batu Khan, Lord of the Golden Horde
and of the Tartars of the West (as Marco Polo calls them), was at that time administering the regions of the empire along the Volga and to the west of that river.

the friar proceed toward the court of Batu, the leader of the Tartars of the West, as Marco Polo calls them, one of the most powerful and influential members of the whole Chinghizide dynasty.[38] He was, moreover, well known in Europe since he had been at the head of the armies that had laid waste part of the continent at the time of their most recent invasion.

Having in mind the imminent project of further Western expeditions, these leaders were now able to obtain precious information about the situation in the Mediterranean and the Christian world represented by the friar. It was probably for this reason that the great Batu in turn made him move on to Karakorum, the capital of the empire, seat of the Great Kaan and center of the government, which Friar William reached after an exhausting journey of more than three months in the company of a rich and insolent Tartar. He did in fact arrive at Mangu (or Möngke) Kaan's encampment, which was only a few days' march from the capital, on December 27, 1253, and he stayed there until Easter of the following year. He was then allowed to proceed to Karakorum, whither the imperial court had in the meantime returned, with its immense retinue of wives, concubines, princes, dignitaries, and slaves of all classes.

Karakorum had originally been a military camp of the leader of the Kerait tribe, which numbered many Christians among its members.[39] At the time of Chinghiz, this camp became the nucleus of the empire's military power and new administration; and by Ogudai, Chinghiz Khan's successor, it was transformed into an urban center, which was vividly described by the friar and is briefly mentioned by Marco Polo.[40]

Thus, while we are indebted to Friar John of Pian del Càrpine for the first description of a Mongolian imperial encampment,

---

Sarai marked the first stage of Niccolò and Maffeo Polo's long journey into the Asian interior at the time of Berke Khan, Lord of the Golden Horde, in 1260.

[38] For this sovereign cf. Spuler, *Die Goldene Horde,* pp. 10 ff. and *passim.*

[39] Cf. P. Pelliot, "Note sur Karakorum," *Journal Asiatique,* Vol. CCVI, 1925, pp. 372 f.

[40] The city was in two divisions, the one Saracen, the other Chinese. The latter was inhabited especially by craftsmen, the former by merchants. In the middle were situated the palaces of the imperial administration, with twelve temples for the idolaters, two mosques, and at the edge of the city a Nestorian church. Cf. *Sinica Franciscana,* Vol. I, pp. 285 ff.

Friar William gives us the first account of an Asian city, which was certainly new, and of a particular type, but characteristic in its structure, population, life, and activities. He looks at it with disdain, through the eyes of a man accustomed to life at Paris and the court of the King of France, and describes it as smaller than the famous Parisian suburb of Saint-Denis; the celebrated palace there, according to him, was ten times superior to those of the Tartar emperor with their sumptuous halls and various buildings for public and private use, erected, after Chinese models, outside the city walls.[41] Thus there disappeared from geographical literature the concept of golden palaces with crystal columns and gem-studded walls, confirmed only fifteen years previously by Friar Julian, which tradition attributed to the sovereigns of Asia; it was replaced by reliable architectural descriptions written by travelers who were guests in the pavilions and palaces of their capital cities. Friar William had found at Karakorum a small, European, Catholic colony among the conspicuous foreign element, especially Chinese and Persian, resident there and in part in the service of the court or government. The native population, on the other hand, unwilling as ever to settle in urban centers, and remaining faithful to its habits as nomads of the steppes, was encamped outside the walls, to the south of the city.

The missionary was therefore able to observe and describe Asian life in its most diverse aspects, concentrated in one place, and to obtain extensive information from fellow believers and compatriots, brought to Mongolia by the Tartar armies as privileged slaves, who took part in the life of the court and the city.[42] And they, in turn, profited in this distant land from the presence of

[41] For a more detailed description of the imperial palaces at Karakorum, also mentioned by Marco Polo, and a bibliography of the subject, cf. the present author's work, *Guillaume Boucher* (cited in note 23 above), pp. 45 ff. For a plan of the ruins of Karakorum, on which is still to be found the Lamaist monastery of Erdeni-tso, cf. A. Herrmann, *Historical and Commercial Atlas of China*, Cambridge, Mass., 1935, p. 54.

[42] For Christian life in the capital, described at length by the friar, cf. *Guillaume Boucher*, loc. cit., and the article by Jean Dauvillier, "Guillaume de Rubrouck et les communautés chaldéennes d'Asie Centrale au moyen âge," *L'Orient Syrien*, Vol. II, 1951, pp. 223–242, in which Dauvillier makes no distinction between Jacobites and Nestorians, the latter being the only ones mentioned by the friar and kept quite distinct by Marco Polo.

two friars who, by renewing the rites and sacraments of the Roman Church in these pagan surroundings, could give them the solace of a common faith for the first time in their many years of exile.[43]

For the rest, and in spite of six baptisms administered by Friar William in Mongolia, his political-religious mission was a failure at the imperial capital, as it had been in the other places of residence of the Chinghizide princes; and King Louis, having suffered yet another humiliation and disillusionment in his attempts to come to a spiritual and political understanding with the Tartars, must have regretted having sent him. The only concrete—indeed, immortal—result of this mission is to be found in the pages of the *Itinerarium,* which is one of the most original and interesting masterpieces in the whole of medieval Latin literature.[44]

Whereas Friar John's *Historia Mongalorum* took on its character mainly from the political mission that inspired it, it was the fundamentally religious task of Friar William that directed the latter's attention toward the ecclesiastical aspects of Asian life as they appeared in court circles and among the cosmopolitan population of the capital. Moreover, even as Friar John competently described the military and political organization of the Tartar empire, so Friar William was able to make known for the first time to ignorant Westerners the Buddhist cults, and Buddhist rites as practiced especially by the resident Tibetan lamas. He also described the heretical aberrations of the Nestorians and the exorcisms of the shamans. But he made no attempt to penetrate the spiritual depths and doctrinal substance of the various cults. On the other hand, he gives a vivid picture both of the religious rivalries around the imperial throne and of the enlightened policy followed by the sovereigns and governments of the empire in order to maintain peace and tolerance amid so much dogmatic ferment and so many latent conflicts. The description of the

[43] Friar Bartholomew of Cremona remained at Karakorum by special permission of the authorities, and probably ended his days there at some date not known to us; he was certainly the first friar to be buried in Tartar territory.

[44] Cf. W. W. Rockhill's translation, with detailed commentary, *The Journey of William of Rubruck,* London, Hakluyt Society, 1900,

public discussion held between the friar and representatives of
Oriental religions records the first direct Catholic contact with
Asian clergy in an age of fierce universal religious controversies,
and it has no equal for vivacity and exactitude in all the medieval
literature that stemmed from it.[45] It was through this report that
the Western world learned for the first time dependably some
of the fundamental principles of Buddhist doctrine, which Tibetan Lamaism had diffused in Mongolia from the time of
Chinghiz Khan.[46]

Friar William's geographical revelations are no less important,
for he was first to realize that the Caspian is an inland sea, and to
recognize in the Chinese the equivalent of the ancient Seres.[47]
He is in no way interested in Asian flora, though he does occasionally cast a glance about him to note the peculiarities of a
landscape; on the other hand, his excellent description of the
Siberian ox reflects a typically medieval realism in the representation of animal life, which we shall encounter on a larger scale in
Marco Polo's book.[48]

For the rest, the Friar's *Itinerarium* is a mine of varied information about the Asiatic life of his times as manifested in the courts,
sanctuaries, tents, customs, folklore, everyday practices, and exceptional happenings, too, as observed by him or learned through
continuous personal contact with peoples so varied in race, language, faith, and culture. Whereas his companion, Bartholomew
of Cremona, who was sick, was allowed by the authorities to remain in the capital, and to care for the souls of the few resident
Catholics, Friar William was sent back to the West as "persona
non grata," and left Karakorum on August 16, 1254. The authorities of the empire and the Great Kaan himself displayed notice-
able haste and energy in their desire to be rid of a man who had
upset the religious peace of the empire by engaging heatedly in
theological discussions and, perhaps, by his very presence. It is

[45] Cf. this famous episode in *Sinica Franciscana*, Vol. I, pp. 289 ff. At present,
no history exists of the religious controversies and disputations of the Middle Ages.
The disputations are one of the characteristic and vivid aspects of the universal
civilization of the XIIIth century, and the occasion recounted by Friar William is certainly the most typical, on account of the variety of faiths represented.

[46] Turn to chap. vii, § 3, of the present work.

[47] *Sinica Franciscana*, Vol. I, p. 108 and p. 152.

[48] *Ibid.*, pp. **233 f.**

in fact likely that his expulsion was solicited by the Nestorians at court and in the government, who refused to tolerate the presence of troublesome Catholic monks in the capitals of the empire.[49]

When he arrived at Acre after a journey of more than a year, the friar compiled and sent to King Louis his report, which transcends in every way the task assigned him by the French monarch. It is a work of obvious improvisation, personal and rhapsodic, without literary pretensions but adorned with Biblical and classical tags, erudite references, and humorous touches, and with some solemn, gracious passages; and the whole is pervaded by the bitter disgust that this barbaric pagan world must have aroused in the soul of our enthusiastic missionary, who was everywhere betrayed and disappointed by his experience of men and things. Nor does his account lack the traditional element of fantasy, and he transfers this time to China the story of towns with walls of gold, as well as the fable of deformed pygmies who were supposed to live in the inaccessible rocky mountains of eastern Cathay.[50]

So, too, he takes up again the reports of Herodotus, Pliny, and Pomponius Mela about the cannibals living in the heart of Asia, and applies them to the Tibetans, of whom Marco Polo also relates many strange things.[51] The story of the cannibals, which

---

[49] Turn to chap. vi of the present work.

[50] *Sinica Franciscana*, Vol. I, pp. 236 f. Friar William was the first (and only) one to make Chinese writing known in the West. Otherwise, it is not mentioned either by Marco Polo or by any of the medieval missionaries to China (cf.. *Sin. Franc.*, Vol. I, p. 271), but it was well known to the Arabs since the Xth century. Cf. Ferrand, *Relations de Voyages,* as cited in note 9 to § 1 above, Vol. I, pp. 135 f.

[51] *Sinica Franciscana*, Vol. I, pp. 234 ff. A similar story about Tibet is recounted by Friar John (*ibid.*, pp. 60 ff.). The idea of cannibalism was traditionally associated with the ancient and medieval concept of the Far East, so that even the Mongols were suspected of this practice, as is learned from Friar John (*ibid.*, p. 47) and from an allusion of Friar William's (*ibid.*, p. 171). This tradition goes back to the ancient geographers (cf. A. Herrmann, *Das Land der Seide und Tibet im Lichte der Antike,* Leipzig, 1938, pp. 31 ff.); and confirmation of it appears in the romances relating the feats of Alexander the Great, in connection with the legend of Gog and Magog, for which see A. R. Anderson, *Alexander's Gate, Gog and Magog, and the Inclosed Nations,* Cambridge, Mass. (Mediaeval Academy of America), 1932, with bibliography of the subject. Mention of these anthropophagi is also to be found in doctrinal vernacular literature (cf. Langlois, *op. cit.*, pp. 128 and 168) and in medieval chronicles (cf. Wright, *Geographical Lore,* as cited in note 1 to § 1 above, p. 330), as well as in the works of Arab geographers, for which see Ferrand, *Relations de Voyages,* Vol. I, pp. 25, 36, 37, and *passim.* The most recent publication on the subject is that by G. Hogg, *Cannibalism and Human Sacrifice,* London, 1958. Neither Marco Polo nor

had a place in the traditional fanciful geography of the Orient, could not fail to make its appearance here, since what was said of certain macabre Lamaist cults, about which the friar may have heard at Karakorum, could certainly have given new though unwarranted life to these fables.[52] Thus, when he asked a Chinese monk for information about the nature of the fabulous monsters of Asia, the friar would sooner suspect the good faith of his informant than accept his candid declaration that he had never heard of them.[53]

Nevertheless, these are but a few scattered anecdotes, in comparison with the mass of authentic information, realistic reports, and critical observations which forms the substance of the book. The friar is certainly not inspired by charitable sentiments in his judgment of the peoples and lands of Asia. Even as Friar John had gone thither in the footsteps of the invaders, which were marked by the bleaching bones and other pitiful remains of their victims, so Friar William was unable to forget the memory of his fellow religionists massacred in Poland and Hungary by the hordes of that same Batu before whom he had to humiliate himself by genuflecting in front of his throne.[54]

As opposed to Marco Polo, who everywhere exalts the power, splendor, and greatness of the Chinghizide empire and its sovereigns, these missionaries disliked the Tartars so much that, in the words of Friar William, they went to so great lengths as energetically to preach war against them.[55] Unlike our great Venetian, these friars had only seen, apart from the countries lying in ruins along their route, the kingdom of the steppes and some evidences of the rudimentary civilization of the nomads, which, all in all, could hardly have been expected to excite their fancy or attract their interest. The splendor of the Chinghizide

---

any other Western traveler of the Middle Ages ever penetrated into Tibet, then under Mongolian sway. Odoric of Pordenone (d. 1331) described it extensively (*Sin. Franc.*, Vol. I, pp. 484 ff.) without a personal knowledge of the country.

[52] Cf., e.g., B. Laufer, *Use of Human Skulls and Bones in Tibet* (Anthropological Leaflets, No. 10, Field Museum, Chicago), to which can be added the so-called *ts'a ts'a*, ornaments made up of earth and pulverized human bones, described by Giuseppe Tucci, *Indo-Tibetica*, Vol. I, Rome, Accademia d'Italia, 1932.

[53] *Sinica Franciscana*, Vol. I, p. 269.

[54] *Ibid.*, pp. 211 ff.

[55] *Ibid.*, p. 244.

courts was in too great contrast with the miserable life led by the Altaic tribes. Their ceremonial rites seemed to be diabolical manifestations, and the theological, ecclesiastical, and magical aberrations of the paganizing Nestorians deeply wounded Friar William's pious soul, and, above all, his sentiments as a Catholic and a missionary.

The strength of spirit shown by the friars is all the more admirable for the way in which they kept as far as possible an open mind in observing and conscientiously portraying an exotic, impenetrable world. With the failure of their apostolic mission, their reports of their travels form the only concrete results of so much effort and so many privations. Their statements formed a sure basis for all plans of defense against further invasions, and informed the Western sovereigns and ecclesiastical authorities of what was happening in the immense hinterland of Asia, at the same time that they transformed the traditional picture of this continent into a vivid, exact description of its lands and peoples.

Marco Polo, who followed them at a distance of some two decades, was left with the task of encircling this vision with his own experiences in the Far East and Greater India, marshaling them to the service of his "Description of the World." His book represents the first great achievement of modern empirical geography and has achieved outstanding popularity among the host of travel books that delight their readers and foster an ever-increasing knowledge of the physical world and universal history.

He had in this task other precursors, who were less cultured than the missionaries and less conscious of their responsibility toward the authorities and the public of their age, but who were certainly not inferior in either courage or experience; namely, those Italian merchants in the East who traded with the Tartars between the Volga and the Caspian Sea, and of whom Niccolò and Maffeo Polo are the most illustrious and successful representatives.[56]

[56] To the group of Marco Polo's Western precursors may be added the figure of Rabbi Benjamin of Tudela, who, having set out from Spain in 1159, proceeded farther than any other Western explorer into the Middle East, where he made a prolonged stay and collected information about the rest of Asia and its peculiarities. (Cf. M. N. Adler, "The Itinerary of Benjamin de Tudela," *Jewish Quarterly Review*, Vol. XVII, 1905, pp. 304 ff., 522 ff.). He relates his experiences in concise form, with the main purpose of making known the contemporary Hebraic diaspora to his

NICCOLÒ AND MAFFEO POLO

Before Niccolò and Maffeo Polo set out in 1260 from Soldaia in the Crimea upon their first transcontinental venture, no other Western merchant seems to have penetrated into Asia, challenging the Mohammedan bloc and the uncertainties of a journey fraught with danger and all too likely to be fruitless. In fact, Friar Julian of Hungary does not mention any in the border regions of the Volga and the Urals, on the edge of the Tartar empire; and those famous merchants, many of them Italian, whom Friar John of Pian del Càrpine met at Kiev in 1247 must certainly have traded in the Ukraine, setting forth from their emporia at Constantinople and from other commercial centers.[57]

In the ten years that had passed since the journeys of our first missionaries, this region had been invaded by the Mongols of Batu Khan, who, after having retreated once more beyond the banks of the Dnieper in 1242, maintained their sovereignty there, which was recognized and accepted by their Russian and Ruthenian vassals. Indirectly, their political power extended to Cracow and reached the confines of the still Latin Byzantine empire, via Bulgaria, a tributary state. Before the constant menace of their armies, ever ready for battle and pillage, the princes and lords of these vast fertile regions accepted a secular yoke which made possible the preservation of their dynastic, feudal, and religious traditions. Moreover, it is well-nigh certain that international trade was of greater interest to this aristocracy, which was partly urban and partly rural, than to the Tartar invaders, nearly all of whom were soldiers or state officials, not traders, and whose occasional wealth was the fruit rather of tribute money and booty than of regular commercial practice.

---

co-religionists; hence, the book attracted little or no notice outside of medieval Hebraic communities until the XIXth century. It will be mentioned on several occasions in the present volume. For its geographical value cf. Beazley, *op. cit.* (in note 1 to § 1 above), Vol. II, pp. 218 ff. Benjamin's *Itinerary*, published by A. Asher, London, 1840, has recently been republished by the Hakesheth Publishing Company, 927 Broadway, New York. For other editions and biographical data cf. the *Encyclopaedia Judaica*, relevant article.

[57] *Sinica Franciscana*, Vol. I, p. 129. They are the Genoese Michele and the Venetians Bartolomeo Manuel, Jacopo Reverio (Venerio), and Niccolò Pisani, with others not clearly identified. The friar also asserts that in this same town of Kiev there were many other Austrian and Polish merchants.

It is therefore very likely that the merchants whom Friar John met at Kiev in 1247 had no direct information or notion of the immense variety of Asiatic life although they were experts in Tartar methods of conquest, dominion, and administration. We are, however, sure of one fact: that these pioneers of Euro-Asian trade served the exchange of goods, on the one hand, by wholesale acquisition of the products of the rich Ukrainian soil and its vast northern hinterland, and, on the other, by providing both the local chieftains and the invaders with hard currency.[58]

Venetian and Byzantine gold and silver coins were used for this purpose, since their purchasing power extended even into the interior of Asia, where the Chinghizide princes of the Golden Horde and of Turkestan had learned to mint money.[59] The export of products from the Ukraine and its outlying regions toward the Mediterranean was primarily directed to Byzantium and, in the second half of the century, to the ports of the Crimea, whence they were sent in every direction on Venetian, Genoese, and Byzantine ships.[60] These western regions of the Tartar empire produced nothing of great rarity, but they offered vast quantities of skins and cereals, salted fish, metals, and various kinds of merchandise; trade thence did not include such treasures as gold, precious stones, or cloths, which could excite curiosity and stimulate the imagination by renewing the memory of the wonders of the Orient.

The Polos cannot have specialized merely in precious objects in their ancestral shop at Constantinople, as is generally believed. Instead, it is probable that this happened at a later date, after they had begun to export some of the ordinary goods listed above. Europe, indeed, did not produce precious stones, but imported them from the East through the agency of Mohammedan merchants and their emporia.[61] At this time the moribund Latin empire was too poor to import large quantities of precious metals and other objects. In fact, from what Marco recounts in the pro-

[58] Cf. the article by Valentino Sciugaevsky, "Monete veneziane del secolo XIII scoperte nell'Ucraina," *Numismatica*, Vol. XVII–XVIII, 1951–52, pp. 1 ff.
[59] Cf. von Heyd, *op. cit.* in note 15 to § 1 above, Vol. I, pp. 51 ff.
[60] For the merchandise and produce from those regions cf. Spuler, *Die Goldene Horde*, pp. 388 ff.
[61] Cf. von Heyd, *op. cit.*, Vol. II, pp. 10 f.

logue to his book, it seems that the two Venetians liquidated their store in the Eastern capital, when the political and economic situation became precarious owing to the imminent return of the Greeks to the Byzantine throne.[62]

The brothers invested the proceeds of this sale in a "great quantity of most beautiful gems," which were easily transportable and readily traded. It may be stated that this initiative had been favored by the general conditions of the markets in those years, when, in the decadent and unsettled capital, luxury articles had increased in purchasing power with respect to goods of prime necessity and immediate utility.[63] However this may be, they must have made the fortune of the Polo brothers, once they had arrived at their store at Soldaia with the intention of finding a market for them at the Tartar court nearest to their base.

This move has historical importance because hitherto the Crimean ports had been used exclusively for the export of merchandise and foodstuffs from Tartar territories toward the West at the same time that the nomads of the steppe demanded few if any Western goods. The Polo brothers' plan was therefore an ingenious one: to introduce into these territories the sole merchandise eagerly desired by their rulers, which in the raw state originated from these same Eastern countries, such as Persia, India, and Central Asia. And it was certainly from these regions that the gems came which the Polos acquired at Constantinople and in the Crimea and which were probably imported by Egyptian and Anatolian merchants, with whom these emporia were in constant commercial contact.

This commerce seemed particularly lucrative since—as was certainly known to the merchants of the area—the Chinghizide princes bought up large quantities of gems, not merely from vanity or greed of possession, or to satisfy the desires of their women, but also as a basis for their fluctuating economy, which

[62] *Il Milione*, cr. ed., p. 4; M.P., p. 74. As is known, Michael VIII Palaeologus took Constantinople in 1261, annulled Venetian privileges, and confiscated much of the property of the Venetian subjects, who were forced to abandon the city. For the chronology of the various moves made by the Polo family during these years cf. Moule-Pelliot, *Marco Polo: The Description of the World*, Vol. I, pp. 22 ff.

[63] For the economic situation of Byzantium at that time cf. von Heyd, *op. cit.*, Vol. I, pp. 427 ff. For bibliography of the subject cf. G. I. Bratianu, "Les Études byzantines d'histoire économique et sociale," *Byzantion*, Vol. XIV, 1939, pp. 497 ff.

was still in large part founded on barter or on a rudimentary monetary system.[64] With the prospect of good business before them, the two Venetians set out from Soldaia to the court of Berke Khan, who then resided in the two centers of his dominion, Sarai and Bulgar, on the lower and middle stretches of the Volga, respectively, holding court there in Tartar fashion according to the seasons, and governing from thence the Western territories of the empire, which extended from the Carpathian Mountains to the northern frontiers of Persia.[65]

On their way thither the Polos must have followed more or less the same route as that explored and described by Friar William of Rubruck some six or seven years previously. Having left this same town of Soldaia on June 1, 1253, he had arrived at the Isthmus of Perekop after twelve days, making his way from camp to camp to the banks of the River Don (July 20) and finally reaching, after two months of travel, the residence of Sartach, not far from the lower stretches of the Volga.[66]

The obstacles and hardships overcome by the friar give us an idea of the journey along this same way a few years later by the two Venetians, who enjoyed fewer privileges than an emissary of the King of France and were exposed to greater dangers on account of their precious, secret load.[67] Having arrived at Sarai, according to Marco's account, they were joyfully and honorably welcomed by the sovereign, to whom they "presented all the gems they had brought with them," receiving in return twice the amount of their actual worth.[68] Note the characteristic form of the quoted expression; Marco thereby draws a discreet veil over the commercial character of this first transaction and transforms it into an act of courteous exchange between persons of the same rank, with the obvious intention of representing the two Vene-

[64] Cf. Spuler, *Die Goldene Horde*, pp. 330 ff. and 388 ff. The Chinghizide princes' eagerness to possess jewelry is well illustrated in the famous letter of Arghun Khan, sovereign of Persia, to Philip the Fair, King of France, in 1289, which asked him, with the promise of adequate reward, to send "(precious) stones of diverse colors"; for which see A. Mostaert, "La Lettre de l'Ilkhan Argun à Philippe le Bel," *Harvard Journal of Asiatic Studies*, Vol. XVIII, 1955, pp. 200 ff.

[65] Spuler, *Die Goldene Horde*, pp. 33 ff.

[66] Cf. the picturesque description of the journey in *Sinica Franciscana*, Vol. I, pp. 164 ff.

[67] For communications in those regions cf. Spuler, *Die Goldene Horde*, pp. 409 ff.

[68] *Il Milione*, cr. ed., p. 4, chap. iii; M.P., p. 75 and n. 1.

tians not as merchants but as gentlemen engaged in a nobler activity—a characteristic trait, which, at the beginning of the book, foreshadows Marco's silence about the family's commercial activities in the Orient during almost half a century of travel and residence on the borders or in the interior of Asia.

One can, however, concede to Marco that his report of the sovereign's joyful and honorable welcome is truthful. Brother to the great Batu, first of the Chinghizides to have gone over to Islam, and powerful lord of the Tartars of the West, Berke Khan delighted in bedecking himself with precious stones, and was certainly open-handed with these toward his consorts and the ladies of the court who appeared with him at feasts and ceremonies.[69] However, it is not possible to doubt that the chivalrous exchange of courtesies mentioned by Marco was in fact no more than one of those commercial transactions between merchants and a ruler which from time immemorial had been a common feature of Asian life—though it was perhaps exceptional in the sense that there is no record of other Italians then trading in the Tartar territory of the Volga region;[70] and this, as we shall see, may in large part account for the Polos' later success at the court of Kublai Kaan.

The details of this transaction remain to be considered, so far as they are disclosed in Marco's laconic allusions. They are primarily concerned with the merchandise itself, inasmuch as these jewels presented as a gift to the wealthy Berke were, according to the best reading of the *Milione,* "sent to be mounted in various places."[71] From this assertion one assumes that the jewels were in their natural state and not yet cut or set. But some doubt remains of the fact, and therefore of the reliability of the text. It is certainly true that in all the Chinghizide residences there existed Mohammedan and Western craftsmen who worked for the

[69] Cf. Grousset, *L'Empire des steppes,* p. 477.

[70] Before the Genoese and Venetians obtained permission from the Tartars to establish themselves in the Crimea—after 1266, it would seem,—trade in these regions was carried on by Mohammedans of varying origin, as well as by Armenians, Greeks, and Jews. Cf. Spuler, *Die Goldene Horde,* pp. 392 ff.

[71] "Il les envoia a parer en plosor partie et furent mout bien parés": *Il Milione,* cr. ed., p. 4, chap. iii. Cf. also Moule-Pelliot, *Marco Polo: The Description of the World.* Vol. I, p. 75 n.

court; [72] hence it is quite probable that some were also employed by Berke Khan who must have been expert in satisfying his predilection for gems and, as it would appear from Marco's text, the technical and aesthetic exigencies of the two Venetians.[73]

Moreover, the account of the commercial transaction remains incomplete since it leaves us in doubt of the Polos' further activities during their year's stay in those regions, and indeed of the very aim of their undertaking. What form of payment did they in fact receive for the gems, to twice their value? Certainly it was not ready money, since gold coinage was never used in the territory of the Golden Horde, and silver coins were rare and not replaced, as in China and later in Persia, by paper money in enforced circulation.[74] More probable, therefore, is the version relating that Berke rewarded the offer of gems with regal gifts which, once they were sold in various quarters, yielded twice their value. The chivalrous exchange of courtesies would thereby be reduced to what it must in fact have been, namely, an excellent piece of business. This, in one way or another, reveals the intentions of the two Venetians in organizing the venture. They never thought of establishing permanent residence among the Tartars, whose power of conquest and dominion made itself felt as far as the Crimea.[75] Most probably the jewels were destined to restock the Polos' store at Soldaia, and perhaps also the one at Constantinople, with goods from Tartary which came, indeed, from the immense territory subject to the primary Islamic branch of the Chinghizide dynasty, called Qipchak from the name of its native population, or the Golden Horde (*altan ordu*) from that of its

[72] Cf. the present author's *Guillaume Boucher*, esp. pp. 16 ff.

[73] The versions VA3 and VL of the *Milione* (cf. Benedetto's Introd. to his cr. ed., pp. c ff.) have, respectively, "which things they sent to be sold in those parts were well sold" and "which gifts they sent to be sold in various parts," while Benedetto accepts the Franco-Italian reading, which he translates as "and he sent them to be mounted in several places and they were very well mounted" (*Il libro di Messer Marco Polo*, p. 4). Cf. also Moule-Pelliot, *Marco Polo: The Description of the World*, Vol. I, p. 75, n. 1; and Marco Polo, *The Travels*, translated into English by A. Ricci from the text of L. F. Benedetto, New York, 1934, p. 3.

[74] Paper money was introduced into China after Kublai's coming, and into Persia only in 1293, with disastrous effects. For this cf. Spuler, *Die Mongolen in Iran*, pp. 300 ff. The Golden Horde does not seem ever to have used paper money.

[75] Spuler, *Die Goldene Horde*, pp. 390 ff.

sovereign's residence.[76] Berke's "gifts" to the Polos were probably
invested in merchandise destined for their stores at Soldaia and
Byzantium, even as some Genoese merchants at these centers
traded in the Ukraine in order to export to the West the various
products of that region.[77]

As we have already mentioned, the Polos' originality consists
in their intelligent courage, whereby they transferred their trading activity to the regions of the Volga, entering into direct contact with the powerful and wealthy ruler himself and thereby
eliminating intermediaries, and at the same time offering an
outlet for the produce of the area.[78] It was probably the organization of a more extensive trade that made them decide to prolong
their stay in the two most important centers of the dominion:
first Sarai, and then Bulgar, the temporary residences of this same
sovereign, who maintained the tradition of the other Chinghizide
princes as nomad lords of the steppe, transferring his place of
residence from one part of his territories to another according to
the season.[79]

In 1260, when the Polos arrived there, Sarai, which means
'seraglio' or palace, was a town made up of pavilions, tents, and
chariots near a branch of the lower Volga. Founded some ten
years previously by Batu, it centered around a walled palace,
probably of Chinese architecture and structure, which resembled
the one at Karakorum; and, like that capital, it was provided with
markets, the sanctuaries of various religions, and, in deference to
Mohammedan custom, public baths, which were unknown to
Mongols of the old order and were abhorred by them.[80] Bulgar,
on the the other hand, formerly the capital of the Volga Bul-

---

[76] *Ibid.*, pp. 10 ff.

[77] It can also be supposed that Berke Khan's gifts consisted of various kinds of
cloth (brocades, silks, etc.), such as those which the Chinghizide sovereigns were
wont to bestow as largess on those they wished to honor or reward. Cf. the *Milione*,
cr. ed., chap. xc; M.P., p. 225.

[78] I.e., furs, hides, cereals, and especially slaves. These last were for the most part
sent to Egypt and Byzantium; their exportation to Italy began only at the end of
the century, and it does not seem that the Polos participated in this traffic. See note 29
to chap. v, below.

[79] This was the custom of Mangu in Mongolia, Kublai in China, Hulagu and his
successors in Persia—all more or less in the same way as described by Marco; cf.
the *Milione*, cr. ed., pp. 62 and 76 f.; M.P., pp. 185 and 211

[80] Cf. Spuler, *Die Goldene Horde*, pp. 264 ff.

garians, and conquered by the Tartars in 1237, had been for centuries an important urban center, situated a few miles from the middle course of the river and inhabited by an Altaic population, converted to Islam in the Xth century, which, according to Friar William of Rubruck, was fanatically attached to that faith.[81]

In the course of their year of residence in these centers the Polos had occasion to become acquainted with aspects of the Tartar world that were still completely unknown to the West. It was a world in which the Mongol element already prevailed, on account of its numbers and influence, over the native population of various Turkish tribes, which preserved, although beneath Mohammedan dress and direction, authentic customs of Asian life. Here the two Venetians, who already knew, apart from the *lingua franca* of the Mediterranean and Levantine merchants, the Greek of the Aegean, Byzantium, and Anatolia, must have learned the language that was, and continued to be, the regional tongue: the Turkish dialect of the Comans, which, according to Friar Pasquale of Vitoria, was still in the following century, together with Persian, the language spoken or understood throughout the Tartar empire from Persia to Cathay.[82] This certainly must have been one of the various languages Marco claims to have learned before entering the service of the Great Kaan at the end of his journey across the continent.[83]

Although, as Marco asserts, they were "wise and prudent," the two brothers had not taken into account all the possibilities of the situation and they found their way blocked; moreover, they had with them all the merchandise they had accumulated at Bulgar with the intention of transporting it to the family stores. These years, from 1260 to 1262, were to witness events of great historical

---

[81] "Et illi Bulgari sunt pessimi sarraceni, fortius tenentes legem Machometi quam aliqui alii" (*Sin. Franc.*, Vol. I, p. 212).

[82] *Sinica Franciscana*, Vol. I, p. 503. Friar John of Pian del Càrpine had already noted the diffusion of the "Coman" language in Turkestan (*Sin. Franc.*, Vol. I, p. 113), whereas William of Rubruck observed (*ibid.*, p. 234) that among the Uigurs was found the "fons et radix" of the Turkish Coman tongue. For this subject cf., apart from the works cited above, E. Bretschneider, *Mediaeval Researches from Eastern Asiatic Sources*, London, 1910, 2 vols., Vol. I, pp. 236 ff.

[83] *Il Milione*, cr. ed., p. 10, chap. xvi; M.P., p. 86. Marco here asserts that he knows, apart from several languages, four different kinds of writing. The reading, however, is doubtful. For a hypothetical identification of these languages cf. Yule-Cordier, *The Book of Ser Marco Polo*, Vol. I, pp. 28 ff., and below, chap. iii, n. 8.

importance precisely in these regions on the extreme western
borders of the immense Tartar empire when this same Berke
Khan mobilized his armies against his cousin, Hulagu, who had
just brought to a succeessful conclusion the Mongol conquest of
Persia, Mesopotamia, and Syria.[84] This long drawn out and
bloody war was brought on because both cousins aspired to
dominion over the Caucasus, originally assigned to Persia but
claimed by the Golden Horde, on account of its strategic value
and immense wealth. Moreover, Berke, a convert to Islam, was
also inspired by resentment against the Ilkhans of Persia, who
some two years previously had destroyed the Abbasid caliphate
and followed an openly anti-Mohammedan policy.[85] Finally,
Berke decided to oppose Kublai, who had proclaimed himself
Lord of China and Great Kaan of the Tartars in this same year,
1260, whereas Hulagu and his successors governed their vast
dominion of the "Tartars of the Levant" as his loyal vassals, although independent in practice from the central government of
the empire.

The adventures of the Polo brothers depended on these complex circumstances, an immediate result of which was the inter-
ruption of navigation on the lower Volga, a waterway which
served to transport merchandise as far as the Caspian Sea and,
to the west of Sarai, toward the Black Sea and the Crimea where
it touched the Caucasian region contested by the two adversaries.
The two Venetians were able to proceed only as far as Ukek, an important caravan center halfway between Bulgar and Sarai, near
present-day Saratov, which according to Marco marked the western limits of the kingdom of the "Lord of the West"—in other
words, the immediate dominion of Berke.[86] This was the starting point for the caravan route which, crossing the Uralsk steppe

[84] For these events cf. Grousset, *L'Empire des steppes,* pp. 470 ff., and Spuler, *Die
Goldene Horde,* pp. 33 ff.

[85] Until Ghazan Khan's conversion in 1295, the Ilkhans of Persia more or less
openly protected Christianity and Buddhism as well as the animistic religion of their
forebears, in spite of Islam, which did, however, eventually gain supremacy for political reasons and by virtue of cultural prestige.

[86] *Il Milione,* cr. ed., p. 5, chap. iii; M.P., p. 75. Marco's statement is obscure,
unless the western borders toward Russia are meant by "la fin dou reigne." Russia,
however, was also politically dependent on the Lord of the Golden Horde, through
his Russian Christian vassals. For this subject cf. Spuler, *Die Goldene Horde,* pp.
274 ff., and G. Vernadsky, *The Mongols and Russia,* Yale Univ. Press, 1953.

and Khwaresm desert to the north of the Caspian Sea, led to the Amu Darya, the ancient Oxus, and to Turkestan and Central Asia.[87] It was along this road that the two merchants set out toward Bokhara, the capital of this rich historic region.

Unfortunately, the information given us by the *Milione* about this Asian digression of the Polo brothers is laconic and confused. It is nevertheless certain that, since they were unable to proceed directly to their destination, they must have decided to make their way there by an immense detour that would take them from Bokhara to Persia along the ancient caravan route which, to the south of the Caspian Sea and across northern Persia, linked Turkestan with the Black Sea.[88] Since they supposed that the war between the two Chinghizide states would last a long time—as did in fact happen,—they were left with no other alternative than to make their way round the territories contested for years with varying fortunes.

However, the journey from Ukek to Bokhara must have taken longer than the seventeen days assigned to it by Marco. Nor can the two brothers have crossed nothing but a desert bereft, as he says, of towns and castles and inhabited only by Tartars with their tents, who lived off their cattle.[89] In fact the caravan route touched, among others, the ancient town of Urgench, to the south of the Aral Sea, a busy commercial center which was described by various travelers of the next century as one of the most active in western Asia and the principal town in the vast empire of Khwaresm, which was conquered and destroyed by Chinghiz Khan in 1220.[90] Since Marco does not even mention the town of Khiva, or other minor centers along the route, we must con-

---

[87] For communications in the dominion and at the time of Berke cf. Spuler, *Die Goldene Horde*, pp. 409 ff.

[88] This caravan route linked Bokhara with Merv, Nishapur, Sultaniyeh, and Tabriz, and thence, through Erzerum, reached the Black Sea ports, leaving the territory of the Golden Horde far to the north. See the map in Spuler, *Die Mongolen in Iran*, 1955.

[89] *Il Milione*, cr. ed., p. 5, chap. iii; M.P., p. 76.

[90] The best, though succinct, medieval account of this itinerary is to be found in the *Pratica della Mercatura* of Francesco Balducci Pegolotti, ed. Allan Evans, Cambridge, Mass. (Mediaeval Academy of America), 1936, p. 21, where "Organchi" is described as a "fruitful land for trade." The treatise was composed about 1340, but the author had been in the Levant many years previously, when Marco Polo was still alive.

clude that he knew little about it. Here, as elsewhere, he seems
to wish to dictate his description of the world by making use
of his own experiences rather than those of his relatives, precursors, and masters. Hence these latter appear in his book as
pale, evanescent, secondary figures, who are infrequently mentioned as companions of fortune in spite of the fact that their
common enterprises brought them all together in ceaseless activity.[91]

For example, Marco merely indicates that the Polo brothers
arrived by this road at the "great and noble" city of Bokhara, "the
best in the whole of Persia; where, since they could go neither
forward nor back," they had to remain for three years, in the reign
of King Barac, the lord of the region.[92] When they arrived there,
presumably between 1261 and 1262, both the city and the region
were in a state of unrest as a result of the civil and dynastic wars
that embroiled the whole of Asia after the proclamation of
Kublai as Great Kaan of the Tartars and the transference of the
capital of the empire into Chinese territory.[93] Local feuds, moreover, among the Chinghizide princes of Central Asia, with their
guerrilla warfare and surprise raids, further complicated the political situation that traditionally disturbed the life of the historic
cities of Transoxiana by interrupting the development of their
vast trade and drying up the basis of their rich intellectual flowering.[94]

"King" Barac, or Buraq Khan, a secondary figure in the same
dynasty, governed this province in accordance with Tartar usage
for his powerful cousin Caidu (or Qaidu), Lord of Central Asia
—then called Chagatai from the name of its first Chinghizide

[91] Marco mentions his father's and uncle's stay at "Campiciu" (Kanchow, in Kansu
province) and their more than problematical participation in the taking of the town
of "Saianfu" (Hsiang-yang, in Hupeh); cr. ed., pp. 138 f.; M.P., pp. 316 f. The
two are always mentioned together as companions of travel and commerce, except
at Foochow, where Niccolò appears alone with Marco at the time of a stay of which
we know neither the aim nor the duration (cr. ed., p. 168 n.; M.P., pp. 347 ff.).

[92] Politically, Bokhara then formed part of the Central Asiatic empire, of which it
marked the extreme western boundary toward the Persia of the Ilkhans, who incorporated it in their dominion only in 1273.

[93] For these facts and their consequences cf. Grousset, L'Empire des steppes, pp.
352 ff. and 474 ff.

[94] Ibid., p. 410.

sovereign.[95] During the years of the Polos' stay at Bokhara the
surrounding fertile region, which was rich in towns, schools,
and commerce, had been invaded by the armies of Aric Buga (or
Ariq-bögä), Kublai's brother and his inveterate rival, who was
soon afterward defeated and exiled to his ancestral, decadent
Mongolia.[96]

Then, threatened in the west by the armies of Hulagu, Khan
of Persia, encamped at Khorasan, not far from the Amu Darya,
for the protection of his empire, Bokhara found itself isolated
from the rest of Asia, of which it was the most important transcontinental emporium. After its total and bloody destruction
by Chinghiz' hordes in 1220, the city had been rapidly rebuilt
under the new Tartar administration, which, as often happened
in Chinghizide history, was in the hands of a woman, the famous
Organa, the widow of Chagatai, first Khan of Central Asia.[97]
The civil war, however, complicated and fed by religious conflicts and dynastic rivalries, paralyzed the cultural and commercial
activities whereby already in the IXth century Bokhara had become one of the most famous capitals in the whole continent.
When the Polos arrived there, without being able to proceed any
farther, these activities were limited by circumstance to a regional

[95] *Ibid.*, pp. 404 ff.

[96] Ariq-bögä (i.e., the 'strong one'), otherwise known as Aric Buga, died in Mongolia in 1266, after having been exiled there by his victorious brother. Until his
capitulation in 1264 he had represented and inspired the Mongolian nationalist party
against the Sinization and decentralization of the empire favored by Kublai, rather
from force of circumstances than from conviction.

[97] Cf. Arminius Vámbéry, *History of Bokhara*, second edition, London, 1873, pp.
119 ff., on the basis of Persian sources of that century. While the historical descriptions and accounts of the city abound in trustworthy information so far as preceding
ages are concerned (cf. esp. Richard N. Frye, *The History of Bukhara*, Cambridge,
Mass., Mediaeval Academy of America, 1954, and his "Notes on the History of
Transoxiana," *Harvard Journal of Asiatic Studies*, Vol. XIX, 1956, pp. 106–125),
we have little precise information about the Mongol period, but it seems certain
that the recovery was a rapid one, that the city prospered as a commercial center,
and that it was favored by the invaders. Chinese coins minted in this region at the
time of Ogudai (1229–1241) point to the existence of a Chinese governor. Cf. W.
Barthold's article, "Bukhārā," in the *Encyclopaedia of Islam*. For the period after the
conquest of this city by the Persian Ilkhans in 1273 the data become more numerous
and more reliable; but at that time the Polos were on their way to China by other
routes, described in the *Milione*, which, by their proceeding from Nishapur toward
Balkh in Bactriana, passed to the south of Transoxiana, which was never visited,
although briefly described, by Marco Polo.

sphere, which transformed this pan-Asiatic caravan center into an agitated provincial bazaar.

Its population, however, which had been decimated by massacre at the hands of the Tartars, had been replenished with Persian, Afghan, Mongol, Kirghiz, Chinese, and other elements. Hence the Polos were able to come across the most disparate ethnic groups and to gather information about almost every region and aspect of Asia. They learned about Asiatic methods of commerce, among other things, and this knowledge proved of use to them on more than one occasion during their stay in the continent.[98] Moreover, three years spent by them in these surroundings must have given them a basic acquaintance with Oriental culture and have made them familiar with the languages spoken around them. These were translated by professional interpreters in the marketplaces, which, even in times of misfortune, were numerous at Bokhara.[99]

The trading idiom of the region was the Persian language, and it must have been here that the two Venetians learned this tongue with which Marco became so familiar and which he mainly spoke in China, where foreign merchants and officials commonly used it for purposes of business and trade.[100] It is therefore possible to assume that Marco learned it as a boy from his

[98] Marco never revealed the type of trade carried on by them at Bokhara or elsewhere in Asia, although it must be supposed that the three men also did some business on their own account.

[99] For the population of the region cf. the writings by Vámbéry and Barthold already cited. For the language spoken in the region cf. J. Benzing, *Einführung in das Studium der altaischen Philologie und der Turkologie*, Wiesbaden, 1953, esp. pp. 114 ff. For the Jewish element cf. Walter J. Fischel, "The Leaders of the Jews of Bokhara," in *Jewish Leaders*, ed. Leo Jung, New York, 1953.

[100] Cf. Yule-Cordier, *The Book of Ser Marco Polo*, Vol. I, p. 380 n., and Vol. II, p. 5 n. For Persian toponymy of China in the *Milione* cf. Cordier, *Addenda*, p. 74. It should be mentioned that the Persian spoken in China in Marco's times was that used by all kinds of foreigners in the service of the Mongol court or government, but was not an official language, whereas Turkish Uigur, and Coman, were placed on the same level as Mongolian in edicts and documents. See below, n. 8 to chap. iii and n. 18 to chap. iv. We may mention that the inscriptions added to the paintings which decorated the first Catholic cathedral at Peking, erected at the end of the century by Friar John of Montecorvino, were written, according to his letter of February, 1306, in Latin, Turkish (probably Uigur), and Persian (cf. *Sinica Franciscana*, Vol. I, p. 352), with a characteristic exclusion of Chinese, a language that not even Marco ever learned. Kublai himself never mastered the language of his subjects, as we learn from H. Franke, "Could the Mongol Emperors Read and Write Chinese?" *Asia Major*, n.s., Vol. III, 1953, pp. 28 ff.

father and uncle, even as it seems certain that it was from them that he obtained the scanty information given in the *Milione* about the region of Samarkand, which he never visited.[101]

In these circumstances, far from their emporia and with all export trade at a dead stop, the two Venetians were unable to carry on in Bokhara anything but a local commercial activity, of which it is not possible for us to establish either the quality or the quantity. It must have provided a sufficiency to keep them alive, but it was certainly not enough to satisfy the ambitions that had made them decide to develop their Asian trade in the Crimea so as to provide a greater affluence of goods in their stores in the Levant and at Venice.

It was obviously this particular psychological and historical situation that made them decide to abandon, at least temporarily, their customary trading and to attempt a quite different venture, thus leaving with glory and profit a restricted activity in the narrow, dangerous region of Bokhara, which was then isolated from world trade. As Marco recounts, while the two Venetians were perforce at a standstill in this city, there arrived from Persia on his way to Kublai Kaan's residence in China an envoy from Hulagu, Lord of the Levant, who, since he had never seen a "Latin" before, was greatly amazed to find two of them in that region, and invited them to follow him, with the promise of a comfortable, safe journey, and honors and wealth besides.[102] In a very few words Marco has here expressed a great deal that illumines this famous episode in his sober, yet vivid, prologue. The fact itself reveals that, although a state of war could immobilize for years those merchants who wished to return home via Persia and Anatolia, an ambassador of the sovereign of these lands could journey unharmed across the whole of Asia, making his way through regions contested by various chieftains and temporarily occupied by soldiers of varying origins and loyalties. Indeed, as all three Polos were to learn from experience on several occasions in the course of some twenty years in the Mongol empire, each imperial envoy was protected by the so-called "tablets" or

---

[101] *Il Milione,* cr. ed., pp. 40 f.; M.P., p. 144.

[102] *Il Milione,* cr. ed., p. 5, chap. iv; M.P., p. 76. The term "Latin" should be interpreted as "Italian," as in Dante, *Inferno,* XXII, 65.

"piasters" of gold or silver, which by imperial command rendered his person inviolable, under pain of death and terrible reprisals against any who should disregard them.[103] Moreover, princes, officials, and imperial or "khanal" envoys and couriers traveled by the famous Tartar posts, organized all over Asia in the way described by Marco, which made possible the safe, speedy transmission of messages and persons, while merchants, excluded from this privilege, followed—generally in convoys of men and camels—roads which in part were guarded by Mongolian soldiers, but which provided at best a slow and difficult means of communication.[104] In spite of the continuous state of war between the rival lords of Asia, their contacts with one another do not seem to have been broken off for long, as were those of traders on the caravan routes.

In this way, after a year of traveling on roads unknown to us, the two Venetians arrived at Kublai's court, probably at the summer residence at Shangtu, which is vividly described by Marco in one of the most famous episodes in his book.[105] Ac-

[103] For this subject cf. Yule-Cordier, *The Book of Ser Marco Polo*, Vol. I, pp. 351 ff., note, and N. Poppe, *The Mongolian Monuments in hP'ags-pa Script*, second edition, trans. and ed. J. R. Krueger (*Göttinger asiatische Forschungen*, Vol. VIII), Wiesbaden, 1957, pp. 6 ff. and pls. VII–IX. These piasters of various metals, described in the *Milione* (chap. lxxxi, cr. ed., p. 71), are called *p'ai-tzu* in Chinese, *gerege* in Mongolian (cf. Francis W. Cleaves in *Harvard Journal of Asiatic Studies*, Vol. XVI, 1953, pp. 255 ff.). The golden piasters were granted to men holding military rank of head of 10,000 foot-soldiers or *toman* (*Il Milione*, cr. ed., p. 55; M.P., p. 172).

[104] Cf. Spuler, *Die Goldene Horde*, pp. 409 ff., and, for the means of communication with China, Peter Olbricht, *Das Postwesen in China unter der Mongolenherrschaft*, Wiesbaden, 1954. One of the principal sources of our knowledge of the Asiatic postal system is to be found in the *Milione*, esp. chap. xcix, cr. ed., pp. 94 ff.; M.P., pp. 243 ff.

[105] Cr. ed., p. 62; M.P., p. 185. Marco, however, has not specified the locality, as he did for his arrival at Kublai's court in or about the year 1275. If we presume that he would not have failed to mention the capital if the two Venetians had arrived there after their first journey across the continent of Asia, we may suppose that Kublai likewise received them at one of his provincial residences on the first occasion. After his accession to the Chinghizide and Chinese throne the court found a temporary residence in a large encampment—a true mobile city—near the Great Wall, whence it moved toward Shangtu, or Chemenfu (Kemenfu), as Marco calls it, which is in the territory of the Öngüt on the border between Manchuria and Mongolia, more than 200 miles to the north of Peking. It was only in 1264, shortly before the Polos' arrival, that this city became the principal seat of the court and government, with the Mongolian name of Daidu, Tai-tu in Chinese, Khanbaliq in Turkish, and Cambalu or Cambaluc in the *Milione*. In fact, as we read in the *Milione*, this was the imperial residence in the winter, whereas for the summer months the court regularly returned to Shangtu in the way described by Marco (cr. ed., chaps. lxxv and xcv; M.P., pp. 185 ff. and 234 ff.). For the chronology of the Polos' travels cf. Moule-Pelliot, *Marco*

cording to him they were the first "Latins" to appear at the Chinghizide court. Far more than any of the Great Kaan's other informants they were experts on the things of both Europe and Asia, and were able to discourse with him in his own tongue, which they had learned while at Bokhara, where the idiom of the Mongol conquerors had imposed itself alongside the local Turkish dialect, the Arabic of the mullahs and other educated persons, and the Persian of the marketplaces and schools.[106]

It was a time-honored tradition of Asiatic sovereigns to receive wandering merchants in private audience and to learn about other countries from them. This historic meeting was, however, exceptional, inasmuch as the two Venetians had no merchandise to offer and could hardly have had the idea of opening up the markets of Europe to China, since they were too far distant to make it profitable. It is true that later there were some Italians who established themselves permanently in China for their business, and we know the names and places of residence of a few of these. But this cannot have been the Polos' intention, since on both occasions when they found themselves in those parts they always thought of their return home.[107] They made their appearance at the imperial court exclusively as informants, and fate willed it that thenceforward they ceased to be merchants, to become, as is known, Kublai Kaan's ambassadors to the Roman Pontiff. The Mongol leaders had for some time past been aware of the Pope's existence, without having any clear idea of the particular character of his sovereignty or of his effective political power.[108]

The information requested from the two Venetians by the

Polo: The Description of the World, Vol. I, pp. 24 ff. For a conjectural plan of Shangtu (in modern Chinese, K'ai-p'ing) see above, chap. i, n. 46.

[106] That Niccolò and Maffeo spoke with the sovereign in Mongolian is indicated by Marco, cr. ed., chap. xv.

[107] *Il Milione,* cr. ed., p. 11, chap. xviii; M.P., p. 187. For Italian merchants in the Far East, especially in the XIVth century, cf. the article by R. S. Lopez, "Venezia e le grandi linee dell'espansione commerciale" (as cited above in note 15 to § 1), esp. pp. 50 ff., and the complete list of the names that can be reconstructed today in the article by R. Gallo, "Marco Polo, la sua famiglia e il suo libro," in the commemorative volume *Nel VII centenario della nascita di Marco Polo* of the Istituto Veneto di Scienze, Lettere ed Arti, Venice, 1955, pp. 147 ff.

[108] Cf. P. Pelliot, "Les Mongols et la Papauté," *Revue de l'Orient Chrétien,* third series, Vol. II, 1923, pp. 3 ff.

"Great Lord" was almost exclusively on political, military, and religious matters. They were asked about the way in which the emperors of the West governed their states, about kings, princes, and other rulers, about the Pope and the state of the Roman Church, as well as the usages of the Latins, i.e., the Italians. After this, Kublai did not ask his informants for an increase in trade between their countries, but sent them as his ambassadors to the Pontiff, with the request that His Holiness should send him one hundred teachers of the seven liberal arts, capable, as Marco says, of demonstrating by force of reason that the Christian law was superior to that of his idolatrous subjects. This request finds its place in the complex political and religious system which had been organized and put into practice by Kublai and which will form the object of special study on our part.[109] One may justifiably doubt the good faith behind such a request. The Great Kaan certainly did not intend to Christianize his peoples, but wanted to obtain some able counselors and learned foreigners to govern his empire, since he distrusted the numerous Moham- medans in his service and at court and was well aware of the resistance offered by many of the Chinese mandarins, who were impatient of the yoke imposed by Mongol barbarians on their highly civilized country.[110]

This time, the tone of the message was quite different from the insolent challenges sent a few years before to the Pope and the sovereigns of Europe by Kublai's predecessors on the Chin- ghizide throne, e.g., Küyük and Mangu (or Möngke) Kaan. In the ten years since their last message the situation of the Mongol empire had changed into one unfavorable to the continental bloc, either owing to internal dynastic struggles or because the con- quest of the world—proclaimed on various occasions by their large and small potentates—now appeared to them less feasible than they had expected. Indeed, the Tartar advance toward the West had been definitely arrested in Syria, in September, 1260, by the troops of the Mamelukes of Egypt, who with their mili- tary victory initiated the recovery of Mohammedan power in

[109] See chap. vi of the present work.
[110] For this subject cf. O. Franke, *Geschichte des chinesischen Reiches*, Vol. IV, Berlin, 1948, pp. 470 ff.

the East, after the destruction of the Abbasid caliphate only two years previously. Moreover, these same Mohammedans had come to regard the Pope, as William of Rubruck asserts, as the potential head of a European, Christian—and possibly also Mohammedan—coalition against the Tartar invaders.[111]

Seen in this light, the mission with which Kublai entrusted the Polo brothers appears not only as a political, cultural, and religious move to the advantage of his sovereign power in China, but also as an attempt to pacify and tempt the Pontiff with the possibility of Christian triumphs in Asia. The oil from the lamp burning at the Holy Sepulcher in Jerusalem, which was also requested by the Great Kaan, probably at the suggestion of the powerful Nestorian minority at his court, was intended not only to serve the magical practices of this sect but also to seal the sovereign's Christian intentions with a supposed act of faith. Kublai was, however, at this time more than ever engaged in furthering Lamaist propaganda, which was in fact gaining supremacy over every other religious teaching in the empire.[112]

The Polos were the instruments of this lofty and far-reaching policy, but with only the meager results related by Marco, owing to the fact that, after their return to Italy some four years later, the Pontiff, Clement IV, was dead and the Papal throne remained vacant for the next three years.[113] Hence, instead of the hundred teachers of the seven liberal arts the two Venetians took with them to Kublai's court young Marco, who was destined by his activity and experience to replace the Papal legates, who never reached their destination.[114]

These circumstances have helped to erase every trace of this historic mission undertaken by the two brothers. It is understandable that there is no mention of it in Chinese or Papal sources, which do not record similar exchanges of ambassadors between Chinghizide sovereigns and the Holy See. But the arrival of two men from regions so far distant and with so important a mission was an event unique in history, which cannot

---

[111] Cf. *Sinica Franciscana*, Vol. I, p. 195.

[112] Cf. O. Franke, *loc. cit.*

[113] *Il Milione*, cr. ed., p. 7; M.P., p. 80.

[114] Namely, the two Dominicans, William of Tripoli and Nicholas of Vicenza (*Il Milione*, cr. ed., p. 8, chap. xiii; M.P., p. 83), with whom we shall deal later.

have failed to arouse comments and observations of every kind
in Venice and elsewhere. We know nothing about this; and even
the cloth of asbestos has been lost which was sent by Kublai to
the Pontiff for the preservation of Veronica's Veil at St. Peter's.[115]
If, as Ramusio relates, the three Polos' return to Venice in 1295
caused such a stir that it was remembered for centuries to come,
the impression made by the two envoys in 1269 cannot have
been less great since the veracity of their accounts was guaranteed
by the "golden tablets of command" and the imperial credentials.
Some three years later, the newly elected Pope, Gregory X, then
at Acre, was apprised in season of the Polos' imminent return to
China, this time taking Marco with them, and he made them his
envoys to the Great Kaan.[116]

As informants of the Pope, and certainly of the public at large,
it would be hard to overestimate the role of Niccolò and Maffeo
as Marco's precursors, and then as his teachers, regarding the
things of Asia. They had likewise preceded him in offering a
summary picture of the political situation in Europe and of its
religious and administrative institutions. Little can have been
known about all this at the Chinghizide court, although the
Mongol leaders who had led their armies as far as Vienna, after
their conquest of Hungary in 1240, were directly acquainted with
central and eastern Europe as far as the Adriatic. They must
thus have formed a geographical picture put together from information gathered from merchants and prisoners whom they
interrogated as they advanced. But the idea they had built up
must have been quite vague, if, for example, the dignitaries who
spoke to William of Rubruck could ask him whether the Pope
was really five hundred years old, or whether there were many
sheep, cattle, and horses in the friar's country. This questioning,
of course, seemed ingenuous, but was intended to elicit whether
there existed conditions that would make possible or favor the
conquest of the Western regions destined to be subjugated by the
Tartars.[117]

The learned Mohammedan cosmographers who were to be

[115] *Il Milione,* cr. ed., p. 47; M.P., p. 157, where Marco speaks of "le saint suder de
nostre seignour Jesucrit." See below, chap. v, n. 64.
[116] *Il Milione,* chaps. xii and xiii; M.P., pp. 83 ff.
[117] Cf. *Sinica Franciscana,* Vol. I, p. 222.

found in such numbers at the court of the Great Kaan, and who constructed terrestrial and celestial globes for him, could have instructed him in this subject by referring to the wealth of Arabic geographical literature diffused and studied all over Chinghizide Asia,[118] but even they would have been unable to reply to the specific questions Kublai set the Venetians. Even less was known about the subject by the Chinese scholars at his court, although Chinese cartography and geographical literature had achieved by the first centuries of our era a remarkable stage of development, superior to that of geography in the West during the Middle Ages.[119] Their first-hand experience of men and things did not extend beyond Central Asia, which had once formed part of the Chinese empire—especially when the so-called empire of the Karakhitai had united all of Turkestan as far as the borders of Persia under the Chinese Liao dynasty, and had laid the Shah of Khwaresm, their neighbor, under tribute.[120]

Therefore, in spite of the traditional contacts between China and Persia, and in spite of this recovery of Chinese prestige in Asia in the XIIth century, the geographical knowledge of medieval China never extended beyond Syria, and very occasionally reached Egypt and Byzantium in vague terms only and with a quasi-total ignorance of the Mediterranean world.[121] An exception to this rule is afforded by the so-called *Description of the Barbarian Peoples* (*Chu-fan-chih*), compiled in the first

[118] The great Persian scientist Nasiruddin remained at Karakorum as Mangu Kaan's cosmographer and astrologer. For the observatory erected at Peking by Kublai with the coöperation of Mohammedan scholars cf. Yule-Cordier, *The Book of Ser Marco Polo*, Vol. I, pp. 446 ff.

[119] For the well-nigh complete absence of information about the West in the official historiography of the empire cf. H. Franke, "Europa in der ostasiatischen Geschichtsschreibung," *Saeculum*, Vol. II, 1951, pp. 65 ff. Cf., moreover, the present author's article, "1254: Venezia, l'Europa e i Tartari," in the volume *Nel VII centenario della nascita di Marco Polo*, pp. 298 ff; and n. 130 below.

[120] For this Central Asiatic episode in Chinese history cf. O. Franke, *Geschichte des chinesischen Reiches*, Vol. IV, pp. 192 ff.

[121] For this subject cf. Bretschneider, *Mediaeval Researches*, Vol. I, pp. 180 ff., and A. Herrmann, "Die ältesten chinesischen Karten von Zentral- und Mittelasien," in *Festschrift für Fr. Hirth*, Berlin, 1920, p. 185; also Éd. Chavannes, "Les Pays d'Occident d'après le Heou Han Chou," *T'oung Pao*, second series, Vol. VIII, 1907, pp. 153 ff. The subject has received exhaustive treatment by Kurakichi Shiratori: "The Geography of the Western Regions Studied on the Basis of the Ta-Ch'in Accounts," *Memoirs of the Research Department of the Tōyō Bunko*, ser. B, No. 15, Tokyo, 1956, pp. 73–163. An extensive Chinese geographical bibliography is offered by Herrmann, *Atlas of China*, pp. 85 ff., and H. Franke, *Sinologie*, Bern, 1952, pp. 194 ff.

decades of the XIIIth century from oral and literary information
by Chau Ju-kua, an inspector of maritime trade at the port of
Chüanchow, in the province of Fukien, Marco Polo's Zaiton.[122]
This work, which is in part doctrinal, has a certain affinity with
contemporary Western geographical treatises, with which Marco's
description of the world likewise has certain links.[123]

Chau Ju-kua, who was related to the imperial Sung family, had
had recourse to Chinese literary sources; and he filled these out
with information gathered in the ports of southern China, which
teemed with Mohammedan merchants and seamen in a continuous exchange of trade with Indonesia, India, and the Persian
Gulf, and—via the Red Sea—as far as the port of Alexandria in
Egypt, to which came much Oriental merchandise that was to
be sent on to the markets of Genoa, Venice, and farther afield.[124]
However, apart from Asia Minor, the only places in the Mediterranean known to our author were Egypt, Sicily, and perhaps
southern Spain, obviously from accounts he had received from
Mohammedan seafarers, who considered these lands as belonging to their faith.[125] The account of these countries and their
products to be found in his book is in some parts correct, in
others fanciful, like the reports of the Orient in the related doctrinal and geographical literature of the West.[126] Hence, Kublai
and his government could not have drawn any useful informa-

[122] Cf. *Chau Ju-kua: His Work on the Chinese and Arab Trade in the XIIth and XIIIth Centuries,* translated into English and annotated by Fr. Hirth and W. W. Rock-hill, St. Petersburg, 1911. And see note 15 to § 1 above.

[123] For the sources of this work cf., apart from the introduction and notes to the translation just cited, the article by Kazuo Enoki, "Some Remarks on the Country of Ta-Ch'in as Known to the Chinese under the Sung," *Asia Major,* n.s. Vol. IV, 1954, pp. 15 ff.

[124] Chau Ju-kua, *ed. cit.,* pp. 146 f. For the best contemporary description of Alex-andria cf. *The Travels of Ibn Jubayr* (trans. R. J. C. Broadhurst, London, 1952, pp. 29 ff.), a famous account by a Spanish Moor written in 1183, the era of Saladin.

[125] Chau Ju-kua, *ed. cit.,* p. 142. For the description of the Etna region cf. the present author's article, "1254: Venezia, l'Europa e i Tartari," as cited in note 119 above, pp. 299 ff.; and his article "L'Etna nelle tradizioni orientali del medio evo," *Rendiconti dell'Accademia nazionale dei Lincei,* Classe di Scienze morali, ser. VIII, Vol. XIV, 1959, pp. 356–369. Fr. Hirth's identification of Mediterranean countries in Chau's treatise is conjectural and dubious.

[126] We do, in fact, find in this treatise some of the most common geographical fables then current in the whole of the ancient and medieval world, combined with precise data about the produce of the various regions and trade with China. For China see the comprehensive article by K. Shiratori cited in note 121 above, pp. 24–72.

tion from it to find out about the things in Europe that were of most interest to them. The importance attributed by them to the information obtained from the two Venetians is obvious when one considers that which an imperial envoy was able to report to the Mongolian authorities about the Western world shortly before the Polos arrived at the imperial court. This was the Chinese Ch'ang Te, sent to Persia in 1259 by Mangu Kaan, Kublai's brother and predecessor, immediately after his other brother, Hulagu, had extended his dominion as far as Syria and the Mediterranean.[127] His *Report on the Lands of the West* (*Si Shi Ki*) was compiled in 1263 by the Chinese scholar Liu Yu, who probably belonged to the imperial administration. It was dedicated to Kublai, who had meanwhile succeeded his brother on the Chinghizide throne.[128] This concise description of western Asia, which is often vague and at times quite fanciful, extends as far as Egypt and Byzantium, and includes some mention of the supposed customs of France, which presumably were learned from members of the French colony at Karakorum, whence this historic embassy had set out.[129] Kublai and his counselors could not be satisfied with these anecdotes, and were the more pre-

[127] Cf. Bretschneider, *Mediaeval Researches*, Vol. I, pp. 109 ff., with subsequent translation of the Chinese text.

[128] Möngke Kaan died on August 11, 1259, in his military encampment near Kialing-kiang in the western Chinese province of Szechwan, which had been conquered in part by his armies six months after the departure of the above-mentioned embassy from Karakorum in February of the same year.

[129] Liu Yu is interested, *inter alia*, in feminine headgear in France, which, according to him, was similar to that of the most venerable Bodhisattva of the Buddhist cult; also in masculine apparel, and he notes the custom of the "Franks" who sleep with clothes on. Cf. Bretschneider, *Medieval Researches*, Vol. I, p. 142. On the other hand, the Ilkhans of Persia were far more extensively, though not more correctly, informed about life in France. Beginning with Ghazan Khan (1295), they had as their historical and geographical informer the great minister Rashiduddin, whose extensive description of Europe takes in the whole of Italy although this country is included in the kingdom of the "Franks" and is never singled out by its geographical name. Cf. *Histoire universelle de Rašid-al-Din*, Vol. I: *Histoire des Francs,* texte persan avec traduction et annotations par K. Jahn, Leiden, 1951. The author must have acquired much of his information about European customs, and especially those of Italy, from merchants and residents at Tabriz, the seat of court and government in Chinghizide Persia. We cannot exclude the possibility that the Polos may have contributed to this picture—sometimes correct and sometimes fanciful—of the lands of Europe, with which, in any case, the political and commercial contacts had remained constant and active. For this see Spuler, *Die Mongolen in Iran*, pp. 430 ff.

pared to appreciate the information received from the Venetians, according to Marco's own assertion, which it is no longer possible to doubt.[130]

[130] Despite possible political or warlike contacts (cf. F. J. Teggart, *Rome and China: A Study of Correlations in Historical Events*, Univ. of California Press, 1939, with extensive bibliography), the Chinese dynastic annals and chronicles offer only vague and mostly fabulous allusions to the Western world (cf. J. J. M. de Groot, *Chinesische Urkunden zur Geschichte Asiens*, 2. Teil: *Die Westlande Chinas in der vorchristlichen Zeit*, Berlin and Leipzig, 1926, and Friedrich Hirth, *China and the Roman Orient: Researches into Their Ancient and Medieval Relations*, Leipzig and Munich, 1885. Chau Ju-kua (*ed. cit.*, pp. 102 ff.) and his main source, Chou Ch'ü-fei's *Ling-wai-tai-ta*, written in 1178 (*ibid.*), show that the few allusions to the easternmost provinces of the Roman Empire contained in the dynastic histories were not forgotten at the eve of the Mongolian conquests in China. On this subject cf. also J. J. L. Duyvendak, *China's Discovery of Africa*, London, 1949, esp. pp. 6 ff.

thRee

MARCO POLO AND HIS BOOK

Nowadays, if anyone were asked to describe the kind of man Marco Polo was, the reply would be: a Venetian merchant, who, having made his fortune in Kublai's China and having returned to his native land in 1295, after an absence of some twenty-five years, dictated his reminiscences in the prison at Genoa, and then ended his days in his native city in the year of grace 1324.

From the renaissance of Polan studies, at the beginning of the XIXth century, down to the present day, the image of Marco Polo as a merchant venturer has dominated the judgment of interpreters and readers of the *Milione*. Since this conception makes of Marco a type and not an individual, a professional and sociological cliché rather than a historical personage, it affects both appraisement of the man and critical evaluation of his book. And while a marked commercial mentality is attributed to him, he is nevertheless surrounded by the poetic prestige that supposedly ennobles the daring trader "in times when life was full of adventure, when trade meant the heroic seeking out of new channels, the arduous conquest of nature and men." [1]

This romantic interpretation of the medieval merchant, so well expressed by the modern reformer of Polan criticism, must be reëxamined in the light of the facts, with more balanced criteria, and in an attempt to arrive at more correct and comprehensive conclusions. Indeed, if one looks at the facts, it is

[1] Cf. Benedetto's preface to *Il Libro di Messer Marco Polo*, Milan and Rome, 1932, p. xv. For a sober judgment cf. Gino Luzzatto, *Storia economica d'Italia*, Rome, 1949, Vol. I, pp. 321 ff. and 343 f. (bibliography). Cf., moreover, A. Sapori, *Le Marchand italien au moyen âge*, Paris, 1948, and G. Luzzatto, "Il mercante veneziano del tempo di Marco Polo," in the commemorative volume of the Istituto Veneto, *Nel VII centenario della nascita di Marco Polo*, Venice, 1955, pp. 243 ff.

very difficult to discover in Marco Polo a merchant in the professional and romantic sense of the word. He never presents himself
so in his book, in which, indeed, commercial information is given
only in passing; it never predominates, nor does it ever reveal a
particular attitude in his judgment of the things and men of the
Orient.

We need only compare the *Milione* with the famous *Pratica
della Mercatura* of Francesco Balducci Pegolotti, a commercial
agent for the Florentine Bardi in the Levant at the time of Marco
Polo, in order to recognize the wideness and variety of Marco's
horizons as opposed to the exclusively commercial vision of an
Italian merchant of the XIVth century.[2] In Pegolotti there is no
fictional hint of distant treasure, no interest in the nature and
civilization of exotic peoples, no description of landscapes, cities,
ports, or customs—not even any mention of the curious or
salacious stories diffused from time immemorial by merchants,
together with their goods, as is attested by both Marco and
Giovanni Boccaccio.[3]

Nevertheless, Pegolotti bestowed upon his commercial guide
to the Orient—from Morocco to Peking—a title similar to the
original of the *Milione,* calling it *Libro di divisamenti di paesi
e di misure di mercatantie,* after the manner of Marco Polo's
"Divisament dou Monde," with the specific addition that determines its character and aim.[4] For the Florentine, the whole earth
is but one vast market. For the Venetian, the world is a spectacle,
which he portrays as best he may and recalls in great variety and
a multiplicity of manifestations.

Amid this mass of information of all kinds the commercial
data contained in the *Milione* make only an occasional appearance, illustrating some particular aspect of life, and are never of-

---

[2] Ed. by Allan Evans, Cambridge, Mass. (Mediaeval Academy of America), 1936.

[3] Tenth Day, Third Story. For Boccaccio's stories dealing with merchants cf. Vittore
Branca, "L'epopea dei mercatanti," *Lettere Italiane,* Vol. VIII, 1956, pp. 9 ff. Pegolotti
obtained his information about Asian trade from merchants he met in the course of a
prolonged stay in Cyprus, after 1324, and probably at Ayas in Armenia, which were
two important centers for the sorting of goods in the exchange between East and
West at the time of Marco Polo.

[4] For the various titles of the *Milione* cf. Benedetto's cr. ed., pp. 245 f. For the complete title of Pegolotti's work cf. *ed. cit.,* p. 8. Cf. also Moule-Pelliot, *Marco Polo: The
Description of the World,* Vol. I, pp. 31 ff.

fered as professional information, as always in Pegolotti's book. Thus, for example, When Marco tells us that in the town of "Tiungiu" in southern China it is possible to buy three magnificent porcelain bowls for the price of one Venetian *grosso*, he thereby wishes to indicate the local abundance of these objects, which were so rare and costly in every other part of the world.[5] Likewise, when he reports the amount of dues levied by customs officials of the Great Kaan in the ports of China, he certainly has no intention of instructing Italian merchants concerning the taxes the state would levy from them, as Pegolotti systematically does, but he makes use of these figures to illustrate the immense wealth that flowed into the imperial coffers from these ports.[6] Marco's remarks on the value of merchandise, the types of currency, and the practice of trade in the countries visited by him are always indicators of their activity and prosperity, or of their particular customs, and are offered without any apparent intention of opening up those lands to Western merchants.

In his youth Marco Polo did not receive any mercantile training, nor was he a merchant in later life. When his father Niccolò and his uncle Maffeo returned to Venice in 1269, Marco was just fifteen years old, and could not then have received any commercial instruction apart from what was common for all boys of that era. At most, they could add up accounts, and had learned some commercial jargon in a prevalently mercantile atmosphere such as that obtaining in the Venice of his times.

We do not know if he learned the small amount of crude Latin that was taught to youths destined for a merchant's career in the maritime towns of the peninsula, as Christopher Columbus did two centuries later (when this was purely a result of tradition, since the vernacular language had by then replaced Latin in nearly all commercial transactions).[7] There is no trace of this

[5] *Il Milione*, cr. ed., p. 160, and Yule-Cordier, *The Book of Ser Marco Polo*, Vol. II, pp. 235 ff. Export of porcelain vessels from southern ports of China was important from early times; cf. Chau Ju-kua, ed. Hirth-Rockhill, pp. 19, 49, 53, and *passim*. For the value of the *grosso* (see below, n. 20) cf. F. C. Lane, "Le vecchie monete di conto veneziane," *Atti dell'Istituto Veneto di Scienze, Lettere ed Arti*, 1958–59, Vol. CXVII (Classe di Scienze morali), pp. 49–78.

[6] Especially in the passages descriptive of Quinsai and Zaiton.

[7] Cf. R. Menéndez Pidal's fundamental study, "La lengua de Cristobal Colón," *Bulletin Hispanique*, Vol. XLII, 1940, pp. 1 ff. For the instruction ordinarily received

in the *Milione*. In any case, it would have been of little help to
Marco, who had to acquaint himself not only with the *lingua
franca* of the merchants of the Levant but also with various
Asiatic languages, which he undoubtedly learned to speak, read,
and perhaps also to write.[8]

During his father's absence his family does not seem to have
engaged in any trade, except for a restricted local activity. The
Polos' "brotherly company" had branches at Constantinople and
in the Crimea, but Marco never participated in this enterprise.[9]
Even Niccolò and Maffeo no longer took a truly active part in
the business (after 1260) when they set out on their first transcontinental journey to China and then returned to Venice, not
as merchants of the Orient, but as ambassadors of the Great Kaan,
armed with letters patent and the imperial golden insignia that
conferred upon them sovereign rank and inviolable protection
throughout the continent of Asia.

Young Marco, who had been instructed by them, accompanied

---

by a medieval Venetian merchant cf. Sapori, *Le Marchand italien au moyen âge*, pp.
xxi ff., and Luzzatto, *Storia economica d'Italia*, Vol. I, pp. 326 f.

[8] It is not possible to ascertain precisely how many languages and ways of writing
Marco had learned in Asia, since the text is corrupt in which he speaks of this (cr. ed.,
chap. xvi; M.P., p. 86). However, they were at least three, of which the writing also
was known to him. Besides those already mentioned (see above, chap. ii, nn. 83 and
100), he must also have been acquainted with the official writing invented by the
Tibetan Phags-pa, "Master of State," which had been imposed by Kublai as early
as 1269 for chancellery and literary use in the whole empire, and especially for coins,
inscriptions, and the piasters of command, which Marco read correctly. For this subject
cf. N. Poppe, *The Mongolian Monuments in ḥP'ags-pa Script*, second edition (*Göttinger asiatische Forschungen*, Vol. VIII), Wiesbaden, 1957. Marco's knowledge of
Chinese seems to have been limited to a few words and ideograms of practical use.
Cf. Yule-Cordier, *op. cit.*, Vol. I, pp. 28 ff., note. Paul Pelliot's observations will be
read in his forthcoming commentary to the *Milione*, announced in 1938 but not yet
published. As for "Marco Polo's Bible," as B. Szcześniak misleadingly calls it in a short
article on the famous Laurentian manuscript (cf. *Journal of the American Oriental
Society*, Vol. LXXV, 1955, pp. 173 ff.), it undoubtedly belonged to a Franciscan
missionary in China in the XIVth century; hence it is unavailing, if not absurd, to
attribute its Latin annotations to the hand of Marco Polo, who was ignorant of Biblical
Latin, as of the Scriptures. A. M. Biscioni, in his *Bibliothecae Medico-Laurentianae
Catalogus*, Florence, 1752, Vol. I, p. 121, had already put forward the supposition that
the manuscript, covered with ancient Chinese silk, had been taken to China by
Marco Polo "aut quivis alius Europeus." The subject is also treated by A. C. Moule,
Christians in China before the Year 1550, London, 1930, p. 85.

[9] The expression "brotherly company," to designate the commercial association of
the Polo brothers, occurs in Maffeo's will. Cf. Moule-Pelliot, *op. cit.*, Vol. I, p. 29. For
this type of commercial undertaking cf. Luzzatto, *Storia economica d'Italia*, Vol. I, chap.
vii.

them on their journey to the imperial court, certainly not as a commercial apprentice, but as an "attaché" to this historic imperial and papal embassy, which was to make of him an official, emissary, and ambassador of the most powerful sovereign on earth. Thus, too, the concrete reality and fabulous wonders of all the Asian continent, from Peking to Trebizond and from Mongolia to Indonesia, were opened up to his mature experience and natural curiosity.

He was presented to the emperor as his "man": that is to say, simply as his subject. This feudal term, however, also designates the lowest grade in the hierarchy of chivalry, corresponding to the *homme lige* of the French and the *nököt* of the Mongols, who was bound to his lord by "homage." The lord, according to the custom of Chinghizide feudal society, assumed the obligation of protecting, sheltering, feeding, and clothing him for so long as he remained in his immediate service. Without this title and these privileges young Marco would never have been able to carry out the first delicate mission entrusted to him by Kublai, of inspecting the distant, semiwild regions on the borders between Tibet and Yunnan, which the Mongolian administration of the empire had difficulty in supervising.[10]

Thereafter, the emperor conferred upon Marco, who was then little more than twenty years old, the title equivalent to *messere* —a term that probably translates the Mongolian title of *nöyök,* which bound the holder even more closely to the sovereign's person. Kublai thus elevated Marco to the rank that was his due as the ruler's informant and personal ambassador to all the peoples of his empire.[11]

[10] The act of "homage" to the sovereign is mentioned in chap. xv of the *Milione,* cr. ed., p. 9. At the time of carrying out the first mission entrusted to him by Kublai, Marco bore a title corresponding to that of "Bachelor" (*ibid.,* chap. xvi, p. 10). which in European medieval terminology indicated the lowest grade in feudal and chivalric society. For the corresponding title in the Chinghizide régime cf. B. Vladimirtsov, *Le Régime social des Mongols* (the translation by M. Carsow), Paris, 1948, pp. 91 ff., 113 ff., and *passim;* and for the institutions characteristic of Mongol feudalism cf. L. Krader, "The Cultural and Historical Position of the Mongols," *Asia Major,* n.s., Vol. III, 1953, pp. 169 ff.

[11] Marco asserts (*Il Milione,* cr. ed., chap. xvii; M.P., p. 87) that he enjoyed this rank in the Great Kaan's service during the whole of his seventeen years' stay in Asia. We should like, moreover, to point out that Niccolò and Maffeo Polo must already have been elevated to a high rank in the Mongolian feudal nobility at the time of their first stay at Kublai's court in 1265, since this dignity was automatically connected with

All these dignities certainly excluded him from trading, which Niccolò and Maffeo had also given up—though they did occasionally indulge in private transactions, as was the custom among the many foreigners in Kublai's China and probably even among his own dignitaries.[12] In his book, as he himself points out,[13] Marco always appears with this title of *messere*, and the Venetian documents that mention him describe him as *nobilis vir* or *Ser* Marco Polo, thus fusing together in his person the corresponding Venetian and Mongolian nobiliary titles of the times.[14] Nowhere is he described as a merchant, nor is any

---

the conferring of the golden piasters and all the courtly privileges that were granted to the two Venetians—as later, also, to Marco. This circumstance explains the fact mentioned in the *Milione* (cr. ed., chap. xv, p. 10; M.P., p. 85) that Maffeo and Niccolò stayed at court "honored above the other barons." Unless we wish to see nothing but an idle boast in Marco's words, we must interpret them in the manner indicated, remembering among other things that Kublai sent his dignitaries to meet the Polos as far as forty days' traveling time would take them from the imperial residence, an honor usually granted only to sovereigns and persons of particular distinction. Cf. the *Milione*, cr. ed., chap. xiv, p. 9; M.P., p. 84. We may presume that Kublai honored the Polos in their "character indelebilis" as papal ambassadors, which was sanctioned by the letters patent of Pope Gregory X. The custom of conferring official rank and title upon foreigners for special merit in promoting commercial intercourse and fiscal profits is attested for the late Sung era by J. Kuwabara, "On P'u Shou-kêng," *Memoirs of the Research Department of the Tōyō Bunko*, ser. B, No. 7, Tokyo, 1935, pp. 42 ff.

[12] The Mongols did not engage in any form of trade. Hence the merchants in their various territories were foreigners, for the most part Mohammedans, and were excluded from their social régime, whereas in Cathay they had at least the lowest place in the social hierarchy, after craftsmen, peasants, and men of letters. Under the Mongol régime rich foreign merchants, especially Mohammedans and Jews, were employed—as Marco Polo may have been—in the administration of the state monopolies. Cf. H. Franke, *Beiträge zur Kulturgeschichte Chinas unter der Mongolenherrschaft (Abhandlungen für die Kunde des Morgenlandes*, Vol. XXXII, Pt. 2), Wiesbaden, 1956, p. 42.

[13] Cf. cr. ed., chap. xvii, p. 10; M.P., p. 87.

[14] The terms *Messere* or *Ser* are appellatives rather than true nobiliary titles, and are applicable to men of military rank as well as to officials of the civil administration. Marco was probably also elevated to a higher rank in the Mongol-Chinese bureaucratic and aristocratic hierarchy, which he described competently in the *Milione*, cr. ed., chap. lxxxvi; M.P., p. 219. Cf. the comments by Yule-Cordier, Pauthier, and Charignon on this description, which reveals the fundamentally military and feudal character of this hierarchy, discussed in Vladimirtsov, *op. cit.*, and briefly for the peripheral regions of the empire by B. Spuler, *Die Mongolen in Iran*, esp. pp. 263 ff., and *Die Goldene Horde*, pp. 293 ff., 303 f., and *passim*. The golden piasters elevated Marco to the rank of head of 10,000 foot-soldiers, or *toman*, as he himself relates in chap. lxx, cr. ed., p. 55; M. P., p. 172. The Chinese nobiliary titles taken over or created during Kublai's reign were far more numerous than those of the Mongols. The honorary civil titles alone numbered forty-two, and were divided into various sections. Cf. Francis W. Cleaves, "The Biography of Bayan," *Harvard Journal of Asiatic Studies*, Vol. XIX, 1956, p. 207 n. 26. Moule-Pelliot, in their Introduction to *Marco Polo: The*

mention made of his having taken up once more—after his return to Venice—the commercial activity of his ancestors, and indeed of a large number of the Venetian nobility of his times. In fact, we learn from documents that the ancient "brotherly company" of the Polos at Constantinople and in the Crimea had been liquidated after the death of Andrea Polo, who was, at least until 1280, its only manager and representative at Soldaia.[15]

The information to be found in Jacopo da Acqui's *Imago Mundi,* that Marco was taken prisoner at Laiazzo (Ayas) and transported to Genoa after a naval encounter between the Genoese and the Venetians that took place at that port in 1296, is therefore hardly trustworthy.[16] It would imply the resumption of the Polos' business in the Levant immediately after their final return home, a resumption of which there is no trace and which, in any case, could only have lasted a very short while, if we find the family permanently established in Venice after Marco's return from the prison at Genoa in 1299.[17]

Nevertheless, some measure of credence may be given to the more heroic version, which makes him a prisoner of the Genoese after a battle which need not necessarily be that of Laiazzo, and in which Marco seems to have participated not as a merchant but as a Venetian nobleman. His motives were both the defense of personal and family interests and the defense of his native city and of Venetian commerce in the Levant or in the Adriatic.[18] Noble rank

---

Description of the World, pp. 19 ff., hesitate to affirm that the Polos belonged to the Venetian nobility. This is, however, asserted with great emphasis by Ramusio in various passages of his preface to his edition of the *Milione.* Although part of the biographical information offered by him is not trustworthy, yet it must be admitted that he was better informed about the Venetian scene than most historians of his age, since he had at his disposal, and had often consulted, the authentic documents, which later in part disappeared. Indeed, those that have been saved serve on various occasions to demonstrate the trustworthiness of some local news, as opposed to the legendary passages in his account. For this cf. Yule-Cordier, *op. cit.,* Introd., pp. 4 ff. The first German edition of the *Milione* (Nuremberg, 1477) presents Marco in a famous woodcut (cf. cr. ed., facing p. clii; M.P., fig. 1) as "der edel Ritter."

[15] Cf. Yule-Cordier, Introd., pp. 64 ff., and Moule-Pelliot, *loc. cit.*

[16] For this subject cf. the passages quoted by Yule-Cordier, Introd., pp. 64 ff., and Moule-Pelliot, pp. 26 ff. See, moreover, the text and observations of Benedetto in his cr. ed. of the *Milione,* pp. cxciii ff.

[17] Jacopo da Acqui asserts in his *Imago Mundi* that Marco was then on board a ship with some merchants, although he was marked off from them by the title *dominus.*

[18] The dates mentioned by Jacopo da Acqui and Ramusio do not agree, either with

certainly did not exclude—indeed, in Venice it almost infallibly implied—the practice of trade, which was quite in accordance with the traditions of this maritime and mercantile republic. However, it is with melancholy surprise that we read in Marco's will and those of the other members of his family, as well as in the existing authentic documents, that the fabulous wealth commonly attributed by legend to our three enterprising travelers was in reality reduced to far more modest proportions, which no successful commercial activity ever seems to have increased in any way.

A further proof, *inter alia,* is provided by the building, which has now disappeared, near the present-day Corte del Milion by San Giovan Grisostomo, which for centuries remained the spacious seat of the Polo family while more sumptuous palaces of other Venetian nobles sprang up one after the other in the Rialto quarter and along the Grand Canal. Some of these nobles were related to the Polos, but, as owners of galleys, emporia, and lands in which they invested their large profits, they had found quite a different type of wealth in their trade with the Orient and with home markets.[19] There is no sign of this prosperity in the documents that attest in an authentic manner to the amount of the Polos' property, even after the return of Marco and his elderly companions from Kublai's Asia.

And, truly, the return home of the ambassador of the wealthiest sovereign in history makes a pathetic spectacle, when, in 1311, we find him suing a certain Paolo Girardo from the parish of Sant' Apollinare, his agent, for having failed to make payment for one and a half pounds of musk, at a price of six pounds of Venetian *grossi*—quite a considerable sum for those times.[20]

---

the historical facts to which they allude or with certain biographical data, as has been clearly proved by Moule-Pelliot, *op. cit.,* Vol. I, pp. 34 ff. Nevertheless the question remains a controversial one.

[19] Cf. Yule-Cordier, *op. cit.,* Vol. II, pp. 510 ff., and Moule-Pelliot, *op. cit.,* Vol. I, pp. 35 ff., where the history of the Polos' house property is discussed and illustrated, on the basis of cadastral and notarial documents, as well as with sketch maps. For this cf. R. Gallo, "Marco Polo, la sua famiglia e il suo libro," in the commemorative volume of the Istituto Veneto. According to this author (cf. *Atti dell'Istituto Veneto di Scienze, Lettere ed Arti,* Vol. CXVI, 1957–58, p. 31), the Polos bought the dwelling after their return from China in 1295 or 1296.

[20] Cf. the relevant document published by Yule-Cordier, *op. cit.,* Vol. II, p. 511. The approximate value of the transactions, as well as of Marco's property in Venice,

Likewise, when he went bail for a certain Bonocio or Bonvecio da Mestre, who was later condemned by the Grand Council for fraudulent importation of wine.[21] The few other commercial transactions known to us are also of little account; they were conducted within the family circle, and were destined to guarantee a small sum of money inherited by his money-minded wife, Donata Badoer, and the three daughters mentioned in Marco's will.

From the inventory of his possessions drawn up after his death, of which there exists an authentic copy of 1366, we learn that almost thirty years after his return home Marco still owned a quantity of cloths, valuable pieces, coverings, hangings, and brocades of silk and gold, exactly like those mentioned several times in his book, together with other precious objects—among which we come across his "golden tablet of command" that had been given him by the Great Kaan on his departure from the Tartar capital, and which elevated him to a high rank at the court there.[22] We need not include certain curios, which were then of little or no commercial value, such as an apparently Buddhist rosary, the silver belt of a Tartar knight which he

---

has been calculated on the basis of the pound sterling by these scholars (*ibid.*, p. 591), who have nevertheless taken into account the fluctuating value of Venetian currency in that epoch. But if a purely approximate evaluation was already difficult at the time of their researches and calculations, it is impossible now to form an exact idea of the values then obtaining, and we are obliged to resign ourselves to a vague, relative evaluation, according to which it would appear that Marco was a man of means but not an enterprising merchant intent on actively increasing his patrimony.

[21] Cf. the documents collected by G. Orlandini, "Marco Polo e la sua famiglia," *Archivio Storico Tridentino*, Vol. IX, 1924, pp. 12 ff., known in part to Yule-Cordier, *op. cit.*, Vol. II, pp. 510 ff., and discussed by Moule-Pelliot, *op. cit.*, Vol. I, pp. 523 ff. The document referring to Bonocio has also been interpreted as concerning Marco Polo senior, our author's uncle; hence its attribution is still doubtful. Cf. the article by R. Gallo already cited. For other similar transactions in Marco's century that attest to a characteristic Venetian custom cf. R. Morozzo della Rocca and A. Lombardo, *Documenti del commercio veneziano nei secoli XI–XIII*, esp. Vol. II.

[22] This document is reproduced in Moule-Pelliot, *op. cit.*, Vol. I, p. 554. It merits extensive study, which has not so far been undertaken. From it we learn, among other things, that Marco never would or could part with a great number of objects of Asiatic origin, of which he seems to have been rather a collector than a merchant. The lack of data about precious stones, pearls, and other valuables of that kind suggests what may at one time have formed the objects of his trade, whereas he had kept for himself a considerable number of cloths, articles of jewelry, and various other objects, although these were still tradable. This, however, can only be ascertained by a careful examination of the varied information contained in the document.

probably wore as a sign of his rank, and some feminine headgear (*bochta*) adorned with gold and "precious stones and pearls" which must have belonged to some Tartar princess, perhaps that same Cocachin who, according to Marco's account, shed copious tears on parting with the three Venetians, to whose care she had been entrusted.[23]

These are the objects with which he neither could nor would part, but which he made over to his daughters, who married into the leading Venetian families, two of them respectively the Bragadin and the Querini, whilst the third married first a Dolfin and then a member of the Gradenigo family. However, in spite of these treasures, the family patrimony was somewhat limited if, for example, its various members had recourse to reciprocal loans of average size. These did, however, yield interest to Marco, which he seems to have exacted with a degree of efficiency that reveals a certain acrimonious pedantry and lack of generosity toward his father and uncle, who had been the initiators and companions of his great adventure.

These transactions therefore indicate a limited fortune, although set in noble surroundings, and a temperament that was meticulous rather than imaginative, parsimonious rather than

[23] That the rosary was not a Christian one is deduced from the fact that it is mentioned in the list as of boxwood "*in the manner of* a paternoster," the latter being the term by which the Christian rosary was commonly designated. The belts of various materials, all more or less valuable, were the most important distinguishing mark among the Mongols of their military and feudal rank. As for the *bochta*, it was the ceremonial headdress of Mongol ladies, and is described at length by Friar William of Rubruck in his *Itinerarium* (*Sinica Franciscana*, Vol. I, pp. 182 ff.; cf. the commentary on this passage by W. W. Rockhill, *The Journey of William Rubruck*, London, Hakluyt Society, 1900, pp. 73 f., and see our fig. 8); also, in accordance with Friar William's testimony, by Vincent of Beauvais in the *Speculum Historiale*, Bk. XXIX, chap. 85. This headdress was called *bogtak* by the Mongols, whence the *bocca* of those Franciscan missionaries who make mention of it, and the *bochta* of the Polan passage quoted. The custom of offering a royal garment as both a parting gift and a sign of affection and esteem was very common, although it was always a sign of particular distinction, among Oriental sovereigns and princes. For this see the present author's note, "Ölün's Chemise," *Journal of the American Oriental Society*, Vol. XVII, 1947, pp. 54 ff. The hypothesis that the *bochta* mentioned in the document was the ceremonial headdress of Princess Cocachin therefore appears to be well founded. Those who drew up the list of objects belonging to Marco on the occasion of his death must have learned from him the Mongol name for this headgear, as well as the Oriental terms for the cloths and other objects mentioned in the same inventory, of which the only existing copy is that written in Venetian dialect (which makes difficult reading), of July 13, 1366.

avid for gain—in a word, that of a conscientious administrator more diligent than ambitious, and spurred on by circumstance rather than by initiative, "unusually careful and prudent," as he himself makes Rustichello define his character in the prologue to the *Milione*. Thus, he was both a careful observer of life in its various aspects and an ingenuous admirer of the wonders of this world. Satisfied with his exceptional fortune, he was just as ready to adapt himself to the modest sphere of local transactions; and, while proud of his fame as an explorer and author, he was perfectly willing to leave the limelight and to live with the memories of a glorious past, surrounded by the gossip of his parish and the women of his family.[24]

These qualities, which show forth clearly enough from the documents of both family and state, confirm his natural adaptability to every kind of surroundings and need, as well as the trustworthiness of his account. It is that of a practical man not gifted with much imagination but endowed with a natural curiosity which was at times led astray by a superficial culture but was never at any time impaired by false literary ambition.[25] And even if the choregraphic display of wealth in cloths and precious stones described by Ramusio, in order to color the return of the three Venetians to their homeland, be somewhat exaggerated, it is nevertheless quite certain that these precious materials and jewelry formed the most conspicuous part of their baggage.[26]

During their long period of absence the Polos had lived chiefly at the expense of Kublai Kaan, and had undoubtedly accumulated a large patrimony. This, presumably, consisted of cloths

[24] He is so presented by the documents and records of undoubted authenticity. In the prologue to his book he described himself as a man who from the time of Adam's creation onward had no equal for his knowledge and experience of the earth, "be he Christian or pagan, Tartar or Indian, or of any other nation whatsoever."

[25] This is, on the other hand, characteristic of Rustichello, who on several occasions altered Marco's account in order to give it an epic tone that would accord with the literary phraseology and tastes of the times. Cf. Benedetto, cr. ed., Introd., pp. xiii ff.

[26] This episode is especially exploited in the romanticized biographies, which must already have originated by Marco's times, as is revealed by the story recounted by Marco Barbaro in his *Genealogia delle famiglie venete* (cf. Yule-Cordier, *op. cit.,* Vol. I, Introd., p. 25 n.). This tells of a threadbare garment belonging to one of the three travelers which was given to a beggar by his wife, who was unaware of the treasure sewn therein, and which was later recovered in the Rialto quarter, thanks to a stratagem devised by the woman. There is as yet no collection of ancient anecdotes about the Polos.

and precious objects of all kinds, of which the sovereign was always lavish whenever he wished to honor or reward his "barons" and the officials of his court.[27] Precious stones, together with gold, were an absolute monopoly of the imperial treasury as the basis of Chinese public economy and monetary policy. The system of exchange was founded, as Marco himself tells us, on paper money, of which some rare examples have come down to us;[28] and it was precisely in the year when the three Venetians left Asia for their return to Venice that this system had been extended to Persia, with disastrous results throughout the whole continent.

Consequently, the importing and exporting of precious stones, which were legally considered to belong to the sovereign, was strictly controlled by special authorities, although within the country it was permissible to buy gems with paper money.[29] Strict prohibition against their exportation would also explain Ramusio's account, according to which the Polos are supposed "with great cunning" to have sewn "a large quantity of most precious gems" in their most tattered clothes to protect themselves from both taxation and robbery.[30]

---

[27] Cf. the *Milione*, cr. ed., p. 92, and M.P., pp. 238 ff., as well as the extensive commentary by Yule-Cordier, *op. cit.*, Vol. I, pp. 424 ff.

[28] Yule-Cordier, *op. cit.*, Vol. I, p. 443 n. It should be noted that all the princes and dignitaries of the empire were in the habit of hoarding precious stones, thereby protecting themselves from the dangers of inflation, which more than once ruined the economy of continental Asia from China to Persia. Cf. O. Franke, *Geschichte des chinesischen Reiches*, Vol. IV, 1948, pp. 383 ff., and Vol. V, 1950, pp. 187 f., as well as B. Spuler, *Die Mongolen in Iran*, pp. 88 ff., 300 ff. Cf., too, K. Jahn, "Das iranische Papiergeld," *Archiv Orientální*, Vol, X, 1938. For Chinghizide China cf. H. Franke, *Geld und Wirtschaft in China unter der Mongolenherrschaft*, Leipzig, 1949, and the critical bibliography of the subject by the same author in *Sinologie*, Bern, 1953, esp. pp. 149 f. For the printing of these notes cf. Walter Fuchs, "Der Kupferdruck in China vom 10. bis 19. Jahrhundert," *Gutenberg Jahrbuch*, 1950, pp. 67 ff., with bibliographical supplement, and the brief note (with illustrations) by L. Rintchent, "A propos du papier-monnaie mongol," *Acta Orientalia* (Budapest), Vol. IV, 1955, pp. 159 ff.

[29] *Il Milione*, cr. ed., pp. 92 f. Francesco Balducci Pegolotti (*Pratica della Mercatura,* ed. Evans, p. 23) asserts one generation later, but certainly not from personal experience, that "the merchandise is not overpaid, because your money is of paper," thereby confirming Marco's statements. The latter, however, although already in his times there existed in the Levant a credit system that was fairly well developed, never fully understood the economic principles on which the use of paper money was based in China. Indeed, he considered it to be the result of a purely arbitrary decision on the part of the sovereign, who is presented by him as "the most accomplished of alchemists."

[30] The list of the precious objects brought back to Venice by the Polos, which is reproduced by Yule-Cordier, *op. cit.*, Introd., pp. 79 f., is based on an obvious forgery.

From the sale of part of these valuable objects Marco and his elderly companions were undoubtedly able to lead an honorable life, if not in extravagant fashion, after their return to Venice. As opposed to the considerable quantity of cloths, Oriental products, and various objects that remained in Marco's home until his death, we find that no will or document makes any mention of the numerous gems of all kinds bestowed upon our Asian explorers by popular tradition, which was echoed by Ramusio. This silence is the more remarkable if we consider that Niccolò and Maffeo Polo already specialized in the gem trade when, in 1260, they set out to cross the Tartar steppes on their way to the Chinghizide courts, where they were truly destined to make their fortune.[31]

If, however, these valuables were really sold on the Venetian market, with the exception of a few pieces of jewelry that Marco wished to leave to his wife and daughters, it is nevertheless certain that only a fraction can have reached Venice with them. For, after they had voyaged unharmed for two years in the train of Princess Cocachin, the future bride of Arghun Khan, Lord of the Tartars of the Levant, in the China Sea and the Indian Ocean; after having crossed the whole of Persia with this royal caravan and its many treasures; no sooner had they set foot on Christian soil at Trebizond, having passed the border of Tartar dominion in Anatolia, than the Polos were robbed of a large part of their possessions, probably by subjects of this minute empire. The Venetian Republic did indeed hold the sovereign himself responsible for the robbery, and intervened on several occasions in behalf of the Polos, who were, however, indemnified only slowly and in part for their losses, after lengthy negotiations of which we have the records in the family papers.[32]

[31] *Il Milione,* cr. ed., p. 4, chap. ii. For the trade in valuables in Marco's times cf. W. von Heyd, *Histoire du commerce du Levant au moyen âge,* édition française par F. Raynaud, Leipzig, 1886, Vol. II, pp. 651 ff., and Pegolotti, *La Pratica della Mercatura,* ed. Evans, pp. 304 ff. (especially for the market at Constantinople, where the Polos had begun to trade in these precious objects).

[32] Cf. Moule-Pelliot, *op. cit.,* Vol. I, pp. 28 f. Trebizond was in Marco's times the principal port for the Black Sea–Persia trade, via Erzerum and Tabriz. Cf. Spuler, *Die Mongolen in Iran,* esp. pp. 435 ff. Competition between the Genoese and Venetians made itself felt, with bitter results, under various circumstances in this port (cf. von Heyd, *op. cit.,* Vol II, pp. 92 ff.). For a historical study of the port and its surrounding territory see the works quoted by A. A. Vasiliev, "The Empire of Trebisond in History and Literature," *Byzantion,* Vol. XV, 1940–41, pp. 316 ff. The Genoese always en-

The part that was saved still represented a considerable patrimony, although it was never profitably administered and at most helped to maintain the vast family in a state of average prosperity, which the original documents allow us to appreciate in accordance with historical reality, noticeably different from the romantic fables invented in later ages.[33] Indeed, it seems evident that the Polos, after their return from the Orient, did not engage in merchandising in the grand style of the Venetian nobility; and we feel quite sure that Marco did not busy himself in retail trade, which, according to the sentiments of the age, would have dishonored him and excluded him from his class. Rather than turn his attention to business affairs, Marco chose to give the rest of his life to protecting the family patrimony and diffusing the book which brought about his rapid rise to fame, popularity, and immortality. It is therefore natural to suppose that he now nourished ambitions of becoming a famous author rather than a great merchant.

Direct evidence of this is to be found in the note inserted in a copy of the *Milione* destined for Charles de Valois which his emissary, Thibault de Chépoy, received from Marco's hands in 1307.[34] Our author must have made a wide acquaintance at Venice in these years, and his book must have been transcribed on various occasions, under his own supervision, in an attempt to satisfy the curiosity of a public ever more hungry for information as the links with the Far East became more strongly forged in this century and the attempts to reach it by land and sea became more frequent.[35] This editorial activity explains in part the nu-

joyed a marked supremacy over the Venetians, and the three Polos, on their return from China, may well have been the victims of this circumstance, as is mentioned *supra*. For the itinerary from Trebizond toward the Orient cf. Pegolotti, *op. cit.*, pp. 29 ff.

[33] Cf. R. Morozzo della Rocca, "Sulle orme di Marco Polo," *L'Italia che scrive*, Vol. XXXVII, 1954, p. 121, col. 1, and note.

[34] For this version of the *Milione* cf. Benedetto's Introd. to his cr. ed., pp. lvi ff. The text of this version, in a literary French of the times, has been published by M. G. Pauthier, 2 vols., Paris, 1865, followed by A. J. H. Charignon, 3 vols., Peking, 1924–1928.

[35] See the well-known, but certainly exaggerated, assertion by Pegolotti, *op. cit.*, p. 2, that "the route from Tana (in the Crimea) to Cathay is most safe, by day and night, according to the reports of the travelers who have used it." For the development of Franciscan missions in China in the XIVth century cf. the Introd. to *Sinica Franciscana*, Vol. I, pp. lix ff., and for Venetian merchants in China in the same century

merous variants in the various versions of the book that bear the author's imprint in their style and subject matter.[36]

Hence, it could not be as a merchant that he won fame among his contemporaries; The renowned Petrus de Abano, who taught medicine at Padua, knew him personally only as a traveler and explorer. The most objective and mature judgment of his personality was that expressed in a few words by Francesco Pipino, of Bologna, who produced a successful Latin translation of the *Milione* while Marco was still alive, and who may have met him at Venice on the occasion of his departure for the Holy Land.[37] This learned Dominican chronicler presents him to his readers as a man universally esteemed for qualities of wisdom, honesty, and devotion, and endowed with those civic virtues that made him worthy of trust and respect.[38] For Pipino, the author of this edifying and entertaining book is not a merchant or an adventurer, but rather a champion of the Faith, who teaches his readers to admire with compunction "the variety, beauty, and immensity of creation," awakening in them a feeling of gratitude toward their Lord for having drawn them forth from the darkness in which dwell not only the pagan peoples but also those wicked Christians who are "more forgetful of the true God than the former are of their idols."

Since Pipino had been entrusted with this translation by the supreme Council of his Order, in which not only scholastic organization but also popular preaching and instruction were then concentrated, his judgment represents, as it were, the official interpretation of the *Milione* in Marco Polo's own day. Hence, too, that factor which, together with the straightforward uni-

---

cf. R. Morozzo della Rocca, "Catay," in *Miscellanea in onore di Roberto Cessi*, Rome (Ediz. di Storia e Letteratura), 1958, pp. 299 ff.

[36] These variants are recorded in Benedetto's cr. ed., and are also to be found in the *variorum* edition by Moule-Pelliot, *ed. cit.*, Vol. I.

[37] For Pipino see the bio-bibliographical data in the cr. ed. of the *Milione*, Introd., esp. pp. cxxxiii and cxlvii. Pipino went to the Holy Land in the year 1320, and may therefore have seen Marco Polo in Venice on that occasion, without, however, mentioning the fact in this proem.

[38] The proem quoted is reproduced in the original text by Benedetto in his cr. ed. of the *Milione*, Introd., p. cliv, and in an Italian translation by Ramusio. The incunabulum containing the first published edition of this widely known version (Antwerp, 1485) has been photomechanically reproduced, with notes by Professor Shinobu Iwamura, Tokyo, National Diet Library, 1949.

versal Latin of his translation, gave to his version of Polo's text a lead over all others, however much more full and faithful.[39] We can be certain that this expurgated and consecrated edition of his—as Pipino himself would have it—inspired Dominican preachers, when, according to the usage of the times and their Order, they illustrated from their pulpits the "exempla" drawn from the best-known and most engaging books in contemporary didactic, anecdotal, and romantic literature, and thereby helped to instruct the faithful.[40] It is certain that the work also corresponded to the intention openly expressed by Pipino of stimulating the diffusion of the Faith in the Orient by contributing to the success of the missions which the religious orders were then organizing on a vast scale while profiting from the experiences of the first explorers of the Asian continent.

In a way, this ecclesiastical sanction of the book was perfectly justified. Marco had, indeed, started on his way to China accompanied by the Pope's blessing and a pontifical embassy that was not taking any merchandise to the Great Kaan, but—apart from the gifts of the newly elected Pontiff—a portion of the oil that burned constantly before the Holy Sepulcher in Jerusalem.

Niccolò and Maffeo Polo were, then, traveling as ambassadors of the Great Kaan Kublai, equipped by him with the necessary credentials, the "golden tablets of command." At the same time, the dignity of pontifical legates was conferred by Gregory X, immediately after his election, on two learned Dominicans mentioned by Marco, namely, Nicholas of Vicenza and William of Tripoli, who were entrusted with a special embassy from the Pope to the Great Kaan, and were endowed with ecclesiastical privileges that could not be extended to their lay companions.[41] However, since these learned monks lacked the necessary courage to venture so far among such a multitude of hidden dangers, the three Venetians not only became a substitute for these pontifical legates, within the limited powers of their lay state, but also for those hundred masters of the liberal arts requested of the Pontiff by Kublai, as we read in the prologue to the

[39] *Il Milione,* cr. ed., Introd., p. cxxxiii.

[40] Cf. J. Th. Welter, *L'Exemplum dans la littérature religieuse et didactique du moyen âge,* Paris, 1927.

[41] *Il Milione,* cr. ed., p. 8, chap. xiii.

Milione, in order to show "clearly to the idolaters . . . by force of reason that the Christian law was superior to theirs." [42]

This apologetic interpretation of the Polos' mission also expressed in some degree the intentions of the Great Kaan, who was the pagan son of a Nestorian mother and was surrounded at his court by servants and dignitaries belonging to this Christian sect that had recently been reintroduced into China by the Mongol dynasty.[43] Kublai himself was closer to Tibetan Lamaism than to any other Asiatic religion; moreover, he was opposed by the Nestorian clergy in every attempt to come into contact with the Roman Church, and he was always ready to procure political advantage from every church and sect in his immense dominions. He showed no inclination toward the Catholic faith, nor any desire to understand its doctrines and practices, but he had a certain respect for the practical manifestations of Western civilization, which, rightly or wrongly, he identified with the dominant religion.[44] Indeed, if we accept what we read in the prologue to the *Milione,* the astute ruler immediately recognized, both in the Venetian and in his older companions, the representatives of a civilization superior to that of his Mongols, and certainly more trustworthy than the Chinese literati and monks, whom he had every reason to mistrust.

Marco Polo is certainly not indulging in idle boasting when he asserts in the prologue to his book that the Great Kaan preferred him to all his other ambassadors, who were "vain and ignorant" and were incapable of providing him with information about the customs and usages of other countries, only reporting, like all good bureaucrats, those things that concerned their specific missions. This was so far true that Chu Ssu-pen, the great Chinese geographer who was a contemporary of Marco Polo and who, after 1311, produced for the court a topographical map of China, bewailed in his preface that he could not offer trustworthy information about foreign countries, because those who arrived

[42] *Ibid.,* p. 6, chap. viii.
[43] Cf. P. Pelliot, "Chrétiens d'Asie Centrale et d'Extrême-Orient," *T'oung Pao,* Vol. XV, 1914, pp. 623 ff.; and, by the same author, *Mongols et Papes aux XIIIe et XIVe siècles,* Paris, 1922, as well as "Les Mongols et la Papauté," *Revue de l'Orient Chrétien,* Vol. XXIII, 1922–23, pp. 3 ff. and cont.
[44] See chap. vi of the present volume.

at court, bearing tribute with them, either had nothing precise to say or else could not be believed.[45]

The three Venetians, who ingenuously interpreted the sovereign's wish as a promise of his own conversion and that of all his subjects, and who accepted literally the Papal mandate of diffusing the Faith in those regions, always regarded themselves as lay apostles, and even entered into religious discussions with Kublai himself, whom they hoped to lead into the fold of the Roman Church. In this the Polos were truly the continuators of the first missionaries who had been the guests of the various Mongol courts of Asia and the pioneers of those who afterward established themselves in China with full ecclesiastical powers and episcopal dignity.[46]

Hence, during the whole of their stay in Asia, Marco and his father and uncle were always seeking out Christian communities, and noted down with documentary precision the seats of the various sects, their churches, sanctuaries, and monasteries, and pointed out the Nestorian groups in Persia, Turkestan, Mongolia, in the various provinces, in India, at the imperial court, and elsewhere in the range of the Christian diaspora, which is known to us through his continual references to it in his book.

To appreciate how deeply and intensely Marco's feelings were engaged in this discovery of Christian Asia, we need only read those lively chapters of the *Milione* which recount the triumphs of the Faith over the pagans of every land and sect, whether the book sets forth at length and in model hagiographic style the miracles worked by some saint or by direct divine intervention,[47] or dramatically reports the discovery and official recognition of a supposedly Christian community in the capital of the Province of Fukien in southern China.[48]

These manifestations of Oriental Christianity require separate study; and we shall return to them. On the whole, they arouse

[45] Cf. the Chinese text, with English translation, bibliography, and critical data, in Walter Fuchs, *The "Mongol Atlas" of China by Chu Ssu-pen and the Kuang yü-ju* (Monumenta Serica, Monograph Series, VIII), Peking, 1946.
[46] Cf. *Sinica Franciscana*, Introd., pp. lix ff.
[47] *Il Milione*, cr. ed., pp. 20 ff., 41 ff. (miracles of the mountain and the pillar).
[48] For this episode, which is narrated only in the Z version of the *Milione* (cr. ed., p. 158; M.P., p. 349) see the present author's article, "Manichaeism, Buddhism and Christianity in Marco Polo's Asia," *Asiatische Studien*, Vol. V, 1951, pp. 1 ff.

in our author expressions of an ingenuous, unwavering devotion, coupled with that sense of meticulous conscientiousness which was a salient feature of his character and was united with a missionary zeal that explains the attitude of the Dominican Order toward the book and its success in ecclesiastical and lay circles of the XIVth century.

Consequently, the Polo brothers are portrayed dressed as monks in some XIVth-century manuscripts of the *Milione,* at times as Franciscans, for example in the Royal Manuscript 19 D 1 of the British Museum, at others in Dominican habit, as in the famous *Livre des Merveilles,* franç. 2810 of the Bibliothèque Nationale in Paris.[49]

Francesco Pipino undoubtedly did much to make this devout interpretation of Marco's book gain wide acceptance. He emphasized its apologetic value, suppressed episodes that might arouse a heretical curiosity in its readers, and increased the excitations to aversion and disgust that present themselves now and then in descriptions of the practices of the idolaters and of the Christian struggle against Moslems and pagans.[50]

It was indeed this devout tendency toward propaganda that transformed the commercial adventure of Niccolò and Maffeo Polo, which had begun among the Tartars of the Volga and the Mohammedans of Turkestan, into a task of Christian conquest for the greater glory of Church and Faith. The two Venetian merchants, who had set out for the court of the Great Kaan from Bokhara with an embassy from his brother Hulagu,[51] did not have any merchandise to offer him; nor was it possible for them to set up an emporium at Peking, where the merchants of central and western Asia, after 1260, had centralized the transcontinental trade in silk and other commodities.[52]

[49] The present author has expressed the opinion that the three Polos are represented in the famous fresco by Andrea di Buonaiuto in the Spanish Chapel of the Church of Santa Maria Novella in Florence, which was painted between 1366 and 1368 (cf. our fig. 2 and the Italian version of this book, Florence, 1957, pp. 113–115). This conjecture is open to discussion.

[50] Cf. *Il Milione,* cr. ed., Introd. p. clv.

[51] *Il Milione,* cr. ed., chap. iv, p. 5; M.P., p. 77.

[52] After the capital of the Tartar empire had been transferred from Karakorum to Peking (Khanbaliq), and because of the greater security in transportation, the city became a flourishing commercial emporium "to which merchants betake themselves and where there is a clearance of trade," as Pegolotti asserts, *op. cit.,* p. 22.

Thus, immediately after their arrival at the court of Kublai for a brief stay, they "would at times speak some words about the Christian faith," as we are told in a characteristic passage of the Ramusian version of the *Milione*.[53] They also solicited the conversion of the sovereign, who, as a mark of respect for his Nestorian relatives and subjects, had the Gospel censed when the great ceremonies of the empire were held, and, together with his barons, would devoutly kiss the Book.[54] According to this version, which is worthy of both credence and study, it was precisely the brothers' solicitations that made him choose them as ambassadors to the Papal court. On the other hand, the newly elected Pope, Gregory X, did not allow to escape him this opportunity of inaugurating his pontificate with an enterprise that not only revealed the bold scope of his political vision but also imposed on the three Venetians an apostolic task of unwonted proportions.

Marco relates in the prologue to the *Milione* that, no sooner had he set out from Acre with his elderly companions, bound for China, than Theobald of Piacenza, a member of the historic Visconti family and Archdeacon of Lièges, then residing in the Holy Land, called back the three Venetian travelers immediately upon receiving the news of his election as Supreme Pontiff. The election had taken place on September 1, 1271, when the Chair of Peter had remained vacant for almost three years.[55] The importance placed by the new Pope on this projected embassy to the Great Kaan, shortly before leaving Acre for Rome, must be measured not only in terms of the more or less successful missions "ad Tartaros" of his predecessors, but, more especially, by a consideration of the extraordinary political vision that ruled the four brief years of Gregory X's pontificate. In fact, he not only succeeded in reuniting at the new Council of Lyons in 1274 all the discordant European powers, which he ably reconciled, but even managed to persuade the Byzantine Emperor, Michael Palaeologus, to accept the supremacy of the Roman Church and proclaim in solemn act the union of the two churches. Thus, al-

[53] Cr. ed., pp. 70 ff.; M. P., p. 202.

[54] *Ibid.*, and A. C. Moule, *Christians in China*, London, 1930, pp. 128 ff.

[55] Cr. ed., pp. 7 f., chaps. x ff. For this episode see M. H. Laurent, "Grégoire X et Marco Polo," *Mélanges d'Archéologie et d'Histoire* (École Française de Rome), Vol. LVIII, 1941–46, pp. 132 ff.

FIG. 2. *Part of a fresco by Andrea di Buonaiuto da Firenze, painted between 1366 and 1368, on the right wall of the Spanish Chapel of the Church of Santa Maria Novella, Florence. Three of the men in the central standing row who face the beholder seem to represent, beginning at the left, Maffeo (in dark Oriental dress), Niccolò (with a white beard), and Marco Polo (who carries his book). The interpretation of all the lay figures in this section is, however, conjectural. They certainly represent the lay contribution to the militant Church through the Dominican Order. For the fresco as a whole see Raimond van Merle,* The Development of the Italian School of Painting, *Vol. III (1924), pp. 425 ff., and Millard Meiss,* Painting in Florence and Siena after the Black Death, *1951, pp. 94 ff.*

FIG. 3. *Kublai Kaan presenting to the Polo brothers the "golden tablets of command"; from an illuminated page of MS Reg. 19 D 1, in the British Museum.*

though it was to be for only a short time, he brought together into one kingdom of peace the whole of Christianity, which he wished to unite in a definite crusade against the unbelievers.[56] With this design and his experience of the Orient gained in the Holy Land, the Pope certainly thought of extending his influence as far as the political center of the great Asian empire. He therefore made the three Venetians instruments of this ecumenical idea, which, with intentions of defense rather than of propaganda, had already occurred to Innocent IV at the moment when Tartar expansion in the West had reached its zenith.[57] We must therefore believe that the new Pope gave to his lay legates— either directly or by means of the two Dominicans who soon turned back—the same mission that Innocent had already entrusted to Friar John of Pian del Càrpine, namely, to inform the Papacy about the situation of Oriental Christianity, which had been a constant topic of discussion in Europe for more than a century. Some definite news had been brought into the West by Franciscan and Dominican missionaries, and especially by William of Rubruck, who had stayed at Karakorum, once the capital of the Mongol empire;[58] but more, much more, was wanted.

Marco, who had been prepared for the task by the Christian sentiments of his family and the preceding experiences of his father and uncle, proved always worthy of this Papal assignment. Moreover, in his book he offered to the entire West the fullest and most faithful picture of that medieval Asiatic Christianity which was to crumble and disappear hardly more than a century after his departure for China.[59] Nevertheless, by transforming

---

[56] See the concise exposition of these events, with bibliography of the subject, in A. Fliche, *Histoire de l'Église depuis les origines jusqu'à nos jours,* Vol. X, Paris, 1950, pp. 494 ff.

[57] See above, chap. ii.

[58] Cf. *Sinica Franciscana,* Introd., pp. lix ff.

[59] All the foreign cults that flourished in China during a century of Mongol domination were radically suppressed on the advent of the national Ming dynasty (1368–1628). Indeed, when the first Jesuit missionaries arrived, at the end of the XVIth century, no trace remained in China of Nestorian Christianity or of the Franciscan missions of the XIVth century. On the other hand, a few Jewish communities—which had become almost totally Sinicized (cf. W. C. White, *Chinese Jews,* 3 vols., Toronto, 1942)—still remained and continued to survive, as did also a group of Manichees at Fukien (in southern China), for whom cf. P. Pelliot, "Les Traditions manichéennes au Foukien," *T'oung Pao,* Vol. XXII, 1923, pp. 193 ff.

Marco Polo from a merchant into a missionary one would certainly replace a unilateral judgment by an exaggerated evaluation. Although his desire to serve the Christian cause never left him, it was not this task that led him to observe the world with a no less constant and ardent mundane curiosity. Nowadays we laugh at those of his interpreters who, not only in the XIVth century, but even in XIXth, presented him as a Venetian cleric.[60] For a man of his times mundane interests and devout tendencies were in no way irreconcilable—just as for a modern explorer a geographic expedition may be at one and the same time a scientific undertaking and an act of homage to one's country. This indissoluble twofold attitude is also characteristic of the greatest medieval enterprises, such as the Crusades and the four expeditions of Christopher Columbus.

Asiatic history records various examples of missionary merchants of various faiths, from the time when the king of the Mongolian Keraits was instructed in the rudiments of Christian law by some Nestorians of Central Asia, who at the beginning of the XIth century were trading in those regions.[61] Hence, Marco Polo was neither a merchant nor a missionary, strictly speaking, and least of all an adventurer, as many still like to call him.[62] It is true, however, that he, like so many of his contemporaries, participated in that spirit of adventure which is so characteristic of his age, when—in real life, as in fiction—the roads everywhere were filled with travelers of all kinds: prelates and monks, teachers and students, merchants and knights, minstrels and architects, pilgrims and soldiers. Thus Marco was something of both man of the world and man with a mission, according to circumstances, and adapted himself empirically to becoming expert in various activities, without any particular vocation, without professional instruction, and without any specific task, amid the thousand and one vicissitudes of a long and varied career.

The proof is that, whereas the clerical interpretation of his book represented him essentially as a champion of the Faith,

[60] Cf. Yule-Cordier, *op. cit.*, Introd., p. 116 n.

[61] Cf. G. Messina, *Cristianesimo, Buddhismo e Manicheismo nell'Asia antica*, Rome, 1947, pp. 83 ff.

[62] Among others, H. H. Hart, *Venetian Adventurer*, Stanford Univ. Press, 1942 and subsequent editions.

the most expert cartographers of the age began to make systematic use of Marco's report in order to trace a picture of the earth in accordance with his geographical experiences. Indeed, the Catalan Map, inspired in its Asiatic section by the *Milione* and probably preceded by other maps of the same kind, dates from 1375.[63] And while the book's apologetic interest declined as a result of the progressive secularization of lay culture during the XVth century, its practical, scientific value increased proportionately. This is definitely attested by the authority of the Florentine, Paolo Toscanelli, and Don Henrique, Infante of Portugal.[64]

Marco's versatility reveals his natural dexterity, coupled with the simplicity of a virgin mind, which was open to all the most varied impressions but closed to logical deduction and hypothetical generalizations and unprepared to find by theory or simply by intuition the relationship between things seen and thought. Columbus was to be, like him, explorer and missionary, adventurer and dignitary, merchant and soldier; but, wishing to be too much in too many fields, he became the personal victim of his haphazard culture, passionate temperament, and the messianic ambitions that occasionally betrayed both his practical spirit and his scientific experience.[65] Marco, on the other hand, a man without literary pretensions, regards his unexplored world as a spectacle in which light and shade alternate, together with

[63] Described (with illustration) in Yule-Cordier, *op. cit.*, Introd., p. 134, and in all the textbooks of medieval geography already mentioned.

[64] Cf. R. Almagià's succinct essay, *La figura e l'opera di Marco Polo secondo recenti studi*, Rome, 1938, together with his article on Marco Polo in the commemorative volume of the Istituto Veneto, *Nel VII centenario della nascita di Marco Polo;* also his article, "A proposito di recenti studi su Marco Polo e i suoi viaggi," *Rivista Geografica Italiana*, Vol. LXII, 1955, pp. 81–100. For further biographical data, and various information, cf. Rodolfo Gallo, "Marco Polo, la sua famiglia e il suo libro," in the volume *Nel VII centenario*, pp. 65–193. G. B. Ramusio, in his "Discorso sopra la 1ª e 2ª Lettera di Andrea Corsali," in *Navigationi & Viaggi*, second edition, Vol. I, p. 194ᵛ, relates that "the book of the Magnifico Messer Marco Polo, a Venetian nobleman, which was taken back to Lisbon by the Most Illustrious Infante, Don Pedro, when he visited the city of Venice . . . after having been translated into their language, caused all those illustrious kings to wish passionately to discover Oriental India, and of these none was so fervent as the king Don João." The Infante Don Pedro was the guest of the Republic of Venice in 1426 and received as a gift from the government a copy of a map attributed to Marco Polo (cf. Yule-Cordier, *op. cit.*, Introd., p. 110 n.).

[65] Cf. Cesare de Lollis, *Cristoforo Colombo nella leggenda e nella storia*, third edition, Rome, 1923, pp. 227 ff.

miracles and reported events, natural phenomena and human fortunes. And behind this moving, varied scene the author so far disappears as to lose himself in a neutral objectivity, which is colorless at times without being dispassionately scientific or unadornedly doctrinal. His culture is limited to reminiscences of the minstrels, who would punctuate their recital of the feats of Alexander the Great with some rudimentary treatise of popular doctrine.[66] At times he draws material, also, from the accounts of Mongolian rhapsodes, whose language he understands, and he tends to follow their dynastic or patriotic leanings,[67] sometimes reflecting poetic visions of Chinese origin,[68] or, as when the legend of the Buddha is his subject, local interpretations of the history and civilization of India and of other Oriental regions.[69] As for the system of classification and order that defined the structure of his book, the determining factor was the positive, methodic element in his character. Marco's psychological make-up is, indeed, a guarantee of the authenticity of his reminiscences, even when they cannot be made to agree with the reality of historical and natural facts. A man so devoid of imagination and literary ability could never have produced and kept up without betraying himself a fiction so varied and on so vast a scale.

Undoubtedly, people were very eager to hear from him, and probably from his older companions, an account of the wonders of the world, after his return and during his term of imprisonment at Genoa. That which later informers have to say about the matter is confirmed by similar instances that are well documented.[70] Rustichello of Pisa, a professional author who knew his public and followed the doctrinal tendencies of the age, helped our illiterate author to transform the ponderous mass of his recollections into an orderly account, written in that Italianized French or Gallicized Italian which, for want of a better idiom,

[66] See chap. ii, § 1, above.

[67] Especially when he is narrating the feats of Chinghiz Khan, cr. ed., pp. 50 ff.

[68] Particularly in the description of the city of Quinsai, cr. ed., pp. 143 ff.; Yule-Cordier, Vol. II, pp. 184 ff.; Moule-Pelliot, Vol. I, p. 162. (Cf. A. C. Moule in *T'oung Pao,* Vol. XXXIII, 1937, pp. 105 ff.; also his *Quinsai, with Other Notes on Marco Polo,* Cambridge Univ. Press, 1957.

[69] Cf. cr. ed., pp. 193 ff.; Yule-Cordier, Vol. II, pp. 316 ff.; Moule-Pelliot. pp. 408 ff.

[70] See note 17 to chap. ii, § 2, above.

was then, between Genoa and Venice, the literary language of the most cultured readers.[71]

The book's success, as is well known, was commensurate with the general interest in works of this sort, which at one and the same time were entertaining, instructive, and edifying, and which abounded in the European literature of those centuries.[72] It excited men's imaginations, and satisfied their desire for knowledge of the world, by offering to the spirit of adventure, the scientific interests, religious engrossments, and practical endeavors of his contemporaries all that the world could present as worthy of admiration and sacrifice, and it harmonized the whole with that view of the cosmos which doctrinal and scholastic literature had already set forth.

All this is obvious, if the book is set by us in the civilization of its times and considered in the light of its initial success among the laymen and clerics who helped to make it universally known. However, a perhaps insoluble problem still requires our attention in this general account of our traveler's career and fortune. In the last chapter of the prologue to the *Milione* he tells us that when he, together with his father and uncle, took his leave of their lord, Kublai Kaan, the sovereign entrusted them with an embassy to the Pope, the kings of France and Spain, and the other sovereigns of Europe, accrediting them with the golden piasters that served as a safe-conduct throughout the empire, and, according to the usage of the times, with special letters patent of which both the structure and the style are known to us.[73] The golden piasters arrived at Venice and were preserved, as we

---

[71] No history of Franco-Italian literature yet exists that expounds the phenomenon in a systematic, satisfactory way. It is competently treated in the well-known works by Gaspary, *Storia della letteratura italiana,* trans. N. Zingarelli, Turin, 1900–1914, Vol. II, and Giulio Bertoni, *Il Duecento,* second edition, 1930, pp. 72 ff. See too, A. Monteverdi's contribution to the commemorative volume of the Fondazione Giorgio Cini di Venezia, *La civiltà veneziana del secolo di Marco Polo,* Florence, 1955, pp. 19 ff., within the framework of the history of medieval Italian literature.

[72] Especially *L'Image du Monde* in its various versions (from *ca.* 1250 onward), Brunetto Latini's *Trésor* (*ca.* 1260–1264), and other minor works (cf. Ch. V. Langlois, *La Connaissance de la Nature et du Monde au moyen âge,* 1927); for Italy, before Dante's *Convivio,* Ristoro d'Arezzo's *La composizione del mondo* of 1282 (Narducci ed., Rome, 1859).

[73] Cr. ed., pp. 12 ff.

know, in the family treasury.[74] However, it is not known whether
the Great Kaan's mission was carried out. Although the letters
of Kublai's predecessors and of his own vassal lords have been
preserved in the Vatican archives and at Paris, those intended
for the Pope and the sovereigns of Europe which were entrusted
by him to the three Venetians have never come to light. It seems
likely that they were never delivered. Yet it is difficult to explain
how the Polos could have abandoned their lord's mission to the
Pope, not only because Niccolò and Maffeo, departing from Acre
some twenty-five years earlier, had set out with a precise assignment from a great Pope, designed for the benefit of all Christendom, but also because, a few years after the Polos' return from
their later travels, Boniface VIII, in 1302, received a direct political embassy from Ghazan Khan—that is to say, from that same
Lord of the Levant who so short a time before had received, we
may say, from Marco's hands, the Tartar Princess Cocachin, who
had been entrusted to the care of the three Venetians by Kublai
and who, as Ghazan's spouse, had become for a brief while a
Queen of Chinghizide Persia.[75]

The Polo brothers had returned to Italy, with Marco, soon
after the election of Boniface VIII, who had been consecrated
in St. Peter's on January 23, 1295. Perhaps "the Prince of the
new Pharisees—waging war near the Lateran," [76] and being occupied in consolidating his power within his dominions before
extending it to include the whole world—thereby incurring
Dante's wrath—gave no thought to distant Oriental lands. It was
just at this time that Friar John of Montecorvino arrived in the
Mongol empire, having been sent by Nicholas IV, the first Franciscan Pope, and invested by him with ample ecclesiastical privileges which allowed the friar to build in Peking, at the expense
of a rich Italian merchant, the first Catholic church edifice in
the Far East for a cleric of episcopal rank.[77] Is it possible that
Boniface did not hear anything of so extraordinary an embassy

[74] See above, n. 22.
[75] Cf. A. Mostaert and Francis W. Cleaves, "Trois documents mongols des Archives
secrètes vaticanes," *Harvard Journal of Asiatic Studies*, Vol. XV, 1952, pp. 419 ff.
[76] Dante, *Inferno*, XXVII, 85–86.
[77] Cf. *Sinica Franciscana*, Vol. I, pp. 335 ff.

as the Polos'? Marco's imprisonment at Genoa, shortly after his return, would not have prevented this, since his father and uncle had remained at Venice, safe and sound, and they, no less than he, were invested with the imperial office and charged with the exceptional mission.

This embassy was to have brought to the Pontiff, among other things, precious gifts from the Great Kaan, of which no other trace or mention has remained than those in the *Milione*.[78] Were they perhaps stolen, with other treasures, by the Greeks of Trebizond? Did they remain in Venice, or were they sent to the Pope by a private channel? The mystery is all the greater inasmuch as the imperial mission and gifts to the Pontiff had been announced *urbi et orbi* in Marco's book as early as 1298, when Boniface VIII was at the apogee of his power and would certainly have welcomed the homage of the most powerful sovereign on earth, who was also his possible ally against the Mohammedans of the Levant.

Not even the kings of France and Spain seem to have paid any attention to the mission, although Marco's book was addressed, as we read in the Paduan manuscript, to "kings, dukes, marquises, counts, knights, princes, and barons, and all those interested in learning about the various conditions of men."

Have we, then, yet another manifestation of the tendency often attributed to Marco, of magnifying the importance of his mission and his rank at Kublai's court? There is certainly no doubt that he was fully conscious of his extraordinary adventure and liked to surround his reminiscences with a nimbus of courtly splendor. Nor can it be denied that he wished always to appear as a nobleman and official of the highest rank, rather than as a subordinate employee of the imperial administration, as some of his biographers would have him, or as an occasional merchant, as in some circumstances he could have been in the Orient, as at Venice in the ways already mentioned and documented. Nevertheless it is

[78] Cf. the *Milione*, cr. ed., p. 47; M.P., p. 157; and chap. v of the present volume. It is well known that the dispatch of gifts was customary in all medieval embassies, both in the West and in the East. Perhaps the letters entrusted to the Polos by Kublai were sent indirectly to the Pontiff and other sovereigns of Europe, and they may one day come to light, like the documents recently discovered in the Vatican Archives.

obvious that, having set out for China in 1271 in the train of a Papal embassy, he returned to Italy in 1295 as Kublai's and Ghazan's ambassador to the leading courts of the West.

Marco's good faith in insisting, here as elsewhere, upon his dignity and the importance of his mission, is evidenced by the simple fact that his father and uncle, who shared in his fortune and glory, could have given the lie to such boastful exaggeration, or else have become his accomplices in bombast and public fraud. Niccolò and Maffeo Polo, however, although they appear in the penumbra of such glory, were by common verdict simple, worthy persons to whom one could not possibly attribute such an attitude. The skepticism that Marco's account is supposed to have aroused in his contemporaries and fellow countrymen was far less widespread than might be thought from the anecdote narrated by Jacopo da Acqui. The latter presents him on his deathbed, surrounded by his incredulous friends, to whom Marco solemnly confirms the truth of the things recounted in his book, however incredible they may appear.[79]

In fact, his good faith and the authenticity of his account were accepted by men outstanding for their rank and wisdom, such as Francesco Pipino, Petrus de Abano, and Thibault de Chépoy. Admittedly, they were few. But his detractors tell us nothing that really justifies Marco's reputation as a vain braggart, or rightly casts doubt upon the final mission of the three Venetians.[80] It is therefore impossible to deny this embassy, which brings the Asiatic career of these men to a brilliant close, or to detract from the value of the *Milione* as a source of historical and autobiographical information.

The lack of documentary, extrinsic proof of this assertion has no effective contradictory value. We find repeated in this episode the experience that scholars have more than once undergone when they have searched in vain in the abundant Chinese sources

[79] Cf. the complete text of the anecdote in the Introd. to the cr. ed. of the *Milione,* pp. cxciii ff. It hardly seems likely that the title of the work reflects the impressions of Marco's contemporaries about his character and the trustworthiness of his information. Moreover, the word *milione* ('a million') never appears in his text. On this controversial question see Benedetto's note to his cr. ed., pp. 245 f.

[80] For Marco's fame among his contemporaries cf. the information gathered by Yule-Cordier, *op. cit.,* Introd., pp. 104 ff., and Benedetto, cr. ed., Introd., pp. ccxii ff. R. Gallo, in his essay cited in note 64 above, has little to add.

for a confirmation of events and a mention of personages described more or less circumstantially in the book. Honesty and good faith have several times—even recently—been denied to Marco Polo because his name never occurs in the Annals of the Empire (*Yüan Shih*), which record the names of foreign visitors far less important and illustrious than the three Venetians. However, this argument *ex silentio* is not valid, so far as we are concerned with delineating and reëvoking Marco's personality with the intention of arriving at an objective evaluation of the man and his book. If his name does not occur in Chinese historical records, the reasons for this silence may be manifold; not least, the fact that the three Venetians were known in the Orient by names unknown to us and certainly having nothing in common with their family name.[81] Who nowadays could recognize the name of the great XVIth-century missionary Matteo Ricci in his Chinese name of Li Ma-tu, without ample, reliable contemporary documentation? And so far as the Western sources are concerned, every medievalist is aware of their sobriety and their habit of ignoring news reports; so much so, indeed, that we should not know anything about the sensational return of the Polos from the Far East to Venice in 1269 and again in 1295, if Ramusio had not mentioned the second homecoming after centuries of tenacious, universal silence. Yet people in Venice and Rome cannot have remained unaware of these events, in a century when the whole of Europe looked at the Orient with an intensity unknown to the preceding ages of Western history.

[81] In the Chinese annals of the Chinghizide dynasty, which were drawn up after 1368 from authentic sources, mention is made of several persons named Po-lo. It is, however, impossible to identify any one of them with any one of the three Venetians. In the Orient the Polos would certainly not have been called by their surname, but —if at all—by their Christian names, more or less faithfully rendered, since these were fairly common in the Christian Asia of their times. For the names they may have had at the Mongol court of China and for the history of this still unsolved problem cf. the present author's article, "Poh-lo: Une question d'onomatologie chinoise," *Oriens,* Vol. III, 1950, pp. 183 ff. Nevertheless, it is certain that the Poh-lo who is recorded in the Annals of the dynasty (*Yüan Shih*) as Vice-President of the Imperial Council, and who held various high offices of state at the time of Marco's visit (cf. P. Pelliot in *T'oung Pao,* Vol. XXV, 1927, pp. 156 ff.), is not to be confused with our Venetian. In fact, he was a Mongol far older than Marco. On the other hand, the Chinese sources do record the names of the Tartar dignitaries who took part in the same embassy. For this subject cf. the note by Yang Chih-chin and Ho Yung-chi in *Harvard Journal of Asiatic Studies,* Vol. IX, 1945, p. 51.

Hence the lack of extrinsic confirmation must not be allowed to distort the picture of our traveler as it appears, more or less clear-cut and coherent, in the pages of his book, in which it is reflected against the background of his experiences. Study of the things he saw and narrated will help to bring this figure into greater relief, and it will become more lifelike and real once it is set in that world-scene which he described to the best of his ability, and the essential features of which are faithfully reproduced by the professional writer, Rustichello of Pisa, who wrote down Marco's account.

four

ASPECTS OF ASIATIC CIVILIZATION
IN MARCO POLO'S BOOK

Marco Polo himself revealed the intentions and circumstances that determined the writing of his book. Even had he not been constrained every day, as Ramusio tells us, to relate laboriously his adventures,[1] he knew that it would have been "a great loss not to have put down in writing the great wonders he had seen or heard to be true," since before him no one had known and explored "as much of the various parts of the world . . . as was known and explored by Messer Marco."[2]

It is obvious that he had returned to his native land with the intention of informing his contemporaries of his extraordinary experiences gained over a period of twenty-six years spent in various unexplored countries. Indeed, according to the Venetian traditions collected by Ramusio, in the course of those years he is supposed to have taken a number of notes to assist him later in the dictation of his memoirs. These same notes are later supposed to have helped the author and the compiler of the *Milione* to prepare the volume at the time of the incarceration at Genoa, which was to be the last adventurous and romantic event in our traveler's harassed existence.

However plausible we may think Ramusio's account of these notes sent from Venice to Genoa expressly for this purpose, the anecdote is nevertheless enveloped by the same doubt that clouds the authenticity of almost all the biographical information supplied by him. If Marco had truly taken notes with a view to com-

[1] *Navigationi & Viaggi*, Vol. II (1559), p. 7.
[2] *Il Milione*, chap. i.

piling his own book, his data would have been more precise, the names more correct, the omissions less numerous, and the discrepancies between historical facts and some of the contents of the *Milione* less irreconcilable than they appear to the perplexed critics of Marco's story.[3]

On the other hand, all this can be explained to our satisfaction if we consider that the book, though well thought out and constructed, had no other immediate source than its author's memory. This, on the whole, served him faithfully, but occasionally it gave way under the mass of reminiscences acquired from so long, vast, and varied an experience of men and things. And if so tenacious a memory may seem—as perhaps it did to Ramusio— an incredible, superhuman faculty, it should be remembered that it would not seem nearly so exceptional to one otherwise acquainted with the extraordinary memory of the men of the Middle Ages. They were less bound than we to the written page, and were trained to retain and develop on all occasions a fabulous number of ideas acquired from life and by study, through a natural disposition or a mnemo-technical apprenticeship that was commonly begun in infancy.[4] At the most, it may be possible to find in the itineraries and the geographical and ethnographical data of the *Milione* an echo of the reports to the Mongol emperor, which were perhaps written down in the Tartar language, and which are recorded with well-deserved pride in the prologue to the book.[5]

In spite of its architectural structure, the *Milione* is at times rhapsodic rather than systematic. This was natural to the author, as he was himself aware; and he meant his book to be recited as well as read, and addressed it to discerning though unlettered laymen rather than to gownsmen easy in Latin and masters of the liberal arts, for whom, however, he felt great respect.[6] Hence it was, and quite in accordance with the author's intentions, that

[3] For this subject, as well as the frequent discussions in the commentaries by Pauthier and Yule-Cordier on the respective passages, see the remarks by Moule-Pelliot in *Marco Polo: The Description of the World*, Vol. I, Introd., pp. 22 ff.

[4] It would seem that this subject was last treated by Francesco Cancellieri, *Dissertazione intorno agli uomini di gran memoria*, Rome, 1815.

[5] An example of these reports, compiled by one of the sovereign's informants, is to be found in the Chinese text by Liu Yu mentioned above, chap. ii *ad fin.*

[6] *Il Milione*, chap. i.

the *Milione* found its rightful place in the Franco-Italian vernacular literature of Marco's times, which was then recited in public and in private for the education and entertainment of a public that was excluded from the methodical instruction offered by the schools.

Nevertheless, even for this apparently more modest task Marco could never have done without the collaboration of a professional writer such as Rustichello of Pisa.[7] And it was a blessing for our author and his readers that in Rustichello he found one who was neither so learned as to alter with erudite additions the ingenuous character of our traveler's account, nor so fanciful as to weigh it down with too many trappings of rhetoric and the clichés of contemporary literary and pseudo-scientific phraseology. Hence, Marco's personality and something of his simple, concrete style, which rarely resorted to images or to emotional force, manage to pierce through the artificial, hybrid jargon in which the book was originally written.

Marco could not have done better. Ignorant of Latin, he had left for the Orient with the Venetian vocabulary of an adolescent, and had then learned at least four exotic languages. It is therefore obvious that, far from home, he was unable to develop the expressive possibilities of his native dialect, especially since his father and uncle, as a result of an even longer stay in the Levant, had become Orientals so far as language and customs were concerned.[8] Rustichello therefore gave the most nearly adequate form possible to the raw material of facts and reminiscences that he obtained from the Venetian by preserving both their substance and their character.

While attesting on various occasions to its veracity, which is also confirmed by the elderly companions of his adventures and experiences,[9] Marco clearly indicated not only the aim of his book but also the extent and limits of the information contained

---

[7] Cf. L. Foscolo Benedetto in the Introd. to his cr. ed., pp. xiii ff. Cf. also the same author's "L'Art de Marco Polo" in *Mélanges Hoepffner*, Paris, 1949, pp. 313 ff.

[8] Cf. the biographical data on Maffeo and Niccolò Polo in Yule-Cordier, *The Book of Ser Marco Polo*, Vol. I, Introd., pp. 15 ff., and Moule-Pelliot, *op. cit.*, Vol. I, pp. 19 ff.

[9] Cf. the preface by Fra Francesco Pipino to his Latin version of *Il Milione*; also cr. ed., Introd., p. cliv; M.P., p. 60.

in it. In addressing those who wished to "learn about the various human races and the peculiarities of the various regions in the world," his intention was to create an original work; considering it "wearisome to tell that which is neither necessary nor useful, or that which others do all day long," [10] he refused to set forth facts that already were universally known about foreign lands and peoples, or to mention details that could not be understood or appreciated by his fellow citizens and contemporaries.[11]

Geographically and substantially limiting his task in this way, Marco declares at the culminating point in his book that he has treated of "peoples, beasts, and birds; gold, silver, precious stones, and pearls; merchandise and many other things." [12] And, concluding his description of continental Asia with this retrospective yet programmatic observation, he then goes on to evoke his reminiscences of insular and tropical Asia, dominated by the wonders of India, "which do not exist in any other part of the world." [13]

As is clearly to be seen from his enumeration, Marco's interest was primarily directed toward the customs of the peoples he visited; then toward the fauna of the various regions; and then the precious metals, gems, and the like, to be found there. These last he tells of rather for their intrinsic beauty and rarity than for their value as objects of trade; and therefore he mentions merchandise as a separate subject, and merely hints at the "many other things" he has neglected to specify. The "other things" are in fact so numerous that those he does mention seem of minor, almost negligible importance. "Merchandise" is last among the superior subjects treated in his book.

A critical study of these topics will not only group together in an ordered presentation the aspects of Marco Polo's Asia that

[10] Cf. the undoubtedly authentic epilogue, preserved in the "Crusca" version, ed. D. Olivieri, second edition, Bari, 1928, p. 248; M.P., p. 489.

[11] So Marco asserts, when treating of Chinese spices unknown in the West (cr. ed., p. 114; M.P., p. 276). This would also explain the fact that tea is never mentioned—an omission which has given rise to much speculation (cf. Yule-Cordier, Introd., pp. 110 f.).

[12] *Il Milione,* cr. ed., p. 160; M.P., p. 353. It is strange that this, however fragmentary, classification of the subjects treated in the *Milione* has never been noted by its commentators, although it is indispensable to any attempt to find one's way through the mass of data and miscellaneous information contained in the book.

[13] *Il Milione,* cr. ed., p. 161; M.P., p. 354.

relate to man and nature, but will also reveal a more precise, faithful image of the personality of one who explored and described them with a versatility of interests and an acuteness of observation that, in spite of the sober style of writing, have no equal in the vernacular literature and science of the age. On the other hand, even the characteristic lacunae and limitations of this eclectic curiosity help to trace the historical portrait of this extraordinary personage against the background of contemporary civilization, both in Europe and in Asia.

The main object of his curiosity was, as we have just seen, the customs of the various peoples, of which the Christian West had not yet formed a direct conception.[14] By his brief reference Marco designated all that we call their civilization, manifested in the most diverse spiritual, intellectual, artistic, moral, and political expressions, as well as the complex mass of popular traditions and usages that are commonly understood in the concept of the national and local folklore of any people.

This exotic world, which was almost entirely dominated or inhabited by Mohammedans or pagans, extended from Armenia, a feudal tributary of the Tartar empire, to Korea, and from the borders of Mongolia and Siberia to the tropical regions of India and Africa. In the immense territory personally explored by him, and in those regions beyond that were known to him through direct and trustworthy information, Marco observes, above all, the various aspects of life, while he neglects precisely that subject for which his book is now universally famous, namely, the systematic geographical description of the various countries.[15]

Indeed, the general geographical perspective of his book is rather vague and in some degree conventional; and the various data about the configuration of the lands visited are nearly always generic, not specific, and are often blurred or arid. At times they are repeated with monotonous insistence, and with inaccurate names and figures, and on the whole the information they offer is more accidental than systematic, inasmuch as it is connected with personal undertakings and travel experiences rather

[14] The text of the cr. ed. reads, quite simply, "jens." However, since it then goes on to refer to the "customs" of the peoples, both Yule-Cordier and Foscolo Benedetto take it to mean "the customs of various peoples."
[15] Cf. Yule-Cordier, *op. cit.*, Introd., p. 109.

than coördinated by methodical observations and scientific curiosity.[16] The geography of the *Milione* is therefore, in the main,
that of its author's itineraries, and hence is a personal construct
derived from his direct experiences and his occasionally vague
reminiscences. His remarks on climate are generally more precise
than those on topo-chorography. Moreover, while he has little
or nothing to say about his means of getting from place to place
on his many long continental journeys, he, as a Venetian and
hence familiar with maritime matters, lingers over a detailed
description of Chinese ships in the ports and on the high seas of
the Orient.[17]

Intent, then, on observing life, Marco outlines what is primarily
a human geography of Asia, far richer, far more precise and
alive, than his physical geography, which by comparison constantly appears as an accessory or background to the vast picture
painted by him of contemporary Oriental civilization. This
attitude, which is more humanistic than scientific, inclines him to
survey the most varied phenomena of Asiatic life—a life which
is always extraordinary even when it is normal, and always fascinating even to one acquainted with its less picturesque sides and
trivial or repugnant manifestations. All this represents those
customs of the various peoples to which Marco primarily gives
space in his book without ever progammatically defining this
ethnographic concept. All that goes to make up the character and
habits of those who live in the lands mentioned or described by
him is included in this term.

In order to differentiate between them in their great variety
and in their essential or common traits, he makes use of some
characteristic manifestations that occur wherever ethnic groups
exist as nations, peoples, or tribes. These are, first of all, religion,
with its cults, rites, and institutions; next, human activities, with
their usages and products; then, the most notable aspects of political, social, and private life; and, finally, language, which he

[16] All this is especially characteristic, because of the mention of his itineraries and
the descriptive phraseology of the regions of central Asia and southern China.

[17] *Il Milione,* cr. ed., p. 30; M.P., p. 124 (Persian ships), 161 f., 354 (Chinese
ships). Cf. Yule-Cordier, *op. cit.,* Vol. II, pp. 249 ff. Cf., too, U. Bertuccioli's essay,
without scientific claims, "Marco Polo uomo di mare," *Ateneo Veneto,* Vol. CXLVI,
1955, pp. 23 ff.

FIG. 4. *The Polo brothers, accompanied by the young Marco, presenting to Kublai Kaan their credentials from Pope Gregory X and a container of oil from the lamp of the Holy Sepulcher; from an illumination in the Oxford MS (XIVth century) of the Book of Ser Marco Polo.*

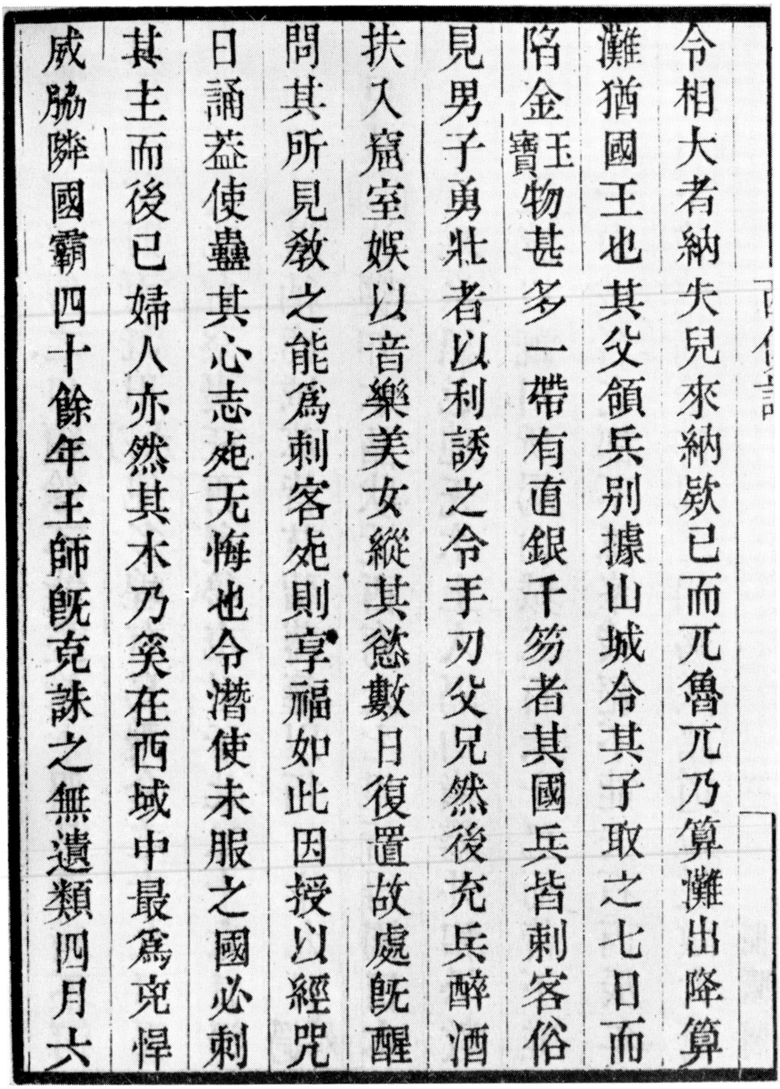

令相大者納失兒來納欵已而兀魯兀乃算灘出降算
灘猶國王也其父領兵別據山城令其子取之七日而
陷金玉寶物甚多一帶有直銀千笏者其國兵皆剌客俗
見男子勇壯者以利誘之令手刃父兄然後充兵醉酒
扶入窟室娛以音樂美女縱其慾數日復置故處既醒
問其所見敎之能爲剌客兀則享福如此因授以經咒
日誦蓋使蠱其心志㐫无悔也令潛使未服之國必剌
其主而後已婦人亦然其朮乃奚在西域中最爲克悍
威脅隣國霸四十餘年王師既克誅之無遺類四月六

FIG. 5. *Description of the country and customs of the Assassins of Persia in the Report on the Lands of the West (Si Shi Ki) of the Chinese general Ch'ang Te compiled by Liu Yu.*

never fails to mention so as to distinguish the inhabitants of a particular region.

These elements are always present in Marco Polo's "description of the world." They are often repeated in the monotonous formulas of an arid, vague phraseology—as in the enumeration of the towns in Persia and Turkestan with their Mohammedan, Christian, or idolatrous inhabitants, all of them subjects of the Great Kaan, who have "their own language" and make a living from commerce or art, and so forth;[18] likewise, in the long list of the populous Chinese centers from Peking to Quinsai (Hangchow), in which other idolatrous subjects of this same sovereign plied their various trades, burned their dead, and used paper money, with few individual variations that have especially to do with products of the soil or the peculiarities of the region. This does, in fact, lead one to believe Marco's oft-repeated assertion that he has nothing else to say, precisely at the moment when he has aroused the reader's curiosity.[19]

On the other hand, the same elements are also to be found in elaborate forms of description and enumeration. These offer an abundance of ethnographic details and a variety of correct, concrete information of all kinds set out in a clear scheme of disposition, interspersed with anecdotes, as in the chapters dealing with Persia, Cathay, Tibet, and India, or in the mention of some Chinese cities and the evocation of the insular world of the tropics, swarming with peoples of different faiths, barbaric tongues, strange customs, and mysterious civilizations. Moreover, this vast assemblage of data, brief mentions, and reminiscences

---

[18] Lingajes por soi" in the Franco-Italian text (cr. ed., chap. xlix, p. 38, and *passim;* M.P., p. 39). This expression was understood by Frampton, the English translator of the Elizabethan age (ed. N. M. Penzer, London, 1929, chaps. 35 and 37, and *passim*) as if it meant the "Persian language"; his version thereby gave the impression that all Asia spoke this idiom, which is too broad a statement. Frampton followed a Spanish version of the Venetian text of the *Milione* (cf. Penzer, *op. cit.,* p. 164).

[19] Examples of this are to be found at the end of nearly all the topographical and descriptive chapters of the *Milione*. For this subject cf. the present author's *Storia letteraria delle scoperte geografiche*, Florence, 1937, pp. 133 ff. This preteritional phraseology is especially frequent, and irritating, in the chapters dealing with central and southern China, which are monotonous and conventional, and which fail, moreover, to satisfy even the most modest curiosity. The phenomenon was noted in particular by G. Dainelli, *Marco Polo*, Turin, 1939, pp. 147 ff., but it is still in need of a more convincing explanation. Cf. P. Demiéville, "La Situation religieuse en Chine," in *Oriente Poliano*, Rome, 1957, pp. 223 ff.

is collected within the plan of Marco's itineraries, which lead to the discovery of a world that was either completely unknown or had been distorted for centuries by traditional fables.

Before systematically bringing together all this mass of information, in an attempt to evoke Marco Polo's Asia in its various aspects, we shall do well to take a sweeping view and make note of those features which for him were most worthy of mention and for us are of most historical interest. First on the list is the religious topography of the continent, which his book portrayed with a greater wealth of detail than is to be found in the works of the missionaries who had attempted the same task half a century before him.[20]

Marco's detached but not impassive attitude is manifest both in this field and in his contemplation of the political aspects of Asian life. With the same conscientious diligence with which he noted all along his route the centers and seats of the various religions, sects, and churches, he likewise indicated the political affiliation of each country, tribe, and city. The latter task was certainly far the easier, since all the regions of continental and part of insular Asia were either subject to the Great Kaan or were his tributaries, and the conquest or submission of the rest was planned. Marco found it not difficult to combine his "denominational" geography of the Orient with a compendium of political geography, vague and provisional as far as territorial boundaries and the various forms of sovereignty were concerned, but correct in the few essential data that reveal the effective power, the principal institutions, and their relationship with the central authority.

Whereas Marco considered the religions of Asia with typically Christian sentiments, although he never attacked or discussed them, he accepted the political conditions in the countries subject to the Chinghizide dynasty with loyalty toward the sovereign and his vassals, without examining too closely the feelings of the oppressed or judging the rights of the rebels. He constantly maintained the legitimist attitude of a scrupulous, obedient subject, and that devotion to his overlord which was typical of the spirit and forms of the feudal *fidelitas*.

[20] See chap. vii of the present work.

After having held for seventeen years various offices in the imperial administration in lands subject to the conqueror, attaining one after another the ascending grades of the courtly and bureaucratic hierarchy, Marco, like many other foreigners residing in China, considered himself an adoptive son of this new country and a faithful servant of its sovereign, in spite of some feelings of nostalgia for his homeland.[21] He looked after Kublai's interests on all occasions with a distrust of natives that was typical of the government official's attitude toward subject peoples, even to the detriment of some just causes, and obviously was indifferent to the resentment and suffering of highly civilized nations smarting under the yoke of a barbaric tyranny that had deprived them of all political authority and brought about their cultural disintegration.[22]

This attitude of total legitimism on the part of Marco and his elderly companions, who were champions of the Faith and lay missionaries for the Christian cause in the Orient, may appear to be incoherent, opportunistic, and servile, even as their extreme subordination to the rigorous feudal hierarchy of the Mongol empire seems to contradict the republican traditions of their Venetian homeland. The explanation of this attitude should, however, be sought for in the general framework of medieval society, which did not differ essentially in the two extremes of the contemporary world.

Indeed, in Marco's century the primitive nomad feudalism of the Mongols had been transformed, through contact with the agricultural and urban civilizations of the great countries conquered and subjected by them, into a political, military, and administrative feudalism. In this system, as in the rest of the medieval world, the right of conquest was consecrated as a result of the divine concept of sovereignty personified in the emperor and, indirectly, in the dynasty and the dominant nobiliary caste.[23]

---

[21] Cf. the *Milione,* cr. ed., chap. xviii, p. 11; M.P., p. 87.

[22] As is clear from his book (cr. ed., pp. 70 and 143), Marco was aware of the national feelings of the peoples subject to the Chinghizide dynasty. For the relations between these peoples and the central authorities cf. O. Franke, *Geschichte des chinesischen Reiches,* Vol. IV, pp. 470 ff., and Vol. V, pp. 234 ff.

[23] Cf. B. Ya. Vladimirtsov, *Le Régime social des Mongols,* Paris, 1948, chap. ii.

This is the principle which is constantly and explicitly expressed
in the letters sent by the Chinghizide sovereigns to the Pope and
the princes of Europe, from Muscovy to France.[24]

The Polos had accepted it not only because of their elevation
in the imperial hierarchy but also from a natural adaptation to a
political and social system that was similar in part to the one
then existing in the West. The Venetian state, apparently, was an
exception since the privileges of the doges were detached from
the republican institutions of the city. However, through the
medium of the nobility, to which the Polos seem to have belonged,
this state did in practice exert its rights of conquest like every
other medieval power, following the customary feudal system
of sovereignty and vassalage in its continental, maritime, and
colonial expansion; and, as in the city itself, there was no interference on the part of those local republican elements which were
characteristic of the Italian communes.[25]   .

This is the source of the Polos' legitimism and legalism which
determined their unconditional devotion to Kublai and their
enthusiastic admiration for the methods of government and
military administration of the dynasty celebrated in those chapters of the *Milione* that deal with its history.[26] And, since the
Mongol court and administration in China and the rest of the empire had retained the feudal, military character given them by
Chinghiz Khan and strengthened by his descendants and successors, Marco drew in his book an authentic picture of the Mongol
military organization, which reveals direct experience of the
system and even today offers the most complete and trustworthy
description of it.[27]

Friar John of Pian del Càrpine had accomplished something

[24] Cf. E. Voegelin, "The Mongolian Orders of Submission," *Byzantion*, Vol. XV,
1940–41, pp. 378 ff.; also A. Mostaert and Francis W. Cleaves, "Trois documents
mongols des Archives secrètes vaticanes," *Harvard Journal of Asiatic Studies*, Vol. XV,
1952, pp. 445 ff.

[25] For these interferences between republican institutions and feudal methods, characteristic of the Italian communes in the Middle Ages, cf. R. Cessi, *Storia della Repub-
blica di Venezia*, Vol. I (1944).

[26] Cr. ed., pp. 50 ff.; M.P., pp. 161 f.; also the chapters dealing with Kublai Kaan
and his methods of government and conquest, cr. ed., pp. 70 ff., and M.P., pp. 202 f.

[27] *Il Milione*, cr. ed., pp. 78 ff.; M.P., pp. 216 f.

similar, half a century earlier, in order to inform Pope Innocent IV of the situation in Asia after the consolidation of the new Mongol empire.[28] His description of this military system, like the Emperor Frederick II's famous letter to the King of England, was intended to help in the defense of Western Christianity against the Tartar expansion toward the Mediterranean and central Europe.[29] In the *Milione,* on the other hand, the subject is treated with a wealth of detail, but at the same time simply as a characteristic aspect of contemporary Asiatic civilization, without any political intentions or exhortation to counterattack. Marco knew that this mighty military organization was the basis and fulcrum of his lord's power. He therefore described it with the fullness and coherence of detail that the character and importance of this grandiose institution merited. Thus, after having mentioned the arms and armor of these soldiers, praised their courage and powers of endurance, and remarked upon the docility and schooling of their horses, he describes the organization of the huge armies themselves. These were so disposed as to provide a captain for every ten, hundred, thousand, and ten thousand men, so that each group had a leader responsible for supplying to his superiors the number of men required by strategic and tactical necessity.[30] We also learn that armies on the move were always preceded and followed by two hundred scouts, who protected them from possible surprise attacks, and that they were governed by a system of revictualing which guaranteed their fighting efficiency in every season and circumstance, even during campaigns over vast distances. Marco further provides us with a vivid, precise account of the Mongolian conquerors' characteristic tactics, based on the mobility of their cavalry, whose impetus both in feigned flight and in frontal attack never failed them in

---

[28] *Sinica Franciscana,* Vol. I, pp. 76 ff.

[29] For this celebrated document cf. *Monumenta Germaniae Historica,* Scriptores, Vol. XXVIII.

[30] With regard to this, Friar John observes (*loc. cit.* in note 28, above) that this system also prevented the defection of any single warrior, who for his wrongful act would be killed, with the rest of his company, by the phalanx next coming up. In this as in all else the Mongol military hierarchy as organized by Chinghiz Khan always acted in groups based on a decimal order, which was also characteristic of other Asiatic peoples. See Yule-Cordier, *op. cit.,* Vol. I, p. 264.

out-maneuvering and overwhelming even their most warlike enemies.[31]

✧   ✧   ✧

Religions and their rites, the state and its functions, the dynasty and its history, are therefore the main themes to receive frequent, systematic treatment in the *Milione*. The descriptions of the characters and customs of the peoples are, of course, numerous and varied, but for the most part they tend toward curious, exceptional manifestations, which are noted here and there as if by accident, with an obvious preference for folklore and its strangest aspects. Hence we find little in the *Milione* about the spiritual life of such highly civilized nations under Mongol domination as Persia and China, and, outside its boundaries, pagan and Mohammedan India. Marco Polo, who, as he himself asserts, had learned the language and customs of the Tartars, their method of writing, and military practices, had also come to share their feelings of contempt for the subject populations and the conquerors' suspicion of the representatives of the various national civilizations.

The men of letters who for centuries had constituted the Chinese governing caste and the administrative system of the old empire were widely replaced by adventitious foreign visitors, who, like Marco, had to use and impose the Mongol language; and by the year 1269, instead of the traditional Chinese ideographic writing, they were employing a special script of recent creation, and, in place of the refined phraseology of the native officials, an uncouth, artificial jargon, which still further alienated the intellectual life of the Chinese empire from that of its conquerors and governors.[32] This is the main reason why Marco

[31] Marco does not mention the firearms used by the Chinese armies (see O. Franke, *Geschichte des chinesischen Reiches*, Vol. IV, p. 287, and Vol. V, p. 155) and recorded in the annals of the Chinghizide dynasty. Cf., too, K. Huuri, "Zur Geschichte des mittelalterlichen Geschützwesens nach orientalischen Quellen," *Studia Orientalia*, Helsingfors, Vol. IX, No. 3, 1941.

[32] Cf. O. Franke, *op. cit.*, Vol. IV, pp. 475 ff., and the essay by E. Haenisch, *Die Kulturpolitik des mongolischen Reiches*, Berlin, 1943. Cf. also H. Franke, *Beiträge zur Kulturgeschichte Chinas unter der Mongolenherrschaft* (*Abhandlungen für die Kunde des Morgenlandes*, Vol. XXXII, Pt. 2), Wiesbaden, 1956, and, for the official script, N. Poppe, *The Mongolian Monuments in ḥP'ags-pa Script*, second edition (*Göttinger asiatische Forschungen*, Vol. VIII), Wiesbaden, 1957.

intentionally ignored its culture. Indeed, for him—a foreigner lacking in any literary or spiritual initiative—this would always have remained inaccessible, even in more fortunate circumstances. Marco, since he had not learned the Chinese language, remained isolated from its cultural sphere. In his inevitable contacts with the natives he would make use of the interpreters who abounded in the Mongol administration throughout the Great Kaan's dominions, or of foreigners, for the most part Arabs and Persians, who resided in the great political and commercial centers.[33]

Such, too, was Marco's attitude toward the Persia of the Mongol Ilkhans, although a knowledge of their language and familiarity with the usages and customs of the Mohammedan population could have led him to a deeper appreciation of the native civilization, which was beginning to recover from the destruction and slaughter incident to the Tartar invasions and the abolition of the Caliphate.[34] Although hardly fascinated by the greatness and wealth of the national civilizations of Persia, China, and India, Marco was at least conscious of their importance; but he chose rather to exalt to the greater glory of his sovereign their external aspects, and especially the manifestations of urban life, little understood or appreciated by the Mongol conquerors, who were still bound to the traditions of nomadic life and unwilling to adapt themselves to the habits and exigencies of sedentary populations.

Amid this barbaric or exotic world, Marco always remained a true Venetian, a European. This is revealed in his often emphatic admiration for those which he calls the "noble" cities of Asia, from Tabriz in Persia to Balkh in Afghanistan, still imposing in its desolate ruins;[35] from Karakorum, the first capital of the

[33] These intermediaries were most often Mohammedans residing in the commercial centers of the empire and its outlying provinces. We have a typical instance in the Z version of the *Milione* (cr. ed., p. 158 n.; M.P., p. 349), which relates that a "sapiens saracenus" acts as a guide to Maffeo and Marco Polo in the town of Foochow. For the vast Mohammedan group in medieval China and the relevant literature see the article "China" in the *Encyclopaedia of Islam*.

[34] For these events and the background cf. B. Spuler, *Die Mongolen in Iran,* Leipzig, 1939, pp. 167 ff.

[35] Briefly described in the *Milione,* cr. ed., p. 35; M.P., pp. 134 f.; Yule-Cordier, *op. cit.,* Vol. I, pp. 151 ff. For further data cf. W. Barthold's well-informed work, *Turkestan Down to the Mongol Invasion,* second edition, London, 1928 ("Gibb Memorial" Series, n.s., V), chap. ii.

Chinghizide empire, with its castle and the governor's "most beautiful" palace, to the immense town of Khanbaliq, the new and magnificent imperial seat; from the rich, populous, industrious, and ornate cities of Cathay to the great historic, artistic, and commercial centers of southern China. He was never tired of admiring and describing these last, both in limited and extensive, even fantastic, detail, but at the same time considering them as conquered places which the emperor exploited by means of taxes and tribute money, levied by his emissaries who were protected by a powerful army and a well-organized police force.

The architectural aspects of all these centers, and sometimes also of the smaller towns, are especially recorded in the *Milione:* namely, the palaces, monasteries, towers, walls, bridges, castles, and characteristic monuments and buildings. Mention is usually made of their dimensions and the building materials employed, and occasionally of structural and ornamental details that make possible their identification.[36] This mass of architectural data which refers to buildings of all kinds throughout the whole of Asia, both sacred and profane, monumental and utilitarian, military and civic, is so abundant that it would seem to deserve critical coördination. It does at least reveal Marco's preference for architecture in comparison with every other artistic activity of the Asiatic peoples. Thus, paintings, which were so characteristic, especially in China, and were even appreciated in the circles of the Chinghizide court, are only rarely and vaguely mentioned by him, perhaps as a result of the artistic interests prevalent in the Venice of his times, where architecture dominated all the other arts.[37] Nor does Marco seem to have been interested in Asiatic music. He merely mentions the stringed and wind instruments which accompanied with their pleasant tones the chants of the Tartar warriors preparing for battle, until their harmony was interrupted by the powerful "naccara."[38] It is certainly

[36] *Inter alia,* the descriptions of the imperial palaces of Shangtu and Khanbaliq (cr. ed., chaps. lxxv and lxxxv; M.P., pp. 185 and 211), and of the residence of Facfur, "king of the Mangi," at Quinsai (cr. ed., chap. cliii, pp. 150 f.; M.P., p. 338), which have no equal in medieval vernacular literature.

[37] For the arts in Oriental Asia during the Mongol period, and for the bibliography on the subject, cf. R. Grousset, *La Chine et son art,* Paris, 1951, and *Les Civilisations de l'Orient,* 4 vols., Paris, 1929–1930.

[38] *Il Milione,* cr. ed., pp. 68 ff.; M.P., p. 198. In this and other passages in which

strange that he should have treated of music only in its connections with military usage or the practices of therapeutic magic,[39]
when, as is well known, it represented one of the most characteristic expressions of contemporary Oriental life, both in the variety
of instruments used and as an indispensable element in many
social circumstances and in court ceremonial.[40]

He reveals an equal lack of sensitivity to other cultural manifestations. They had no part in Mongol tradition; and as for
those of the highly civilized subject peoples, he regarded them
with the same suspicious indifference as did their conquerors,
who in Persia had destroyed the most flourishing centers of culture, from Samarkand to Tabriz, and in China had eliminated
from public life the ruling cultured class.[41] Moreover, that passage of descriptive prose which, according to the *Milione,* enabled
the last empress of the Sung dynasty to save her magnificent
capital from the fury of the Tartars, and helped Marco to describe
the city, appears in the book merely as a historical document, and
certainly not as a literary monument.[42] Likewise, the songs of
the Mongol rhapsodes, of which we catch some echo in his epic
biography of Chinghiz Khan, are used by Marco—as formerly
by the Tartar chroniclers and Oriental annalists—as a historical
source and narrative prelude.[43] Hence, we find in his book no

music is even more briefly and vaguely mentioned, Marco always refers to Tartar
music, without ever recalling the Chinese variety.

[39] Especially in the wild province of "Zardandan," on the border between China
and Burma (cr. ed., chap. cxxi; M.P., pp. 281 ff.).

[40] Cf. R. Wilhelm, *Chinesische Musik,* Frankfurt a. M., 1927, as well as A. C.
Moule, "A List of Musical . . . Instruments of the Chinese," *Journal of the North
China Branch of the Royal Asiatic Society,* 1908, pp. 1–160.

[41] See above, note 34.

[42] Cf. *Il Milione,* cr. ed., p. 143, chap. cliii; M.P., pp. 326 f.; Yule-Cordier, *op. cit.,*
Vol. II, pp. 193 f.; also A. C. Moule, "Marco Polo's Description of 'Quinsai,'" *T'oung
Pao,* Vol. XXXIII, 1937, pp. 105–128, and his *Quinsai* etc. (1957).

[43] *Il Milione,* cr. ed., pp. 50 ff. The epic motives that make up the poetic background of the *Secret History of the Mongols (Manghol un niuča tobča'an,* ed. E.
Haenisch, 2 vols., Leipzig, 1937–1939), which was compiled in 1240 at the court of
Ogudai, the son and successor of Chinghiz Khan, have been illustrated in the Russian
edition of the Mongol text with translation (ed. S. A. Kozin, *Sokrovennoe Skazanie,*
Moscow and Leningrad, Akad. Nauk SSSR, 1941, Vol. I). It is now accessible in the
complete German translation by E. Haenisch, *Die geheime Geschichte der Mongolen,*
second edition, Leipzig, 1948, and in the partial translation by P. Pelliot, *Œuvres
posthumes,* Vol. I, Paris, 1949. Reflections of this poetical history of the Mongols are
to be found, apart from *Il Milione,* in *La Flor des estoires de la terre d'Orient* by the
Armenian Hayton, published in Latin and French in the year 1307 (cf. *Recueil des*

trace of the flourishing literatures of China, India, and Persia,
whereas he does not fail to note some of the characteristic
manifestations of what he considered to be the natural sciences
and liberal arts most studied in those lands, especially "necromancy, 'physics,' astronomy, geomancy, and physiognomy." [44]
In particular, he mentions two of the most important centers
for these disciplines: Baghdad, the capital of Iraq and formerly
the seat of the Abbasid caliphate; and the "noble" city of Soochow
in southern China, where he observed "philosophers and healers
well versed in the secrets of nature." [45] Even today it is possible
to assert that between Anatolia and the China Sea there were at the
time no other cultural centers that could compete with these two
cities for the study and practice of every science.[46]
But first of all we should consider what Marco understood by
these ideas. We may be sure that his *fisica* had nothing to do with
what is nowadays understood by the term "physics." In those
times it designated "physic," the science of medicine, even as the
modern English word "physician" still signifies a doctor, the
fisicale of medieval tradition.[47] Similarly, Marco's "astronomy"
was, as for his contemporaries, a synonym for astrology, of which
frequent mention is made in his book, both with regard to the
scientific or magical horoscopes of medieval usage, and as the
basis for the compilation of the Chinese "almanacs," which set
forth, together with the prediction of the year's outstanding

Historiens des Croisades, Documents arméniens, Vol. II, Paris, 1906), and, indirectly,
in Giovanni Villani's *Cronaca,* as well as in the historical encyclopedia by the Persian
Rashiduddin (cf. E. Blochet, *Introduction à l'Histoire des Mongols de Fadl Allah Rashid-
ed-Din,* "Gibb Memorial" series, Vol. XII, 1910, and the Persian text with introduction in the subsequent volumes of this series). The same motives recur in the official
Chinese history of the Chinghizide dynasty (*Yüan Shih*), compiled in 1368 ff., and
even in modern Chinese poetry—for this see William Hung, "Three of Ch'ien
Ta-hsin's poems on Yüan History," *Harvard Journal of Asiatic Studies,* Vol. XIX,
1956, pp. 1–32.
   [44] *Il Milione,* cr. ed., p. 18, chap. xxv, n.; M.P., p. 102.
   [45] *Il Milione,* cr. ed., p. 142, chap. clii; M.P., p. 325.
   [46] The great and glorious centers of Mohammedan culture in Khorasan and Turkestan
(such as Merv, Balkh, Nishapur, Samarkand, etc.) had been annihilated by the
Mongols of Chinghiz Khan, and never rose up from their ruins to any further intellectual activity.
   [47] The term *fisica* for medicine is also found in ancient Italian texts (*Novellino,*
Aldobrandino da Siena, etc.), cited in the Vocabolario della Crusca under this word-
heading.

phenomena, the sovereign's highest civic function and religious and dynastic responsibility.[48]

All the disciplines enumerated or mentioned in the *Milione* are nothing but the components or adjuncts of this most important science of astrology. While they always border on natural or occult magic, they represent its systematic, theoretical, and rational aspect, as a basis for medical practice or else as an empirical instrumentality for every sort of divination. Such, indeed, are necromancy, as the evocation of spirits; geomancy, as the determining of auspicious and inauspicious places, for example, to build upon; and physiognomy, "which makes men known at sight," practiced, and observed by Marco, in the most civilized countries of the Asian continent.[49] He made a distinction between these disciplines, considered to be sciences, and the exorcistic magic of the Mongol shamans, the *bacsi* (or *bakhshi*) of Tibet and Kashmir, and the enchanters of India.[50]

His interest in these things was owing to their familiarity: they did not greatly differ, in method, substance, or popular appeal, from the forms and tendencies of Western civilization. Indeed, if there was a common meeting ground for East and West at that time, it was determined precisely by the common interest

[48] For the importance of the official almanac in Chinese public life cf. M. Granet, *La Civilisation chinoise*, Paris, 1929. For Marco Polo's allusions to this cf. Yule-Cordier, *op. cit.*, Vol. I, pp. 448 ff.

[49] Besides the allusions to these disciplines in the descriptions of Mesopotamia, Persia, and China, cf. the references contained in the chapter relating to the "great province of Maabar" and the numerous details offered on the subject by the Z version (cr. ed., *loc. cit.*). The most important treatise on "physiognomy" of Marco Polo's times, written in Paris in 1295 and printed at Padua in 1474, was that of Petrus de Abano (cf. Lynn Thorndike, *A History of Magic and Experimental Science*, Vol. II, p. 877), who was preceded by Michael Scott, the celebrated astrologer of Frederick II (*ibid.*, p. 328). The widely known *Secretum Secretorum*, of Oriental origin but attributed to Aristotle, in its various vernacular versions (cf. *ibid.*, pp. 267 ff., and Ch. V. Langlois, *La Connaissance de la Nature et du Monde*, pp. 117 ff.) established the popularity of this discipline, which is recorded in various other encyclopedias of medieval science. For these pseudo-sciences in China cf. H. Franke, *Sinologie*, Bern, 1953, chaps. vii and xii; Joseph Needham, *Science and Civilisation in China*, Vol. II, §§ 14 ff.; and the article "Fêng Shui" in S. Couling, *Encyclopaedia Sinica*, London, 1917. For Western geomancy in Marco's times see Th. Ebneter, "Poème sur les figures géomantiques en Ancien Provençal" (with bibliography), in *Bibliotheca Helvetica*, Olten and Lausanne, Vol. II (1955).

[50] When mentioning the tricks of the quacks, or those of Christian heretics on the island of Socotra, Marco seems to have refrained from describing them in detail because they disgusted him. Cf. cr. ed., p. 205, and M.P., p. 427; also chap. x of the present work.

in these more or less esoteric disciplines, even as nowadays it is almost exclusively in the natural and applied sciences that Europe and Asia agree with and understand each other.

At the time of Marco Polo, Italy was the land where all these pseudo-sciences flourished under the direct protection of the courts, republics, and cultured classes; they became, indeed, the most characteristic expression of scientific and philosophical interest.[51] Guido Bonatti, Francesco Stabili, and Petrus de Abano, to name three among Marco's contemporaries, were popular and active although they were suspected, persecuted, and condemned by the ecclesiastical authorities on account of the heretical doctrines and diabolical practices that were attributed to them.[52] And since these were, in their various manifestations, the adaptation, development, and logical outcome of ancient Asiatic traditions, which had been taken over and renewed by the Mohammedans of Persia, Syria, Egypt, Spain, and Sicily, they too did not differ greatly from those that Marco observed in the great cultural centers of the Asian continent and at the court of Kublai, who had in his train a whole army of Mohammedan, Christian, and pagan astrologers.[53] In fact, Marco speaks of them with the seriousness that was their due as representatives of that which was regarded in both Europe and Asia as the most noble of the sciences and the end of all practical philosophy.[54]

[51] Cf. Thorndike, *op. cit.*, esp. Vol. II.

[52] Guido Bonatti is mentioned by Dante, *Inferno*, XX, 118; and Cecco d'Ascoli (Francesco Stabili), famous for his vernacular *Acerba*, is remembered also as a victim of the Inquisition; he was burned alive in 1327.

[53] Five thousand, according to Marco (*Il Milione*, cr. ed., p. 100 n.; M.P., p. 252), including Christians, Saracens, and "idolaters." Cf. Yule-Cordier, *op. cit.*, Vol. I, pp. 446 ff. They were controlled by a special ministry that was divided into various sections according to the respective races and religions; cf. H. Franke, *Beiträge zur Kulturgeschichte Chinas*, p. 72.

[54] In distinguishing astrology from magic all his medieval masters were theoretically in agreement, from the time of Michael Scott (cf. Thorndike, *op. cit.*, Vol. II, p. 319), and so, too, Dante (cf. E. Moore, *Studies in Dante*, Third Series, Oxford, 1903, pp. 19 ff.), although in practice it was well-nigh impossible to limit the respective fields of these pseudo-sciences. Hence, Dante's condemnation of him who "sorrows at God's judgment" (*Inferno*, XX, 30), and the fate of Petrus de Abano and Cecco d'Ascoli, both of whom were condemned by the Inquisition in spite of the fact that astrology was commonly practiced even in the ecclesiastical medieval world. Marco's attitude is very like that of all his contemporaries, at the same time that he shows an ingenuous curiosity for the impious, condemned magical practices. His interest shows through, even in the midst of occasional expressions of disgust aroused by the Christian's horror for the pagan cults with which the practices of Oriental magic, such as the

Moreover, he was not aware of making scientific observations on those few occasions when he directed his attention toward natural phenomena; for example, when in the tropical seas he measured in his own way the height of the stars and described the southern constellations.[55] As we know, it was Petrus de Abano, a professional scientist, who profited from these observations. So, too, in the High Pamir, Marco had no idea of the scientific value of his discovery that fire does not burn there as elsewhere and cooks less well; mistakenly, he attributed the fact to the intense cold of those altitudes.[56] Again, when on more than one occasion he treated of the medical practices of various peoples, he regarded them rather as curious works of the Devil, though he was not unaware of their relationship with complementary disciplines that were thought to be proper subject matter for science and recondite doctrine.

His interest, therefore, is primarily directed toward popular traditions, and he consequently felt himself more attracted by the fossilized, primordial forms of Asiatic civilizations than by their more elevated and refined expressions. This is the characteristic attitude of the uncultured man when confronted with the most obvious manifestations of the spiritual and intellectual life of any land and people. Hence, his book is an inexhaustible mine of information about the usages and customs of the Asiatic world as they appear in everyday life: modes of clothing and adornment, funeral and matrimonial rites, the superstitions attaching to religion or magic, the more or less barbaric practices of tattooing, the couvade, and cannibalism; the conservation of age-old ceremonies, of which the original significance had already been lost; strange cults; and singularities of all kinds in domestic life, food, drink, and erotic practices. The whole is spiced with anecdotes, almost always accompanied by remarks that indicate the ethnographic differences of the various peoples and tribes, and by mention of their more or less curious inclinations, both attractive and repellent, which go to make up the Asiatic folklore

evocation of spirits and of secret natural forces, were closely connected. Geomancy, physiognomy, and necromancy are disciplines complementary to astrology in the works of the authors cited.

[55] See above, chap. i, § 2.
[56] *Il Milione,* cr. ed., chap. l, p. 40; M.P., p. 142.

discovered and commented upon by Marco for the first time in history.

All this information, which invites systematic investigation, forms the complex mass of Marco's observations on the customs of the people of the whole continent, considered in their major expressions and most characteristic, curious, popular manifestations. As a whole, they constitute one of the main aspects of his book and the constant object of his insatiable curiosity. Admittedly, they are not very profound; but they are always reliable and valuable as a starting point for further research on the Asia of his times. Indeed, in themselves they provide sufficient justification for considering Marco Polo as the pioneer of a new ethnographical science that must always look upon him as a guide and master.

ƒIVE

ASPECTS OF NATURE—ANIMAL, VEGETABLE, MINERAL—IN MARCO POLO'S BOOK

In his list of the main themes treated in his book, Marco Polo follows the manifestations of the life and civilization of Asiatic peoples with sober mention of those aspects of nature—animal, vegetable, or mineral—which especially attracted his attention in the course of his journeys about the continent and his voyages in the surrounding seas. He himself tells us that he was interested, above all, in beasts and birds; a simple calculation of the number of times he mentions these in his "Description of the World" would alone afford proof of his constant interest in every kind of animal. He classified them in only two categories, quadrupeds and winged creatures, omitting fishes and reptiles, of which, however, he makes opportune mention in various parts of his book.[1]

The importance he assigns to the fauna of the continent is the more noteworthy because preceding explorers of Asia had rarely

[1] E.g., sturgeons and salmon of the Caspian Sea (*Il Milione*, cr. ed., p. 16), the seasonal fish in Georgia (*ibid.*, p. 17), the trout of Badakhshan (*ibid.*, p. 38 n.), the fish in the imperial parks at Khanbaliq (*ibid.*, pp. 75 and 86), in the waters of the distant province of Gaindu (*ibid.*, p. 114), in Yunnan (*ibid.*, p. 116), in Lake Kao-yu to the north of Quinsai (*ibid.*, p. 136, chap. cxliii); without counting the various references to the whales of the Pacific and Indian oceans (*ibid.*, pp. 203, 206, 208) and the "serpents" that designate the crocodiles of Carajan (*ibid.*, pp. 116 ff.), and, finally (*ibid.*, p. 214) the dried fish from the Arabian Sea. (For references in the English translations of the *Milione*, consult their indexes at the items mentioned above.) Venice imported great quantities of salted fish from the Black Sea, where the industry flourished. This is often mentioned as an article of trade by Pegolotti, *La Pratica della Mercatura*, ed. Evans, p. 22 etc. See also B. Spuler, *Die Goldene Horde*, pp. 388 ff. It may be pointed out that Brunetto Latini places fish and amphibious creatures at the beginning of the zoölogical section of his *Trésor*.

mentioned this category of things seen by them. As a Venetian, Marco in his youth was hardly familiar with the animal world that was variously represented in his city in sculptural forms rather than in flesh and bones and in the practices of daily life;[2] but from the time of his adolescence he probably shared in the general curiosity shown by his times in the animal kingdom— a curiosity evidenced by a vast doctrinal zoölogical literature that not only resulted in the famous traditional bestiaries but also contributed to the extraordinary popularity of Aristotle's *Historia Animalium,* which, for this field of interest, was the book of the century.[3] This same interest is further documented by the vogue enjoyed by the *Roman de Renart* throughout Europe, with its poetical and satirical humanization of the animal world;[4] and, finally, by the innumerable works of sculpture and miniatures that reflect in realistic and fantastic shapes the particular interest of medieval society in every form and aspect of animal life.

The practical interests of falconry and the chase should be added to the scientific, poetic, artistic, moralistic, and didactic expressions of this curiosity. In particular, they stimulated the compilation of numerous books, beginning with the famous treatise by Frederick II and his collaborators which represents a courtly, literary, and scientific manifestation of a fashion and discipline that were characteristic of lay interest in the XIIIth century.[5]

---

[2] The representation of every kind of animal is a characteristic phenomenon of Romanesque and Gothic art, especially of the XIIIth century. As is well known, this subject is one of the most important in Oriental, and especially Chinese, art, and is often recorded by Marco Polo as a decorative theme ("bestes et osiaus"). Various typical examples are offered by William Cohn, *Chinese Art,* London, 1930, and in the well-known works on Oriental art by O. Sirén and R. Grousset.

[3] For the influence of this treatise, translated into Latin between 1221 and 1223 by Michael Scott, the astrologer at the court of Frederick II in Sicily, cf. Lynn Thorndike, *A History of Magic and Experimental Science,* Vol. II, pp. 380 ff.

[4] For the text and illustrations cf. the present author's *Romanische Literaturen des Mittelalters,* 1929, esp. pp. 139 ff. This zoöepic was especially popular in the Venetian region, as can be learned from the note in E. Monaci, *Crestomazia italiana dei primi secoli,* p. 387, and Adriana Caboni, "Note e correzioni al Rainardo e Lesengrino," *Rendiconti della Reale Accademia dei Lincei,* classe di scienze morali, sixth series, Vol. XI, 1936, pp. 936 ff.

[5] Cf. the extensive bibliography of the subject compiled by F. Werth, "Altfranzösische Jagdlehrbücher," *Zeitschrift für romanische Philologie,* Vol. XII, 1888, pp. 146 ff. and 381 ff., Vol. XIII, 1889, pp. 1 ff. (this also includes Italian treatises). For the *De Arte Venandi cum Avibus* by Frederick II and his son, King Manfred, cf. *The Art*

This spirit and this familiarity with the animal kingdom are reflected just as much in the *Divine Comedy* as in the *Milione;* and it is only rarely that the two works and their authors seem to meet against the common background of contemporary civilization.[6] However, when Marco, who was then barely seventeen years of age, left Venice for the East in 1271, none of the works in the vernacular dealing with the world of animals and nature had yet been compiled and diffused in Italy. Brunetto Latini's *Trésor,* with its imaginary and traditional bestiary, which contemporary readers were already beginning to find dull and lacking in interest, had been compiled in French some years previously and was not yet accessible in the Tuscan translation by Bono Giamboni.[7] It is therefore hardly likely that Marco was familiar with the chapters on birds used for hunting; and the *Trésor* is the only medieval encyclopedia to have dealt with both the scientific and the practical ends of the noble discipline which engaged in its praise the imperial leisure of Frederick II and the poetic ingenuity of Daude de Pradaz.[8] Hence, Marco's intense interest in every kind of hunting animal, and even more his constant curiosity about the domestic and wild beasts of Asia, must have been developed on another basis, although some treatises designed for the instruction of the uncultured, such as the *Image du Monde* and

---

of Falconry, trans. and ed. C. A. Wood and F. M. Fyfe, Stanford Univ. Press, 1943, profusely illustrated and with a full bibliography of the subject. In this manual Frederick rejected the authority of Aristotle's *Historia Animalium* in this field, although it was translated for him by Michael Scott, even as his contemporary Albertus Magnus refused to follow the *Physiologus* and its derivative bestiaries when describing the various aspects of animal life. Cf. Thorndike, *op. cit.,* Vol. II, pp. 541 ff. Cf. the *Physiologus Latinus,* with introduction and bibliography by Francis J. Carmody, Paris, 1939, and University of California, *Publications in Classical Philology,* Vol. XII, No. 7, 1941, pp. 95 ff., and the essay by Pauline Aitken, "The Animal History of Albertus Magnus and Thomas of Cantimpré," *Speculum,* Vol. XXII, 1947, pp. 204 ff.

[6] For the animals in Dante's poem see M. Lessona, *Gli animali nell'opera di Dante,* Turin, 1893, and Francesco Neri's book with the same title, Pisa, 1896, as well as other articles on this subject to be found in the Dante bibliographies by Passerini, Evola, and Vallone.

[7] Cf. the text with introduction and bibliography, ed. F. J. Carmody, Univ. of California Press, 1948.

[8] Brunetto Latini, *Trésor,* chaps. cxxxxvi ff. (*ed. cit.,* pp. 137 ff.), preceded by the treatise by Albertus Magnus, *De Falconibus,* which is in large measure modeled on Frederick's work (cf. Thorndike, *op. cit.,* Vol. II, pp. 562 f.). For *Lo Romans dels Auzels cassadors,* by Daude de Pradaz (*ca.* 1220) cf. A. Pillet, *Bibliographie der Troubadours,* Halle, 1933, pp. 110 f.

the well-known *Secretum Secretorum* in the vernacular, commonly associated the erudite and teratological zoölogy with geographical data.[9]

Apart from these literary records and the general tendencies of his age, two things in particular contributed to the importance he accorded to Asiatic domestic, wild, and cynegetic fauna. First of all was the common psychological, animistic stimulus that makes us discover in animals a reflection of human feelings and attitudes, and between vegetative life and our own a number of similarities and affinities. These had already been asserted in this century, of which, indeed, this artistic and literary symbiosis was one of the most characteristic phenomena.[10] The *Secretum* itself, which in various languages was used for popular instruction and served as source material for the *exempla* of the preachers, makes Aristotle tell Alexander the Great—the most famous figure in medieval Asiatic history—that man carries within himself all the qualities of the animals, since he is bold like the lion, simple like the lamb, lazy like the bear, base and stupid like the ass, lustful like the pig, and so forth, in a sequence of moral allegories connecting with the wisdom of the ancients and the Orient the feats of the Macedonian and popular cosmography.[11]

To this general stimulus of human curiosity should be added the fact that Marco, as he traveled over the Asian lands and seas, found there all the creatures, more or less fabulous to the West, which, like the lion, tiger, elephant, camel, bear, whale, and in unexpected forms the unicorn and the gryphon, were then the living symbols of an exotic world. Here, too, he discovered as yet unknown varieties of animals common in the West, such as the big-horned sheep of the Pamir (*Ovis poli*), the wild buffaloes of "Erginul," the Mongolian deer, the papions of the imperial preserves (leopard-like beasts used in hunting), the various cranes

[9] For these vernacular treatises cf. Ch. V. Langlois, *La Connaissance de la Nature et du Monde au moyen âge*, Paris, 1927. As for *La composizione del mondo*, by Ristoro d'Arezzo, it was completed in 1282, when Marco was in China, and treats mainly of the influence of the stars on every creature and substance, although it does record some observed phenomena in a spirit akin to Marco's.

[10] Especially in the *Roman de Renart* and derivative works, as well as in the figurative arts and in scientific and didactic literature, for which see Thorndike, *op. cit.*, Vol. II, pp. 56 ff., etc.

[11] This passage is reproduced in the French text by Langlois, *op. cit.*, p. 112.

of Cathay, and the featherless chickens of Fukien, which were similar to the snow-white hens that Odoric of Pordenone was later to admire in the capital of this southern Chinese province.[12]

His interest in these zoölogical discoveries is so inclusive that he has instant words of admiration for even the varieties of the most familiar types of animals, such as the horses of the Turcomans and of Badakhshan, the wild asses and humped oxen of Persia, the falcons of Mongolia, the pheasants of western China, the musk-gazelle, dried head and hoofs of which he seems to have taken back to Venice; and many more.[13] Indeed, we can almost feel him trembling with joy at the sight of all the extraordinary wild game of the Orient, which he never tires of describing, enumerating, and exalting, in his style which is so concise and sober that a single epithet is enough to reveal the feelings that inspire him.

Our Venetian traveler acquired this familiarity with Asiatic fauna, about which he was to become so knowledgeable, especially in the Mongol environment. The Mongols, who were shepherds and hunters, had developed a keen understanding of animal psychology and an infallible expertness in dealing with beasts of all kinds. In their age-old experience with animals, these nomads had learned to exploit them to the utmost and to protect them with a minimum of trouble and expense. This familiarity with the fauna of the forests and steppes is manifested in their life and poetic history, and survived even when the Tartar nobility became sedentary in the capitals of the Golden Horde, of Persia, Mongolia, and China; that is to say, when the Chinghizide sovereigns and princes maintained near their residences immense parks filled with wild beasts and birds, and organized great

[12] Cf. *Sinica Franciscana,* Vol. I, p. 461, and A. C. Moule, *Quinsai, with Other Notes on Marco Polo,* Cambridge, 1957, pp. 54 ff. and 61 ff., which offers the fullest treatment of the subject, and discusses also Marco's "papiones."

[13] Some references to Marco Polo's zoölogy are to be found in V. Carus, *Zoologie,* Munich, 1872, pp. 197 ff. Marco notes as regions especially rich in all kinds of game: Armenia, Persia, northern Mongolia, the Chinese provinces of Kansu and Shantung, and the vast province of Szechwan; the territory of Laos; and various parts of India, without counting the imperial estates described at length (cr. ed., pp. 85 ff.; M.P., pp. 227 f.), and the many regions named on this account but only in passing. For large-scale crocodile hunts cf. cr. ed., pp. 116 f.; M.P., p. 279. For all kinds of animals in Ethiopia, cr. ed., p. 212; M.P., pp. 442 ff. For those in the arctic territories of Russia, cr. ed., pp. 231 and 232; M.P., pp. 474 ff.

hunts there, almost military in style, and imported from all over Asia exotic and rare animals which they passionately added to the more valuable specimens of their native fauna.[14]

No Asian or Western author has given us a more vivid and sharply detailed picture of this than Marco, who to his own interest in the subject added that of his hosts, assimilating himself with them even in this characteristic aspect of their attenuated barbaric civilization.[15] And so we find that this Venetian, who as a boy must at the most have hunted cats, gnats, and rats, had now mastered the secrets of the chase and of falconry, conforming to the ideal soldier and courtier of the Great Kaan, who required his vassals regularly to take part in his colossal hunts. These would simulate vast military maneuvers, and a multitude of men and animals were deployed in them with great pomp and circumstance. All this is extensively described by Marco; yet it is only with difficulty that we can imagine the scene without an excess of fantasy.[16]

[14] Especially elephants. The king of Champa had to supply to the Great Kaan each year twenty of these beasts from among the finest specimens (cr. ed., p. 168; M.P., p. 367), and each of the Kaan's other vassals was obliged regularly to replenish his preserves with every kind of animal or other game killed, or, instead of these, to send hides properly prepared and tanned. Cf. the cr. ed., p. 85; M.P., pp. 226 f. For the beasts of the imperial menagerie cf. cr. ed., chap. xcii; M.P. pp. 227 f. For the tame lion, cf. cr. ed., chap. xc. With the term "lion" Marco and his contemporaries also designated tigers, which were better known in China than lions. The latter, imported from Persia, were rare, and the beast's appearance was known mainly through the stylized forms of sculpture.

[15] The *Secret History of the Mongols,* of 1240, offers many examples of their familiarity with animal life. It is well known that the civilization of the Tartars was based especially on an exploitation of those domestic and wild animals which met every need of their nomadic life.

[16] Marco gives three chapters (xcii–xciv) to a description of these great hunts, which he saw as a follower in the emperor's train, and thereby makes known to us the various methods of hunting with falcons, eagles, leopards, tigers (always called "lions"), lynxes, and the 5,000 hounds trained for the task. All were unleashed to pursue bears, wild boars, stags, deer, and wild asses, while with the various kinds of hawk the hunters caught cranes, quail, and other winged creatures that abounded in the preserves. For treatises on Asiatic falconry cf. J. von Hammer-Purgstall, *Falknerklee: bestehend in drey ungedruckten Werken über die Falknerey,* Pest, 1840, with references to Marco Polo; and on the same subject, with special reference to China, Edward H. Schafer, "Falconry in T'ang Times," *T'oung Pao,* Vol. XLVI, 1958, pp. 293 ff. St. Mark's National Library in Venice possesses the unique manuscript of two French treatises on falconry (CIV, 7) attributed to Persian authors, first translated into Latin by Master Theodorus, philosopher, astrologue, and secretary of the Emperor Frederick II; cf. Langlois, *op. cit.* (note 9, above), p. 207.

Such was the school in which he learned to distinguish and record many varieties of continental, tropical, and insular fauna, of which some specimens had reached the court of Kublai, an ardent collector of every kind of animal. As he describes them in his book, in relation to his journeys to these distant, hitherto unexplored lands, Marco's heedfulness is also influenced by reminiscences of the medieval teratological zoölogy of legendary and literary tradition. This, for example, makes him discover the mythical unicorn in the rhinoceros of Sumatra; although he does observe that this animal appeared "quite different from that which we imagine him to be," and thereby gives an indication of his Western culture under stress of personal experience.[17] Certainly his surprise must have been very great when, instead of the lithe, agile animal depicted by medieval artists, he discovered in the tropical jungle the monstrous, massive mammal that had usurped its name and characteristic attribute. Likewise, his stay in the kingdom of Lambri, in Sumatra, gives him an opportunity of recalling the legendary men with tails that never failed to appear in medieval representations of the Orient; here, they served to designate the anthropoids of Indonesia.[18] These same reminiscences make him recognize the ancient Cynocephali in the savage inhabitants of the Andaman Islands,[19] or induce him to repeat, in his efforts to describe the great vultures or other birds of prey which are to be found in the coastal and insular

[17] *Il Milione*, cr. ed., p. 171; M.P., p. 372. The description of this animal is one of the most minute in the book. For stories about the unicorn, which never fail to turn up in medieval bestiaries and are often recounted in various Oriental texts, cf. R. Ettinghausen, *The Unicorn*, Washington, D.C., 1951. The rhinoceros described by Marco is differently recorded by the Chinese Chau Ju-kua (trans. and ed. Hirth and Rockhill) for those regions, and his horn as an object of trade all round the Indian Ocean.

[18] For this Western teratology and its sources cf. the article by R. Wittkower, "Marvels of the East: A Study of the History of Monsters," *Journal of the Warburg and Courtauld Institutes*, Vol. V, 1942, pp. 159 ff. See, too, the same author's already cited essay, "Marco Polo and the Pictorial Tradition of the Marvels of the East," in *Oriente Poliano*, Rome, 1957, pp. 155 ff. The "Corpus Teratologicum" of Thomas of Cantimpré was translated into French in the XIVth century and has been published by A. Hilka, "La Manière et les faitures des monstres qui sont en Orient," *Abhandlungen der Gesellschaft der Wissenschaften zu Göttingen*, phil.-hist. Klasse, third series, No. 7, 1933, pp. 23 ff. Cf. L. F. Flutre in *Zeitschrift für romanische Philologie*, Vol. LXXI, 1955, pp. 422 ff.

[19] *Il Milione*, cr. ed., p. 176; M.P., p. 378.

regions of tropical Africa, the famous story of gryphons capable of lifting up an elephant in their talons.[20]

Hence, anyone who might have wished to group together the data on exotic fauna scattered throughout the *Milione,* classify the beasts and birds, and add a zoölogical and literary commentary, could have compiled a small encyclopedia of the animal world of Asia which would have been more inclusive and more reliable for precision and wealth of detail than any far more voluminous treatise on natural history available in that century. It seems strange that Marco did not stress with equal emphasis his no less important contribution to the science of Oriental flora. Psychological and professional prerequisites would not have been lacking, since the vegetable kingdom included both herbs, with their more or less secret virtues, and spices, which, together with cereals, are one of the commonest subjects in his description of Asia. Medicinal herbs and spices from the Orient appeared also in the vast medieval didactic literature in Latin and the vernacular, although both products are usually accorded less frequent mention than animals and precious stones. Thus, Brunetto Latini does not treat of them in his *Trésor,* though he supplies an abundance of data on the other natural kingdoms. Albertus Magnus, who compiled a famous treatise *De Vegetabilibus,* preferred, like

---

[20] *Il Milione,* cr. ed., p. 206; M.P., p. 431. Here is mentioned the fabled roc (*ruc, rukh*), for which see Yule-Cordier's commentary on this passage (*The Book of Ser Marco Polo,* Vol. II, pp. 415 ff.), and, for the Arabic sources, G. Ferrand, *Relations de Voyages,* Vol. II, pp. 456 ff. For its iconography cf. R. Wittkower's note, "Miraculous Birds," *Journal of the Warburg and Courtauld Institutes,* Vol. I, 1938, pp. 253 ff. This is the famous *p'êng* of the Chinese, already mentioned by the Taoist classics Lieh Tzŭ and Chuang Tzŭ; cf. L. Wieger, *Les Pères du système taoiste,* Paris, 1950 (reprint), pp. 133 and 209 (Chinese text and French translation). Among the fauna of Africa, in part imaginary, recorded as to be found in "Mogdasio" (Madagascar) and Zanzibar (Somali Coast), which were never visited by him, Marco describes the giraffe with precision and admiration (cr. ed., p. 208; M.P., p. 432). Very likely he had seen one in Kublai's zoölogical park; he designates it as "mout belle couse a veoir" (a very beautiful thing to see). This animal is recorded in like terms by the Chinese Chau Ju-kua (ed. Hirth-Rockhill, p. 128) in his references to the same region. If the hypothesis put forward by the editors of his text is correct, that the Chinese name for giraffe (*tsu-la*) is of Persian origin (*zurnāpā*), it would then be possible to confirm the supposed importation of this animal into China in Marco Polo's times. Cf. B. Laufer, *The Giraffe in History and Art,* Chicago (Field Museum of Natural History), 1928, esp. pp. 43 and 70 ff., and J. J. L. Duyvendak, *China's Discovery of Africa,* London, 1949, pp. 32 ff. In Marco's times, also, the Mameluke sultan of Egypt possessed some giraffes in his preserves near Cairo; cf. M. Esposito, "The Pilgrimage of Symon Semeonis," *Geographical Journal,* Vol. LI, 1918, p. 86.

the other encyclopedists of the Middle Ages, to study plants from books rather than in their natural surroundings.[21] The *Milione* is not lacking in allusions to the erudite and doctrinal traditions of contemporary zoölogy, especially when Marco contradicts its assertions in the light of facts directly observed by him; but no link can be discovered between the herbaria of his times and his frequent mentions of Asiatic vegetation in connection with the regions visited and recalled. Here, too, his interest transcends the practical preoccupations of a medical man or merchant, and is directed toward the most varied aspects of the vegetable world, with the same relationship between vernacular literary culture and direct experience of natural phenomena that we have pointed out as characteristic of his description of Asiatic fauna.

In fact, although his mention of the legendary *Arbre sec* in the plain of Tunocain in Persia was inspired by the tales of the minstrels who sang of the feats of Alexander the Great in the squares of Italian towns, he was the only one to note the most characteristic features of this tree, which later made it possible for botanists to identify it.[22] And, whereas the Franciscan missionaries who preceded him in the discovery of Asia hardly men-

[21] Cf. the critical edition of this treatise published by E. H. F. Meyer in 1867, and Meyer's *Geschichte der Botanik,* Vol. IV, Königsberg, 1857, pp. 38–78. For other medieval authors of this branch of knowledge cf. Thorndike, *op. cit.,* Vol. II, pp. 472 ff., 555 ff., etc. A large part of the interest shown by medieval naturalists in the vegetable kingdom is directed toward medicinal plants and herbs. In this field medieval science did not go beyond Pliny (*Historia Naturalis,* Bks. XIII–XIX), for whose Oriental and Greek sources cf. the article in Pauly-Wissowa, *Realencyclopädie der classischen Altertumswissenschaft,* Vol. XLI, Pt. 1, 1951, coll. 319 ff. The short treatise in hexameters *De Viribus Herbarum* by Floridus Macer, otherwise known as Odo Magdunensis or Eudes de Meung, of the XIth century, was also read (see M. Manitius, *Geschichte der lateinischen Literatur des Mittelalters,* Munich, 1923, Pt. 2a, pp. 539 ff.); and it is reproduced almost word for word in Vincent of Beauvais, *Speculum Naturale,* Bks. IX–XV. The pseudo-Aristotelian treatise *De Vegetabilibus,* and mention of the fundamental work in botany by Dioscorides, may conclude our references to the vast medieval literature on the subject, for which see G. Sarton, *Introduction to the History of Science,* Vol. II, and Herrmann Fischer, *Mittelalterliche Pflanzenkunde,* Munich, 1929.

[22] Cf. *Il Milione,* cr. ed., pp. 25 and 32; M.P., pp. 116 and 128. Under the name of Arbre Sol, it designated a province of northern Persia (cr. ed., p. 222; M.P., p. 456), mentioned by Marco with some references to the legend of Alexander the Great connected with the tree and its region. For this cf. the commentary by Yule-Cordier, Vol. I, pp. 128–139; also, the curious interpretation offered by Stanislao Franchi, *L'itinerario di Marco Polo in Persia,* Turin, 1941.

tion one plant in the whole course of their travels, which took them deep into the heart of Mongolia, Marco notes in his book, with keen interest, and for their own sake, the luxuriant forests of box trees in Georgia, the oases of palms in Persia, the fir trees of Mongolia, the huge tracts of forest in Shangtu near Kublai Kaan's summer residence, the extensive plantations of mulberry trees and canes in China, the rows of umbriferous trees which the same sovereign had caused to be planted along the roads of his empire for the comfort of travelers and as a warranty of long life to him who put them there, as Marco comments.[23] Then, there are the forests of exotic plants and trees in the kingdom of Champa and on the island of Sumatra; the exuberant artificial gardens of Alamut in Persia; the imperial parks at Peking and Quinsai; the orchards of Khorasan and beautiful vineyards of Kashgar; the bamboo of Tibet; and various single plants of insular Asia, and of India and other countries on the continent.[24] All this exotic vegetation is part of the landscape and life of these regions, and Marco recalls it, with admiration expressed in sober terms, as the chief natural aspect typical of the lands he visited, and indispensable to the activity and wealth of their various populations. As for spices, it is possible that he considered them as "merchandise" rather than vegetal products. In fact, we find them all mentioned in Francesco Balducci Pegolotti's *Pratica della Mercatura*. However, Pegolotti never expressed that botanical interest which Marco continuously reveals in his observations of those vegetal products for which there was then so great a demand in Europe, and which reached the consumer indirectly via the Arab buyers of tropical Asia and then the emporia and markets of Venice.[25] Since for this reason they were surrounded by an air of mystery, and were prized not only for their monetary value but also for their marvelous medicinal and magical virtues, spices were for all Westerners the fragrant,

---

[23] *Il Milione,* cr. ed., p. 98, chap. ci and note; M.P., p. 248. For this symbol cf. the present author's *Guillaume Boucher,* pp. 68 ff.

[24] For Chinese flora in the *Milione* cf. E. Bretschneider, *History of European Botanical Discoveries in China,* London, 1898.

[25] Cf. W. von Heyd, *Histoire du commerce du Levant au moyen âge,* Vol. II, pp. 563 ff., and Adolf Schaube, *Handelsgeschichte der romanischen Völker im Mittelmeer,* Munich and Berlin, 1906, and some references in Gino Luzzatto, *Storia economica d'Italia,* Rome, 1949, Vol. I, chap. vii, with bibliographical data.

living symbol of that exotic world from which they did indeed come. No Westerner had ever visited this world before Marco. When he returned home, therefore, he was consulted on this matter by the learned Paduan physician Petrus de Abano, to whom he revealed the places of origin of these miraculous, legendary substances.[26]

Before Marco supplied this information, the merchants of Venice, Genoa, and Pisa already knew that the spices and gems of tropical Asia—generally called "India"—were brought up the Persian Gulf and the Tigris to Baghdad, which was a sorting center, as was Alexandria for merchandise coming via the Red Sea.[27] The *Milione,* however, was the first account to localize them precisely, thereby making it possible to reach directly the places of production, whence export had for centuries been monopolized by Arab commerce that ranged from the Mediterranean to the ports of southern China. Thus it came to be known in the West that the aloe plant grew profusely in the kingdom of Champa in Indochina, and that cinnamon abounded in both Tibet and Malabar; that galingale and ginger were characteristic products of southern China, that cloves flourished especially in the impassable mountains of Kienchang, pepper in Bengal, Greater Java, and elsewhere in tropical India, and rhubarb in Tangut, "where merchants buy it and then transport it all over the world."[28]

Not even the names of these regions were known in Europe. It is therefore likely that Marco's trustworthy revelations encouraged merchants and governments to break the Arab monopoly of this lucrative produce by directing their ships and

[26] See chap. i, § 2, n. 68, above.

[27] Cf. *Il Milione,* cr. ed., p. 18, M.P., p. 101 (for transport from Basra to Baghdad and beyond), and cr. ed., p. 23, M.P., p. 104 (for Baghdad as a forwarding port, which Pegolotti, *op. cit.,* frequently mentions at length for every type of merchandise). On this subject cf. von Heyd, *op. cit.*

[28] Among all the spices of the Orient, pepper was the most important both for import and for commercial profit. The Genoese had specialized in the pepper trade. Nevertheless, Marco is repeatedly interested in the acquisition and consumption of this condiment in the China of his times, especially at Quinsai (cr. ed., p. 145, and M.P., p. 340) and Zaiton (cr. ed., p. 159, and M.P., p. 351); and he mentions also its production in India (cr. ed., pp. 125, 197, etc.) and the forwarding market at Alexandria, in Egypt, which was the principal Mediterranean emporium for spices (cr. ed., pp. 199, 212 f.). Cf. Chau Ju-kua, *ed. cit.,* p. 258.

their trade toward the as yet unexplored regions of tropical and continental Asia. Moreover, these indications, which were not to be found elsewhere, inspired the Portuguese to navigate the open seas eastward as far as Macao, and Christopher Columbus "to seek out the Orient via the west."[29]

But Marco could neither have foreseen nor comprehended all this. After his return home, it never occurred to him to organize an expedition toward regions that were blocked by Mohammedan merchants. Even if his seagoing experiences had suggested to him the possibility of the circumnavigation of Africa, he would doubtless have judged that such an enterprise would not be worth the hazard. He was content to be the first botanical explorer of our modern era, freeing all those herbs and spices from their sacks, warehouses, dispensaries, and books, that he might contemplate them in their natural surroundings as fine, living vegetable entities, which had grown up beneath the sun of distant lands.

We should see, for example, in the Franco-Italian text of the *Milione* with what loving attention and precision he describes the cloves of the province of Gaindu or the coconut palm of the island of Sumatra.[30] That he foregoes describing the types of spices which, in his own words, "are not brought to our countries" does not in the least diminish his merit of having empirically initiated the method of descriptive and applied natural history,

---

[29] See Ramusio's remark on the *Milione* quoted above, chap. iii, n. 64. As is well known, the commercial aims of Columbus' expeditions included gold, spices, and slaves; indeed, all the principal products of Asia, both real and fanciful. Slaves were imported in large numbers from the Crimea to Venice, from the end of the XIIIth century until the Ottoman conquest of Byzantium in 1453, which made this trade difficult and hardly profitable. Columbus, when he reached the "Indies," as we read in his *Letters,* did in fact seek out these "goods" in order to supply the markets of the West. After his return to Venice, Marco also had a "Tartar" slave in his service, to whom Venetian citizenship was granted in 1328, namely, after his master's death, "pro bono suo portamento" and also because he had been so long in Venice. See the document published by Yule-Cordier, Vol. II, p. 517 n. 13. In his book Marco Polo did not mention the slave traffic, which was very active—in Venice especially—during the XIVth and XVth centuries. For this see R. Livi, *La schiavitù domestica in Italia,* Padua, 1928, and Ch. Verlinden, "La Colonie vénitienne de Tana," in *Studi in onore di G. Luzzatto,* Milan, 1950, Vol. II, pp. 1–25, and Iris Origo, "The Domestic Enemy: The Eastern Slaves in Tuscany in the XIVth and XVth Centuries," *Speculum,* Vol. XXX, 1955, pp. 321–366; also, the present author's article, "Asiatic Exoticism," *Art Bulletin,* Vol. XXVI, 1944, pp. 95 ff.

[30] Cr. ed., pp. 114 and 172; M.P., pp. 276 and 374.

a systematic examination of which would reveal its extent and importance.

✧ ✧ ✧

To return to the list of subjects which, according to Marco himself, he emphasized in his book, we find in the third place metals and precious stones. These were, of course, traditionally associated with the legendary literary and geographical vision of Asia and especially of those vast regions which in medieval conceptions of the Orient were wont to be designated by the name of "India." [31] As may be seen in contemporary Latin and vernacular encyclopedias, both scientific and popular, this name alone was sufficient to evoke all these treasures, so alluringly described in the celebrated *Letter of Prester John,* the legendary sovereign of the Orient mentioned more than once in the *Milione.*[32]

The literary mirages of Oriental gold, at times substantiated by actual trade in this metal, had such power over the medieval mind that they still excited in Christopher Columbus the frenzied vision of "the gold of Cipango," the existence of which he never doubted until the day of his death.[33] Explorers can, indeed, be divided into two categories, the realists and the romantics; and for one as for the other, wonders and fabulous treasures always exist beyond the bounds of their experience and are always present to their minds.[34] It is true that, in spite of the special emphasis with which Marco enumerates these treasures, he does not

[31] For this geographical concept, which included the lands from Ethiopia to China, cf. John Kirtland Wright, *The Geographical Lore of the Time of the Crusades,* New York (American Geographical Society), 1925, pp. 272 ff., with full bibliography of the subject.

[32] For this subject cf. chap. ix, § 2, of the present work.

[33] For the gold trade in the Levant and beyond in the first half of the XIVth century cf. Pegolotti, *La Pratica della Mercatura,* ed. Evans, p. 424. It is hardly conspicuous. As is well known, the same mirages attracted and inspired the conquistadors and colonizers of both the Indies and the Americas until the second half of the XVIth century.

[34] For this vision of the Orient and the discovery of gold in the supposed Indies see the most reliable biographies, as, e.g., Cesare de Lollis, *Cristoforo Colombo,* third edition, Rome, 1923, and Samuel Eliot Morison, *Admiral of the Ocean Sea,* 2 vols., Boston, 1941. A warning must be sounded against the unfounded interpretations of certain less serious biographers.

mention them in his descriptions of continental Asia from the Mediterranean to the Yellow Sea. In all this immense territory the only pearls mentioned by him are those taken by his father and uncle from Soldaia to Sarai at the time of their first commercial venture in Tartar territory in 1260, and those that were imported from India to Baghdad through the Persian Gulf and thence by river to this center, where they were pierced and sent to all the markets. Moreover, although Marco had occasion to mention in passing the silver mines of Armenia, Badakhshan, and Chahar, it is only beyond the boundaries of Cathay that he mentions gold for the first time—in order to evoke the riches of Japan, where he had never set foot. This circumstance is all the more strange since one of the vastest territories of the Chinghizide empire was called the Golden Horde (*altan ordu*), and the Tartar dynasty of the Jurchen, dethroned by Chinghiz Khan in China in 1215, had taken from gold its historical Chinese name, *Kin*.

Marco's silence is explained by the fact that gold never played a very important role in the economy and, especially, in the monetary system of China; its rather meager production in the outlying provinces of the empire served mainly to finance imports from countries with hard currencies, such as India, Persia, and Byzantium, whose coins sometimes turned up as far away as Mongolia and Central Asia.[35] At every stage of their history the

---

[35] A complete list of the currency circulating in the Levant at the time of Marco Polo is to be found in Pegolotti, *op. cit.*, pp. 287–292 and 436 ff. For moneys mentioned by Marco cf. Yule-Cordier, Vol. II, pp. 590 ff. They were not, however, in regular use for commercial dealings in the Tartar dominions, where barter was most customary. In the various regions this took, respectively, the form of hides, cloth, porcelain, salt, shells, and metals. Paper money was in circulation in China and, later, in Persia. Basic for money in the Mongol states were the silver "sommi," which were also used in commercial transactions, and were called, in Turkish, *yastuq* (William of Rubruck, *Itinerarium*, in *Sinica Franciscana*, Vol. I, p. 237, refers to them as *iascot*, for which see P. Pelliot in *T'oung Pao*, Vol. XXVII, 1930, pp. 190 ff.). Gold was never minted in the Tartar-Chinese dominions. The quality of Byzantine coins was determined by their smell after they had been vigorously rubbed, according to Friar William, *op. cit.*, p. 192. For the monetary system and production of Chinese gold in Marco's times cf. H. Franke, *Geld und Wirtschaft in China unter der Mongolenherrschaft*, Leipzig, 1949, and J. J. L. Duyvendak, *China's Discovery of Africa*, London, 1941, pp. 17 ff., who emphasizes the prohibition against exporting Chinese coins in the Sung era. They were scattered all over southern Asia and westward to Zanzibar and the Somali Coast, but became scarce in Marco's times when printed money was

Chinese accumulated reserves of gold, more or less legally, but these were never great; and tributes of this metal required from subject countries that produced it were always relatively slight in quantity. The administration in Cathay was therefore periodically obliged to produce paper money as legal tender in Marco Polo's China. In one of the few flashes of wit in his book he asserts, when discussing from personal experience the currency of the Great Kaan, that Kublai "has the perfect alchemy" because he is able to transmute even the bark of mulberry trees into gold. A paper made of bast from these trees, and stamped, was used for trade in "pearls, gold, silver, and precious stones, and generally for all other things." [36]

Thus Marco Polo, far from being a prey to lust for gold—as he is sometimes wrongfully presented,—limited himself to mentioning those regions that produced it and the use made of it by the various peoples of his time, and restricted his account to what he knew from personal observation. Moreover, even when the idea of this bright metal evoked for him bewitching visions of the fabulous Cipango, the stimulus proceeded from the environment of Kublai's court when preparations, described at length in the *Milione,* were being made for the conquest of Japan, a project that was not successful.[37] The imaginary palace of the Japanese sovereign, with its roof of solid gold and halls studded with gems, closely recalls those described in the *Letter of Prester John* [38] and resembles the palaces portrayed at that time by the Chinese official Chau Ju-kua in his description of the wonders of Ceylon.[39] At the time of Marco Polo's stay the tales of Japanese

---

substituted for specie. For Persia and Russia cf. Spuler, *Die Mongolen in Iran* and *Die Goldene Horde,* with a full bibliography of the subject.

[36] Quoted according to the Polan text of the Accademia della Crusca, ed. D. Olivieri, second edition, 1928, pp. 102 ff.

[37] For these military and naval expeditions cf. O. Franke, *Geschichte des chinesischen Reiches,* Vol. IV, pp. 432 ff., Vol. V, pp. 211 f., etc.

[38] Cf. the text published by F. Zarncke, "Der Brief des Presbyters Johannes," *Abhandlungen d. k. Sächsischen Gesellschaft der Wissenschaften,* phil.-hist. Klasse, Vol. VII, No. 8, Leipzig, 1879, pp. 917 ff.

[39] Chau Ju-kua, *ed. cit.,* pp. 72 f. These imaginary palaces are not recorded by Marco among the wonders of Ceylon, which he visited when on his voyage homeward from China (cr. ed., pp. 176 ff., and M.P., pp. 379 ff.); but they are mentioned in similar terms by Odoric of Pordenone in *Sinica Franciscana,* Vol. I, chap. xiii, with regard to the island of Java.

gold were being used to further the imperial propaganda, as justifying with visions of glittering plunder the ruinous military undertakings of the régime.[40]

Just as rarely does Marco yield to the literary and legendary fascination of pearls and precious stones, of which he enumerates, as occasion presents itself, and with the competence he acquired from his expert older companions, the places of production and principal markets throughout the course of his continental and maritime journeys.[41] It was not merely familiar tradition and the instrinsic value of these precious objects that determined this diligent inquiry. In the medieval world they were even more greatly prized than they are now, both because they were then rarer and because of the "virtues" then attributed to them. Even a realistic merchant like Pegolotti, when treating of "the innate qualities of pearls," distinguishes between the ornamental variety and the medicinal, currently used in medical practice of those times in the Orient as well as in the West, adding that "from one carat and upwards they are at present in great demand for the lords and people of the Levant."[42] This is precisely what Marco reveals from direct experience; for he lived in the Mongol-Chinese courtly and nobiliary circles which amassed spectacular quantities of the choicer pearls, while those of lesser value were used, apart from medicinal purposes, as adornment for the rich-

---

[40] Some gold was imported into China from Japan (cf. Chau Ju-kua, *ed. cit.*, p. 170), more from Persia (B. Laufer, *Sino-Iranica*, Chicago, Field Museum, 1919, p. 509) and from Tibet (*ibid.*, p. 516). Cf. Lien-shêng Yang, *Money and Credit in China*, Cambridge, Mass., 1952, esp. chap. v. For paper money on a gold basis, as well as for the gold-producing regions of (especially southern) China, see H. Franke, *op. cit.*, pp. 119 ff. Cf., too, Yule-Cordier, Vol. I, pp. 496 ff.; and, likewise, for the Sino-Mongol military ventures in Japan, Vol. II, pp. 260 ff., and below, chap. viii.

[41] It should be noted that these precious stones are mentioned in the *Milione* only as products of southern and insular Asia. Pearls were found, according to Marco, in a lake in Gaindu, a semi-legendary region between Yunnan and eastern Tibet (Kien-chang); in Japan, which produced roseate pearls; and in India (provinces of Maabar and Soli). A flourishing trade in these objects was carried on at Mosul in Iraq and at Hormuz on the Persian Gulf; also, in the various residences of the Mongol and Indian sovereigns and vassals, who competed in the collection of unimaginable quantities of the most beautiful varieties. Cf. the Persian treatise on pearls by Shaikh ʿAlī Ḥazīn, ed. and trans. S. Khan Khatak and O. Spies (with introduction and bibliography) in *Beiträge zur Sprach- und Kulturgeschichte des Orients*, Heft 7, Wiesbaden, 1954. For the production of pearls in China, which is not specifically mentioned by Marco, cf. the exhaustive article by Edward H. Schafer, "The Pearl Fisheries of Ho-Pu," *Journal of the American Oriental Society*, Vol. LXXII, 1952, pp. 155 ff.

[42] *La Pratica della Mercatura*, ed. Evans, p. 304.

est garments, or were worked into the precious cloths described by him.[43] Moreover, the number of gems and precious stones mentioned in the *Milione* is significant, and the list includes, apart from those prized in every part of the world—namely, diamonds, rubies, turquoises, sapphires, topazes, amethysts, and the like,—the various qualities of jade that were unknown in Europe and therefore were incorrectly named by Marco according as they appeared to have affinities with stones current in the West such as jasper and chalcedony.[44]

All these gems, with their secret properties as revealed by Pliny, by the famous pseudo-Aristotelian "Book of Stones," [45] and by many other medieval works derived from it, were part of the common requisites for the fabulous representation of the Orient. By virtue of their miraculous powers they were also used by those Christians of the Middle Ages who practiced Mariolatry, and by pagans as ornaments for their "idols" and statues of the Buddha wherever he was venerated and represented.[46] This, indeed, was the intellectual, spiritual, and cultural realm wherein the religious and scientific traditions of East and West most commonly met and blended together, being helped along in these tendencies by the Arab-Persian and Arab-Indian literature which from the Xth century onward was diffused in all directions and especially in the great centers of eclectic civilization in Khorasan and Transoxiana, where it was particularly flourishing.[47]

[43] Cr. ed., pp. 18 and 61; M.P., pp. 101 and 183. Marco, however, does not say that these brocades, which he calls *nassit* and *nac*, were generally interwoven with pearls, as has been shown by P. Pelliot in *Journal Asiatique*, Vol. CCXI, 1927, p. 269 n. 1 and p. 278. This is also mentioned by Pegolotti, *op. cit.*, p. 423. For the decorated cloths, set with pearls, of the period cf. the present author's *Guillaume Boucher*, pp. 18 ff.

[44] See the note in Yule-Cordier, Vol. I, p. 193. Odoric of Pordenone (*Relatio*, in *Sinica Franciscana*, Vol. I, p. 473) calls jade *merdicas*, a term of obscure origin studied by Yule-Cordier, *Cathay*, Vol. II, pp. 219 f. For the whole subject cf. F. de Mély, "Lapidaires chinois," in *Les Lapidaires de l'antiquité et du moyen âge*, Paris, 1896, Vol. I; also, E. Bretschneider, *Mediaeval Researches*, Vol. I, pp. 173 ff.

[45] Cf. J. Ruska, *Das Steinbuch des Aristoteles*, Heidelberg, 1912, and Thorndike, *op. cit.*, pp. 260 ff.

[46] For the use of gems in the Christian cult see A. Salzer, *Die Sinnbilder und Beiwörter Mariens*, Linz, 1893, pp. 71 ff. and *passim*. For the Buddhist cult of the age see the description of the gigantic "idol" in the *Relatio* by Odoric of Pordenone cited above, *Sinica Franciscana*, Vol. I, p. 143. The notorious profusion of jewels on the statues of the Buddha had already been noted in the famous *Fihrist* by Abulfaraj in the Xth century (cf. G. Ferrand, *Relations de Voyages*, Vol. I, p. 119).

[47] See the numerous examples collected by Ferrand, *op. cit.*, and, for Western di-

We can therefore understand why Marco localized in Japan the legend of the stone that makes warriors invulnerable, which was immortalized by Ariosto in various passages of the *Orlando Furioso*.[48] In this he showed himself more credulous than the contemporary adapter of the *Secretum Secretorum,* who relates the same anecdote with a certain degree of skepticism.[49] However, mental habits are tenacious, and they dominated the minds of far more learned authors. Hence it should not surprise us that Marco, who is so precise in specifying the sites of the mines from which diamonds were extracted, repeats the ancient fable of the eagles that brought these precious stones to hunters who, as a bait, would throw down pieces of meat into the depths of inaccessible ravines.[50] This fable is narrated in medieval Arabic, Persian, Chinese, and Armenian texts, as well as in the more or less moralizing lapidaria of the West.[51] Its universality is to be explained by the fact that no one then had any precise idea of whence or how diamonds originated. The trade in them had always been carried on by intermediaries whose interest it was to keep this hidden. Marco never set foot in any of the diamond-producing regions; he therefore relates what he had heard from Mohammedan merchants who dealt in these precious stones in India.[52]

---

dactic literature of the Middle Ages, the works of Thorndike and Langlois already cited. The most nearly complete list of real, fabulous, and symbolical gems is certainly that offered by the *Letter of Prester John* in the various versions published by F. Zarncke, *op. cit.*

[48] *Il Milione,* cr. ed., p. 166; M.P., p. 363. The same legend is mentioned by Odoric of Pordenone with reference to islands of Indonesia (*Sin. Franc.,* Vol. I, p. 449). He asserts that this stone was extracted from certain bamboo canes or palms, and that it conferred invulnerability on its bearers. We are thus still within the sphere of insular romanticism, to which even our skeptic Marco occasionally succumbed (cf. the present author's *Storia letteraria delle scoperte geografiche,* pp. 34 ff.).

[49] Cf. Langlois, *op. cit.,* p. 108.

[50] Cr. ed., p. 186. As is known, this story is part of the Sindbad episode in the *Thousand and One Nights,* which must have been recounted for centuries in the Arab world before its appearance in that famous book. It is repeated, even earlier than in the *Nights,* by Niccolò de' Conti when treating of Mount Albenigerus (?) in India; cf. his *Viaggi,* ed. M. Longhena, Milan, 1929, pp. 177 ff. Cf. B. Laufer, "The Diamond," *Field Museum, Anthropological Series,* Vol. XV, 1915, pp. 7 ff.

[51] Cf. Yule-Cordier, *The Book of Ser Marco Polo,* Vol. II, pp. 362 ff.

[52] For the importation of diamonds into China at the time of Marco Polo cf. Chau Ju-kua, *ed. cit.,* p. 111, whose information is somewhat scant. See, too, B. Laufer, *Sino-Iranica,* p. 521, and Otto Maenchen-Helfen, "Diamonds in China," *Journal of the American Oriental Society,* 1950, pp. 187 ff. Pegolotti does not even mention them, and Brunetto Latini merely refers to them as a symbol of virtue, together with other precious stones with a moral function. Cf. *Trésor,* ed. Carmody, p. 175.

However, he was the first author to liberate the other precious stones from the ancient fables and charms, while nevertheless recording them as among the wonders of Asia as well as the most sought-after products of its remotest regions. His contemporaries were not satisfied with these discoveries and the sober account that Marco gave of them; indeed, they not only magnified the treasures of pearls, gems, and precious stones that the three travelers brought back with them to Venice, on the occasion of the second return, but also used them, so to speak, as a prompter's cue for further legends, in which the leading roles were imposed upon their three famous fellow citizens.[53]

All the other subjects considered by Marco Polo in his book are comprehensively designated by him as "merchandise" and "many other things," extremely vague terms that embrace an incalculable number of heterogeneous aspects of Asiatic life, whether described at length, or merely recorded, or here and there no more than hinted at. Only an orderly classification, so far as that is possible, can give some idea of the range of our traveler's empirical culture, which is rather connected with the places visited by him than grouped together according to scientific or didactic criteria. Many of the things lumped by him in the brief list of subjects dealt with in his book were then, and still are, objects of trade, and a number of those hidden away in the mass of "various products" are of particular interest and among the most important in the whole book.

Let us take, for example, the raw materials recorded in it. It is well known that the *Milione* contains the first reference in Western literature to petroleum, which is mentioned as a combustible and for medical properties that are correctly attributed to it.[54] Marco's observations cover the essentials. It is, of course, true that the *Image du Monde* of Gossouin de Metz, and its Latin sources a century earlier, already make mention of the boiling pitch used by the necromancers of Persia, which is also recorded

---

Infrequent mention is likewise made of them by Arab geographers and travelers when treating of the Far East; see Ferrand, *Relations de Voyages,* Vol. II, p. 700.

[53] Cf. the Polan legends collected by Ramusio, *Navigationi & Viaggi,* Vol. II, proem.

[54] Cr. ed., pp. 15 ff.; M.P., p. 97 (on the border between Armenia and Georgia).

in the *Mirabilia Descripta* of Friar Jourdain de Sévérac; [55] but in Marco's text we have not only a more precise allusion to the authentic product but also the data that enable us to identify its source in the Baku peninsula, on the Caspian Sea.[56] And further, by pointing out that it is not a comestible, he clearly distinguishes it from the other oils produced in the mountains of Badakhshan and Kashmir, which are extracted from sesame and nuts.[57] On the other hand, we do not find any clear distinction made between vegetable and mineral oils, which latter were then unknown in the Western world.[58]

No less remarkable is the description in the *Milione* of fossilized carbon (coal), which though unknown in the West was so abundant in every part of China that anyone there could indulge in three hot baths a week, and one every day in winter, "provided they are able to," while the nobles and other wealthy citizens had their private baths in their own homes.[59] And Marco adds at this point that wood, though plentiful there, would never have sufficed.

These observations are characteristic of his attitude toward the civilization of the Far East. He does not hint at the important part played for centuries by fossilized carbon in the economy and the metallurgical production of China; [60] instead, coming from a

[55] Cf. Langlois, *op. cit.*, p. 171. Friar Jourdain's Latin text (ed., with French translation, by H. Cordier, Paris, 1925, p. 111 and p. 59) asserts that "in ista Persida sunt aliqui fontes de quibus scaturit unum genus picis quae *ķic* vocatur (*pix*, dico, seu *pegua*)." The term *pegua* is reminiscent of Dante's "pegola spessa," *Inferno*, XX, 17.
[56] In Marco's times, and for many centuries to come, this territory was part of the Persian dominions, then under the sway of the Ilkhans.
[57] *Il Milione*, cr. ed., pp. 37 and 177; M.P., pp. 138 and 379. Walnut oil was commonly produced and used in medieval Europe as well as in China (cf. Laufer, *Sino-Iranica*, pp. 265 ff.). The plant was introduced from Persia in the first centuries of the Christian era. For fish oil and whale oil mentioned by Marco see the cr. ed., pp. 30, 162, and 204 n.; M.P., pp. 123, 355, and 425.
[58] Pegolotti was acquainted with various types of vegetable oils (*La Pratica della Mercatura*, p. 423), but never makes any reference to petroleum, which must then have been used solely for local purposes as described by Marco.
[59] Cr. ed., p. 99, chap. ciii; M.P., p. 250. The story of the baths, which is certainly authentic, is to be found only in the Ramusian text. Fossilized carbon was very common in China and, according to Marco, very cheap. It is not mentioned as an article of export in the treatise by Chau Ju-kua, *ed. cit.*, or in the Arab texts collected by Ferrand in *Relations de Voyages*, and can therefore be considered as unknown outside of Chinese territory. Nor was it a state monopoly, as were most of the products of the Chinese soil.
[60] Cf. H. Franke, *Geld und Wirtschaft in China*, esp. pp. 119 ff. (although insufficient so far as the production of coal is concerned).

land that produced neither coal nor iron, and where a hot bath was a costly luxury and the privilege of the upper classes, and finding himself among the Mongols of Asia, who were always reluctant to contaminate the sacred element of water by contact with the human skin, our Venetian traveler was greatly impressed by the use of fossilized carbon for hygienic purposes, on the part of a people whom he considered to be unwarlike and effeminate.[61] We also find in the *Milione* the oldest and most extensive record of the extraction of asbestos. It was described to Marco by an intelligent Turkish expert who was his colleague in the imperial administration and was charged by Kublai with the exploitation of the metalliferous soil of the remote province of Chingintalas in the Altai region.[62] Hence the Venetian was finally able to reveal the true nature of this substance, already known to Pliny and his Hellenic sources, but in the Middle Ages generally considered to be an animal product, more precisely, the wool of the incombustible salamander.[63] He was interested in this fibrous mineral because of its reputedly miraculous qualities, and because it was universally prized—so much so, in fact, that the Great Kaan sent a "sheet" (*toaille*) of it to the Pope for the preservation of "the shroud of Our Lord."[64] All trace of the "sheet," however, was soon lost.[65]

[61] No exhaustive study of Italian balneology in Marco Polo's times appears to exist. The subject is well worth investigating. See chap. x, n. 21, in the present work.

[62] *Il Milione*, cr. ed., p. 47; M.P., pp. 156 f. For the specification of the region cf. Cordier, *Addenda*, p. 52.

[63] Pliny treats of the salamander and asbestos separately; hence the association of the fabulous amphibian which lives in fire with the incombustible fibrous metal is a later notion, which perhaps resulted from a simple metaphor in which the two concepts were fused—in the sense that the name of the salamander, a creature legendarily resistant to fire without harm or pain (as was still professed by Brunetto Latini, *Trésor*, ed. Carmody, p. 135: I, 144, 2), had now come to designate asbestos because this virtue was possessed by the latter. Cf. B. Laufer, "Asbestos and Salamander," *T'oung Pao*, Vol. XVI, 1915, pp. 299–373, the most extensive study on the subject.

[64] *Il Milione*, cr. ed., p. 47; M.P., p. 157. Marco here says that there is found in Rome "une toaille que le gran can envoie a l'apostoille por grant present." The Z version adds that there was said to have been inscribed on it "Tu es Petrus et super hanc petram edificabo ecclesiam meam" (Matt. 16: 18). However, Marco does not state clearly whether the gift was entrusted to him personally or to his older companions, nor when or how it arrived in Rome. Nevertheless he considers the gift to be of exceptional value.

[65] An old fragment of asbestos cloth was preserved in the Vatican collections, but it would seem to have dated from classical antiquity. Cf. Yule-Cordier, *The Book of Ser Marco Polo*, Vol. I, p. 216 n.; also Laufer, *op. cit.* in note 63 above, pp. 302, 308 f.

In this famous passage of his book Marco was able to inform his contemporaries that "the salamander is not an animal," as the medieval encyclopedias and the *Letter of Prester John* on the wonders of the Orient had held it to be, but a silicate from which a fiber like that of wool was made.[66] It seems strange indeed that although certain deposits of this mineral existed in Italy, as well as in other parts of Europe, the true nature of asbestos was empirically established so late and in one of the least accessible regions of the Old World;[67] and it goes without saying that with his discovery our wandering naturalist expelled from the animal world the legendary salamander, which supposedly could live in fire[68]—whereas the real salamander, which he does not mention, is a lizard-like creature that lives either in water or on land.

Besides, Marco gave the West a first report on the manufacture of porcelain, which was produced in "Tiungiu," a town—not yet identified—in the province of Fukien, for a long period the center of production and export of Chinese pottery. He reports that "those of the city gather, as from a mine, clay and crumbly earth and make great mounds of it, and leave them thus in the wind, rain, and sun for thirty or forty years. By that time the

[66] In the *Letter of Prester John* of 1167 mention is made of various garments of this "wool" belonging to the imaginary sovereign, which is probably a reminiscence of that attributed to Charlemagne (cf. Thorndike, *op. cit.*, Vol. II, p. 242). Vincent of Beauvais (*ibid.*, p. 473) asserts that Pope Alexander III (1159–1181) owned a garment woven in "salamander wool" (*Speculum Historiale*, XXI, 63). Chinese sources also attribute an asbestos garment to the Buddha. For the use of this substance in Asia cf. Laufer, *Sino-Iranica*, pp. 498 ff. The *Letter of Prester John* (ed. Zarncke, p. 915: 89) explains that the salamander produces this substance, even as "alii vermes" produce silk. It is woven by the ladies of the palace who prepare the legendary sovereign's garments. By the Chinese, asbestos is counted among the marvels of the West. It is first mentioned in the *Hou Han Shu*, compiled in the Vth century A.D. (cf. E. Chavannes, "Les Pays d'Occident," *T'oung Pao*, second series, Vol. VIII, 1907, p. 181). Asbestos is also mentioned in the same sense in the famous Nestorian inscription of Hsinanfu (Shensi); cf. A. C. Moule, *Christians in China*, p. 40 and note. Asbestos cloths are mentioned by Chau Ju-kua (*ed. cit.*, p. 140) as a product of "Wu-ti-li," i.e., Mosul.

[67] We may, however, assume that the experts on the subject, although few in number, were acquainted with the origin and character of asbestos in spite of the fact that they designated it by the name of "salamander."

[68] For superstitions and legends connected with this amphibian cf. Bächtold-Stäubli, *Handwörterbuch des deutschen Aberglaubens*, Vol. VI, pp. 455 ff. (with full bibliography). For the Arabs, too, the salamander was one of the wonders of India, as is apparent from the anonymous text of uncertain date (Xth century?) published by Ferrand in *Relations de Voyages*, Vol. II, p. 587.

same earth is brought into such condition that the bowls made of it have the color of azure, and they are very shiny and most beautiful." [69]

On the other hand, we find in the *Milione* no mention of alum, whereas Pegolotti gives several pages to it,[70] and Friar William of Rubruck had mentioned it almost half a century earlier, in his *Itinerary*, as the chief product of Turkey, exploited exclusively by Genoese and Venetian merchants in Asia Minor.[71] We must assume that Marco did not mention this rich product of the Asian soil because he found no trace of it in all the Chinghizide empire.

Iron, considered at all times a metallurgical ubiquity, he records in its varieties, and names the regions where it is extracted and prepared for one or another use. It is found in great quantities, he tells us, in the Persian province of Kerman, where steel mills already long in operation then produced weapons for the Mongol army of the Ilkhans;[72] then, in the region of "Cobinan" (Kuhbanan), which specialized in the manufacture of metallic mirrors;[73] and, too, in the mountains of Chingintalas, near the western borders of Mongolia, one of the most important mining centers of the Asiatic continent.[74] On the other hand, Marco

[69] This·passage of the Ramusian and Z versions of the *Milione* (cr. ed., p. 160 n.; M.P., p. 362) was considered an interpolation by Yule (*The Book of Ser Marco Polo*, Vol. II, p. 242 n. 5) and others. "Tiungiu" seems to be "Ja-chau fu," according to Penzer, *The Travels of Marco Polo*, p. 237. With the same name of "porcelaine" Marco designates also cowry shells, used as money in the province of "Caragian" and other parts of southern China (cf. cr. ed., pp. 115, 116, 119, etc.; M.P., pp. 276, 277, 282, etc.). The alternate use of the term might be explained by the similarity of the iridescent brilliancy noticed by Marco. Cf. Pegolotti, *La Pratica della Mercatura*, ed. Evans, pp. 427 f.

[70] *La Pratica della Mercatura*, ed. Evans, pp. 411 f.

[71] *Sinica Franciscana*, Vol. I, p. 328. The Genoese merchant Nicola di San Siro, who exploited this monopoly at Conia (Iconium) in Asia Minor, was associated with the Venetian Bonifacio da Molendino. For this trade cf. W. von Heyd, *Histoire du commerce du Levant*, Vol. I, p. 302, and Schaube, *op. cit.* (in note 25 above), Index. From Asia Minor, alum was exported as far as China via Persia and then by sea, cf. Laufer, *Sino-Iranica*, pp. 474 ff.; but we learn from Chau Ju-kua (*ed. cit.*, p. 78) that there was a market for this product in Java, which was an active center for exchange merchandise in the Middle Ages. However, this is not mentioned in the Arab texts collected by Ferrand in *Relations de Voyages*.

[72] *Il Milione*, cr. ed., p. 27; M. P., pp. 118 ff. See also Yule-Cordier's commentary on this passage, which gives a list of the objects manufactured in this region.

[73] Cr. ed., resp. p. 32 and p. 125; M.P., p. 127.

[74] Cr. ed, resp. p. 47 and pp. 214 ff.; M.P., p. 156. Cf., too, Cordier, *Addenda*, p. 51. "Chinese" iron is mentioned as rustproof by the Arab poet Abū Dulaf Misʿar ibn al-

makes no mention of the iron mines of India, which perhaps from the most ancient times were the most celebrated for the manufacture of swords that were a byword for excellence throughout the Islamic world and highly commended also in Chinese texts.[75] Obviously, Marco's interest in iron does not extend beyond the boundaries of the Chinghizide empire. Moreover, the fact that he set little store by copper, and even less by tin, which was then, and had been since prehistoric times, one of the most sought after of the products of eastern Asia, proves yet again how little he allowed himself to be guided by mercantile considerations in satisfying his own and others' curiosity for the things of the world.[76] His interest in this, as in many other subjects, was determined by the circles in which he moved and by the demands of the régime he served with the same honesty with which he was later to inform his fellow citizens.[77]

Muhalhil (Xth century); cf. Ferrand, *Relations de Voyages*, Vol. I, p. 224. The wealth of fossilized carbon favored the iron industry in China, which exported it both by land and by sea. A brief mention is made of iron imports into China in the *Milione*, cr. ed., p. 140 n.

[75] Cf. Yule-Cordier, *The Book of Ser Marco Polo*, Vol. I, pp. 92 ff., for the type of iron repeatedly called "ondanique" by Marco Polo, for which see Cordier, *Addenda*, p. 19.

[76] For Indian trade in iron and steel at that time cf. Ferrand, *Relations de Voyages*, Vol. I, p. 177 and *passim*, as well as Chau Ju-kua, *ed. cit.*, pp. 84, 111, etc. The information contained in Ludwig Beck, *Geschichte des Eisens*, second edition, Braunschweig, 1891, pp. 270 ff., is insufficient. Marco notes the copper of Tana and "Canbaet" (the ancient settlement of Cambay on the gulf of the same name), where various metals were traded, as in the kingdom of Champa, according to the Z version, cr. ed., p. 167 n. Frequent mention of tin is found in the texts collected by Ferrand, *op. cit.*, Chau Ju-kua, *ed. cit.*, with other, more ancient, Chinese texts listed on his p. 59, n., and Pegolotti in various passages of the *Pratica della Mercatura*.

[77] Marco never alludes to the production of copper in China, where for centuries past it had been used for the minting of coins of small denomination, even during the Chinghizide period, when paper money was in circulation and gold and silver were prohibited for every kind of commercial transaction. See Lien-shêng Yang, *Money and Credit in China*, Cambridge, Mass. (Harvard-Yenching Institute, Monograph Series, Vol. XII), 1952, pp. 62 ff., and the full bibliography on pp. 110 and 113. For centuries the exportation of copper coins had been a capital crime, but nonetheless they circulated everywhere in the East, even to India and Africa; cf. Duyvendak, *China's Discovery of Africa*, p. 17. The smelting of bronze, which is nowhere mentioned by Marco Polo, had reached a remarkable degree of technical proficiency in the Far East even before the introduction of iron. Henceforward, bronze was to remain the most prized material for the uses of Chinese sculpture, of which our traveler must have seen innumerable masterpieces in Chinese temples and the imperial palaces. He showed little interest, however, in the fine arts of the country; his silence perhaps reflects the indifference and incapacity of the Mongols for this branch of metallurgical technique, which had been only slightly developed in medieval Venice.

Until the time of Chinghiz Khan's great conquests the material civilization of the Mongol tribes was founded on felt, which is fittingly mentioned more than once in the *Milione*,[78] and on leather, which, as Marco observed, was used especially for military purposes.[79] It was only after they had come into contact with forces that had arms and armor of iron and steel that the nomads of the steppes exchanged for these a good deal of their leather battle-harness, thus advantaging their hordes with yet greater offensive and defensive strength. Before that, metal armor had been very rare, and was correspondingly valued, among Altaic warriors. The Emperor Frederick II, writing to King Henry III of England, describes how "they are handsomely fitted out with the choicer equipments taken from the conquered Christians." [80]

Indeed, the Tartars built up great stocks of every kind of ferrous metal during their invasions of both the Orient and the West, and, where possible, forced tributes of it from the conquered. In their nomad life as shepherds and hunters, however, they had not learned how to treat it. They therefore respected artisans in iron as exceptional beings, and created the legend, recounted even by Giovanni Villani, that Chinghiz Khan had been, as he says, "a humble smith" before becoming the conqueror of Asia and head of a historic dynasty.[81]

The exploitation of metalliferous lodes was therefore entrusted

[78] With reference to the manufacture of the tents or *yurts* of the Mongols (*Il Milione,* cr. ed., p. 53; M.P., p. 168) and the making of idols (cr. ed., p. 54).

[79] *Il Milione,* cr. ed., p. 55; M.P., p. 171. These two materials recur in Chinese literature as typical manifestations of the civilization of the nomads, who were considered to be barbarians and therefore despised. For the Tartars' leathern arms and breastplates, see Friar John of Pian del Càrpine in *Sinica Franciscana,* Vol. I, pp. 77 ff.

[80] Cf. Matthew Paris' *Cronaca* in *Monumenta Germaniae Historica,* Scriptores, Vol. XXVIII, p. 211.

[81] This legend is of eponymic origin and comes from the original name of Chinghiz Khan, who was called Temudjin (from *temur* = 'iron') before his election as lord of the world. For the origin of this name, which was that of a Tatar leader defeated by his father at the time of his birth, cf. B. Ya. Vladimirtsov, *The Life of Chingis-Khan,* trans. Prince Mirsky, London, 1930, pp. 9 ff. Marco does not record this, nor was the legend known to the official *Secret History of the Mongols,* of 1240, or to Chinese and Persian chroniclers of the XIVth century. Villani (*Cronica,* Bk. V, chap. xxix) took the story from the *Flor des estoires de la terre d'Orient* of Hayton, an Armenian prince who dictated his narrative at Poitiers in 1307. This valuable work was also widely known in Italy and was sometimes added to the *Milione* in medieval manuscripts (see cr. ed., Introd., *passim*); it is rich in Oriental legends and historical data, taken directly from native tradition in the course of the author's various sojourns in the Tartar dominion and at its courts.

by the Chinghizide administration to foreigners who were transferred from various regions of the empire, such as Mohammedans
from Turkestan, who were transported *en masse* by Chinghiz
Khan into recently conquered Chinese territory,[82] or the Christians of the Caucasus, known as the Alans, who were great ar-
morers and experts in the metallurgy of iron and steel, and who
soon became the strongest and most loyal mainstay of the
dynasty.[83]

Already at the time of the emperors Küyük and Möngke, German slaves who had been taken prisoner by the Mongols advancing in 1240 toward central Europe were working in the
iron mines of Zungaria, which were among the most important
in the whole continent.[84] The "Turk" who supplied Marco with
information about the iron of the Altai was certainly one of the
many Uigur Christians employed by Kublai. The possibility cannot therefore be excluded that Marco, to whom so many different
tasks were entrusted in the long years of his stay in the farther
part of Asia, was also attached to this branch of the imperial
administration—certainly not as an adept in this field, but rather
as an administrative expert at certain mines which were a part
of the state monopolies, and which the Great Kaan felt he could
not leave entirely in the hands of native technicians and officials.[85]

[82] Cf. P. Pelliot, "Une ville musulmane dans la Chine du Nord sous les Mongols,"
Journal Asiatique, Vol. CCXI, 1927, pp. 261 ff. The forced migration of entire populations from one end of Asia to the other is a fairly common feature of the Tartar
régime, at times inspired by political reasons, at others by need of labor for the development of crafts unknown to the civilization of the nomads.

[83] They are mentioned as loyal soldiers in the *Milione*, cr. ed., p. 142; M.P., p. 324.
Cf. the note in Yule-Cordier, *The Book of Ser Marco Polo*, Vol. II, p. 179. Friar
William of Rubruck also notes that they are excellent artisans and manufacturers of
arms (*Sin. Franc.*, Vol. I, p. 317). The Alans, who belonged to the Greek Church,
are often mentioned in reports by Franciscan missionaries. For bibliographical data
see Spuler, *Die Goldene Horde*, pp. 456 ff. (under the name of "Osseten"). Kublai's
imperial guard was made up of soldiers from this people.

[84] Cf. William of Rubruck's *Relatio* in *Sinica Franciscana*, Vol. I, p. 224, and
W. W. Rockhill's comment in his translation, p. 137. These "Teutons" also worked in
other parts of the Mongol empire, especially in the gold mines and for the manufacture
of arms, always as slaves or prisoners.

[85] Marco Polo makes various references to this (cr. ed., pp. 78 ff., 157, etc.; M.P.,
pp. 214 f. and 348), revealing the rebellious feelings harbored by the Chinese people
against the Tartar régime and the foreigners who governed the country. The Chinghizide Mongols took over from preceding dynasties the monopoly, or official control,
of metals; see Lien-shêng Yang, *op. cit.* In Marco Polo's times, the fiscal system of

The like did happen on other occasions, as we shall see, and this explains the Venetian's special interest in the natural products of Asia, which were politically, economically, and fiscally of great importance to the régime served by him. Salt was outstanding among these. Indeed, few products play so important a role in the *Milione* as this humble chloride of sodium, which abounded all over Asia in its most diverse edible and medicinal varieties, and certainly was never regarded by Marco as merchandise or a commodity for export. He found it in the deserts, lakes, and streams of Persia, and so abundant in the mountains of "Taican," on the borders of Badakhshan, "that there would be sufficient for the whole earth, until the end of the world." [86] He therefore studied its production in the various provinces of China, its marketing, the use made of it by some Oriental peoples as money, and the fabulous sums that the state received from it as the most universal, important, and fruitful monopoly.[87] It is this circumstance, more than anything else, that concentrates his attention on the salt marshes—so exclusively, in fact, that he takes into account only those found in territories subject to the Great Kaan, without a word about the immense production of salt in India and in the parts of tropical Asia visited by him.[88] It is quite clear

---

the Chinghizide empire in China was divided into two categories: the first, entrusted to the native bureaucracy, perpetuated the administration that had existed before the conquest; the other, of Mongol origin and superimposed on the traditional scheme, exacted tributes and personal or collective taxes of a purely feudal sort, which were paid directly to the sovereign or to his vicegerents and vassals. For this subject see H. F. Schurmann, "Mongolian Tributary Practices of the Thirteenth Century," *Harvard Journal of Asiatic Studies,* Vol. XIX, 1956, pp. 304 ff.

[86] *Il Milione,* cr. ed., p. 36; M. P., p. 135. This is, in fact, the region of Talikan, now part of northeastern Afghanistan, and at that time part of the dominion of Chagatai, which took its name from that of the son of Chinghiz Khan to whom this historic region was allotted upon the division of his father's empire. Cf. W. Barthold, *Turkestan,* pp. 437 ff., etc. Marco's observations have been confirmed by modern experience, as is revealed in the fundamental work by Baron J. Ottokar von Buschman, *Das Salz,* Leipzig, 1906, Vol. II, pp. 185 ff. The inexhaustible supplies of salt in Persia are likewise specified in this book (*ibid.,* pp. 169 ff.), which also considers the relevant geological, technical, commercial, and historical data, although these now deserve fuller and more precise treatment. For this subject see the detailed study by H. F. Schurmann, *Economic Structure of the Yüan Dynasty,* Cambridge, Mass. (Harvard-Yenching Institute Studies, Vol. XVI), 1956, pp. 166 ff.

[87] *Il Milione,* cr. ed., pp. 136, 137, 140, 152 f.; M.P., pp. 314, 315, 322, 341 f. See Yule-Cordier's notes to the corresponding passages in the text.

[88] The province of Gaindu, where the natives (Lolo) used salt as money, worth its weight in gold, is situated between Yunnan, in China, and the upper Irrawaddy, on

that he looked on this product with the eyes of an imperial servant; here, he is not the curious empirical naturalist. The mention of salt in his book is so frequent, and the calculation of the fiscal revenue derived from it is so precise in facts and figures, as to lead us to believe that he was employed for some time in this very important branch of the imperial administration.[89] Marco did indeed spend three years at Yangchow in the saliferous Chinese province of Kiangsu, certainly not as governor, as we read in the current versions of the *Milione,* but in an official position which he can have held with success while still a young man.[90] He may well have been in charge of the imperial salt marshes, a post as important as it was unpopular in Chinghizide China, which received its greatest revenues from this monopoly and jealously watched over its exploitation, while putting out to contract the production of the salt.[91]

the border between Burma and Tibet, regions which were then subject to, or tributaries of, the Great Kaan, and were explored by Marco on his orders. See the full description of this journey in the Ramusian text (cr. ed., p. 114; M.P., p. 275) and, besides Yule-Cordier's commentary in *The Book of Ser Marco Polo,* Vol. II, pp. 57 f., the numerous data collected by the explorer Joseph F. Rock, *The Ancient Na-khi Kingdom of Southwest Asia,* Cambridge, Mass., 1947, at the points mentioned in the Index, Vol. II, pp. 521 f.

[89] The opinion that Marco was engaged for years in the administration of the salt marshes or the Chinese salt monopoly has already been expressed by Pelliot (*T'oung Pao,* Vol. XXV, 1928, pp. 156 ff.), who found in the annals of the Chinghizide dynasty (*Yüan Shih*) a certain Poh-lo, superintendent of the salt administration in the province of Yangchow at the time when Marco was supposed to have been its governor. However, it has recently been demonstrated that Marco was never called by his family name in China, but probably by the Chinese form of his Christian name, which was familiar to the Christian Nestorians of Mongolia and China, as were those of Maffeo and Niccolò; cf. the present author's article, "Poh-lo: Une question d'onomatologie chinoise," *Oriens,* Vol. III, 1950, pp. 183 ff.

[90] Cf. *Il Milione,* cr. ed., p. 137; M.P., p. 316. The reading "gouverna" instead of "séjourna" is more than doubtful, not only because this reference is completely lacking in two versions of the *Milione* (cr. ed., Introd., p. clxxviii, n. 2), but especially because it is unthinkable that a young man, less than thirty years old and only recently arrived from the West, could have been made governor of one of the most important cities and provinces of China, which had only been conquered by Kublai in 1276 and was notoriously unreconciled to the Tartar régime—so much so, that in Marco's times a powerful garrison was stationed there, ready to put down any attempt at rebellion. According to the Mongol custom described by Marco (cr. ed., pp. 93 f.; M.P., pp. 241 f.), a province of such importance was always administered by a son or relative of Kublai, or by one of the most able and expert Mongol military leaders. The few passages in his book in which Marco could be accused of boasting are suspect and are contradicted by the reputation for honesty accorded by well-informed persons both to him and to his older companions (see above, chap. iii, n. 80).

[91] Marco treats of this at length, cr. ed., pp. 152 f.; M.P., pp. 341 f. For salt produc-

The monopoly of salt was, like that of iron, an ancient Chinese tradition continued by the Chinghizide dynasty, which already by about the middle of the XIIIth century had extended it throughout the whole continent as far as the mouth of the river Don.[92] Apart from its incalculable value as a source of revenue, this monoply was of great political importance in that immense empire, above all in China, where provinces, towns, and rural communities were on the whole self-sufficient so far as many essential goods were concerned, but—especially in the interior—had to obtain outside supplies of this indispensable commodity.[93] The central administration was thereby able to keep in subjection the populations fiscally exploited, by elaborating a special, powerful bureaucracy within the first ranks of the state hierarchy.[94]

tion in ancient and modern China cf. von Buschman, *Das Salz,* Vol. II, pp. 3 ff. The unpopularity of the salt monopoly, which was always associated with that of iron, is clearly revealed in an interesting dialogue in the *Yen T'ieh Lun* (*Discourses on Salt and Iron*) by Huan K'uan, a Chinese scholar of the Ist century B.C., trans. Esson M. Gale, Leiden, 1931, and fundamental for the history and theory of Chinese political economy. The salt trade of the Chinghizide period is hardly touched upon in H. Franke, *Geld und Wirtschaft.*

[92] This is attested by Friar William of Rubruck (*Sin. Franc.,* Vol. I, p. 171), who asserts, in 1253, that the Chinghizide sovereigns of the Golden Horde, such as Batu Khan and Sartach, derived enormous incomes from the salt marshes of the lower Don, which had already been exploited in antiquity by the Greeks. The reason given by the friar is that the whole of Russia obtained its supplies from this region, paying two sheets of cotton for each cartload, which were worth half an *yperpera.* According to Rockhill, in his translation of Friar William's *Journey,* p. 52, the *yperpera* was about the equivalent of 10 shillings sterling. For further data offered by the missionaries cf. *ibid.,* p. 36 (salt marshes of the Uralsk steppe) and p. 92 (reference to the Tartar monopoly of foodstuffs in western Asia). For these salt-producing regions cf. von Buschman, *op. cit.,* esp. Vol. I, pp. 23 ff., and Vol. II, pp. 118 ff.

[93] Von Buschman, *op. cit.,* Vol. II, pp. 3 ff.; and for Tibet and Mongolia, where it is especially abundant, pp. 14 ff. For the economic and political history of salt in China cf. W. Hirth's article on this subject in the *Journal of the North China Branch of the Royal Asiatic Society,* Vol. XXII, pp. 55 ff., and the recent studies by Denis Twitchett, "The Salt Commissioners after An Lu-shan's Rebellion," *Asia Major,* n.s., Vol. IV, 1954, pp. 60 ff., and Ho Ping-ti, "The Salt Merchants of Yang-chou," *Harvard Journal of Asiatic Studies,* Vol. XVII, 1954, pp. 130 ff.; also, the works indicated by O. Franke, *Geschichte des chinesischen Reiches,* Vol. V, p. 185. Moreover, important contributions by contemporary Chinese scholars exist, which are accessible only to specialists.

[94] For this subject cf. Pierre Hoang, S.J., "Exposé du commerce public du sel," in *Variétés Sinologiques,* no. 15, Shanghai, 1898. The legislation and administration governing this monopoly at the end of the Chinese empire in 1911 were still similar to those handed down by the Ming dynasty (1368–1628), which had taken them over from the Chinghizide sovereigns. Thus, roughly speaking, the hierarchic order of the mandarins in charge of this commodity, still flourishing at the beginning of the present century, was essentially the same as that of Marco Polo's age. It was still

Since the peoples restless under the Tartar yoke did not offer sufficient guarantees of administrative and political loyalty, the government entrusted the administration of this, as of other public enterprises, to foreigners, for example the Turk Zurficar, who supervised the Altaic mines,[95] Mar Sargis, the Nestorian with the Syrian name who governed the industrious town of Chinkiang,[96] the Saracen "Achmach" (Achmet), the all-powerful minister of the imperial finances,[97] and many others whose names are recorded in the annals of the dynasty, or of whom we have some indirect mention.[98]

Though the age-old imposition of a tax on salt, which has nowadays disappeared from almost all civilized countries, was then a common usage, the Sino-Mongolian system of putting the salt tax to both fiscal and political use was very similar to the Venetian one, which, especially after the conquest of the saliferous regions of Istria in the first decades of the XIIIth century, remained for a long time a means of Venetian domination and influence, not only in the Adriatic, but above all in the adjacent territories on the mainland, from the Alps to the Romagna.[99] Owing to his earlier Venetian environment, Marco was suited for appointment to high office in this administrative and political

---

headed by the emperor himself, to whom the Mongol viceroys or governors of the provinces had annually to report the amount of salt produced and sold in their respective jurisdictions, according to information received from their subalterns in the thirteen hierarchical grades of this monopoly. It can be presumed from the precise information on the salt trade and its revenues contained in the *Milione* (cr. ed., *loc. cit.*) that Marco had obtained at Yangchow an office equivalent to that of prefect of the salt-producing region, or *yen-t'i-ƙiu*, which would in some way have justified his feeling of having "governed" this province. Indeed, these officials did at times act as local mandarins in handling the affairs of the people.

[95] *Il Milione*, cr. ed., p. 46; M.P., p. 157.

[96] Cr. ed., p. 141; M.P., p. 323. Also, A. C. Moule, *Christians in China*, pp. 139 f., etc.

[97] *Il Milione*, cr. ed., pp. 78 ff.; M.P., pp. 214 f.

[98] Cf. O. Franke, *Geschichte des chinesischen Reiches*, Vol. IV, pp. 471 f., 475 f., etc., and Vol. V, pp. 235 ff. For the names recorded in contemporary Chinese sources cf. the important article by L. Carrington Goodrich, "Westerners and Central Asians in Yüan China," in *Oriente Poliano*, Rome (Istituto per il Medio ed Estremo Oriente), 1957, pp. 1–21.

[99] Cf., apart from works on the general history of the Venetian republic such as Kretschmayr's *Geschichte von Venedig*, Vols. I and II, and, for the technical part, von Buschman's *Das Salz*, esp. Vol. I, pp. 281 f. and 490 f., the article by C. Bauer, "Venetianische Salzhandelspolitik bis zum Ende des XIV. Jahrhunderts," *Vierteljahrs-schrift für Sozial- und Wirtschaftsgeschichte*, Vol. XXIII, 1930, pp. 1 ff.

branch of the Chinghizide government, which had officials of a rank and power analogous to those of the salt commissioners of the Venetian Republic. This explains the interest shown by him in those distant salt-producing regions, and reveals to us the personal background and starting point for his observations on the products of the Asiatic soil.

He never disregards these, even when faced with all the wonders of the Orient, and thus offers us data that suffice to establish their distribution and use in all the continent. He makes frequent allusion to the cereals grown and consumed in the various regions.[100] He also makes mention of foodstuffs and of commodities in common use such as cotton, wool, hides and furs, silk and fabrics, with various other industrial products and merchandise, of which he brought back some samples to Venice.[101] Thereby, indeed, Marco taught his contemporaries not to limit themselves in their contemplation of this exotic world to its fabulous, mysterious aspects, but to come to know it also in those of its human and material manifestations that make possible the discovery of the affinities and ubiquity of human life in all climes and in its manifold national and local varieties.

[100] In accordance with its importance in Asiatic life, rice is mentioned in the *Milione* more often than any other cereal as the characteristic food of Asia's peoples, especially in China (cf. cr. ed., chap. xcix n., cxiv, cxix, etc.), and in Indonesia (*ibid.,* chap. clxviii), Ceylon, and India as well (*ibid.,* chaps. clxxiv, clxxv, clxxvii, clxxxi). Rice is also mentioned as used in the production of a popular wine, made aromatic with various spices, which was full-bodied and universally appreciated in Cathay (*ibid.,* chap. cii; cf. the corresponding chapter in M.P.). As for wheat, Marco mentions that it grew abundantly in Persia, where every kind of grain flourished (cr. ed., chaps. xxxiv, xxxvi), in the region of Hormuz, in Badakhshan, and in China, where, according to his reports, it grew but sparsely and was used for making various kinds of paste but not wheaten bread, which was not eaten by the Tartars and Chinese (cr. ed., p. 95 n., and chap. cxix). Hence the legend that it was our traveler who introduced "spaghetti" into Italy. Marco also offers some data on the distribution of barley and panic grass, and he seems to be aware of the large-scale use that the Chinese and Tartars then made—as they still do—of millet, which was especially abundant in the provinces of northern China and Manchuria, for which see S. Couling, *Encyclopaedia Sinica*, p. 366. Marco, however, keeps silent about the methods of cultivating grain. These are mentioned on several occasions by Chinese travelers of his times: Ch'ang Ch'un (cf. A. Waley, *The Travels of an Alchemist,* London, 1931) and Ch'ang Te (cf. E. Bretschneider, *Mediaeval Researches,* Vol. I, pp. 122 ff.). For references in the English translations cf. the respective Indexes at the articles mentioned above.

[101] We shall merely observe that Marco noted the abundance of cotton and hemp in central Asia and mentioned their scarcity in China (cr. ed., p. 91 n.), where, on the other hand, the production of silk is limitless owing to the great number of mulberry trees, which are referred to by him on various occasions. For the production of fibrous materials in medieval Asia cf. the relevant chapters in Laufer, *Sino-Iranica*.

SIX

POLITICS AND RELIGION IN
MARCO POLO'S ASIA

Marco Polo's intention of conferring upon his journey the character of a religious mission is immediately evident in the first
part of his book. Ecclesiastical and pious motives abound, from
the moment when the three Venetians procured some oil from
the lamp of the Holy Sepulcher in Jerusalem and departed with
the Pope's blessing (*benedictio finalis*); then in the description
of the Christian sects in western Asia;[1] in the narration of the
miracles worked by the Faith in the struggle against the infidels;[2] and in the account of the homage paid by the Magi to
the Christ Child, which opens his description of Persia.[3]

At the same time, our traveler notes the most striking manifestations of the Mohammedan faith, notably in his description
of the end of the Abbasid caliphate, and in his still more dramatic
account of the sect of the Assassins in Persia, which, in Marco's
times, caused a stir throughout the Old World from China to
Spain.[4] Nor does he fail to mention the "fire-worshipers," the
last followers of Zoroaster.[5] Further on, in his description of the
peoples of Asia, Marco's attention is everywhere directed toward
what may be called a denominational topography of the Orient;
and his is the most extensive and most nearly complete portrayal
of it that is to be found anywhere in the geographical and ecclesiastical literature of the Middle Ages.[6]

[1] *Il Milione*, cr. ed., pp. 17 ff.; M.P., pp. 99 ff.
[2] Cr. ed., pp. 20 ff. and 40 f.; M.P., pp. 105 ff.
[3] Cr. ed., pp. 24 f.; M.P., pp. 113 ff.
[4] Cr. ed., pp. 18 ff. and 32 ff.; M.P., pp. 101 ff. and 129 ff.
[5] Cr. ed, p. 24; M.P., p. 115.
[6] Rabbi Benjamin of Tudela preceded him in this by more than a century; from

To a faithful, devout Catholic unconcerned with theological inquiry or metaphysical conflict the coexistence of so many religions and their sects in an empire ruled by a single and still secure dynasty must have appeared at first sight a disconcerting and incomprehensible spectacle. Addressing a Europe in which Catholic orthodoxy had been restored with patience and wisdom, and with violence too, and dictating his book at the end of a century agitated by bitter religious struggles, Marco begins one of his best versions by explaining to his readers a phenomenon that distinguishes the Asiatic world in its essence from the Christian community of the West. "These Tartars," he says, "do not care what god is worshiped in their lands. If only all are faithful to the lord Kaan and quite obedient and give therefore the appointed tribute, and justice is well kept, thou mayest do what pleaseth thee with thy soul. They will not that thou speak evil of their souls; nor fail thou to assist at their doings. But do thou what thou wilt with God and thy soul, whether thou art Jew or pagan or Saracen or Christian who dwellest among the Tartars. They confess indeed in Tartary that Christ is Lord, but say that he is a proud Lord because he will not be with other gods but will be God above all the others in the world. And so in some places they have a Christ of gold and silver and keep him hidden in some chest, and say that he is the great and supreme Lord of the Christians." [7]

This adequate description of the religious situation in the Chinghizide empire at the time of Marco's stay in Asia could not have been composed by anyone but him. It sums up all his long and varied experience of this facet of Oriental civilization. This frank, unruffled judgment was undoubtedly suppressed in the current versions of the *Milione* because of its disturbing novelty; for, among other things, it clearly indicated the insurmountable barrier that divided both the Roman and Greek Orthodox churches, with their equally rigid, dogmatic pretensions, from the civilization of Asia, which was apparently indifferent to denominational and ecclesiastical questions. [8]

1159 to 1173 he traveled through the lands of the Mediterranean, the Levant, and the Middle East in search of Jewish communities. See note 56 to chap. ii, § 2, above.

[7] Cr. ed., p. 14 n.; M.P., p. 96 (quoted here).

[8] The conclusion of the passage quoted is openly blasphemous. It should be noted

When the three Polos left Venice for China in 1271, the fervor
of the mendicant orders and enlightened Papal policy had certainly restored religious unity to Europe. Nevertheless, the struggle against the heretics was not yet at an end. As late as 1276,
in near-by Verona, one hundred and fifty "Patarins" were im-
prisoned and many of them were burned alive, and new sects
continued to spring up here and there until the death of Fra
Dolcino, the tough rebel mentioned by Dante. All this kept the
thought of contemporary heresies present in Marco's mind as he
made note of the various religions of Asia.[9]

To the weak, unsuccessful crusades of the Emperor Frederick
II and King Louis IX of France, and the conquest of the Levant
by force of arms, there had now succeeded the conquest of souls
by means of missions and public religious disputations. The
latter, indeed, represent one of the most characteristic manifestations of the civilization of that age, from Morocco to China.
Eloquent symptoms of it are to be found even in a book like this,
inspired by its author's lay sentiments and interests.[10] Hence, it
is to the "holy strife of disputatious men" that we must look for
the expression of the passions and tendencies that then dominated
the religious field, and that are reflected in Marco Polo's activity and feelings.

Two noteworthy examples help to illustrate the different attitudes assumed in religious controversy by those who best represent his age, respectively in the West and the East, and reveal
the contrast between the two worlds, as well as Marco's ability
to adapt himself without conflict to either. Joinville relates in his
biography of King Louis that, on the occasion of a theological
dispute between the monks of the abbey at Cluny and the learned

---

that Francesco Pipino systematically suppressed in his Latin version those passages in
the *Milione* which might suggest some heretical or heterodox reflection, or any that
could appear favorable to the Christian or pagan sects of Asia.

[9] The Patarins are mentioned in the *Milione* in the sense of heretics among the
pagans only. For the heretics of Sirmione, burned alive at Verona in 1276, cf. L. A.
Muratori, *Dissertazioni sopra l'antichità italiane*, Vol. III, p. 238. For other victims
in Marco's times, such as Segarelli, condemned to the stake in 1296, and Fra Dolcino,
burned in 1307, cf. G. Volpe, *Movimenti religiosi e sette eretiche nella società medievale
italiana*, second edition, Florence, 1926. For the facts cf. Cesare Cantù, *Gli eretici
d'Italia*, 3 vols., Turin, 1865–1867, and S. Runciman, *The Medieval Manichee*, Cambridge, 1947.

[10] Cr. ed., p. 70 n.; M.P., pp. 201 f.

"grand master" of the Jews in France, a knight who was present, on hearing Christ's divinity and Mary's virginity brought into question, put an end to the discussion by cracking the unbeliever's head. The abbot protested, whereupon King Louis replied that the best way for a Christian layman to defend his faith against those people was "to thrust his sword into their entrails, as far as it would go." [11] Such sentiments were then permissible to a king, a saint, famous down the ages for his piety and justice.[12]

Later on—precisely, on May 31, 1254,—when Friar William of Rubruck, who had been sent to Mongolia by this same king, St. Louis of France, allowed his feelings to get the better of him in a celebrated theological dispute with the representatives of the religions of Asia who had gathered for the occasion in Karakorum, he was called into the presence of the Great Kaan of the Tartars, who had already decreed his expulsion.[13] This all-powerful sovereign, who was already making preparations for the conquest of southern China and the Mongol advance to the shores of the Mediterranean, expressed his displeasure to the kneeling friar at this attempt to disturb the religious peace of his empire, and gave him a lecture: "We Mongols," he said, "believe that there is only one God, by whom we live and by whom we die, and for whom we have an upright heart. . . . But as God gives us the different fingers of the hand, so he gives to men divers ways. . . . God gave you the Scriptures, and you do not abide by them; he gave us diviners, we do what they tell us, and we live in peace." [14]

[11] Joinville, *Histoire de Saint Louis,* chap. x.

[12] It should be remembered that Frederick II, while finding pleasure in religious discussions and surrounding himself with men of every faith, so that he was considered a heretic and irreligious, was perhaps even more systematic and resolute than his pious French contemporary in violently suppressing the heretical groups in his empire. He exercised every sort of pressure on the Mohammedans and Jews of his Italian dominion in order to bring them into the fold of the Catholic Church, which, as is known, he fiercely opposed in the person of the Supreme Pontiff and as a militant political power.

[13] Cf. *Sinica Franciscana,* Vol. I, pp. 298 ff.

[14] *The Journey of William of Rubruck,* trans. W. Rockhill, London, Hakluyt Society, 1900, pp. 235 f. In the later Buddhistic interpretation of this famous profession of faith, which had nevertheless already been included in the Chinese treatise *Pien Wei Lu* published in 1291 by order of Kublai, his brother Mangu was supposed to have explained that the palm of the hand represented the Buddhist faith and therefore the

The sovereign's profession of faith is famous in Asiatic history and literature, and corresponds exactly to the attitude manifested by this brother of Kublai in all his religious policy. For the Chinghizide rulers from China to the Crimea, the Christian faith was only one religion among the many professed in their immense empire; as Marco justly observed in the passage quoted, even those who recognized Christ's divinity denied Him supremacy over the other divinities of Asia and the claims of His church to spiritual sovereignty over the whole world.[15]

These sentiments were also expressed by Kublai when he discussed religious questions with the Polo brothers. "There are four prophets," he said, "that are adored and revered by the whole world. The Christians declare their God to have been Jesus Christ, the Saracens Mohammed, the Jews Moses, the idolaters [i.e., the Buddhists] Sagamoni Borcan [i.e., Sakyamuni, the Buddha], who was the first god among the idols; and I honor and revere all four; that is to say, the one who is greatest in heaven and most true, and I pray that he may help me." [16]

basis of every other religion. Cf. E. Chavannes, "Inscriptions et pièces de chancellerie de l'époque mongole," *T'oung Pao,* second series, Vol. VI, 1905, pp. 1 ff. It is, however, doubtful that the emperor did really express himself in this way, even in the audience granted to William of Rubruck, or that the latter suppressed this phrase in his report to King Louis. Indeed, Friar William (*loc. cit.*) makes us understand that Mangu seemed annoyed at being considered a "tuin," i.e., a Buddhist. Evidently, the sovereign did not wish the religious peace of his empire to be disturbed by these preferences. For Mangu's supposed monotheistic declaration cf. N. Pallisen, "Die alte Religion der Mongolen," *Numen,* Vol. III, 1956, pp. 178 ff.

[15] As is well known, the Chinghizide sovereigns aspired to this universal sovereignty; they expressed their intention clearly and insistently, with obvious polemical and programmatic intent, in their letters and proclamations to the Roman pontiffs, as can be seen in E. Voegelin's article, "Mongol Orders," *Byzantion,* Vol. XV, 1940–41, pp. 378 ff. For more recent documents, with a complete bibliography of the subject, see A. Mostaert and F. W. Cleaves, "Trois documents mongols," *Harvard Journal of Asiatic Studies,* Vol. XV, 1952, pp. 419 ff.

[16] The account of Kublai's speech to Niccolò and Maffeo Polo, on the occasion of their first visit to his court in 1265, is found only in the Ramusian version (cr. ed., p. 70 n.) and was probably suppressed in the current versions and by Pipino for the reasons discussed further on. The authenticity of Kublai's speech is confirmed by the fact that a Chinese Buddhist treatise (cited later) attributes a similar profession of faith to him. It seems contradictory, or at least confused, that the four "prophets" are also described as "gods." Kublai evidently regarded them as emanations of the same supreme divinity, of which he was the representative and executor on earth, even as various Buddhist and Taoist sects in China had considered Buddha, Lao-tzŭ, Manes, and even Jesus, to be reincarnations, emanations, or manifestations of the supreme godhead. For this subject cf. E. Chavannes and P. Pelliot, "Un traité manichéen retrouvé en Chine," Paris, 1912 (extract from the *Journal Asiatique*).

The contrast between the attitude of the Christian rulers and that of the pagan emperors sets off the rigid intransigence of the former and the considerate tolerance of the latter. The toleration of various cults in the Chinghizide dominion follows from this idea of their metaphysical equivalence and their political value, which Marco clearly expressed in his simple style; as did also both of the Tartar emperors in their serenely figurative speech, which in a way foreshadows the parable of the three rings, inspired by Oriental tales and immortalized by Boccaccio.[17]

Which of the four prophets of one and the same god was preferred by him, Kublai, wise and calculating, never revealed either to Marco or to anyone else, thereby leaving to the faithful of each sect the illusion of his secret inclination toward their preference and the certainty of his equable protection. Our Venetians were indeed under the impression that he considered "the Christian faith to be the most true"; whereas, in fact, at that moment his Buddhist subjects had even more valid grounds for thinking that Kublai was one of them.[18] And the Mongol shamans must have been equally sure of this same imperial privilege; for in all the Chinghizide courts they still represented the pagan traditions of the Tartar tribes, which were never given up by the sovereigns and ruling classes of the empire.[19]

It was to these traditions that there belonged the god "who is greatest in heaven and most true"—namely, that supreme impersonal divinity of whom, according to Kublai, Jesus, Mohammed, Moses, and Sakyamuni are emanations, incarnations, and prophets, and equally worthy of worship and respect. This paramount divinity, whom the Tartars designated with the Turkish and Mongol name *Möngke Tängri,* or "Eternal Heaven," cor-

---

[17] The *Decameron,* First Day, Third Story. For the sources cf. M. Landau, *Die Quellen des Dekameron,* Stuttgart, 1884. Cf. also M. Penna, *La parabola dei tre anelli e la tolleranza nel medio evo,* Turin, 1953.

[18] For the penetration and supremacy of Lamaist Buddhism in Kublai's entourage cf. O. Franke, *Geschichte des chinesischen Reiches,* Vol. IV, pp. 331 ff. and *passim.* This trend had been begun by his brother, Mangu, at Karakorum, as is demonstrated by the monumental stupa of Tibetan design which Mangu had caused to be built there in 1259. For this cf. the present author's *Guillaume Boucher,* esp. p. 24.

[19] These are the *divinatores* mentioned by Mangu in the passage cited above (n. 14), of whom his brother Kublai also kept a large number at his court, as Marco Polo relates (cr. ed., p. 100 n.). For the doctrines and practices of the shamans referred to in the *Milione* see chap. vii, § 3, of the present work.

responding to the *T'ien* of the Chinese, of whom the emperor was supposed to be the son, was always invoked in imperial seals and proclamations, in order to signify that the sovereign was his representative on earth and the executor of his will.[20]

If the demotion of Jesus Christ to the rank of prophet, the equal of Moses, Buddha, and Mohammed, must have sounded blasphemous to Marco, a good Catholic, the idea of an impersonal supreme divinity, so characteristic of the peoples of the Far East, must certainly have remained quite incomprehensible to him, as indeed to all who had and have grown up in the atmosphere of Biblical revelation. This is, indeed, the insurmountable barrier between the Orient and the West, which was already recognized by Mohammed when, in a famous passage in the Koran, he made the distinction between the Biblical peoples (*Ahl al-Kitāb*), who were more or less tolerated in Mohammedan communities, and the idolaters, who were to be either converted or exterminated.[21]

This intransigence on the part of the Biblical peoples, which is in contrast with the tolerance of the Oriental pagans, is above all to be explained by the fact that only monotheistic religions can be, and always have been, exclusive and irreconcilable to the point of fanaticism, whereas the pagan Pantheon readily opens its doors to all concordant divinities, generally fusing them in a pantheism that is simultaneously tribal, national, eclectic, and universal, such as developed in the Roman Empire and, conformably to Chinese traditions, in Chinghizide Asia.[22] In both these empires

[20] The formula that expresses this concept is invariably, for all the Chinghizide rulers of Asia, *Möngke tängri-yin Küčündür* (= 'by the power of eternal heaven'), concerning which see the article by Mostaert and Cleaves cited in note 15 above, esp. pp. 485 ff. The formula became known in the West because it occurred at the beginning of the letters and proclamations of the rulers addressed to the Popes and other European sovereigns; a fairly correct account of this is to be found in the famous and imaginary *Travels* of Mandeville (cf. the edition by M. Letts, London, Hakluyt Society, 1953, Vol. II, chap. xxiv, pp. 359 ff.).

[21] Cf. A. S. Tritton, *The Caliphs and Their Non-Muslim Subjects,* London, 1931. The term *Ahl* in the famous Koranic expression (sura xci) has neither an ethnic nor a political significance, but renders rather the genetic concept of *people*. The phrase expresses a relative solidarity among the Biblical religions opposed to the idolaters of every kind and country. As is well known, none of the native Chinese religions—and certainly none of the Buddhistic sects—admits the existence of a god who is creator of the world and director of its fate. See below, chap. vii, § 3, n. 114.

[22] For the national universalism of ancient China and its influence on the Mongol expansion cf. O. Franke, *op. cit.,* Vol. IV, pp. 76 ff. and 496 ff., who is perhaps inclined to overestimate the importance attributed to Confucian doctrines.

the sovereign was in constant communion with the universal, impersonal divinity, together with its other emanations and incarnations, which he himself could create and multiply through the exercise of his own will and inspiration.[23]

The Chinghizide dynasty only made use of this privilege in order to deify itself when Kublai, for reasons of state, formally took up again the traditional imperial ceremonies in the ancient national temples of China, assuming with these the dynastic cult of his ancestors.[24] At the same time, he associated all the other cults of the subject peoples, of which hitherto the various Turkish and Mongol tribes of Upper Asia had known nothing, with his traditional shamanistic animism of Turko-Mongol origin, which was characteristic of the nomads of the steppes. With his Mongols, who dominated the whole continent, he remained faithful to the practices of their shamans; for the Chinese, he revived the cult of their rural divinities; from the Tibetans, subjects or tributaries of his empire, he took over the Lamaist worship of the Buddha. And, while he exploited the ability and experience of the Mohammedans, who were both powerful and numerous in his dominions, either directly, or by means of his vassals in the West, he entered into friendly relations with the Papacy and other Christian powers, with a view to a common assault against Islam, which was an obstacle to further Mongol expansion in the Mediterranean.

Thus, religion in the Chinghizide empire took on a markedly political function that was completely foreign to the Chinese tradition and even opposed to it.[25] With the suppression of the Confucian caste the new dynastic cult ceased to be what it had

---

[23] This is a characteristic aspect of the official Chinese cult, unknown to the Mongols but taken over by Kublai as emperor of China, thereby fusing the universalism of the Chinghizide dynasty with this traditional concept of the classical Chinese dynasties, for which see J. J. M. de Groot, *Universismus,* Berlin, 1910.

[24] Cf. O. Franke, *op. cit.,* Vol. IV, pp. 498 f.

[25] Religion had become political on other occasions in the history of China, especially in the T'ang era (618–905 A.D.), when the religions of foreign extraction (Manichaeism, Christianity, and Mohammedanism, as well as Buddhism) developed vigorously until their violent suppression in the year 845. For religious struggles in China cf. J. J. M. de Groot, *Sectarianism and Religious Persecution in China,* 2 vols., Amsterdam, 1903. Thus, the introduction of the doctrines and practices of Lamaist Buddhism at the Mongol court in the first decades of the XIIIth century was an eminently political event, connected with Chinghiz Khan's first attempts to subjugate Tibet and its monastic theocracy, personified in the great Saskya Pandita (Ānandadhvāja). The latter yielded in the political field, only to regain the advantage in the spiritual realm

always been in China, namely, national and exclusive. Instead, it now became a manifestation of that universal sovereignty for which it considered itself to be destined from the times of its founder. Thus, Kublai added the elements of imperial Chinese worship to the Mongol ceremonial, fusing the two traditions in the spectacular "epiphanies" described by Marco Polo as gigantic bacchanalia.[26]

By accepting the worship of one's ancestors and that of the native agrarian deities, Kublai intended to create in his Chinese subjects the same illusion as that of which Marco Polo was for a time a victim; for Marco, as a result of certain of the sovereign's apparent tributes of devotion to Christian symbols when the great ceremonies were held, nourished the hope that the emperor might one day be baptized, if not by him, at least by one of the many Nestorian priests attached to the court—the same who may have suggested the idea of obtaining the oil from the lamp of the Holy Sepulcher, which the Polos did, in fact, convey to Peking by order of the Kaan himself.[27] This also left the three Venetians with the illusion that they would later be able to carry out the Papal mandate entrusted to them by inducing him to become an apostolic Roman Catholic.

The condition placed on his conversion by Kublai had been expressed by him in person to Maffeo and Niccolò Polo at the time of their first visit to his court, in 1265, little more than ten years after the last Franciscan mission to Tartary had, by order of King Louis, explored the probability of converting the Chinghizide rulers. As is well known to readers of the *Milione,* after the two Venetians had begun to say "a few words about the Christian faith" and asked the sovereign why, since he considered it the best, he did not "become a Christian," they received the reply

by assuring to his sect for a century and a half the favor and conversion of the Chinghizide dynasty. For these dramatic events cf. Giuseppe Tucci's observations, based on new documents and direct information, in *Tibetan Painted Scrolls,* Rome, 1949, Vol. I, pp. 6 ff.

[26] *Il Milione,* cr. ed., chap. lxxxix; M.P., pp. 217 ff. For the Chinese texts that confirm and describe this cult cf. P. Pauthier's commentary to this passage.

[27] P. Pelliot ("Chrétiens d'Asie Centrale et d'Extrême-Orient," *T'oung Pao,* Vol. XV, 1914, pp. 623 ff.) supposes that this mission was promoted by Nestorian ladies of the court, which would mean that the oil would have been used for superstitious practices rather than for divine worship; other occasions of such use have been noted by the present author in *Guillaume Boucher,* pp. 24 f.

that "the Christians who are in these parts are so ignorant that they do nothing and can do nothing," whereas "these idolaters do whatever they wish" and might kill him with their secret, superhuman powers if he should turn toward the faith of the inept. The emperor concluded that if the hundred men he had requested from the Pope, "in the presence of these idolaters, reprove them for their actions, and tell them that they, too, are able to do such things, but do not wish to because they are done by the help of diabolic art and evil spirits, and so constrain them [the idolaters] that they have not the power to do such things in their presence; then, when we see this, we shall reprove them and their law; and so, I shall be baptized, and, when I am baptized, all my barons and nobles will be baptized, and then their subjects will receive baptism, and so there will be more Christians here than there are in your parts." [28]

This conclusion, which sounds like the epic finale of a *chanson de geste* or a joke played by the wily emperor, bears a touch of authenticity, and becomes a characteristic expression of the Asiatic civilization of that age, when considered within the framework of the continent's religious and political history and in relation to the expansion of the Chinghizide regime. The whole of Kublai's speech to the Venetians already reveals a preference, which is more practical than doctrinal, for Lamaist Buddhism; and this, in fact, was to prevail over every other religion during his reign and in the further development and decline of the dynasty.[29] Moreover, he openly declares his conception of religion as the mere instrument of his political power, which evaluates its merits according to the practical results and occult forces mastered by the respective clergy.

The powerful emperor, as Marco relates, had the three Venetians sit in his hall with ten thousand other persons while the *bacsi* with their art made the goblets full of wine, fermented

[28] Cf. *Il Milione,* cr. ed., p. 70 n.; M.P., pp. 201 f. (The whole passage is found exclusively in the Ramusian text.)

[29] The reference to Lamaist Buddhism is clear because Marco uses the term "Idolaters," which recurs in this passage and elsewhere to designate the followers of this sect; and it is known that from this time (*ca.* 1265) onward Kublai openly favored Lamaist Buddhism to the detriment of Taoism and every other organized and recognized religion in his dominions.

milk, and other beverages, rise from the floor, where they had been lined up in the Mongol fashion, and come to Kublai without anyone's touching them, and then return empty to their point of departure.[30] Similarly, Marco was able to watch the feats of the representatives of Buddhistic Tantrism from Tibet and Kashmir. When the Great Kaan was at his summer residence, "by will power and by means of their spells, they would keep all clouds and bad weather away from the palace." [31]

Marco and his older companions, who undoubtedly saw these tricks and were ingenuously amazed by them, could not imagine that behind them lay hidden not only a religious faith but also a farsighted cultural policy, formulated by a sovereign who had only just emerged from the barbaric practices of the steppes and the forests. This policy was served not only by the representatives of all the great religions of Asia but also by the Christians of the Oriental Nestorian sect. These latter, as opposed to the orthodox of the various Eastern churches and the few Roman Catholics residing in the empire, had for centuries past adapted themselves to the native religious practices and claims, renouncing, as Marco himself tells us, an effective supremacy of Christ over the other divinities revered by the Asiatic peoples.[32] The supremacy to which the Nestorians at the imperial court truly aspired was that of their sect over every other Christian church, while they contented themselves with being treated as the equals of the other religious groups represented and recognized at the court of the Great Kaan.[33]

Kublai's promise to receive baptism, though aleatory, was not so misleading as it may seem at first sight. Nor was it altogether absurd for him to suppose that, once he should be baptized, the

---

[30] *Il Milione*, cr. ed., p. 64 and note; M.P., p. 189. Cf. also Yule-Cordier's comment in *The Book of Ser Marco Polo*, Vol. I, p. 301 and note. The *bacsi* (or *bakhshi*) are the lamas. For the ceremonial of these libations cf. the Chinese document translated by M. G. Pauthier, *Le Livre de Marco Polo*, Vol. I, pp. 291 ff.

[31] *Il Milione*, cr. ed., and M.P., *loc. cit.*

[32] Summary, but reliable, information on Christianity in ancient and medieval Asia is to be found in G. Messina, *Cristianesimo, Buddhismo, Manicheismo nell'Asia antica,* Rome, 1947.

[33] Cf. A. C. Moule, *Christians in China*, pp. 216 ff.; and, for the court of Karakorum, the description given by Friar William of Rubruck, *Sinica Franciscana*, Vol. I, pp. 245 ff.

whole hierarchy of his vassals, and perhaps even the peoples of his dominion, would be converted to the Christian faith. Indeed, a large part of the evangelization of central and eastern Asia, and at the same time the expansion of other foreign cults throughout the continent, had been accomplished for almost a thousand years by peaceful conquest of the courts and of the nomadic or sedentary aristocracy, though these but rarely showed any determined interest in imposing the new faith on those among their subjects who preferred to remain faithful to the superstitious practices of the religion they already had.

Buddhism was introduced into Tibet in the VIth century as a result of the conversion of King Srong Tsan Gampo, who was influenced by one of his Chinese consorts and by another from Nepal.[34] The court followed his example, and from that time Tibet became, as is known, the center of a Buddhist sect which in the XIIIth century extended itself to the Mongol aristocracy and then gained preponderance in Kublai's religious and cultural policy at the time of Marco Polo. Moreover, already in the first centuries of the Christian era, the impetus to the diffusion of Buddhism in China had come from the rulers and their courts. Since the age of Chinghiz Khan, the infiltration of Lamaist Buddhism in the Mongol court and aristocracy had been a phenomenon essentially political in character and consequences, which, on the one hand, led to the submission of the Tibetan monastic theocracy to the Chinghizide power, and, on the other, determined the esoteric, temporal tendencies of their great Lamaist convents and the political power of their spiritual and

---

[34] It can be presumed that a first, tentative expansion of Buddhism in Mongolia was accomplished by Uigur missionaries from Turkestan or the region of Turfan, an outpost of that doctrine, thus paving the way for the sending of missionaries directly from Tibet in the XIIIth century, and the definitive conversion of the Mongols to Lamaism in the XVIth century. The official Tibetan history of this expansion, dictated by Jigs-med nam-mk'a, has been published by G. Huth, *Geschichte des Buddhismus in der Mongolei,* Strassburg, 1892, 2 vols., with text and translation. The circumstances of Buddhist penetration in the Chinghizide court during the first decades of the XIIIth century are illustrated with new and impressive documents by Giuseppe Tucci, *op. cit., loc. cit.* For pre-Buddhistic religions in Tibet, in part absorbed by Lamaism and by it diffused abroad, cf. Helmut Hoffmann, *Quellen zur Geschichte der tibetischen Bon-Religion,* Wiesbaden, 1950, and the same author's *Die Religionen Tibets,* Freiburg and Munich, 1956.

administrative head.[35] In the same way, and unmotivated by any practical reason, in the VIIIth century the *Khakhan*, or king, of the Khazars, a powerful Altaic tribe that had settled between the Volga and the Crimea (a region called Gazaria by Marco Polo and his contemporaries), embraced Hebraism as the state religion. Together with the governing classes of that people, he thus came to represent the last ethnic conquest registered by the Law of Moses in its millenary existence.[36]

All these conversions were the work of missionaries of the respective faiths and, it would appear, the fruit of theological discussions, which, as we know, were more than ever active in Marco's age.[37] Kublai's request to the Pope is in harmony with this long Asiatic tradition; hence our lay missionary was not completely wrong in charging against the Christians the failure to convert Kublai. Like Christopher Columbus some two centuries later, Marco certainly believed that Kublai's conversion, and that of all his vassals, would have been accomplished if the hundred clerics requested from the Supreme Pontiff had duly arrived at his court.[38]

This claim does, indeed, appear less absurd if it is remembered that, at the beginning of the XIth century, Syrian merchants and Nestorian priests respectively instructed and baptized the king of the Keraits, a Mongol tribe which became, and remained, Christian, as well as a number of neighboring Naiman nobles, of the Turkestan Uigurs and the Öngüt, who had settled in the region of the upper reaches of the Yellow River, in Chinese ter-

[35] This evolution is noted with various historical and documentary data by Tucci, *op. cit., loc. cit.*
[36] For this cf. D. M. Dunlop's well-informed work, *The History of the Jewish Khazars*, Princeton Univ. Press, 1954 (with full bibliography).
[37] Unfortunately, no monograph exists on this important aspect of medieval civilization in the West and the East, and the specialized studies on this subject are few and insufficient. Cf. M. Steinschneider, *Polemische und apologetische Literatur in arabischer Sprache*, Leipzig, 1877 (simple bibliography). For religious discussions, frequent and important at the courts of Mongolia and China in Marco Polo's times, cf. E. Chavannes, "Inscriptions et pièces de chancellerie de l'époque mongole," *T'oung Pao*, second series, Vol. V, 1904, pp. 357 ff., and Vol. VI, 1905, pp. 1 ff.
[38] Cf. the logbook of the first voyage, where it is said of the "Great Kaan . . . how on many occasions he and his predecessors had sent to Rome to ask for doctors in our holy faith, so that they might instruct them in this, and that the Holy Father had never provided them, and so many peoples were lost, falling into idolatry." The original text is found in *Raccolta di Documenti e Studi pubblicati dalla R. Commissione Colombiana*, Rome, 1893, Vol. I, Tome I, p. 2 (prologue).

ritory, having infiltrated by marriage and their contacts with the nomadic life the aristocracy of the Mongol steppes, the Turkish and Tartar tribes, and then the Chinghizide dynasty itself.[39] Mangu Kaan, the grandson of Chinghiz Khan and his third successor to the imperial throne, his brother Hulagu, the conqueror of Persia and first of the Ilkhans, and Kublai himself, all had a Christian mother and Christian wives.

Moreover, it was then asserted that Chagatai, the son of Chinghiz Khan, lord of Central Asia and one of the greatest figures of this powerful dynasty, had more or less openly adhered to the Nestorian Church, without, however, conferring any lasting prestige on this sect in his prevalently Mohammedan dominion.[40] The Catholic Church registered only one success in those times which would make it possible in retrospect to confirm the hopes and forecasts of the three Venetians, who were then already homeward bound on their return journey. Two

[39] Cf. R. Grousset, *L'Empire des steppes*, pp. 243 ff., and A. C. Moule, *Christians in China*, pp. 216 ff.

[40] For this branch of the Chinghizide dynasty cf. Grousset, *op. cit.*, pp. 397 ff. His territory was called the Middle Empire since it included Central Asia, and is not to be confused with the historic title of the Chinese empire (the Middle Kingdom), which had already been abolished before the Mongol conquest. Hence, when in his commentary on Dante's poem (*Inferno*, I, 105) we learn of a story which Boccaccio asserts was recounted by merchants coming from the Middle Empire, we should take it to mean the empire of Chagatai rather than China. We may even suppose that this name indicated the territory of Almaliq, a great commercial center of Central Asia, where numerous Italian merchants and monks had taken up their abode. Cf. V. Rondelez, "Un évêché en Asie Centrale au XIV⁽ᵉ⁾ siècle," *Neue Zeitschrift für Missionswissenschaft*, Vol. VII, 1951, pp. 1 ff. (with full bibliography). The tradition of Chagatai's baptism is documented by a miniature in the Paris MS (Bibl. Nat., Suppl. persan 1113) of the celebrated universal history by Rashiduddin, compiled in the early years of the XIVth century and probably also illuminated in this same century, although neither he nor any other Mohammedan historian refers to the event, which is positively asserted only by Marco Polo, *Il Milione*, cr. ed., pp. 40 f.; M.P., p. 144. Perhaps this baptism is merely a legend, inspired by the severe treatment inflicted by this sovereign on the Mohammedans of his vast dominion (cf. C. d'Ohsson, *Histoire des Mongols*, Vol. II, pp. 100 ff., and the article "Chagatai" in the *Encyclopaedia of Islam*). This dominion is called by Marco Great Turkey (cr. ed., pp. 216 ff.), and approximately corresponds to Turkestan. The miniature represents a group of priests beside the sovereign's bier, which is, however, covered in the Mongol fashion by a pall of felt with the inscription in Arabic ("As-Sultān al-'ālim al-'ādil Khāqān al-a'ẓam," that is to say, "The wise, just Sultan, the great Khaqan"). The whole expresses the characteristic political-religious syncretism of his age (1227–1242). Cf., apart from Grousset, *op. cit.*, pp. 397 ff., E. Blochet, *Introduction à l'histoire des Mongols de Fadl Allah Rachid ed-Din*, Leiden ("Gibb Memorial" series, XII), 1911, pp. 165 ff., as well as the present author's *The Myth of Felt*, Univ. of California Press, 1949 (with illustrations).

years after their departure from Khanbaliq, the Taidu of the
Tartars with its Turkish name, this capital received its first
Catholic bishop, Friar John of Montecorvino.[41] In a short space
of time he was successful in bringing into the bosom of the
Roman Church King George, lord of the Öngüt, of ancient
Nestorian stock, and, according to Marco, a descendant of
"Prester John." This son-in-law and vassal of Kublai was evi-
dently known to our Venetian prior to his Catholic baptism as
a result of more than one stay in his country.[42]

In accordance with ancient Asiatic usage, King George's immediate entourage and part of his people followed his example,
arousing the wrath of the Nestorian clergy. A palace conspiracy
inspired by the latter put an end to the life of this first and last
Catholic sovereign of eastern Asia, and brought about the destruction of the splendid church built by him in the capital, while
it restored to the Nestorian sect the dynasty, the court, and all
the converts in the land.[43] All this took place in Chinese territory
in the year 1298, when Marco was dictating the *Milione* in the
prison at Genoa.

The foregoing examples make it possible to connect the Polos'
mission and Marco's activity with these traditions in the religious
and political history of Asia—a history which, though it appeared relatively tranquil at the time of their stay in the Far
East, nevertheless was not devoid of ferment and conflict, as the
Milione itself indicates. Indeed, behind the apparent tolerance so
well described by its author a vast religious drama was stirring,
in which Marco's mission was only a minor though significant
episode.

Contrary to what may appear at first sight, the relationship

[41] Cf. *Sinica Franciscana*, Vol. I, pp. lxix ff., 348 f. Friar John began his activities
in China in 1294, immediately after Kublai's death, which occurred in February of
that year, as first apostolic legate in the Far East.
[42] This subject will be discussed at greater length in chap. vii, § 1. The territory of
the Öngüt along the bend of the Yellow River had a prevalently Christian population,
of which numerous archaeological traces have come to light. Cf. besides Moule,
Christians in China, pp. 174, 284 ff., etc., and P. Y. Saeki, *The Nestorian Documents
and Relics in China*, second edition, pp. 423 ff., the work by H. Bernard, S.J., *La
Découverte de Nestoriens mongols aux Ordos et l'histoire ancienne du christianisme en
Extrême-Orient*, Tientsin, 1935.
[43] Friar John of Montecorvino does not refer to King George's violent death, but
the circumstances of his end confirm this.

between politics and religion in the Chinghizide empire was a close and continuous one, jealously guarded by church and state, and dependent on events and tendencies which, though information on the subject is scant, may nevertheless be clearly made out. The Mongol conquests of that age were never inspired by religious aims or pretexts as the Mohammedan advance in Persia and India had been, from the VIIth century on, or the Crusades that extended far beyond the Holy Land with the French territorial conquests and the commercial ventures of the Genoese and Venetians. The abolition of the Caliphate, the destruction of the Ishmaelitic sect of the Assassins, and the degradation of the cult of Confucius by the Mongols were, from one end of Asia to the other, exclusively political acts, inspired by the peril that these spiritual organizations, whether aggressive or not, represented for the conquerors. On the other hand, the rulers were well aware of the political value that the religious groups could acquire, once they had been made a part of, and were controlled by, the dynastic and administrative system of the empire.

Moreover, this political centralization offered new scope to the missionary activities of the organized cults of Asia, which had never ceased to expand and develop in the age-old, relentless competition between the various churches and sects: Christian, Buddhist, Mohammedan, Hebraic, Manichaean, and Zoroastrian. To these must be added, within the vast confines of the Chinese empire, its most ancient national religions: Taoism and Confucianism. The last to participate in this sectarian contest was the Catholic Church, with its Franciscan and Dominican missions, from 1247 to 1368, and, in the interval between 1265 and 1292, its no less active lay missionaries: Niccolò, Maffeo, and Marco Polo from Venice.

Whereas the Chinghizide sovereigns sought to advantage themselves through each of these ecclesiastical and cultural groups, considering them on all occasions to be the instruments of their policy and upholders of their dynasty, so, too, the respective churches tended to avail themselves of both policy and rule as instruments for their own propaganda and support for their clerical, doctrinal, and monastic organizations. In other words, the churches attempted to secure privileges for themselves, especially those of a fiscal, protective, or apologetic sort; and the rulers, on the other hand, endeavored to absorb and exploit the churches, as the circumstances and the political and practical value of the various doctrines and communities might warrant. The administrative vigilance to which the faiths were subjected enabled their more important representatives to exert an influence, in turn, on the emperor and his government—not unlike that attempted by the Polos, as a reward for their services, in favor of Christianity.

This characteristic aspect of Marco Polo's Asia—an effect, as we have seen, of the dynastic if not always the administrative centralization of the continent—was originated by Chinghiz Khan, the founder of the empire and its first lawgiver, and was maintained with the participation of the clergy and laymen of all faiths until the end of the medieval Catholic missions in the Far East. From the very beginning the Mongols entrusted the more important civic offices to representatives of foreign religions. Thus, the first chancellor of the new empire and civilizer of the nomadic barbarians called to govern the world was a Turkish Uigur, probably a Christian,[44] who was followed by the "prothonotary" Chingai, who died in 1251, a Nestorian like his successor, Bulgai, the prime minister and head of the political police at the time of Mangu Kaan, Kublai's brother and predecessor on the imperial throne.[45]

It was from two Mohammedan dignitaries from Central Asia that Chinghiz Khan received instruction in the art of governing towns and cities, after he had destroyed forever, with unparalleled cruelty, the flourishing centers of Islamic culture in Khorasan, the inheritors of Hellenic civilization in those historic regions and the diffusers of scientific knowledge throughout the Mohammedan and Christian worlds.[46] One of these

[44] Known only under the Chinese name of *T'a-t'a-t'ong-a*.

[45] For all these Christian personages cf. P. Pelliot, "Chrétiens d'Asie Centrale et d'Extrême-Orient," *T'oung Pao*, Vol. XV, 1914, pp. 623 ff., and the works cited by R. Grousset in *L'Asie orientale*, pp. 307 f. Bulgai is treated at length by Friar William of Rubruck in *Sinica Franciscana*, Vol. I, pp. 265, 275, etc.

[46] This episode in Chinghiz Khan's biography is treated with exemplary sobriety by B. Ya. Vladimirtsov, *The Life of Chingis-Khan*, trans. Prince Mirsky, London, 1930, and with literary exuberance by R. Grousset, *Le Conquérant du Monde*, Paris, 1944, as well as by H. Desmond Martin, *The Rise of Chingis Khan*, Baltimore, 1950.

luminaries, the great Nasiruddin, then appears at the court of Mangu Kaan, as his counselor, toward the middle of the century, at the time when the lamas of Tibet were beginning their successful task of Buddhistic penetration in the same circles at the capital, which led to the triumph of their practices and doctrines in the whole of Mongolia and, thence, in Kublai's China.[47]

Meanwhile, the Chinese religious organizations had also entered the lists, after a thousand years of alternating vicissitudes in their own land.[48] An episode famous both in the history of China and in the life story of Chinghiz Khan deals with the meeting between the great conqueror and the spiritual head of the Taoists, who, leaving his Chinese hermitage in 1221, joined Chinghiz in the Hindu Kush, in Afghan territory, to administer to him, not the drug of immortality, in which neither seriously believed, but the grave and subtle teachings of his sect. On this occasion he was able to insure for his followers not only a dominant position in Cathay but also fiscal and moral privileges never attained by his successors, down to our own times.[49] As a result, the *tuini,* as they are called by William of Rubruck,[50] and the *sensin* described in the *Milione* as the faithful of this religion,[51] abounded at the court at Karakorum and Peking, until this sect was suppressed and its sacred books destroyed by order of Kublai, at the suggestion of Buddhists.[52] Moreover, in

[47] The astronomer, physician, philosopher, and historian Nasiruddin was called from Persia to Karakorum by Mangu Kaan, who wished to put him in charge of organizing an observatory necessary for the astronomical predictions of his "divinatores," who, according to William of Rubruck (*Sin. Franc.,* Vol. I, p. 301), were able to predict solar and lunar eclipses. Another Mohammedan was ordered by Kublai in 1279 to build the famous observatory at Peking, for which see Yule-Cordier, *The Book of Ser Marco Polo,* Vol. I, p. 453, and O. Franke, *Geschichte des chinesischen Reiches,* Vol. V, pp. 273 ff.

[48] Cf. J. J. M. de Groot, *The Religious System of China,* 6 vols., Leiden, 1892–1910, and the same author's *Sectarianism and Religious Persecutions in China,* 2 vols., Amsterdam, 1904; also, L. Wieger, *Histoire des croyances religieuses et des opinions philosophiques en Chine,* 1917, English edition, Hsien-hsien, 1927.

[49] Cf. A. Waley, *The Travels of an Alchemist,* London, 1931.

[50] *Sinica Franciscana,* Vol. I, p. 238.

[51] Cr. ed., p. 65; M.P., p. 191.

[52] This took place in 1281, after long-drawn-out struggles and discussions between Lamaists and Taoists. Cf. Chavannes, "Inscriptions et pièces de chancellerie," as cited in note 37 above. The destruction of the sacred books of the Taoists was instigated by the Tibeto-Mongol Buddhistic lamas, who perceived in their adversaries a dangerous national Chinese element, disliked also by the emperor on account of the political effects of this resistance. The only Taoist text saved was the classic *Tao Tê Ching,*

the reign of Chinghiz Khan a host of Confucian scholars collaborated with their country's conqueror and rose high in the ranks of the Mongol administration and of the court hierarchy, where they finally prevailed, at least numerically, and made the court and native nobility familiar with the fundamental doctrines of their powerful, historic caste, which at last was dissolved by Kublai himself.[53]

The Nestorian churches, the mosques, the Taoist, Lamaist, and Confucian temples, all rose up as near as possible to the imperial residences, both in the capitals and in the vast encampments of pavilions, tents, and chariots where the court spent a part of each year, as Marco describes at length.[54] In this way the various sects, all committed to praying for the sovereign's health and longevity, continually reminded him of their presence, knowing that the prosperity of their institutions and the

---

attributed to Lao-tzŭ. As for the terms *tuin* (perhaps from the Chinese *Tao jen*, according to Ferdinand Lessing, *Ostasiatische Zeitschrift*, Vol. XXII, 1936, p. 199, or, according to Chavannes, *loc. cit.*, p. 366, from the Chinese *tuinan*, Mongol *döin*) and *sensin* (from the Chinese *hsien sheng*, namely, "master"), their etymology is controversial. According to Rockhill (*The Journey* etc., p. 159 n. 1), it seems to be a Uigur term, used also by Hayton for the designation of Buddhist priests. The corresponding Chinese title may be *t'ien-jen*, i.e., 'heavenly man.' Cf. A. Waley, *The Travels of an Alchemist*, p. 101 n. However this may be, all these "religions" were abundantly represented at the imperial court in Marco Polo's times, and were charged with propitiating the divinities in the emperor's behalf and with counseling him on the basis of their magical practices or astrological knowledge.

[53] O. Franke, *Geschichte des chinesischen Reiches*, Vol. IV, pp. 320 ff., 397 ff., is especially insistent on this point, while E. Haenisch, *Die Kulturpolitik des mongolischen Weltreiches*, pp. 10 f., in order to illustrate the proportion between native and foreign officials, offers some eloquent figures, which go back, however, to the first decades of the XIVth century, when the Tartar court at Peking was largely Sinicized. There, the Chinese of Confucian tradition numbered 1,151, as opposed to 938 foreigners; in the administration of the capital, 351 to 155; and in the provinces, 14,236 to 5,689. These figures are not valid for Marco Polo's times, when the Confucian Chinese were still a minority which was more tolerated than welcome. Moreover, it should be noted that their collaboration with the Mongols was more active in northern China (Marco Polo's Cathay), which for centuries had been governed by dynasties of like origin, whereas it was insignificant in the southern China of the Sung (Marco's "Mangi"), which was only incorporated after 1279 into Kublai's empire, on the fall of the Sung dynasty, and never adapted itself to the Tartar rule, which lasted there for almost a century. Cf. P. Demiéville, "La Situation religieuse en Chine au temps de Marco Polo," in *Oriente Poliano*, Rome, 1957, pp. 193 ff.

[54] Cr. ed., pp. 62 ff., 91 ff., etc.; M.P., pp. 185 ff., 222 ff. The situation was the same, though in far more modest proportions, at Karakorum, and in the imperial encampments described by the Franciscan missionaries. Cf. *Sinica Franciscana*, Vol. I, pp. 245 f.

prestige of their doctrines depended on his good-will. Hence, when Friar John of Montecorvino, who arrived at Peking a short while after the Polos' departure, built there the first Catholic bishop's church in the empire, which was financed by the rich Italian merchant Pietro da Lucalongo, he desired it to be erected so near to the emperor's residence that the latter, as the Friar himself tells us, could hear not only its bells but also the divine office chanted by its parishioners. "Et hoc mirabile factum longe lateque divulgatum est inter gentes."[55] The result of all this was that at Karakorum, and then in the other residences, there beat upon the imperial ears, in a contest of sonority and propaganda, the chimes of the Catholics, the reverberation of the Nestorian tablets, the intonation of the muezzin, and the raucous sound of the powerful Lamaistic trumpets, not to mention the drums of the shamans, the gongs of the *tuins,* and, at Peking, perhaps even the shofar of the Jews.[56] And each of these sects offered to the sovereign and his government the wealth of culture and experience accumulated in the course of their millenary traditions.

These were the circles in which the Polos moved when they found themselves at Kublai's court as representatives of the Pope and of Western civilization. They were present at the solemn ceremonies at which the emperor and "all his barons and nobles who attended" devoutly kissed "the book in which the four

---

[55] Friar John of Montecorvino's Letter (*Sin. Franc.,* Vol. I, p. 335). It should be pointed out that the Nestorians, apart from ringing the bells, "pulsant tabulam," that is to say, beat upon a block of wood or iron, as was observed by Friar John of Pian del Càrpine (*Sin. Franc.,* Vol. I, p. 125) and by William of Rubruck in several passages of his *Itinerarium,* who also describes the mobile churches of the imperial encampments, in which the representatives of the various denominations officiated in special tents in the vicinity of the imperial pavilion.

[56] Marco Polo is the only author in his century to mention them as a recognized religious community (cr. ed., p. 70 n.; M.P., p. 201). For this subject see Yule-Cordier, *The Book of Ser Marco Polo,* Vol. I, pp. 346 ff., and R. Loewenthal in *Monumenta Serica,* Vol. XII, 1947, pp. 97 ff. Owing to the affluence of Jews from western Asia, this Pekinese community probably differed from the ancient one at Kaifeng, which had become almost completely Sinicized and was known to Matteo Ricci, who had met one of its most eminent members; for this see P. Pelliot's article, "Le Juif Ngai," *T'oung Pao,* Vol. XX, 1921, pp. 32 ff. Ricci's text is given in P. M. d'Elia, S.J., *Fonti Ricciane,* Vol. II, Rome, 1949, pp. 316 ff. For the community itself, disbanded some hundred years ago, cf. W. C. White, *The Jews in China,* 3 vols., Toronto, 1942. For other information cf. R. Loewenthal, "The Early Jews in China," *Folklore Studies,* Catholic University of Peking, Vol. V, 1946, p. 394. And for a general orientation cf. L. Rabinowitz, *Jewish Merchant Adventurers,* London, 1948.

Gospels are." Year after year these ceremonies were followed, as the principal feast days came round, by acts of homage to the cults of "Saracens, Jews, and Idolaters," apparently in an even-handed manner, confirming the theoretical equivalence of all religions in the public life of the empire.

It will be noted that Marco lists only foreign cults, revealing, among other things, the existence in the capital of an organized Jewish community, which was granted official recognition. It is also certain that his "Idolaters" were not Chinese Buddhists of ancient tradition, in large part monks and scholars, but rather the representatives of the Tibetan Lamaist sect, which was already influential in Mongolia at the time of Mangu, and was now elevated by Kublai to the highest pinnacles of court and state. This preference is to be explained by the prestige enjoyed during the decisive years of his reign by the Tibetan Phags-pa, inventor of the official script of the empire and spiritual guide of its ruler, who, with his help, succeeded in extending Chinghizide sovereignty to Tibet, making it thenceforward a state subject to China.[57]

This was the moment when Lamaist Buddhism contrived after age-long struggles to bring about suppression of the national Taoist religion of China, the sacred books of which were destroyed and the privileges annulled that had been granted by Chinghiz Khan. Hence the ancient and once popular sect, now in abject decline, is not expressly named by Marco as among those honored by Kublai and his court,[58] from which the Confucian men of letters were excluded both as a sect and as a caste. While it is true that they were individually admitted to government office, they were nevertheless relegated as a group to the lowest classes of the social order of the empire.[59]

As we see, the *tregua Dei* described by Marco was not so complete and secure as he would have us believe. The suppression of the Taoists and the humiliation of the Confucians were acts of

---

[57] Cf., besides C. d'Ohsson's classic *Histoire des Mongols,* Vol. II, pp. 487 ff., O. Franke, *Geschichte des chinesischen Reiches,* Vol. IV, pp. 480 f., Vol. V, p. 242, and P. Demiéville, as cited in note 53 above, p. 216.

[58] It is probably to this that Marco refers when speaking of the sect designated by him under the name of *sensin.*

[59] Cf. G. Maspero and J. Escarra, *Les Institutions de la Chine,* Paris, 1953, p. 123, and N. Poppe, *The Mongolian Monuments* in *ḥP'ags-pa Script,* second edition (*Göttinger asiatische Forschungen,* Vol. VIII), Wiesbaden, 1957.

government that were intended to deprive of their spiritual support the Chinese who were subject to the Mongol dynasty. Kublai
himself, probably at the instigation of Buddhists and Christians
at his court, forbade the Mohammedans of the empire their
ritual practices for more than seven years and placed the whole
sect in danger, after having learned of the Koran's precept to kill
all polytheists who would not be converted to the Mohammedan
faith.[60] He only yielded to practical considerations—political,
commercial, or fiscal—when the imperial coffers began to register
the deleterious effects of these measures on the transcontinental
trade by land and sea, which for centuries had been carried on
exclusively by Mohammedan merchants and shipowners from
Persia and China.[61]

The most propitious occasion for giving his peoples a spectacular proof of his denominational policy presented itself to Kublai
in the year 1288, when the most precious relics of the Buddha
arrived in the capital. These were his miraculous bowl, two of his
teeth, and a tuft of his hair, which hitherto had been preserved
in a sanctuary on the island of Ceylon, an ancient center of his
cult.[62] Marco was present and gave a full description of this event,

[60] This act of Kublai's is recited, on the basis of Oriental and Western sources, by
C. d'Ohsson, *Histoire des Mongols,* Vol. II, pp. 490 ff., and is reported in like terms
in the works of H. H. Howorth, R. Grousset, and O. Franke, cited earlier. The enemies
of the Mohammedans at Kublai's court must have read to him the ninety-first sura
of the Koran, which contains the explicit statement referred to.

[61] The development of the Chinese navy in Marco's times had already made a
breach in this Mohammedan maritime monopoly, as can be seen from Jung-pang Lo's
article, "The Emergence of China as a Sea Power during the Late Sung and Early
Yüan Period," *Far Eastern Quarterly,* Vol. XIV, 1955, pp. 488 ff.

[62] The embassy had left Khanbaliq with great pomp in 1284, as Marco relates; cf.
cr. ed., p. 194, and M.P., p. 411. For the history of these relics, mentioned in the
Milione (cr. ed., p. 194; M.P., p. 380), cf. Yule-Cordier, *The Book of Ser Marco Polo,*
Vol. II, pp. 328 ff., with the bibliography added by Cordier, *Addenda,* p. 111. Dupli-
cates of the relics existed in various parts of Asia, and "Buddha's tooth" is still
venerated, after many vicissitudes, in the celebrated sanctuary of Kandy. This moving
of the Buddha's relics from one place to another recalls the solemn transference of his
finger in the year 819, arousing a violent reaction on the part of the Confucians,
which led to the radical suppression of Buddhism in China in the year 845. For this
cf., apart from the literature cited, Edwin O. Reischauer, *Ennin's Travels in T'ang
China,* New York, 1955, pp. 221 ff. The "beautiful bowl of green porphyry" admired
and described by Marco (*loc. cit.*) was certainly not authentic; cf. the present author's
article, "The Crib of Christ and the Bowl of Buddha," *Journal of the American
Oriental Society,* Vol. LXX, 1950, pp. 161 ff. For the simultaneity of cults and relics
in Ceylon cf. Cesar E. Dubler, "Alte arabische Berichte über den Fernen Osten,"
Asiatische Studien, Vol. VIII, 1954, pp. 51 ff.

on which the emperor conferred a special solemnity by requiring the entire population of Peking and the representatives of all the religions to turn out for the processional entry of the relics into his capital.

This would seem to represent the triumph of Buddhism over the other religions of the empire. And such indeed it was, especially since the acquisition of the treasures, at a high price, as Marco points out, was undoubtedly inspired by the powerful lamas of the court after the suppression of Taoism. However, the Saracens, together with the Christians of the East, who were no less active in their propaganda, looked on them as relics of Adam, who was unknown to the Buddhists, and venerated them as of that origin not only in Ceylon and the rest of India, but—as Marco insinuates—also at Peking, although he entertained some doubts of their authenticity.[63] However this may be, on this unique occasion the Biblical religionists agreed to associate with the "Idolaters" of the Chinese or Tibetan sect in worshiping these objects, which, taken with the oil from the lamp of the Holy Sepulcher, made manifest the religious unity of the empire while leaving to each worshiper the right, as noted by Marco, to interpret and venerate them in his own way.

The fact is all the more characteristic inasmuch as the transference of these relics is merely an episode in the Chinghizide policy of expansion, then aimed at the conquest of Indochina and Burma, and of Ceylon and other islands of the Indian Ocean, which in some degree were already tributaries of the Tartar empire.[64] These universally revered relics became a vehicle for, and a symbol of, that centralization of spiritual and political power

---

[63] *Il Milione,* cr. ed., p. 194; M.P., p. 407. The supposition of Benedetto (cr. ed., in note) that in this context (line 71) *Borcan* (Mongol appellation for the Buddha), instead of *Adan* (for Adam), should be read, is untenable, not only because this term never stands alone in Marco's text, but also because Kazwini, apart from the versions of the *Milione,* confirms this attribution of the relics to Adam. Cf. Ferrand, *Relations de Voyages,* Vol. II, pp. 307, and the article quoted in the preceding note. Moreover, it is certainly an error on Ramusio's part to suppose that the Saracens had suggested to Kublai the transference of these relics (cf. the *Milione,* cr. ed., *loc. cit.,* note), thereby doing a service to the "Idolaters," who were far more interested in the Buddha's relics than the Mohammedans and Christians in those of Adam. According to Hebraic and Christian tradition, to which Marco expressly refers (*loc. cit.*), Adam's tomb was supposed to be found in the Holy Land, perhaps on Golgotha itself.
[64] Cf. O. Franke, *Geschichte des chinesischen Reiches,* Vol. IV, pp. 461 ff.

which Kublai claimed for himself and his dynasty in the sense of Chinghizide universalism rather than in accordance with the national traditions of ancient China.[65]

In the years of Marco's stay in the Far East all the recognized religions passed under state control.[66] A special commission was set up for each one, which supervised its activities and finances, and watched its leanings, without interfering in questions of doctrine. Freedom of worship was therefore limited, and even if, as Marco asserts, everyone could dispose of his soul in the manner he willed, the religious congregations not approved by the police ran grave risks and had to meet in the greatest secrecy.

Of the existence of these secret communities the *Milione* offers us a few examples, which are all the more valuable since the official Chinese sources of the period do not deal with religious questions except to record fiscal and administrative affairs. The first reference to the secret cults concludes Marco's observations on religious liberty in the Tartar empire, and concerns those Christians, probably of the Greek rite, who kept hidden in their places of worship crucifixes of gold and silver representing, as the text has it, "the supreme lord of Christianity."[67] These precautions were due, not to the worth of the sacred objects, but rather to the well-known fact that the Nestorians, who were still influential in the empire, did not permit the use of crucifixes, either because the doctrines of the sect forbade it, or because they feared lest the horror and divine and human degradation of the Agony should appear repugnant and inauspicious to the pagans and therefore harmful to the prestige of their faith.[68] Indeed, none of the numberless Christian crosses found in central

[65] Cf. the works by J. J. M. de Groot cited in note 48 above; also *Universismus,* Berlin, 1910. This concept was limited in ancient China to the national territory and, at most, to the Far East, whereas for the Chinghizide sovereigns it signified the submission of all the peoples of the earth to the Great Kaan. It was expressed again in 1276 in the report of Bayan, the Mongol general, mentioned by Marco (cr. ed., p. 134 f.; M.P., p. 311), for which see F. W. Cleaves, "The Biography of Bayan," *Harvard Journal of Asiatic Studies,* Vol. XIX, 1956, p. 249.

[66] For Mongol-Chinese ecclesiastical legislation in Marco Polo's age cf. P. Ratchnevsky, *Un code des Yuan,* Paris (*Bibliothèque de l'Institut des Hautes Études Chinoises,* Vol. IV), 1937, pp. lxviii f.

[67] *Il Milione,* cr. ed., p. 14 n.; M.P., p. 96.

[68] All this had already been noted by William of Rubruck in his *Itinerarium* (cf. *Sin. Franc.,* Vol. I, pp. 203, 264, and 275).

and eastern Asia bears the figure of Christ, who, according to the Nestorian interpretation of the Passion, was crucified as man and not as God.[69] And so great was the distaste of the pagans for this instrument of torture and death that the Emperor Kublai, although he respected and favored the Christian faith of every rite, nevertheless—as Marco tells us—"would in no wise suffer the Christians to carry the cross before them; this was because so great a man as Christ had been scourged and had died on it," words that clearly reveal the Nestorian conception of the Crucifixion and the authenticity of the text in which they are found.[70]

The Nestorian clergy's jealousy of Catholic influence in Asia is confirmed by an event, related by Friar William of Rubruck, which is characteristic of the cold war waged by the various churches aspiring to supremacy, or at least to special privileges, in the circles of the Chinghizide court. When the French sculptor Guillaume Boucher made a crucifix for a high official of the imperial government, a Nestorian who was courted by different groups of Christians in the capital, the sacred object was stolen by the Nestorian clergy of the court and was never returned to the person for whom it was intended—who, by a stroke of irony, was also the head of the political police of the empire.[71] Moreover, we may suppose that in the open struggle between Nestorians and Catholics at the court of Peking, during the reign of Kublai's successors to the Chinese throne, the crucifix played an important part as a symbol unworthy of Christ's divinity and an object detested by the ruling classes of the empire.[72]

Marco Polo participated in this secret struggle between the religions and sects of Asia so far as he could do so both as a good Christian and as his sovereign's zealous servant. Thus, he once happened to discover a secret religious community in the city

---

[69] Cf. Saeki, *The Nestorian Documents* etc., pp. 425 f. The Nestorian heresy was little known in the West. Friar William, who despised the Christians of Asia for many reasons, asserts among other things that "male sentiunt de Passione . . . et erubescunt ea," without however going into details about their doctrinal dualism, which attracted more or less all the Asiatic faithful of the most diverse religions except that of Islam, always opposed to metaphysical dualism of every sort.

[70] *Il Milione*, cr. ed., p. 70 n.; M.P., p. 201.

[71] Cf. the present author's *Guillaume Boucher*, pp. 32 ff.

[72] Friar John of Montecorvino has some bitter words to say about this situation in his letter of January 8, 1305 (*Sin. Franc.*, Vol. I, pp. 346 f.).

of Foochow, a populous commercial center of southern China, which with obvious joy he recognized to be a Christian congregation.[73] It was, however, a Manichaean community, the residue of an ancient secret cult that according to tradition had been kept alive since the time when this dualistic religion, which in its various ramifications extended from China to Spain, had been dissolved and prohibited throughout China by the edict of Wu Tsung in the year 843 A.D.[74]

Marco's mistake is to be explained not only by his zeal, but also by the fact that this sect, persecuted since its origins in every part of the world, associated its heretical cult of an impersonal and mythical Christ with doctrines and rites derived from Buddhism and various Zoroastrian sects connected with gnosis and with the Gospels and other sacred books of the East.[75] According as their environment in the respective countries demanded, the Manichaeans concealed their practices beneath the more or less authentic appearances of the religions tolerated, now emphasizing the Christian element, and now, especially in their liturgical and symbolical iconography, bringing to the forefront the pagan aspects of their religion. Thus, in their isolated community at Foochow, they had managed to elude the vigilance both of the other denominations in this great city and of the political authorities, who were unaware of its existence until the arrival of Marco and his uncle Maffeo in the course of one of their journeys through those distant regions of the empire.

Once their attention had been drawn by a learned Saracen to this indeterminate religious group, the two Venetians began insistently to interrogate its members, who were terrified by this inquest, which, they felt, might deprive them of the practice of their faith and bring down upon them the sovereign's wrath. Their terror shows that they belonged to a prohibited sect, ev-

[73] *Il Milione,* cr. ed., p. 158 n.; M.P., p. 349.
[74] For this group and the literature on the subject cf. the present author's article, "Manichaeism, Buddhism, and Christianity in Marco Polo's China," *Asiatische Studien,* Vol. V, 1951, pp. 1 ff.
[75] For the relationship between Manichaeism and the other Asiatic cults cf., besides the classic study by E. Chavannes and P. Pelliot, "Un traité manichéen retrouvé en Chine" (extract from *Journal Asiatique*), Paris, 1912, the compendious work by H. Ch. Puech, *Le Manichéisme,* Paris, 1949, p. 61 and the copious notes. See, too, Edward H. Schafer, *The Empire of Min,* Rutland, Vt., and Tokyo, 1954, p. 102.

idently Manichaean, which already on several occasions had been
denounced to the authorities of the past régime of the Sung without the latter's having been able to suppress it entirely.[76]

However, since they found a psalter among the books of this
community, and had observed three images in one of its temples,
which, according to Marco, represented three of the Apostles, the
two Venetians thought they had discovered a Christian fellow-
ship and advised its members to send two messengers to the Great
Kaan in order to obtain his recognition and protection for their
practices and beliefs. Marco's circumstantial account almost permits us to hear the debates between the head of the Christians
and the leader of the Buddhists at court, who upheld in turn their
arguments in favor of their respective confessions and jurisdictions.[77]

These arguments can easily be reconstructed because the psalter,
included in the sacred texts of the Manichaeans, belonged also
to the traditional cult of Jesus (though this may have degenerated
into a form blasphemously heretical), and so could testify in favor
of the Christians. On the other hand, the fundamentally Buddhistic substance of their homiletic literature and the three images
in their temple, interpreted as representing the three hypostases
of the Buddha, which were common in his Chinese cult, argued
for that faith.[78] Driven to extremities by the emperor, who had
intervened in these inconclusive discussions, the emissaries of the
secret community at Foochow preferred, as Marco tells us, to
make an official declaration that they belonged to the Christian

[76] Cf. the Chinese texts collected, translated, and annotated by Chavannes and Pelliot
in the study cited in the preceding note.

[77] This episode in Marco's biography can be dated with sufficient precision because
the central office for supervision of the Christian cult was organized by Kublai in
1289, who replaced by it the various provincial offices scattered throughout his empire. The discovery and denunciation of this congregation, described in the Z reading
of the *Milione* (*loc. cit.*), must have occurred in that same year, or soon afterward.
For this institution cf. A. C. Moule, *Christians in China,* pp. 225 ff., and Saeki, *The
Nestorian Documents and Relics in China,* pp. 497 ff. We find men of various religions in charge of this office, which affords proof of its purely administrative character. The head of the ministry for the supervision of the Buddhist church held a
similar official position and presided over the Council of the Wise, or *Chi hsien yüan,*
which also controlled the activities of the Taoist church.

[78] This so-called Buddhistic trinity of the Mahayana sect, which is characteristic of
Upper Asia and China, is composed of Amitabha, Kuan-yin, and Ta-shih-chih. These
were frequently represented in the Chinese art of those centuries.

faith, most probably in order to escape the vigilance of the powerful Buddhistic church, which had persecuted them for a long
time past, and—as the Manichaeans had always done, at all times
and in all places—in order to continue under false appearances
the actual practices of their community and its ancient cult. This,
indeed, maintained its secret existence until the XVIIth century
in the same center, the last outpost of a universal faith that had
reached its zenith in Europe in Marco Polo's age, in Central Asia at
the time of the ephemeral Uiguric empire (IXth century), and in
China in the golden age of the T'ang dynasty.[79]

The authenticity of this account is beyond doubt. No one in
those times, or for many centuries to come, could have possessed
or invented such definite information of this congregation lost
among the various religious communities of the populous Chinese
city. Odoric of Pordenone, who visited Foochow in 1324, or
thereabouts, admired its "cocks, the biggest in the world," and
the "chickens white as snow," but found no trace of Christians
or Manichees.[80] Nor could anyone but Marco have been so well
acquainted with the procedure of the imperial ministry of cults
at the time of Kublai, who had set it up as part of the political
organization of his empire.

Undoubtedly a pious exaggeration, however, is the *Milione's*
total of Christian families—700,000—who were supposed to have
settled in southern China. Even if we admit that the statistics of
the *Milione* are nearly always inexact, and often differ in its
various versions, we cannot possibly attribute this reckoning to
Marco. If it is not due to the slip of a scribe's pen, it is perhaps
a pious invention on the part of the compiler of this authoritative
version, who, greatly interested in the religions of Asia, probably
wished to rekindle the diminished fervor for the missions to the
Orient.[81]

Marco, indeed, was perfectly well aware of how small, among
the general population, was the scattering of Christians in Chin-

---

[79] For the later history of this secret community cf. P. Pelliot, "Les Traditions
manichéennes au Foukien," *T'oung Pao*, Vol. XXII, 1923, pp. 193 ff.

[80] Cf. *Sinica Franciscana*, Vol. I, p. 461.

[81] For this reading cf., besides the data offered by Benedetto in the Introd. to his
cr. ed. of the *Milione*, pp. clxiii ff., Moule-Pelliot, *Marco Polo: The Description of the
World*, Vol. II (Latin text) and Vol. I, pp. 47 ff. (English translation and notes).

ghizide Asia.[82] According to an approximate calculation, at the
height of its power the whole Chinese empire did not number
more than 100,000 Christians among its inhabitants. These included Nestorians or Christians of the Greek rite, and the Armenians, who were then a part of the Chinghizide empire, the numerous Alans of the imperial guard, the Catholics of the Franciscan
missions, and the merchants with their families, who, it would
seem, were for the most part Italians.[83] The imperial ministry
whose task it was to supervise their groups and cults was organ-

---

[82] Concerning this and the respective groups cf. Moule, *Christians in China*, pp. 240 ff.
and *passim*.

[83] We have little information—and that indirect—about the residence of European
merchants in the large Chinese commercial centers. However, it seems certain their
number was small, in spite of the opening of a store at Zaiton by the Frescobaldi
family and references in Genoese notarial documents of the XIVth century, for which
see R. S. Lopez, "China Silk in Europe in the Yüan Period," *Journal of the American
Oriental Society*, Vol. LXXII, 1952, pp. 72 ff. Friar John of Montecorvino attests to
the presence in Peking of a merchant, Pietro da Lucalongo, who traveled with him
and made a fortune there, and speaks also of a Lombard physician who came to the
same city in 1303 and broadcast incredible slanderous reports about the Roman Curia,
the Franciscan Order, and conditions in the West—perhaps he was one of the
Lombard heretics of that time, and in order to save himself journeyed to the ends
of the earth; cf. *Sinica Franciscana*, Vol. I, resp. pp. 352 f. and 349 f. A sculptured
funerary inscription discovered at Yangchow, in Kiangsu, pertaining to the tomb of a
certain Caterina de Viljonis, who died in 1340, is briefly discussed by M. Roncaglia,
O.F.M., in *Neue Zeitschrift für Missionswissenschaft*, Vol. VIII, 1952, p. 293. She was
probably the wife of an Italian merchant in that city, of which Marco is supposed
to have laid claim to being governor for three years (see chap. v, n. 89) and in
which Odoric of Pordenone mentions a contemporary Franciscan monastery. Cf. *Sinica
Franciscana*, Vol. I, p. 385, etc. This would be the only European woman recorded in
China in that century. Pegolotti observes in his "Avvisamento del viaggio del Gattaio,"
in *Pratica della Mercatura*, ed. Evans, pp. 21 f., that "if the merchant does not wish
to bring any woman with him from Tana [in the Crimea], he need not . . . if he
does bring one, he will be thought of higher station than if he did not." Pegolotti,
however, probably alludes to one of the slaves then bought and sold in large numbers
in the ports of the Crimea (cf. R. Livi, *La schiavitù domestica in Italia*, Padua, 1928).
It may certainly be presumed that the Caterina at Yangchow belonged to the Viglioni
family from Venice who had settled at Tabriz in Persia toward the middle of the
XIIIth century, as we learn from Pietro Viglioni's will of December 10, 1264, published in the *Archivio Veneto*, Vol. XXVII, pp. 161 ff. For this family, with whom the
Polos probably came into contact, cf. W. von Heyd, *Histoire du commerce du Levant*,
Vol. II, p. 110. For Caterina Viglioni's tomb see Francis A. Rouleau, S.J., "The
Yangchou Latin Tombstone as a Landmark of Medieval Christianity in China,"
Harvard Journal of Asiatic Studies, Vol. XVII, 1954, pp. 346 ff., and R. Morozzo
della Rocca, "Sulle orme di Marco Polo," *L'Italia che scrive*, Vol. XXXVII, 1954, p.
120. The Christian colony at Yangchow must have been of more recent formation,
since it is not mentioned by Marco, who resided for three years in that city without,
as usual, mentioning his co-religionists, including heretics (cf. *Il Milione*, cr. ed.,

ized only in 1289, undoubtedly as a result of the influx of Christians into China and the increasing importance of the empire's relations with Byzantium and the Mediterranean world.[84]

In fact, no trace remained of the ancient Nestorian colony founded at Hsinanfu in 635 by Christians from Syria and Persia, who had fled from the Arab invasion of their lands after their suppression in China, which occurred in September, 845.[85] The first Christians to return were those who followed the Mongolian conquerors of the northern provinces of China, from the year 1215 onward. They were Turks of varied stock, who mainly came from the regions on the borders of northwestern China which were affiliated to the new Chinghizide empire. The Christian infiltration from western Asia was accomplished for the most part by individuals, if we except the Alans, who from the time of Chinghiz Khan represented, as we know, the élite of the imperial army.[86]

In the same year in which he arrived at Peking (1275), two Nestorian monks, native-born residents of the capital and important figures in the history of Oriental Christianity of those times, moved in the opposite direction—toward the western

---

p. 137, chap. cxlv). The tombstones of Catholic and Nestorian Christians recently discovered at Zaiton (i.e., Chüanchow, modern Tsinkiang) in Fukien (cf. *Il Milione,* cr. ed., pp. 159 ff.; M.P., pp. 350 f.) also belong to the later XIVth century. Among these is that of Friar Andrew of Perugia, the suffragan bishop of that diocese (who died *ca.* 1330), for whom see S. Foster, "Crosses from the Walls of Zaitun," *Journal of the Royal Asiatic Society,* 1954, pp. 1–25, and L. Carrington Goodrich, "Recent Discoveries at Zayton," *Journal of the American Oriental Society,* Vol. LXXVII, 1957, pp. 161 ff., Vol. LXXVIII, 1958, p. 118. Marco never mentions a Christian colony in this city and region that were well known to him.

[84] In fact, the official report mentions an interpreter, as well as two annalists, among the members of this authority (cf. Saeki, *Nestorian Documents,* p. 497). It should be noted that at that time Christian prestige had risen at the court of the Ilkhans in Persia, partly as a result of the marriage of Abaqa, the Mongol sovereign of this land (1265–1282) and Kublai's nephew, with a daughter of Michael Palaeologus, the Byzantine emperor.

[85] For these famous episodes cf. Moule, *Christians in China,* pp. 27 ff., and Saeki, *Nestorian Documents,* which presents the various imperial acts that illustrate the vicissitudes of Christianity in China (Chinese texts and translation).

[86] For the latter cf. Moule, *loc. cit.* Marco himself mentions that before the year 1278 there were no Christians living in the city of "Cinghianfu," present-day Chinkiang, in the province of Kiangsu, which was conquered by Kublai's armies in 1276. For the toponymy of Marco Polo's China cf. Hope Wright, *Geographical Names in Sung China,* Paris (École Pratique de Hautes Études), announced.

regions of the Chinghizide empire bordering on the Christian lands of the Levant—on a politico-religious mission inspired by Kublai. The shrewd emperor wished to make his authority felt as head of the dynasty and protector of the Christians of Asia, since the great Baibars, the Mameluke sultan of Egypt, was harassing Kublai's vassals in Asia Minor, with the result that Abaqa, the Chinghizide sovereign of Persia, had determined to solicit an alliance with the Pope and the kings of France and England against the common Mohammedan enemy.[87]

The imperial mission met with success. One of the two Turko-Chinese monks, Marc by name, arrived at Baghdad and, in 1281, was elected patriarch of the Nestorians there, with the name of Jaballaha III.[88] His companion, Rabban Sauma, who wrote a fascinating account of his embassy, continued in 1287 his historic mission to the West, which led him to Rome, Genoa, and France, where he met Philip the Fair and Edward I of England—the two sovereigns who, on account of their avarice and pride, aroused the noble wrath of Dante Alighieri.[89]

The age was that of the greatest expansion of Christianity in the Ancient World, when the contacts between the Asiatic sovereigns and the Papacy were most frequent, and the mendicant orders most active in creating new episcopal and suffragan seats in Central Asia and China, where they attracted to their churches and monasteries the heterodox elements of the Asian continent rather than individual followers of other doctrines.[90] In Marco's times, that which united all Christians from the Yellow Sea to the Atlantic was more than anything else their common front against Islam, which likewise extended from one end to the other of the Ancient World; but as a practical measure it was

[87] For these events cf. Sir E. A. Wallis Budge, *The Monks of Kûblâi Khan*, London, 1928, Introd., and R. Grousset, *L'Empire des steppes*, pp. 442 ff.

[88] The political character of this election, which is obvious for a variety of reasons, is emphasized by the fact that this Turko-Chinese monk, elected head of the Nestorian and Jacobite churches, did not understand the Syriac language of their liturgy and theology. The vicissitudes of his patriarchate, which was quite eventful, are related in the works cited in the preceding note.

[89] *Paradiso*, XII, 118–123. The account of this embassy has been translated by Budge, *op. cit.* For other translations cf. his bibliography.

[90] Cf. *Sinica Franciscana*, Introd., esp. pp. lix ff.

a political solidarity, and therefore contingent and of short duration.

In the Levant the Mohammedans finally prevailed, when, upon Ghazan's conversion, the Mongol dynasty in Persia embraced the religion of Mohammed.[91] In the Orient, Lamaist Buddhism gradually consolidated its strong position at the court of Kublai's successors.[92] However, these dominant religious groups were less violent against the Christians than the Nestorians were against their Catholic and Greek brethren in the empire. Hopes of securing political, courtly, fiscal, and social privileges were always more decisive than doctrinal or denominational ambitions.

All the Catholics admitted at court or protected by the Chinghizide sovereigns had to suffer the resentment, jealousy, and persecution of the native Christians who were opposed to the propaganda of the Franciscan missionaries in China.[93] As a layman, Marco was not directly affected, although even before his arrival in those far-off lands he represented with obvious pride not only his faith, but also that Christian civilization which, even when surrounded by the wonders of the Orient, he considered superior in its doctrines, moral worth, and practical realizations.

When, however, the official collaboration of the various faiths and laws came to an end in 1368 with the collapse of the dynasty and its rule, however nominal, over the whole of Asia, the weak Christian diaspora of Central Asia and the Far East was forced to yield to the pressure exerted by the native religions and na-

[91] Ghazan, formerly a Mongol Buddhist, expelled from Persia the lamas who had arrived there in the wake of the dynasty, but protected the Nestorians while following a coherent policy for the Islamization of his court and the rest of the country. Cf. Grousset, *L'Empire des steppes,* pp. 453 ff., who follows C. d'Ohsson, *Histoire des Mongols,* Vol. IV, pp. 143 ff., where the Oriental sources are faithfully given. Baron von Hammer-Purgstall's vivid account of the events is still of interest, in his *Geschichte der Ilkhane,* 2 vols. in 1, Darmstadt, 1842–43. B. Spuler's *Die Mongolen in Iran,* Leipzig, 1939 (1955), is well informed about the sources, throughout.

[92] Even in these circumstances, as the Franciscan missionaries in China were able to observe, the last Chinghizide rulers were lavish in their favors to the Christian communities while still limiting their prestige. Cf. Moule, *Christians in China,* pp. 216 ff.

[93] Cf. Friar John of Montecorvino's bitter comments on this, *Sinica Franciscana,* Vol. I, pp. 346 f. Elsewhere this antagonism lasted for centuries, as can be seen in L. W. Brown's *The Indian Christians of St. Thomas,* Cambridge, 1956, and R. Almagià's article, "G. B. Britti Cosentino, viaggiatore in Oriente," *Archivio Storico per la Calabria e la Lucania,* Vol. XXV, 1957, pp. 99 ff.

tional tendencies. Hence, when at the end of the XVIth century the first Jesuit missionaries visited these lands, the Christianity of the medieval Orient was but a vague memory.[94]

[94] Cf. P. M. d'Elia, S.J., *Fonti Ricciane*, Vol. II, 1949, esp. pp. 316 ff.; A. C. Moule, *Christians in China*, esp. pp. 7 ff. That Jews and Mohammedans—the latter in large numbers—survived the revolution of 1368, which substituted the Ming for the Chinghizide dynasty and suppressed foreign religions, is perhaps to be explained by the protection which the Mongol dynasty of the Yüan had accorded to Christianity as a religion of national scope, hence abhorrent to the new dominators, who did, on the other hand, tolerate Jews and Saracens on account of their political neutrality, their abstention from all proselytism, and their advanced cultural assimilation into the Chinese system.

seven

THE RELIGIONS OF ASIA IN
MARCO POLO'S BOOK

I. ORIENTAL CHRISTIANITY IN
MARCO POLO'S TIMES

In the course of his travels across Asia, Marco Polo came into contact with various communities of the Christian dispersion which extended from one end of the continent to the other; and he recorded them so conscientiously that his book offers the fullest and most accurate documentation of their expansion in medieval Asia, an expansion that was greatest at the time of the Polos' journeys in the Orient. His account includes not only the sects of ancient Asiatic tradition, but also the churches of Europe to which the political or dynastic unity of the Tartar empire had opened its gates for more than a century.[1]

Small groups of Catholics were already to be found before the arrival of the Franciscan missionaries at the Chinghizide court of Karakorum, where some Hungarian clerics were living, probably as interpreters—"scientes latinum et gallicum," who, together with other Europeans of French, English, and German origin, had been swept far by the Tartar flood that had temporarily

A synopsis of the subject is to be found in J. Witte, *Das Buch des Marco Polo als Quelle für die Religionsgeschichte*, Berlin, 1916, which is well-nigh unobtainable (a copy was placed at the present author's disposal by the University Library at Münster i. W., Germany). The work does not consider Oriental Christianity, and follows almost exclusively Yule's text of 1903.

[1] Cf. A. C. Moule, *Christians in China*, London, 1930, and the articles by P. Pelliot, "Chrétiens d'Asie Centrale et d'Extrême-Orient," *T'oung Pao*, Vol. XV, 1914, pp. 623 ff., and "Les Mongols et la Papauté," *Revue de l'Orient Chrétien*, Vols. XXIII, 1922–23, XXIV, 1924, and XXVIII, 1928; P. Y. Saeki, *Nestorian Documents and Relics in China*, second edition, Tokyo, 1951; and K. S. Latourette, *A History of the Expansion of Christianity*, 7 vols., London, 1937–1945, esp. Vol. II.

submerged central Europe about the year 1240.[2] With the conquest of Georgia and the submission of Russia, with the prudent
and loyal vassalage of the kings of Armenia to the Great Kaan,
the representatives of the national churches of the Eastern rite
established themselves in all the courts of the empire, with functions that were more political than ecclesiastical, though to be
sure they ministered to their fellow believers exiled in those far-
off lands.

None of these churches ventured on a systematic proselytism,
which their very character excluded—to the advantage of Roman
Catholic universalism. Hence, without paying overmuch attention to this particular aspect of Christian expansion in Oriental
Asia, Marco Polo takes note of these national Christian churches
and of the ancient sects of Asiatic tradition which had never met
with success in the West and were completely unknown there
until the time of the Crusades.

First of all, he mentions the Nestorians, the only Christian
sect in Asia to possess an organized ecclesiastical hierarchy and to
enjoy the privileges accorded to a church recognized and protected by the lay and pagan authorities of the Chinghizide empire. He notes their preferred position at the very beginning of
his description of Asia, where he treats of those various regions
of the empire in which the Christian communities were more
compact, and even dominant; Georgia, for example, with its
capital, Tiflis, and numerous castles and hamlets situated among
impassable mountains, inhabited, with a few Saracens and Jews,
by Christians of the national Armenian rite.[3] When he mentions
the kingdom of Mosul, to the south of Greater Armenia, Marco
points out that it is inhabited by Nestorians and Jacobites who
follow, as he says, the religion of Christ, but not in the way prescribed by the Church of Rome, since they err on various points
of doctrine—which, however, he does not specify.[4]

As on other occasions, he is indifferent to the doctrinal aspects
of these sects, whereas he does describe the Nestorians' organization, which is similar to the Roman Catholic inasmuch as they

[2] For the Catholic colony at Karakorum cf. the present author's *Guillaume Boucher,*
pp. 16 ff.
[3] *Il Milione,* cr. ed., pp. 16 f.; M.P., p. 98.
[4] *Il Milione,* cr. ed., pp. 17 f.; M.P., p. 100.

have a patriarch who from his seat at Baghdad appoints archbishops, bishops, abbots, and other ecclesiastical dignitaries, whom
he sends as far as India and Cathay. At this point Marco warns
the reader that all the Christians mentioned in the description of
his travels were either Nestorians or Jacobites. Thereafter, however, from one end of the continent to the other, all the Christian
communities noted by him belonged to the Nestorian church.
It is indeed a fact that all the Turks and Mongols who were converted to the Christian religion from the XIth century onward
and, as a result of the Tartar invasions, were dispersed as far as
the eastern limits of the empire, belonged exclusively to this
church; whereas the Jacobites, who adhered to the Monophysite
belief and took their name from that of their founder, the bishop
of Edessa, left no trace to the east of Persia, where they were
only an exiguous minority even before the Arab invasion in the
VIIth century, which destroyed the dynasty and civilization of
the Sassanids.[5]

On the other hand, in Marco's times, the Nestorian church had
reached the culminating phase of its history under the protection
of the Chinghizide dynasty, which was affiliated to it. Accorded
temporary protection by the Ilkhans in the common struggle
against the Mohammedans of Persia, Mesopotamia, Syria, and
Asia Minor, this Christian renaissance exactly coincided with
Marco's visits in their lands. He crossed Persia twice, in different
directions, in 1272, and a third time, on his way home, in 1294,
respectively at the time of the Ilkhan sovereigns Abaqa (1265-
1282) and Gaikhatu, when, throughout the Levant, a rare truce
prevailed among the national Christian churches under the active
protection of the new and powerful dynasty.[6] In that period all
these territories were restocked with churches and convents,
which had not been allowed to flourish during the long centuries
of Mohammedan rule; and the fervor of a spiritual rebirth gave
to the various sects and communities a final period of expansion,

[5] By ancient tradition the patriarch of the Nestorians also acted as head of the
Jacobite church, under the political and administrative control of the Mohammedan
authorities, who had encouraged or imposed this personal union to the detriment of
the Christian minority in Mesopotamia and Persia. Cf. C. d'Ohsson, *Histoire des
Mongols,* 4 vols., The Hague and Amsterdam, 1834–35, Vol. III, pp. 278 ff. (from
Oriental sources).

[6] For these itineraries see above, chap. i, § 1.

which still shines forth in the history of Oriental Christianity. At
that time, Jaballaha III, who had come to Baghdad from Kublai's
China to testify to the Christian unity of the empire, had just become patriarch of the Nestorians; and the head of the Syrian
Jacobites was the great Abulfaraj, an outstanding philosopher,
theologian, and historian, whose origin is revealed by the name
Bar-Hebraeus whereby he was celebrated throughout the West.[7]

Marco Polo is distinguished from the missionaries who preceded him in Asia by a lack of rancor against these heretics,
schismatics, and heterodox Christians with whom he came into
contact during his stay in the Orient. We need only remember
the violent language employed, for example, by William of
Rubruck in his dealings with the Nestorian prelates of the Chinghizide courts, calling them corrupt, vicious, ignorant, liars, simo-
niacs, and drunkards, to appreciate this attitude which is characteristic of our traveler.[8] Marco not only offers a picture of peaceful
coexistence between the Eastern churches of the Tartar dominion,
but shows us that God works miracles through them also, and
protects all who recognize Him and offer up their prayers to Him
according to their lights.

This attitude was not dictated by Christian solidarity, since—
as is well known—the repression of heterodox sects in the West
was far more violent and bloody than the religious wars against
the pagans; and furthermore, the contemporary history of the
Levant records more than one alliance between Christians and
Saracens against rulers and captains of their own faith.[9] Marco's
benevolent neutrality toward the schismatic and heterodox
churches of the East results from the fact that he, an official and
knight of the Tartar empire, recognized in the Nestorian sect a
national Mongol church, and in the Christians of Cilicia, Syria,
Georgia, and other regions, loyal subjects of the same sovereign.

Such, indeed, they were. The victorious captain, Kitbuka, for

---

[7] Cf. B. Spuler's brief references in *Die Mongolen in Iran*, pp. 198 ff., and R. Grousset,
L'Empire des steppes, pp. 448 ff. For Bar-Hebraeus and the Christian renaissance in
Persia cf. Ugo Monneret de Villard, *Il libro della peregrinazione nelle parti d'Oriente
di Fra Ricoldo da Montecroce*, Rome, 1948. For the Patriarch Jaballaha III (Rabban
Marcos) cf. Sir E. A. Wallis Budge, *The Monks of Kûblâi Khan*, London, 1928, pp.
42 ff., and Moule, *Christians in China*, pp. 94 ff.

[8] *Sinica Franciscana*, Vol. I, pp. 238, 265, and *passim.*

[9] Cf. S. Runciman, *A History of the Crusades*, 3 vols., Cambridge, 1951–1954.

example, who conquered Persia and Syria for the Chinghizide dynasty amid the enthusiasm of the Levantine Christians, was a Naiman Nestorian from Mongolia, even as, at the courts of Tabriz and Peking, some of the sovereigns' wives and most powerful ministers were likewise of Christian origin.[10] Nor could Marco ever forget that he had crossed the Asian continent with a Papal mission, or that he had accompanied from Peking to Tabriz the princess who was destined to become the wife of Arghun, nephew of Kublai and lord of the so-called Tartars of the Levant, who was famous throughout the Christian world for his benevolence toward the faithful of every rite.[11]

Thus, Marco does not mention the advances made by Buddhism at some Mongolian courts when the three brothers of the preceding generation—Hulagu in Persia, Möngke in Mongolia, and Kublai in China—had inclined ever more markedly toward that religion, which had been extinct for centuries in the western regions of the continent.[12] Instead, his description of the dominion of the Ilkhans in the first part of the *Milione* is in the main an anecdotic history of the triumphs of the Christians over their adversaries, a history narrated on a heroic or hagiographical level as "gesta Dei per Tartaros," with little or no comment on their orthodoxy.[13]

Indeed, even as mention of the kingdom of Mosul prompted Marco to describe the organization of the Christian churches of Asia, so, too, when his subject is the city of Baghdad, the ancient seat of the Abbasid caliphate, he improves the opportunity to

[10] Grousset, *op. cit.,* pp. 435 ff.

[11] *Il Milione,* cr. ed., pp. 7 f. and 12 f.; M.P., pp. 81 and 90 f. For the events referred to cf. the next section of the present chapter.

[12] For the expansions and decline of Buddhism in pre-Islamic western Asia cf., apart from the fundamental work by Arthur Christensen, *L'Iran sous les Sassanides,* second edition, Paris and Copenhagen, 1944, the two volumes by A. Foucher, *La Vieille Route de l'Inde de Bactres à Taxila,* Paris, 1942–1944, and B. Spuler, *Iran in früh-islamischer Zeit,* Wiesbaden, 1952; also, Karl Jahn, "Kamālashri: Rashid al-Din's Life and Teachings of Buddha," *Central Asiatic Journal,* Vol. II, 1956, pp. 81 ff. The Buddhist recovery in Persia under the reigns of the first Ilkhans was limited to court circles, inasmuch as the Chinghizide princes, before their Islamization, favored the national religions of Mongolia. This was especially true of the courts at Karakorum and Peking.

[13] Marco discusses in the last chapters of the *Milione* (cr. ed., pp. 222 ff.; M.P., pp. 456 f.) the political history of the Ilkhans, considering the Tartars of the Levant (Persia and Asia Minor) and those of the West (Golden Horde) from the Russian steppes to Great Turkey (Turkestan) and the western borders of Mongolia.

exalt the glory of Hulagu, who destroyed it. He recounts in detail Hulagu's humiliation of Mustassim Billah, the last of the Caliphs, who starved to death when the conqueror bade him "eat his store of treasure."[14] The story is not authentic, but it is used by Marco to illustrate the triumph of the Tartar armies over the inept Saracens, of virtue over avarice, and of divine justice over the wickedness of the infidels, thereby making the Tartars appear to be an instrument of the divine will.[15]

He relates as occurring in the same region a miracle that proved the power of the faith that moves mountains. The Caliph had imposed upon the Christians the alternative of abjuring their faith or of suffering death—unless they should cause a near-by mountain to move. A cobbler renowned for his saintly life thereupon offered up a prayer, the mountain moved, the Christians were saved, and the Caliph and many of the Saracens were converted.[16] Though the hagiographical motif was not rare, we may nevertheless suppose that Marco heard this exemplification of it from Christians in those regions, probably at Tabriz since it seems certain that he never set foot in either Baghdad or Mosul.[17] However, in the form narrated by him the miracle was certainly not occasioned by Catholics but by the heterodox Christians of those parts.

The like also happened at Samarkand. The Saracens of that city wished to recover from the Christians a stone, once theirs, on which now rested the column that supported the roof of the great church dedicated to St. John the Baptist in memory of the

---

[14] *Il Milione*, cr. ed., pp. 18 ff.; M.P., pp. 101 ff.

[15] The last of the Caliphs was killed in the manner reserved by the Mongols for the execution of sovereigns or princes of royal blood. The victim was enveloped in carpets of felt or other material, and then run over by Mongol horsemen at full gallop, or else was tossed one way and another until he was dead. Marco records and explains this barbaric custom on the occasion of the execution of the Christian rebel Nayan (cr. ed., p. 69; M.P., pp. 199 f.).

[16] *Il Milione*, cr. ed., pp. 20 ff.; M.P., pp. 105 ff.

[17] As we have already stated above, from Tabriz the three Polos proceeded directly toward the great caravan center of Kerman, following the route to the Persian Gulf, and in 1294 returned by the same track in reverse, at all times far away from Mesopotamia and Iraq. For the history of the hagiographical legend cf. Yule-Cordier's note, *The Book of Ser Marco Polo*, Vol. I, pp. 73 f. The motif harks back to the legend of St. Patrick (cf. C. Grant Loomis, *White Magic*, Cambridge, Mass., Mediaeval Academy of America, 1949, pp. 89 and 200), and is connected with the numberless miracles that attest to the power of the spirit and of prayer over matter.

baptism of Chagatái, son of Chinghiz Khan and lord of that country.[18] The Great Kaan ordered the return of the stone; the Christians besought divine help; the stone was then found moved; and though the column now rested on air, the church did not collapse.[19] The story of this miracle was also known to the Nestorians of China, and Marco may have heard it from his father and uncle, since he himself never visited Samarkand.[20] It is a characteristic illustration of the unity of this Christian sect, which obviously could lay claim to divine protection as well as that of the emperor of the Tartars and his most powerful vassals and servants.

It might be thought that Marco recounted these edifying stories, which with others were current throughout Christian Asia, because he had nothing else to tell his Western audience about the continent's most famous cities. However, a great part of his description of Persia is also given over to the religious aspects of that land, which was the center for the Asiatic expansion of every faith and the cradle of ancient cults. Indeed, while his description of Azerbaijan concludes with pious mention of the Jacobite monastery of Bar-Sauma, the apostle of the Monophysites,[21] his description of Persia opens with an account of the journey of the Magi which accords with local tradition in the Saveh region, where Marco saw their supposed tomb, preserved in a quadrangular building with a dome of beautiful craftsmanship.[22] The building was not, however, used for Christian worship; hence its origin and significance were not known to the Mohammedan population of that important commercial and cultural center of Persia. In the near-by village of Cala Ataperistan, Marco

[18] *Il Milione,* cr. ed., pp. 40 f.; M.P., pp. 143 f.

[19] For Chagatai's supposed baptism see above, chap. vi, n. 40.

[20] Cf. Moule, *Christians in China,* p. 146. This phenomenon is also known to Western hagiography, as may be seen from the examples offered by Loomis, *op. cit.,* p. 48.

[21] *Il Milione,* cr. ed., p. 23 n.; M.P., p. 105. The "blessed Barsam" of the Ramusian version worked miracles with girdles of consecrated wool, made by the monks of the monastery.

[22] *Il Milione,* cr. ed., p. 24, chap. xxxii; M.P., pp. 114 f. This episode, both evangelical and pagan, was suppressed by Francesco Pipino and was therefore little known in the Middle Ages, evidently because, as the S version of the *Milione* (not found in the cr. ed., *loc. cit.*) asserts, "it is full of the common errors of a people without faith, who add lies upon lies." Cf. M.P., Vol. I, p. 32. It should, however, be remembered that the story is related at length in the vernacular versions of the book and that Marco insists on its veracity.

learned that this temple was venerated by the fire worshipers, who, as a result of the religious syncretism characteristic of the region, ascribed the origin of their cult to the Child Jesus.[23] The account of the Magi and their symbolic exchange of gifts with the Child Jesus is, in this version, one of the most notable contributions offered by the *Milione* to the history of the religions of Asia. It is too complex in its doctrinal and allegorical counterpart to be treated here in detail.[24] For the present it will suffice to note that Marco not only narrated at length a heterodox, and even pagan, version of one of the most popular episodes in the Gospels —a version unknown to Western Christianity,—but also revealed the tenacity of evangelical tradition in a region inhabited, in the main, by orthodox Mohammedans and isolated groups of Zoroastrians. The latter had not taken part in the emigration of the so-called Parsees to India, where they still maintain their ancient rites and customs.[25]

This is the only mention of the Zoroastrian cult to be found in the *Milione*.[26] Indeed, no trace had remained in Central Asia or China of this ancient fire worship, the expansion of which toward the East had moved outward from the religious metropolis of Balkh.[27] Moreover, Marco's reference to it in this account tends to connect it with Jesus rather than Zoroaster. In this he is substantiated, it appears, by some ancient Christian traditions of Central Asia revealed by a Turkish text probably of the XIth

---

[23] For ample bibliography of this subject and the region, cf., besides the older works, which are still fundamental, the list offered by B. Spuler and L. Forrer in *Der Vordere Orient in islamischer Zeit*, 1954, pp. 76 ff.

[24] Cf. Ugo Monneret de Villard's broad critical treatment of the subject in *Le leggende orientali sui Magi evangelici*, Città del Vaticano, 1952 (Studi e Testi, no. 163), and the present author's study, "The Wise Men of the East in Oriental Traditions," in *Semitic and Oriental Studies*, Univ. of California Press, 1951, pp. 375 ff.

[25] A residue of these ancient Zoroastrian communities has remained until our times in this same region. For the history of the rites and communities cf., besides the latest edition of M. N. Dhalla's *History of Zoroastrianism*, New York, 1938, B. M. Tirmidhi's article, "Zoroastrians and Their Fire Temples," *Islamic Culture*, Vol. XXIV, 1950, pp. 271 ff., which does, in fact, consider the fire temples of Marco's age.

[26] For another cult of fire in the *Milione* see § 3 of the present chapter.

[27] Fire worship, together with the other foreign cults, was suppressed in China in the year 845 (cf. P. Y. Saeki, *Nestorian Documents*, p. 475). For the Zoroastrian diaspora in Asia cf. the articles "Madjūs" and "Pārsen" in the *Handwörterbuch des Islam* (with bibliography) and its English edition, as well as scattered information on Central Asia in W. Barthold's *Turkestan Down to the Mongol Conquest*, London, 1928.

century which are very close to the account found in the *Milione.*[28] Although various records, both literary and iconographic, of the cult of the Magi in Christian Asia exist down to Marco's times,[29] this sacred fire had been spiritually and materially extinguished for some time in the rest of Asia.[30]

Hence, of all the pre-Islamic universal religions diffused throughout the continent, there remained only the Christians of the Nestorian sect, whose traces Marco noted wherever he could do so. He would certainly not, we believe, have been capable of discovering among them—as William of Rubruck had done, a generation before him—some residue of the Manichaean doctrines that had captivated the Uigurs of Turkestan and Mongolia at the time of their greatest political expansion.[31] However this may be, Marco never denies to the Nestorians the dignity of Christians, calling them at times by this name, at others specifically by that of their sect. They were never more than a small minority exposed to the influences of their local surroundings, which eventually absorbed them, destroying, as we have seen, all vital traces of their cult.

Though he mentions their churches along his route from one end of Asia to the other, Marco never exaggerates their importance; but he does conceal the fact—sorrowfully remarked by his predecessors—that the Nestorians were now Christians more in name than in deed. This was so far true that William of Rubruck at times did not distinguish between the customs of their clergy and those of the bonzes and lamas.[32] Marco portrays the Christians at Kublai's court as associated in magical practice with the pagans and competing with them in order not to be humiliated

[28] Published by F. W. K. Müller in "Uigurica," *Abhandlungen d. k. Preussischen Akademie der Wissenschaften,* phil.-hist. Klasse, Berlin, 1908. Cf. on the subject Monneret de Villard, *Le leggende orientali sui Magi evangelici,* esp. pp. 71 f.

[29] Cf. G. S. Assemani, *Bibliotheca Orientalis,* Vol. III, Pt. 2, Rome, 1728, p. 500, and J. Bidez et F. Cumont, *Les Mages hellénisés,* 2 vols., Paris, 1938, Vol. I, pp. 117 ff.

[30] For its influence on other cults on the western borders of China cf. Chavannes-Pelliot, "Un traité manichéen retrouvé en Chine" (extract from *Journal Asiatique*), 1912.

[31] Cf. *Sinica Franciscana,* Vol. I, pp. 273 f. and 295; W. W. Rockhill, *The Journey of William of Rubruck,* pp. 150 n. and 231.

[32] *Sinica Franciscana,* Vol. I, pp. 277 ff. and 231 n. 1.

before those in power, if not indeed before God himself,[33] as had already occurred, according to the *Milione,* at the time of Chinghiz Khan, when the Nestorian priests, like the emperor's astrologers, performed similar mysteries with their psalms and spells even to the detriment of their fellow believers.[34] And Friar William tells the same thing of the Nestorian clergy at the court of Mangu Kaan, where every religion acquired prestige and credit by virtue of its magical powers and accomplishments.[35]

It is therefore no wonder that Kublai kept alive this tradition, as is attested by Marco, who saw the Christian astrologers at work at his court, together with their Saracen and pagan colleagues.[36] It would seem, however, that the emperor did not esteem them overmuch, since he declared them to be inept and lacking in control over their familiar spirits and, especially, over his most powerful courtiers.[37] Similar judgments were also expressed on other occasions by Mohammedans and Jews, as the *Milione* reveals with its account of the defeat suffered by Nayan, a Christian Chinghizide prince, who rebelled against Kublai and was severely punished by him.[38]

Marco, as no one else in the West, was aware of the ties that united the dynasty to the Nestorian church. He recorded the conversion of Chagatai, son of Chinghiz Khan and the first, powerful sovereign of Central Asia, the ancient territory of the so-called Karakhitai, which, as we have already observed, was somewhat ambiguously called "the Middle Empire." [39] Moreover, he noted the traditional kinship that united his sovereign with the Christian dynasty of the Öngüt on the western borders of China,

---

[33] *Il Milione,* cr. ed., pp. 51 and 100 n.; M.P., pp. 166 and 252.

[34] *Il Milione,* cr. ed., p. 52, chap. lxvii; M.P., p. 166.

[35] Cf. *Sinica Franciscana,* Vol. I, p. 238.

[36] Cf. *Il Milione,* cr. ed., p. 100 n; M..P., p. 252.

[37] *Il Milione,* cr. ed., p. 70 n.; M.P., pp. 201 f.

[38] *Il Milione,* p. 70; M.P., p. 200. Saracens, idolaters, and Jews mocked the Christians, according to Marco, because the cross displayed by the Christian rebel Nayan did not save him from defeat and death. For these events cf., besides the commentaries of Yule-Cordier and Charignon, O. Franke, *Geschichte der chinesischen Reiches,* Vol. IV, pp. 463 ff., and Vol. V, pp. 233 f.; and, for the Chinese versions, J. A. M. de Moyriac de Mailla, S.J., *Histoire générale de la Chine,* Vol. IX, Paris, 1779, pp. 433 ff., and F. W. Cleaves, "The Biography of Bayan," *Harvard Journal of Asiatic Studies,* Vol. XIX, 1956, pp. 265 ff. (translation from the *Yüan Shih,* with notes).

[39] Marco Polo's "Great Turkey"; see n. 40 to chap. vi above.

which was already known to the Armenian High Constable, Sempad, who visited its capital in 1245, and known too, though vaguely, in Europe, as having issued from the legendary Prester John.[40] Likewise, Marco was also acquainted by direct experience with the history of Christianity in Persia, where this religion was then still favored by the Ilkhans of Chinghizide stock. And, while nourishing some hope of a future fusion of all this princely Christian diaspora within the bosom of the Roman Church, he never fell a prey to the illusions entertained by Louis IX and the papal and regal envoys, who exaggerated its power, numbers, and faith.[41]

The first Christians that Marco came upon as he traversed the interior of the continent were in the town of Kashgar, beyond the Pamir and on the western borders of present-day Chinese Turkestan. They were few in number and of Turkish origin, according to him, and were surrounded by a prevalently Mohammedan population in that immense region of sandy deserts and small urban oases. We may assume that they were Nestorian Uigurs recently arrived in Kashgar, which the Turko-Chinese monk, Rabban Sauma, found depopulated and in ruins soon after our traveler's brief stay there.[42] Even in the ancient metropolitan center of Yarkand, an important emporium in this same territory, the Christians were few, and Marco saw not one in Khotan, the capital, which was so important in the religious history of that immense region.[43]

At "Caracocio" (Karakhodja), on the other hand, the capital of the extreme eastern province of Turkestan (which Marco calls Icoguristan), there were, according to him, numerous Christians

[40] *Il Milione,* cr. ed., pp. 60 f.; M.P., pp. 181 f. For these happenings and legends see chap. ix, § 2, below, on Prester John. For this cf., apart from the literature mentioned in note 2 above, Namio Egami's article, "Découverte d'une 'Église romaine,' établie au XIII° siècle, en Mongolie, par Monte Corvino," in *Conferenze* of the Istituto Italiano per il Medio ed Estremo Oriente, Rome, 1955.

[41] See chap. ii, § 2, of the present work.

[42] Cf. Budge, *The Monks of Kûblâi Khan,* p. 139. Marco must have passed through this important caravan center in Chinese Turkestan in 1274, the same year in which the Turko-Chinese monk left Peking for Jerusalem; hence it would seem that the monk must have visited Kashgar in 1276 at the latest.

[43] *Il Milione,* cr. ed., pp. 40 and 42; M.P., pp. 143 and 147. For this region cf. Sir Aurel Stein, *On Ancient Central-Asian Tracks,* London, 1933, pp. 49 ff. and *passim,* referring to other works by this great explorer, among which is *Ancient Khotan,* 2 vols., Oxford, 1907, with frequent mention of Marco Polo's remarks.

of the Nestorian rite among the "Idolaters," who formed the
majority of the population, larger than the Mohammedan element.[44] However, their tendency to marry with the pagans,
which he reveals, already indicates the decadence and disappearance of an ancient Christian center whose artistic monuments,
discovered half a century ago, still attest to the faith and zeal of
the Nestorians of that region, which was esteemed by the Venetian
for its customs and for the wisdom of its inhabitants.[45]

The reason for this decadence should not be sought for in the
frequency of mixed marriages alone, but rather in the fact that
from the beginning of the XIIIth century the best elements in the
population of that region emigrated to Mongolia and China,
where they became powerful and indispensable servants of the
new Chinghizide emperors. The region around Karakhodja,
which included the commercial, cultural, and religious center of
Turfan, belonged to the Uigurs, a people who distinguished
themselves throughout the Middle Ages among the Turkish tribes
of Asia, owing to the relative superiority of their clergy and the
intensity of their religious interests. Marco Polo notes that even
the "Idolaters" of this region busied themselves unceasingly with
the study of the liberal arts.[46] This had been an accomplishment
of the Christians, who, before making their way to the courts of
the Mongol sovereigns, to become there the most influential
teachers, officials, and military leaders, formed the most highly
developed element in the whole of Upper Asia. Deprived of this
cultural élite, the Uigurs became an easy prey to Lamaist prop-

[44] *Il Milione,* cr. ed., p. 46 n.; M.P., pp. 155 f. "Icoguristan," or Uiguristan, is the
region of Turfan, mentioned only in the Z version of the *Milione.* The correct identification of Caracocio (not to be confused with Carachoto) is to be found in N. M.
Penzer, *The . . . Travels of Marco Polo,* pp. xliii ff., and Sir Aurel Stein, *On Ancient
Central-Asian Tracks,* pp. 256 ff. It should be noted that "Jogoristan" is mentioned,
undoubtedly modeled on a similar version in the *Milione,* in the XVth-century *Mappamondo di Fra Mauro,* ed. Tullia Gasparrini Leporace, with a foreword by Roberto
Almagià, Rome, 1956, plates xxxviii and xxxix. See the geographical index of this
splendid publication.

[45] *Il Milione, loc. cit.*

[46] *Ibid.* For the history and civilization of the Uigur Turks cf., besides E. Bretschneider, *Mediaeval Researches from Eastern Asiatic Sources,* Vol. I, pp. 236 ff., the
numerous writings cited by B. Spuler and L. Forrer, *Der Vordere Orient in islamischer
Zeit,* pp. 92–95. For the evangelization of the Uigurs cf. G. Messina, *Cristianesimo,
Buddhismo, Manicheismo nell'Asia antica,* pp. 63 ff., with a bibliography of the
subject.

aganda, which had taken on fresh vigor in that century and had come into competition with the Christian beliefs in the various courts of the Chinghizide sovereigns.

Only beyond the Gobi Desert, in Chinese territory, did Marco discover dense groups of Christians among the populations of varied stock, language, and faith scattered in the outlying provinces of Cathay. First of all, among the Buddhists of the vast Tangut region, were the usual Turks "who follow the Nestorian law," concentrated in the town of "Saciu" in what is now the Chinese province of Kansu.[47] This town more or less corresponds to the existing village of Tun-huang, near which was discovered, in 1908, the remarkable library that, with the wealth and variety of its records in prose and verse, attests to the intensity of the religious and intellectual life of that distant and isolated region about the year 1000.[48]

Little of it was visible when Marco Polo stayed there, and he tells us that he saw nothing noteworthy in a further ten days of travel in those desolate surroundings, where the sand of the ages covered over the caves which in other times had been transformed into ornate and solemn Buddhist temples.[49] He names a few Christians in the village of Suchow at the end of this stage of his long journey. And as he gradually made his way toward the interior of Cathay, along the wall that follows its western borders, the traces of their presence became ever more marked.

During the next stage, in Kanchow, which he calls Campiciu, (still in present-day Kansu), he saw "three fine large churches" besides the populous monasteries and rich "abbeys" of the "idolaters," which are described by him with a wealth of detail.[50] However, even though the importance of the Christian element in

[47] *Il Milione,* cr. ed., pp. 47 f.; M.P., p. 158. This is the "province of Succiu" of Polo's text, on the western borders of the Chinese empire near its frontier with Sinkiang or Chinese Turkestan.

[48] There is now a vast specialized literature on this artistic, religious, and bibliographic center, for which see H. Franke, *Sinologie,* Bern, 1953, pp. 30 f. and *passim.* For the region cf. Stein, *On Ancient Central-Asian Tracks,* pp. 145 ff., and *passim.*

[49] These are the famous caves of the thousand Buddhas, with their colossal figures and statues, which in Marco's times were closed, hidden, and inaccessible. Mention of them is made by Stein, *op. cit.,* esp. pp. 193–237, and others. See also Irene Vongehr Vincent, *The Sacred Oasis,* Univ. of Chicago Press, 1953, and Basil Gray, *Buddhist Cave Paintings at Tun-huang,* London, 1959 (with photographs by J. B. Vincent).

[50] *Il Milione,* cr. ed., p. 48, with the mention of various types of idols; M.P., pp. 158 f.

these places is sufficiently documented by the three churches, we do not learn anything, either here or elsewhere, about their interiors or exteriors. This information is not even obtainable from other sources; and so, in spite of some noteworthy fragments brought to light by learned explorers, it is difficult to imagine their architectural structure or interior decoration. The latter certainly cannot have been wholly canonical, since the Nestorian rite did not permit this.[51] Indeed, these churches seen by Marco, although beautiful, may perhaps have been lacking in ornaments, as most probably was the one visited by Friar William of Rubruck in the ancient capital of Karakorum.[52]

Hence, drawing ever nearer to the eastern limits of this great desert province of Kansu, where the Yellow River begins its great bend, our traveler finds Christians in all the urban centers of the various small feudal states into which it was divided, and especially in "Erginul," where they seem to have formed the majority of the population.[53] Three more churches at Calachan, the Mongol name for present-day Ning-hsia on the upper bend of the Yellow River, announce the proximity of the Christian kingdom of Tenduc, which was governed by King George in the name of Kublai, his father-in-law.

We shall have to discuss at length on some future occasion the history and fable surrounding this supposed descendant of the legendary Prester John, who, like him, was both king and priest. Here we shall merely record his name among those of the warriors and personages who, like Nayan, rebel and cousin to Kublai, still belonged to the native Christian tradition and represented among the Christians of other sects, come from other parts of the

---

[51] We have two sources of evidence for the decoration of two Christian churches in the Far East: one is William of Rubruck, who speaks of a Nestorian oratory in an imperial encampment in Mongolia, which was adorned with splendid tapestry, the gift of King Louis IX of France to the Emperor Küyük (cf. the present author's *Guillaume Boucher*, pp. 18 ff.); the other is Prince Sempad of Armenia, who saw a representation of the Magi and a portrait of Sorhahtani, Kublai's Christian mother, in a church in the kingdom of Tangut. Cf. Assemani, *Bibliotheca Orientalis*, Vol. III, Pt. 2, p. 500. For ornamental motifs in Nestorian liturgy cf. Saeki, *Nestorian Documents*.
[52] Cf. *Sinica Franciscana*, Vol. I, p. 279.
[53] For Marco Polo's Christian itinerary cf. Moule, *Christians in China*, pp. 128 ff. Erginul (or Erguiul) seems to correspond to present-day Liangchow. The text is to be found in the cr. ed., p. 58; M.P., p. 180.

empire, the last bulwarks of a national faith which was to disappear completely after one last reawakening in Marco Polo's China.[54]

All these Nestorians of the Far East were either Turks or Mongols of the surrounding regions, Uigurs, Öngüt, Keraits, or Naimans. Marco does not mention them again anywhere in Cathay, apart from those in the service of the court who resided in the capital and were clearly distinguished by their beards, as well as by their language and customs, from the natives of the country.[55] They, too, originated from those regions, like the rest of the Nestorians who had immigrated into Yunnan and the other provinces of southern China, where, as Marco asserts, there was "no one who believed in Christ, until the year 1278," when the land was decisively conquered from the Sung.[56]

In fact, this new Christian expansion in those regions followed upon the conquest achieved by Kublai's armies in those years and consolidated by the importation of foreign nationals, who settled there permanently.[57] Some religious fervor and pious zeal must certainly have inspired these new Christian communities, lost among the pagans and Mohammedans, who bore them nothing

[54] For these vicissitudes cf. Moule, *Christians in China*, pp. 216 ff., and Saeki, *Nestorian Documents*, pp. 448 ff. The most compact Christian population of Mongol origin was found in the great bend of the Yellow River in the region of the Ordos. The most recent bibliography of the subject is that offered in J. van Hecken, "Les Réductions catholiques du pays des Ordos," *Neue Zeitschrift für Missionswissenschaft*, Vol. XI, 1955, pp. 105 ff. Louis Hambis ("Deux noms chrétiens chez les Tartars au XIe siècle," *Journal Asiatique*, Vol. CCXLI, 1953, pp. 473 ff.) attempts to prove that Nestorian Christianity had already reached Manchuria in the XIth century, justifying the Christian standard displayed by the rebel Nayan as the ensign of his nation, as Marco relates in the *Milione*, cr. ed., pp. 66 f.; M.P., pp. 193 f.

[55] *Il Milione*, cr. ed., p. 79 n. (Ramusian text); M.P., p. 215. Marco here observes that the native Chinese of Cathay were all clean-shaven, whereas Tartars, Saracens, and Christians all wore beards.

[56] *Il Milione*, cr. ed., p. 141; M.P., p. 322. See also above, chap. vi, n. 86.

[57] Cf. Moule, *Christians in China*, p. 138, n. 17, who refers his readers to some specialized studies on the foreigners in the province that Marco calls Caragian (cr. ed., p. 115; M.P., p. 278). This "province" is in western Yunnan around its chief city of Ta Li. For the name of the region cf. P. Pelliot, "Deux itinéraires de Chine en Inde," *Bulletin de l'École Française d'Extrême-Orient*, Vol. IV, 1904, pp. 158 ff. The sole Christian church at Quinsai (Hangchow) mentioned by Marco (cr. ed., p. 152; M.P., p. 326) and by Odoric of Pordenone (*Sin. Franc.*, Vol. I, p. 465) was of recent foundation, for which see A. C. Moule, *Quinsai, with Other Notes on Marco Polo*, 1957, p. 36.

but hatred while tolerating them only under constraint of the imperial vigilance which forbade open religious conflict, of whatever origin or intention. Marco mentions Mar Sargis, who was the temporary governor of the great city and province of Chinkiang and who built there two churches, which are referred to in the *Milione* as the first in that land.[58]

The Christians who attended them were not many, but they were numerous enough to justify the construction of a Nestorian monastery, the history of which comes to us from other sources.[59] From the little that is known we learn that the monks led there much the same life of meditation and asceticism as that admired by Marco in the Buddhist and Taoist monasteries mentioned by him on several occasions. Evidence of this is offered by the biography of Rabban Sauma, in which we read of the clergy and faithful of those parts who remained inconsolable after he went away accompanied by Rabban Marcos. The two were greeted with enthusiastic devotion by the Christian congregations they found along their route, which took them from one end to the other of the Chinese empire. We also learn that the Nestorian population of the vast region of Tangut described by Marco Polo was everywhere inspired by religious ardor and the ideals of a pure life.[60]

It is certainly difficult to doubt this as one reads Rabban Sauma's pages studded with Biblical quotations and sacred references; and yet, the very presence of the apologetic style invites one to form a more prudent judgment of the value of these and similar expressions of religious enthusiasm, which are lacking in Marco Polo's description of these same regions. It is indeed true that recent discoveries of innumerable metallic crosses strengthen the evidence from Oriental sources, and from the *Milione,* concerning these populations;[61] but we do not know precisely what use was made of them. At the same time, the influence of Buddhist and Taoist doctrines and phraseology is equally clear in the

[58] Cr. ed., p. 141; M.P., p. 322. For the Nestorian Mar Sargis and the Christians of Chinkiang (Marco Polo's Cinghianfu) see Moule, *Christians in China*, pp. 145 ff., and Saeki, *Nestorian Documents*, pp. 511 ff.

[59] Cf. Moule, *loc. cit.*

[60] Cf. Budge, *The Monks of Kúblâi Khan.*

[61] Cf., besides Saeki, *Nestorian Documents,* pp. 423 ff., H. Bernard, S.J., *La Découverte de Nestoriens mongols aux Ordos,* Tientsin, 1935.

Chinese Nestorian texts which have come to light,[62] though these are poor and scant in comparison with the number of books, documents, and monuments of those religions that were preserved in places where the Christian population appears to have been more numerous and important.

The decline and eventual disappearance of the Nestorians were inevitable. Separated from their spiritual and cultural centers in Mesopotamia and Syria, opposed by Christians of other sects, and isolated in small groups divided by impassable mountains, barren deserts, and lands continually ravaged by war, their traditions allowed them to vegetate for centuries without the emergence of any man renowned for piety, ability, or fortune who could save them from swift and total ruin.

Such, too, was the position of the Christians of India, who are mentioned in the *Milione* in connection with the famous sanctuary of St. Thomas the Apostle, near Madras on the Coromandel Coast.[63] The shrine is portrayed as isolated in a small village, remote from everything, but the goal of continual pilgrimages consecrated by ancient and recent miracles. From Marco's references we understand that it was then one of the characteristic Asiatic sanctuaries which, like the supposed tomb of the Magi in Persia, the Manichaean temple at Foochow, Adam's sepulcher in Ceylon, and others not mentioned in the *Milione,* had from time immemorial served the purposes of the various successive cults there, which rose and fell in a tangled mass of traditions, legends, and reciprocal influences now well-nigh impossible to unravel or specify. They are reflected in Marco's data and observations with regard to this dispersed Indo-African Christianity, of which

[62] Cf. Saeki, *Nestorian Documents,* pp. 311 and *passim.* Cr. ed., pp. 181 f. and 187 ff.; M.P., pp. 397 ff. See Yule-Cordier's extensive commentary, *The Book of Ser Marco Polo,* Vol. II, pp. 355 ff.

[63] Cr. ed., pp. 181 ff. and 187 ff.; M.P., pp. 397 ff. A Christian diaspora seems to have existed in India, from the IIId century onward, and Cosmas Indicopleustes already mentions in his *Peregrinatio* (Migne, *Patrologia Graeca,* Vol. LXXXVIII, p. 70) the community described by Marco. He does not, however, mention the apostle, whom the legend—which only came into being in the IXth century—substituted for a merchant with the same name, a benefactor of this isolated Christian center, which remained ecclesiastically autonomous. For the history of this cult and the legend associated with it see L. W. Brown, *The Indian Christians of St. Thomas,* Cambridge, 1956, chap. ii, esp. pp. 56 and 82, with a full bibliography of the subject. Also, Eugène Cardinal Tisserant, "Eastern Christianity in India," Calcutta, 1957 (from the *Dictionnaire de Théologie catholique*).

almost nothing is known from other sources but which is still worthy of study.[64]

The authenticity of St. Thomas' tomb at Mailapur is almost as doubtful as that of Adam in Ceylon. However, while the latter arouses Marco's suspicions because, as he asserts, the Holy Scriptures place it elsewhere, his critical faculties are lulled by the evidence of the miracles that the apostle continued to work in favor of the Christians of that region. He therefore accepted the opinion of the Nestorians of India, who venerated St. Thomas as the patron of Asiatic Christianity, and was unmindful of those numerous fellow believers who, with more legitimate reasons, had set up a whole mythology about his legendary tomb at Edessa.[65]

The first to describe this celebrated Indo-Christian sanctuary and to spread its fame abroad with his book, Marco transformed a place of pilgrimage not very widely important into a center for Christian piety and propaganda, almost a far eastern peer of Santiago de Compostela at the far western limits of the European world, with the difference that the tomb of St. Thomas was guarded by Christians opposed to the Church of Rome. The monks who dwelt near by, according to Marco's account, lived on the coconuts "which the land there freely produces." These religious must have been fairly numerous if, thirty years later, when the cult was already in its decline, Friar Odoric of Pordenone counted some fifteen buildings about the sanctuary. This had in the meantime become a Hindu temple filled with idols, lacking any visible trace of its ancient Christian cult.[66] Friar John of Montecorvino, on the other hand, after having passed some thirteen months in that region almost contemporaneously with Marco's visit, says nothing of the apostle's tomb, and

[64] For this complex subject cf., besides the works cited, R. Hennig, "Das Christentum im Mittelalter," *Historische Vierteljahrsschrift*, Vol. XXIX, 1934, pp. 238 ff., and U. Monneret de Villard, *Le leggende orientali sui Magi evangelici*, pp. 65 ff., 153 ff., 220 ff., with many other references *passim*.

[65] For this cult and its various ramifications cf. Monneret de Villard, *op. cit.*, Brown, *op. cit.*, and B. J. Lamers, "Der Apostel Thomas in Südindien," *Neue Zeitschrift für Missionswissenschaft*, Vol. XIV, 1958, pp. 15–28.

[66] *Sinica Franciscana*, Vol. I, p. 442. Friar Odoric presents the Nestorians of the place as "nequissimi heretici," and it is probably for this reason that he does not add other details to his description of their monasteries and the church of St. Thomas.

mentions the church only in passing, most probably owing to the disgust he felt for the Nestorians, of whom he nevertheless succeeded in baptizing a considerable number according to the rite of the Roman Church.[67]

Marco relates that the saint constantly worked miracles there. One particle of the earth where he lay buried would cure quartan or tertian ague, and other fevers.[68] When Marco took some with him to Venice, it had a beneficial effect on many to whom he administered it. Moreover, we also learn from him of the first attempt known to us to suppress this cult, which was carried out a few years later by the sovereign of that kingdom. Indeed, when the pagan ruler of the region filled with rice the church and monasteries of Mailapur, in order to put an end to the Christian practices of the Nestorian rites, the apostle threateningly appeared to him in a dream and made him so far change his ways as to exempt the faithful from all tribute and to safeguard the church from violation.

This miracle is a rather conventional bit of hagiography, of the sort common to all the Asiatic faiths. It recalls the legendary dream of the Emperor T'ai Tsung who is supposed to have invited the first Mohammedans to settle in China in the VIIth century.[69] Or again, that of Buqu Khan, lord of the Uigurs, who, as the result of a similar apparition, was converted to the Manichaean faith.[70] Marco's account, then, is rather a token of the more or less open religious war at that time being waged even in this region, where, as he himself relates, both Christians and Saracens seemed united in a common resistance against the pagans, who were superior both in numbers and power.

[67] Other curious legends about the church and the cult of the apostle in that place are offered by Friar Giovanni de Marignolli, who is fascinated by extravaganza as well as by miracles, in his *Relatio;* cf. *Sinica Franciscana,* Vol. I, pp. 544 f., and Brown, *op. cit.,* pp. 83 f.

[68] For the hagiographical motif of the curative virtues of earth consecrated by a saint cf. the examples given by Loomis, *White Magic,* pp. 104 f.

[69] Cf. *Encyclopaedia of Islam,* art. "China." This motif is probably modeled on the legend of the Chinese emperor Ming Ti, who, following upon the apparition in a dream of an image of the Buddha, introduced the Buddhistic cult into his empire, *ca.* 63 A.D.

[70] Cf. W. Bang and A. von Gabain in *Sitzungsberichte der Preussischen Akademie der Wissenschaften,* phil.-hist. Klasse, 1929, pp. 411 ff., and a brief note in G. Messina, *Cristianesimo, Buddhismo, Manicheismo* etc., pp. 248 f.

On the other hand, the story of the apostle's martyrdom as
narrated to Marco by the people of the country is far more
original, and is probably of local origin.[71] According to the
ancient, though apocryphal, version of the saint's biography, he
was killed by the lance-thrusts of a legendary king of India whom
he was supposed to have tried to convert to the new Christian
faith.[72] However, we read in the *Milione* that St. Thomas ended
his days as the victim of a hunting accident when the arrow of
a native pagan, aimed at a peacock, pierced the apostle's right
side while he was absorbed in prayer.[73] The explanation of this
strange episode may perhaps be found in Indian mythology,
which is rich in stories of the hunt and symbolic legends of the
peacocks which abound in those regions and are otherwise connected with St. Thomas in Oriental hagiographical legend.[74]

No less noteworthy is the reference to Thomas' apostolate in
Nubia, which, according to information gathered by Marco at
this sanctuary, was supposed to have preceded the saint's sojourn
in Coromandel;[75] this would make Thomas the apostle of India

---

[71] *Il Milione,* cr. ed., pp. 187 ff.; M.P., pp. 397 ff.

[72] For these traditions and legends cf. the literature cited by P. A. van den Wyngaert
in *Sinica Franciscana,* Vol. I, p. 442, n. 2, and by Moule, *Christians in China,* p. 18 n.,
as well as Brown, *The Indian Christians of St. Thomas,* pp. 48 ff.

[73] Cr. ed., p. 188; M.P., p. 398. According to this version, the apostle's death was
supposed to have been accidentally brought about by a people whom Marco calls *gavi*
(cr. ed., pp. 181, 182; see § 3 of the present chapter), perhaps corresponding to the
pariahs of modern India. In his description of Maabar, Marco relates that as a punishment the people of this caste were not permitted to set foot in the church of the
apostle, not even should twenty men attempt to compel the entry of only one (cr. ed.,
p. 182; M. P., p. 388). Thus, St. Thomas was supposed to have been a victim but not
a martyr—which would add further complications to the already tangled mass of
fables concerning his apostolate and his end. Cf. also Moule, *Christians in China,*
pp. 18 ff.

[74] The peacock is common to the region and is associated by Friar Giovanni de
Marignolli with the history of the apostle, who, he tells us, wore a cloak of peacock
feathers (cf. his *Relatio* in *Sin. Franc.,* Vol. I, p. 544). For the Christian symbolism
of the peacock cf. H. Lother, *Der Pfau in der altchristlichen Kunst,* Leipzig, 1929.
For peacock legends in folklore cf. Bächtold-Stäubli, *Handwörterbuch des deutschen
Aberglaubens,* Vol. VI, cols. 1568 ff. The local origin of the legend of the peacock
hunt, with respect to St. Thomas' apostolate in India, is argued by G. M. Rae, *The
Syrian Church in India,* Edinburgh, 1892, pp. 29 ff. For Indian mythology see H.
Zimmer, *Myths and Symbols in Indian Art and Civilization,* New York, 1945 (Bol-
lingen Series, VI), pp. 48 and 72. For the peacock in the religion of the Mandaeans
cf. G. Furlani's article, "Il pavone nella religione dei Mandei," *Rendiconti dell'Istituto
Lombardo di Scienze e Lettere* (Classe di Lettere e Scienze morali e storiche), Vol.
89/90, 1956, pp. 79 ff.

[75] Cf. Ugo Monneret de Villard, *Storia della Nubia Cristiana,* Rome, 1938 (Pon-

and Africa, contrary to the legend that represents him as the evangelist of China.[76] Marco certainly does not perceive any connection between the scattered Christianity of the Indian Ocean and the Nestorian diaspora of Cathay.[77] Instead, he reveals the close ties of faith and rite that unite the Christians of the island of Socotra with the Church of Baghdad and its patriarch,[78] a Christianity which is, according to him, degenerate and desecrated by the barbaric rites and customs of its members. However, he was only acquainted with it from hearsay. It is more than doubtful that he ever set foot on this island, which is nevertheless described at length and with a wealth of colorful detail. But the numerous references to the power and expansion of the Nestorian church which he offers precisely at this juncture reveal the lucid geographical vision that Marco had, not only of the Asiatic continent, but also of the whole of Oriental Christianity observed by him in its various regional aspects.

This probably corresponded to the wishes of Pope Gregory X, who desired to be informed on the matter, even as his predecessors had been by the reports of their missionaries, the first explorers of Christian Asia. Thus, the description of the island of

---

tificio Istituto di Studi Orientali). Marco does not refer to St. Thomas' apostolate in China, although he met numerous Nestorians there. The legend is evidently of later origin, as appears from A. C. Moule's analysis, loc. cit. The apostolate in India, on the other hand, is generally admitted, even though not extended to include Malabar and the region around Madras, by J. N. Farquhar, "The Apostle Thomas in North India," *Bulletin of the John Rylands Library,* Vol. V, 1926, p. 80, and A. Mingana, "The Early Spread of Christianity in India," *ibid.,* pp. 435 ff.; cf. L. W. Brown as cited in note 63 above.

[76] This legend is not referred to by any of the Franciscan missionaries in China. The Oriental ubiquity of St. Thomas' apostolate is explained by the fact that the geographical term "India" included, apart from the subcontinent of this name, the lands washed by the Indian Ocean as far as the China Sea in the east and the Arabian peninsula, Ethiopia, and the African coast in the west. Marco Polo distinguishes Greater India—in his words, "the largest and best that exists" (*Il Milione,* cr. ed., p. 177; M.P., p. 381)—from Lesser India, which included insular Asia from Indochina to Madagascar, and from Middle India, which is Ethiopia or Abyssinia (Abasce); cf. *Il Milione,* cr. ed., pp. 209 f.; M.P., pp. 434 f. For these geographical concepts cf., besides the commentaries already cited, especially Yule-Cordier, *The Book of Ser Marco Polo,* Vol. II, p. 431 n., and John Kirtland Wright, *The Geographical Lore of the Time of the Crusades,* pp. 272 f.; also the literature cited by Monneret de Villard, *Le leggende orientali sui Magi evangelici,* esp. p. 220 n.

[77] Marco did not designate the Nestorians of India by that name, as did the Franciscan missionaries who visited or mentioned those places.

[78] *Il Milione,* cr. ed., pp. 203 ff.; M.P., pp. 425 ff.

Socotra closes the cycle of information on Christian Asia, of
which Marco gave, scanty as it is, the most nearly complete and
reliable picture in all medieval ecclesiastical and lay literature.[79]

2. THE MOHAMMEDANS

Whereas the Christian dispersion in Marco Polo's Asia was made
up of isolated communities that were prevalently of Turkish or
Mongolian origin, the Mohammedans throughout the continent
formed a compact unit which exceeded in numbers, extent, and
vitality every other religious organization in the Orient. From
the moment when Marco went ashore with his father and uncle
at Ayas, in 1271, until their return to Trebizond in 1295, he was
almost constantly in contact with Mohammedans, individually
or in groups, especially in those centers where he tarried longest.

In spite of the Mongol advance as far as the Holy Land, the
Mohammedans were dominant, at least numerically, throughout

[79] *Il Milione* (cr. ed., pp. 209 ff.; M. P., pp. 434 ff.) afterward refers to the three
Christian kingdoms of Ethiopia, a country never visited by Marco, but of which he
gives a description which is as lengthy as it is fanciful, based on the tales of merchants
and seamen, in large part Mohammedans, who sailed the Indian Ocean. Some information about this country, which is called "une terre maldite" in the *Chanson de
Roland* (v. 1916) and is mentioned by Dante on more than one occasion, but was
never referred to by Marco under this classical name, had even reached China (cf.
Chau Ju-kua, ed. and trans. Hirth and Rockhill, St. Petersburg, 1911, pp. 128 ff., and
J. J. L. Duyvendak, *China's Discovery of Africa,* London, 1949). Marco knew that
the population of Abasce, or Abyssinia, was composed of Christians, Mohammedans,
and Jews, but attributed to the first a kind of baptism by fire that left three marks
on the face, made by a red-hot iron, as a sign of nobility and token of good health
(cr. ed., p. 209; M.P., p. 434). For this fable and its history cf. the notes to this
passage in Yule-Cordier, *The Book of Ser Marco Polo,* Vol. II, pp. 432 f. For the
religions of Abyssinia cf., besides the fundamental work by C. Conti Rossini, *Etiopia
e genti d'Etiopia,* Florence, 1937, J. S. Trimingham, *Islam in Ethiopia,* Oxford, 1952, chap.
ii. Finally, Marco also records the Russians as Christians of the Greek rite (cr. ed.,
p. 232; M.P., p. 474). One of the most curious passages in the *Milione* (cr. ed., p 203;
M.P., p. 424) has to do with the fabulous islands called, respectively, Male and
Female, of universal legendary tradition, the populations of which, according to
Marco, were supposed to be baptized Christians but faithful to the customs and
precepts of the Old Testament. This Christianization of the fabled islands, which bore
some relation to the ancient myth of the Amazons, is certainly not of Marco's invention, but is perhaps bound up with the classical and Christian traditions of the island
of Socotra, which was long a Greek colony and was evangelized by Greeks in the
early centuries of the Christian era. Islands with these names may possibly have
existed in the vicinity. Cf., besides Yule-Cordier, Vol. II, pp. 405 f., Chau Ju-kua,
ed. cit., pp. 151 f., and R. Hennig, *Terrae Incognitae,* second edition, Vol. IV, pp.
51 f. A. Herrmann's *Historical and Commercial Atlas of China,* Cambridge, Mass.,
1935 (not always reliable), map 50–51, D 4, places the Male and Female islands off
the southeast coast of the Arabian peninsula.

western Asia and among the Turkish populations of the Golden Horde and Central Asia, right up to the borders of Tibet and China.[1] The effects of Chinghiz Khan's destruction of all the greatest centers of their civilization, and afterward those of the Abbasid caliphate, were fatal to the declining Mohammedan culture of Khwaresm, Persia, and Mesopotamia. There remained, nevertheless, the commercial monopoly enjoyed by the Mohammedan merchants, which throughout the duration of the Chinghizide dynasty was the most powerful instrument of their religious expansion.

In comparison with the volume and extent of this age-old internal and intercontinental trade, organized by the Mohammedans of western and central Asia and developed under Tartar rule, the traffic of the Christians in those regions was almost insignificant in the economic history of the Orient. Moreover, the limited and temporary development of any specialized branch of commercial activity depended on Mohammedan merchants both for the production of the merchandise and the methods of supply and communication. These traders acted as intermediaries and traveled in large convoys along the ancient caravan routes that connected the various centers of their religion.[2]

The commercial preponderance of the Moslems in China depended on the circumstance that Persians and Arabs were expert

[1] W. Barthold, *Turkestan Down to the Mongol Conquest,* London, 1928 ("Gibb Memorial" series, n.s., V) is still fundamental for the Islamization of Central Asia. For the Golden Horde cf. B. Spuler, *Die Goldene Horde,* pp. 219 ff., etc. Friar William of Rubruck, who traveled in 1252 among the Mohammedans of the Volga in so-called Great Bulgaria, asserts that they were markedly fanatical, and asks himself which devil can possibly have carried the law of Mohammed to those regions (*Sinica Franciscana,* Vol. I, p. 212)—a question that is still debated. Cf. Spuler, *loc. cit.* And see also a survey of the early religious, commercial, and cultural Arab expansion through central and eastern Asia by S. A. Huzayyin, *Arabia and the Far East in Graeco-Roman and Irano-Arabian Times,* Cairo, 1942 (with maps and bibliography).

[2] No systematic study exists on the caravan routes of medieval Asia (A. Henning's work, *Wege des Verkehrs,* Leipzig, 1939, is inadequate), but information can be collected from the four volumes of Yule-Cordier, *Cathay and the Way Thither,* second edition, and *The Book of Ser Marco Polo* (their commentary to the *Milione*); from Penzer's Introd. to his edition of Marco's *Travels;* and, besides the writings of the great modern explorers, von Richthofen, Sven Hedin, and Owen Lattimore, from the various works of Sir Aurel Stein, especially *On Ancient Central-Asian Tracks,* 1933, with frequent references to Polo's text. See, too, the classic *Histoire du commerce du Levant* by W. von Heyd, the works dealing with the silk trade (e.g., W. F. Leggett, *The Story of Silk,* New York, 1949), and A. Herrmann, *Historical and Commercial Atlas of China,* Cambridge, Mass., 1935.

sailors in epochs when the Chinese neglected their maritime expansion and commercial intercourse with foreign nations. Moreover, trade could not develop in a Confucian society, in which
it was considered an inferior, almost sordid, activity. The Tartar
rulers held a similar attitude toward merchants and granted a
sort of monopoly to foreigners whom at one and the same time
they despised, exploited, and protected.

An Arabized Persian was the *lingua franca* of the continent,
from the Black Sea to Peking, and the corrupt Arabic of the
seamen and merchants was used for commercial purposes from
the ports of China to the Red Sea, across tropical and insular
Asia, India, and Ethiopia, as far as the Egypt of the Mamelukes.[3]
Marco Polo was able to speak their language, which his father
and uncle had already learned in the markets of the Orient. The
majority of the geographical names occurring in the *Milione*
are those used by the Mohammedans of Persia.[4] We also find
them, with few variants, in older and contemporary accounts by
medieval travelers and geographers.[5] From the VIIth century onward, the Arab advance and Islamic propaganda had won over
one by one all the regions of central Asia, undermining the Nestorian element there, and destroying within the space of two or

---

[3] Cf. H. Cordier, *Addenda to the Book of Ser Marco Polo*, New York, 1920, p. 74.
For further data and examples see G. Ferrand's two volumes, *Relations de Voyages*
etc., Paris, 1913, and the Introd. by Hirth and Rockhill to their edition of Chau
Ju-kua.

[4] For the Mohammedan toponymy of medieval Asia cf. Ferrand, *Relations de Voyages*,
as well as V. Minorsky's commentary to his exemplary edition of *Hudūd al 'Ālam*,
London, 1937 ("Gibb Memorial" series, n.s., XI). It appears that in particular the
names of the towns and regions of southern China referred to by Marco are the same
as, or similar to, those used by contemporary Persian authors (e.g., Rashiduddin)
and by Mohammedan travelers such as Ibn Batuta and others, in part a corruption of
Chinese names, for example Mangi, Pulisanghin, Quinsai, Zaiton, etc.; cf. O. Franke,
Geschichte des chinesischen Reiches, Vol V, pp. 213 ff., as well as the major commentaries. The name of Quinsai derives from the Chinese *Hsing-tsai*, i.e., 'temporary
residence' (cf. A. C. Moule, *Quinsai*, pp. 7 ff.), and refers to the transfer of the old
capital to this southern town during the barbarian domination of northern China. As
for Zaiton (or Zaitun), the name renders the Chinese *Tzu-t'ung* which, according to
Ferrand, *Relations de Voyages*, Vol. I, p. 11, and Vol. II, p. 455 n. 6, should be
pronounced and written *Zītūn;* it has been confused with Arabic *zaytūn*, 'olive.'
Some Turkish and Mongol names used by Marco, such as Khanbaliq for Peking (or
Taidu), Zardandan for Yunnan, and others quite independent of Chinese toponymy,
appear in Persian forms that are found in texts of western Asia.

[5] Cf. Ferrand, *Relations de Voyages*, and the well-known series by M. J. de Goeje,
Bibliotheca Geographorum Arabicorum, in large part without translations.

three centuries every trace of Buddhist expansion in Afghanistan, Sogdiana, Eastern Turkestan, and even in Kashmir, which had become the most active center for its propaganda to the north of the Himalayas.[6]

The wealth and variety of Arabo-Persian geographical literature of the Middle Ages reveals the extent of that knowledge. Marco profited greatly from this, and frequently observed the men and things of Asia through the eyes of his Saracen informants. He collaborated with these subjects and guests of the Great Kaan in the course of his travels throughout the various parts of the empire, where they formed a ubiquitous element. The destructive fury of the Mongol warriors who, in the XIIIth century, had crushed the brilliant Mohammedan civilization of Asia in the havoc of their conquests, had in its turn become an instrument of Islamic expansion precisely in those countries where its propaganda had not until then taken hold.

This paradoxical phenomenon took place in two ways. Even as the Mongols swept countless numbers of nomads from their various tribes and regions into Mohammedan territory, thereby exposing them to a rapid and total process of Islamization, so, too, they transferred entire Mohammedan populations to many parts of Upper Asia, and especially China. These large groups formed a stable though not assimilable element that was added to the fluctuating foreign colonies of merchants, caravaneers, and sailors.[7] So, for example, in the first capital of the Mongol em-

---

[6] Marco Polo already refers to this phenomenon (*Il Milione,* cr. ed., pp. 38 f.; M.P., p. 140).

[7] Examples of the displacement of entire populations in the Mongol period are offered by Rashiduddin in the French translation by E. M. Quatremère, *Histoire des Mongols de la Perse,* Paris, 1836, Vol. I (the only one published), and—a typical and specific instance—by P. Pelliot, "Une ville musulmane dans la Chine du Nord," *Journal Asiatique,* Vol. CCXI, 1927, pp. 266 ff. No exhaustive study yet exists of this phenomenon, which recurred recently with the transference of the Armenians in Asia Minor, and of the Crimean Tartars to Siberia. It should be noted that the people of present-day Azerbaijan, and especially of its urban centers, are still prevalently of Turco-Tartar origin, descendants from the hordes that immigrated there in the XIIth century and later. Nevertheless, Marco Polo does not so specify them in the long list of the various ethnic groups that made up the contemporary population of Tabriz (cf. *Milione,* cr. ed., p. 23; M.P., p. 104), in which town, according to his account, the Mohammedans were especially ill-disposed and treacherous. The versions V and Z, both trustworthy, explain this severe judgment by adding that they "do a great deal of harm to the Christians and all the others who are not of their faith." This attitude of theirs is extended to the whole of Islam, but the special mention made of it

pire, which in Ogudai's times had developed from a simple military camp into the first urban center of that vast country, half the population consisted of recent Mohammedan immigrants, who had been drawn thither by commerce and the various activities which the court and central administration of the empire had suddenly revived amid the steppes and pastures of Mongolia.[8] Similarly, the transference of the capital of the Tartar empire from Karakorum to Peking in 1260 attracted to this center and to other Chinese cities the mass of Mohammedan merchants, artisans, engineers, officials, astrologers, adventurers, soldiers, and slaves who made up the colonies of Islam in the Far East.[9] At the same time, dense groups of Islamized Uigurs penetrated into the western provinces of Sung China, Marco Polo's "Mangi," when the Mongol armies of Mangu and Kublai Kaan, reinforced by

---

with respect to a capital of the Tartars of the Levant is perhaps to be explained by fierce commercial competition between the native Mohammedans and the resident Italian merchants, who formed a rich and influential colony in that city.

[8] The population of Karakorum, the early Mongol capital which Marco described and perhaps visited, had already been mentioned by William of Rubruck half a century before (*Sin. Franc.*, Vol. I, pp. 285 f.) as half Mohammedans, half Chinese, whereas the Mongols lived in their tents or *yurts* outside the walls since they could not adapt themselves to even so modest a form of urban life. Indeed, according to the friar, this capital was inferior to the hamlet of Saint-Denis, near Paris. Cf. P. Pelliot, "Note sur Karakorum," *Journal Asiatique*, Vol. CCVI, 1925, p. 372.

[9] It may indeed be assumed that a large part of the Mohammedan population of Karakorum followed the court into China, where the Great Kaan had his principal seat of power. This fact is clearly asserted (in spite of the doubts of Moule-Pelliot, *Marco Polo: The Description of the World*, Vol. I, p. 161, n. 3) in the reliable Venetian version of the *Milione* (cr. ed., p. 49, chap. lxiv, n.), where it is stated—admittedly in somewhat obscure fashion—that the whole population of the former capital followed the emperor to his new residences (Shangtu or Peking). Karakorum was, in fact, almost exclusively inhabited by foreigners and officials in the service of the court or government. For the Mohammedans employed in the Chinghizide administration cf. E. Bretschneider, *Mediaeval Researches*, Vol. I, esp. pp. 264 ff. The complex and lengthy history of Mohammedan China, from its origins in the VIIIth century to the bloody revolts of the XIXth, and down to our own times, has not received adequate treatment. Cf., besides M. Hartmann's article in the *Encyclopaedia of Islam*, M. Broomhall's study, *Islam in China*, London, 1910, and I. Mason, "How Islam Entered China," *Moslem World*, Vol. XIX, 1929, pp. 249 ff. The annals of the empire (*Yüan Shih*) contain a reliable biographical list of the most important Mohammedan personages at court, in the public administration, and in the army, at the time of Marco Polo. A brief summary is given by Bretschneider, *op. cit.*, pp. 268 ff. For these foreigners, who were mainly Mohammedans, cf. L. Carrington Goodrich, "Westerners and Central Asians in Yüan China," in *Oriente Poliano*, Rome, 1958, pp. 1 ff. For influential Mohammedans in Sung China before the Mongol conquest cf. J. Kuwabara, "On P'u Shou-kêng," *Memoirs of the Research Department of the Tōyō Bunko*, ser. B, No. 2, 1928.

Saracen elements, conquered after 1259 the vast and wealthy province of Yunnan, and founded there the most powerful Mohammedan stronghold in the whole of China—one that has lasted to the present day.[10] In Marco's times they formed the dominant element in the homonymous capital of this province, although the resident viceroy was Essen Timur, Kublai's nephew, who is exalted in the *Milione* as a great and powerful prince possessing both riches and wisdom.[11]

If we also take into account that the maritime towns of China held far older Mohammedan colonies in direct and continuous contact with India, Arabia, and Persia, we may conclude that the whole of that immense land was well-nigh encircled by these foreign colonies which remained for a long time to come, and in all fields of human activity, the sole active intermediary that connected the civilization of China, withdrawn and inaccessible, with the rest of the ancient and medieval world. The whole of Asia was affected, and in large part converted, with the exception of Tibet and Mongolia. There the religion of the Prophet and his followers never succeeded in obtaining a foothold, most probably because the civilization and spiritual organization of Islam was always prevalently urban and therefore alien to the way of life of the nomads, who hated and destroyed all the towns conquered by them from one end to the other of Mohammedan Asia. The absolute, fanatical monotheism of Islam was, moreover, incompatible with the crude animism and paganism of all the native religions of Upper Asia and the Far East. Marco was, at least on one occasion, quite conscious of this fundamental Mohammedan urbanism; when he visited the island of Sumatra he made a clear distinction between the population of the capital of the kingdom of Ferlec, which had been Islamized by the

---

[10] Cf. Yule-Cordier, *The Book of Ser Marco Polo*, Vol. II, pp. 104 ff., and, for a rapid survey of the main events, R. Grousset, *L'Empire des steppes*, pp. 349 ff. For a more detailed exposition see O. Franke, *Geschichte des chinesischen Reiches*, Vol. IV, pp. 316 ff., 434 ff., and *passim*.

[11] Cr. ed., p. 115, and M.P., p. 276, where Essen Timur is described as Kublai's son. Cf. the note by E. H. Parker in Cordier's *Addenda*, pp. 68 f., and L. Foscolo Benedetto, *Il libro di Messer Marco Polo*, p. 443. The most famous warrior and dignitary of the region was Nasreddin, who was descended from a family of Bokhara in Turkestan, which gave a number of administrative experts to the Chinghizide dynasty. Marco refers to him, *loc. cit.*, as a great soldier and expert captain, without, however, specifying that he was a Mohammedan.

numerous merchants trading there, and the barbarians who inhabited the surrounding countryside.[12]

It was as a result of this characteristic tradition that Islam never
became a national faith in Mongolia, like Nestorian Christianity,
and never introduced there that fanatical proselytism which won
over the urbanized Turks of Central Asia, the Altaic tribes of the
Golden Horde, and a part of the peoples of India. Tibet and
Mongolia are therefore, in the *Milione,* the only regions in the
whole continent where Saracens do not appear. It was not difficult for Marco to make them out in the other parts of Asia, not
only because of the familiarity he had acquired with this characteristic Oriental element, but also because in China they were
grouped together in autonomous organizations dating from the
time of their first appearance, in the T'ang era, at the country's
maritime centers, where they still abound today.[13]

This segregation made them doctrinally impenetrable and im-
mune to the influences of their surroundings, which sooner or
later overcame the groups of Christians, Jews, and folk of other
faiths.[14] The Chinese knew them as a people who, by refusing to
eat pork, physically and symbolically deprived themselves of the
country's national food.[15] For Marco, they were simply the worshipers of Mohammed. This conception reveals his abysmal ignorance of the most elementary principles of this religion—an
attitude which at first sight seems incomprehensible, when we
consider that he came into contact with Saracens of every sort in
the course of his travels in Asia, and was familiar with their
language and customs.[16]

The mystery is somewhat lessened if we remember how little

---

[12] *Il Milione,* cr. ed., p. 171; M.P., p. 371.

[13] See above, note 1. For Islam in India cf. *Cambridge History of India,* Vol. III,
1928 ("Turks and Afghans," by Sir Wolseley Haig); also, M. T. Titus, *Indian Islam,*
London, 1930, and the various reviews dedicated to the Mohammedans of India and
present-day Pakistan.

[14] For the Mohammedan cult there does not appear to have been in Marco's times
a special government commission corresponding to the *Ch'ung fu ssu* for the Christians
and *Chi hsien yüan* for the Buddhists, although the Saracens of the empire were more
numerous than the Nestorians. The autonomy of the powerful Mohammedan groups
in present-day Kansu is a characteristic phenomenon of recent Chinese history. In
the course of centuries, many Chinese in the outlying provinces were converted to
Islam and followed the fate of their communities in the various rebellions against the
central power.

[15] Cf. P. Y. Saeki, *The Nestorian Documents and Relics in China,* 1951, pp. 448 ff.

[16] Cf. the present author's *Storia letteraria delle scoperte geografiche,* pp. 183 ff. It

was known about this people by other Christians who had lived for a long time in that environment.[17] Even the learned compiler of a history of the Orient, Jacques de Vitry, after having lived for many years in the Levant as Bishop of Acre, asserts, together with many other crude fables, that "Machomet est deus et Calyphas est Papa,"[18] while the most serious contemporary student of Islam—the same Friar William of Tripoli who was chosen by the newly elected Pope Gregory X to accompany the Polos as far as China—gives utterance to comments and judgments that reveal a hardly less superficial knowledge of the most obvious and fundamental doctrines of Islam.[19]

However, these and other learned medieval Catholic writers only mention this faith in their historical and didactic writings in order to combat it, without taking pains to understand it; whereas, the curiosity that enlivens the pages of Marco Polo's book is sometimes halted before the impenetrable mystery of heterodox doctrines. The general feeling toward Islam was that to study and understand it was much the same as to accept it. The medieval attitude is best characterized in a verse from the *Chanson de Roland,* "Paiens unt tort et Crestiens unt dreit"— Paynims are wrong and Christians are right.[20]

Marco had been accustomed to this erroneous judgment by popular opinion, which was reflected and diffused by the whole of medieval epic literature. This represented Mohammed, with

should be noted that the famous Moorish traveler, Ibn Jubair of Valencia (Spain), when describing the island of Sicily, visited by him in 1184–85, repeatedly refers to its Catholic Norman kings as "polytheists," and this in spite of close contacts with Christian civilization and the fact that he was a man of outstanding culture and experience. Cf. *The Travels of Ibn Jubair,* trans. R. J. C. Broadhurst, London, 1952, pp. 341 and 349.

[17] Cf. Ugo Monneret de Villard, *Lo studio dell'Islàm in Europa nel XII e nel XIII secolo,* Città del Vaticano, 1944 (Studi e Testi, no. 110), esp. pp. 59 ff.

[18] *Ibid.,* p. 61.

[19] Cf. the text published by H. Prutz, *Kulturgeschichte der Kreuzzüge,* Berlin, 1883, pp. 575 f. Ricoldo of Montecroce's *Libro della peregrinazione nelle parti d'Oriente* has the same shortcomings and does not represent any advance on William of Tripoli's work. See Monneret de Villard, *Il libro della peregrinazione,* Rome, Istituto Storico Domenicano, 1948. For biographical data on Ricoldo cf. Stefano Orlandi, *Necrologio di Santa Maria Novella,* 2 vols., Florence, 1955, Vol. I, pp. 308 ff.

[20] V. 1015. This verse is paraphrased in the *Milione* (cr. ed., p. 224, chap. ccvi, lines 21 f.; M.P., p. 460), where it is perhaps the work of Rustichello, who was familiar with this medieval epic phraseology. It refers to the struggle between the Ilkhan Arghun—the pro-Christian ruler of Persia—and his Saracen rival Acomat (or Achmed), who was quite naturally worsted after an apparent victory.

the Apollo of the ancients and the mysterious Tervagant, as a member of a triad of idols, opposed to the Holy Trinity. To be sure, the unholy triad belonged entirely and exclusively to the kingdom of fables and poetic fancy,[21] but the belief was nonetheless potent. Moreover, the hatred the popular tales inspired, with their evocation of imaginary Christian triumphs over the Saracens, had so fixed itself in Marco's mind that it altered his vision of a most obvious reality and the result of his long experience of the men and things of Islam.

These sentiments were further nourished by the instinctive aversion entertained by the Mongols for this sect, which in Marco's times was as useful to them as it was dangerous.[22] He does, in fact, mention them more than once, after having established at the very beginning of his description of Asia "that all the Saracens in the world feel a great hatred for all the Christians," and that, since they are everywhere treacherous and disloyal, they persecute whomsoever is not of their faith, and especially Christians. They do this all the more readily because, according to him, the facile absolution they receive from their "priest" at the end of their life favors all their iniquities and encourages the conversion of the "Tartars" and other peoples to their faith.[23]

This is one of the rare references in the *Milione* to the practices of the Mohammedan religion, as if their profession of faith actually sufficed to redeem them from all sin. It is, of course, possible to believe that the simple, picturesque Mohammedan eschatology contributed to the success of their propaganda, even as it seems certain that the popularity of Buddhism in China was helped by the mirages of a better life which the mythology of the Great Vessel (*Mahāyāna*) promised to the faithful.[24]

---

[21] On Tervagant, which Marco Polo never mentioned, cf. the present author's essay in *Rendiconti dell'Accademia Nazionale dei Lincei,* Classe di Scienze morali, ser. VIII, Vol. XIV, 1959, pp. 202–215. For Western legends of Mohammed cf. Alessandro d'Ancona, "La leggenda di Maometto in Occidente," *Giornale Storico della Letteratura Italiana,* Vol. XIII, 1880, pp. 199–281, and A. Mancini, "Per lo studio della leggenda di Maometto in Occidente," *Rendiconti della R. Accademia dei Lincei,* Classe di Scienze morali, ser. VI, Vol. X, fasc. 5–10, 1934.

[22] See above, chap. vi.

[23] *Il Milione,* cr. ed., p. 23 n.; M.P., p. 112.

[24] Cf. E. Chavannes, *Cinq cents contes et apologues extraits du Tripitaka chinois,* 4 vols., Paris, 1910–1934, Vol. I, Introd. For Mohammedan casuistry cf. the *Handwörterbuch des Islam,* pp. 307 ff.

It is indeed likely that this promise of eternal life attracted the rude Tartars who had settled in Persia and Russia, as well as the Turks of Central Asia, and lent more efficacious support to the religious propaganda than the complex Mohammedan theology, which, like that of strict Buddhistic philosophy, was only accessible to the elect who dedicated themselves to studying and meditating upon these mysteries. Nothing new or great, however, and no original contribution to Islamic civilization, resulted from this tardy conversion of Turks and "Tartars," who seem to have been unacquainted with Islam's most outstanding monuments and successful doctrines.[25] Marco, therefore, was right in speaking of those barbarians as a people of superficial culture whose sole preoccupation was to survive in an afterlife that gave the illusion of salvation. In fact, this essentially Christian concept was undoubtedly foreign to their religious sentiments and was materialized only in the crude, spectacular, and sensual eschatology of the Koran and the *Miraj,* which substituted and realized for them, in a transcendent reality, the vain search for a magical longevity that should know no ending.[26]

This was the concept and aspiration that had always drawn Turks, Tartars, and Chinese toward acceptance of an animistic cult of natural forces—an animism which betrayed them, both as a religion and as a science. It is noteworthy that when Chinghiz Khan asked the great Taoist sage Ch'ang Ch'un for the drug of immortality which the alchemy of the pagans promised to their credulous sects, this honest teacher denied both its existence and its effect, thereby arousing in the bloodthirsty emperor the admiration his candor deserved.[27]

[25] No record of Islamic art or literature has been found in the archaeological discoveries in the marginal regions of western China, amid the numberless documents and relics of Buddhistic, Christian, Manichaean, and other civilizations unearthed in the present century. The Turks and Afghans had developed, as is known, a magnificent Mohammedan civilization in India, and stimulated its rebirth in Central Asia in the Timurid era (XIVth century).

[26] For this Mohammedan eschatology, which has been so much discussed on account of its supposed relationship with Dante, cf. E. Cerulli, *Il Libro della Scala e la questione delle fonti arabo-spagnuole della Divina Commedia,* Città del Vaticano, 1949, (Studi e Testi, no. 150). For the possible influence of this eschatology on Chinese literature cf. J. J. L. Duyvendak, "A Chinese 'Divina Commedia,'" *T'oung Pao,* Vol. XLI, 1952, pp 255 ff.

[27] Cf. A. Waley, *The Travels of an Alchemist,* London, 1931, p. 101.

For his skeptical or ignorant barbarian subjects, however, the promise of eternal salvation offered them by Mohammedan propaganda lent seeming assurance of posthumous life, a metaphysical mirage which satisfied to the full their religious sentiments and their faith in an easily acquired bliss. This, at least, was Marco's opinion, and we must believe that with this expedient the Mohammedan missionaries readily induced the barbarians to accept the Prophet's law.[28]

Thus, too, the hatred of the Saracens for the Christians is, for Marco, sufficient reason to explain the attempts to exterminate them and the tricks thought up by some Saracen chieftains in order to humiliate and harm them, as at Baghdad and Samarkand, where the Christians were in the minority and therefore more exposed to persecution.[29] It was to this same feeling, and not to a desire for conquest, that Marco attributed the Sultan of Yemen's attack against the town of Acre, which, in 1291, led to the Egyptian conquest of this ancient Christian outpost in the Levant.[30] This situation, indeed, has renewed itself repeatedly down to the present day, when psychological and political factors, rather than territorial or economic interests, succeed in uniting the discordant nations and tribes of the Mohammedan East beneath the banner of the Prophet.

This feeling is extended by Marco to his judgment of the attitude of the Saracens toward other faiths. Hence, his explanation for the malversations and crimes of Achmet, Kublai's Mohammedan finance minister, is that Achmet's "accursed sect" allows its faithful to kill whomsoever is not of their beliefs and, without sin, to injure those who oppose them. For Marco, the misdeeds and extortionate abuses of all kinds that incited the Chinese to rebel against this bloodthirsty and vicious exploiter of their homeland are an expression of Saracen hatred for the infidels and a characteristic trait of the "accursed doctrine" that inspired it in all times and places.[31] Marco therefore sees the hand

[28] On the other hand, Mohammedan propaganda met with little success in China, where the fundamental dualism of the native religions made the cult of Allah incomprehensible; and it was considered even more repugnant for its practice of circumcision and its dietetic precepts.

[29] See § 1 of the present chapter.

[30] *Il Milione*, cr. ed., p. 213; M.P., p. 441.

[31] *Il Milione*, cr. ed., p. 80; M.P., p. 216. The same observation is made by Marco with respect to the Saracens of Persia: cr. ed., p. 23; M.P., p. 105.

of God in the fate of this infamous tyrant and betrayer of his sovereign's trust, who was killed by Chinese in rebellion against his crushing severities; it is the only time that Marco expresses any sympathy, admiration, or pity for the Chinese who struck back at Chinghizide domination and paid dearly for the attempt to free themselves from this Mohammedan overlord's oppression.[32]

Marco, who had been an eyewitness to these events, had understood that hatred of the infidel cemented the unity of the Mohammedan world, which otherwise was at that time even more divided and troubled than it is now. Indeed, in the Z version of the *Milione* we read that "those peoples were then without unified rule and were discordant in mind and will," as if he wished to contrast with the characteristic division of the Mohammedan peoples the unity, however precarious, of the Chinghizide empire.[33] But whereas that unity was maintained, in any degree, apparently as a result of the Mongol sovereigns' religious tolerance, it was precisely the traditional fanaticism of the followers of the Prophet that guaranteed the cohesion of the Mohammedan peoples against both Christians and pagans.

However, Marco had only a vague, limited knowledge of the numerous sects that divided Islam at that time. There is no trace in his book of the intense antagonism between Sunnite orthodoxy and the schismatic Shi'ites, either because he was never interested in the spiritual background of Asiatic religions, or because Mohammedan expansion in the Far East was accomplished mainly by traditional orthodox elements lacking in theological conflicts and doctrinal preoccupations.[34] Thus, on the only oc-

---

[32] For the events connected with this revolt, which Marco witnessed in part, cf. O. Franke, *Geschichte des chinesischen Reiches,* Vol. V, pp. 237 f. and 244 f.

[33] Cr. ed., p. 34; M.P., p. 132.

[34] It does not appear that the Mohammedan rulers and peoples of the Chinghizide empire accepted or protected Shi'ite doctrines or other mystical teachings that were still active at the time of the Mongol invasions in the East and West. Berke Khan in the Golden Horde, Ghazan Khan in Persia, and their successors, down to Tamerlane and beyond, all remained faithful to the practical norms of the tradition which, with the Koranic name *Sunna,* was derived from Mohammed himself and his dogmatic interpreters, and which is the only one known to Marco as the "Saracen law." For a brief survey and bibliography of the Mohammedan sects of that time see the relevant articles in the *Handwörterbuch des Islam,* as well as B. Spuler, "Geschichte der islamischen Länder," *Handbuch der Orientalistik,* Vol. VI, 1952, and the same author's work (in collaboration with L. Forrer) *Der Vordere Orient in islamischer Zeit,* 1954, esp. pp. 27 ff.

casion that he expressly mentions a sect heretical "according to
the Saracen law," that is, when he treats of the Assassins of Persia,
Marco sides against them, presenting them rather as a criminal
association than as a political and religious order.[35] It was thus
that he was able to justify their extermination by Hulagu,
Kublai's brother and the scourge of Islam, accepting without
further inquiry the version of the acts of the Assassins given by
their orthodox victims of the region.[36]

This episode will be considered separately, as one of the most
complex and noteworthy manifestations of the Mohammedan
civilization described by Marco Polo. However, the references
to the orthodox beliefs and practices of the Saracens scattered
throughout the *Milione* give us an idea of his acquaintance with
them and with his readers' interests. Generally speaking, our
author mentions concrete aspects rather than the moral precepts
of that law, and especially those which have always aroused the
curiosity of Christians and still today form the center of popular
interest in this religion. First and foremost is Mohammed's
tantalizing Paradise, abhorred and perhaps envied in the West,
since the Prophet, as Marco asserts, "made the Saracens believe
that those who go to Paradise will have beautiful women at will,
and will find there rivers of wine, milk, honey, and water,"
exactly following that which the Prophet had taught and which
Mohammedan theology had accepted and interpreted in the
spirit and according to the letter of the Koran.[37]

As far as wine is concerned, Marco knows that it is theoretically
forbidden to the followers of the Prophet, but he affirms that it is
possible to boil it and make it sweeter, and then to drink one's
fill without violating the law that forbids it.[38] This is correct and

---

[35] This is the famous sect of the Assassins, whose Persian territory in Mazandaran is
designated by Marco with the name *Muleete* (*Il Milione*, cr. ed., p. 32, chap. xli;
M.P., p. 128), which does, in fact, mean 'heretics' or 'impious,' and had already been
used by William of Rubruck (*Sin. Franc.*, Vol. I, pp. 210 and 277) and, as he himself
affirms, was commonly used by the Mohammedans of that region. The subject will be
treated at greater length in chap. ix, § 1.

[36] As is well known, the description Marco gives of the practices of this sect is the
most detailed to be found in any Western Christian or Mohammedan text, although
they had already been known for some time past.

[37] Sura XLVII, 14 ff. For the theological discussions and further details cf. *Handwörterbuch des Islam*, art. "Djanna," etc.

[38] *Il Milione*, cr. ed., p. 26 n. (version Z and Ramusian); M.P., pp. 117 f.

corresponds to the observations on the subject to be found in Mohammedan literature.[39] As for the loophole offered by this religious casuistry, it may be taken to refer to the more orthodox groups, since the prohibition of wine has never been applied with severity in Persia, as we learn from its most celebrated poets and as appears from the practices of the sects that did not recognize it.[40] Indeed, the current interpretation of the Koranic precepts tolerated the moderate use of wine, and was mainly opposed to drunkenness.

Marco was acquainted with other famous Islamic usages and precepts. First of all, polygamy, which, according to him, the Saracens had in common with the "idolaters," and which allowed them to take as many as ten wives and to beget "an infinite number of children."[41] This phenomenon gives him the opportunity to make a noteworthy demographic observation, which still holds good in certain respects. He compares the relative scarcity of population in the West with the high birth rate in the Orient, which allowed the sovereign to have vast armies and to employ innumerable persons in his service and that of his subjects without affecting the general condition of the country or the organization of the state.[42] There is no doubt that the resistance and importance of the Mohammedan element in China from those times until the present are certainly not due to any special intellectual or moral qualities on the part of this strong minority, but rather

[39] For this subject cf. *Handwörterbuch des Islam*, art. "Khamr," p. 300, and "Nabīdh," p. 563.

[40] Sufficient proof of this is to be found in the *Rubáiyat* of Omar Khayyám and the works of the poet Hafiz. It should be noted that, according to various statements of the Persian historian Mirkhond, or Mirkhwand (cf. *Notes et Extraits des Manuscrits de la Bibliothèque Impériale*, Vol. IX, 1813), spectacular bacchanalian revels were sometimes held at the abode of the Old Man of the Mountain, where at other times the most severe asceticism was observed. William of Tripoli, Marco Polo's temporary companion, observed the like in Egypt (cf. *De Statu Sarracenorum*, in Prutz, as cited in note 19 above, chap. xxi, p. 528). The different varieties of wine produced and used by the Arabs and accepted by the casuistry of their faith are listed by Marco, who distinguishes wines made from sugar, rice, and dates ("very good," according to him), as well as the much rarer ones, made from grapes (cf. *Il Milione*, cr. ed., Index, "Vino," and Yule-Cordier, *The Book of Ser Marco Polo*, Vol. II, Index, "Wine."

[41] *Il Milione*, cr. ed., p. 95 n. (Ramusian text); M.P., p. 244.

[42] For Chinese polygamy, to which Marco alludes in the passage cited, cf. M. Granet's extensive study, *Études sociologiques sur la Chine*, Paris, 1953. For polygamy in more recent times cf. E. T. Williams, *China Yesterday and Today*, 2 vols., third edition, New York, 1932, and Pierre Hoang, *Le Mariage chinois au point de vue légal*, Shanghai, 1898 (*Variétés Sinologiques*, no. 14).

to their numbers and vitality, limited, as is well known, mainly
by infant mortality, which throughout the whole of Asia and the
rest of the Mohammedan world assumes proportions that are
inconceivable to us.

Marco was also acquainted with practices of ritual slaughter,
often distasteful to both Christians and pagans alike.[43] Chinghiz
Khan, indeed, prohibited these rites, and Kublai imitated him
half a century later when the refusal of some Mohammedan merchants to accept certain dishes he offered them aroused the emperor's wrath against the whole of that sect, which had already
incurred his disapproval for other reasons. For a number of
years the Mohammedans residing in the empire were obliged,
according to Marco, to slit the animals' bellies in the Tartar way
instead of cutting their throats as the Semites did.[44] The Buddhists
and Taoists were both more consistent and more radical in this
matter since they forbade the eating of animal flesh, or at least,
as Marco tells, the slaughter of animals for food. We read in
the *Milione* that when the Buddhists of Kashmir or the Brahmans
of India wished to evade this prohibition and "feed upon sheep
or other beasts, or birds," they would employ the services of the
Saracens or others who did not follow their rites and customs,
without too nice an examination of the methods of slaughter
used.[45]

For the Tartar emperors, the ritual slaughter practiced by the
Mohammedans was not a matter of either religion or sentiment,
but rather a foreign custom and therefore despicable and illegal.
Hence, at Kublai's order it was replaced by the Tartar method,
which was certainly no less cruel, and no less ritualistic, than the
Saracen. We also know from other sources that the emperor
might never have paid attention to the question if the Mohammedans' religious adversaries had not found in it a pretext to
incite him against these powerful competitors at his court and in
the state administration.

[43] For the system of slaughter prescribed for the Tartars in the ordinances of the
empire (*Yassaq*) cf. C. d'Ohsson, *Histoire des Mongols*, Vol. I, p. 94, and Vol. II, p.
410, and B. Ya. Vladimirtsov, *The Life of Chingis-Khan*, pp. 74 ff.

[44] *Il Milione*, cr. ed., p. 80 n. (Ramusian text) and p. 181; M.P., pp. 216 and 388.
For Mohammedan dietetic practices cf. the *Handwörterbuch des Islam*, art. "Maita."

[45] *Il Milione*, cr. ed., p. 39 n. (Ramusian text) and p. 182; M.P., pp. 140 and 389.

However, Marco says nothing of the numerous representatives of Islamic culture gathered about the imperial throne, among whom were to be found experts in science, medicine, practical mechanics, and the art of war. As he watched them at work, his thoughts may well have turned with rancor toward those hundred Christians versed in the seven liberal arts whom Kublai had requested from the Pope through his father and uncle, and for whom, as a young man, Marco had become by force of circumstances a substitute.[46] His is an eloquent silence, then, as eloquent as the reference to the "accursed sect," inspired by the wrongdoing of its most influential follower at the court of Kublai Kaan.

All this is typical of how his account is affected when the mutual hatred between Christians and Saracens flares up in our author's staid prose. Moreover, in order to give vent to these feelings and attune his "description of the world" to those of his contemporaries, he narrates at length and in the epic forms dear to Rustichello, his scribe, the struggle that began in 1288 between the Christian king of Abyssinia and the Saracen sultan of Yemen.[47] Marco called this story a "fine" one, although it is not authenticated either by the Ethiopian chronicles or by the geographical data. It tells how an Abyssinian bishop who had set out on a pilgrimage to the Holy Sepulcher was forcibly circumcised by the hirelings of the Sultan of Aden, because he refused to adhere to the law of Mohammed.[48] As was only to be expected, the Christian king declared war upon this enemy of his faith and defeated him, together with two other sultans who had hastened to the aid of their fellow believer, invading their territories in order to destroy them and slaughter a vast number of Saracens, the whole incident conforming to the ideal scheme of the *chansons de geste* and according with the spirit of the

[46] *Il Milione*, cr. ed., p. 6; M.P., p. 78.

[47] Cr. ed., pp. 210 ff.; M.P., pp. 436 ff.

[48] As has already been observed by Yule-Cordier, *The Book of Ser Marco Polo*, Vol. II, pp. 431 f., Marco's geographical vision of these regions is somewhat confused. Hence it is not clear whether these events took place in Ethiopia, Somaliland, or Arabia, countries never visited by him and which were then well-nigh inaccessible. The story may perhaps reflect some legend concerning the frequent Ethiopian pilgrimages to Jerusalem (for which see E. Cerulli, *Gli Etiopi in Palestina: Storia della comunità etiopica di Gerusalemme*, 2 vols., Rome, 1947–48), such as that undertaken by Negus Yāgbe'a Ṣyōn in 1290, to which Marco possibly refers (cf. J. S. Trimingham, *Islam in Ethiopia*, Oxford, 1952, p. 69 n.).

times. The outcome of this legendary struggle, so different from those actually fought in the Levant at that time, could not be otherwise either in fable or in poetry, for the simple reason that, according to Marco, "the Christians are worth far more than the Saracens," and it is not just, as he adds, that these "Saracen dogs" should get the better of the Christians.[49]

This is not only a judgment with which Marco concludes the fabulous episode in the *Milione;* it is also a view held after twenty-five years of continuous contacts with the Mohammedan world in every part of the Asian continent. It is therefore small wonder that he portrays the wars between the various branches of the Chinghizide dynasty as religious struggles, with the obvious intention of discrediting the Mohammedan peoples and conferring fresh glory on those who combat them in every quarter of the known world. Nevertheless, the victors are not Christians, but Tartars who had remained faithful to the traditions of their race, striving against other Tartars who had adapted themselves to the Mohammedan environment and had accepted its customs and faith.

Marco thus interprets the complex and turbulent vicissitudes of the two branches of the Chinghizide dynasty which between them had taken over the whole of western Asia: the one, with the name of Qipchak, called Golden Horde, extending from the Ukraine to Mongolia, and rapidly converted to Islam from the year 1257 onward;[50] the other, including Persia and Asia Minor, politically oriented toward the Christian world and, until the end of the century, denominationally neutral according to Tartar tradition, and so well described by Marco at the beginning of his description of those lands.[51]

Hence, the long and bloody war between these Tartars whom Marco designates as those of the Levant and the others from the West is for him but another episode in the age-old struggle be-

---

[49] *Il Milione,* cr. ed., pp. 210 f. See also a similar expression on p. 224, with regard to Achmed, who rebelled against Arghun, the Ilkhan of Persia. M.P., pp. 459 f.

[50] Cf. the works of d'Ohsson, Howorth, Spuler, and Grousset, already cited, and, though it is somewhat dated, the *Geschichte der Goldenen Horde im Kiptschack* by J. von Hammer-Purgstall, Budapest, 1840.

[51] Cr. ed., p. 14 n.; M.P., p. 96.

tween Christians and Mohammedans in the Orient, in which the latter are always worsted in his account, despite the final historical outcome that marked the total submission of these Chinghizide dynasties to the law of Mohammed. Indeed, returning to the Levant from China, our author saw these contests in the light and spirit of the Crusades; whence the epic tone of his account and the leading role played by religion, even when he refers to dynastic or political moves made under provocation of sheer violence or in defense of legitimate sovereign interests.[52] The real issue in this revolt, which is described in detail in the *Milione,* was the question of succession that had already prompted more than one Chinghizide prince to take arms against his sovereign.[53] A trial of strength was now to decide whether, after Abaqa's death in 1282, the throne of Persia was to pass to his brother Tekuder or to his son Arghun. Tekuder, though originally baptized a Christian, was a Mohammedan hater of Christians; whereas Arghun was always well disposed toward the Roman Pontiff, the other sovereigns of Europe, and his faithful Christian subjects of the Nestorian or Jacobite rites.[54]

It is therefore understandable that Marco saw the hand of God in the final triumph of Arghun, who, though beaten on the field of battle and taken prisoner by his rival, nevertheless ascended

[52] *Il Milione,* cr. ed., pp. 223 ff.; M.P., pp. 458 ff. The commentaries by Yule-Cordier, Pauthier, Charignon, etc., pay slight attention to these episodes in the book. In his narration of them Marco was able to disentangle, although in a rudimentary form, the personal and dynastic motives, as well as the religious ones, in the struggle between the various members of the Chinghizide dynasty of western and central Asia. These events and Marco's interpretation of them will be treated in greater detail in chap. viii, below.

[53] For these dramatic occurrences cf. B. Spuler, *Die Mongolen in Iran,* R. Grousset, *L'Empire des steppes,* and their Persian sources, to which have recently been added the editions of Rashiduddin prepared by Karl Jahn (*Geschichte der Ilkhane Abaga bis Gaihatu, 1265–1295,* Prague, 1941, and *Geschichte Gazan-Hans,* Prague, 1940), which deal with precisely the period described by Marco Polo and include the time of his stay in Persia.

[54] The rivalry for the succession between the brothers and sons of a Chinghizide sovereign, recorded by Marco in these chapters of his book, is characteristic of that dynasty, especially from the time when a successor was no longer elected according to the constitutional and traditional diet of princes and vassals (*kuriltai*), but came to power, as did Kublai in 1260, by means of a military pronouncement, or by a palace revolution (especially in Persia), or simply by the use of military force, as described by Marco on various occasions. The last constitutional election was that which placed Möngke (or Mangu) on the throne in 1251.

his father's throne as the result of a palace conspiracy, and, albeit for a short period of time, inaugurated a Christian dynasty.[55] Hence, too, Marco makes him incite his vassals and knights to fight Tekuder by telling them how shameful a thing it would be for them if the Saracens should manage to overcome the Tartars, and a renegade Christian, a worshiper of Mohammed, should seize his father's throne.[56]

Marco reached Persia from China after the death of Arghun, to whose land the Polos had escorted the Princess "Cocachin," sent to be Arghun's bride by Kublai, the nominal head of the dynasty.[57] This was in the year 1294, which was to witness the Great Kaan's death and, across all Asia, portentous events that meant the final decline of the Chinghizide tradition. Our traveler, on his way home, remained awhile in Persia, on the eve of the total Islamization of continental Asia from the Pamir to the Mediterranean. He was still in time to enjoy the hospitality of Gaikhatu, the last of the Ilkhans, who, for a further brief period, effectively protected the Christian cause on the western boundaries of the Chinghizide empire.[58]

Just before Marco's departure for Venice, in the autumn of

[55] The internal and foreign policies of this ruler, who has Marco's complete sympathy, tended to free the throne, the court, and the whole country from Mohammedan pressure and from the danger of being encircled by the aggressive Egypt of the great Baibars, the Golden Horde (already Islamized), and, on the east, by Great Turkey (*Il Milione,* cr. ed., pp. 216 ff.; M.P., pp. 447 ff.), which was wholly Mohammedan, in a continual tumult of territorial and religious conquest against neighbors and the central power. Hence, the pro-Christian policy of this period and the frequent contacts between the Ilkhans and the Holy See and the sovereigns of Europe, who associated themselves in a platonic anti-Islamic alliance with the Tartars but did not in practice react to Arghun Khan's requests for common action against the Mohammedans of all sects and lands. Cf., apart from the works already cited, the article by A. Mostaert and F. W. Cleaves, "Trois documents mongols des Archives secrètes vaticanes," *Harvard Journal of Asiatic Studies,* Vol. XV, 1952, pp. 448 ff.

[56] This was the same Achmad who abjured the Christian religion of the Nestorian rite immediately after his ascent to the throne of Persia in 1282, a decision for which Marco Polo eloquently reproaches him through the mouth of Arghun, his conqueror and successor. Cf. *Il Milione,* cr. ed., p. 224, lines 15 f.; M.P., p. 459.

[57] *Il Milione,* cr. ed., p. 13; M.P., p. 93. The princess became the wife of Ghazan, Arghun's son, who was then in Khorasan, on the eastern borders of the dominion, and who succeeded Gaikhatu in 1295, about a year after Marco left Persia on his way home to Venice.

[58] However, as Marco Polo himself affirms (cr. ed., pp. 229 f.; M.P., pp. 467 f., chap. ccxvi), the sovereignty of this brother of Arghun was contested as illegitimate by powerful elements in his kingdom who favored in his stead Ghazan, Arghun's son, and who killed him in 1295 after little more than four years of ruinous government.

1295, the violent death of this sovereign and of Baidu, his successor, had put an end to the ancient hopes and illusions entertained by the Christians of the Orient, which inspired this epic account in the *Milione.*[59] With Ghazan Khan, who married Cocachin and, as Arghun's son, was the legitimate lord of the Tartars of the Levant, the law of Mohammed triumphed anew in Persia, as it had already done in the Golden Horde of the Tartars of the West; and it was to find in his successors, until the coming of Timur Lenk (Tamerlane), the most powerful and successful champions of Islam. Everywhere, Marco noticed the weakness of Christianity, which was confronted by the successes achieved in every part of the continent by its rival faith. This only served to heighten his anger against the indomitable enemies of his religion, whose tenacity, power, and ability in every field of human activity he had been forced to recognize during twenty-five years of contact with them.

Marco was convinced that, with adequate means, it would have been possible to convert the Great Kaan to the faith of Christ. But we should look in vain in the pages of the *Milione* for the slightest reference to the hope of winning over one single Mohammedan. He thereby annuls the pious optimism expressed by his former traveling companion, Friar William of Tripoli, who, together with the more learned but certainly less expert contemporary students of Islam, such as Ramón Lull or Ricoldo of Montecroce, entertained the illusion of being able to convert the followers of Mohammed "simplici sermone, sive philosophicis argumentis sive militaribus armis."[60] Not one of them had

[59] Baidu, the last of the Christian Ilkhans, and so designated by Marco (cr. ed., p. 230, chap. ccxvii; M.P., p. 468), reigned for only a few months (April–October, 1295). The most eloquent testimonies in favor of these two last protectors of Asiatic Christianity come from the two leading representatives of the Nestorian and Jacobite churches in Marco's time: Jaballaha III, the Turko-Chinese patriarch, faithful to the dynasty and always involved in the fortunes of its members; and Bar-Hebraeus, the spiritual head of the Church of Syria, and an illustrious historian, as we have mentioned earlier.

[60] Cf. *De Statu Sarracenorum,* ed. Prutz (*Kulturgeschichte der Kreuzzüge,* pp. 597 f.). A large part of this treatise is intended to prove that there is a fundamental agreement between Christians and Saracens, and hence that they could meet on a common theological basis. Theology, however, did not determine, as was thought by both Ricoldo da Montecroce and Ramón Lull, his contemporaries, the force of cohesion of the Mohammedan peoples and the tenacity of their faith. On these missionaries and their writings see Monneret de Villard, *Lo studio dell'Islām,* esp. pp. 75 ff., and for

divined the secret power of this universal religion, which had culturally and spiritually destroyed itself with the conquest of barbarian peoples, and which Marco had learned to fear rather than esteem. Marco's experiences find their counterpart in those of Friar John of Montecorvino, the first Bishop of Peking, who —while saving many souls in those far-off regions—openly confessed that it was a hopeless task to attempt to baptize even one Mohammedan. In such circumstances, Marco's only hope was that of seeing this hated sect destroyed by the Tartars, who, however, were willing to exploit the abilities and recognize the tenacity of the Mohammedans.

3. PAGAN ASIA

In the course of his long stay in the Orient, Marco Polo came into contact with the most diverse aspects of Asiatic paganism, which ranged from the lowest manifestations of animistic superstition to the highest intellectual aspirations of metaphysical knowledge, and from the crude practices of black magic to the highest moral and philosophical experiences. However, he was not always able to distinguish these varieties and differences, and the picture drawn by him is far more confused than those he offers of Christian and Mohammedan Asia.

Nevertheless, his interest in this exotic and then unknown world is always lively, and is free from the prejudices that cloud his judgment of the Mohammedan cult and rites. Thus, his description of pagan Asia is not impaired by the hatred he entertained against Mohammed's religion, which at times caused him to give vent to his feelings in violent outbursts of invective. This attitude of Marco's marks him off from his precursor, Friar William of Rubruck, who was the first traveler from the West to have an opportunity of observing the various idolatries of Asia and of entering into discussions with their clergy.[1] In such circumstances the friar found himself, in a sense, in parallel with the Mohammedans since their monotheism, while not sufficing to

---

the fortunes of Islam in the sense referred to cf. B. Spuler and L. Forrer, *Der Vordere Orient in islamischer Zeit,* Bern, 1954 (in the form of a systematic bibliography), as well as Spuler's studies in *Geschichte der islamischen Länder,* I: *Die Chalifenzeit,* Leiden, 1952, and II: *Die Mongolenzeit,* Leiden, 1953.

[1] *Sinica Franciscana,* Vol. I, pp. 292 and *passim.*

procure for them his understanding or esteem, at any rate distinguished them substantially from the pagans of every kind and land.[2]

In the *Milione* these pagans are always idolaters, *ydres* in the French terminology used by Marco's scribe, but never the *paiens mescréans* whereby French and Franco-Italian literature of Marco's times usually identified both pagans and Saracens in a common expression of hatred and ignorance.[3] Though Marco knows that they belong to different sects, practice various rites, and are grouped in independent religious organizations, he nevertheless attributes all these diverse manifestations of Asiatic idolatry to a common founder, identified in the person of the Buddha.[4] This is considered to be an interpretation peculiar to our author and apparently without parallel in the rest of Oriental and Western literature, whether erudite or popular, and hence originating from a misunderstanding that his interpreters have had difficulty in explaining. However, already about the year 1225 the learned Chau Ju-kua, following a Chinese source of more than half a century earlier—i.e., the *Ling-wai-tai-ta* of Chou Ch'ü-fei,—uses the name of Buddha (Chinese *Fo*) to designate every kind of divinity and even Mohammed himself[5]—an attitude no less absurd than the common medieval representation of Mohammed worshiped as an idol by his followers, together with Apollo and Tervagant.[6] However, anyone acquainted with Marco's Asiatic environment and the medieval attitude toward such religious manifestations will certainly find this idea of the Buddha as originator and head of all the idols less strange and arbitrary.

Although Marco expresses this opinion for the first time when

[2] In the theological discussion at Karakorum in May, 1254, between religious of the various sects represented at this capital, the Franciscan missionary refused to debate with the Mohammedans on the grounds that the latter were fundamentally akin to the Christians by virtue of their monotheism. His opposition was therefore limited to the pagans, in particular to the Buddhists. Cf. *Sinica Franciscana*, Vol. I, p. 293, § II.

[3] This is characteristic of the *chansons de geste*, which extend the appellation "Saracens" to include all pagans, even the Romans.

[4] *Il Milione*, cr. ed., pp. 70 and 194; M.P., pp. 201 and 410.

[5] Cf. Chau Ju-kua, ed. and trans. Hirth and Rockhill, St. Petersburg, 1911, pp. 90 n. 5, 116, 124, 135, etc.

[6] See above, n. 21 to § 2 of this chapter.

referring to Buddhism on the island of Ceylon, which he visited in 1293,[7] it seems certain that his conception derived from what he had learned about Buddhism in the Mongol environment of Kublai's court. He never refers to the Buddha by that title, but designates him by the Mongol name Sagamoni Borcan,[8] of which the first part is the Mongolized form of the original appellation of Sakyamuni, who was to become the "Enlightened One," and the other (Borcan) an Altaic word which among the Turkish and Mongol tribes of Upper Asia was used to describe not only a divinity, but also, as has been shown by Berthold Laufer, its image, or, as Marco has it, its idol.[9]

This concept was no longer connected with the historically consecrated figure of the Buddha, who had first of all abandoned and then overcome the native divinities and their idols, while setting up his humanity as the most noble and effective cosmic force. What Marco saw and understood of his doctrines and worship in the regions where Buddhism had become the dominant religion was restricted to the shamanist interpretation of the Turks and Mongols, who had been converted to this cult in the XIIIth century by the Uigur and Tibetan lamas who flocked to

---

[7] *Il Milione*, cr. ed., pp. 176 and 192 ff.; M.P., pp. 379 and 407 ff.

[8] Marco at this point (cr. ed., p. 70 n.; M.P., p. 201) reports Kublai's words.

[9] Cf. B. Laufer, "Burkhan," *Journal of the American Oriental Society*, Vol. XXXVI, 1917, pp. 390 ff. Marco expressly translates this term, saying that it "means 'saint' " (cr. ed., p. 194, line 63; M.P., p. 410). The term recurs more than once in the ancient Mongol text (cf. E. Haenisch, ed., *Manghol un niuča tobča'an*, Vol. II: *Wörterbuch*, at this article), especially to describe a sacred mountain in Mongolia, thereby implying its divinity. It was probably after the composition of the so-called *Secret History of the Mongols* (1240), and probably as a result of Lamaist influence, that this word acquired the specific meaning of 'supreme divinity,' hence the Buddha. In the sense of 'divinity' this term is also to be found in the extensively Christianized region of the Öngüt, or Ordos, which is described in detail by Marco under the name of Tenduc (*Il Milione*, cr. ed., pp. 60 ff.; M.P., pp. 181 ff.). Cf. A. Mostaert, *Folklore Ordos*, Peiping (*Monumenta Serica*, Monograph XI), 1947, p. 597. The common use of *burqan* for the Buddha among the Mongols of Marco's times is attested *inter alia* by a Mongol Buddhistic treatise of the year 1311, discussed by F. W. Cleaves in *Harvard Journal of Asiatic Studies*, Vol. XVII, 1954, pp. 1 ff., esp. p. 90 n. 29. L. Hambis (*Journal Asiatique*, Vol. CCXLI, 1953, p. 224) is of the opinion that the term *borkan*, whereby the Mongols and Uigurs describe Sakyamuni, derives from the fusion of the Chinese word *fo* for Buddha with Altaic *han*, 'sovereign.' This hypothesis, however, does not seem convincing. The Mongolist P. K. Kozlow, in his book *Mongolei, Amdo und die tote Stadt Chara-choto* (German translation from the Russian, Berlin, 1925, p. 50), asserts that the Mongols use the term *burchan* in the sense of 'idol.' This would explain the specific use of it made by Marco and consequently by the Buddhists of Upper Asia, from whom he must have learned it either directly or indirectly.

the Chinghizide courts.[10] As a result of their teachings, the nomads, who were fundamentally irreligious in a metaphysical and moral sense, transferred to the historical and mythical Buddha the term *borcan,* repeated by Marco, which they used to describe a person who possessed the magical powers whereby the shaman became a mediator between mortal beings and the world of the spirits. The latter, in their turn, were understood as natural divinities infused into the cosmic forces, the five elements and their derivative phenomena.[11] Having become a *borcan* among

[10] As we have already noted in chap. vi, Lamaism was introduced at the Chinghizide court only toward the middle of the century; but the Mongol conquerors' contacts with Buddhism date from the conquest of the neighboring territories of Tangut and Turfan, accomplished by Chinghiz Khan in 1226. In these lands, inhabited by Turks mixed with Tibetan and Chinese elements, there had existed for hundreds of years strong Buddhistic groups whose religious and cultural influence was limited to the urban oases of those vast desert regions without extending beyond the borders of Mongolia. No mention of this is made in the *Secret History,* which is wholly pervaded by the characteristic, savage animism of the nomads. The foundation of the first Mongol urban center, in the reign of Ogudai (1227–1240), Chinghiz' successor to the imperial throne, encouraged the first immigration of lamas from Tibet and even earlier from the conquered regions. They followed the various ramifications of the Chinghizide dynasty, especially in Persia (for which see B. Spuler, *Die Mongolen in Iran,* 1939, pp. 198 ff.) and in Kublai's China, after 1260. For these events cf., besides H. H. Howorth's classic *History of the Mongols,* Pt. IV, 1927, the documents and information from Tibetan sources in G. Tucci, *Tibetan Painted Scrolls,* Rome, 1949, Vol. I, pp. 8 ff., where we read of Chinghiz Khan's interest in the rites and magic powers of the Tibetan lamas already associated with his court and empire.

[11] For the various aspects of shamanism among the Mongols and other Altaic peoples cf., besides Howorth's *History,* Vol. IV, pp. 90 ff., and the relevant article in the *Encyclopaedia of Religion and Ethics,* the work by Wilhelm Schmidt, *Die asiatischen Hirtenvölker,* Vol. X of his series on *Der Ursprung der Gottesidee,* Munich, 1952 (the general thesis put forward by this learned writer occasionally prejudices his conclusions, which are not always founded on an exhaustive study of the sources and literature pertaining to the subject); his volume contains a critical summary of the unpublished dissertation by N. Pallisen, "Die alte Religion der mongolischen Völker," Marburg, 1949, of which I have been able to see a microfilm. Cf., too, the same author's article, "Die alte Religion der Mongolen und der Kultus Tschingis Khans," *Numen,* Vol. III, 1956, pp. 178–229. It should be noted that the name *burhan* is never applied to the shamans (or diviners, sorcerers, etc.), who are designated by other terms, most frequently by the word *cham,* which was already known to Friar John of Pian del Càrpine (*Sin. Franc.,* Vol. I, p. 41). Their practices are also described by Friar William of Rubruck (*ibid.,* pp. 301 ff.), for whom see W. W. Rockhill, *The Journey* etc., p. 246. According to Pavel Poucha, "Mongolische Miszellen," *Central Asiatic Journal,* Vol. I, 1955, p. 285, the term *burqan* was also applied to the sovereigns of Tangut, probably in order to designate their divine power, which was implicit in the concept of sovereignty held by the Asiatic peoples. As for the elements that form the basis of the cosmological system of the peoples of the Far East and influence the theories and practices of their medicine and of shamanistic or priestly alchemy, in China they were five: earth, water, fire, metal, and wood. These were most probably accepted by the Mongol diviners in the Chinese cultural sphere, whereas Buddhistic

these Altaic peoples, the enlightened and clairvoyant Buddha of ancient India was thereby transformed into a concrete materialization of a supernatural power that was vaguely apprehended and never specified, and finally became a supreme divinity worshiped in the images which represented it.

The success enjoyed by Tibetan Buddhism from the beginning of the Chinghizide dynasty in Mongolia and among the Tartars in China is essentially to be explained by the notion of this "Sagamoni Borcan" as the sovereigns and ruling classes of the new empire conceived him. He was regarded as a transcendent miracle-worker who was obeyed by gods and devils alike, natural and occult forces, and the spirits of the departed— a barbaric and grotesque caricature of the Enlightened One, who wished to free man from the servitude of his passions, from his instincts that lead him astray, and from pain which harries him relentlessly from the cradle to the grave.[12]

Marco had a vague idea of the moral greatness of this remarkable man, but only after having learned something about the historical Buddha in the sanctuaries of Ceylon, on his way home at the end of his great adventure; he could then say, as we read in the Florentine version of the *Milione,* that "for a certainty, if he had been baptized a Christian he would have been a great saint before God."[13] In spite of this, however, the Buddha remained for our traveler the Sagamoni Borcan of the Mongols, and hence the first and foremost of all idols, as Marco had considered him when observing his more or less spurious cult among the Tartars and Chinese.[14]

This thaumaturgic conception of the Buddha had been impressed on his mind in the most authoritative way by Kublai him-

physics and metaphysics recognized only four elements (earth, fire, water, and air), which, however, varied with the different schools of thought. For their relationship with Greek cosmography and its derivatives cf. W. Kirfel, "Die fünf Elemente," *Beiträge zur Sprach- und Kulturgeschichte des Orients,* fasc. 4, 1951.

[12] Cf. the recent attempt to evoke the historical Buddha, in A. Foucher, *La Vie du Buddha,* Paris, 1949.

[13] Ed. Olivieri, Bari, 1928, p. 205.

[14] The supposed universality of the Buddhistic cult seemed to Marco to be documented by the fact that he came across its images in often similar forms in all the countries of the Far East and the islands of the Indian Ocean visited by him. For the Buddha's name in the various versions of the text cf. L. Foscolo Benedetto's critical edition of the *Milione,* p. 70 n., and p. 193 n.

self in the profession of faith, handed down to us in the Ramusian version of the *Milione,* in which the sovereign, after having numbered Sagamoni Borcan among the four "prophets" or founders of the universal religions, designated him as "the first god among the idols," by virtue of whose sanctity and power his priests performed the portents and miracles witnessed by Marco on the various occasions described by him.[15]

The idea of this primacy, so much emphasized in his book, was less absurd than might be thought without further reflection. As is common knowledge, the Indian and Chinese mythologies existed long before the birth of Sakyamuni; the one, poetic in form in the great epic cycle that makes up its sacred books; the other, popular in its natural and esoteric pantheism. The Buddha, as it were, theologically overcame all those divinities, because he alone, with his disciples, was able to free himself from the anthropomorphism that was their indelible characteristic. In this sense, the Buddha—under the name of *Fo* in China, *Sakya Tub'pa* in Tibet, and *Burhan* in Mongolia—was spiritually deified and hence a superior creature and head of the crowded Oriental pantheon.[16]

Although Marco attempted to see further into the mystery of this idolatry, so often described or mentioned by him, he was never able to penetrate to those speculative depths that were the ultimate concern of the meditations and doctrines of Sakyamuni's followers and that determined the transcendental humanity of the Buddha. These were not understood even in the court and government circles where Marco had observed the manifestations of the cult. Hence, the Buddhism that he knew and portrayed in his book is essentially different from the Buddhism of the Chinese; and different also, in certain respects, from Lamaistic teaching, which had been imported into Cathay from Mongolia in the wake of the court, together with the other foreign cults protected by the dynasty in its various ramifications.[17] This

[15] *Il Milione,* cr. ed., pp. 62 ff. and p. 70 n.; M.P., pp. 185 ff.

[16] The Tibetan name for the Buddha is a compound of two terms, the second of which is an appellative: *Sākya* the powerful (*tub'pa*). The Mongols preserved the entire form *Sākyamuni,* adding an appellative the connection of which with the Tibetan language can only be studied by a competent specialist.

[17] Although organized by two eminent monks mentioned in Chinese sources as Watochi and Namo, respectively, both immigrants from Kashmir, and although as-

Lamaism had more in common with the demonology of the nomads of Upper Asia and the magical practices of its wizards than with the ancient Chinese traditions of faith and doctrine. At Karakorum, Mangu Kaan practiced the scapulomancy of his diviners, while at the same time, before undertaking the conquest of Yunnan and southern China, he built a monumental stupa which was probably intended to further the success of his undertaking in the name of the "Sagamoni Borcan" of the Mongolian Buddhists.[18] Moreover, although in 1289 Kublai commanded a republication of the so-called Buddhistic canon—the collection of sacred and philosophical texts inspired by this religion—he nevertheless offered public protection to the sect that followed, though in the name of "Sagamoni Borcan," the magic practices of Mongolia rather than the moral precepts and doctrinal speculation of the monks and scholars, and thereby alienated an essential number of the intellectuals of the land.[19]

sociated with the temporal and spiritual head of Tibetan Buddhism in the person of the "abbot" of Saskya in Tibet, the Lamaism originally practiced in Mongolia was essentially magical, as is confirmed by Friar William of Rubruck, who describes the contests between the priests of the various religions in their practice of medicine and necromancy. In this form the degenerate Buddhism of Mongolia remained limited to court circles and the Mongol nobility of local origin as well as those who had emigrated with the court to China in 1260. The general spread of Buddhism in that country and among neighboring peoples only took place in the XVIth century after the thorough reorganization of Lamaism accomplished by the celebrated Tsong Kha-pa. Cf. the classic history of Buddhism in Mongolia written in the XVIIth century by a tardy Chinghizide and new apostle of this faith, Ssanang Ssetzen (or Sagang Sečen); see the text and German translation by I. J. Schmidt, *Geschichte der Ost-Mongolen und ihres Fürstenhauses,* St. Petersburg, 1829, as well as Sagang Sečen, *Erdeni-yin Tobči: Mongolian Chronicle,* Cambridge, Mass. (Harvard-Yenching Institute), 1956, with a critical introduction by A. Mostaert and a foreword by F. W. Cleaves. The history is narrated from the Tibetan point of view by Jigs-med nam-mk'a; see the German translation (with the original Tibetan text) by G. Huth, *Geschichte des Buddhismus in der Mongolei,* Strassburg, 1893.

[18] For the scapulomantic practices of Mangu, Kublai's brother, cf. William of Rubruck in *Sinica Franciscana,* Vol. I, pp. 261 ff., and for this kind of divination, very common in Asia, the relevant article in the *Encyclopaedia of Religion and Ethics,* and C. R. Bawden, "On the Practice of Scapulomancy among the Mongols," *Central Asiatic Journal,* Vol. IV, 1958, pp. 1–31. Marco never records these practices. For the Buddhistic stupa erected by Mangu (Möngke) Kaan in his capital, about the year 1259, cf. P. Pelliot, "Note sur Karakorum," *Journal Asiatique,* Vol. CCVI, 1925, p. 372. This monument bears witness to the Chinghizide dynasty's leanings toward Lamaistic Buddhism, which then spread to Persia and Anatolia. For this phenomenon cf. U. Monneret de Villard, *Il libro della peregrinazione nelle parti d'Oriente di Fra Ricoldo da Montecroce,* Rome, 1948, pp. 47 ff.

[19] For the political consequences of this evolution cf. O. Franke, *Geschichte des*

During the first centuries of our era, Chinese Buddhism exerted a lasting, if not unopposed, influence on the literary culture and philosophical and religious trends of China, but it was never able to regain those heights after the violent and systematic suppression of its monasteries and the persecution of its adherents that followed upon the imperial edict of the year 845.[20] Nevertheless, it was so deeply rooted in the intellectual life of a large part of the population that it would not be extirpated as radically as Manichaeism, Christianity, and the other foreign religions.[21] Thus, when Cathay became the center of the Chinghizide dynasty some few years before Matteo and Niccolò Polo first arrived there, Buddhism still represented one of that region's indigenous moral and social forces, with a long tradition, a large number of wealthy monasteries, a vast literature, and numberless followers among all classes.[22]

More than Taoism, which had already fallen away to the level of vulgar superstition, and more than Confucianism, which had been reformed as a state religion with a certain moral and social basis, Chinese Buddhism satisfied the metaphysical needs of those who aspired to know the reasons for the existence and destiny of man, alone and suffering and surrounded by the mysteries of the world about him.

chinesischen Reiches, Vol. IV, pp. 480 ff., and for the influence of Buddhism on Kublai see chap. ix, § 3, of the present work. On the enormous power gained by the lamas in China under the Mongol régime cf. P. Ratchnevsky, *Un code des Yuan,* Paris, 1937, pp. lxxix ff.

[20] A brief but masterly characterization of Chinese Buddhism is offered by the lamented Henri Maspero in *Les Religions chinoises,* Paris, 1950, pp. 65 ff.; and cf. other writings by this author on the same subject, which has also been fully treated by orientalists already cited. For this vast scattered literature cf., besides the *Bibliographie bouddhique,* the list of principal works in Kenneth Scott Latourette, *The Chinese,* third edition, New York, 1947, and H. Franke, *Sinologie,* Berlin, 1953, pp. 101 ff.

[21] Especially in southern China during the Sung era. This region, which Marco calls "Mangi," from *Man-tzŭ,* a popular term in contemporary usage, became a part of the Chinese empire in 1279, and until this date was less exposed than Cathay (northern China) to foreign religious and intellectual influences. Here Marco was able to observe the native traditions of ancient Chinese Buddhism, which, however, he did not distinguish with any sense of precision. Similarly, he was not aware of the decisive Confucian renaissance in this land after the reform brought about by the great Chu Hsi (XIIth century), whom Pelliot justly calls the Chinese Aristotle.

[22] For the principal Chinese Buddhistic texts see L. Wieger, *Bouddhisme chinois,* 2 vols., Hochienfu, 1910–1913, and, for legends and popular hagiography, E. Chavannes, *Le Tripitaka chinois,* 3 vols., Paris, 1910–1911. On the Buddhistic canon cf. Prabodh Chandra Bagchi, *Le Canon bouddhique en Chine,* Paris, 1926.

This doctrine had the advantage over the others of expressing itself in concrete forms of art and worship, and of logically elaborating a moral system that culminated in an eschatology which rationally admitted not only the dissolution of existence in the non-being of *nirvāna,* but also the possibility of participating outside the limits of time in a kind of eternal purgatory. It is therefore permissible to suppose that the success of this faith with all the Chinghizide rulers, and especially those in Mongolia and China, was due in large measure to this vision of eternal life, sought for and claimed by them as the elect of their "eternal heaven," their supreme divinity.[23]

It was, then, this late Far Eastern deviation of Buddhism with which Marco Polo came to be acquainted in its various aspects, contaminated by doctrines, practices, and traditions of other origin, and ill distinguished from the forms of idolatry more or less arbitrarily superimposed by Tibetan Lamaism and Mongolian shamanism. Hence is explained why he insists in attributing to the Buddha original supremacy over all the numberless idols that he saw on his wanderings through Asia and described with mixed feelings of respect and repulsion. Very likely, this supposed primacy was confirmed for him by the colossal statues of the Enlightened One, seen by him in various parts of the empire, which seemed to signify monumentally the peculiar rank enjoyed by Buddhism at the courts of Peking and Tabriz—as was observed by Friar Ricoldo of Montecroce at almost the same time.

This concept and this attitude find their justification in the fact that Marco became acquainted with Buddhism in the late phase of the teaching called *Mahāyāna,* or "Great Vessel," which leads to salvation all those who practice the moral virtues of charity, abstinence, and devotion to the incarnate and figurative

[23] Longevity and survival after death were concepts and aspirations that obsessed this society even in remote times and under the various national and foreign dynasties in China (numberless examples in L. Wieger, *Textes historiques,* 2 vols., third edition, Hien-hien, 1929). The sovereigns surrounded themselves with sages and adventurers of every sect, who promised them health, longevity, and immortality by the practice of magical arts or medical alchemy, or by resort to mere trickery, as had already been described at length by Friar William of Rubruck. This was one of the chief reasons that induced the Chinghizide rulers to put the powers of the various religions to the test, and finally to favor Buddhism in its magical forms, as developed in the later phases of this doctrine.

divinities that form the main object of their worship.[24] These divinities were, and are still, conceived as hypostases of the Buddha, endowed with eternal life in the transcendent world of the blessed, whose favor may be propitiated by worship and offerings at their sanctuaries. In this sense, Marco's assertion that the Buddha was first and foremost of all the idols is understandable and justified, since these so-called "bodhisattvas," by personifying his illumination, thereby became participants in his divinity.[25] According to what we read in the *Milione,* the idols were supposed iconographically to derive from a golden statue, adorned with pearls, which the king, Sakyamuni's father, erected in his memory in order to fix his features for all time and to have him honored as a god by the king's subjects.[26]

This is a fable that Marco seems himself to have added to the biography of the Buddha as narrated by him, since it is not only historically absurd, but also unconnected with the numerous legends illustrating the terrestrial and posthumous life of the Enlightened One which were current throughout Oriental Asia.[27] Everyone knew that Sakyamuni had died after his eightieth year, and everyone thought that his cult had been originated within his lifetime, and not merely after his death. It is certainly not clear how Marco reconciled his assertion with his account of

[24] Cf. J. J. M. de Groot, *Le Code du Mahāyāna en Chine: son influence sur la vie monacale et sur le monde laïque,* Amsterdam, 1893.

[25] Marco never mentions them either by this or by any other name. These mythical figures, characteristic of Mahayanic Buddhism, represent those followers of the Buddha who renounce his way to perfect salvation, in order to help the world along this way until it shall be liberated from immanent physical and moral suffering. It would, however, be superfluous to examine this doctrine in detail since Marco only perceived its external aspects without being able to understand its significance and attributes.

[26] *Il Milione,* cr. ed., p. 194; M. P., p. 410.

[27] It may be presumed that a certain episode in the Buddha's posthumous life was narrated to Marco by his informants in Ceylon or other parts of eastern Asia; namely, that Sakyamuni's father first worshiped him while listening to the prediction of his son's mission, and later after having witnessed his first transfiguration. This legend is part of the canonical cycle in the Buddha's biography, and therefore commands as much respect as the famous episode from his childhood narrated in its genuine form in the *Milione,* cr. ed., pp. 193 f., M.P., p. 408, without the Christian interpolations found in the medieval romance of Barlaam and Josaphat, which was also known in Italy through the French versions of the celebrated hagiographical account by St. John Damascene (see M.P., p. 410. n. 2; and below, n. 114). This account, like Marco's, portrays the infant Siddhartha as a Christian saint. The episode included in Jacopo da Varazze's *Legenda Aurea* may have been known to Marco in this Christian version before he became acquainted with its Indian origin. Cf. the note by Yule-Cordier in *The Book of Ser Marco Polo,* Vol. II, pp. 323 ff.

the idols in China "with the heads of oxen, pigs, dogs, sheep, and other animals," not to mention those that had, according to him, one head with four faces, or three heads on two shoulders, and others with four, ten, or even a thousand hands, which were more highly esteemed by the faithful.[28] It is obvious that these monstrosities could not possibly have derived from a supposedly authentic portrait of the Buddha, like that mentioned in the *Milione*.[29]

Marco Polo lacked the preparation that might have enabled him to extricate the authentic doctrines of Buddhism from the refuse and sediment that other beliefs, practices, and traditions had heaped about it in the course of seventeen centuries of internal and external evolution in the various communities and cultures of Asia. Not even Friar William of Rubruck, equipped with far better intellectual training and with more direct experience of the religious phenomena of the Orient, was able to see more deeply into the mysteries of that ecclesiastical and doctrinal system.[30] Even for the modern specialist who is an expert in the methods of historical and philological criticism, and is advantaged by the direct exploration of lands and contact with peoples, the problem of separating all the elements that go to make up the various manifestations of Asiatic paganism is still a most difficult one, and sometimes quite hopeless. Nevertheless, the confused, at times inextricable, account of it offered by the *Milione,* of which we have just seen a characteristic example, does in the last analysis reflect the reality of the various aspects

[28] *Il Milione,* cr. ed., p. 166; M.P., p. 364. For this Buddhistic iconography cf. A. Grünwedel, *Buddhistische Mythologie,* Leipzig, 1900, and Paris, 1904; W. Kirfel, *Symbolik des Buddhismus,* Stuttgart, 1959; and below, n. 122.

[29] We find Marco saying (*Il Milione,* cr. ed., p. 166) that this image was made in his likeness, whereas Buddhistic monumental iconography actually originated, two centuries after Sakyamuni's death, in northern India and its neighboring regions, as Marco had already noted when describing Kashmir (*Il Milione,* cr. ed., p. 38; M.P., p. 140). On his return journey he probably allowed himself to be convinced by the local guides in Ceylon that the Buddha had lived there in the flesh and not only through his cult, contrarily to tradition and history, which make the cult date from the time of Asoka, ruler of India, who introduced it to the island.

[30] It should, however, be noted that the information offered by him in his *Itinerary* is on the whole more precise and more abundant, especially concerning the monuments, rites, customs, vestments, ceremonies, images, etc. (cf. *Sin. Franc.,* Vol. I, pp. 224 ff., 300 ff., etc.), to which should be added the first mention of a child endowed with all the traits of an incarnate lama or living Buddha (*ibid.,* p. 245).

of this same religious life as practiced by the peoples and groups of that century, when none of the primitive Asiatic cults, and least of all Buddhism, had kept its original doctrinal basis unaltered.

In making the whole of Oriental paganism derive from the Buddha, in its most noble as well as most repellent forms, Marco merely followed his monotheistic prompting, which invariably reduced the complex mass of respective faiths, laws, and doctrines to one single "prophet" and master, be his name Jesus, Moses, Mohammed, or Sagamoni Borcan. In this he found himself in agreement with Mangu and Kublai, who as sons of a Christian mother were inclined toward a fundamental monotheistic tendency that was lacking in the true pagans of their race.[31]

Nevertheless, this did not prevent our Venetian from observing the diverse manifestations of this cult in the various parts of Asia that he visited. In the monasteries described in the *Milione* he saw those who, in order to reach the salvation of nirvana, mortified themselves in the practices of contemplative monachism. He watched the devout following the way of the active life, carrying out good works, worshiping the "Three Venerable Ones," making offerings before the images of their saints, going on pilgrimages to the most famous sanctuaries, studying the arts and sciences, offering prayers, and putting into practice the moral, dietetic, and social precepts characteristic of their faith—all, indeed, that saved them from the sorrows of life and the horrors of hell by drawing them nearer to the deified Buddha, or by transubstantiating them in his eternal and transcendent essence.

On the other hand, Marco noted with especial curiosity and

---

[31] Wilhelm Schmidt, in accord with the general thesis of his *Asiatischen Hirtenvölker*, and with some difficulty, insists on asserting the fundamentally monotheistic tendencies that he attributes to these pagans. Pallisen, as cited in n. 11 above, is less explicit in this sense. However, neither of these scholars has thought of connecting the imperial professions of monotheistic faith, recorded by the Franciscan missionaries as well as by Marco Polo, with the Nestorian (and possibly Saracen) influence, which was exceedingly strong and sometimes decisive, especially on the ruling classes of the nomad tribes affiliated with the Chinghizide dynasty (such as the Merkits, Öngüt, and Naimans) and of the urban oases in Eastern Turkestan. In contrast with Mangu's and Kublai's assertions on the subject, the Buddhists of the court, when speaking to William of Rubruck, emphatically denied the existence of an omnipotent god, creator and supreme judge of the world (cf. *Sin. Franc.*, Vol. I, pp. 296 ff.).

wonder the exaggerations, aberrations, and superstitions that Taoism in China and shamanism in Mongolia had grafted upon the great trunk of the Tree of Illumination, emphasizing and falsifying the magic power of the idols to the detriment of their doctrinal and religious value, and insisting on the picturesque, grotesque demonology into which the Lamaism of Tibet, the Tantrism of Kashmir, and the Hinduism of Ceylon and Burma had transmuted the worship and doctrines of primitive Buddhism.

Since he could not separate the elements constituting the religious syncretism or eclecticism characteristic of the Far East, and was not acquainted with the national "religions" of China then in the process of philosophical and ecclesiastical renewal, Marco attributes a false unity and universality to Buddhism, identifying it moreover with idolatry. In this he was certainly influenced by seeing it favored in the sympathies and leanings of Kublai and the ruling classes in the Sino-Tartar society of his times, the more because the emperor's military and political conquests extended to the places where Buddhism was then most flourishing: Japan, Indochina, Burma, and the island of Ceylon, which Kublai dreamed of being able to include in his empire, together with the Sunda Islands and Tibet, the spiritual homeland of the lamas in his service.

The complex mass of idolatries described in the *Milione* cannot therefore be analyzed by reference to the standards of Buddhism.[32] Even though it is possible to justify Marco's attitude, it is certainly not permissible for the modern critic to consider beneath this one aspect the manifold cults, rites, doctrines, superstitions, and ethnographical and magical data that are scattered through the pages of the *Milione*. In order to form an adequate and relatively precise idea of all this it is necessary to follow the author in his wanderings and study his attitudes and observations as occasion warrants; only thus may one arrive at a comprehensive vision and a historically correct interpretation.

[32] As was done by J. Witte in a study now well-nigh unobtainable, *Das Buch des Marco Polo als Quelle für die Religionsgeschichte,* Berlin, 1916 (see above, the introductory note to § 1 of this chapter), of which the section on Buddhism has appeared separately as a dissertation of the Faculty of Theology of Berlin University, 1916.

It is strange that we find no record in the *Milione* of the Buddhist temples in eastern Anatolia and Persia which Ricoldo of Montecroce mentioned in his *Libro della peregrinazione nelle parti d'Oriente,* written only a few years subsequent to the *Milione,* and which were still in existence when Marco visited those regions in the year 1272 and again on his return journey in 1294.[33] Certainly, their priests cannot have escaped his eye, since they were easily recognizable in appearance and dress at the court of the Ilkhans, and Marco must have noticed the rich sanctuaries built by Hulagu and Abaqa, which were adorned with statues and paintings, and were still used for purposes of worship when the three Venetians were the guests of Gaikhatu as the ambassadors of the Great Kaan Kublai.[34]

Marco's silence is all the more strange since the Buddhists of Persia and Armenia were no different from those observed by him at Kublai's court and in other parts of Asia, and practiced the same rites and exorcisms, and observed the same customs, which he faithfully and vividly described in his book.[35] The Buddhism at Tabriz was in fact an almost exclusively courtly manifestation, intended to propitiate the inherently adverse divinities to the sovereign's advantage. And so, indeed, it remained during the Chinghizide era in Mongolia and China, where it enjoyed neither widespread favor nor opportunity to permit its expansion beyond the circles of the court and the Tartar administration.[36] This recovery of Lamaist Buddhism in the Chinghizide empire in Marco's times remained a phenomenon intimately connected with the expansion of the dynasty, and

[33] Cf. Monneret de Villard, *Il libro della peregrinazione nelle parti d'Oriente di Fra Ricoldo da Montecroce,* esp. pp. 47 ff.

[34] *Il Milione,* prologue, cr. ed., p. 12; M.P., p. 91. For Buddhism at this court cf. the scant information offered by B. Spuler, *Die Mongolen in Iran,* pp. 198 ff., and Monneret de Villard, *Il libro della peregrinazione,* pp. 47 ff., who comments upon Ricoldo da Montecroce's valuable observations on this subject.

[35] In fact, Ricoldo da Montecroce (*op. cit.,* pp. 50 f.) saw the same *bacsi* in Persia as those described by Marco in the *Milione,* cr. ed., pp. 64 f.; M.P., pp. 189 f.

[36] Lamaism died out in China with the passing of the Chinghizide power and the triumph of the Ming dynasty, which originated in 1368 with Hung Wu (secular name: Chu Yüan-chang), formerly a Buddhist monk of Chinese tradition and hence both spiritually and politically opposed to the Tibetan sect. The only trace of the latter remaining in China is that afforded by the two Lamaist temples at Peking, for which see Ferdinand Lessing, *Yung-Ho-Kung: An Iconography of the Lamaist Cathedral in Peking,* Vol. I (the only one to have appeared), Stockholm, 1942.

disappeared with it for some centuries, returning to the inaccessible land of Tibet, whence a century before it had made a triumphal advance coinciding with the advent of this dynasty.

And it is no less curious that Marco, after having kept silent when he had an excellent opportunity to discuss it, mentions this form of idolatry for the first time when describing some regions of central Asia never visited by him. He does, however, refer to the characteristics and practices of the idolaters when treating of the regions neighboring on northern India, between Afghanistan and Tibet. He calls them respectively "Pasciai," from the name of the language of Aryan stock spoken by the peoples of Kafiristan as far as the Indus, and "Chesciemur," in the characteristic form that designates present-day and historical Kashmir.[37] These regions were then, as they are now, a prey to furious religious struggles and to violent national and political agitation.[38]

At all the Chinghizide courts, and in various parts of Asia, Marco had seen these men, whom he describes as dark-skinned and slender, very wise and possessed of special powers over devils, able to perform all kinds of prodigies, and endowed with the highest moral virtues. He relates that "for love of their idols" they scrupulously observed the precepts of abstinence and chastity. Some, he says, dedicated themselves to a life of solitude in their hermitages, while others submitted to an exceedingly severe

[37] *Il Milione*, cr. ed., p. 38; M.P., p. 139. For the geo-topographical identification of those regions see Yule-Cordier, *The Book of Ser Marco Polo*, Vol. I, pp. 164 ff., 168 ff., and Cordier, *Addenda*, pp. 22 ff., 34 ff. The form "Keshimir" is already found in the *Secret History*, sections 262 and 269 (ed. Haenisch), in connection with plans of conquest attributed to Chinghiz Khan. The region was in fact invaded several times by the Mongols, as Marco was aware (cf. *Milione*, cr. ed., pp. 28 f., M.P., pp. 121 f.; also the article by Sir Aurel Stein, "Marco Polo's Account of a Mongol Inroad into Kashmir," *Geographical Journal*, 1919, pp. 92 ff.). Modern Kafiristan, which is a region in the northeast of present-day Afghanistan (cf. R. Fazy, "L'Exploration du Kafiristan par les Européens," *Asiatische Studien*, 1953, pp. 1–25), lends its name to description of the "infidels," even as the "Muleete" of Marco Polo (cr. ed., p. 32; M.P., p. 128) and the Franciscan missionaries (cf. *Sin. Franc.*, Vol. I, pp. 206, 207, 489) describes in various forms the "heretics" of Mazandaran in Persia, commonly known as the Assassins.

[38] Mohammedan penetration in Kashmir in Marco's times was notably advanced without yet having assumed, with respect to Hinduism and other native cults still alive today, the religious and political importance that was to play so prominent a role in the destiny of this legendary land. According to the *Milione* (cr. ed., p. 39 n.; M.P., p. 140), the Buddhists made use of these Saracens to slaughter the animals whose flesh they ate.

form of monasticism in their numerous "abbeys," and were distinguished by a tonsure like that of "our Dominicans and Friars Minor." [39] These are the religious of Kashmir, who, Marco asserts, are the leaders of all the pagans of Asia because it was from their country that all the idols had originated of which the Buddha was supposed to be the father and head.

This is a brief but eloquent reference to the decisive part that Kashmir played in the history of Buddhism down to Marco's own times, namely, from the era when Asoka, its king, and some of his successors, from the IIId century B.C. onward, made that land a center for the renewal and expansion of Buddhism, the cradle of its religious art, and a school for its doctrines.[40] Moreover, he correctly differentiates priests (regulars), hermits, and teachers (lamas), whom he elsewhere calls *bacsi,* using the Altaic term of obscure origin that was already known to Ricoldo of Montecroce, who saw lamas in Persia in those very same years and described them in similar terms.[41]

[39] *Il Milione,* cr. ed., pp. 38 f.; M.P., pp. 140.

[40] As is known, Asoka, a convert to Buddhism, toward the middle of the IIId century B.C. helped to spread this faith throughout much of India, and his son and successor brought it to the island of Ceylon. It met with especial success in the northern border regions, which were governed by Greco-Indian dynasties, and in the Ist century A.D. spread with renewed vigor (owing to the favor of Kanishka I, the king of the Kushanas) beyond the borders of India, toward Bactriana and Turkestan. This expansion gave rise to new styles of Buddhistic iconography, which have been systematically studied in numerous recent publications following upon A. Foucher's *L'Art gréco-bouddhique du Gandhara,* 2 vols., Paris, 1905–1908, which are listed in the already cited *Bibliographie bouddhique.* For these iconographical ramifications cf. G. Tucci, *Tibetan Painted Scrolls,* Vol. I, chap. iii, and other passages in that fundamental work.

As can be seen from the extract quoted, Marco was aware that these border regions, e.g. Gandhara, Kashmir, and Afghanistan, were the cradle and center of expansion for the Buddhistic "idols," although he later made them derive from Ceylon (cf. *Il Milione,* cr. ed., p. 193; M.P., p. 410) and observed their late manifestations and traditions in the Buddhistic temples of Turkestan, Tangut, and China.

[41] Cf. Monneret de Villard, *Il libro della peregrinazione,* pp. 47 ff. The origin of the term *bacsi* (pronounced *bakhshi* in Mongolian and Uiguric), perhaps from Sanskrit *bhikshu,* is still debated, as can be seen *loc. cit.,* n. 168; but that it signifies a Buddhistic priest is beyond doubt. According to A. von Gabain, *Alttürkische Grammatik,* second edition, Leipzig, 1950, p. 300, the term *bakshi* would derive from Chinese *pāk-shi,* but this etymon does not seem convincing. Ricoldo describes the *baxi* seen by him in Persia and Anatolia as "nigri et adusti," in terms similar to those used by Marco with respect to the people of Kashmir ("brun et maigri"; *Il Milione,* p. 38). It is therefore possible to assume that these "indiani homines valde sapientes," who according to the friar were well versed in all the magic arts, came to the various Chinghizide courts from Kashmir, and hence that Marco designates them by this name when describing their practices at Kublai's court (cr. ed., p. 64; M.P., p. 188).

These were the three types of Buddhist clergy observed by
Marco in the course of his travels through Asia, and at that
time dominating those remote regions not yet invaded by Turks,
Afghans, Mongols, or Indians of other faiths, or, especially,
Mohammedans, who, as Marco noted, had nevertheless begun
to infiltrate the region.[42] It was here that in the first millennium
of our era the most celebrated Chinese missionaries of Buddhism
had searched for the authentic sources and studied the decisive
phases of the Buddhist doctrine, which already was so important
an element in the civilization of their own country.[43] Here, too,
in the inaccessible valleys which, with the name of "Bolor" in the
Milione, rise up from the great bend of the upper Indus to the
Pamir, there still lived tribes of savages, whom Marco also describes as idolaters, but who undoubtedly adhered to the crude
rites of a native paganism which had not yet been refined and
superseded by the doctrines and precepts of Buddhism.[44]

All this topography of the religions practiced in the region
between the Hindu Kush and the Karakorum range, with the
massive heights of the Pamir at its center, is traced out in the
Milione in summary fashion, but with a precision of essential
data derived from information probably had from the Mohammedan merchants of Badakhshan, a land of transit for the age-old
trade between Bactriana and Eastern Turkestan, in the historic
country between the Oxus and the Indus.[45] In this province,
which he describes with a wealth of detail, Marco had spent a
period of convalescence after a year-long illness that he had con-
tracted in the less salubrious parts of this territory, which once
marked the western limit of Buddhistic expansion toward Persia.[46]

---

[42] *Il Milione,* cr. ed., p. 39 n.; M.P., p. 140.

[43] These famous texts, of capital importance for the geography, history, ethnography,
botany, etc., of those regions, are collected in part in an annotated English translation by S. Beal, *Si-yu-ki: Buddhist Records of the Western World,* 2 vols., London,
1906.

[44] *Il Milione,* cr. ed., p. 40, chap. 1; M.P., pp. 141 f. For the name of this region
cf. the lengthy discussion in Yule-Cordier, *The Book of Ser Marco Polo,* Vol. I, pp.
172 ff., and for the practices of these peoples, which were probably akin to those
of the pre-Buddhist populations of Kashmir and Tibet, cf. Cordier, *Addenda,* pp. 42 f.,
and V. Minorsky, Ḥudūd al 'Ālam, § 19 and pp. 369 ff.

[45] *Il Milione,* cr. ed., pp. 36 ff. (Balascian); M.P., pp. 136 ff.

[46] See chap. i above. The town of Taican (Talikan), mentioned by Marco (cr. ed.,

Marco was therefore well prepared for his first direct contact with the pagan world of Asia, though he still had to journey a great distance before those personal experiences should begin. Indeed, it was only in Chinese territory—the historic region of Tangut—that he was able to observe the rites and customs of the idolaters, as he continues to call them, in the various aspects which Buddhistic practice had developed there in direct dependence upon Tibetan Lamaism, absorbing the popular cults and traditions of the sedentary and nomad peoples scattered throughout this vast expanse of desert, urban oases, arid mountains, and meager pastureland.[47]

✧ ✧ ✧

Before reaching Tangut, Marco spent months in crossing the immense, deserted regions that extended from Talikan, in Badakhshan, across the Pamir, to present-day Sinkiang and the Great Desert, as far as the borders of China. For some centuries this land had been a center of Buddhist faith and culture, as we know from the Chinese missionaries who visited the small courts of its regional nobility and the monasteries and holy places of this faith, as well as from the archaeological remains recovered and described within the past fifty years by explorers from various nations.[48] No trace of Buddhism, however, was found by our traveler: a proof of the total Islamization of those regions that had been accomplished in his century with swift and lasting success. Marco, who was always so careful to mention even the minor religious characteristics of the localities visited by him, would certainly not have failed to indicate the presence of

p. 35; M.P., p. 135), would appear to have marked the western limit of Buddhist expansion until the Mohammedans came, although temporarily Buddhism was known as far westward as Balkh, the flourishing capital of Bactriana down to the time of the Mongol invasion, for which see B. Spuler, *Iran in früh-islamischer Zeit*, Wiesbaden, 1952, pp. 217 ff., with an extensive bibliography.

[47] *Il Milione*, cr. ed., pp. 44 ff.; M.P., pp. 150 ff. A topographical and archaeological description of this region is to be found (apart from the commentaries already mentioned) in the works of Sir Aurel Stein, especially *Ruins of Desert Cathay*, London, 1912; *Serindia*, 5 vols., Oxford, 1921; *Innermost Asia*, 4 vols., Oxford, 1928, and *On Ancient Central-Asian Tracks*, London, 1933 (which sums up the author's various other studies and offers a lucid account of his travels).

[48] Cf. Beal, *Si-yu-ki*, Vol. II, pp. 296 ff.

"idolaters" among the then exclusively Mohammedan populations.[49]

Having therefore arrived at "Saciu" or "the going out of the
desert," on the western borders of the present Chinese province
of Kansu, he found himself for the first time in a land inhabited
almost exclusively by idolaters, and was the first European
traveler to set foot there, so far as we know.[50] This afforded him
an opportunity to describe at first hand their rites and customs,
with an enumeration of ethnographic data valid not only for
this population of very mixed origin but also for those of other
regions where the cult of the Buddha and his idols prevailed.

The ancient kingdom of Tangut, conquered by the Tartars in
1227, was inhabited in its urban oases by Turks of various tribes,
especially Uigurs, as well as by Mongols, Chinese, and Tibetans.
These last spoke a dialect and preserved the language of their
Lamaist cult's sacred texts in their crowded monasteries and rich
sanctuaries. As agriculturalists they were marked off from the other
ethnic groups that inhabited this vast province, who busied themselves with trade, as did the majority of the Mohammedan and
Christian Turks mentioned by Marco, or with hunting and pastoral occupations, like the nomad Tartars.[51]

These idolaters had built there, as we read in the *Milione,* a
great number of abbeys and monasteries, filled with idols of all
shapes and sizes to which they offered sacrifices, honoring them
with reverence and devotion. However, the only rite that Marco

[49] The description of Eastern (or Chinese) Turkestan occupies chaps. li–lvii of the
Milione, cr. ed., pp. 40 ff.; M.P., pp. 143 ff. It is one of the most laconic accounts
in the whole book. For the extinction of Buddhism in this vast region and its subsequent and total Islamization cf. W. Barthold, *Turkestan,* pp. 254 ff., 387 ff., etc., and the
relevant articles in the *Encyclopaedia of Islam.*

[50] The Armenian High Constable Sempad passed through it, about the year 1248,
without, however, describing it in his famous letter, reproduced by Assemani in
Bibliotheca Orientalis, Vol. III, p. 500. "Saciu," on the edge of the desert, which is
nowadays known as Tun-huang, has for the past fifty years been renowned for its
"grottoes of the thousand Buddhas," which we have mentioned earlier. (See note 49
to § 1 of this chapter.)

[51] The Chinese element in those border regions was chiefly composed of soldiers
and officials. With their families and followers they formed, so to speak, a human
wall along and beyond the "Great Wall" in its last western stretches and isolated
outposts, which in Chinese lyric poetry of past ages are often mentioned as inhos-
pitable places of exile. The agricultural and urban groups were limited to the oases
that broke the monotonous solitude of those immense deserts.

describes at any length is in no way characteristic of Tibetan Lamaism or any other Buddhistic cult, but rather of practices in use among the Chinese, which were repeated with less pomp and significance among the nomads of the steppe, led by their shamans, whom Marco elsewhere refers to as "enchanters" inspired by the Devil.[52] He tells of the sacrifice of a ram in honor of the idols, which, according to him, "eat the substance of the flesh," which is afterward cut up and consumed with great reverence by the family of the person who ordered the propitiatory ceremony; the head, feet, entrails, and skin of the animal are left for the priests, and its bones are gathered with much care and stored in a sack.[53]

Although it is true that the degenerate Buddhism of the Middle Ages offers examples of exorcisms or sacrifices intended, like the one just described, to propitiate the deities whom man thus succeeds in dominating and directing, nevertheless this kind of priestly *agape* is completely alien to that religion, whereas it is very similar to the Tartar rites already described half a century before Marco by Friar John of Pian del Càrpine.[54] The precept prohibiting the killing of animals and feeding upon their flesh was followed more or less strictly by the Buddhist monks of every sect. Moreover, the images of their deities which they kept in great numbers in their monasteries, as Marco states, were not idols in the realistic and popular sense of the word, but symbolic figures that were supposed to intensify and direct the meditations which they felt would enable them to achieve the ultimate in spiritual

[52] For these sacrifices among the Mongols and other peoples of Upper Asia cf. Howorth, *History of the Mongols*, Pt. IV, pp. 99 ff. Following the excellent work by P. Pallas, *Sammlung historischer Nachrichten über die mongolischen Völkerschaften*, 2 vols., St. Petersburg, 1776–1801, the author asserts that the lamas had taken over these rites in order to please the native population, and had also imitated the shamans and their practices. For Chinese rites cf. J. J. M. de Groot, *The Religious System of China*, Leiden, 1892–1910, esp. Vols. IV and V.

[53] Cf. *Il Milione*, cr. ed., p. 44; M.P., pp. 150 f.

[54] *Sinica Franciscana*, Vol. I, p. 37; for other references cf. Rockhill, *The Journey of William of Rubruck*, p. 59. These rites must have been commonly practiced not only in the outlying region of Tangut, where Marco observed them, but elsewhere as well, since, as is noted by P. Demiéville, "La Situation religieuse en Chine au temps de Marco Polo," in *Oriente Poliano*, p. 266, the slaughtering of oxen and rams for these Buddhistic feasts of barbaric origin was prohibited by Kublai in 1291 as contrary to that religion.

enlightenment and the control of natural and spiritual forces—conditions necessary for their salvation.[55] On the other hand, the family atmosphere so warmly described in the *Milione,* the reference to the New Year and other feasts of the Chinese calendar, and the affinity with rites still practiced among the Chinese in recent times, and perhaps even today, are all clear indications of the national and popular character of this ceremony, which was inspired rather by Taoist traditions than by the doctrines and traditions of Buddhism.[56]

Even if Marco was not able to distinguish them from similar Tartar practices and other pagan rites of the Far East, he nevertheless supplies details that permit us to recognize them. Thus we may conclude that, immediately after having crossed the borders of the ancient Chinese empire, in the first place where he set foot he not only found the first Buddhistic monuments, but was able also to make out among the mass of peoples and religions in those parts the most characteristic aspects of Chinese national civilization, which was based, as is well known, on the unity of the family and the worship of the domestic deities that protected it, these being represented by the traditional images of their sanctuaries.

The preponderance of the Chinese element in the life of that distant province is clear from the lengthy description that Marco offers in this same chapter of the funeral rites observed there, which he erroneously extends to all the idolaters in the world.[57] Guided by these first impressions of pagan life, he describes the

[55] The offerings to the idols consisted mainly of flowers and incense. The complex symbolism of the images was known only to the monks of higher rank and culture. Many of them, as we have already mentioned, adapted themselves to popular superstitious practices which dated from the period before the expansion of Buddhism throughout the Far East.

[56] The province of Kansu, which for a long time was an independent kingdom, and in which Marco observed the rite described, had—like every other Chinese province and locality—its own regional divinities or genii, as well as deified mountains, rivers, and trees, and the cult of famous local personages. Kansu is renowned, moreover, for its numerous artificial and sculptured grottoes and the wealth of its Buddhist monuments.

[57] For these funeral rites, which are still practiced today in every part of China, cf. Henri Doré, S.J., *Recherches sur les superstitions en Chine,* Tome I (*Variétés Sinologiques,* no. 32), Shanghai, 1911. There is available also in English a translation by P. M. Kennelly. Father Doré has also published a short *Manuel des superstitions chinoises,* Shanghai, 1926, intended for the use of missionaries, but serviceable as a brief introduction to these ancient and modern practices.

observances on the basis of the traditions and religious customs practiced in Tangut, mentioning in detail the essential elements of the complex ritual that is so characteristic of the Chinese people and their popular religion.[58] The participation of the "diviners," also called astrologers by Marco, in these ceremonies is proof, as eloquent as rare, of the adoption of various popular rites and customs by all the religions practiced in China in Marco's times, namely, both by Taoists and by Buddhists of national tradition, as well as by the lamas who had settled in the country in the Chinghizide era, and who favored more than any other sect the practice of magic and the exorcism of spirits, in the way described by our author at this point.[59]

Leaving this study to more competent and systematic investigations of Polo's ethnography, and following the data in the *Milione* concerning the western regions of Cathay, we find ourselves in the province of Camul, which is recorded by Marco as a territory wholly inhabited by idolaters famous for the generous hospitality they extend to strangers, to the point of yielding up to them their women—"beautiful, and of a happy and entertaining disposition." [60] However, our traveler was not able to enjoy the benefits of this hospitality since he himself never visited this uncommon province, which was limited to the oasis of Hami on the edge of the Great Desert, on the caravan route that led from the town of

[58] *Il Milione,* cr. ed., p. 45; M.P., p. 151. This information forms part of the ethnographical, rather than the religious, data contained in the book, and should be studied accordingly.

[59] This religious eclecticism is characteristic of the Chinese peoples, even as their doctrinal syncretism is well known; hence it is more difficult to delimit the various denominational aspects in their religious practices than in their doctrines. The phenomenon is common to all advanced stages of paganism. Thus, the three ancient national religions of China (*San Chao*) have in practice been fused into one single magical, propitiatory cult, as has been shown most recently by H. Maspero, *Les Religions chinoises,* especially pp. 111 ff. This evolution was already well under way in Marco's times, and our author does in fact consider Oriental idolatry in the totality of its superstitious practices.

[60] Cr. ed., pp. 45 f.; M. P., pp. 154 f. Even though it may be possible to connect this custom with certain "rites" of sacerdotal defloration practiced among a few Asiatic tribes and as a Buddhist rite (cf. H. Franke, *Sinologie,* p. 105 and n.), it is nevertheless totally unrelated to the religious traditions observed in those regions, and may be associated with Marco's account of the province of Gaindu (cr. ed., p. 113; M.P., p. 273) in upper Yunnan, which was inhabited by the Lolos, who yielded up their wives, daughters, sisters, and other women to foreigners in order to propitiate their gods and idols. For this region and its customs cf. J. F. Rock, *The Ancient Na-khi Kingdom of Southwest China,* 2 vols., Cambridge, Mass., 1947.

Suchow, mentioned by him, to Turfan, the capital of Uiguristan.[61]

This vast region of mountains and deserts lay along the western foothills of the Celestial Mountains, the Chinese T'ien Shan, and included the metalliferous district of Chingintalas, as well as the oases of Hami and Karakhodja. It was inhabited by a mixed population of prevalently Uigur origin, presented by Marco as idolaters engaged in agriculture or dwelling in towns and fortified places, now ruined but rich in the relics and documents of an ancient regional civilization.[62] Here Marco was able to locate important Buddhistic communities, which dated from this faith's first period of expansion toward northern Asia. Whether or not they were seen by Marco in person, his description of them presents quite different aspects from those observed by him in the Chinese territory of "Succiu."

Their isolation among impassable mountains and limitless deserts, in a climate described by Marco as extremely severe in winter, and by other rare travelers as lethal in summer, helped to keep intact the doctrines, liturgy, literature, and art which the first Buddhist missionaries from Eastern Turkestan had introduced there from the Xth century onward, and especially at the time when the Mohammedan advance in Central Asia had intensified the exodus of all the pagan groups toward more hospitable regions. The Altaic peoples of those parts were quite free from religious prejudice and had formerly welcomed both Manichees and Christians without disturbing their practices. Indeed, with the favor of their lords, they had freely accepted these doctrines, which were more or less faithfully understood and followed by them.

Marco portrays the idolaters of this land as a wise people, who devoted themselves unceasingly to the study of the liberal arts and therefore were superior in culture and customs to the Saracen and Christian minorities with whom they lived in concord.[63]

---

[61] For the topography of these regions cf. Stein, *On Ancient Central-Asian Tracks*, pp. 240 ff.

[62] The monuments of Turfan and its neighboring regions have been studied systematically as a consequence of the expeditions organized by the German archaeologists A. Grünwedel and A. von Le Coq from 1902 onward. Cf. Stein, *On Ancient Central-Asian Tracks*, pp. 256 ff.

[63] *Il Milione*, cr. ed., p. 46 n.; M.P., p. 156.

Just what he meant by these liberal arts that were so earnestly cultivated by the pagans is not immediately obvious. Grammar, logic, and rhetoric—the Western *trivium* of medieval times— must of course be excluded; we should consider rather three disciplines of the *quadrivium*—arithmetic, geometry, and astronomy,—which were of practical utility even in those lands.

Indeed, it would appear that these latter, in their Oriental forms, were professed by the most learned monks and teachers not only in serving princes and sovereigns but also in attending the commonest circumstances in the daily life of the people; several examples are offered in the *Milione*. These "sciences" were learned and applied exclusively for purposes of divination; and it was because their counterparts were at times used similarly in Europe that Marco applied the term "liberal arts" to the studies and practices to which the pagan sages so diligently applied themselves.[64] In those regions, as elsewhere, nothing was undertaken without the help, advice, or direct participation of these wise men, of whom he speaks with such respect, and who, under the name of *bacsi,* were differentiated by their culture, however rudimentary and esoteric, from the Mongolian sorcerers and illiterate Turks.

By means of their astrological and geometric practices they established the dates, places, and circumstances most favorable to every undertaking in both peace and war; in daily life, the births, weddings, funerals, and all that could take place according to the will or grace of the divinities propitiated or exorcized. Convinced of the superiority of Christian civilization, as we have seen, Marco was here able to make a comparison between these arts of the Orient and the disciplines of the West, and wished to teach European scholars ways in which they could compete with the

[64] Geomancy, practiced in China for centuries, under the name of *fêng shui,* and in Italy in Marco's times, was employed in the Orient for determining the most propitious site for the erection of a town, cemetery, sepulcher, house, etc., for the protection of families and individuals against evil spirits and influences. An excellent introduction to the theory and practice of geomancy in China is to be found in J. J. M. de Groot, *Universismus,* pp. 364 ff. For the same sort of divination practiced with essentially similar aims and methods in the West at the time of Marco Polo cf. Bartholomew of Parma's unpublished treatise, which was composed at the bidding of the Bishop of Reggio Emilia in 1288 and is briefly discussed by Lynn Thorndike in *A History of Magic and Experimental Science,* Vol. II, New York, 1923, pp. 835 ff. See, too, the works quoted in n. 49 to chap. iv of the present volume.

pagans in exercising the powers of knowledge and of faith. More-over, while he praised these Altaic monks for their mastery of the "liberal arts," he clearly distinguished them from those who practiced magical arts with the help of the Devil.[65]

The diviners, astrologers, and skilled necromancers whom Marco saw at Kublai's court, and whose practices he described on various occasions, came only in part from those border regions. The missionaries who successfully introduced their Buddhism at the Chinghizide court were Tibetan lamas and magicians from Kashmir, who thereby contributed to the expansion of Mongol rule over the whole of continental Asia.[66]

It was precisely because of the historical and contemporary importance of the Buddhistic element among the Uigurs of these neighboring regions in Mongolia and China that Marco wished to make clear what it was that so differentiated its members from both the shamanist nomads and the Taoist monks of Cathay. The Altaic "idolaters" had indeed preserved Buddhist religious and literary traditions in relatively genuine form; and this conservatism was owing not merely to their isolation, which protected them from the influences of other pagan sects, but to their life on the land, which had assured their preservation until then but was to do so for only a short while to come.

According to Marco, they not only engaged in trade, which in the towns was so often the business of Christians and Saracens, but also grew grain and made wine and, on occasion, added pastoral produce.[67] Thus, the stability of this town and country life in the oases of that immense desert region naturally helped to maintain, together with curious local customs, the traditions of Buddhistic culture and art. These have recently been brought to light by systematic archaeological explorations which confirm their importance and variety as well as the information handed down to us by our traveler.[68]

By proceeding along the main route that led toward Cathay, he was able to supplement these secondhand reports with many

[65] *Il Milione*, cr. ed., resp. pp. 6 (chap. viii) and 70 n.; M.P., pp. 79 and 202.
[66] See above, n. 25 to chap. vi.
[67] *Il Milione*, cr. ed., pp. 44 and 48; M.P., pp. 150 and 159.
[61] For the topography of these regions cf. Stein, *On Ancient Central-Asian Tracks*, 238 ff., 256 ff.

details observed or learned through personal experience in the
course of a year spent with his father and uncle at Kanchow
(which he calls Campiciu), the capital of the ancient kingdom of
Tangut, which had become the Chinese province of Kansu.[69]
Marco fails to specify the reasons for their protracted stay there,
but we may assume that the three men used this important political, military, and caravan center as a base for excursions in
various directions, thereby giving a general impression of that
vast and historic border region and the various kinds of paganism
that flourished in the urban centers of those oases and the steppes
of the nomads on the edge of Greater Turkey (Turkestan) and
Mongolia.[70]

Here, too, the dominant element in the mixed population of
the provincial capital of China was made up of idolaters who
professed the Buddhistic faith. Our author again mentions their
monasteries and abbeys. This time, however, he notes the infinite
number of images, and refers to the rule of life followed by both
monks and laymen. For the first time, moreover, he looks at the
statues with a sense of artistic appreciation; probably because in
this town, which he describes as large and noble, they stood out
more than elsewhere on account of their numbers, craftsmanship,
and splendor. He saw them covered with gold, and beautifully
sculptured in wood, clay, or stone, either in the colossal forms of
the reclining Buddha or in those of the minor idols, in attitudes of
reverent humility, which were found in the local sanctuaries,
temples, and monasteries, as well as in caves consecrated to this
cult.[71]

[69] *Il Milione,* cr. ed., p. 48, chap. lxii; M.P., p. 159; and Stein, *op. cit.,* pp. 243 ff.
(with various references to Marco Polo's itinerary).

[70] Marco does not specify the localities personally visited by him in these regions.
Nevertheless, his topographical, ethnographical, and denominational data are equally
reliable for all of them. He notes that the Buddhist population of Tangut has its own
language and is thereby distinguished from the Saracens of the region and the Christians,
who probably spoke Uigur. Until the Mongol conquest this vast territory had preserved its own language, which has been studied by B. Laufer, "The Si-hia Language," *T'oung Pao,* Vol. XVII, 1916, pp. 1–126; it was probably still spoken at the
time of Marco's visit, but his reference is vague.

[71] These enormous statues of the reclining Buddha, which Marco says were as much
as 10 feet long—but which at Kanchow and at other places in China and Mongolia
were as much as 100 feet in length,—are especially characteristic of the numerous
sacred grottoes carved out of the rock on those bare mountainsides. The first to record
them in the West was Friar William of Rubruck (*Sin. Franc.,* Vol. I, pp. 228 f.), who

This, as is well known, is a typical scene of Buddhistic iconography to be found throughout the Orient, which signifies the Enlightened One's entry into nirvana, attended by his saints, whom Marco compares to those of the Christian religion, and who perpetuate his teachings and example in the world. Indeed, Marco immediately follows these iconographic observations by what he knows or imagines to be the moral and ecclesiastical rule of these faithful worshipers. As often in his account, it is the sins of the flesh that excite his curiosity; hence, while on the one hand he notes the chastity observed by the religious, on the other he embarks upon a casuistic inquiry into the sexual relationships between lay members of that faith,—an excursus that is nearer to the penitential distinctions of the confessional than to the concepts of Buddhistic morality.[72] In this same context, Marco makes a more precise distinction between the extreme abstinence practiced by the religious and the temporary abstinence observed by laymen, who deprived themselves of animal food for brief periods indicated by their calendar, which marked the special feast days celebrating their various "idols," the fast days, and those of special devotion when they lived "more virtuously than usual." [73]

Directing his glance northward—as probably his steps also,— Marco made his way through the desert separating the Chinese oases already mentioned from the southern borders of Mongolia. Here he came upon the caravan town of Etzina, the Mongol name for the Turkish city of Karakhoto, which was situated in one of the most desolate regions of the continent, but was famous in the

---

describes a reclining Buddha found in a temple at Karakorum "even as we portray St. Christopher" and refers to a statue in China described to him as so high that it could be seen "a duabus dietis" (from two days' journey away). These statues were generally made of clay, although, as Marco states, they were also carved in stone. The "minor idols" mentioned by Marco are evidently "bodhisattvas."

[72] "Il se gardent de luxurie, mes ne l'ont pas por grant pechiés," as Marco asserts (*Il Milione,* cr. ed., p. 48; M.P., p. 159) with apparent justice, while it is not possible to confirm his statement that they condemned to death "aucun home que aie jeu con feme contre nature."

[73] This detail accords with the practices (current even today) of the Buddhist faith, as well as those of every other official religion, whether organized or popular, in China. A well-nigh complete list is to be found in Doré, *Manuel des superstitions chinoises.* For these traditions cf. M. Granet, *Fêtes et chansons anciennes de la Chine,* second edition, Paris, 1929, and W. Eberhard, *Chinese Festivals,* New York, 1952. For the feast days of the Tibetan ecclesiastical calendar, also observed elsewhere, cf. L. A. Waddell, *The Buddhism of Tibet,* second edition, Cambridge, 1934, pp. 501 ff.

political and religious history of Upper Asia.[74] Indeed, it marked the northern limit of the first wave of Buddhistic expansion among those Turkish tribes, and its ancient ruins revealed its importance as an agricultural center and military station from the remotest antiquity down to the coming of Chinghiz Khan in 1226. In Marco's times, its population, as he asserts, was completely idolatrous. This last reference to its existence is confirmed by the number of polyglot texts and documents, buildings, statues, and relics of every kind that have come to light in the past fifty years of scientific exploration.[75]

The history of the Chinghizide conquests beyond the borders of near-by Mongolia begins at this point in the *Milione,* as it had done in the reality of recent history, and, with this, the description of the customs and religion of the Tartars with which this celebrated chapter opens. Here, for the first time, Marco specifies a particular aspect of Asiatic paganism, clearly distinguishing it from the Chinese or Lamaist Buddhism which he had treated hitherto in his denominational topography of Asia.[76] While describing the rites and beliefs of the Tartars, he notes that the genuine traditions of their "law" have given way to more refined manifestations of worship and civilization owing to the influence of the "idolaters" of Cathay, their vassals and neighbors.[77]

Marco therefore wished to give an authentic picture of this cult, as he was still able to observe it far from the great centers and courts, where, as we shall see later, some of these traditions did nevertheless remain alive. Thus Marco was the last Western author to witness those practices before they were, as he himself relates, corrupted by such contacts and overcome by the doctrines that had won over the ruling classes in the empire. Since they

---

[74] Cf. Cordier, *Addenda,* pp. 53 ff., and Stein, *On Ancient Central-Asian Tracks,* who offers detailed descriptions of these regions, their urban centers, and civilization, frequently quoting Marco Polo.

[75] As has already been mentioned in the first section of this chapter, the other towns mentioned by Marco—Shachow (Tun-huang) and Kanchow, as well as the Uigur center of Karakhodja (Turfan)—at that time still possessed Christian populations, and were thereby differentiated from Etzina (Karakhoto), which was inhabited only by "idolaters."

[76] *Il Milione,* cr. ed., pp. 54 ff.; M.P., pp. 170 ff.

[77] Marco justly observes (cr. ed., p. 56; M.P., p. 174 f.) that, whereas the Tartars who had settled in China had accepted the local customs and idols, those of the Levant followed the beliefs and practices of the Saracens.

were characteristic of the rude, primitive civilization of the nomads, they were preserved more or less intact especially beyond
the northern limits of Mongolia, among the Buriats, Tungus,
and other tribes of central and eastern Siberia, where the ancient
animist cult of the shamans has continued down to our own
times. Indeed, their ritual and the beliefs that govern it still serve
to illustrate Marco's acquaintance with their religion as it was
still preserved in its genuine forms among the peoples of Chinghizide Mongolia.[78]

The same subject had been treated in even greater detail by the
two Franciscan missionaries who had visited these countries
before him.[79] At that time, Lamaist Buddhism had not yet influenced or supplanted these declining traditions in any decisive
manner; hence the picture offered by the two friars serves to confirm and supplement our author's precise yet sober account. The
latter is all the more important since we have no other Oriental
or Western document, from the time of Kublai down to the end
of the dynasty, which illustrates the character and history of
that aspect of Tartar life.[80]

Our author, then, tells us that the Tartars had two chief divinities: a celestial one, to whom they daily offered up incense,
and from whom they entreated health of both mind and body;
the other, a terrestrial one called Natigai (or Nacigai), portrayed
in idols made of felt and cloth, who, when propitiated by means

[78] This is fully treated by Wilhelm Schmidt, *Die asiatischen Hirtenvölker*, on a basis
of information mainly gathered from Russian explorers and anthropologists of the
XIXth century. For popular traditions and the chants of the Mongol shamans, which
may still be heard today, see N. Poppe, *Mongolische Volksdichtung*, Wiesbaden, 1955.
[79] Cf. Friar John of Pian del Càrpine in *Sinica Franciscana*, Vol. I, pp. 36 ff., and
William of Rubruck, *ibid.*, pp. 174 f., etc.
[80] The Chinese documents relating to the religions professed in eastern Asia consider questions of almost exclusively practical and administrative interest, and are
therefore of little help in illustrating the rites and beliefs of the nomads. Since these
have never been systematically codified, and few traces of them are to be found even
in Mongol literature before it was altered by Buddhist and Chinese influences, it is
not possible to examine them in the light of exhaustive evidence. Hence, the various
interpretations of even the fundamental aspects of these traditions are at times widely
divergent: for example, the concept of divinity and professions of monotheism, dualism, or polytheism, which were reported, not without misunderstanding, by medieval
travelers including Marco. Hence, once again, this subject enters into the category of
anthropological problems and folklore, for which the *Milione* offers much valuable
material.

of various rites, protected their families, herds, and corn.[81] He found these same leading divinities among the inhabitants of Cathay, but there venerated by them with different rites from those practiced in Tartary.[82] Thus Marco recognized the fundamental dualism which, in quite different forms and doctrines, the Tartars had in common not only with the Chinese people but also with all the natives of Asia that had not been won over to the Mohammedan faith.[83]

The celestial divinity, universal and impersonal, of whom the sovereign was the emanation, the living image, and the omnipotent executor of his will, was fundamentally the same as the one to whom the Altaic peoples gave the name of Tängri, and the Chinese that of T'ien; that is to say, the immutable and inscrutable heaven, in whose name the Chinghizide sovereigns conquered and governed the world.[84]

The terrestrial divinity appears in the *Milione* only in a domestic context, as the protector of the home among the Chinese, of the tent among the nomads, and represented with a wife and children in a family group honored with domestic rites among the Tartars, who made these idols take part in their meals by smearing their mouths with the fat of the meat that had been prepared for the table.[85]

[81] *Il Milione*, cr. ed., pp. 54, 102 n., 230 (for the variants of this name cf. the notes to the passages quoted); M.P., pp. 170, 254, 469. The latest study concerning the name of this divinity is that by A. Mostaert, in *Oriente Poliano*, Rome, 1957, pp. 56 ff., where preference is given to the form "Naçigai," which also occurs in Francesco Pipino's Latin version of the *Milione*. This form would lend itself to a more satisfactory interpretation of the name, which has been variously explained by the most competent commentators.

[82] It is only in the Ramusian version that Natigai is mentioned at this point (cr. ed., p. 102 n.; M.P., p. 254). This is justly considered spurious by Yule-Cordier, *The Book of Ser Marco Polo*, Vol. I, p. 458 n. 3. Marco was aware that the Chinese never used felt, which they considered to be a barbaric material, unworthy of the godhead. Cf., besides Laufer, *Sino-Iranica*, the present author's work, *The Myth of Felt*, pp. 14 ff.

[83] For example, Zoroastrianism and Manichaeism, which have more or less influenced all the religions of Asia, as had already been observed by William of Rubruck (*Sin. Franc.*, Vol. I, pp. 273 ff. and 295 ff.). Cf. G. Messina, *Cristianesimo, Buddhismo, Manicheismo nell'Asia antica*, and, for more detailed study, the fundamental work by E. Chavannes and P. Pelliot, "Un traité manichéen retrouvé en Chine" (extract from *Journal Asiatique*), 1912.

[84] See above, chap. vi, nn. 15 and 20.

[85] Marco therefore noted the essential difference between the divinities of the Buddhist

Natigai and this same rite are also correctly mentioned by
Marco in his account of the Tartars of Siberia, who, according
to him, lived like animals in a northern region which it is impossible to specify but undoubtedly was outside the sphere of
Chinese and Persian influence and therefore more faithful to
the genuine traditions of the nomads of the steppe.[86] Indeed,
Marco at this point confirms the fact that their "law" was common to all the Tartars; he mentions once more the idols made
of felt which were characteristic of their civilization.

A great deal of discussion has centered on the name and function of this Natigai, who is mentioned only in the *Milione* and in
a form that is undoubtedly altered.[87] It is, however, unlikely

sanctuaries and the Tartar idols, which latter were also recognizable by the material
of which they were made. Moreover, he described the domestic cult of the Chinese,
which mainly consisted in censing the votive tablets (cr. ed., Ramusian text, p. 102 n.,
M.P., p. 254), which was not a custom of the illiterate Tartars, who would raise
their hands and "grind their teeth." On this expression, which is probably incorrect,
cf. Yule-Cordier, *The Book of Ser Marco Polo*, Vol. I, p. 461. The practice of smearing the mouths of their idols with grease (also blood) was fairly common throughout
Upper Asia. Late, but specific, evidence is offered by the anonymous *Lettera di rag-
guaglio del Granducato di Moscovia*, Milan, Bologna, Florence, 1657 (reprinted in
Documenti che si conservano nell'Archivio di Stato in Firenze, ed. M. Boutourlin,
Moscow, 1871, pp. 143 ff.), in which it is stated that in so-called Greater Hungary—
i.e., in western Siberia,—in proximity to the Tartars, as the letter has it, there existed
a stone idol representing an old woman with a child in her arms (?), called *Zolotobaba*
—the Russian for "old woman of gold,"—whose mouth and other parts of the body
were anointed with the blood of slaughtered deer.

[86] This is the region Marco calls "Canci" (*Il Milione*, cr. ed., p. 230; M.P., p. 469),
situated in the "Tramontaine" district, and so called from the name of a Chinghizide
prince who reigned in western Siberia, beyond the boundaries of the Golden Horde,
or Qipchak, whose ambassadors Marco may have seen at Gaikhatu's court in Persia in
the year 1293 (cf. Yule-Cordier, *The Book of Ser Marco Polo*, Vol. II, p. 481). However this may be, the passage in the *Milione* is of great interest and value owing to
the rarity of authentic, or direct, information about the religious practices and customs
of this region beyond the Urals (cf. Spuler, *Die Goldene Horde*, pp. 241 ff.), which
corresponds to that described in the Letter cited in the preceding note. We may believe Marco's statement that this territory was still inhabited by pagan nomads, hunters,
and suppliers of furs to the courts and merchants of the empire. The nobles or merchants would then transmit more or less exact information about these peoples, like
that contained in the already mentioned Letter. Already in 1238 the Hungarian Dominican, Julian, had written a letter to the Bishop of Perugia, pontifical legate in Hungary,
wherein he briefly described the territories situated between the Volga and the Urals,
i.e., that same "Greater Hungary," which had just been conquered by the Mongols.
Cf. László Benfedy's article, cited earlier (chap. ii, § 2, n. 31), in *Archivum Europae
Centro-Orientalis*, Vol. II, pp. 1 ff.

[87] Cf. Yule-Cordier, *The Book of Ser Marco Polo*, Vol. I, pp. 258 f. P. Pelliot (*T'oung
Pao*, Vol. XXV, 1927, p. 148) identifies it with Ätügän, "vieille déesse mongole de la
terre." See above, n. 81.

that he represented the Mongol divinity of the earth, invoked under the name of Ätügän (or Itügän) by Temudjin, the future Chinghiz Khan, according to the *Secret History of the Mongols,* which was compiled in 1240 and based on authentic documents and the poetic history of the conqueror.[88] This is in fact a female divinity, and in that character is mentioned as a cosmic element in that greatest Mongol literary document of the Chinghizide era.[89]

Marco Polo's Natigai, on the other hand, appears as the supreme domestic idol of Altaic nomad tribes described by him as people who lived on milk and meat but did not practice agriculture. This is therefore no agrarian divinity, but a male idol who, according to Marco, has a wife and even children of his own. In this way Natigai comes to resemble the head of the domestic divinities that were found in every Chinese home. Moreover, the sons that Marco attributes to him are not other than the minor deities of the hearth, which, like all the other numerous domestic gods in the popular religion of those peoples, are subject to him.[90] Hence Marco was mistaken in giving him the name, however altered, of the terrestrial divinity of the Mongols, whereas he does on the other hand offer some correct information about his cult, which

[88] Section 113 in the Mongol text edited by Haenisch, as well as in the German translation by the same author and the French translation by P. Pelliot, *Œuvres posthumes,* Vol. I, pp. 29 and 151.

[89] Cf. what Schmidt (*Die asiatischen Hirtenvölker*) has to say about it with respect to Itoga, Vol. X, pp. 62 ff.; also, N. Pallisen in the dissertation cited in n. 11 above. The whole question, however, is in need of a reëxamination based on A. Mostaert's article (mentioned in n. 81). It would seem that one should rather recognize in this Mongolian female divinity the corresponding Chinese cosmic principle which represents the earth as existing in harmonious discord with heaven, and the sovereign as moderator and intermediary between the two.

[90] Cf. H. Maspero, *Les Religions chinoises,* pp. 111 ff. For these individual domestic divinities and the god of the hearth, as well as the ceremonies and rites universally and traditionally practiced in China, see H. Doré, S.J., *Recherches sur les superstitions en Chine,* Vol. XI (*Variétés Sinologiques,* no. 46), Shanghai, 1916, pp. 901 ff. We are not so well informed concerning Tartar and shamanist rites, although these have been studied by W. Radloff, *Aus Sibirien,* Leipzig, 1893, and by Pallisen in the dissertation cited. Various aspects of these practices have recently been studied by Russian anthropologists. Yule (*The Book of Ser Marco Polo,* Vol. I, pp. 258 f.) identifies Marco's Natigai with the Öngüt—also called Nogait, Ongotai, etc., by related and neighboring tribes in Siberia,—a term which designates the minor deities or spirits. This interpretation would certainly appear to be more credible than the confused data offered by our author. According to him, the wife is placed on the left, as in fact she is in Tartar court ceremonial.

may have been observed by the Venetian in the course of his travels.
The other rite described in the *Milione* in his discussion of this
religion is the custom of pouring some broth outside the entrance
to a house, as an offering to the other "spirits." [91] It is difficult to
interpret this offering as an act of homage to the divinity of the
soil; it should be connected rather with the animistic demonology
of the Altaic peoples, as intended to placate the spirits that held
sway outside the dominion of the domestic divinities. The world
is full of these spirits, according to beliefs that are still current in
the Far East. Inspired by these local legends, Marco felt their influence at work, terrorizing the travelers who crossed the deserts
on the northwestern borders of China.[92]

This was in fact their favorite spot, and the memory of their
threatening voices and the sound of drums and other musical
instruments occasioned by them at night in those desolate deserts
afforded good proof of their reality. Similar references are frequently to be found in travel literature from eras long past, and
are echoed in Arab and Chinese texts down to Marco's own
times.[93] Nor could they fail to turn up at this point; especially
since, already convinced of the existence of demons as a result of
his Christian upbringing, our traveler not only heard the mysterious sounds on a number of occasions, but also accepted the
most common local explanation of them.[94]

---

[91] This rite not only recalls Friar John of Pian del Càrpine's account of this method
of making the "spirits" participate in meals at court and in the home (cf. *Sin. Franc.*,
Vol. I, p. 37), but is also reminiscent of the Chinese imperial rite minutely described
by J. J. M. de Groot, *Universismus*, pp. 155 ff. The latter, however, does not allow the
presence and worship of idols, which the Confucian tradition replaces by votive
tablets. For reasons of state, Kublai restored these grandiose ceremonies in the temples
of Heaven and Earth in the capital, whereas in his summer residences he maintained
the Tartar usage in the way described by Marco (*Il Milione*, cr. ed., p. 63; M.P., p.
187). The aspersions were also made with *kumis*, or *cosmos*, i.e., fermented mare's milk,
the national Tartar drink, which was also described by the Franciscan missionaries
who visited Mongolia, as may be seen in *Sinica Franciscana*, Vol. I, pp. 175 ff., 179,
etc.

[92] *Il Milione*, cr. ed., pp. 43 and 58; M.P., pp. 150 and 178.

[93] Examples in Yule-Cordier, *The Book of Ser Marco Polo*, Vol. I, pp. 201 ff.

[94] Namely the belief, prevalent throughout pagan Asia, in the existence of spirits
essentially adverse to the life and work of man. These demons, who populate the air
and every other element and aspect of life, persecute travelers, as Marco tells us, by taking them so far out of their way "that they are never found again." They do this,
however, as a result of their natural "evil will," as Dante (*Purgatorio*, V, 112) defines
it, and not in order to tempt their victims.

It is of course true that not everyone yielded to this terror. The great Taoist prelate, Ch'ang Ch'un, who crossed the deserts of Mongolia by marching at night, in 1221, on his way from China to the Hindu Kush, comforted his companions and exhorted them not to give way to fear. He said to them: "Do you not know that ghosts and evil spirits fly from the presence of honest men? There are many instances of this in books which I am sure you have all read. And if this is true of ordinary folk, the followers of Tao ought surely not to be afraid." [95] And we may assume that, as a good Christian, Marco thought himself similarly protected from these adverse forces that were a part of Oriental demonology.

Although the Tartars also worshiped images, they are not, for Marco, the same idolaters; clearly, he recognized that the Asiatic peoples had different forms of paganism, distinct according to the race and country. The total absence of any "church," collective worship, or liturgy likewise served to mark off this rude and popular paganism from Lamaist Buddhism, which had absorbed or tolerated it for social or propagandistic reasons rather than from doctrinal conviction. In the course of its renewed expansion in Mongolia and China, the Lamaist missionaries, as always, limited their conquests to the court circles and ruling classes, leaving the people to their ancestral superstitions. They knew that by bringing about the suppression of Chinese Taoism they would extirpate or at least paralyze this ancient popular religion in China, of which Ch'ang Ch'un had been the last and worthy reformer. [96]

Consequently, it was at the court of the Great Kaan Kublai that Marco could see at work all the practices of contemporary Asiatic paganism, and inquire into their institutions, rites, and to some degree even their fundamental doctrines. Their practices were evidently performed with greater pomp and frequency at the sovereign's summer residence, where he was not only less burdened by affairs of state and court but also more inclined to cultivate the traditional forms of life and worship, which the

---

[95] Cf. A. Waley, *The Travels of an Alchemist*, p. 79. Here we learn that it was the custom to anoint the horses' heads with blood in order to keep these spirits at a safe distance.

[96] This did in fact take place in Kublai's reign; see above, chap. vi.

cosmopolitan atmosphere of the capital naturally tended to alter and restrict.

Marco was in fact able to observe the entire varied pageant of those idolatries in the grandiose pavilions of "Ciandu" (Shangtu), which stood in a region of lakes and forests (where the present Chinese province of Jehol borders on Mongolia) that preserved in its scenery, and in the language and customs of its inhabitants, the characteristic aspects of the emperor's homeland.[97] It is not therefore by mere chance that the first mention of the rites practiced at court refers to the custom of sprinkling the fermented milk of consecrated mares in the air and on the ground before the emperor's departure from his summer residence on the twenty-eighth day of the August moon.[98] The idolaters told him on this occasion that the sacrifice was "necessary, so that the spirits should preserve all his property, men and women, beasts, birds, corn, and everything else." This, as we see, corresponds to what was described as a characteristic Tartar rite practiced with the same forms and intentions, though in more modest surroundings, at the other end of Mongolia. The "idolaters" who imposed and directed this propitiatory rite and exorcism at Kublai's court were therefore Mongolian shamans, like those seen by William of Rubruck at the court of Karakorum, who were always eager to sprinkle the soil and their idols of felt with mare's milk according as their calendar and the ceremonial of the imperial court required, as well as on the days considered favorable to one or another undertaking, whether normal or extraordinary.[99]

Whereas these imperial shamans and their rites represented the Mongol element in the Great Kaan's religious circus, his enchanters and astrologers from Tibet and Kashmir, whom Marco calls *bacsi,* as we have already seen, belonged to that sect of

[97] *Il Milione,* cr. ed., pp. 62 ff.; M.P., pp. 185 ff. It was in this now legendary locality of "Xanadu" that Niccolò and Maffeo Polo were presented to the emperor in the summer of 1265. See above, n. 105 to chap. ii, § 2.

[98] Aside from the dates fixed every year by the court astrologers for the official calendar, which regulated the entire life of the empire and was imposed on tributaries, the most propitious days were assigned, as occasion arose, for determining the times of arrival and departure for the sovereign and his court; hence for these events there were both fixed and variable dates.

[99] The Chinese did not use fermented milk; their ritualistic and magical aspersions were made with animal or vegetable broth, in the solemn imperial celebrations as well as in the domestic practices described by Marco.

Lamaist Buddhism which had been especially successful in those lands, and was characterized by magical practices more or less arbitrarily inserted into the ancient system of worship.[100] Marco's attitude is far more critical toward these professional miracle-workers who brought both good and bad weather to Kublai's court, and made goblets fly through the air to the sovereign's lips without the help of human hands.[101]

For our Venetian, who had nothing to say when the shamans exorcized the spirits of the desert or propitiated those of the earth and the air, all the practices of the *bacsi* were works of the Devil. On their part, to be sure, the sorcerers averred that their unearthly feats were made possible by their own priestly sanctity and by divine help; and thus they succeeded in obtaining from the sovereign all that they desired in order to honor and propitiate their idols on their respective feast days, censing them with fine spices, offering up sacrificial viands, sprinkling the temples with broth, and organizing illuminations and festivals of song.[102]

It is in this context that Marco makes us understand the great ascendancy that the *bacsi* had over the emperor, and their power over the dignitaries of the court. While it is possible to believe that the uncleanliness which he attributes to them is to be referred rather to the sorcerers of Tartary, it is not possible to doubt that the ritual cannibalism referred to by him was practiced in special circumstances and in a more or less symbolic form by these same lamas, whom he portrays as clothed in more honorable fashion than the others and recognizable by their closely shaven heads and faces.[103]

[100] Cf. the *Milione,* cr. ed., pp. 64 n., 65, 78; M.P., pp. 189 f. and 219. See n. 41 above.

[101] *Il Milione,* cr. ed. and M.P. as cited in the preceding note. These practices have been exhaustively described by Yule-Cordier, *The Book of Ser Marco Polo,* Vol. I, p. 314, and it is not possible to add anything else from authentic sources.

[102] *Il Milione,* cr. ed., p. 64; M.P., p. 189.

[103] The reference to the uncleanliness of the court *bacsi* is found only in the Ramusian version, at the end of a passage that praises the power of these "sages homes," expert in the art of magic. The remark is strange since cleanliness has never been a virtue of the Mongols, who have always been reluctant to contaminate the element of water and its spirits. It is a known fact that their stench was one of the things that most terrified the European armies in their struggle against the Mongol hordes. It is, however, doubtful that Marco would speak of so common a trait with reference especially to Buddhist magicians, particularly since Ricoldo da Montecroce, his contemporary, does not mention it when describing them at even greater length in his *Libro della*

Marco distinguishes, moreover, those who lived in the populous monasteries, as large as towns, from those who were allowed to take a wife and beget a large number of children. Indeed, it was only after the reform of Tsong Kha-pa, at the end of the XIVth century, that the strict rule of celibacy observed in Chinese Buddhistic monasticism was also imposed, at least theoretically, on the religious, while setting free the lay brothers from the obligations of their monastic life, to which, however, they could return if and when it so pleased them.[104] Thus Marco was able to note that, in spite of various similarities in ritual and way of life, Lamaist monasticism was less rigid than the Western kind, although in the Orient there were to be found excesses of renunciation and sacrifice, which were becoming far more rare in Europe.

By a careful reading of the text we realize that Marco made some fundamental distinctions between the several sects and practices of Oriental paganism. He marked off from the great mass of idolaters of all kinds those religious who practiced strict abstinence. They were considered to be heretics by the other monks, owing to the different images they worshiped, the hard life they led in total celibacy, their meager, insipid fare, their distinctive yellow and black dress, and the name of *sensin* by which they were called.[105] In China this appellation was used to designate

---

peregrinazione (cf. the edition by Monneret de Villard, pp. 47 ff.). The observation, therefore, may well be out of place in the passage cited from the Ramusian text and may refer to others—perhaps the shamans, who were notorious for their neglect of bodily hygiene. So far as ritual cannibalism is concerned, it would seem that it was practiced at least symbolically in Tibet as a relic of the rites and sacrifices of the pre-Buddhist religion there (cf. L. A. Waddell, *The Buddhism of Tibet*, pp. 516 f.), but it does not appear among the rites practiced by the shamans (Schmidt, *Die asiatischen Hirtenvölker*, Vol. X, pp. 722 ff., etc.). It was, however, attributed to all the Oriental peoples, whether historical or fabulous, by classical, Hellenistic, medieval, Arabic, and Christian geographical literature. Hence, Marco's remark may be merely an echo of this literary cliché or of local legend. Cf. the relevant article in the *Encyclopaedia of Religion and Ethics*, and Garry Hogg, *Cannibalism and Human Sacrifice*, London, 1958; also note 51 to chap. ii, § 2, above.

[104] Seclusion, extreme asceticism, and the most extravagant practices of mortification and self-obliteration are, as is well known, characteristic and frequent aspects of the Oriental religions to which Marco gave a few lines in his description of India, where various sects still observe these practices in their most repellent forms (cf. *Il Milione*, cr. ed., pp. 190 f.; M.P., pp. 405 f.).

[105] *Il Milione*, cr. ed., p. 65; M.P., p. 191. It would seem that Marco refers to particular Taoist practices. Cf. H. Maspero, *Les Religions chinoises*, pp. 49 ff., Waley's

masters of the Tao, the doctrine of Lao-tzŭ, which had in fact developed a system of teachings, use of idols, liturgy, and monastic organization comparable to their respective Buddhistic models, yet concentrating all these manifestations of a national Chinese religion in a kind of hereditary papacy, and at the same time cultivating, apart from popular magic in its lowliest practices, a system of natural science that culminated in an esoteric alchemy of a mystical and moral sort which found its most illustrious exponent in the age of Chinghiz in the person of the sage, Ch'ang Ch'un.

The affinities that existed, from the first centuries of our era, between this national religion and Chinese or Lamaist Buddhism justifies the term "Paterins" that Marco applies to the Taoists, especially since in his times the Buddhists of the court described by him represented an official religion, whereas the Taoists were considered a rebellious sect, which was combated with methods not unlike those used in the West to persecute and exterminate the heretics referred to as Paterins or Cathars.[106] Nevertheless, Marco perceived the difference in the representatives of this

---

introduction to *The Travels of an Alchemist*, pp. 9 ff., and, besides the works by J. J. M. de Groot already cited, L. Wieger's *Taoisme*, 2 vols., 1911–1913, with its list of the sacred texts and literature of this cult, and W. Eichhorn, "Bemerkung zur Einführung des Zölibats für Taoisten," *Rivista degli Studi Orientali*, Vol. XXX, 1955, pp. 297 ff. As will be noted, Marco was only acquainted with the animistic and naturalistic aspects of the Tao, but not with the philosophical, mystical, scientific, and moral doctrines developed by its classics into a complex universal system. The fire worship that Marco attributes to them is independent of Zoroastrianism; it is more reminiscent of the Chinese cult, similar to that of the Turkish and Mongol shamans, for which see N. Poppe, "Zum Feuerkultus bei den Mongolen," *Asia Major*, Vol. II, 1925, and Schmidt, *Die asiatischen Hirtenvölker*, Vol. X, 1925, pp. 70 ff. As for the food eaten by these ascetics, which Marco describes as bran soaked in hot water, it is difficult to equate it with the Mongol-Tibetan *tzamba*, which is instead a compound of barley meal mixed with melted butter and dissolved in warm tea. Marco is always precise in his identifications of the cereals used in Asia, and would hardly have mistaken wheat for barley. This detail helps to make an important distinction between the *sensin*, or Chinese Taoists, and any other Tibetan or Mongolian sect that Marco might mistakenly have designated with this name. The Chinese do not in fact drink the beverage described in the *Milione* (*loc. cit.*). We must therefore regard it as an extreme example of the dietetic abstinence practiced by this sect, and not as a national drink like the *tzamba* of Upper Asia, which is still used today. Everything therefore points to the identification of Marco's *sensin* with the *hsien sheng* of the Chinese, who thus designated those who strove in the way described by Marco to achieve that physical, moral, and metaphysical incorruptibility which was the goal of their daily sacrifices.

[106] See chap. vi above.

ascetic fanaticism, which by means of a systematic apprenticeship of renunciation gave to its followers the absolute spiritual
integrity necessary to bring about in themselves the primordial
perfection and perfect understanding of the Tao that is the vital
principle of the universe and, at the same time, as the word
(='way') itself reveals, the way to grasp and realize it in the
human microcosm in harmony with the eternal and natural
macrocosm.[107]

However, the only one of the doctrines concealed behind the
various rites and customs of Chinese idolatry to be revealed by
Marco is that of the transmigration of souls. For the rest, he asserts
with some exaggeration that the inhabitants of Cathay, whose
"law" is briefly treated by him, have no care either for their
consciences or for their souls. But since in the same chapter he
discusses with admiration the high moral qualities of this people,
noting among other things the filial love which, as is well known,
under the name of *hsiao* was at the basis of the whole social and
political structure of ancient China, it may be taken for certain
that these words should be understood in the Christian, theological
sense.

Marco thereby differentiates the Christian concept of an individual, redeemable soul and conscience from that of the pagans,
who do not believe in a personal god or creator to whom man is

[107] The description of the practices of this sect closes with an obscure remark that
deserves critical examination. The most reliable text of the *Milione* (F in the cr. ed.)
asserts at this point (*ibid.*, p. 65, lines 104 f., M.P., pp. 190 f.) that "lor moistier et
lor ydres sunt toutes femes, ce est a dire qu'il ont toutes nons de femes." This reading
makes no sense and is certainly corrupt; hence, several authoritative versions of Polo's
text omit the word for 'monasteries' and refer only to the idols, while still declaring
that they are all female. (For the various readings cf. M.P., p. 191, n. 5.) It is not
possible to believe that Marco attributed feminine names to the monasteries and idols
of the Far East, especially since, when discussing those of India (cr. ed., p. 184, M.P.,
p. 393), he divides them into "masles et feme," after having stated earlier (cr. ed.,
p. 166, M.P., p. 364) that the idols of the Far East are "d'une mainere," that is, all
of one fashion. Moreover, the explicative tag "ce est a dire . . ." is quite unusual in
Marco's style and would appear to be a gloss which, albeit an old one, was interpolated
in the text in order to explain an incoherent phrase. In fact, we know that throughout the pagan Orient there existed not only male, female, and and androgynous idols,
but also both monasteries and convents which are duly so registered in the imperial
annals as a result of the fiscal and other privileges enjoyed by these institutions when
permitted to function at all. Therefore we may, and perhaps ought, conjecture an
original reading as follows: "Lor moistier et lor ydres sunt d'homes et femes," thereby
abandoning the explicative gloss, which is superfluous and in open contradiction to
other and genuine remarks by Marco on this subject.

accountable for his actions, and do not accept the immortality of single souls in a dogmatically defined ultramundane system.[108] Hence, he received the impression that the Chinese could concern themselves merely with the material satisfactions of life while still applying themselves with diligence to studious pursuits and in the belief that when the time should come for them to be born again in the eternal cycle of life their future existence would depend upon their good or bad behavior on earth.[109]

In this way Marco recognized that the basis of the Buddhist religion was more moral than metaphysical, and that the religious interests of the Chinese tended to be practical rather than transcendent. Hence even his conception of this transmigration is essentially social, so far as it is morally determined. According to Marco's account, the moral worth of a person is measured by the various steps that he ascends in the social hierarchy, from the most abject squalor to divine perfection, through successive reincarnations in the womb of a gentlewoman, and then of a princess, and so rising until he is one with the Deity. The reverse is the descent from nobility to agrarian servitude, and thence to the animal kingdom, from dogs downward, to the lowest forms of existence and at last the Devil.[110]

A metaphysical leap is thereby implied from the princely state to the divine, to which is opposed the other from a man, be he but a simple peasant, to a beast and, to complete the series, to the infernal monsters admitted by Buddhistic eschatology in direct

---

[108] According to Taoist teaching, immortality is gained by ascetic practices, to which Marco refers, accompanied by alchemistic and magical tricks, in such a way as to liberate man from his physical body and transform him in life and death into a perfect being, possessed of freedom and happiness. The concept of the soul, which is so clear in its Christian definition, is one of the most obscure in the whole Buddhistic system and one generally avoided by its apologists, although it is the subject of endless, inconclusive speculation and controversy among the various sects. Unlike the soul with which the Christian is born, the Buddhistic soul is rather an acquired character and therefore mutable according to its various incarnations, which correspond to so many deviations from the main road to salvation revealed by Sakyamuni, the Buddha. For the Chinese concept of the soul cf. D. H. Smith in *Numen*, Vol. V, 1958, pp. 165–179.

[109] *Il Milione*, cr. ed., p. 102 n.; M.P., p. 254.

[110] For Buddhist demonology, especially in its popular, mythological, and artistic aspects, as developed within the framework of the Buddha's teachings, cf. Waddell, *The Buddhism of Tibet*, pp. 475 ff., and G. Tucci, *Tibetan Painted Schrolls*, at the respective chapters; also, H. Hoffmann, *Die Religionen Tibets*, pp. 83 f.

contrast to the divine.[111] This natural, social hierarchy of reincarnation, which recalls the caste system of Brahmanic India, was
alien to Chinese Buddhism, although it was an ancient custom to
confer nobiliary titles on Buddhistic idols and gods.[112] Moreover,
nowhere in Marco Polo's account do we find mention of the
fundamental concept of *nirvāna* as a willed and definitive libera-
tion from this cycle of rebirths, a cycle determined by moral
qualities and conduct in secular life, but especially by the systematic sacrifices of the monastic life.[113]

Marco was also unaware of the other fundamental principles
of Buddhism that were a part of the philosophical, cosmological,
contemplative, and mystical system of this religion and were dis-
regarded by, or even unknown to, the laymen of the Oriental
world in which our Venetian found himself. In that world, as in
his book, the highest grade in the hierarchy of beings was represented by the divinity conceived as an idol—that is to say, as the
image of a sovereign being with occult powers who held sway
over even the highest dignitaries in the social hierarchy described
in Marco's pages.[114]

[111] There are various types of demons in Buddhist demonology, which was largely
taken over by Taoism. However, they remain distinct from those of the Christian
system inasmuch as this latter does not accept a metaphysical and theistic opposition
of good and evil in the dualistic sense. The Buddhist demons represent the adverse
forces immanent in nature and in humankind which tempt man and may even
destroy him. They may be put to flight by the practice of magic, but are overcome
only when man has freed himself from desire according to the methods taught by the
Buddha. As Marco Polo himself pointed out, the individual soul does not exist in
the Buddhistic system as a created and lasting entity.

[112] Cf. the works quoted above on Chinese religions, especially H. Maspero, *Les
Religions chinoises,* pp. 71 ff.

[113] Marco, although in somewhat rudimentary fashion, made a valid distinction between the monastic and lay virtues as understood and practiced in the Orient, but
he was not aware of the belief that it is possible to be freed from the cycle of reincarnation. He implicitly considered the next existence to be perpetual and pro-
portional to the creature's social rank, conceived by him in accordance with the
feudal system in the West. There, the villein occupied the lowest place; and the
Chinese peasant's condition under the Mongol dynasty was in fact similar; see W.
Eberhard, *Chinas Geschichte,* Bern, 1948, pp. 263 ff. The Mongols were not acquainted
with the social status of peasants, but had to take it into account after their conquest
of China, where agricultural production differed greatly in the various regions, rice
being the principal crop in the southern provinces, whereas other cereals were cultivated in the north.

[114] For Marco, the Buddha's death does not represent his entrance into, or return
to, nirvana, nor the definitive cessation of the cycle of earthly existences referred to
by our author, but rather a return to "him who never dies and who had created him"
(cf. *Il Milione,* cr. ed., p. 194, line 43; M.P., p. 409). This, according to Marco, was what

This feudal interpretation of the *samśara,* or cycle of existence, most probably stems from the conception of it formed by those members of the Chinghizide court who had been won over to Lamaist Buddhism. It corresponds not only to the hierarchic system of the society and administration of the Chinghizide empire, but also to ancient Chinese traditions preserved in classical texts and in the terminology of the popular religion. It was in this way that a Buddhist monk residing at Karakorum half a century before had explained to William of Rubruck the system of divinities accepted there, comparing it to a feudal hierarchy that set up a supreme, though not omnipotent, chieftain with numerous vassals and a potentially infinite number of earthly deities.[115]

his Sagamoni Borcan had sought to attain in life; and he thereby attributed to him Christian concepts and aims that were foreign to Buddhism but were associated with it in the medieval romance of Barlaam and Josaphat, for which see F. Dölger, "Der griechische Barlaam-Roman," *Studia Patristica et Byzantina,* 1953. Some extracts from the Italian XIVth-century translation of this famous text are to be found in Don G. de Luca, ed., *Prosatori minori del Trecento,* I: *Scrittori di religione* (in the series *La Letteratura italiana: Storia e Testi,* Vol. XII, Tomo I), Milan and Naples, 1954, pp. 383–395. See above, note 27. According to what Marco learned in Ceylon (*loc. cit.*), the Buddha, before being deified, had died eighty-four times, successively becoming an ox, horse, dog, or other animal. This crude interpretation of his reincarnations is probably of Mohammedan origin and therefore quite different from the concept held by Mongolian Buddhists. The canonical accounts of the former lives of the Buddha are contained in the *Jataka,* one of the most popular books of Buddhist literature.

[115] Cf. *Sinica Franciscana,* Vol. I, p. 296. This passage is of great importance for an understanding of Marco's attitude and for the history of the religions then practiced in Upper Asia and China. A Buddhist, probably a Uigur from Karakorum, told Friar William: "There is one god in the sky who is above all others, and of whose origin we are still ignorant, and there are ten others under him, and under these latter is another lower one"—a purely Mahayana doctrine referring to the primordial or Adhi-Buddha and his personifications called Dhyani-Buddhas, or, in Tibetan, Jinas, generally seven in number and not ten as the friar stated. Shortly before, this same *tuin,* or Buddhist priest, had asserted: "Fools say that there is only one god, but the wise say that there are many. Are there not great lords in your country, and is not this Mangu Kaan a greater lord? So it is of the gods, for they are different in different regions." However, the sect or school of the Mahayana, which practiced its beliefs in Upper Asia and China, and of which the *tuin* here mentioned is an authentic and well-informed representative, admitted the deification of cosmic principles and natural forces; indeed, going so far as to personify the Supreme Reality in the popular figure of Amitabha, the Buddha's celestial hypostasis, variously interpreted by the different schools. This Supreme Reality is the universal essence in whose depths the individual being merges in his attempt to enter into perfect harmony with it. This is the most likely interpretation of the statement reported by William of Rubruck, who naturally contrasts this profession of faith with the revelation of a personal God, creator and redeemer of the world, which was incomprehensible to his opponents.

This concept, which probably helped to transform Lamaist Buddhism into the official religion of the Chinghizide dynasty in Mongolia and China, was readily understandable to our Venetian traveler—who had become an official in the hierarchy of the imperial administration—without being aware of how remote his interpretation was from the authentic doctrines that prevailed among the native Chinese. Indeed, he was not acquainted with the most characteristic and common religious expression of those tenets, namely, ancestor-worship—domestic, priestly, and political,—which was later professed by the emperor himself in homage to the founders of his dynasty and his subjects' traditional beliefs.[116]

Marco's limitation of the number of idols worshiped in China to eighty-four is just as arbitrary.[117] This number exactly corresponds to that of the supposed reincarnation of the Buddha and to the eighty-four teachers of the Tantric sect of magic Buddhism, or *Vajrayāna,* which was better known to Marco than any other.[118]

---

[116] Marco notes the Chinese custom of affixing an inscription in which he sees the name of the domestic "idol" and which, according to him, replaces it. It may, however, be supposed that this was the customary votive tablet that recorded the ancestors of every Chinese family and was accorded the place of honor on the domestic altar. Kublai introduced into the official cult this characteristic form of Chinese worship, which had been unknown to the illiterate Mongols and was neglected by Marco, and thereby initiated the worship of his own ancestors in accordance with Chinese usage of both Taoist and Confucian origin. For the ceremonial connected with this cult cf. J. J. M. de Groot, *Universismus,* pp. 128 ff., 148 ff. For the subject in general see P. Demiéville, "La Situation religieuse en Chine au temps de Marco Polo," in *Oriente Poliano,* pp. 193 f.

[117] *Il Milione,* cr. ed., p. 131 n. (Z version); M.P., p. 305. This passage and the entire chapter come after the description of the city and region of Tandinfu (probably modern Yenchow in the province of Shantung), and are found only in the Z version, which we already know to be rich in information about the religions of the East.

[118] *Il Milione,* cr. ed., p. 131; M.P., p. 305. This figure is not indicated in other versions, but its authenticity is assured by its peculiarity, and it therefore merits consideration. The number of Buddha's existences (cr. ed., p. 194; M.P., p. 490) varies among the sects or schools that practice his cult. However, the number 84 and its multiples are found in Buddhist literature in a variety of combinations. It should also be remembered that there are 84 elements in the rosary still used today in the popular cult of Siva, a pre-Buddhistic Hindu divinity of India. According to A. Grünwedel (*Mythologie du Bouddhisme,* p. 4), the number 84 may be derived from a calculation of the various divine, human, and animal existences of the Buddha. W. Kirfel ("Der Rosenkranz," *Beiträge zur Sprach- und Kulturgeschichte des Ostens,* fasc. 1, 1949, pp. 21 ff.), on the other hand, connects this figure with the mystical numbers of Hinduism, in which it plays a prominent part in the geography, history, and mythical eschatology of that faith, in various combinations which also recur in Buddhism. In fact, the famous Mahasiddhas or Great Miracle-Workers of the latter cult were 84 in number; they

To each of the idols, which were in fact potentially unlimited in numbers, a special virtue is assigned by the god of heaven, which is specified in part by Marco when he lets it be understood that in the China of his times—as still today, and as formerly in pagan Italy—every aspect of life and nature was made subject to a divinity distinguished by its own particular name and power, which the practices of the cult or the supplications of an inspired person can succeed in actuating in favor of the faithful.[119] Marco once determined to test the power of these idols, on the occasion of having mislaid a ring. Learning of the existence of a divinity capable of restoring any lost object to its rightful owner, he managed, with the help of an old sorceress, the guardian of a Chinese temple, to recover the ring. He did not, however, make any oblation to the idols, thereby salving his conscience while re-

were supposed to have originated its Tantric sect, which had been so much in evidence at the time of Marco's stay in China and had comprised those whom he calls *Chesciemur* and *Tebet* from its places of origin. His "eighty-four idols" (*loc. cit.*) are therefore the founders of the Tantric sect, of whom Marco had some knowledge— a fact that substantiates the authenticity of the passage and the version of the *Milione* wherein it is found. These 84 masters are listed by G. Tucci in *Tibetan Painted Scrolls*, Vol. I, pp. 226 f., and Vol. II, pp. 333 ff. For their legends cf. A. Grünwedel, "Die Geschichten der vierundachtzig Zauberer (Mahāsiddhas) aus dem Tibetischen übersetzt," *Baessler Archiv*, Vol. V, 1916, pp. 137–228. In order to understand the significance of this number and its repeated mention in the *Milione*, we shall quote the remarks on the subject to be found in the quasi-canonical text of the *Mahāvastu* (trans. J. J. Jones, London, 1949, Vol. I, p. 52): "This Sublime One [i.e., the Buddha] with his eighty-four thousand disciples lived in eighty-four cycles of the dissolution and evolution of the world. In each of these dissolutions the Sublime One, together with his eighty-four thousand disciples, penetrated into the kingdom of the Abhāsvara deva," etc. From this we see that Marco Polo followed fairly reliable sources, even though he did not apply them in accordance with more serious and adequate criteria. It should, moreover, be noted that he was not so precise in reporting the number of parts that make up the Hindu rosary, to which he attributes 104 beads (cr. ed., p. 179; M.P., p. 384) instead of the ritual 108 of the Vishnu cult, which serve the purpose described by him. This, too, like 84, is a mystical pre-Buddhistic Indian number, for which see Kirfel, "Der Rosenkranz," p. 22, and Yule-Cordier, *The Book of Ser Marco Polo*, Vol. II, p. 357. The number 104 is doubtless a mistake on the part of some copyist, and we may assume that Marco originally quoted the correct figure, which was already known to Friar William of Rubruck (cf. *Sin. Franc.*, Vol. I, p. 230 n. 2, and Rockhill, *The Journey* etc., p. 146 n. 1), from whom we also learn that the 108 beads of the Lamaist rosary, used as they repeat their invocations (*Om mane padme hum*), correspond to the "108 gates of the Law," or Truth, according to the Mahayanic interpretation. With regard to the 84 Mahasiddhas, mentioned by Marco, and who seem also (in a special context) to number 85, see the work soon to be published by Toni Schmid, *Eighty-five Mahāsiddhas*, Uppsala.

[119] Cf. H. Maspero, *Les Religions chinoises*, pp. 111 ff., and a complete list of Chinese idols, with their specific functions and activities, in Doré, *Manuel des superstitions chinoises*, esp. pp. 122–131.

gaining his property.[120] This delightful anecdote is handed down
to us, in a sincere and vivid telling, in one sole and valuable version of the *Milione* which, in spite of its Latinization, reveals to
us Marco's half curious, half wily, attitude toward the idolatry of
Asia, that for two decades surrounded him on all sides without
his ever investigating its doctrinal background.

He does, however, give a comprehensive description of these
idols, which he thought everywhere to be the same, portraying
them with various animal heads, multiple heads, or human faces,
and with four, ten, or a thousand hands, while he was satisfied to
attribute these "extravaganzas and devilries" to inveterate custom
without searching for more recondite meanings or speculative
fantasies, an account of which, in his opinion, would have been
"too dreadful to be heard by Christians." [121] Hence the cult of
these images, which were mythologically and symbolically so
diverse, is not even located with precision; for though they appear
in Hindu, Burmese, and Tibetan sanctuaries, they do not, on the
other hand, correspond to the Chinese iconography, which was a
more rational, human, and restrained manifestation of Oriental
idolatry.[122]

[120] This idol is akin to the popular Yuen-kuang, to whom recourse is had even today when the petitioner wishes to discover thieves and other evildoers; cf. Doré, *Manuel*,
p. 105. The anecdote is related only in the Z version of the *Milione*, cr. ed., p. 132 n.;
M.P., pp. 305 f.

[121] Il Milione, cr. ed., p. 166 (M.P., p. 366): "Now, you must know that the idols
of Cathay, of Mangi, and of these islands are all of one fashion." The description of
them is included in the chapter dealing with Japan, almost as if Marco wished his
readers to understand that this country, which was only known to him by hearsay,
worshiped the same divinities as the other peoples of the East.

[122] Nevertheless, the monstrosities to which Marco refers are in fact present. The
religious iconography of the Far East is treated especially in works dealing with
the sculpture and painting of those peoples; among these, O. Sirén, *Chinese Sculpture
from the Vth to the XIVth century*, 4 vols., London, 1925, and G. Tucci, *Tibetan
Painted Scrolls*, are of especial value and illustrate all the monstrous divinities to which
Marco refers, *loc. cit.* See, too, A. K. Coomaraswamy, *Elements of Buddhist Iconography*,
Cambridge, Mass., 1935. There is also a *Dictionary of Chinese Mythology* by E. T. C.
Werner, Shanghai, 1932; and L. Wieger, *Histoire des croyances religieuses et des
opinions philosophiques en Chine*, Hochienfu, 1917, is still valuable for the material
it contains. It is not for us to identify the individual divinities mentioned in the
Milione, *loc. cit.*; we therefore leave this task to a monographic study of the subject.
It should, however, be noted that the term "a thousand hands" may also be taken
literally, since a statue with a thousand hands and eyes, as Marco records it, remained
for a long time a monstrous ornament in the Forbidden City of Peking. This is the
most excessive figuration of the popular Chinese divinity which, under the name of
Kuan-yin, represents the main hypostasis of the Bodhisattva Avalokiteśvara as a symbol

It must be that Marco had but a vague and rudimentary conception of these divinities; for he neither could nor would make a distinction between the images he had observed in various Chinese monasteries, as for example the great one of "Caigiu" (Kwachow) in the province of Kiangsu, and the others, male and female, that were to be found in the temples of Greater India, whose strangest and coarsest rites, especially the more salacious practices, were described by him with obvious enjoyment.[123]

This notwithstanding, and in spite of his instinctive Christian aversion for all these active manifestations of paganism, Marco recognized the high moral worth of Buddhism and its contribution to the civilization of the Far East. Moreover, he attributes to its teachers and sages the merit of having civilized the Great Kaan by making him understand the virtue and power of charity, though it was practiced, as he himself confirms, in the name of pagan idols and offered up to them in atonement.[124] He denied the Tartars this virtue, since he imagined—or knew—that their barbarous society regarded the poor as contemptible, accursed beings, who fully de-

---

of the infinite compassion that is expressed in this manner, portraying the essence of Buddhism. For this subject see H. Maspero's article in *Mythologie asiatique illustrée*, Paris, 1928, pp. 239–362, and Ferdinand Lessing, *Yung-Ho-Kung*, as cited in n. 36 above; also Dietrich Seckel, *Buddhistische Kunst Ostasiens*, Stuttgart, 1957.

[123] The Chinese monastery that Marco describes as situated in the middle of the Yangtze-Kiang, opposite the great city of Kwachow in the province of Kiangsu, was, according to him, the chief of many other monasteries of "idolaters," corresponding to one of our archbishoprics, and possessing a great number of idols, which are not specified by him. In this passage Marco reveals that there existed at that time in China, as in Tibet, a hierarchy of such institutions, which he at times describes as being "as big as towns" (cr. ed., p. 65; M.P., p. 190). Nevertheless, the monastery mentioned by Marco then had only two hundred monks, according to his calculations. This would confirm that these institutions had not yet taken on the gigantic proportions they were to assume at a later date, especially in Tibet. On the other hand, we know from official Chinese sources that in Kublai's times there were 215,000 Buddhist monks within the limits of China proper, all of whom were exempt from taxation and military and civic duties. Cf. P. Ratchnevsky, *Un code des Yuan*, pp. lxviii–lxxxvi. As for the gay damsels whose task it was to attend to the entertainment of the idols in the temples of India (cr. ed., p. 184; M.P., p. 393) and to offer their services in order to test the resistance of the initiate to sensual temptation, they evidently represent a phenomenon characteristic of Indian religions. Moreover, it is only with some difficulty that Marco can have obtained authentic information about this branch of Oriental paganism. The "courtesans of Buddha" are already recorded by the Arab merchant Suleiman in 851 (cf. M. Reinaud, *Relation de voyages faits par les Arabes et les Persans dans l'Inde et à la Chine*, Paris, 1845, Vol. I, pp. 134 ff.). Idrisi mentioned them in his famous *Kitāb Nuzhat* in 1154 (*ibid.*, Vol. II, p. 33, n. 112).

[124] *Il Milione*, cr. ed., p. 100 n.; M.P., p. 254.

served their wretched state. Thanks to the "idolatrous law," Kublai became, according to Marco, a good, liberal ruler, offering daily proof of the compassion he felt for his people, who in their gratitude revered him as a god.[125] It may be supposed that this charity of his made Marco forgive his protector for not having become a Christian.

[125] *Ibid.;* and, for his cult, see cr. ed., pp. 83 f.; M.P., pp. 223 f.

SUMMARY OF
THE CHINGHIZIDE GENEALOGY

SUMMARY OF THE CHINGHIZIDE GENEALOGY
(Seniority runs from right to left.)

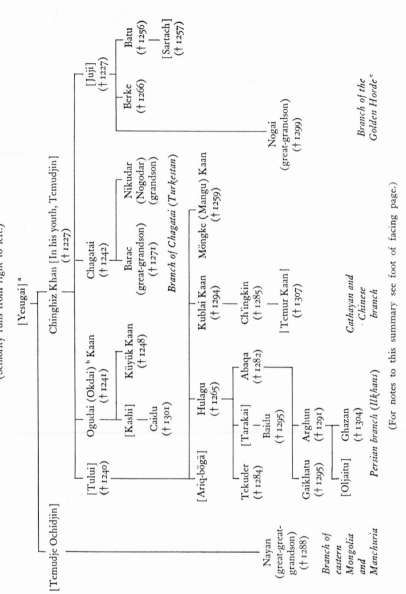

(For notes to this summary see foot of facing page.)

€ight

ASIATIC HISTORY IN
MARCO POLO'S BOOK

Many chapters of Marco Polo's book are given over to the history of ancient and contemporary Asia, and always with more or less mention of the political events that determined the shaping and ultimate dismemberment of the Mongol empire. This constant interest of his in the political fortunes of the continent was owing to his participating, directly or indirectly, in portentous events or in minor and local happenings, either as an instrument of the imperial power, or as an eyewitness, or as no more than a chance victim of circumstances. Hence, his description of Asia in the *Milione* is everywhere commingled with the history of the Chin-

Readers not acquainted with Asiatic history of the XIIIth century are advised to cast a preliminary glance at the genealogical tree of the dynasty which, in its various ramifications, dominated almost the entire continent. The expansion and geographical distribution of this dynasty will help to give a fairly clear idea of its power and the origins of the internal and external conflicts to which Marco refers in various parts of his book. (See opposite.)

[a] The names in square brackets are not mentioned in Marco Polo's book. The names in this summary vary according to the different versions of the *Milione* and its translations, as well as according to the historians of the Chinghizide dynasty and its separate branches. For the phonetic varieties of some of these names cf. P. Pelliot, "Notes sur l'Histoire de la Horde d'Or de B. Spuler," in *Œuvres posthumes de Paul Pelliot*, Paris, Vol. II, 1950. For the official Mongol-Chinese genealogy of the Chinghiskanides cf. L. Hambis, "Le Chapitre CVII du Yuan che," in *T'oung Pao*, supplement to Vol. XXXVIII, 1945, with additional notes by P. Pelliot. For the complete genealogy of the branch of the Golden Horde cf. B. Spuler, *Die Goldene Horde*, appendix to p. 452; and for the Ilkhans of Persia, the same author, *Die Mongolen in Iran*, p. 533. An ample summary of the entire genealogy to the end of the XIIIth century is offered by Yule-Cordier, *The Book of Ser Marco Polo*, Vol. II, p. 505.

[b] This form is a striking conjecture by Professor L. Foscolo Benedetto (*Il Milione*, cr. ed., p. 53 n.). The text reads "Altou" or "Alton," which make no sense.

[c] To this branch belong also Tuda-Mangu (Tudai Möngke) (†1230), Toktai (†1212), and Tulabuga (†1291), all mentioned by Marco Polo.

301

ghizide dynasty and of its separate regions, and thus is an inexhaustible source of historical information which, while it does
not maintain a uniform level of reliability and authenticity, is
always interesting, valuable, and symptomatic.

The reader's interest is intensified by the author's actual or
assumed participation as revealed in his judgments of men and of
all sorts of matters, in his choice of episodes, in the varied style
that lends them life, and in the sources and traditions used by
Marco whenever he does not relate his personal experiences. The
Milione belongs, indeed, to both Western and Oriental medieval
historiographic literature. It reveals the characteristic styles and
tendencies of both, while yet remaining unique in its polymor-
phous genre, which is at one and the same time realistic and
imaginary, personal and objective, epic and anecdotic in form.

The two great missionaries who preceded Marco had made
brief mention of the history of Chinghizide Asia: Friar John of
Pian del Càrpine, concisely yet systematically, in his *Historia
Mongalorum,* and, on occasion, Friar William of Rubruck in his
Itinerarium.[1] Marco was not acquainted with these works, and
would not have been capable of profiting from them. His conception of history is the same as that shared by his untutored contemporaries, to whom his book is addressed. They interpreted it
as a sort of epic after the pattern of the French and Franco-Italian
chansons de geste, or of other and simpler forms of vernacular
literature popularized by minstrels and recited in the circles of
the nobility and middle classes throughout Europe.[2] Hence,

[1] See, in the historical section of Friar John's book, especially chap. v, on the origins
and development of the Chinghizide empire. Cf. *Sinica Franciscana,* Vol. I, pp. 51–76,
with bibliographical footnotes—although little is known about the friar's sources. His
information is, on the whole, more nearly correct than that offered by Marco on the
same subject, but it reveals a completely different frame of mind and a hostile attitude toward the Mongols. A comparative study of the two outlooks would be interesting. It would of course examine the folklore reported by these two authors, and the
legendary traditions relating to personages and events of Tartar history. The historical
names that appear here and there in Friar William's *Itinerarium* (*Sin. Franc.,* Vol. I,
pp. 147–332) are usually connected with contemporary events about which the friar
was directly informed when he lived among the various "hordes" and in the capital,
where a number of Europeans resided. The historical elements in his book could
usefully be coördinated and examined in a detailed study, which might also include
a comparative analysis of the historical element contained in the *Flor des estoires de
la terre d'Orient* by the Armenian Prince Hayton, compiled some ten years after the
Milione.

[2] This is one of the least-studied aspects of Italian literature of the Middle Ages.
Still unsurpassed are the judgments and data to be found in A. Gaspary, *Storia della*

though Rustichello of Pisa, the first editor of the *Milione,* while employing the narrative phraseology of the times, may well have heightened the literary tone of Marco's account by adorning it with the customary epic flourishes, this must nevertheless have been the way in which our author understood history and enjoyed hearing it narrated.[3]

He underwent his historical initiation in Asia rather than in the West, and more especially in the Mongol and Persian environments that surrounded him for some twenty-five years, at Kublai's court and in the colonies of Mohammedan merchants and adventurers from every land that flourished in its surroundings. In this Asiatic world, interest in historical matters had undergone an extraordinary development in Marco's century, giving rise to a Mongolian, a Chinese, and a Persian literature, each of which abounded in historiographic and poetic masterpieces notable for their variety and intrinsic worth.

As in the West, various parts of Chinghizide Asia had produced not only erudite, official, and courtly historiography, but also popular histories that were epic and rhapsodic in style. The latter were broadcast among the Mongols and Turks, who now ruled over the whole continent, by their rhapsodes, who, as in Europe, entertained the courts, the warlike conquerors, and the families of the nomads of the steppe.[4] This extraordinary flowering of historical interest in Persia, Mongolia, and China in Marco's times undoubtedly represents a literary, philosophical, political, and psychological reflection of the portentous changes that swept

---

letteratura italiana, trans. N. Zingarelli, Vol. II; T. Casini, *Grundriss der romanischen Philologie,* Vol. II, Pt. 3, Strassburg, 1901, pp. 13 ff.; and G. Bertoni, *Il Duecento* (in *Storia letteraria d'Italia*), second edition, Milan, 1930, chap. iv. Cf. also the article by A. Monteverdi in the commemorative volume of the Fondazione Giorgio Cini di Venezia, *La civiltà veneziana del secolo di Marco Polo,* Florence, 1955, pp. 19 ff.

[3] For Rustichello's stylistic contribution to the *Milione* cf. L. Foscolo Benedetto's remarks in the Introduction to his critical edition, pp. xix ff. It is especially apparent in historical and narrative passages. See, too, the remarks and bibliographical notes by B. Terracini, "Analisi del concetto di lingua letteraria," *Cultura Neolatina,* Vol. XVI, 1956, p. 29.

[4] Cf. B. Laufer, "Skizze der mongolischen Literatur," *Keleti Szemle,* Vol. VII, 1907, pp. 165–261, and the more nearly complete Russian edition, Leningrad, 1927, as well as N. Poppe, *Mongolische Volksdichtung,* Wiesbaden, 1955, and W. Heissig, "Ein moderner mongolischer Beitrag zur mongolischen Literaturgeschichte," *Central Asiatic Journal,* Vol. II, 1956, pp. 44 ff. Echoes of this poetical history are to be found in the collection by A. Mostaert, *Folklore Ordos,* Peiping (*Monumenta Serica,* Monograph XI), 1947, pp. 181 ff.

across the whole of Asia in a saga of blood and glory. The desire
to record and celebrate these experiences arose from an awareness
of their significance. This in turn found expression in chronicles
and in poetic history, the relationship of one to the other being
similar to that which in the West distinguished Latin historiography from the *chansons de geste,* which were indirectly inspired by the Crusades and the great political events of medieval
Europe.

That Marco Polo was fully taken up by this apologetic, heroic,
and communicative spirit, typical of his contemporaries in the
Oriental world, is proved by the important role played by history
in his book, which is seen to reflect the characteristic trends and
styles of both courtly and popular Asiatic historiography. This,
too, reveals how intense the general participation was in the
great happenings of this epoch, which was indeed fateful for the
whole continent, from Anatolia to Japan. Thus, like its French
counterpart, medieval Mongolian literature opens with a masterpiece of national history, more or less poetic: the *Secret History
of the Mongols,* compiled in 1240 at Karakorum by order of
Ogudai, son and successor of Chinghiz Khan.[5]

This work, in its brief chapters, fused the narration of events
with the chants of the Mongol rhapsodes, and dynastic legends
with the history of Chinghiz Khan; the chronicler's style was
heightened by occasional outbursts of savage poetry, and the
bare narration of facts by a rudimentary, and therefore sincere,
metaphorical language. It gave to a proud people of illiterate
nomads, hunters, and shepherds the prestige conferred by a
national literary monument which glorified and spiritually consolidated their conquests.[6] Marco was not directly acquainted with
it, since it was preserved as a secret treasure in the archives of the
court (hence its official Mongol and Chinese title) and was

[5] See, besides the original text, *Manghol un niuča tobča'an,* edited with glossary by
E. Haenisch, Leipzig, 2 vols., 1937–1939, the German translation by the same author,
second edition, Leipzig, 1948, and the partial translation into French by P. Pelliot,
Histoire secrète des Mongols, Paris, 1949.

[6] This is the interpretation given to the Mongol title—and its Chinese counterpart,
Yüan Ch'ao Pi Shih—of this famous work, an edition of which, with a translation into
Russian, and various versions of the text, has been published by S. A. Kozin, *Sokrovennoe Skazanie,* Vol. I, Moscow and Leningrad, Akad. Nauk SSSR, 1941. The typog-
raphy of this edition distinguishes between the prose narrative and the epic passages
inserted into the text.

accessible only to a few Uigur, Persian, and Chinese scholars who received an assignment or permission from the emperor or the Ilkhans to consult and exploit it to the greater glory of the Chinghizide dynasty.

Even though Marco could not have been directly acquainted with it, he did, as we shall see, make use of episodes and legends from ancient and recent Mongol history made known to him through the same oral traditions that had in large measure inspired this book.[7] The grandiose nature of these events, which had awakened in the nomads of Asia a sense of history and a desire to give expression to it, also aroused our author's interest and adapted his vision to the continental and universal dimensions of his new experiences, which would otherwise have remained closed to a Venetian youth of his times. Thus, Marco obeyed the same impulses that inspired the extensive writings of contemporary historians in Persia, who were to a greater or less degree impartial observers of these apocalyptic events.

Indeed, Marco was the contemporary of the greatest Mohammedan historians in medieval Asia, all of whom were fascinated, as he was, by the Chinghizide saga and the spectacle of the grandeurs and atrocities for which it is still remembered. The first was Juwainī, governor of Baghdad, who in 1260 dictated his *History of the Great Conqueror,* i.e., Chinghiz Khan;[8] then, the great Rashiduddin, physician and minister to Ghazan Khan, and author of the leading universal chronicle of medieval times, whom Marco must certainly have seen when he made his last stay in Persia, between 1294 and 1295;[9] and finally, with other and minor

[7] This was also done by Prince Hayton of Armenia, who in the years he spent among the Mongols and Turks collected popular Asiatic traditions, which he included in his *Flor des estoires* written at Poitiers in the year 1307. The Florentine chronicler Giovanni Villani and others made use of this work; hence, subjects celebrated by Mongol rhapsodes in the first decades of Tartar expansion in Asia reached XIVth-century Italy by diverse routes.

[8] *The Ta'rīkh-i-Jahān-Gushā,* Vols. I and II, ed. Mírzá Muḥammad, London ("Gibb Memorial" series, XVI), 1913–1917; Vol. III, text with Introd. by Sir E. Dennison Ross, London (Royal Asiatic Society), 1931. C. d'Ohsson made extensive use of this work (and others cited *infra*) for his *Histoire des Mongols,* which is still fundamental for the history of Tartar Asia. The first Western translation of Juwainī's work is that by J. A. Boyle, *The History of the World-Conqueror,* 2 vols., Manchester Univ. Press, 1957.

[9] Cf. E. Blochet, *Introduction à l'Histoire des Mongols,* London ("Gibb Memorial" series, XII), 1910, and the subsequent parts of the Persian text now published in its

figures, the eloquent "panegyrist of the court," Wassaf, younger and somewhat less reliable, but, together with the others just mentioned, indispensable to anyone who wishes to clarify the data and possible sources of the *Milione*.[10]

All these Persian chroniclers had been, like Marco, in the service of the Chinghizide sovereigns whose deeds they relate. They were men of wide Asiatic and cosmopolitan culture, and far more expert than he in the vicissitudes of Asian affairs; and they not only had access to immediate sources of documentary information, but also a connected view of events which made it possible for them to group together, almost always in a geographical context, the same historical data that in the *Milione* are more or less fragmented. Marco's observations should therefore be studied within this framework, especially since the historical and geographical names occurring in his text reflect, in the forms he employs for them, their local origins and, consequently, the cultural environments from which he drew his information about the men and events of his age. Thus, in the chapters of his book that deal with the history of Asia we cannot help noticing the fusion of traditions and trends of Mongol inspiration with second-hand reports of Persian origin, vague Chinese reminiscences, and Turkish and Mohammedan legends from various sources, the whole being set down in a subjective and undiscriminating manner, or in the epic tone of the *chansons de geste* and the novels of chivalry.

It is in this way that Marco records the history of Chinghizide Asia, at times narrating the principal events in order, at others making sporadic mention of more or less relevant facts and figures. It will therefore be useful to summarize before embarking upon a critical examination, if we are to have some idea of the richness of the historical element contained in the *Milione,* and to

---

entirety in six volumes of the same series, the last with a useful introduction and summary by K. Jahn (n.s., XIV, 1940). Cf. the latter's *Geschichte der Ilhâne Abâgâ bis Gaihâtü,* Prague, 1941; also, Rashiduddin's history in the French translation by E. Quatremère, *L'Histoire des Mongols de la Perse,* Paris, 1836, Vol. I only.

[10] There is a partial edition with German translation by J. von Hammer-Purgstall. For this and other editions, cf. the data collected by Mírzá Muḥammad in the Introd. to his edition of the *Ta'ríkh;* cf. also, for the whole subject and pertinent bibliography, B. Spuler, *Die Mongolen in Iran,* Leipzig, 1939, pp. 14–21, and E. G. Browne, *A History of Persian Literature,* Vol. III, Cambridge, 1920, pp. 62 ff.

appreciate the constant relationship that exists between the geographical data and the events narrated.

The book opens with an account of the historical reasons for Niccolò and Maffeo Polo's first expedition among the Tartars in 1260. On that occasion, a long and bloody war between Berke, lord of the Golden Horde, and Hulagu, the conqueror and ruler of Persia, both of whom sought possession of the Caucasus, made it impossible for the two Venetians to return to their commercial base in the Crimea and obliged them to make a detour toward Central Asia and then toward the Far East.[11] The fierce rivalry between the two Chinghizide rulers naturally impaired the dynastic unity of the empire and had a bad effect on trade that passed through the Caspian and Black seas.[12]

Again, the continuous state of dynastic and civil war at the time of the Polos' second Asiatic adventure, and the difficulties and obstacles encountered by them, made Marco decide to set his scanty biographical data within the framework of those events, from the time when the three Venetians ran the risk of falling victims to the Egyptian invasion of Anatolia in 1271 until their homeward journey from Peking to the West in 1291–1295. As we read in the prologue to the *Milione,* they were at last compelled to voyage by sea, as a result of the wars between Tartar princes which were then raging in Central Asia.[13]

Against the background of these dates and events, each step

[11] Cf. the prologue to the *Milione,* and above, chap. ii, § 2.

[12] The causes of conflict between the Tartars of the Levant, as Marco calls them, and those of the West, or Golden Horde, were various, as we have already seen, and all were strong enough to keep the two Chinghizide sovereigns in a continuous state of war. For details of the conflict cf. Spuler, *Die Mongolen in Iran,* pp. 63 ff., and R. Grousset, *L'Empire des steppes,* esp. pp. 470 ff.

[13] The undertaking embarked upon by the Polos and the two Dominicans who accompanied them for a short distance was almost cut short by the advance of the Mameluke general, Baibars (who originated from Qipchak), on Damascus and into Cilicia in the year 1271. The Polos' return journey was begun overland, but was interrupted after eight months, as we read in the Ramusian version. We can therefore calculate that our travelers were delayed in Turkestan, and then sent back to China, owing to the war waged by Caidu—the ruler of Central Asia, who was well known to Marco—on the borders of Mongolia against Kublai, so that not even dignitaries provided with "tablets of command," as were the Polos, were certain of being able to cross Transoxiana and Persia by the overland route. For the date of the Polos' first departure from Kublai's court with the Princess Cocachin, and for the Tartar dignitaries who accompanied them, cf. the note by Yang Chih-chin and Ho Yung-chi in *Harvard Journal of Asiatic Studies,* Vol. IX, 1945, p. 51.

of their journey and each step in Marco's narrative has reference to political and military moves which illustrate conditions in Asia at that time and the instability of the vast Chinghizide empire. Moreover, this contemporary history is interspersed with accounts of happenings both recent and remote. For example, when he tells of their going through the Derbend Pass on the western shores of the Caspian Sea, the strategic gateway to the Asian interior, Marco digresses in order to evoke the legend of the "Iron Gate" that Alexander the Great was supposed to have set there to defend the West against the "Tartars." In reality, a long wall with towers, and a fortress, had at some time been built to guard the narrow way through the well-nigh impassable Caucasus Mountains.[14]

This passage in the *Milione* represents the fusion of fact and local legend which the poetical story of the Macedonian conqueror in its Greco-Latin, Biblical, and Mohammedan versions had spread abroad, from the IXth century onward, from Spain to China and from Scandinavia to Ethiopia.[15] From the most ancient times the Derbend Pass had been the gateway for invasions in both directions, and was so recognized by Alexander, who made it of vital importance to his whole strategic system in the Orient. Later it became a point of attraction and sorting center for all the legends dispersed throughout the Old World concerning the more or less imaginary limits between the Orient and the West, first of all the Biblical legend of Gog and Magog, which was repeated and diffused by the Koran. The concept of a divided world was extended to include, as a rampart between nations, even the Great Wall of China; and Marco may have

[14] The best commentary to this interesting passage in the *Milione* is still that by Yule-Cordier, *The Book of Ser Marco Polo*, Vol. I, pp. 55–57, to whose bibliography should be added the important study by Arturo Graf, "Le leggende di Gog e Magog," in *Roma nelle memorie e nelle immaginazioni del medio evo*, Turin, 1893, Vol. II, pp. 507 ff.; also A. R. Anderson, *Alexander's Gate, Gog and Magog, and the Inclosed Nations*, Cambridge, Mass., 1932, with full bibliography, and G. Cary, *The Medieval Alexander*, Cambridge, Eng., 1956, pp. 135 f. and notes to pp. 295 ff.

[15] In historic times the legend of Gog and Magog, connected with that of the Iron Gate, has been variously localized in different parts of Asia. However, it seems that it originally referred to the exploits of Alexander the Great in this region around Derbend, on the Caspian Sea, which is described by Marco, and which corresponded to the *Portae Albanae* of the Romans. Marco did, however, separate the two complementary legends of the Iron Gate and of Gog and Magog, since he localized the latter in the "Tenduc" region on the upper Yellow River.

designated the Wall by his reference to Gog and Magog, a name as suggestive as it was geographically ill-defined.[16]

In this he follows contemporary Persian toponymy. However, in his topographical descriptions of the region between the Caucasus and the Caspian he makes use of a method of historical criticism which he applies with conscientious discernment. He does in fact tell the reader here that Alexander the Great did not hem in the Tartars among those mountains, behind the so-called Iron Gate. The people concerned were not Tartars, he says, since Tartars did not then exist; rather, they were Comans. These were Turkish nomads from southeastern Russia who in the early Middle Ages established themselves in a vast territory to which the ancients had vaguely assigned the barbaric Scythians.[17]

This characteristic distinction between Tartars and Comans was evidently determined by the error then commonly made in designating the Altaic peoples.[18] The term "Tartars" used by Marco on this and other occasions is itself incorrect. He took it from Western phraseology, which, by analogy with the classical underworld, Tartarus, had thus altered the ancient name of the Tatars who lived on the eastern borders of Mongolia.[19] In fact,

[16] These legends have already been discussed above; see Index. The frequent passage of invading armies through the region of Derbend had helped to keep alive there the memory of Alexander's exploits, which Marco may have come across when rounding the Caspian Sea. Otherwise, he may have heard them celebrated in Venice, where the legend of the Macedonian was illustrated on monuments and in the recitation of episodes from the *Romans d'Alexandre* and its various adaptations. See above, chap. i, § 2, n. 44.

[17] Cf. P. Pelliot, "A propos des Comans," *Journal Asiatique*, eleventh series, Vol. XV, 1920, pp. 115 ff.

[18] Thus, for example, in the Venetian and Florentine documents that register the Oriental slaves imported into Italy from the Black Sea ports, they are described as "de genere Tartarorum," as can be seen from the lists published by R. Livi, *La schiavitù domestica in Italia*, Padua, 1928, and Charles Verlinden, "La Colonie vénitienne de Tana," in *Studi in onore di G. Luzzatto*, Vol. II, Milan, 1950, pp. 1–25. The Coman language, which, according to Friar Pasquale of Vitoria, was spoken "in all the kingdoms and empires of the Tartars, Persians, Chaldeans, Medes, and Cathayans" of his times (cf. his letter from Almaliq of 1338 in *Sin. Franc.*, Vol. I, p. 503), possessed some literary monuments, for which see K. Grønbech, *Komanisches Wörterbuch*, Copenhagen, 1942, Introd.

[19] The name "Tatar" belonged to the Tungus tribes that had their pastures in eastern Mongolia on the borders of China, with which country they were both in alliance and in conflict from the XIIth century onward, until they were destroyed by Chinghiz Khan. The name was applied to the Mongol conquerors after their victorious leader, who had become lord of all the nomads of Asia, extended to these peoples

Marco's term, apart from being incorrect, was a source of irritation to the Chinghizide conquerors, who wished to be called *Mohal* (Mongols), and not by the name of a tribe that had been exterminated by them after long and violent conflicts.[20] This confusion of the various names of the Altaic tribes was owing to affinities in language and customs among these nomads of the Asiatic steppes, which had greatly helped the assimilation and fusion of the different tribes in many parts of the empire even before its definitive constitution.[21] Marco, on the other hand, came to know these peoples separately over a long period of time. Hence, in the sequence of events that took place in that region he did not wish the Turkish Comans to be confused with the Tartars.

This slight pedantry on the part of our author is symptomatic of his desire to see to it that his readers are correctly informed, while at the same time respecting their habits and the traditions to which he himself remained bound. No one would have understood him if he had spoken of Mongols instead of Tartars.[22] However, in describing the Scythians of Alexander the Great as Comans he was merely following a common usage of medieval historiography, whereby, down to Machiavelli's times, the ancient Gauls were treated as French and the Latins as Italians. Like all his Western contemporaries, Marco tends to evoke the past in the light of more recent events. Far more eloquent proof of this is afforded by the subsequent chapters in which he treats

---

the name of his own tribe (*Manghol,* or *Mohal,* or *Mongol*). Whereas this name was unknown in the West for a long time to come, the Mongols appear in the documents and records of European chancelleries, in literary allusions, and in Marco's text, as "Tartars." This form, which was both popular and learned and included the vague reminiscence of a vanquished tribe, was associated with the legend of the classical Tartarus (Hades), from which, because of the horrors evoked by that name, they were supposed to have sprung. The Franciscan missionaries clearly distinguished the various Mongol tribes. For this see W. W. Rockhill, *The Journey of William of Rubruck,* Introd., pp. xiii, xix, and *passim,* as well as the commentary to the relevant passages in Friar John's and Friar William's texts, *Sinica Franciscana,* Vol. I (see index, p. 610). It is strange that Marco never used the name "Mongol" in any of its forms.

[20] William of Rubruck mentions this; cf. *Sinica Franciscana,* Vol. I, p. 205.

[21] A short historical list of the Mongol tribes is to be found in E. Haenisch, *Die geheime Geschichte der Mongolen,* pp. 182 f. Cf. the article "Mongoli" by P. Pelliot in the *Enciclopedia Italiana.*

[22] The name Mongols occurs in the Florentine form *mòccoli* in F. Balducci Pegolotti's *Pratica della Mercatura,* ed. Evans, p. 5.

of Mesopotamia and Persia. Here, the historical element, together with its religious counterpart, dominates over every other, and reveals fresh aspects of Marco's historiography which are certainly worth careful consideration.

✧ ✧ ✧

Marco Polo never visited Mesopotamia. This country was then subject to Mongol domination, but was left to the west of his itineraries, both on his outward journey across the Asian continent and on his return voyage; the information in the *Milione* on Mosul, Baghdad, and the surrounding regions is therefore brief, vague, and indirect. Marco does, however, dwell at length on the history of their subjection and the circumstances that led to the end of the Abbasid caliphate and the political destruction of so large and important a country. The conquest was an event of very great importance, and Marco must have been fully aware of its consequences since he gives so much space and interest to it. He does in fact offer a fairly detailed description of it within the general framework of Tartar policy in the reign of Möngke Kaan (1251–1259), a policy which, as we read at this point in the *Milione,* aimed at subjugating the whole world to the rule of the Chinghizide dynasty; and therefore the event appears here as an episode in the Mongol expansion throughout Asia, which was to be continued by Hulagu, brother of the Great Kaan and of Kublai, his successor.[23]

The magnitude of the conquest is matched by the breadth and precision with which we are informed by contemporary Persian historians who based themselves on Arabic and Chinese sources, and finally by Marco Polo, regarding the circumstances that led to the setting up of the Chinghizide khanate in Persia. Our Venetian knew that the success of the operation was essentially due to the able strategy followed by the Mongol leaders, who attacked the Mohammedan capital and spiritual center of Islam

[23] The fullest description of this advance is contained in the Persian chronicles already mentioned, and especially in the Third Part of Juwainī's *Ta'rīkh-i-Jahān-Gushā* (cited in note 8 above), as well as in the section of Rashiduddin's *Djami el-Tévarikh,* trans. and ed. with original text by E. Quatremère as *L'Histoire des Mongols de la Perse,* Paris, 1836. These events are treated in detail by C. d'Ohsson, *Histoire des Mongols,* and H. H. Howorth, *History of the Mongols,* as well as by more recent authors such as Grousset in his various works already cited, and by Spuler, *Die Mongolen in Iran,* pp. 48 ff.

on three sides, thus bringing about its capitulation. There fol-
lowed the destruction of the city, the wholesale slaughter of its
Mohammedan population, and, finally, the death of Mustassim
Billah, the last of the Abbasid caliphs.[24]

The campaign, which had been carefully planned by Hulagu,
his general Baidu, and the Naiman Kitbuka, a Christian Nestorian from Mongolia, is reduced in the *Milione* to a simple
tactical stratagem which attributes the Caliph's death from starvation amidst his priceless treasures to an act of moral justice
that compelled him to expiate, by a death as cruel as it was ignoble, the ineptitude, apathy, and greed to which he and his
people had fallen prey. The origin of this legend should probably be sought in the fact that the Caliph was obliged to hand
over his boundless treasure to the victor. The popular interpretation, however, satisfied both the Mohammedans, who were deprived of their spiritual head, and the Mongols, who, as Marco
believed, regarded their leaders as executors of the divine will
and legitimate instruments of a moral justice superior to that
enjoyed by any other nation or dynasty. It would seem more
credible that, as other sources inform us, the conquerors accorded
to Mustassim Billah the honor of a death reserved for defeated
princes, who were enveloped in a rug and trampled to death by
the cavalry or crushed by fatal blows.[25] Marco was acquainted
with this torture inflicted "ad honorem" upon enemies and
traitors of high rank.[26] Nevertheless, probably in deference to
Christian public opinion, he did not wish to concede the privilege
to the leader of the "accursed sect" of the Saracens, and instead
attributed to him a legendary death inspired by literary and
homiletic themes.

The same style characterizes Marco's subsequent account of
the destruction of the sect of the Assassins and the death of their

---

[24] *Il Milione,* cr. ed., pp. 18 ff.; M.P., pp. 101 ff. For the various accounts of the
events from Mohammedan sources cf. G. Le Strange, "The Story of the Death of the
Last Abbasid Caliph," *Journal of the Royal Asiatic Society,* 1900, pp. 293 ff.

[25] This is the version recounted by Wassaf and given in English by Yule in *The
Book of Ser Marco Polo,* Vol. I, p. 68 n., while Marco's account of the last Caliph's
death by starvation finds parallels in Hayton of Armenia, Ricoldo of Montecroce, Joinville, and other authors mentioned by Yule-Cordier, *loc. cit.* For the origin and
diffusion of similar legends of a purely popular and apologetic sort, see the examples
discussed by U. Monneret de Villard, *Il libro della peregrinazione,* pp. 83 ff.

[26] See the episode of Nayan the rebel in the *Milione,* cr. ed., p. 69; M.P., pp. 192 f.

leader, the Old Man of the Mountain, which in actuality had preceded the suppression of the Baghdad caliphate in a no less epic and gory struggle. In the *Milione,* this historic event, which was determined by both political and strategic factors, is merely an episode inserted in the description of the various parts of Persia. These included the headquarters of this famous Moham-medan sect, namely, the territory called Mazandaran, in the Elbruz chain of mountains to the south of the Caspian Sea, which was known to Marco and other medieval travelers as the land of the Mulehet, or heretics.[27]

Marco never visited this well-nigh inaccessible region, which was quite out of the way of his Persian itineraries both on the occasion of his outward journey to China and on his return. However, the events that took place there in the year 1256 were related to him by several persons with a wealth of detail that reveals their importance in the history of Asia and the interest they held for Marco. We shall therefore make a special study of these chapters, which will reveal their informative value and literary merit.[28] For the present, this typical example will confirm the fact that our author's historical vision lacked the structural unity that did on the other hand make possible his "description of the world." The chronological sequence and coördination of events are replaced in his book by the narration of single facts, which are isolated in both time and space although always con-nected with the underlying theme of the unity of the Chinghizide dynasty. It is this intrinsic political and historical vision which indirectly creates the over-all view whereby Marco evokes the creation of this great empire, its consolidation toward the middle of the century, and its fateful collapse after Kublai's death.[29]

The relief thus given to the single episodes increases their value and particular interest. Proof of this is afforded by the account of the Chinghizide prince Nogodar, Chagatai's nephew and the leader of a band or tribe of rebel warriors who, at the time of Marco's journey toward the Asian interior, made an armed in-

[27] For further examples of the use of this name to indicate the region of Alamut, where the Old Man of the Mountain had his seat, cf. *Sinica Franciscana,* Vol. I, pp. 210, 286, 287, 488 f.

[28] See below, chap. ix, § 1.

[29] Kublai died on February 18, 1294, two years after the Polos' departure from his court and at the time when they were about to reach Persia as members of his embassy.

cursion into the Punjab, where they slaughtered large numbers of men and cattle and established themselves with their leader in the capital, Lahore.[30] This bold enterprise, which represents the first invasion of India by a Tartar chieftain, was, as Marco leads us to believe and as the rare Persian sources attest, one of the many predatory incursions attributed to this reckless and cruel warrior, who is pictured and condemned by Marco as the head of a rabble of thieves rather than as a fearless conqueror. While recounting these exploits, with various mistakes in the names and dates, our author reveals the resentment he entertained against this adventurer, who betrayed his sovereign, the laws of the empire, and his dynasty's mission of unification by fighting against members of his own family and transforming war into an individual act of brigandage, as well as occupying without his lord's approval a land that had been unlawfully conquered.[31]

This attitude implicitly reveals the way in which Marco judged the facts of contemporary history. In fact, Nogodar's enterprise, in spite of its ignoble and brigand-like aspects, is an important event, for it represents the first Mongol conquest in India at the expense of Mohammedan sovereigns of Turkish stock who had ruled there for two centuries;[32] for example, "Asedin," who was dethroned by Nogodar and mentioned by Marco.[33] Nevertheless, even though the supposed nephew of Chagatai here ap-

[30] *Il Milione,* cr. ed., pp. 28 f.; M.P., pp. 121 f. Marco portrays Nogodar as the chief of the Caraunas, a tribe that has never been satisfactorily identified; according to him, it was made up of brigands of Indo-Tartar origin. This episode has been studied by Sir Aurel Stein, "Marco Polo's Account of a Mongol Inroad into Kashmir," *Geographical Journal,* Vol. LIV, 1919, pp. 92–103. Further information about the rebel prince, who is recorded under the name of *Nikūdār* in Persian sources, and his "Qarāunās" (i.e., mongrels), is to be found in Spuler, *Die Mongolen in Iran,* pp. 69, 75 f., 81 n. 3, and 85. Cf. also Karl Jahn, "A Note on Kashmir and the Mongols," *Central Asiatic Journal,* Vol. II, 1956, pp. 176 ff.

[31] For Turko-Mongol-Afghan incursions into India, of which the episode recorded by Marco is but an obscure example, cf. Sir Wolseley Haig, "Turks and Afghans," in Vol. III of the *Cambridge History of India,* 1928, which does not, however, mention Nogodar or the Caraunas. For Marco, Nogodar's enterprise is limited to an act of felony and insubordination. It was variously judged by the Persian historians of the age, as can be seen by consulting Yule, *The Book of Ser Marco Polo,* Vol. I, pp. 101 ff., and Cordier, *Addenda,* pp. 21 f., as well as Spuler, *loc. cit.*

[32] For the political situation in northern India in Marco's time, cf. Wolseley Haig, *op. cit.*

[33] His name was Ghiasuddin. He reigned as Sultan of Delhi from 1266 to 1286.

pears as the first precursor of Tamerlane and the Great Moguls of the XVIth century, to our Venetian he is nothing but a rebel. It would seem, however, that Marco divined the strategic and political importance of this undertaking, which demonstrated to the Tartar conquerors of Asia that it was possible to overcome the apparently insurmountable obstacles represented by the Hindu Kush and the mountains of the Karakorum range that lay in the path of armies advancing toward Kashmir and the rich plains of northern India.[34] His legitimist view of the Chinghizide cause is nevertheless the criterion that finally determines his judgment of this bold venture as, in general, it affects his historical criticism of such happenings. The same attitude was probably taken by his informants, who supplied him the memoranda and recited the more or less legendary circumstances of events in which he could not have participated. We may be sure that in his description of this, the first Mongol invasion of those lands, our author adhered to the official version, which must have made a great impression on public opinion in the Asia of those times.[35]

The very fact that Marco describes in detail an obscure tangential episode in the great Chinghizide saga, and the severity with which he judges its success, are an indication of the importance attributed to it in the circles in which he moved. He seems to be swayed by moral reasons. In fact, however, the events following that expedition were political, and stemmed from

[34] The first attempt in this direction was made by the army of Chinghiz Khan, in 1222, in his advance toward Kabul in Afghanistan.

[35] The fact that Marco only just managed to escape—as he tells us at this point—from an ambush by thieves, while crossing the borders of eastern Persia, added a personal touch to the contempt he felt for those rebels, though they probably had nothing to do with the brigands that ordinarily infested those regions. We may suppose that the Caraunas were a tribe of Mongol origin which had associated itself with peoples from a different stock in the course of their more or less predatory migrations which took them through Central Asia and as far as India in search of booty and, as Marco says, of slaves. Their leader, Nogodar, is not mentioned in historical texts or official records of the times. He must, however, have been a notorious figure, since in the *Milione* he is discussed at length, as well as his exploits, which are severely criticized. However this may be, he is a typical leader of those groups of Altaic nomads who, though never entering the limelight of history, were continually on the move in search of new pastures and booty. They thus spread out from Mongolia into Turkestan, Afghanistan, Bactriana, and as far as eastern Persia, Kashmir, and India, where they left traces that can still be detected in the respective languages and customs. Nogodar did, in fact, give his name to the Nikudaris tribe (*Nikūdārejān*), for which see Spuler, *Die Mongolen in Iran*, p. 69 and *passim*.

considerations with which our author was undoubtedly acquainted. From the very beginning of the dynasty the conquest of India had been one of its chief aims, and one which Kublai himself tried to achieve and for which he made use of the information offered by our author, *inter alia*.[36] It was these long-term aims that had made Chinghiz Khan and his immediate successors determine to subjugate Tibet and fortify the regions bordering on India, from Persia to southern China. To the Mongol sovereigns and their loyal dignitaries and generals, the adventurers who successively embarked upon those predatory excursions for their personal profit were usurpers and traitors to the imperial cause who must be opposed and condemned; and this is the probable reason for Marco's interest in events that had occurred in distant, inaccessible regions which he had never visited. It must be admitted that the passionate tone of his account is the only basis for our interpretation. Nevertheless, Marco's temperament reveals itself in the style and choice of subject matter, even in the versions of Rustichello and others; in this respect, the data that he gives, which at times are vague and incorrect, or may not now be verified, are less important and expressive.

Marco's legitimist attitude, which we have already noted with respect to religious matters, appears in all the dynastic history that is scattered through many chapters of the *Milione*, from the detailed account of Chinghiz Khan's triumph to single episodes in the story of Chinghizide expansion and the conflicts between the various sovereigns and feudatories of the empire. It appears in his first remarks on the origins of the empire, in connection with his brief description of the former capital of Karakorum, which from a simple military camp became the central seat of the Mongol administration at the time of Ogudai, son of Chinghiz and his first successor.[37] The occasion is well taken, since this

---

[36] Marco expressly mentions a special voyage undertaken by him from China to India "through unknown seas." He gave a full report of this undertaking to Kublai, who had apparently sent him there to gather information. This visit to India was probably undertaken in 1290 (cf. the *Milione,* cr. ed., p. 11; M.P., p. 89), although it is not possible to specify its itinerary or purpose.

[37] In Marco's times the city was the administrative center of Mongolia and an important military stronghold in the struggles among various branches of the dynasty. It is briefly described by Marco as built "of wood and mud" and surrounded by earthworks, with a castle and a "fine palace" which was the governor's residence.

strategic and political center was truly the cradle and pivot of Chinghizide power; and it was already evident in Marco's times that the transference of the imperial seat from Karakorum to Peking by order of Kublai, in 1261, would result in the dismemberment of the empire.[38] It was also this presentiment that induced both Kublai's brother Aric Buga (d. 1264) and his cousin Caidu (d. 1301) successively to contend with him for the imperial dignity, in the name of the centralistic traditions which they purposed to represent in favor of the national, political, and strategic unity of their dynasty and its power—a totality divided among so many families all sprung from the same stock.[39]

Marco, a loyal subject of Kublai and dazzled by the splendor of his court, never accepts or discusses the reasons put forward by these pretenders to the imperial throne, though he was well aware of what was at stake. The important thing for him is the historical continuity of the dynasty, which had remained Mongol in sentiment, tradition, language, and customs, even beneath exotic appearances, in Persia as in China, and was therefore universally bound to its founder's policy in the fraternal government of the empire and plans for world conquest.[40] Hence,

---

The palace is minutely described by Friar William of Rubruck (cf. *Sin. Franc.*, Vol. I, pp. 276 ff.); but to him the city looks smaller than the Parisian suburb of Saint-Denis, and the royal palace there, the Friar adds, is worth ten times more than the imperial residence of the Great Kaan of the Tartars (*ibid.*, p. 285). For Karakorum, which at the time of its greatest splendor (from 1235 to 1259) held a cosmopolitan populace, cf. the present author's *Guillaume Boucher*, Baltimore, 1946. It is doubtful that Marco ever visited it, though the possibility cannot be excluded since he had spent a year with his father and uncle in the Sino-Mongol border region which was crossed by the caravan route that led to the city.

[38] That part of China which had been conquered by the Mongols had first of all been a territorial appanage of Kublai's. He left behind him in the ancient capital a center for the nationalistic tendencies traditionally upheld by the dynasty, which were represented by Aric Buga, Kublai's brother and pretender to the dignity of Great Kaan of the Tartars until his death in 1264.

[39] We shall have occasion to deal at greater length with Caidu, concerning whom the *Milione* gives only scattered information. Cf. the summary account of his exploits given by Grousset, *L'Empire des steppes*, pp. 359 f.

[40] This political testament of Chinghiz Khan was more or less formally adhered to throughout the century by nearly all the members of the dynasty in spite of their bitter conflicts, which in part were begun under the pretext of carrying out the founder's true intentions. The secession was in fact brought about by the conversion of the Tartars of the Golden Horde to Islam, which isolated them from the main pagan and Nestorian stem of the empire as well as from Christian civilization in the West. This occurred in the second half of the XIIIth century, at the same time that the Tartars in China were slowly being absorbed by that country's civilization and con-

Marco gives a whole series of chapters to the feats of Chinghiz Khan, its founder, who is evoked by him not as a symbolic figure but as a person, around whom the dynastic legends and the facts of history are glimpsed only through vague, fleeting allusions.

Since he was not acquainted with his hero's genealogy, or with wonder-tales of his infancy, Marco begins his biography of Chinghiz with the proclamation of his election as "king of the Tartars" by his fellow countrymen, which took place in 1196.[41] While emphasizing the prime element of his future success— namely, his ability to persuade the heads of the various Mongol tribes to participate in his undertakings,—our author exalts his hero's undeniable political and military genius, and, ignoring his savage impetuosity, nefarious crimes, and pitiless rancor, praises him as a good, wise, and upright man.[42]

This account, though hagiographic, nevertheless permits us to discern the factual reality that made possible so grandiose a career. This was the young conqueror's ability to organize by pacts and by force of arms a federation of autonomous tribes. Our author thereby recognizes the national period in Chinghizide history; and then, without entering into details, he proceeds to the second period of Mongol expansion, which, as we read at this point in the *Milione,* was designed to conquer the whole world.[43]

---

verted to Lamaist Buddhism. For this twofold evolution cf. B. Spuler, *Die Goldene Horde,* esp. pp. 209 ff., and O. Franke, *Geschichte des chinesischen Reiches,* Vol. IV, pp. 430 ff.

[41] *Il Milione,* cr. ed., pp. 50 f., chaps. lxv–lxvi; M.P., pp. 162 f.

[42] The main authentic source for Chinghiz Khan's biography before his election as head of the Mongols is the *Secret History* already cited. Cf. B. Ya. Vladimirtsov, *The Life of Chingis-Khan,* trans. Prince Mirsky, London, 1930; R. Grousset, *Le Conquérant du Monde,* Paris, 1944; and H. Desmond Martin, *The Rise of Chingis Khan,* Baltimore, 1950. Marco assigns the election of Chinghiz (hitherto called Temudjin) to the year 1187. Once again, however, his chronology is incorrect, or at best doubtful, and the Oriental sources are just as confused, starting even with Chinghiz Khan's birth, which is ascribed by some to the year 1155, by others to 1162.

[43] Chinghiz Khan's conquests can in fact be divided into four periods. The first includes the struggle for supremacy over the Mongol tribes of the Keraits, Naimans, and other minor groups, a struggle which terminated with the unification of Mongolia in 1206; the second, the conquest of northern China and central Asia (so-called Karakhitai), from 1209 to 1218; the third, which is the period of western expansion, the invasion of Khwaresm, Persia, and Russia, from 1218 to 1225; the fourth, the

Marco thus portrays his hero in terms similar to those used in the most ancient Mongol biography of Chinghiz, which has reached us in a Chinese version that was composed in Kublai's times and is quite independent of the *Secret History* and the sober Annals of the Empire.[44] In this brief work the founder of the dynasty is portrayed as both saint and warrior, and the literary interpretation of his personality is the official one that was currently accepted in Marco's times in the Chinghizide courts of China and Persia.[45] The biographer also insists, as does Marco, that the Mongol chieftains, captivated by the warlike virtues and growing prestige of the great leader, submitted to him of their own volition. Quite to the contrary are the other sources, whether Mongol, Chinese, or Persian: they relate in detail the tempestuous fortunes that, in fact, led to the political unification of the various Mongol tribes, whether this was voluntary or was forced upon them after endless ferocious struggles, defections, killings, reprisals, and bloody fratricidal conflicts.[46]

Marco's brief account, encomiastic, almost idyllic, reads like a plaintive echo of what the official propaganda of Kublai's age emphasized in its teachings concerning the origins of the dynasty. The task of spreading the official story was especially entrusted to the bards who followed the nomads everywhere and were always to be found at public festivals and private gatherings, and even at the solemn assemblies of the Chinghizide courts. Our traveler's version did, however, contain some slight degree of historical truth—enough to persuade us that it is not

last two years of the conqueror's life (he died August 18, 1227), which were taken up by the campaign intended to consolidate and extend his dominion in China, despite the resistance of princes and peoples who would not accept the Tartar yoke.

[44] Cf. *L'Histoire des campagnes de Gengis Khan* (*Cheng-won Ts'in-tcheng Lou*), trans. and annotated by P. Pelliot and L. Hambis, Vol. I, Leiden, 1951. The section of the Annals of the Empire (*Yüan Shih*) that deals with Chinghiz Khan has been published, with German translation and notes, by F. E. A. Krause, *Cingis Han: Geschichte seines Lebens nach den chinesischen Reichsannalen,* 1922. For the poetical history of the origins of the Chinghizide dynasty cf. Pavel Poucha, "Zum Stammbaum des Tschingis Chan," in *Asiatica: Festschrift für Fr. Weller,* Leipzig, 1954, pp. 442 ff.

[45] Pelliot and Hambis, *op. cit.,* p. 1.

[46] Cf. the *Cheng-won T'sin-tcheng Lou* already cited, which is a Chinese translation of a Mongol biographical chronicle. The original text, dating from the first half of the XIIIth century, has been lost. It was, however, translated into Persian by Rashiduddin, who incorporated it into his famous historical work, *Djami-el-Tévarikh.* The Chinese translation was probably made at the time of Marco Polo's stay in the Far East.

merely a creation of Marco's fancy, which was not very produc-
tive, or a romantic invention on the part of his scribe, whose
tampering with the substance of the facts narrated was discreet
and quite rare. Indeed, this grouping of Mongol tribes around
a strong and influential leader, whether it was spontaneous or
opportunistic, was certainly no novelty in their history, but rather
a fairly common phenomenon. Essentially, it meant the creation
of a coterie of families noble in birth and rich in cattle, chariots,
and slaves, in a society the component parts of which, as Marco
correctly points out, "either were ruled by the community or had
each its king and lord." [47]

What marks off Chinghiz Khan from other leaders of ancient
and more recent times in Mongolia was the unwonted extension
of this hierarchic federation of the various chieftains, and its
administrative and military strengthening, by this exceptional
leader. According to Marco, his extraordinary and lasting success was owing to his refraining from injury to any, great or
small, who were incorporated into his system of alliances and
vassalage, while he led them to victory over other peoples and to
conquest of territories that were better suited for pasture and the
hunt. In so saying, however, our author forgets all those powerful
rivals, occasional rebels, and adverse coalitions that his hero had
to overcome by force of arms and by guile before concluding his
epic ascent.

Marco deals with the dynastic progress until it brought Temudjin to primacy over the Mongol chieftains, that is, to his partial
and provisional election to the rank of *han,* or local sovereign,
in 1196. But there the account stops. Marco was thus quite unaware of Temudjin's proclamation as Great Kaan (*Khakhan*)
some ten years later, under the name Chinghiz, and of his
further conquests that made him lord of all Asia from northern
China to southern Russia and from Siberia to the borders of
India. In fact, Marco makes him die of a leg wound six years
after his first election, whereas it was well known that he ended

[47] For the fluctuating social and political structure of the Mongol tribes in the
Middle Ages cf. B. Ya. Vladimirtsov, *Le Régime social des Mongols,* trans. M. Carsow,
Paris, 1948; and for the unification of families and tribes for predatory or simply
political purposes, Grousset, *L'Empire des steppes,* pp. 243 ff., and the same author's
Le Conquérant du Monde, in the various episodes from Chinghiz Khan's biography.

his days some twenty-five years later, in recently conquered Chinese territory.[48]

This account, then, is not merely poetic or fictitious or slanted history, but, quite simply, reflects Marco's ignorance of the salient dates and events in the life of Chinghiz Khan. It seems likely that Marco's informants limited their reports to the national, Mongol, period of Temudjin's rise to power, thereby reserving the imperial glory exclusively to his successors.[49] From this we may conclude that Marco obtained his data in the restricted Mongol environment and from subordinate, or at least illiterate, persons who had as little interest as our author in ascertaining the truth of the matter or in seeking out more authoritative sources.

This circumstance is all the more remarkable since, among the numberless events that led his hero to such power and fame, Marco records at length only his final conflict with Togrul, the Mongol chieftain who is improperly called "Prester John" in the *Milione,* and whose loyal vassal Chinghiz Khan had been for many years, at the outset of his career.[50] The choice of this episode among the innumerable real or legendary happenings in the life of this great warrior finds its justification in the fact that the defeat of this last rival and his people's submission to the victor did in fact mark the last phase of Chinghiz Khan's ascendancy. Until then—in the year 1203,—although engaged in creating his coalition of Mongol tribes, he had remained officially a loyal vassal of this king of the Keraits, a people that in large

[48] The death of Chinghiz Khan in the second Chinese campaign gave rise to various legends, but none of them explains Marco's version. For the historical circumstances cf. the biographies of Chinghiz Khan already cited; also, E. T. C. Werner, "The Burial Place of Genghis Khan," *Journal of the North China Branch of the Royal Asiatic Society,* Vol. LVI, 1925, pp. 18 ff., E. Haenisch, "Die letzten Feldzüge Cinggis Hans," *Asia Major,* Vol. IX, 1933, pp. 503–551, and P. Pelliot in *T'oung Pao,* Vol. XXXI, 1935, pp. 157 ff.

[49] The Chinese annals—of which a summary translation is given in the still interesting work by J. A. M. de Moyriac de Mailla, S.J., *Histoire générale de la Chine,* Vol. IX, Paris, 1779—tend to treat the Chinghizide rulers as a national dynasty with the names, titles, and domestic rites, after the Chinese fashion, that were introduced by Kublai in court and state ceremonial, in contrast to the Mongol traditions which had hitherto prevailed and were preserved in the other branches of the dynasty that had not yet gone over to Islam.

[50] Cf. the *Milione,* cr. ed., pp. 51 f.; M.P., pp. 165 f., and, for the historical facts, the biographies of Chinghiz Khan already quoted.

part had been Christianized from the XIth century onward and were among the most civilized, powerful, and respected among the nomads of the steppe. Their leader, owing to his victory over the Tatars, had been invested with royal rank by the Emperor of China, and hence he added the title of *Wang* (king) to the national, Altaic *Han*, forming the combination *Wang-han*. This is the phonetic basis for the name Unc Can, whereby Marco designates him.[51]

It is not so clear why he identified Togrul, a provincial Mongol chieftain, with the famous Prester John, the imaginary lord of Asia of whose power "the whole world speaks," as we read at this point in the *Milione*. But that problem will be discussed further on, in connection with the legend itself and its derivatives;[52] here, we shall emphasize that by narrating at length only this one among the numberless epic and dramatic episodes in Mongol history our author reveals his awareness of its decisive historical importance.

Indeed, in the struggle for political supremacy, it was the elimination of this final rival, who was also his superior in the feudal hierarchy, that allowed Chinghiz Khan to rise from the rank of vassal of the Wang-han to the dignity of universal sovereign. The circumstances that led to the conflict and to the final victory are revealed and documented by the Oriental sources, which agree with Marco's account in attributing the vassal's bold rebellion against his lawful master to feelings of personal resentment as well as to ambition. We read in the *Milione* that the haughty refusal of "Prester John" to give him one of his daughters in marriage so infuriated Chinghiz that he made war on him, to punish him for the affront.[53] It is indeed well estab-

---

[51] *Il Milione,* cr. ed., p. 50, chap. lxiv; M.P., p. 162, where Marco states that the Tartars of the "Ciorcia" region (i.e., of the Jurchen) in northern Manchuria did not have a ruler of their own, but were tributaries of this Unc Can "que vaut a dir en françois le grant sire." The latter is briefly mentioned by William of Rubruck in his *Itinerarium,* for which see *Sinica Francisana,* Vol. I, pp. 208, 234. His historical name of Togrul is revealed to us by the *Secret History* and its derivative Oriental sources. The specification of his dominions in the *Milione* is incorrect. The Keraits had their central territory in the region of the Orkhon and Tola rivers. For the titles of Mongol rulers cf. L. Krader, "Qan-Qagan and the Beginning of Mongolian Kingship," *Central Asiatic Journal,* Vol. I, 1955, pp. 17 f.

[52] See below, chap. ix, § 2.

[53] *Il Milione,* cr. ed., pp. 51 f.; M.P. p. 163.

lished that Chinghiz in his long career as warrior and ruler would never tolerate treachery or haughtiness, being extremely susceptible to any offense against his dignity; indeed, this supplied material for his poetic history as diffused by the Mongol bards, who even now sing of his exploits.

For the rest, the facts were quite different. It was to Juji (Jöci), Chinghiz' eldest son, that the Wang-han (or Ong Khan) of the Keraits refused the hand of his daughter, while at the same time rejecting a proposal that Qojin, Chinghiz Khan's daughter, should become the wife of one of his grandsons.[54] In a society in which ladies of high rank played their part as an instrument of dynastic policy this double humiliation could have no other consequences than those which, with some incorrectness of detail that allowed free play to his imagination, Marco Polo felt that he should describe at length.

In fact, the episode recounted in the *Milione* does not refer to Chinghiz Khan's victory over Togrul, but to his conquest of the kingdom of Tenduc in Chinese territory, in the year 1209.[55] It seems probable that Marco mistook the name of this province of the Öngüt, governed by Christian kings, for that of Tenduc in Mongolia, properly so called, which was part of the territory ruled by the king of the Keraits, Chinghiz Khan's last Mongol rival.[56] Led astray by the similarity in names, which are sometimes interchanged in the various versions of his text, Marco confused the internal conflict that led his hero to absolute dominion in Mongolia (concluded in 1203) with the victorious expedition led by the newly proclaimed first Great Kaan beyond the national borders toward the conquest and domination of

[54] Although the *Secret History* portrays the rancor felt by Chinghiz Khan at the insults to his dignity, it was probably political jealousy that precipitated the struggle between these two rulers, whose relationship had been harmonious from the time of their childhood until the final conflict in 1203, from which Chinghiz Khan emerged victorious.

[55] This is the region, in the great bend of the Yellow River, which was governed in Marco's times by the descendants of the "Unc Can," who were Nestorians by faith and vassals of the Great Kaan, to whom they were related. The conquest of this immense territory was the aim of Chinghiz Khan's first campaign outside the boundaries of Mongolia.

[56] For the nomenclature and topography cf., apart from L. Foscolo Benedetto's notes to this passage (cr. ed., p. 60), the lengthy discussion on this subject in Yule-Cordier, *The Book of Ser Marco Polo*, Vol. I, pp. 231 ff. and 285.

the Chinese territories along and inside the Great Wall in 1209.

For Marco, these historical episodes are merely a convenient framework for relating others of a warlike nature, which, to judge from the frequency and length of such descriptions in his book, must have appealed both to him and to the public he addressed. It is therefore easy for us to discern in all this martial phraseology an echo of the medieval epic style, which was familiar to Marco and even more so to Rustichello, his scribe. However, the influence of the *chansons de geste* is here, as elsewhere, more apparent than substantial, and affects the style rather than the structure of Marco's book. Suffice it to say that in the *Milione,* as in the facts related, it is the pagan, Chinghiz Khan, who defeats and kills the Christian, Prester John. This is a theme unheard of in the epic legends of the West, in which the unbelievers, whoever they be, are always worsted in the end.

In relating this episode Marco refers to the historical accounts.[57] However, we find in his narrative no trace of the long succession of intrigues, plots, conflicts, and misdeeds that appear in the corresponding passages of the *Secret History of the Mongols.* Instead, we are entertained by a detailed description of how Chinghiz, on the eve of his battle with Prester John, consulted his Christian astrologers, who foretold its outcome: they marked two sticks with the names of the two contestants, and, after their incantations, Chinghiz' stick got above the other—which meant, they said, that he would win.[58] It may be presumed that this legend, which is not to be found in the other sources, was of Nestorian origin and that Marco came across it in the Christian colonies of eastern Asia, although this ancient and popular method of divination was certainly not a monopoly of Oriental Christians.[59] On the other hand, we may rather view this as evidence of our author's desire to associate a Christian victory, however small, with his hero's triumph, and to make it the starting point for a brief history of his dynasty.[60] It is of course well known that astrologers of every sect were employed by the conqueror and all his captains and descendants to foretell the out-

[57] "Or dit li contes que" etc., as we read in chap. lxvii, cr. ed., p. 52; M.P., p. 165.
[58] *Ibid.*
[59] Various examples are offered by Yule-Cordier, *op. cit.,* pp. 242 f.
[60] *Il Milione,* cr. ed., p. 53; M.P., p. 166.

come of their undertakings, often by far more elaborate methods than those supposedly used in this instance.[61]

Marco then makes Chinghiz Khan die prematurely six years after this event, whereas, as we know, he ended his days in 1227.[62] Moreover, when he goes on to list his successors, he fails to include Ogudai, Chinghiz' third son and, from 1229 to 1241, his immediate heir, although it was in Ogudai's reign that the Tartars extended their dominion from Korea to the Adriatic and at the same time succeeded in consolidating the internal structure of their new empire in a compact and solid political and military organization.[63] Küyük, who succeeded him from 1246 to 1248, and Mangu, from 1251 to 1259, respectively, are hardly mentioned, and the regents Törägäna and Oghul Gaimish, who courageously governed the empire during the interregnums, are passed over in silence. These omissions are the more curious since all these powerful members of the Chinghizide dynasty were in contact with the Roman pontiffs and the sovereigns of Europe, who received information about them from the great missionaries "ad Tartaros." All their contemporaries might learn about their deeds in the works of Vincent of Beauvais and other more recent authors.[64] However, Marco himself arbitrarily elevated Batu to the rank of Great Kaan. This son of Juji and grandson of Chinghiz Khan did for a time aspire to that dignity, but later wisely remained satisfied with his position as the powerful ruler of the Golden Horde and invincible conqueror of the West.[65]

[61] For the importance of astrology in Chinghizide policy see below, chap. x, and the *Milione*, cr. ed., index, p. 266, "Divinazione."

[62] *Il Milione*, cr. ed., p. 52, chap. lxviii; M.P., pp. 167 f., where Chinghiz Khan is made to die from a knee wound. Chinese traditions give it instead to Mangu, who died in 1259 when on a campaign in Szechwan. For these legends cf. O. Franke, *Geschichte des chinesischen Reiches*, Vol. V, pp. 170 f.

[63] L. Foscolo Benedetto, *Il Libro di Ser Marco Polo*, notes to pp. 84 and 431, supposes that the names in the list of Chinghizide rulers mentioned by Marco have been altered, and that it is legitimate to read Oktai (i.e., Ogudai, or Okkudai) in place of "Altou" or "Alton," which we find in various MSS of the French text.

[64] See above, chap. ii.

[65] If it is not an error in transcription (*Il Milione*, cr. ed., p. 53; M.P., p. 167), the mention of Batui (Batu) Khan reflects the importance of this first sovereign of the Tartars of the West, who reigned from 1227 to 1255 without ever becoming supreme ruler of the empire. Detailed and accurate information about him is offered by Friar

These gaps and careless mistakes reveal Marco's slight interest in the things of the past, which, indeed, are only introduced in this context in order to serve as a rapid prelude to the subsequent exaltation of Kublai, "the greatest and most powerful of all so far," to whose glory the whole book would seem to be dedicated. Hence, the history of his real and legendary actions calls for special treatment among those of the outstanding personages in the *Milione*.[66] Indeed, all the great historical events that took place in his long reign, from 1260 to 1294, have left some trace in Marco's book. During the quarter of a century spent by him in Asia, he was able to observe or learn of three different aspects in this history: Kublai's conquests in the Far East and their turbulent outcome; the rivalry between the various Chinghizide rulers, which led to the dismemberment of the empire; and, lastly, the national uprisings against the régime, especially in China, until the Mongol dynasty, which in character and habit had become almost totally Chinese, should finally be overthrown.

Each of these diverse aspects of Asian history merits detailed study that would clear away the obscurities and difficulties in Marco's account, in part by means of a comparative examination of the various sources, which offer divergent and at times irreconcilable data and circumstances. It will suffice here, however, to note the facts, throw some light on the problems, and coördinate with the information offered in the *Milione* certain events that are documented elsewhere.

Beginning, then, with the undertakings of conquest and expansion described in the book, we find that the first mention of the Mongol advance in China, before the total annexation of that country in Kublai's times, refers to the expedition organized by his brother, the Great Kaan Mangu, who died there in 1259. While contemplating a widely devastated province, where many a town, castle, and hamlet lay in ruins, Marco describes the bloody conquest of the rich and populous Szechwan region, across which

John of Pian del Càrpine and William of Rubruck, who visited him at his court (cf. *Sin. Franc.* Vol. I, pp. 102 ff., 148 ff., and *passim*). For this powerful sovereign's personality cf. Grousset, *L'Empire des steppes,* pp. 470 ff.

[66] See below, chap. ix, § 3.

his journey led him, amid lofty mountains and savage peoples, far into the southwest.[67] From 1253 onward, the Mongol armies more than once assailed these vast territories, until, after Marco's arrival in China, they were at last subjugated.[68] By the time of his visit there, the havoc wrought by these fierce battles and sieges had not yet been repaired, and was all the more striking to the eye because the wars of conquest organized by Mangu, and continued by the young Kublai, had not been rapid campaigns with massed cavalry, but a succession of local actions against separate strongholds protected by mountains and rivers in regions strange to the invader.

It is certainly to be remarked that these brief references to so distant a part of the empire gave Marco his one opportunity of recalling the China of bygone days, of which he knew so little. He thus mentions, though in a veiled and legendary way, the Three Kingdoms (*San Kuo*) which, from 221 to 265 A.D., succeeded the great Han dynasty, and of which the vast province of Szechwan formed one of the chief dominions.[69] Indeed, at this point in the *Milione,* we read that this great province, which he calls Sindufu, had once been divided, together with its capital, among the three sons of a king, who was the rich and powerful ruler of this land.[70] This is evidently an eponymous legend, or a

---

[67] Marco designates this province "molt gasté" with the name of "Tebet" (cr. ed., p. 110; M.P., p. 268), though he is referring to the western section of the great kingdom of Szechwan ("Sindufu" in Marco's toponymy), which is separated from Tibet proper by various ranges of wild and lofty mountains. Mangu led his armies toward those regions in his last attempt to use this route as well as the one through the neighboring province of Yunnan in order to surround and invade Sung China, a project realized, after a number of failures, by his brother Kublai some twenty years later. For the Szechwan undertaking, cf. O. Franke, *Geschichte des chinesischen Reiches,* Vol. IV, pp. 323 ff., and Vol. V, pp. 170 f.

[68] Marco must have crossed these southwestern regions of China when on his first embassy, soon after his arrival at Kublai's court, or slightly less than twenty years after Mangu's death. A map of the regions then visited by Marco is offered by Yule-Cordier, *The Book of Ser Marco Polo,* Vol. II, pp. 127 ff.

[69] *Il Milione,* cr. ed., p. 109; M.P., p. 266. The "Three Kingdoms" included the territories of Wei, Wu, and Shu, so called after the principal rivers in the respective regions. The third included what was then the capital city Ch'engtu, still one of the largest administrative and cultural centers in China, and the territory toward the west which is briefly described by Marco, *loc. cit.*

[70] This is pure fable. For the origins and development of the Three Kingdoms, cf. O. Franke, *op. cit.,* Vol. I, pp. 422 ff., Vol. II, pp. 1 ff., etc.

fanciful interpretation of an episode in ancient Chinese history, which though of brief duration was certainly famous.[71]

✧ ✧ ✧

Marco's description of these southwestern territories of the empire and his account of the missions that took him as far afield as Burma, and perhaps even into India, give him an opportunity to evoke the circumstances that led to the conquest of those immense border regions and the submission of tribes and peoples of varying civilizations, who hitherto had remained independent of their powerful neighbors. Moreover, since he followed a north-south direction, both when making his journey and in ordering his account, he consequently remains faithful to the chronological as well as the geographical and autobiographical order of things in his description of Kublai's advance into southern China and the neighboring territories incorporated in his empire.

Marco's own experiences made him first of all mention the imperial armies' advance through western Yunnan into Burma and as far as the kingdom of Bengal in the populous region which Marco vaguely located "at the borders of India." [72] This must have been the goal of our Venetian's first reconnaissance of the outskirts of the empire, not long after his arrival at Kublai's court, a journey followed by other visits to those distant parts of

[71] It is still very popular in China, either owing to the dramatic events connected with it or because of the notoriety enjoyed by some of the figures that illustrate its history—including Liu Pei, the ruler to whom the traditions reported by Marco evidently refer. This proves that even after a thousand years his memory was still alive. It was later celebrated in the *San Kuo Chih,* one of the most popular historical romances in ancient Chinese literature.

[72] *Il Milione,* cr. ed., p. 125; M.P., p. 295. It would appear that this realm was situated in the southern part of Burma, in the large delta of the Irrawaddy River, which flows into the Gulf of Bengal. The gulf may have given its name to the region. The identification of the "province of Bengal" with the locality of Peju was first made by Yule, *The Book of Ser Marco Polo,* Vol II, p. 128 n. 6, and is purely conjectural. It is not likely that Marco ventured so far, through impassable jungle and mountainous country, especially since—as he himself points out—that vast land had not yet been conquered by the Great Kaan in 1290. Marco's entire topography of Burmese territory is somewhat confused as a result of vague recollections and fragmentary experiences. The *History of Bengal* published by the University of Bengal (Vol. I, 1943, pp. 651, 655 ff., and 659) includes the regions mentioned by Marco as "at the borders of India" in the territory of Bengal proper, i.e., within the delta of the Ganges and the Brahmaputra; but this interpretation is not convincing.

the Great Kaan's dominions which were ethnically and culturally independent of China proper.[73]

Indeed, the relevant events narrated in the *Milione* refer to the happenings on the Sino-Burmese borders in 1277, two years after Marco's arrival at the emperor's court. The fullness of his account, its epic fervor, and the wealth of detail in each episode all reveal his intense participation in these events, which remained so vividly impressed on his mind that this is one of the most eloquent and remarkable passages not only in this book but in all XIIIth-century vernacular prose.[74] To appreciate its intrinsic interest and literary value we need only consider Marco's account against the historical background as it can be reconstructed from other and authentic, but more laconic, reports contained in the various contemporary Oriental sources. Here, then, is a brief summary of the facts.

Kublai, in that year, had sent one of his armies to the border region between Yunnan and Burma; subjugation was to conclude his conquest of the continental Far East. Marco says it was intended to safeguard these Indochinese kingdoms;[75] but the influence of official phraseology, similar to that used by every conqueror, is evident in the interpretation put forward by our author, who faithfully echoes the imperial propaganda.[76] In fact, the campaign had been forced upon the sovereign and his military leaders by the logic of events, and was demanded by the dictates of strategy, after the capitulation in 1276 of Sung (southern) China and its incorporation into the Chinghizide dominion.[77] The reluctance of such highly civilized peoples to tolerate the yoke forced upon them by conquerors whom they regarded as

---

[73] For these regions in southwestern China cf. J. F. Rock, *The Ancient Na-khi Kingdom*, 2 vols. (profusely illustrated), Cambridge, Mass., 1947. For the chronology of the conquest cf. O. Franke, *op. cit.*, Vol. IV, pp. 475 ff., and for the literature on the subject, Vol. V, pp. 225 ff. Marco designates Burma by the Chinese name "Mien."

[74] *Il Milione*, cr. ed., pp. 121–123, and Introd., p. xxii n. 1; M.P., pp. 266 ff.

[75] Cf. O. Franke, *loc. cit.* (in n. 73 above), and R. Grousset, *L'Asie orientale*, pp. 327 f. (a brief summary of the events).

[76] It should also be remembered that here, as on other occasions, Marco is more directly interested in the strategic situation than in the political circumstances, which escaped him.

[77] This took place in 1276. It was some time, however, before it became effective throughout the land.

barbarians; the state of unrest prevalent in the neighboring regions, with their races and civilizations that were different from both the Chinese and the Mongols who had infiltrated there; the failure of the Mongols' first expedition against Japan in 1274; and, above all, the long-established dynastic project of including India in the immediate dominion of the Chinghizide empire—all these motives sufficed to justify one of the most difficult undertakings ever recorded in the history of the Orient, the conquest of the well-nigh impassable regions between the Salween River and the plains of the Irrawaddy, down to the Gulf of Martaban. And hence it was that Marco dwelt at length on one episode of this long and difficult campaign.[78]

That the Mongol invasion was stubbornly resisted by the king of Mien and Bengal, together with other rulers in Indochina, can be deduced from the fact that, in spite of their military defeat, political pacts, and the formal recognition of Chinghizide supremacy, not one of these kingdoms passively accepted that overlordship during the period of Mongol rule in China, but constantly remained in a state of latent or open rebellion. Hence, in Kublai's times these regions formed what would nowadays be called the nerve center of the empire's political and military organism; and it is here that we must look for the reason why Kublai chose this Venetian youth as his informant concerning a dominion which, more than any other, was a prey to resentment and fear and where hopes of resistance and independence flourished.

Since he could not rely on the native elements or the loyalty of his Chinese advisers, and knew that his Mongol officials were not yet equal to so difficult a task of subjugation, the emperor had reluctantly made use of his Mohammedan subjects in preparing and carrying out the conquest of Sung China, Yunnan, and the neighboring territories, since the Chinese, Tibetan, and Burmese Buddhist sects predominant in their religious life were fiercely opposed by the Mohammedans of the empire. When, however, the Moslems gathered strength and cohesion in Chinghizide Yunnan, and in the XIIIth century began to predominate in the kingdom of Bengal as in the rest of northern India, the grounds

---

[78] Described in the *Milione*, pp. 121–123, chaps. cxxii–cxxiv; M.P., pp. 286 ff.

for suspicion of these collaborators must have influenced the emperor to choose Marco. This foreign Catholic, who was still innocent of all intrigue, was the ideal person to report upon conditions in the territories that were strategically and politically essential for the safety and expansion of the empire.

Here as elsewhere, however, Marco does not appear to take the slightest interest in the political aspects of his adventure. For him, these are confined to a respect for all authority, however acquired, unconditional obedience to the sovereign, and the observance of pacts concluded both within and without the respective dominions. It does not matter to him that the conflict lies between the emperor's aspirations to universal sovereignty and the refusal of the conquered to accept his claims and to remain vassals of the central power—a refusal which, together with the nonpayment of tribute money, was the most common cause of the external wars waged in eastern Asia in Kublai's reign. Marco's historical data, though stated in positive terms, merely reflect the common reality of contemporary events. Here, too, his interest is mainly in the strategic or warlike aspects of the events narrated. For example, he criticizes like a military expert the mistake made by the king of Burma when in the course of the decisive battle he attacked the Tartars while their rear was still protected by a forest, instead of awaiting them in open country where they would have been unable to resist the charge of armed elephants.[79]

This characteristic and highly personal attitude faithfully reflects the spirit that prevailed in his Asiatic environment, where the dominant factor was the military organization of an empire which, as Marco well knew, was kept in being only by the strength of its armies and the ability of its generals.[80] Marco had penetrated far into this order of things and ideas, owing to his

[79] *Il Milione,* cr. ed., p. 123, n.; M.P., p. 291. Benedetto, cr. ed., *loc cit.,* mistakenly considers these tactical observations by Marco—included in the Ramusian version—to be "mere rhetorical ornamentation."

[80] Marco's detailed and correct description of the military organization of the empire (*Il Milione,* cr. ed., pp. 55 f.; M.P., pp. 171 ff.) shows that his constant interest in this particular aspect of contemporary Asiatic civilization was not determined by the picturesque element in the military actions, which he generally wanted Rustichello to present in a deliberately literary style. This is not apparent, however, in this famous episode in the Burmese campaign, in which the methods of combat employed were very different from those usually set forth in the various descriptions of battles contained in the Millione.

employment as an informant and, very likely, his participation in martial operations, which enabled him in his book to present the most important events in ancient and contemporary Asiatic history. The war against Burma, which he describes at length, offers one of the most striking examples of this.

It had been preceded and provoked, as Marco knew, by political pressure and military threats which, as usual, were intended to force the peoples of those regions to recognize Chinghizide sovereignty and to exact costly and humiliating tributes from their rulers. This was a time-honored system that had been employed more or less by all the sovereigns of the preceding Chinese dynasties, whether national or foreign, as well as by the various Turkish and Mongol tribes who in the past thousand years had aspired to sovereignty over the continental Far East. It was the stock resort of a policy which varied with time and place, and in the amount of force applied, but which remained invariable in its methods and aims.[81]

From Marco's account we learn that the king of Burma and pretender to the throne of the neighboring state of Bengal wished to forestall this customary and inevitable move before Kublai should extend his feudal and political sovereignty to the adjacent provinces. Indeed, war broke out, according to our author, before the emperor was able to send one of his sons there to take possession, precisely at the moment when the Mongols from China, aided by others of different races and faiths, established themselves

---

[81] Those interested in studying this characteristic phenomenon of Chinese history in the relevant documents should consult E. Chavannes, *Documents historiques sur les Tou-kioue occidentaux,* Paris, 1942 (reprint), and for more recent epochs the same author's "Inscriptions et pièces de chancellerie chinoises de l'époque mongole," Vol. V, 1904, pp. 357 ff., Vol. VI, 1905, pp. 1 ff., and Vol. IX, 1908, pp. 297–428. Also, the Chinese author Ma Tuan-lin, a contemporary of Marco Polo; the historical part of his encyclopedia has been translated into French by the marquis d'Hervey de Saint-Denys (Geneva, 1876–1883). From ancient times the least that was required of the rulers of subject or conquered nations was—apart from the regular payment of tribute money—an act of personal submission to the emperor, acceptance of the Chinese calendar on the part of the new subjects in order that their private and public life should be regulated according to the set pattern imposed upon the whole empire; and, finally, the use of the Chinese seal in their acts of chancellery. These were the conditions that foreigners always had most difficulty in accepting, since they meant the abasement of native religion and prestige and hence were more humiliating that the mere payment of material tribute.

at strategic points along the frontier for its defense and protection, or, we may add, as an advance guard for further military action which would nowadays be called aggression.[82]

In agreement with the Chinese sources cited by Pauthier,[83] Marco's account informs us that the policy of the king of Burma (or Mien) was to forestall armed incursion by a surprise attack advantaged by the superiority of a regular army specially trained to assault and destroy the small Mongol border garrisons detached from the main body of the imperial forces. Thus the political problem, characteristic of all medieval Asiatic history, was reduced to a military task exceptional for two reasons: first, because two experienced and well-led armies now confronted each other; and secondly, because the adversaries employed means and methods of combat which had not yet been tested in the clash of battle. Against the Mongol light cavalry was pitted an array of two thousand elephants bearing armed turrets. In the outcome, this formidable and novel force was defeated by the tactical genius of Nasreddin, the Mohammedan commander of the Tartar armies in these regions.[84]

The universal aspects of this struggle have conferred military fame upon a subsidiary episode in Chinghizide history. They also inspired Marco's dramatic account, which combines with what he knew of tactics and combat the excitement engendered by a grandiose spectacle. Even today, the battle is worthy of study by anyone acquainted with those localities and interested in the art of war. But at any rate, Marco's text is quite explicit about the essentials. It should, however, be noted that whereas the sole

[82] A state of war had existed in the border regions between China, Tibet, and Burma since the year 1253, as a result of the Mongol advance led by Kublai some years before his ascent to the Chinese, or Cathayan, throne in 1260. Hence, the military actions described by Marco can be considered as the continuation of a traditional plan of conquest. Cf. O. Franke, *Geschichte des chinesischen Reiches,* Vol. IV, pp. 320 ff. For the occasional use of elephants in the Chinese army cf. E. H. Schafer, "War Elephants in Ancient and Medieval China," *Oriens,* Vol. X, 1957, pp. 289 f.

[83] *Le Livre de Marco Polo,* Vol. II, pp. 43 f.

[84] This famous battle is described by P. Armandi, *Histoire militaire des éléphants,* Paris, 1843, pp. 439 ff. For Nasreddin (whom Marco calls Nescradin), born at Bokhara in 1210 and one of the leading personages of the Chinghizide period, see, apart from the commentaries to the *Milione* already cited, Rock, *The Ancient Na-khi Kingdom,* Vol. I, p. 72 n. 11.

Chinese source that records the action describes it simply as a
"frontier incident," [85] Marco makes it a "fine pitched battle,"
fought with varying tactical vicissitudes on a plain that lay between the two vast and swift rivers on the borders between Burma
and the Chinese province of Yunnan.[86] Moreover, it is probable
that in this description, with its lively episodes and picturesque
details heightened by literary embellishments, Marco condensed
his reminiscences of the various campaigns that had taken place
in these regions during the whole of his stay in China, before the
total submission of Burma to the Mongol power.[87]

The conquest of this rich land and its fabulous capital, Pagan,
by Kublai's Mongols was accomplished gradually and after much
internecine strife, which is authentically recorded in the Chinese
and Burmese sources.[88] The critical phase of the operations began
in 1284, when the "king of Mien and Bengal," as Marco calls him,
had the emperor's envoys put to death after they had solicited
humiliating tributes from him.[89] Marco makes no mention
of this episode. Instead, he reveals the contempt felt by his sovereign for that land, the conquest of which, he tells us, the Great
Kaan entrusted to jugglers and acrobats from his court.[90] This

[85] Cf. E. Huber, "La Fin de la dynastie de Pagan," *Bulletin de l'École Française
d'Extrême-Orient*, Vol. IX, 1909, pp. 633 ff.

[86] *Il Milione*, cr. ed., p. 121; M.P., p. 287. The locality is not specified, and Marco's
deploying of armies on a vast and beautiful plain makes it even more difficult to
establish. Nevertheless, since this region is famous for its spacious valleys between
steep mountains and ancient forests, the site seems to have been correctly described
by Marco although the phraseology is Rustichello's, as has been pointed out by Benedetto, cr. ed., Introd., p. xxiii n. 1. However, as can be seen from the present author's
Storia letteraria delle scoperte geografiche, medieval travelers and explorers were wont
to describe exotic landscapes and episodes in accordance with the literary clichés then
in vogue. For the topography of the region see the illustrations in Rock, *op. cit.*, and
the sketch maps included in the second volume of his work.

[87] The impression made on the tribes of those regions by the Mongol conquest
described by Marco was a lasting one, as is proved by the legends they still recount
today, which are to be found in Rock, *op. cit.*, Vol. I, pp. 72 f.

[88] Cf. the article by Huber cited in n. 85 above.

[89] Cf. G. E. Harvey, *History of Burmah*, London, 1925, pp. 64 ff.

[90] *Il Milione*, cr. ed., p. 124; M.P., p. 293. The jugglers at Kublai's court were
probably East Indians, since, according to Chau Ju-kua (ed. Hirth-Rockhill, p. 111),
the most gifted acrobats came from India. This author adds that, although expert at
handling or playing with weapons, they were cowards in battle. It has always been
proverbial to the Chinese that acrobats and buffoons are of Western origin. Cf. F.
Hirth, *China and the Roman Orient*, Leipzig and Munich, 1885, pp. 36 f., for jugglers
who arrived at the Chinese court "from western seas" in 120 A.D. The Franciscan

strange anecdote may well represent the echo of some slighting remark of Kublai's concerning this disloyal sovereign, who was later constrained by the force of the Mongol-Chinese armies to recognize the emperor's supremacy. Kublai, however, as we read in the *Milione,* wished to afford proof of his magnanimity by leaving intact the tomb of gold and silver that the vanquished king had built in his capital.[91]

True, Marco sometimes substitutes for chronicle of actual events an anecdote. But it is precisely in this that the interest of his account lies. Whereas the Oriental annals and documents do not necessarily require doubtful confirmation from Marco, the *Milione* reflects the gossip, legends, and opinions, current in the official circles and foreign colonies of the empire, that would never have been recorded by courtly or erudite historiography. On the factual side, things did not go as easily as Marco and his informants would have us believe, for the final surrender of Burma did not take place until 1301, after the death of Kublai, and after the *Milione* had been published.

❖   ❖   ❖

While these semifabulous incidents were occurring on the outskirts of the empire and, as it were, before Marco's own eyes, some quite different events, actual and far more fateful, had extended Mongol rule in the Far East on the eve of the arrival of the three Venetians at Kublai's court. Linking that story with his own experience of places and affairs, Marco treats of it in his chapters that deal with the regions of southern China which,

---

missionaries mentioned the great number of jugglers at the court of the Great Kaans; cf. *Sinica Franciscana,* Vol. I, pp. 374, 475, 480. In 1223 Ch'ang Ch'un and his retinue were entertained in a Central Asiatic town by tightrope-walking and sword-dancing small boys; see A. Waley, *The Travels of an Alchemist,* p. 91. On the other hand, Marco Polo affirms that Burma supplied to the overlords of the neighboring countries a great number of eunuchs and slave girls. Cf. cr. ed., p. 125, chap. cxxvii; M.P., p. 295.

[91] *Il Milione,* cr. ed., p. 124; M.P., pp. 293 f.; Yule-Cordier, *The Book of Ser Marco Polo,* Vol. II, pp. 110 f. This passage contains Marco's description of the wonderful city of Pagan, the capital of the kingdom of "Mien," or Burma, from the IIId to the XIIIth century. It began to fall away after the first Mongol-Chinese invasion in 1281, and is now a center for tourists and archaeological studies. Cf. Harvey, *History of Burmah.*

until their annexation to the Chinghizide dominion, formed the
national empire of the Sung dynasty. This extended from the
banks of the Yellow River to the northern borders of present-day
Tonkin, and had remained independent of the neighboring state
of Cathay, which for centuries had been dominated by Turko-
Mongol dynasties deeply impregnated by Chinese influences.[92]

This immense and highly civilized territory, extensively described in the *Milione,* is here given the name Mangi, which in its
Chinese form *Man-tzŭ,* meaning "Barbarians," records the contempt in which its people were commonly held by the conquerors.[93] The version Marco gives of the Mongols' victorious advance
and his explanation of their rapid conquest of regions so pros-
perous and so densely populated undoubtedly reflect the opinions
currently held in court circles, and those which official propaganda
imposed upon those who were not in a position to know the
facts. Though Marco does on several occasions mention the
desperate resistance offered by this people to the Mongol advance
through their lands, he nevertheless attributes their eventual submission exclusively to their unwarlikeness, their lack of proficiency
in combat, and finally to the indolent life led by their last effective
sovereign, who had great resources in wealth, lands, and men, but

[92] For the civilization of the late Sung empire cf. O. Franke, *Geschichte des
chinesischen Reiches,* Vol. IV, pp. 351–423. This is followed by the history of the
Khanate of Cathay. Of the foreign dynasties that dominated this country for several
centuries, Marco is acquainted only with that of the Kin, in the person of the Golden
King (*Il Milione,* cr. ed., pp. 105 ff., M.P.; pp. 258 ff.), who was deposed by the
Mongols in 1234 after the Kin had ruled in northern China since 1115. The name of
this Tartar dynasty survives in that of its last sovereign, who is recorded by Marco
as the Golden King since *Kin* does in fact mean 'gold' in Chinese. The long-drawn-out
struggle between the Kin and Chinghizide dynasties is described in all the historical
works already quoted, including the *Histoire des campagnes de Gengis Khan,* ed. P.
Pelliot and L. Hambis, Paris, 1951 (Chinese text with translation and a detailed his-
torical-philological commentary).

[93] This name is generally used by Marco to designate the part of China that lies
to the south of the Yellow River. He does, however, indicate that this immense territory—which, according to him, included nine kingdoms and 1,200 towns and cities
—was called *Chin* in the islands of the China Sea (*Il Milione,* cr. ed., p. 166; M.P.,
p. 365), whereas the classical Chinese name, *Chung Hua,* is applied by Marco in the
form Choncha (cr. ed., p. 156; M.P., p. 347) to the single province of Fukien (Fugiu).
For the term *Mangi* and other names for the various peoples of China in Marco's
age cf. O. Franke, *Geschichte des chinesischen Reiches,* Vol. IV, p. 475, and Vol. V,
pp. 237 f. The more nearly correct form would be *Manzi,* as it appears in the geographical notes by Rashiduddin, who was Marco's contemporary (Cf. H. Yule, *Cathay,*
second edition, 1914, Vol. III, p. 113).

who gave himself up exclusively to women and, as Marco has it, to good works,[94] while he concludes that "if they had been a soldierly race, they would never have lost that province." [95]

It must be conceded that this ruler, Tu-tsong, after handing over the cares of state to one of his all-powerful ministers, did, like many of his predecessors, lead a life of pleasure so unworthy of his rank that, as we know from Chinese sources, he learned of the day's events from his concubines rather than from his officials.[96] For the rest, Marco expresses in his own way the traditional feelings of contempt entertained by the nomads, who were constantly engaged in combat, for all forms of courtly, sedentary, and urban civilization dominated by spiritual interests and given up to the enjoyment of the good things of life.

Marco's severe judgment may also be referred to the neutrality of the Sung dynasty at the time of the Tartar invasions of Cathay, which was swept with fire and sword by the armies of Chinghiz Khan and his generals.[97] Marco is quite right in thinking that if the Chinese of Mangi had united on this and other occasions with those of Cathay, they would have been able to save their independence by offering a common resistance to the Tartar onslaught. The rulers and ministers of southern China did in fact realize—when it was too late—the error they had made by remaining impassive spectators before the bloody spectacle of the violent destruction of the neighboring empire of the Kin, who fiercely opposed the Mongol invasions and the conquest of their capital in 1215.

Indeed, the commonplace, which in times past has been frequently and foolishly repeated, of the unwarlike and effeminate Chinese made Marco forget the episode of heroic, if isolated, resistance offered by the towns and armies of Mangi to the Tartar

[94] Cf. *Il Milione,* cr. ed., p. 134; M.P.., p. 309 (with regard to King Facfur, a Persian translation of the Chinese imperial title *T'ien tzŭ* or "Son of Heaven" which belonged by right to the Sung emperor of southern China).

[95] On the other hand, Marco describes the Chinese of Mangi as able merchants and artisans, while he also states that they were especially gifted in the fields of medicine, natural philosophy, and astrology.

[96] For the persons and events that characterize the dramatic end of the Sung empire see the detailed account in O. Franke, *op. cit.,* Vol. IV, pp. 220–423, with bibliographical information on the Chinese sources and relevant literature in Vol. V, pp. 123 ff.

[97] For these events see O. Franke, *op. cit.,* esp. Vol. IV, pp. 343 ff.

advance through this populous land, which for centuries had
laid aside the practice of arms. Nor does Marco make the slightest
mention of the highly dramatic circumstances that culminated
in total surrender, which took place in 1276, and in the dispersion
of the celebrated dynasty. Instead, his account of these events is
brief, and popular in tone and content. He records the flight by
land and sea of the last emperor, Tu-tsong, and his faithful followers who had vowed to resist to the bitter end. At the same
time, however, he reduces the subsequent capitulation, proclaimed
by the empress governing in the name of the infant Kong-ti, to
a prediction made by her astrologers.[98] According to Marco, they
had predicted that a man with a hundred eyes would succeed in
conquering the kingdom.[99]

The prophecy referred to the Mongol name of Bayan, the
general commanding Kublai's armies for the conquest of the
Sung dominion.[100] When pronounced in the ancient manner,
this name could sound like *Pai-yen,* the exact equivalent of "One
Hundred Eyes." It may be assumed that the astrologers whose
task it was to advise the empress realized the futility of all further
resistance and fabricated the legend so as to induce her to accept
unconditional surrender, which entailed the handing over of her
splendid capital, Quinsai (modern Hangchow), and the numberless other towns in her dominion to this captain, whose victory
was apparently decreed by fate.[101]

In actuality the events were quite different. However, the fable
does succeed in expressing the alarm, confusion, and dismay that

[98] For the child's name cf. the note by O. Franke, *op. cit.,* Vol. V, pp. 176 f. Marco
offers various examples of the civic virtues practiced by this dynasty and especially
by its last ruler.

[99] *Il Milione,* cr. ed., p. 135 (M.P., p. 311): "E quant la raine oi que cestui avoit a
non c oilz, tantost li foi a remenbré de l'astrolomie que disoit que un home que
avesse c oilz devoit elz tolir lo reigne," etc.

[100] Bayan was one of the greatest military leaders of Kublai's age; he was as successful in civil and dynastic wars as in those waged for the conquest of China, Burma,
and Indochina. Marco attributes to him the name "Cincsan" (cr. ed., p. 134, lines
14–15; M.P., p. 310), whereas this term was in fact merely the Chinese title for
minister of state, or *ch'eng-hsiang,* which had been conferred upon the great captain.
For his various campaigns cf. O. Franke, *op. cit.,* Vol. IV, pp. 336 ff., 466 ff., etc., and
F. W. Cleaves, "The Biography of Bayan," *Harvard Journal of Asiatic Studies,* Vol.
XIX, 1956, pp. 185–303.

[101] The interference of astrologers in these military operations is confirmed in the
official Chinese report of the events. Cf. Cleaves, "The Biography of Bayan," p. 218.

overcame the imperial family, the court, and the fainthearted ministers before the advance of the Mongol armies, which came to the gates of the capital without having encountered any organized resistance. Moreover, it recalls others of similar style and intent which by fiction and anecdote accounted for the capitulation of great kingdoms that were powerless to save themselves.[102] It brings to mind the prophecy of the white man whose coming would spell the end of the ancient Carib and Aztec kingdoms, which were in fact conquered by a handful of Spaniards.[103] The only authentic information contained in Marco's account is the pathetic appeal addressed to Kublai by the empress regent, which is written in the florid style typical of Chinese imperial documents and of which we may perceive some reflection in Marco's rhetoric.[104] Kublai is entreated to save from destruction the ancient capital of Quinsai, pearl of cities, described in this famous chapter of the *Milione* on the basis of the poetic picture painted by the historic message. The petition must have been widely circulated in a Mongol or Persian translation, since Marco was able to understand it and transmit it to posterity with its pathetic accents and ornate exaggeration.[105]

Not everything, therefore, is the fruit of Marco's imagination in this circumstantial description of the final conquest of Mangi, which took place after our author's arrival in China. Instead, it is likely that he gathered local or personal interpretations, which also gave rise to the legend of the hundred eyes of Bayan. He was not well enough acquainted with Chinese to indulge in play on words in this language which so readily lends itself to such puns.

[102] Cf. Yule-Cordier, *The Book of Ser Marco Polo,* Vol. II, pp. 149 f, n. 5.

[103] The legend is narrated in the Mexican chronicles that record the conquests of Hernán Cortés, the white man whose coming had been prophesied by native soothsayers for the end of the world (if, indeed, this story is not a later elaboration invented by the conquerors themselves).

[104] Cf. the article by A. C. Moule, "Marco Polo's Description of Quinsai," *T'oung Pao,* Vol. XXXIII, 1937, pp. 105 ff., and the same author's *Quinsai, with Other Notes on Marco Polo,* Cambridge Univ. Press, 1956, and E. Balasz, "Marco Polo dans la capitale de la Chine," in *Oriente Poliano,* Rome, 1957, pp. 133 ff.; also, O. Franke, *op. cit.,* Vol. V, pp. 214 f., and W. Eichhorn, "Züge aus dem hauptstädtischen Leben der südlichen Sung Dynastie," *Zeitschrift der deutschen morgenländischen Gesellschaft,* Vol. CVII, 1957, pp. 161–184.

[105] Cf. the *Milione,* cr. ed., pp. 143 ff.; M.P., pp. 326 ff. For contemporary Chinese descriptions of this capital, which are characterized by their rhetorical style, similar to Marco's, cf. the article by E. Balasz cited above, esp. pp. 136 ff.

Nevertheless, it is true that a historically documented prophecy did in fact precede, and may psychologically have influenced, the capitulation of the empress in the name of her son, not yet of age, and of the nation, wearied of resistance. Indeed, we read that Bayan himself is supposed to have warned the court and government of the Sung that this dynasty, which had come to power in the year 960 with the infant Tsung-hün, would end with another child bearing the same name.[106]

The prophecy was soon realized. The court astrologers, who always had the last word on such occasions, in the Orient as in the West, merely had to refer to the menace of Bayan "of the hundred eyes," and to public opinion, which was in favor of surrender in the face of irremediable defeat. Marco was also aware of the generosity shown by Kublai toward these last representatives of an ancient dynasty which had given to southern China, and indirectly to the whole empire, a national civilization of rare brilliance and lasting fame. The victorious emperor made the entire family of the deposed dynasty welcome at his court, and Marco recalls the Sung princess who was included in the train of the Princess Cocachin whom the Polos accompanied to Persia and most probably was destined for the harem of the Ilkhan Arghun, lord of that empire.[107]

Of those great happenings, Marco's recital and his various apparently legendary allusions offer us a popular account that most likely was the one current among his Mongol acquaintances, who knew little enough about Chinese life and were therefore inclined to misunderstand its expressions. An indication that this interpretation of recent events was of foreign origin is afforded not only by the lack of any evidence in the Chinese sources, but, more than

---

[106] Cf. O. Franke, *op. cit.*, Vol. IV, pp. 341 f.

[107] This "fille au roi dou Mangi" is referred to by Marco in the prologue to the *Milione* (cr. ed., p. 13; M.P., p. 92) as a great lady of the same rank as Cocachin, the Chinghizide princess who was the bride-to-be of Arghun Khan. Kublai's magnanimity toward the deposed Sung family and their subjects after the surrender is especially emphasized by Bayan himself in his eloquent report to the emperor. Cf. Cleaves, "The Biography of Bayan," esp. pp. 254 f. For these episodes and other sources see O. Franke, *Geschichte des chinesischen Reiches, loc. cit.*, and Vol. V, pp. 178 ff., as well as R. Grousset, *Histoire de l'Extrême-Orient*, Vol. II, p. 450, and H. Franke, *Beiträge zur Kulturgeschichte Chinas*, p. 112.

anything else, by the appellation given to the last of the Sung emperors, namely, Facfur, which is a Persian translation of the Chinese title *T'ien-tzŭ,* or "Son of Heaven," which was his due.[108] Indeed, it was with this title that the empress regent greeted Kublai in his hour of victory, in her message of unconditional surrender of 1276, whereby she solemnly and officially invested the Chinghizide sovereign with imperial power over all China. It was therefore only from this time forward that the great Kaan reigned with the Chinese title and assumed all the prerogatives it conferred upon the holder. Marco was obviously unaware that this title was traditional and characteristic of the Chinese sovereigns. Instead, he makes a proper noun of it and thereby reveals the limitations of his linguistic knowledge and the foreign sources from which he drew his information about Chinese history.

These sources are partly identified by a communication contained in the description of the imperial palace at Quinsai, where Marco adds the finishing touches to his picture of the last Sung emperor, who, "owing to his ineptitude and cowardliness," lost his throne and state "to his great shame and infamy." All that concerned his habits and way of life was told to Marco "by a wealthy merchant of that city, now very advanced in years, who had once been on intimate terms" with the king.[109] This merchant must have been one of the many Mohammedans of eastern Asia —especially Persians—who lived at Hangchow, the Sung capital, and in the ports of southern China, with which our Venetian was acquainted as a result of his various periods of residence there.[110]

In Marco, however, we find a definite tendency to judge historical personages and events in accordance with moral criteria, as though he wished to offer an example and a warning to those who rule peoples and read books. Without having a moralist's intentions, he nevertheless judges the facts of history and thereby

[108] For the name Facfur cf. Yule-Cordier, *The Book of Ser Marco Polo,* Vol. II, p. 148.

[109] *Il Milione,* cr. ed., p. 151; M.P., p. 339 n.

[110] For Mohammedan colonies in the ports of southern China in the XIIIth century cf. the information collected by Hirth and Rockhill in the Introd. to their edition of Chau Ju-kua's treatise, already cited, and, with much more detail, J. Kuwabara when dealing with P'u Shou-kêng (see above, chap. i, § 2, n. 61, and chap. iii, n. 11), perhaps the same man described by Marco.

follows the didactic traditions of his Western contemporaries, who regarded and treated history as a lesson rather than as information.[111]

❖   ❖   ❖

Marco mentions only one military episode in this memorable campaign, which lasted from 1268 until 1276 and brought to a close the conquest of the whole of China; and it is the one that proved decisive for the victorious advance of the Mongol army, namely, the surrender of Saianfu (present-day Hsiang-yang) in the province of Hupeh, a stronghold which held out for five years against the Mongol siege and finally capitulated in 1273, in circumstances which Marco minutely describes.[112] This surrender, which opened the way to southern China for Kublai's armies, is famous in Chinghizide annals, and is the object of our author's keenest historical interest. In fact, he attributes this victory, which had until then been vainly sought, to a weapon suggested by the three Polos. They had some great mangonels built on the spot, which, according to Marco, were of a kind unknown to the veteran imperial armies and were capable of hurling rocks weighing three hundred pounds or more over a great distance.[113]

The Chinese annals and Oriental historians who describe at length this memorable siege agree with Marco in attributing the final success to powerful engines, though they say that these were built by skilled military engineers who had been sent expressly from western Asia once the imperial council of war, headed by Kublai himself, had ordered their construction. Moreover, these sources and Marco's account both agree in stressing the important part played by the Nestorian Christians in the reduction of Saianfu. It is even possible to specify this in the person of Alihaya,

---

[111] This tendency is already evident in this same episode, where Marco enumerates, *loc. cit.*, the various measures enacted by the last of the Sung sovereigns for the public welfare and to insure that justice should prevail among his peoples. Likewise, in various part of his book, Marco offers an ideal portrait of the virtues of Kublai as the perfect ruler (see below, chap. ix, § 3). For him, justice and liberality were the principal sovereign virtues, which he also found to be practiced by the kings of Armenia (*Il Milione*, cr. ed., p. 13, chap. xx; M.P., p. 92) and Kashmir (cr. ed., p. 39; M.P., p. 140).

[112] *Il Milione*, cr. ed., pp. 138 f.; M.P., pp. 316 f.

[113] For the various readings of the text cf., besides the cr. ed., *loc. cit.*, Moule-Pelliot, *Marco Polo: The Description of the World*, Vol. I, p. 318, and p. 26 n. 3.

a Uigur general who is expressly mentioned in the Annals of the Empire (*Yüan Shih*) as the originator of the plan.[114]

For the rest, however, the discrepancies between the authentic reports of the historical facts and the account contained in the *Milione* are so great as to have given rise, on the one hand, to malicious insinuations against our author's integrity, and, on the other, to more or less ingenious but always inconclusive attempts to save his honor by reconciling the contradictory versions of the event. Marco postpones it until the last stages of the Mongol advance into China, which, as mentioned above, ended in 1276. If his chronology were correct, the Polos' participation as he describes it would have been possible. But it was only after the siege was concluded—namely, after the surrender of Saianfu in March, 1273—that the Mongol armies were able to proceed with the fairly rapid conquest of southern China.[115] And at that time the Polos had not yet arrived at the court of the Great Kaan and could not have had any part in the undertaking.

Any attempt to ascribe their arrival to the year 1272 would be in direct contradiction to the period of time taken up by their journey from Ayas to Peking, which, according to Marco, lasted three years and a half, that is, until the end of 1274.[116] Nor do we find it easier to accept the suggestion that the responsibility for this military rodomontade, which is contradicted by the facts, should be imputed to Marco's scribe Rustichello.[117] Any such attempt at distortion of the truth would be no less blameworthy, even if Marco had accepted it. Furthermore, little would be gained by supposing that the anecdote should be taken to refer only to Marco's father and uncle, who paid a first, brief visit to Kublai's court in the year 1265. At that time the Mongol advance into southern China had not yet begun and therefore could not have been influenced by the Venetians' counsel.[118]

[114] Cf. A. C. Moule, "The Siege of Saianfu," *Journal of the North China Branch of the Royal Asiatic Society*, 1927, pp. 1–35; 1928, pp. 256 ff., and the same author's *Quinsai*, pp. 70 ff.

[115] For this campaign cf. O. Franke, *op. cit.*, Vol. IV, pp. 334 ff., and Cleaves, "The Biography of Bayan," pp. 185 ff.

[116] For this interpretation, put forward by A. J. H. Charignon (*Le Livre de Marco Polo*, Vol. III, 1928, pp. 52 ff.), cf. the observations by Moule-Pelliot, *op. cit.*, Vol. I, p. 27.

[117] M.P., *loc. cit.*, and Moule, *Quinsai*, pp. 77 f.

[118] It is difficult to admit the possibility that Marco invented the whole episode of

On the other hand, these difficulties, so compromising to the reputation of our author—who is normally sparing in personal allusions,—may be escaped if one turns to those authoritative versions of the text which make no mention of the Polos' participation in the siege of Hsiang-yang.[119] No error then remains except in the dating of the event. Marco's chronology is always uncertain and, even here, should not much disturb the reality of the narration. At any rate, the episode offers further proof of Marco's keen interest in every type of military operation, the use of arms and war materials, and the technical and strategic ability of the leaders of Oriental armies.[120]

The taking of this stronghold gave our author an opportunity to describe the vicissitudes of a long siege, even as the open battle in Burma had prompted him to mention the use of massed elephants in a war of movement. And now, the attempted conquest of Japan offered him the possibility of reporting a series of amphibious operations, unsuccessful so far as Kublai's armies were concerned, but attractive as a subject for animated description. Not only do these two chapters [121] contain the first news of the Japanese empire to have reached the Christian West; they also relate one of the outstanding events in the history of his times and the only manifest defeat recorded in the annals of Kublai's long reign. Marco does not seek to minimize its effects; and he reveals its causes, noting the essential phases and all the catastrophic consequences of this extraordinary undertaking.[122]

his father's and uncle's participation in this siege, for he would have run the danger of being publicly contradicted by them, or of making them accessories to a falsification which would certainly have come to their knowledge, since both continued to live for several years after the composition of the _Milione_. It is nevertheless possible to make out a certain military vanity in other parts of the book. This attitude was characteristic of Marco, who was dazzled by the spectacle of might and splendor offered by Kublai's armies in both peace and war. This does not, however, allow us to assume that Niccolò and Maffeo Polo followed their young companion in these leanings.

[119] Cf. the critical apparatus to the cr. ed. of the _Milione_, p. 128 n., and more especially M.P., Vol. I, p. 318 n. 2.

[120] Cf. L. Foscolo Benedetto, _Il Libro di Messer Marco Polo_, p. 432 (note to p. 234 of the translation). References to military affairs are numerous in the _Milione_, apart from the detailed description of the Mongol armies and their strategy.

[121] _Il Milione_, cr. ed., pp. 162–166; M.P., pp. 357 ff.

[122] For the course of these events see O. Franke, _op. cit._, Vol. IV, pp. 432 ff., and for a bibliography of the subject, Vol. V, pp. 211 f. See, too, K. Enoki's article in _Oriente Poliano_, already cited, pp. 32 f. (with relevant Japanese literature).

He attributes the failure to three different factors. First, as we read in the *Milione,* the ships of the imperial navy were able to land men and horses on one of the Japanese islands, but these forces were then left without protection from town or castle and exposed to attack in open country with the sea at their backs and mountains in front. Second, the situation was further aggravated by the rivalry that existed between the two captains, Abacan and Vonsainchin, whom the emperor had put in command of the expedition: the first a Mongolian chieftain called Argan (in Chinese, *A-la-kan*), known in the military history of the empire, and the other a Chinese general Won or Wong, of the same rank as the famous Bayan but not recorded in the annals of the dynasty. Third, and decisive, was the tempest—the Japanese *kamikase*—which forced the withdrawal of a large part of the imperial fleet and spread dismay among the troops forsaken on one of the islands of the archipelago. In the end, one of the commanders, persuaded that the situation was hopeless, managed to set sail toward the continental mainland, and left thirty thousand of his men to their fate.[123]

Nevertheless, according to Marco, the abandoned troops outwitted the Japanese who came against them, and seized their ships, weapons, and standards. Nay, more, they occupied and held the enemy's capital for some seven months until, on condition that their lives be spared, they surrendered, in 1279.[124] How much truth is there in this dramatic story, recounted with such spirit by our author? It deals with happenings that took place in part while the Polos were in China; and even though it certainly is not an eyewitness account, it nevertheless portrays a series of spectacular events as reflected in the memory and judgment of contemporary observers. On the whole, the Oriental sources offer ample confirmation of this, as may be seen from all the major commentaries to the *Milione* which reproduce the

---

[123] This historic tempest, which decided the outcome of the war, like that which in 1588 wrecked the "invincible armada" of Philip II of Spain, gave rise in Japan to legends which within our own times have developed into a special cult emphasizing a supposedly divine intervention that should protect the Japanese from all foreign invasions.

[124] *Il Milione,* cr. ed., p. 165; M.P., p. 359. Here, too, Marco's dates are unreliable. For the chronology of the events cf. R. Grousset, *L'Asie orientale,* pp. 327 ff. and 528 ff.

essential passages. Some, indeed, have seen in Marco's account a token of his direct participation in these events, or at least in those preceding the last fateful expedition.[125]

However, his fanciful description of the riches of Japan, and the somewhat ingenuous story of the stratagems devised by the shipwrecked soldiers and their temporary conquest of the capital, bear a legendary stamp—which also appears here and there in the authentic records. In fact, some time before the Polos' arrival in the Far East, and before organizing with partial success, in 1274, the first armed expedition against Kyushu, the most southerly of the country's large islands, Kublai had more than once sought recognition of his imperial supremacy by the Japanese regent, Hojo Tokimune. As on other occasions, the emperor was merely subserving the Chinghizide aspiration to universal sovereignty, irrespective of the vision of boundless wealth which in the *Milione* appears as his principal motive.[126]

Some two centuries later, this glittering mirage was to inspire Columbus and encourage those who financed his expeditions; but it played no decisive part in the decisions of the Mongol emperor, who was already sated with riches of every kind, or in the calculations of his counselors. Rather than new treasure, Kublai saw in the lands destined for conquest new dominions to hand over to his numerous sons, who did in fact become viceroys and feudatories in various parts of the empire and in the recently subjugated provinces.[127] The emperor and his dignitaries knew that Japan was a land with scanty natural resources and that its yield of gold was insignificant in comparison with that of con-

[125] This expedition of 1274 had been preceded by various exchanges of embassies between the two sovereigns and by negotiations which concerned the usual condition of personal submission. The second expedition, culminating in the naval defeat suffered by the Sino-Mongol-Korean forces, was undertaken in 1281, when Marco was in China.

[126] The proverbial gold of Cipango, pronounced *Je-pen-kuo* in its original Chinese form ("Land of the Rising Sun"), was, as is well known, the principal motive behind Columbus' expedition, although the hopes of boundless profit were not immediately realized.

[127] This fact is attested by Marco Polo (*Il Milione*, cr. ed., p. 73; M.P., p. 206), who attributes twenty-two sons to Kublai from his four wives and another twenty-five from his concubines. Seven of his legitimate sons were kings of vast provinces, and the others were "great barons" and therefore enjoyed the highest rank in the Mongol feudal, military, and political hierarchy.

tinental Asia subject to Tartar rule.[128] It seems certain that the magnificent palaces of Cipango, gilded without and within, are nothing but fancies, products of that universal insular romanticism which always offers such visions of lands beyond the seas.[129] Indeed, those palaces and the supposed wonders of Japan had long been a topic of Chinese fabulous geography, as we find in old Taoist and Buddhist literature and in several treatises on the marvels of imaginary archipelagoes scattered over the uncharted seas east of the Chinese mainland.[130] Western literature offers, with the saga of Alexander the Great and the *Letter of Prester John,* similar insular and continental examples of this gorgeous architecture, which some rulers of Asia had tried to materialize in their overornamented residences.[131] The riches of the last Caliph of Baghdad, conquered by the Mongols in 1258 in the way described by Marco Polo, seemed to confirm those tales and enhance those expectations.[132] It may therefore be supposed that the legend of the gold of Japan was broadcast by intention, to offer the lure of limitless booty and strange marvels to those soldiers of the motley imperial army who, like the Koreans and the Chinese, felt no enthusiasm for political expeditions intended to increase Chinghizide prestige, but expected advantages of a more direct and concrete kind.[133]

These troops do indeed appear to have been the first to yield, in a surrender which marked the final defeat of the invading Mongol army. At the same time the Japanese, after having successfully repulsed the attempts at invasion, ended by attributing to the intervention of the gods the great storm of the 15th of August, 1281, which scattered the Mongol-Chinese fleet and exposed the remnants of the army to the total defeat that followed. History

[128] Chau Ju-kua (ed. Hirth-Rockhill, p. 171) and his informants knew that the production of gold was limited to only one of the Japanese islands, most probably to the Handa mines in the insular province of Iwashiro.

[129] For this concept cf. the present author's *Storia letteraria delle scoperte geografiche,* Florence, 1937, pp. 14 ff.

[130] Cf. G. Schlegel, *Problèmes géographiques,* Leiden, 1896 (extracts from *T'oung Pao*), who collected the relevant Chinese texts with attempts at a geographical identification, generally rejected by sinologists and geographers.

[131] See above, chap. iv, nn. 36 and 37.

[132] *Il Milione,* cr. ed., pp. 18 ff.; M.P., pp. 101 f.

[133] O. Franke, *Geschichte des chinesischen Reiches,* Vol. IV, pp. 432 ff.

and legend were mingled in the interpretation of these events already accepted by Marco, which must have come to his notice, more than elsewhere, in the well-informed circles of southern China, where this second expedition was organized. He speaks only of those detachments of the imperial forces which set out to attack Japan from the ports of Quinsai and Zaiton, without mentioning the strong Mongol and Korean contingents that on more that one occasion had set sail from Fusan and other ports of those regions nearer to their destination. However, the space and emphasis given to them by Marco are an indication of the importance of these events which limited Chinghizide expansion toward the Orient only a few years after, at the other end of the Asian continent, the armies of the Mamelukes of Egypt had put an end to the advance of the Mongol armies toward the Mediterranean.[134]

These setbacks did not cause Kublai to renounce his dream of world-wide dominion, and Marco himself tells us that the emperor was laying his plans for the conquest of Indochina while his armies were occupied in one direction with the invasion of Japan, and in another with the subjugation of the kingdom of Burma. We read in the *Milione* of a military expedition under the command of Sagatu which attacked the rich kingdom of Champa, in the center of modern Annam, in 1278, or two years after the total annexation of Sung China, at a time when the Mongol armies were harassing the rulers of Cipango, Burma, and Annam with demands for vassalage and tribute to the Great Kaan.[135] In spite of having visited these regions and having remained there for some time in 1285, Marco has little to say about the long-drawn-out struggles, difficult negotiations, palace conspiracies, feigned submission, and popular revolts which these military expeditions and diplomatic pressures stirred up in those years and until the end of the century.[136] Our author is certainly well aware of the wealth of Indochina and the numberless islands near by;

[134] For these events cf. Grousset, *L'Empire des steppes,* pp. 356 ff.
[135] For the diplomatic and military aspects of this action cf. G. Maspero, *Le Royaume de Champa,* Paris and Brussels, 1928, esp. chap. viii.
[136] *Il Milione,* cr. ed., pp. 167 f.; M.P., pp. 366 f.

yet he merely observes that the elderly sovereign of Champa, terrified by the destruction wrought by the Mongols in his small kingdom, eventually recognized Kublai's supremacy and offered him an annual tribute of elephants and miscellaneous produce.[137]

All this more or less corresponds to the facts, though these are simplified in a way that is either merely convenient or ingenuous. The pity which, according to Marco, moved the Great Kaan to content himself with accepting the offer proposed by this elderly king while allowing him to retain his throne and his seignorial rights in all the bridal beds in his kingdom, is a benevolent interpretation; our author is always eager to point out his sovereign's clemency and humanity toward both friend and foe. In actual fact, it was part of Kublai's general policy, which was the same as that of his predecessors on the Chinese throne, to maintain the reigning dynasties in vassal states while reducing their rank and requiring the personal submission of the respective sovereigns, who may possibly have had to perform this act in person in the capital of the empire.

He applied the same pressures to the kingdom of Champa, attempting to obtain the maximum either by threats or by the use of force. If, however, he finally contented himself with simple tributes, this apparently clement decision depended on the difficulties everywhere encountered by his armies in Indochina, which fought back with its lethal climate, its jungles, rebellious population, and the resistance to total submission put up by its officials. Indeed, Mongol supremacy was recognized more in name than in fact, even after Kublai's death, which occurred in 1294, a year before our author's return to Venice.

Marco was well aware of these limitations, even as he was acquainted with the strength of the opposing forces, which virtually saved the independence of the countries destined to be absorbed in the immense political, administrative, feudal, and military machine of the empire. Among other things, he explains how the great distance and dangers entailed by any such expedition prevented the conquest of "Java," the greatest island, as he asserts,

---

[137] Kublai, as usual, demanded an act of personal submission on the part of the aged ruler. The negotiations, and the tributes requested and granted, are described in G. Maspero, *loc. cit.*

in the whole world.[138] However this may be, it is certainly part of the other islands and territories which the Great Kaan claimed for his immediate dominion, although he was never able to realize all his ambitions.[139]

Nor did Marco have any illusions about the stability of this immense empire. He was not only aware of the ferment of rebellion which obliged the Chinghizide rulers throughout Asia to adopt repressive measures, both administrative and military, but was also familiar with their common rivalry, which kept the whole continent in a perpetual state of latent or open warfare. This, indeed, helped to give Marco some expertness in military problems, as can be seen in his account.

This internal history of the empire is dominated by the successive alliances and defections of the various members of the dynasty who put forward territorial claims, rights of succession, and privileges of authority. Moreover, although the understanding that existed between the two great Chinghizide dominions of China in the east and Persia in the west remained undisturbed until and beyond the end of the century, and although the Ilkhans always recognized the nominal supremacy of the Great Kaan of Peking and made use of his seal, this harmony never included the other members of his family, who were likewise vassals of the same Kublai. Thus, while the Ilkhans of Persia were engaged in perpetual combat with the rulers of the Golden Horde or, as Marco calls them, Tartars of the West, or else with Caidu, the lord of Central Asia, the Great Kaan was faced with political and armed rebellion on the part of vassals who allied themselves with Caidu against him in the very years when he was organizing

[138] *Il Milione,* cr. ed., pp. 169 ff.; M.P., pp. 368 f. Marco distinguishes "la grant isle de Java" (variously—and never definitely—identified among the various archipelagoes to the east and south of China) from "Java la menor," which is undoubtedly the present island of Sumatra, where Marco stayed for some time when on his return voyage to Venice. The complex medieval toponymy of these islands has been amply discussed and partly clarified by P. Pelliot, "Deux itinéraires de Chine en Inde," *Bulletin de l'École Française d'Extrême-Orient,* Vol. IV, 1904, pp. 270 ff. Marco asserts that the eight kings on the island all recognized the Great Kaan's nominal sovereignty, without, however, paying him tribute money, although they did send him occasional gifts.

[139] In 1292, Kublai sent an army to conquer as much territory as possible on the large islands of Indonesia, including the northern regions of Sumatra. For this see O. Franke, *op. cit.,* pp. 463 ff.

punitive expeditions or imperialistic forays beyond the confines of his immense domain.[140]

Marco knew that the most stubborn and powerful of his master's internal enemies was his nephew Caidu, renowned for his leadership in politics and war. This indefatigable champion of the Chinghizide and Mongol cause bitterly opposed the Sinization and consequent dismemberment of the empire, for which he blamed his uncle Kublai.[141] It was against this nephew and his ally Nayan that Kublai, as we read in the *Milione,* personally took up arms—the one time that he did so in the course of his long reign. On other occasions he had entrusted the tasks of military action to his sons or generals.[142] Marco thereby makes us understand both the historical importance of this dynastic war and the bitterness with which it was fought. Moreover, in spite of the fact that he emphasizes the part played by the Christian Nayan, our author nevertheless reveals the preponderant role of Caidu, lord of Central Asia, in all these struggles.[143]

This episode in the internal history of the empire was a continuation of those rivalries which had already induced Kublai to make war on his brother Aric Buga, a candidate for the imperial title after the death of the Great Kaan Mangu in 1259. This rival, representing the Mongol national element in the dynasty and the army, declared that Kublai's elevation to the supreme dignity, which had taken place without a proper election, was contrary to tradition and the constitution of the empire as established by Chinghiz Khan in his ordinances. From all the members of his family, Chinghiz had in fact chosen his third-born son Chagatai, the first autonomous ruler of Central Asia, to be the guardian of his decrees and intentions.[144]

[140] For this complex situation and the resulting conflicts cf. C. d'Ohsson, *Histoire des Mongols,* Vol. II, pp. 439 ff., O. Franke, *op. cit.,* Vol. IV, pp. 466 ff., 491 ff., and *passim,* and Grousset, *L'Empire des steppes,* pp. 397 ff.

[141] *Il Milione,* cr. ed., pp. 216 ff.; M.P., pp. 447 ff.

[142] Cr. ed., pp. 66 f.; M.P., pp. 192 f.

[143] Nayan, an ally of Caidu the rebel, was lord of what is now northern Manchuria. His dominions extended from the borders of eastern Mongolia as far as the Chinese territory that was directly subject to Kublai. Nayan, a direct descendant of Uchegin, brother to Chinghiz Khan, was a Nestorian and bore the cross on his standards. See above, chap. vii, § 1, n. 54. He was defeated and slain by Kublai in 1288.

[144] For the Chinghizide succession and his famous ordinances (*Yassaq*) cf. B. Ya. Vladimirtsov, *The Life of Chingis-Khan,* London, 1930, pp. 74 f.

In 1264, Aric Buga had to yield before the *fait accompli* and the military and political supremacy of his brother Kublai, who had contrived to be elected by his generals instead of by the diet of the empire, and who had behind him the enormous arsenal and incalculable masses of his Chinese dominions. This, however, did not put an end to the rivalry or resentment. Caidu, Ogudai's nephew and heir presumptive, successfully organized the opposition, ambitious aims, and claims of the other leaders, and thereby moved the legitimist currents from Mongolia, which had hitherto been their center, toward Central Asia, making this the headquarters for political and military action and resistance against Kublai.

From this new stronghold the rebel's authority spread across the continent. After an unsuccessful attempt to win over to his cause the former capital of Karakorum and its adjacent Mongolian territory, he discovered in his cousin Nayan a warlike ally on the borders of China. This made it possible to launch a formidable coalition of princes, armies, and peoples against the might of the Great Kaan.[145] As we know, Nayan also turned the conflict into a war of religion. Kublai's reaction was vigorous and met with success, and the account we find in the *Milione* of the final battle and the circumstances that put an end to this armed rebellion corresponds, when shorn of its literary finery, to the versions of it offered by the Oriental sources directly informed of these dramatic events.

To learn of their outcome and consequences we need only read the eloquent chapters about them in Marco's account and the elucidations of his best commentators.[146] It should be remembered, however, that whereas Kublai's personal intervention gave fresh impetus and glamour to the exploit that brought about the destruction of Nayan's armies, this victory was made possible by the simultaneous action of Bayan, the famous general "of the hundred eyes," who was keeping at bay the Mongol and Turkish armies united under the leadership of Caidu. The rebel leader was encamped in Mongolia and commanded the eastern wing of

---

[145] M. G. Pauthier, *Le Livre de Marco Polo*, Vol. I, pp. 241 f.; Yule-Cordier, *The Book of Ser Marco Polo*, Vol. I, pp. 335 ff.; Charignon, *op. cit.*, Vol. II, pp. 8 ff.
[146] *Il Milione*, cr. ed., pp. 216 ff.

the massive deployment of forces that extended in an almost unbroken line from Central Asia to northern Manchuria.[147]

Marco mistakenly describes this powerful and energetic rival of his immediate lord as a nephew of Chagatai, most probably because Caidu had inherited and in part conquered the territory in central Asia which, borrowing its name from that of Chagatai, its first Chinghizide ruler, included all the land between Transoxiana and China.[148] With more justification, our Venetian knew that Caidu, like Chagatai before him, was the continuator of Tartar traditions and thus in opposition to the Chinese and Persian branches of the dynasty. "Know then," Marco tells us, "that there has never been any agreement between this Caidu and the Great Kaan: there has always been much warfare between them." [149] This was one of the most serious of the dynastic feuds, not only because it kept Asia in a state of ferment for almost half a century, but for other reasons as well: first, because Chagatai's dominions, though within fluctuating boundaries, were a stronghold at the very center of the continent and controlled the entire system of trade and communication between the Orient and the West; and second, because, as Marco noted, "all his men were good soldiers and expert in war."

Caidu had indeed become the leader of the warlike peoples whose various tribes extended from Western Turkestan eastward as far as the Altai and the Chinese border, and from north to south inhabited the steppes and oases that stretched from Lake

[147] For the official Chinese report of these events cf. Cleaves, "The Biography of Bayan," pp. 265 ff. Caidu had taken part in the conquest of central Europe.

[148] This was the historic territory of the Karakhitai in the heart of Asia, inhabited by nomadic and sedentary Turkish peoples of various cultures who were subject to Persian, Chinese, Christian, and Buddhistic influences, although the Mohammedan religion prevailed there during the Chinghizide epoch. It is likely that the ever-fluctuating boundaries of this immense territory and its turbulent history in the XIIIth century helped to seal it with the name of its first Chinghizide ruler, who also gave his name to the literary language of Central Asia (so-called Chagatai). For these details cf. W. Barthold, *Turkestan*, pp. 130–332, and the corresponding article in the *Encyclopaedia of Islam*. For the Karakhitai cf. K. A. Wittfogel and Fêng Chia-shêng, *History of Chinese Society: Liao, 907–1225*, Philadelphia, American Philosophical Society, 1949.

[149] Benedetto, in a brief note in *Il Libro di Messer Marco Polo*, p. 439, affirms that "Marco Polo slightly reduced the figure of Caidu" by not mentioning the latter's resistance to his great adversary's Chinese leanings. It is, however, doubtful that these feelings of Mongol nationalism were as much alive in him as they certainly were in Aric Buga, his rival for the Chinghizide throne.

Balkhash to the chain of the Kunlun and Karakorum mountains, including a large part of present-day Afghanistan. Marco does not relate the circumstances whereby Caidu became lord of this vast kingdom at the expense of other members of his family, but he does make him the predominant figure in the numerous chapters that make up the final section in his book. This is an exception, inasmuch as the author for the first time abandons his description of the world in accordance with his itineraries and the things seen and heard during these various journeys, in order to give his attention to an epic and anecdotal account of events that kept all western Asia in turmoil for several decades.[150]

Thus, at the end of his work, from being an empirical and eclectic observer of the things of the Orient, Marco becomes a political and military historian. Caidu is his hero, and the wars in which he was involved provide our author with an opportunity to evoke more or less legendary events. This final section of the book is therefore the one that presents Marco Polo almost exclusively as a historian of contemporary Asia who portrays aspects of this world that are characteristic both of his particular way of interpreting them and of medieval historiography in general. In spite of this—perhaps because of it—the last part of the *Milione* has never enjoyed so much favor as the rest of the book. It is lacking in geographical and ethnograpical interest, variety of subject matter, and concrete data, which last are frequently sacrificed to the narrative and literary element. Hence, various authoritative versions of the text since the XIVth century have suppressed or condensed its contents, and modern commentators have taken little interest to it, even discarding entire chapters from this section.[151]

It must be admitted that Marco's account of these happenings in central and western Asia corresponds neither with that given by leading Oriental historians nor with the way in which events actually occurred. Marco's book, however, is not merely to be consulted in order to confirm or deny the statements of other contemporary sources, but also—among other things—to reveal

[150] *Il Milione,* cr. ed., pp. 216–223; M.P., pp. 447 ff.

[151] Yule-Cordier, e.g., suppressed various chapters that mainly contained descriptions of battles. Cf. Benedetto's remarks in the Introd. to his cr. ed. of the *Milione,* pp. xxii ff.

the attitude of medieval man toward every aspect of Oriental life, of which political and military history is but one of the essential manifestations. Moreover, even if in the description of battles and legendary episodes we sense the effects of Rustichello's style, as he seeks to adorn Marco Polo's account with the commonplaces of epic phraseology and vernacular history, we must nevertheless remember that Marco not only must have approved these literary interferences in this part of his book, but probably wished also to ennoble his material according to the canons of the time, so as to make it worthy of being treated and regarded as history. As Brunetto Latini tells us, history has its place between rhetoric and politics, and therefore aspires to a dignity conferred by literary artifice and the nobility of the persons and events with which it deals.[152]

The emphatic, picturesque style that dominates this final section of the *Milione* bespeaks not only Marco's intentions but also the importance of the actors and events concerned. The story centers round the great duel fought between Kublai and Caidu, which played so important a part in the dismemberment of the Chinghizide empire. Marco does, it is true, reduce this great Asiatic drama to a question of protocol when he asserts that the Great Kaan would have been willing to make vast territorial concessions in China to his rebellious nephew if only the latter had agreed to make an act of personal homage, solemnly affirming his submission to the supreme power. Indeed, Marco asserts that Kublai, in spite of his wrath, would have spared the rebel since ties of blood bound the latter to him. This, however, is more than doubtful when we consider the incalculable harm done to the empire by Caidu's policy and actions, and recall the execution of Kublai's relative, Nayan, which was carried out at the emperor's own bidding. As always, Marco here assumes a strictly legitimist point of view, although he knew that Kublai had acquired the dignity of Great Kaan by a ruse and without the consent of the other Chinghizide rulers.[153] However, it may also

[152] Cf. *Li Livres dou Trésor*, cr. ed. by F. J. Carmody, Univ. of California Press, 1948, pp. 317 ff.
[153] We read in the Ramusian version of the *Milione* (cr. ed., p. 79 n.; M.P., p. 215) that "the Great Kaan had not been legally invested with the dominion of the province of Cathay, but had acquired it by force."

be supposed that his version was the official one, accepted and spread abroad by the court and by Kublai's followers, who were constantly made to feel the effects of this fateful rivalry.

Although, according to the official report,[154] the long and bloody campaign was not ungraced by generous acts on Kublai's part, Marco is sufficiently objective to say that Caidu's suspicions of his uncle were justified. He had reason to fear that the Great Kaan might destroy him; for, as the head of a powerful coalition of rebels, he succeeded in keeping at bay large armies which otherwise could have been used by Kublai for territorial conquest. On the other hand, as we read in the *Milione,* Caidu's attitude toward his uncle became ever more arrogant and pretentious. The latter, presumably, would have been only too glad to eliminate this dangerous opponent, who had done so much to undermine his authority and the unity of the empire.

This dynastic conflict served more than once as a pretext for the customary exploits of territorial brigandage which perpetuated the traditional rivalries of armed nomads; yet its dramatic magnitude lent itself to colorful narration like that which suited the tastes of the Mongol rhapsodes and their public; the more so, since Marco was keenly aware of the all too human weaknesses that underlay the emperor's apparently conciliatory attitude and his adversary's tenacious pride. This gave our author and his scribe a starting point for the literary elaboration of the conflict, which was based on Oriental themes gathered by our Venetian in the same way as Prince Hayton of Armenia, while living among the Tartars, obtained from Asiatic minstrels the literary and epic material with which he adorns his famous chronicle.[155]

Thus, after having mentioned the systems of alliances, the methods of combat, and the weapons used in these conflicts, the author of the *Milione* and his scribe added their minute descriptions of battles in their various phases, which are not dissimilar to those recorded in other parts of the book but are here portrayed in a way that would most appeal to their intended public. The heroic, epic tone of these episodes and the obvious intention

[154] Cf. Cleaves, "The Biography of Bayan," pp. 267 ff.

[155] A careful study of this famous chronicle would make it possible to distinguish between the historical sources and the popular traditions which it incorporated and transmitted to posterity in an authentic form.

of emphasizing the courage and valor shown by the armies and their leaders, as well as the fierceness of the fighting, lead us to suppose that Marco obtained his information from native rhapsodes rather than from authoritative sources. This seems the more likely since the story of Aigiaruc, or "Brilliant Moon," the invincibly strong daughter of King Caidu, which is not to be found in any authentic contemporary record, has the characteristics of a popular legend or historical fable based on a theme fairly common in universal literature.[156] Indeed, this episode may well bring to mind the chivalrous motive of the amazons immortalized in Ariosto's epic, who are resolved to be won in armed combat by still more able and valiant knights.

We must therefore see in the literary conventionalism of these chapters a chivalrous and epic refashioning of motifs taken from a poetical history of Central Asia that has left no other trace than those to be found in these passages of the *Milione*. The relationship that here exists between historical fact and epic narration is much akin to that found in the poems dealing with the exploits of Charlemagne, in the various versions of the legendary feats of Alexander the Great, and in Slavic or Turkish epics inspired by real persons and events that were later transformed by popular imagination. All this is reflected in the prose of the *Milione,* which, even if its historical value is not thereby increased, does gain in variety of style and content.

❖   ❖   ❖

Marco then goes on to treat in a similar and no less picturesque way the dynastic history of Chinghizide Persia, which extended its dominions eastward as far as Caidu's central kingdom. We thus learn that the Ilkhans, the rulers of this land, and more

[156] This is the story of a valiant daughter of King Caidu who was promised in marriage to the man who should win her in single combat, but who succeeded in defeating all the rich knights who accepted the challenge. Cf. *Il Milione*, cr. ed., pp. 220 ff.; M.P., p. 454 ff. The official Mongol-Chinese genealogy of the Chinghizide dynasty does not record this supposed daughter of Caidu. See, too, Yule-Cordier, *The Book of Ser Marco Polo,* Vol. II, pp. 463 ff., and G. Ferrand, *Relations de Voyages,* Vol. II, pp. 432 and 452 ff. Both offer some examples of this theme in Oriental traditions. For its diffusion in popular and literary tradition cf. W. Eberhard and P. N. Boratav, *Typen türkischer Volksmärchen,* Wiesbaden, 1953. For similar episodes in Western romances cf. Pio Rajna, *Le fonti dell'Orlando Furioso,* second edition, Florence, 1900, esp. pp. 47 ff. and 593 f.

particularly Abaqa, son of Hulagu the conqueror, maintained a powerful army in order to protect themselves from their dangerous rebel neighbor. These forces were encamped on the plain where the fabulous *Arbre sec* was to be found—"where, according to the people of that region, the battle between Alexander and Darius took place." [157] Which battle, is not specified; nor do we find in the legendary history of the Macedonian any mention of a battle fought in the vicinity of the tree. However, from the account given by Marco and his local informants we must assume that the reference is to a battle decisive for the fate of the East.

Similarly, in Marco's account, the military actions described by him which took place at that time (1285) in this region of northern Persia were to decide the fate of the Chinghizide dynasty and determine the whole of the future political and religious development of central and western Asia. The celebrated tree is therefore not only a geographical indication, but more, a symbol of fateful events. It is so portrayed, indeed, in the famous *Livre de Sidrac,* which was written by one of Marco's contemporaries and is probably to be connected with Oriental traditions in its prophecy that the day will come when the Christians, led by the Pope, will fight a battle on that spot and exterminate the Tartars and all idolaters, whereupon the tree will bloom once more, as a sign of peace and redemption. [158] Marco, however, does not lose himself in such apocalyptic visions. Instead, interested as always in military affairs, he goes on to narrate in his own way the happenings that occurred in that region. According to our author, and certainly in actual fact, it was a position of so great strategic importance that the ruler of Persia had sent there with authority his son Arghun, the heir to the throne and commander of the frontier armies. [159] Not only did the surrounding plain offer

---

[157] This is the region of Khorasan which Marco calls Tunocain, "on the borders of Persia toward the north" (cr. ed., pp. 25 and 32; M.P., p. 116), which was so named from two of its most important centers, Tûn and Qâin, for which see above, chap. i, § 2, as well as Cordier, *Addenda,* pp. 25 f. The events are narrated in the *Milione,* cr. ed., pp. 222 ff.; M.P., pp. 456 ff.

[158] Cf. *Il Libro di Sidrach,* published by A. Bartoli, Bologna, 1868 (Collezione di opere inedite o rare, etc.), pp. 510 ff. See Ch. V. Langlois, *La Connaissance de la Nature et du Monde,* Paris, 1927, pp. 271 f., and the present author's *Storia letteraria delle scoperte geografiche,* pp. 152 f. The passage from Sidrach's book deserves fuller study. The first English translation was published in London in 1530 ("The History of Kyng Boccus & Sydracke," trans. Hugo of Caumpeden).

[159] *Il Milione,* cr. ed., pp. 222 ff.; M.P., pp. 456 ff.

an approach to the rich land of Transoxiana, with its great markets and the principal towns of Turkestan; but thence also led the ways to India and Kashmir, lands that had been the object of Turkish invasion and Mohammedan conquest.

Caidu's enterprising mind planned the annexation of Persia, and he entrusted the military operations to Barac, whom Marco mistakenly describes as brother, instead of cousin, to the rebel. This descendant of Chagatai, and hence the Chinghizide lord of Central Asia, attacked the Persia of the Ilkhans and was defeated by Arghun in an open battle fought some ten miles from the banks of the Oxus.[160] This information opens Marco's account of the contemporary "Tartars of the Levant," from the death of Arghun to the brief reign of Baidu, which ended when the latter was put to death a year after the Polos had left Persia on their way home to Venice.[161]

The account of these happenings centers on a few episodes which, with their descriptions of the speeches and battles exchanged, illustrate the dynastic and territorial rivalries of these sovereigns and their vassals, which were further complicated by questions of religious supremacy. Disputes of that sort were quite absent from the long struggle between Kublai and his Oriental rebels, but were, as we have seen, latent in the legend of the *Arbre sec* and its surrounding region.[162] We therefore find in the *Milione* the concept of religious feuds between the Tartars, who were inclined to adopt the Islamic traditions of the country, and those others who favored the Christian element, represented by the Nestorians, Greek Orthodox, and Catholics who resided in compact communities in various parts of the land.[163]

In this context, however, as in Marco's subsequent chapters, which deal with the Tartars of the West, or Golden Horde, the account of the leading events in contemporary history is once

[160] For these events cf. B. Spuler, *Die Mongolen in Iran,* pp. 67 ff.

[161] *Il Milione,* cr. ed., pp. 228 ff.; M.P., pp. 465 ff.

[162] Abaqa, Hulagu's successor, of Buddhistic leanings but still strongly tied to Mongol traditions, favored Christians of all rites and married a daughter of Michael Palaeologus, the emperor of Byzantium. Tekuder, his brother and successor, who is not mentioned by Marco, initiated the Islamization of the Tartars of the Levant, which was interrupted by his son Arghun. The latter, while protecting Christians and Jews, personally remained faithful to Mongolian Buddhism. For the renewed Islamization of the Chinghizide rulers in the persons of Gaikhatu, Baidu, and Ghazan Khan cf. Spuler, *Die Mongolen in Iran,* and Grousset, *L'Empire des steppes,* pp. 449 ff.

[163] See above, ch. vii, § 3.

again limited to the rhetorical description of a few warlike episodes, with a few references to what was said about them in
circles that were ignorant of the palace intrigues, conspiracies,
and scandals that shook these kingdoms during all the years of
their existence.[164] These deeds and misdeeds were perpetrated
behind the scenes, while the mass of the people hardly participated in court events, which took place in an atmosphere of
constant tension that would alternately rise to the heights of
terror and then wallow in the depths of apathy.

It is therefore no mere chance if the local historians of the
period, whom we have had cause to mention on other occasions,
were all statesmen or officials in the court or public administration: Juwainī, for example, who was governor of Baghdad, or
Rashiduddin, the prime minister and court physician to Ghazan
Khan and his successor Oljaitu.[165] Those who were not directly
concerned could only catch a distant echo of the event; and it is
precisely this which Marco gathered, without being able to verify
the facts. He therefore contented himself with illustrating them
in the way most acceptable to his contemporaries. On the whole,
then, his method of writing Asian history is that of a journalist
who reports the topics and events of the day, local reminiscences,
and current opinions, but finds himself excluded from authentic
sources of information and is therefore obliged to touch up his
account in order to satisfy the curiosity of his public and excite
its imagination. For his own good fortune, and ours, he was
unique in this genre, but already aware of the things which the
public desired to read about and learn. And since this public
shared in the warlike, epic spirit of the times, Marco never tired
of giving it all it could wish in the way of battles. These sections
of his book are filled with the spectacle of arrows darkening the

[164] This background of intrigue and unrest, which is hardly perceptible in the detailed account of the dynastic and civil wars to be found in the *Milione,* is not even
referred to by Ricoldo of Montecroce, who visited the capital, Tabriz, and journeyed
through Persia and Mesopotamia in those years.

[165] Abū Saʿīd, Oljaitu's son, inflicted a horrible and humiliating punishment upon
this great man, who—interested as he was in every aspect of life and history, and
the leading personage at the Mongol court in Persia—most probably met Marco Polo
in person, especially since the Ilkhans were then in contact with the courts of the
West as well as with the Papacy. Mention should also be made of the large Venetian
colony at Tabriz, one of the principal seats of the court and the cultural and religious
capital of Chinghizide Persia.

air, and blows delivered with such force by sword and mace "that the thundering god himself would not have been heard," and the ultimate scene of the battlefield strewn with gashed corpses, and piteous mention of the "many women who were widowed on that day, and many orphaned children"—a touch of humanity that embraces even his enemies and distant peoples, and which, although conventional, seems to us to ring true.[166]

[166] For epic phraseology in the *Milione* cf. cr. ed., pp. xx ff. Although it is often conventional, authentic Oriental touches are not lacking, as, for example, the mention of the warlike drums or "naccara" which sounded the signal for battle wherever Mongol forces were employed (cr. ed., pp. 68, 69, 218, 237), and which are also mentioned in the *Secret History* (trans. E. Haenisch, pp. 25, 26, etc.); or the characteristic leathern breastplates worn by Mongol horsemen (cr. ed., p. 221; M.P., p. 457), as well as other typically Asiatic features, which are not to be found in French or Franco-Italian epic poetry of the Middle Ages. The expression "dieu tonant" (cr. ed., p. 222, line 27; M.P., p. 457) is part of Rustichello's epic phraseology (cf. Benedetto, cr. ed., Introd., p. xxiii n.), but does at the same time correspond to the common Chinese term *lei shen,* of which the Mongol equivalent must have been known to Marco Polo. The "god of thunder" belongs also to shamanist, Lamaist, and Tantric mythology, which was familiar to the Mongol peoples with whose language Marco was acquainted. This coincidence is worth noting, if only as a mere curiosity, because the "god of thunder" is different from "the thundering god."

nine

HISTORICAL AND LEGENDARY FIGURES
IN MARCO POLO'S BOOK

I. THE OLD MAN OF THE MOUNTAIN

The history and civilization of Asia are at times personified by Marco Polo in a few great figures, partly real and partly fanciful, which become in his book the most characteristic expressions of the shape and color of the times. Thus, Mohammedan Asia has its historical and legendary hero in the Old Man of the Mountain, corresponding to the "Sheikh el Jebel," Grand Master of the Ishmaelitic sect of the Assassins; Prester John represents the Christian Orient; and Kublai Kaan, the power and glory of the Chinghizide empire. Marco has lent special emphasis to these great personages by portraying them in a manner befitting their importance and popular celebrity. Two of them belong to the religious as well as the political history of the continent: the Old Man of the Mountain, as head of a Mohammedan sect; and Prester John, as ruler of a heretical Christian people. Undoubtedly, it was the exceptional status of these personages and their

---

For the subject of this section, its history and bibliography, cf. the two excellent articles, "The Old Man of the Mountain," by C. E. Nowell, *Speculum,* Vol. XXII, 1947, pp. 497 ff., and "The Sources of the History of the Syrian Assassins," by B. Lewis, *ibid.,* Vol. XXVII, 1952, pp. 875 ff. For further data cf. the discussion of "Assassins" in Gibb-Kramers, *Shorter Encyclopaedia of Islam,* Leiden, 1953, and in the new edition of the *Encyclopaedia of Islam.* For the internal history of this sect, its theology, and its spiritual and political organization, cf. the comprehensive work by Marshall G. S. Hodgson, *The Order of the Assassins: The Struggle of the Early Ismā'īlīs against the Islamic World,* The Hague, 1955, with an extensive bibliography of the subject. For Western developments of the legend cf. W. Fleischhauer, "The Old Man of the Mountain: The Growth of a Legend," *Symposium,* Vol. IX, 1955, n. 1, pp. 79 ff. These diligent studies do not, however, emphasize the aspects treated in the present section.

renown throughout the Old World that impelled Marco to exhibit them and their exploits in bold relief.

The three chapters that Marco gives to the head of the so-called Assassins occupy a conspicuous part in his description of Persia.[1] Yet neither he nor his older companions ever passed through the region where the Old Man had his principal residence at the Rock of Alamut, in a territory specified by Marco with the name Muleete, 'heretics,' which does in fact describe the true nature of the sect.[2] This district was part of the Persian province of Mazandaran, in the very center of the Elbruz chain of mountains and to the south of the Caspian Sea, but did not represent a politically united or homogeneous territory.[3] The power of the Assassins was concentrated in their fortresses, which were scattered in the mountainous districts of the land and extended, as Marco well knew, as far as Syria and Kurdistan.[4]

By means of their powerful organization the leader of these heretics made his influence felt well beyond the Persian and Levantine borders, and from the XIIth century onward became the terror of the whole of Mohammedan Asia and of all the rulers of the Ancient World.[5] It was precisely this mysterious power that made him famous everywhere, and therefore justified the amount of space given him by Marco, who was less intent on illustrating the doctrines and aims of the sect than on satisfying the curiosity universally felt concerning this outstanding figure and the exploits of his followers. This widespread interest apparently persisted even when Hulagu had destroyed their head-

---

[1] *Il Milione*, cr. ed., chaps. xli–xliii.

[2] This name is derived from the Arabic *Mulahida*, which can also mean 'impious,' 'atheists.' It occurs in the form *Muliec* and *Mulihet* in Friar William of Rubruck's *Itinerarium* (cf. *Sin. Franc.*, Vol. I, p. 210 and n. 4). The name is curiously altered to *Millestorte* by Odoric of Pordenone, who dictated his *Relatio* in 1330 and described the Old Man and his Assassins in terms so closely resembling those used by Marco Polo that we may suppose they were inspired by the *Milione*. Cf. *Sinica Franciscana*, Vol. I, p. 488 and n. 2.

[3] For this territory and its relevant geo-topographical literature cf. A. Gabriel, *Die Erforschung Persiens*, Vienna, 1952, pp. 29 f., 41, 295, 299. Cf. Stanislao Franchi, *L'itinerario di Marco Polo in Persia*, Turin, 1941, for the regions visited by our traveler.

[4] *Il Milione*, cr. ed., chap. xliii, p. 34; M.P., p. 129. For the Assassins of Syria cf. the article by Lewis already cited.

[5] The victims of this sect are listed in the articles by Nowell and Lewis cited above, which also discuss the effects of the Assassins' activities in Europe and Asia.

quarters in 1256, after a three years' siege that ended with the death of their last leader and the dispersion of those of his followers who survived the slaughter.[6]

Westerners had been curious about the Assassins ever since the Crusaders' first contacts with the Mohammedan world in Syria and the Holy Land; that is to say, only a few decades after the founding of this sect in 1090 by Hassan Sabbah, in Persia, which was then ruled by the Seljuk Turks. A generation after Hassan Sabbah's death at Alamut in 1124, and at a time when his followers had reached the zenith of their power, the wandering Spanish rabbi Benjamin of Tudela gave to his fellow Jews in the West their first information about this organization of Mohammedan heretics, who followed not the law of Mohammed but the orders of their leader.[7] Rabbi Benjamin, however, was more interested in the Jews of that region than in the doctrines and practices of the Assassins.

Far more about them was known to the Knights Templars, a military order founded in 1108 in the Holy Land and spiritually organized in France by St. Bernard of Clairvaux, which had rapidly increased its power and prestige in a manner somewhat paralleling that of the Mohammedan sect.[8] Indeed, relations between the two organizations were so close, in spite of frequent tension and bloody incidents, that when the fourth Grand Master of the Assassins of Persia abolished, after the year 1162, some fundamental principles of the Mohammedan law, including those respecting food and wine, the Crusaders in the Levant

---

[6] Marco refers to the leader of the sect as "Alaodin" ('Alā ad-Dīn), which was the name of the penultimate Grand Master of the Assassins, whereas the one who surrendered to Hulagu and closed the series was called Rukn ad-Dīn. He was slain by the Mongols after the capitulation of his stronghold at Alamut.

[7] Cf. the Hebraic text with English translation, ed. by A. Asher, *The Itinerary of Rabbi Benjamin of Tudela*, 2 vols., London and Berlin, 1840 (republished, New York, 1900), Vol. I, pp. 120 f., as well as M. N. Adler, *The Itinerary of Benjamin of Tudela*, London, 1907. Rabbi Benjamin compiled his work between 1164 and 1173. Marco Polo expresses himself in similar terms.

[8] The affinities, which are substantially external, were first noted with little success by J. von Hammer-Purgstall, *Geschichte der Assassinen aus morgenländischen Quellen*, Stuttgart, 1818. For the history of the order and its origins against the background of contemporary events cf. R. Grousset, *Histoire des Croisades*, 3 vols., Paris, 1934–1936, Vol. I, pp. 541 ff. For the extensive literature on the subject cf. M. Dessubré, *Bibliographie de l'Ordre des Templiers*, Paris, 1928, and G. Charpentier, *L'Ordre des Templiers*, Paris, 1945.

were led to hope that the Old Man and his followers would before long be converted to the Christian faith.[9]

It was not these contacts and episodes, however, that determined the keen interest felt by Westerners in the mysterious
and powerful leader and the practices of his sect. There was sheer
panic after the Old Man had sent his hirelings to assassinate
Raymond, Count of Tripoli (1149), and Conrad of Montferrat,
the titular king of Jerusalem, not to mention three caliphs and
numerous Mohammedan dignitaries. Attempts were also made
on the life of Saladin and, a century later, of Prince Edward of
England, in 1272 at Acre.[10] Fear was no less acute in the Asian
interior, especially when, in 1253, a conspiracy was discovered in
the Mongol capital of Karakorum. In spite of strict vigilance on
the part of the authorities, a number of the Old Man's followers
had succeeded in insinuating themselves into the court of Mangu
(Möngke), Great Kaan of the Tartars, intending to murder him
at the first favorable opportunity.[11]

Not long before, Louis IX of France, who was then in Syria,
found it necessary to protect himself lest he too should be a victim;[12] and likewise, the Emperor Frederick II, who was later
suspected by Pope Innocent IV of having adopted to his own

[9] For the relations existing between Assassins and Templars cf. the article by Nowell
already cited, pp. 504 ff.

[10] This last misdeed must be attributed to the Assassins in Syria who survived the
destruction of their order as an association of mercenary cutthroats rather than as
followers of the Old Man or members of a religious sect. Their organization was suppressed after the capture of its castles in Syria by Baibars, the leader of the Mamelukes
of Egypt who conquered that region between 1260 and 1273. Cf. Lewis's article already cited, pp. 488 ff. According to Fleischhauer, as cited above, pp. 84 f., it was
especially the slaying of Conrad of Monferrat that made the sect universally notorious
throughout the West. His assassination was exploited for political purposes in the
struggle that took place in the last decades of the XIIth century between the Emperor,
King Philip Augustus of France, and Richard the Lionhearted.

[11] The conspiracy is mentioned by Friar William of Rubruck in his *Itinerarium*
(*Sin. Franc.*, Vol. I, p. 286); he says that no fewer than forty Assassins had been
sent by the Old Man under various disguises to slay Mangu (Möngke) Kaan, probably in
order to frustrate his planned conquest of Persia and Syria.

[12] The fact is narrated by Joinville, *Histoire de Saint Louis*, ed. Natalis de Wailly,
Paris, 1921, pp. 189 ff., together with some strange and incorrect data regarding the
teachings of the sect which "creoit en la loy de Haali." Although an eyewitness to
the facts, he ascribes certain doctrines to the Assassins which were characteristic of the
Druses (cf. Silvestre de Sacy, *Exposé de la religion des Druses*, Paris, 1838), as, e.g.,
the belief in metempsychosis, which the Assassins did not accept. Cf. Joinville, *op. cit.*,
pp. 104 ff. and 193 f. (with respect to the Bedouins).

ends the practices of the Assassins.[13] These, as we know, always followed the same pattern. Adherents of the Old Man would at his command insinuate themselves in the entourage of the designated victim and would stab him to death as soon as a favorable occasion offered. They, in turn, were usually killed on the spot, blindly sacrificing their lives to the will of their leader.

The curiosity excited in Marco's contemporaries by the secret power of this sect centered especially in its practice of premeditated organized murder. As a result, from the XIIth century onward the term "assassin," which both Latin and vernacular literature of the late Middle Ages applied to the Old Man's followers, was also used of other murderers who planned their crimes. But although Dante's adjective "perfidious" emphasized the underhand scheming that characterized the dark deeds of the heretical Mohammedan fanatics, no one was aware of the origin or meaning of the word which described them as "assassins." [14]

However, in spite of the horror and fear that these practices everywhere aroused, popular interest was not exclusively condemnatory; there was also a general feeling of awe for the astuteness and hardihood shown by the followers of the Old Man, who so unfalteringly sacrificed their lives. Admittedly, they were perfidious assassins; but they were not without moral resolution and unflinching physical courage, and their possession of these highly prized virtues raised them up in the eyes of their contemporaries. Hence, the condemnation of their misdeeds was

[13] This is asserted by C. E. Nowell in his article already cited, p. 511, who follows the statements of J. von Hammer-Purgstall. Frederick was supposed to have availed himself of an Assassin for the killing of the Duke of Bavaria in 1231, even as in 1192 Richard the Lionhearted had already been suspected of plotting the murder of Philip Augustus of France by the same means. It is significant that the act of excommunication decreed against Frederick II at the Council of Lyons follows immediately upon Canon 9, which condemns those who make use of "assassini" for political purposes. Cf. Hefele and Leclercq, *Histoire des Conciles,* Vol. V, Pt. II, pp. 1670 f. Innocent IV had on that occasion formally accused the deposed emperor of having hired assassins of this sect to do away with his political adversaries, and in the year 1280 Jansen Enikel asserted in his rhymed Chronicle and *Fürstenbuch* (publ. in the *Monumenta Germaniae Historica, Deutsche Chroniken,* Vol. III, p. 649) that Frederick had created an organization similar to that attributed by legend to the Old Man of the Mountain. Cf. Fleischhauer, *op. cit.,* pp. 80 f.

[14] *Inferno,* XIX, 50: "lo perfido assassin." For the history of the various interpretations of the term cf. Lewis as cited above, pp. 875 ff.

mitigated by more or less open admiration, which made a distinction between the criminal activities of the Assassins and those of common malefactors.

Political assassination was by no means a monopoly of the sect. It was practiced generally by the pagan, Mohammedan, and Christian societies of those times, as a more or less normal instrument for seizing power; no less therefore in Europe than in Persia, Mongolia, or China. Hence, the popular interest in the sect did not depend merely on the murderous activities of its followers, but rather on the mystery surrounding them and their rule of unconditional devotion and obedience to the orders of their Grand Master, the Old Man of the Mountain. Thus, too, the allusions to them that we find in contemporary Western literature refer to this constancy, which was considered a virtue, rather than to assassination practiced as an instrument of political conquest.[15]

The oldest and most characteristic expression of this attitude is to be found in contemporary Provençal poetry, which created and varied the theme of unconditional devotion to the poet's beloved, comparing this fidelity to that of the Assassin who carries out the orders of his Grand Master:

> Io aissi'm pren con fai als assesis,
> Qe fan tot so qe lurs senhors lur di.
> —Bernart de Bondeilh [16]

For this poet, as for Aimeric de Peguilhan, Giraut de Bornelh, and others of the XIIth and XIIIth centuries, the true lover blindly submits to the orders of his lady, going so far as to offer her his life, and by this sacrifice wins for himself the joys of Paradise. The theme is also to be found, for example, in the second sonnet of the *Fiore* formerly attributed to Dante,[17] wherein

[15] Cf. Frank M. Chambers, "The Troubadours and the Assassins," *Modern Language Notes,* Vol. LXIV, 1949, pp. 245 ff.

[16] This poet flourished toward the end of the XIIth century. Chambers (*op. cit.,* p. 287) points out that, on the whole, the Provençal poets do not refer to the murderous practices of the Assassins in the Dantesque sense—i.e., as common cutthroats,—but choose rather to allude to their devotion to the Old Man.

[17] Cf. *Le opere di Dante,* testo critico della Società Dantesca Italiana, Florence, 1921, App., p. 4. The "Priest" in this sonnet refers to Prester John and his legendary humility and devotion.

the poet, undoubtedly a Florentine of his times, portrays himself
as devoted to Love

More than the Assassin to his Master or the Priest to God.

The total consecration of the Assassins to obeying the behests
of their leader is further illustrated in a well-known anecdote
from the *Novellino,* composed at the same time as the *Fiore,*
which tells how the Emperor Frederick II is supposed to have
visited the Old Man in his mountain stronghold. The latter,
"in order to show him how greatly he was feared, looked up on
high and saw two assassins at the top of the tower. He touched
his beard, and they cast themselves down onto the earth below
and were straightway killed." [18] This story, which had already
been recounted in Arnold of Lübeck's *Chronica Slavorum* (*ca.*
1210), was also applied to other historical and legendary figures;
and in the XIVth century it was taken up once more by the
Venetian, Marin Sanudo the Elder, in order to signify that no
vassal in the West could compete with the Assassins in blind
devotion to their lord.[19] This explains why the Old Man had become, for the poets of the West, the unique symbol of the most
absolute sovereignty.

The amazement created in the medieval world by this human
and political phenomenon was accompanied by an intense desire
to find out the method whereby the Old Man had obtained this
utter subservience from his followers. All the medieval legends
about him reveal such avid interest in this régime and its secret
discipline as to ignore its doctrinal basis and the training actually
undergone by its members. The ferocious courage that was their
hallmark was popularly attributed to a stimulant—the *Cannabis
indica*—commonly found in the East, which was supposed to be
administered to them in the course of a secret initiation directed

[18] Cf. *Le cento novelle antiche,* etc., ed. Letterio di Francia, Turin, 1930, pp. 162 ff.
The same story is in Enikel's *Fürstenbuch, loc. cit.*

[19] The Venetian chronicler's account is given in the note, *loc. cit.* The passage from
Arnold of Lübeck's chronicle is to be found in the English translation by W.
Fleischhauer, *op. cit.,* p. 80. The attribution of the legend to Frederick II is substantiated
by the existence of historically confirmed contacts between the Emperor and the Grand
Master of the Assassins, probably of Syria. Cf. G. Levi della Vida, *Aneddoti e svaghi,
arabi e non arabi,* Milan and Naples, 1959, p. 55.

by their leader. Thus, from this drug, commonly known as *hashish*, his followers were supposed to have taken the name of *Hashshāshīn*, which then became *assassini* in the Latin of that age and the Romance languages.[20]

However, neither this word nor the drug from which it is derived is ever mentioned in the detailed descriptions of the Assassins offered by the most authoritative Mohammedan historians directly acquainted with the sect: for example, Juwainī, the governor of Baghdad and historian of the Mongol conquest; his successor, Rashiduddin, the most universal of the Mohammedan historians of his times; or the philosopher and scientist, Nasiruddin Tusi, who was for a time affiliated with the sect shortly before its destruction.[21] These celebrated authors, all of whom were averse to the Assassins' heresies, would certainly not have failed to reveal the administering of the drug, since thus they would further have discredited the sect, which their Mohammedan orthodoxy exposed to universal contempt. Nor is any mention made of it by later chroniclers, such as the learned Mirkhond or the great Ibn Khaldun, who based their works on the original sources and the most authoritative texts of Oriental historical tradition.[22] The use of hashish was then, as now, so widespread in the Near and Middle East that it could not be regarded by Mohammedan scholars as a specific expedient in the initiation of the followers of the Old Man of the Mountain. This familiarity would, of course, explain their silence on the point.

[20] This, as is well known, is the etymology (sporadically contested) established by the great orientalist Silvestre de Sacy in his famous "Mémoire sur la Dynastie des Assassins et sur l'étymologie de leur nom," in *Mémoires de l'Institut Royal*, Vol. IV, Paris, 1818, pp. 1–85. Cf. the article by Lewis already cited, p. 477 n. 14, and the observations made by Hodgson, *The Order of the Assassins*, pp. 133 ff.

[21] For this author and his treatise cf. the article by W. Ivanow, "An Ismailic Work by Nasiru'd-din Tusi," *Journal of the Royal Asiatic Society*, 1931, pp. 527–564. For the other authors cf. M. C. Defrémery, "Documents sur l'Histoire des Ismaéliens ou Bathiniens de Perse," *Journal Asiatique*, fifth series, Vol. XV, 1860, pp. 164 ff.

[22] Mirkhond's extensive work, which is based on authentic sources, was translated into French by A. Jourdain, "Le Jardin de Pureté," in *Notices et Extraits des Manuscrits de la Bibliothèque Impériale*, Vol. IX, 1813, pp. 142 ff. For other Persian sources cf. E. G. Browne, *A Literary History of Persia*, 1920, Vol. III, pp. 431 ff. and *passim*. Marco was not acquainted with this drug, and attributed the effect described by him to an indeterminate potion (see the *Milione*, cr. ed., p. 31, chap. xxxviii; M.P., pp. 128 f.).

On the other hand, the various Western authors who treat the subject are likewise unaware of the etymology of the name Assassin; hence, too, of that special employment of the drug which apparently was accepted in the Mohammedan world as a popular explanation for the deeds and misdeeds, and the awesome and admirable qualities, of the Old Man's followers.[23] That leader's régime of boundless authority and blind submission had long seemed inexplicable to Mohammedans as well as to Christians. Indeed, in spite of the various forms of autocracy developed in medieval society in both the Orient and the West, no earlier example exists of a political organization that required from its members so extreme a degree of subordination to the will of its ruler. The feudal system was based, in theory at least, on a pact of mutual protection between the lord and his vassal, and between the vassal and his hierarchically organized subjects. In the religious systems, unconditional obedience "perinde ac si cadaver" was still part of a distant future, in spite of the fact that the new orders of chivalry organized in the first decades of the XIIth century—perhaps after the example of the Assassins—had already introduced absolute obedience as one of the fundamental principles of their associations.[24]

It may therefore be supposed that those of their contemporaries who were unacquainted with the novitiate of unconditional obedience imagined it to be the result of secret artifices to which the Old Man resorted in order to exercise his bloodthirsty tyranny, which turned his henchmen into pliable and unfailing instruments of his supreme will. The mystery surrounding his exceptional power gave rise to legendary interpretations and fabulous accounts, which were spread abroad and confirmed by trav-

---

[23] See the chronicle of William of Tyre, in which he asserts that both Christians and Saracens of his times (XIIth century) called the members of that sect "Assassins," but that no one knew how they had come by this name; cf. Guillaume de Tyr, "Histoire des Croisades," in *Collection des Mémoires relatifs à l'Histoire de France,* ed. M. Guizot, Paris, 1823–1885, Vol. XVIII, p. 297. William of Tyre was generally well informed about the sect and the exploits of the Assassins right down to his own times. Burchardus, too, the *vice dominus* of Strassburg, who visited the Levant in 1175 as Frederick Barbarossa's envoy to the Sultan, is not acquainted with the drug or potion mentioned by Marco and other authors, according to Arnold of Lübeck's statements in his Chronicle; cf. Fleischhauer, *op. cit.,* p. 82.

[24] Cf. Grousset, *Histoire des Croisades,* Vol. I, pp. 541 ff., and Henri de Curzon, *La Règle du Temple,* Paris, 1886, chap. i.

elers who had come across them in the course of their visits to the Orient, without the possibility of finding the clue to the secret, or more authentic information, in Mohammedan historical and political literature.

The first person to have informed Westerners about the practices whereby the Old Man of the Mountain transformed his followers into assassins seems to have been the German chronicler Arnold of Lübeck, whose *Chronica Slavorum* tells the story in much the same way as Marco's account.[25] The Venetian, even before his departure for the Orient, must have shared in the general curiosity of his contemporaries about this sect, which had then become—after the destruction of its center—an association entirely composed of men who sold their lives to the highest bidder, or mercenaries who were trained to commit murder as a means of political, or simply criminal, activity.[26] Marco Polo, however, was unaware of these recent developments, and still portrays the sect as a religious and political group whose name was surrounded by an aura of wonder and terror; so much so, indeed, that even when traveling through a part of Persia far from the headquarters of the Assassins, he besought several whom he met for information on what took place in those mysterious surroundings.[27]

He was told that the founder of the sect had transformed a remote and arid valley in the "Muleete" region into a luxuriant garden "like the Paradise promised to the Saracens by Mohammed," in which, around ornate palaces of gold, flowed rivers not

---

[25] *Il Milione,* cr. ed., pp. 32 ff.; M.P., pp. 128 ff. The subject was treated at length and dramatized in an Arabic historical novel (*Memoirs of Hakim*), the date of which has not yet been established. Cf. *Fundgruben des Ostens* (*Mines de l'Orient*), Vol. III, 1813, pp. 201 ff., in which J. von Hammer-Purgstall published the extract concerning the Assassins ("Sur le Paradis du Vieux de la Montagne") from MS 107 of the Imperial Library of Vienna. For Arnold of Lübeck's sources cf. the article by Fleischhauer already cited, pp. 82 f.

[26] This is how they are portrayed by Jacopo da Acqui in his *Imago Mundi*. He did not follow Marco's text, but seems to have obtained his information from another source which has not yet been identified. Cf. Moule-Pelliot, *Marco Polo: The Description of the World,* Vol. I, p. 491 n., and the English translation of the original Latin text. This passage states that the Old Man sold his assassins to those who wished to make use of them in order to rid themselves of their adversaries—a detail unknown to Marco, who merely regarded them as doers of the will of their immediate lord.

[27] *Il Milione,* cr. ed., p. 32, chap. xli ("Or vos conterai tout son afer selonc que je meser Marc oi la conter a plusors homes"); cf. M.P., p. 129.

of water only, but of wine, and milk, and honey. Here the Old
Man held splendid court, leading "a most noble life," entertained
by the singing and dancing of the most beautiful women and
maidens in the world, and gathering about him all the young
men of the land, from the ages of twelve to twenty, who were
able to bear arms. In this artificial paradise a sleeping potion
was given the youths which wafted them as in a dream, amidst
an inexhaustible variety of delights, to the true Paradise which
Mohammed described and promised to the faithful [28]—so en-
thralling was their illusion. When they came back to reality, the
world appeared so unbearable to them that they yearned after the
pleasures they had just quitted, though the price should be their
lives; they therefore gladly accepted the most dangerous, even
fatal, missions whenever the Old Man of the Mountain wished
to make use of their daggers to rid himself of some great personage. And he would so require of them, once they had given
proof of their courage and loyalty by killing other and lesser victims in the neighboring regions. Thus, if he so wished, no one
marked down could escape certain death; and the killer joyfully
sacrificed his own life for his lord, in order that he might the
sooner attain the bliss offered by the true Paradise described in
the Koran, of which he had already had a foretaste in the Old
Man's gardens.

That these ingenuous tales were then current in the Orient
is confirmed by the report on a mission to western Asia which
the Chinese general Ch'ang Te made to Kublai Kaan in 1263
with the help of the Chinese literate, Liu Yu.[29] This document,
only a few years after the destruction of the sect and its posses-

---

[28] Sura LVI. This was the passage from the Koran best known to medieval Christians, as can be seen from the work by Ugo Monneret de Villard, *Lo studio dell'Islām
in Europa nel XII e XIII secolo,* Città del Vaticano, 1944 (Studi e Testi, no. 163).

[29] Cf. E. Bretschneider, *Mediaeval Researches from Eastern Asiatic Sources,* Vol. I,
pp. 135 ff. The passage from this text concerning the Assassins had already been
translated into French by Abel Rémusat (*Nouveaux Mélanges asiatiques,* Paris, 1829,
Vol. I, p. 178) and into English by Yule-Cordier, *The Book of Ser Marco Polo,* Vol. I,
p. 143 n. Another French translation (somewhat incorrect), by M. G. Pauthier, is to
be found in the Introduction to his edition of *Le Livre de Marco Polo,* Vol. I, pp.
cxl f. None of the recent studies on the subject mentions this important text, which
offers the only evidence that the legend was current in the Mohammedan circles in
Persia from which both our Chinese general and Marco Polo obtained their essential
—and similar—data, within little more than ten years of each other.

sions, and therefore more than a decade before Marco Polo's journey through Persia, mentions that the Old Man's dominions included 360 fortified crags and an army composed entirely of sturdy youths who were blindly devoted to their leader.[30] It tells that, in order to bend them so far to his will, this leader first made them drunk with wine, and then had them borne to a cavern where sweet music and beautiful women enchanted them with delights of every sort. Once they had regained their senses, they were told that by becoming faithful followers of the Old Man, and by dying for him, they would enjoy these pleasures for all eternity. Next came a period of indoctrination, with readings of orations and sacred texts each day, until they became so compliant that they would execute their leader's orders without hesitation or fear of death.[31]

The two versions—Marco's and the Oriental's—correspond in their main features, though the Venetian's account is more extensive and detailed than that of his Chinese contemporary. It is to be noted that the latter, after relating that the vision of inexhaustible pleasure takes place in a cave,[32] adds the important detail of the spiritual training undergone by the Assassins, which is ignored by Marco though he must certainly have been aware that their military, religious, and political association was that of a sect.[33] For the rest, the two accounts have all the marks of a fable. They find no confirmation in any of their essential points in the various works by Mohammedan authors which describe at length the doctrines and customs of the Assassins without ever mentioning either the gardens and places of delight or the voluptuous enticements with which the Old Man was supposed

[30] Cf. the Chinese text here reproduced (fig. 5) and the English translation by Bretschneider, *loc. cit.*

[31] The text also mentions the terror inspired by the Assassins throughout all western Asia until their total destruction by Hulagu's Mongols.

[32] It should be noted that, by coincidence, the motif of education in a subterranean place is also to be found in the Platonic myth of the Cave and in a passage of Cicero's *De Natura Deorum,* Bk. II, chap. 37, inspired by one of Aristotle's dialogues which has been lost; this is discussed by Fleischhauer, *op. cit.,* p. 83. Neither the Chinese nor Marco Polo was acquainted with these classical texts.

[33] The spiritual training undergone by the Old Man's youthful recruits was only revealed in the West by Arnold of Lübeck, who reported the statements of Burchardus. Vaguer references are also to be found, however, in the authors mentioned by Fleischhauer, *loc. cit.*

to captivate his followers before sending them to certain death. Our two travelers evidently came across a popular version, the character, origin, and diffusion of which certainly deserve to be considered in the light of the facts.

No one will be so ingenuous as to believe that the expedients described by Liu Yu and Marco Polo can really have prepared a large number of men for a career of sacrifice and discipline without parallel in medieval history. When one considers the power and influence enjoyed by the sect, these naïve accounts seem rather to be fanciful and malicious explanations of a political and human phenomenon of unusual power and interest. It is also clear that they must have originated among orthodox circles in Persia, which were bitterly opposed to the sect and its heretical leader.

According to these fables, then, the Old Man's power over his followers depended on two motives: his imaginary paradise, and the potion that lulled his victims to sleep. Now, the paradise story —which is not found in any of the Asiatic sources—is contradicted not only by the austerity practiced by the sect, but especially by the aridity of the region, which did not permit of any such luxuriant vegetation and elaborate architecture as we find in Marco's description.[34] With a far greater sense of realism, the imperial Chinese envoy had observed that the inhabitants of the region had constructed dikes, wells, and watercourses so as to be able to irrigate their fields on that arid plateau and among the rocky mountains of the province of Rudbar in Mazandaran.[35] We do, in fact, learn from the reliable Persian historian Mirkhond that Hassan Sabbah, the founder of the sect, and his successors had organized in these inaccessible valleys a vast irrigation system intended to make their community autonomous and capable of resisting attack to the last extremity.[36] Those far-

[34] See A. Gabriel, *Die Erforschung Persiens,* p. 299, who gives a brief report of the observations made by the most recent explorers of that region; also, the various references contained in Hodgson, *The Order of the Assassins,* concerning the Rock of Alamut, pp. 48 ff. and *passim.*

[35] Cf. Bretschneider, *Mediaeval Researches,* Vol. I, p. 133, and the Chinese text reproduced here.

[36] Mirkhond, ed. Jourdain, p. 155. Cf. Nowell's article, p. 499. The course of the river Bahir—which supplied the Old Man's stronghold with water—had been specially deflected for this purpose. Cf. Bretschneider, *Mediaeval Researches,* Vol. II, p. 109. The

sighted leaders had transformed their fortresses and villages into artificial oases, which, though of modest proportions as limited by the nature of the soil, nevertheless made an impression on the merchants, soldiers, and travelers who came upon them after crossing the near-by deserts and the limitless steppes of western Asia. Confronted with flowering trees and running waters, their imagination must have transformed these gardens into a fabulous landscape that partook of the mystery and prestige of those who had created it.

It should be remembered that hydraulic engineering has always been a characteristic feature of Mohammedan civilization in Asia and in Egypt, in Sicily as in Spain. When the famous Taoist sage Ch'ang Ch'un, who was journeying from Peking by order of Chinghiz Khan, arrived in the year 1222 at the imperial encampment in the well-nigh inaccessible regions of the upper Hindu Kush, he noted with interest how all along the route the Mohammedans ran canals through their lands in order to irrigate their crops of cereals.[37] In the latter part of his journey, moreover, this great Chinese prelate, who was himself expert in the art of rainmaking with his spells, always associated the memory of the Mohammedan lands visited by him with the simple but efficacious hydraulic contrivances with which the inhabitants transformed their arid soil into cultivated fields. Owing to their special skill, Mohammedan artisans were employed by the imperial administration in Mongolia for the building of the famous Chinese canals, and also for the creation of the magnificent parks in Kublai's new place of residence which are described by Marco.[38]

The enchanted gardens of Alamut were but a modest replica

capitulation of the Rock of Alamut was in fact brought about by hunger, after a long siege. Cf. Hodgson, *The Order of the Assassins,* p. 260.

[37] Cf. the English translation of this text, which is so important for the geography and civilization of the Asia of his times, published with an introduction and notes by A. Waley, *The Travels of an Alchemist,* London, 1931, pp. 72, 92, etc.

[38] Cf. the description of the Grand Canal of China in the *Milione,* cr. ed., p. 141, chap. cxlix; M.P., p. 322; H. Cordier, *Addenda,* pp. 91 and 93; D. Gandar, *Le Canal impérial (Variétés Sinologiques,* no. 4), 1894. For the imperial parks see the *Milione,* cr. ed., p. 75; M.P., p. 210. For their history cf. the commentaries by Yule, Pauthier, and Charignon to the respective passages. Cf. also Frederick P. Bargebuhr, "The Alhambra Palace of the Eleventh Century," *Journal of the Warburg and Courtauld Institutes,* Vol. XIX, 1956, pp. 192–258.

of the numberless pleasure-parks that were built for their sovereigns by Mohammedan architects in many parts of the world, from Granada to Peking, and from Karakorum to Baghdad and the Indian residences of the moghuls and maharajas. In fashioning these ideal landscapes they always kept in mind Mohammed's famous description of Paradise, which was the consecrated model for both the literary and the architectural structure of these princely gardens of delight. It was therefore easy to attribute to the modest gardens of the Old Man these wonders which were in everyone's imagination and which here seemed to be destined for a purpose quite different from the more innocent pleasures generally sought after.

The absurdity of the information obtained by Marco is proved by the fact that the eschatology of this sect accepted Mohammed's paradise merely for the symbolic value of its structure and figures, and not as a concrete reality. Thus, the rivers mentioned by Marco represent, in this interpretation, the various forms of knowledge rather than a further contribution to the natural delights of the place.[39] The Old Man's garden must have existed—if at all—as a retreat for contemplation and edification, and certainly not for the purpose imagined by the uninitiated, who were quite ignorant of the régime of strict austerity imposed on the members of the sect, and were therefore unable to understand the secret forces that were active in the spiritual organization, with its characteristic practices and discipline.

Hence, the use of the sleeping draught which the two travelers assert to have been administered by the Old Man to his victims appears to be a mere fable, in spite of the fact that the use of hashish among the members of the sect cannot be excluded or ascribed to pure legend. This drug was certainly widely used in the Orient, but its effect was quite different from that described by Marco Polo. Hashish is not a narcotic, but rather a treacherous intoxicant, which only for too heavy a price produces those sweet paradisiac visions which Western travelers materialized in the enchantment of the fabulous gardens.[40] On the faith of Charles Baudelaire, who in two famous essays described

---

[39] Cf. W. Ivanow, as cited in n. 21 above, p. 561.

[40] Cf. the observations and bibliographical references in Nowell's article, pp. 499 f.

the effects of this drug, we should suppose that the Old Man would have taken good care *not* to administer it to his followers, who were submitted to a most rigorous military discipline. "Cela ne fait ni des guerriers ni des citoyens," we are told by the great French poet, who knew from personal experience and systematic observation the way in which it annihilates the will, corrupts all discipline, and saps the physical strength of those who use it.[41] It is for this reason that contemporary Mohammedan historians never mention hashish in connection with the Assassins; it was the ignorant masses who thus named them, attributing their extraordinary exploits and the power the Old Man wielded over them to the effects of this drug.

In actual fact, the young men who unconditionally submitted themselves to his orders were not victims of artful tricks, but devotees who gave themselves body and soul to a cause they considered sacred and glorious. Liu Yu acknowledges the generosity of their sacrifice when he designates them by the term *tz'ŭ k'ê,* which in the Chinese of his times did not signify a common murderer, but a zealot who is devoted to a cause and who kills and dies for it.[42] The true nature of this cause was well

[41] Cf. the two essays: *Du Vin et du Haschisch* (1851) and *Les Paradis artificiels* (1860). The effects of this "powder of miraculous virtue" are entertainingly described by Boccaccio in the *Decameron,* Third Day, Eighth Story, when he tells how it was used by an adulterous abbot from Tuscany to send a cuckold to Purgatory.

[42] The term *tz'ŭ k'ê* is found in line 3 at the bottom of the facsimile reproduced here (fig. 5). It recurs in line 6, characters 9 and 10 from the top, but with a misprint which makes it read in the alternate form *la k'ê,* which has the same meaning. The Chinese term means 'devotee' and is an exact translation of the Persian *fidā'ī,* which did in fact designate those of his followers who were trained for political assassination. The original meaning of the Persian term was established by Silvestre de Sacy in a brief note to Jourdain's translation of Mirkhond (*op. cit.,* p. 151, n. 3). In the leading Chinese dictionaries *tz'ŭ k'ê* is always given for one who kills for patriotic motives or out of devotion to a person or cause. Cf. the note by Bretschneider, *Mediaeval Researches,* Vol. I, p. 135, n. 360. The original meaning of the two components of the Chinese term is 'stabbing guest,' which more clearly describes the method adopted by the Old Man's followers than the Persian word *fidā'ī,* for they did in fact introduce themselves under false pretenses into courts which, unaware of their true intentions, received them as experts in various fields and welcome guests. They would thus make themselves indispensable to the sovereign, whose trust they would win while spying out his habits in order to seize the opportune moment to stab him to death; hence the concept of perfidy associated with their name. For the term *fidā'ī,* cf. s.v. in Gibb-Kramers, *Shorter Encyclopaedia of Islam;* and for the various ranks in the sect's hierarchy, Nowell's article, pp. 504 f. Marco Polo and the other travelers were only acquainted with these devotees, who were the material executors of the Old Man's orders. For their organization and training cf. Hodgson, *The Order of the Assassins,* pp. 82 and 133 ff.

known to the Mohammedan historians who treat of its fortunes.
It tended to realize the faith of the Ishmaelites in the coming of
the Imam, the universal Mohammedan leader, a legitimate descendant of 'Alī, Mohammed's cousin and son-in-law, the fourth
of the caliphs who succeeded him and, according to the Shi'ite
interpretation, mystically connected with the godhead.[43]

The Assassins, then, were a religious and military order bent
on realizing for all Islam the mythical Imam's power, and on ac-
complishing by force—by specific acts of homicide—that which
was the aim and prayer of all the Ishmaelites. The deathblows
were not determined by a bloodthirsty inclination on the Old
Man's part, but rather by the fact that his followers were fanatics
with a program. They numbered, at most, sixty thousand, and
were dispersed throughout Persia and Syria in the hilltop fortresses of their order.

The Assassins can therefore be associated with the various
mystical and military groups which, under the name of *futūwwa,*
from the IXth century onward pursued political and religious
aims in the hope of promoting a holy war independently of the
various regular armies maintained by the Islamic states of central
and western Asia.[44] These associations required from their members the practice of civic and heroic virtues, self-denial and strong
resolve, courage and humility; and success in the fulfillment of
the imposed conditions naturally depended on the mettle of the
recruits and hence on individual character.

Hassan Sabbah submitted his subjects and followers to a rigorous military and spiritual training until they became servile instruments of his will in the way described by both history and
legend. The instruction they received had long been a subject
of controversy among the theologians and philosophers of Islam.

[43] For the Ishmaelites in general, as a branch of the Shi'ites of Persia, and for the
Imam and his myth, see the *Shorter Encyclopaedia of Islam* at the respective articles,
with bibliographies. For the sect's theological, philosophical, and moral ideology, with
respect to other religious and mystical Mohammedan groups, we refer our readers
once and for all to Hodgson, *The Order of the Assassins.* As is well known, Dante
mentions 'Alī as a schismatic Mohammedan leader (*Inferno,* XXVIII, 32); so, too,
Joinville, in *Histoire de Saint Louis,* secs. 458 ff.

[44] For this subject cf. G. Salinger, "Was the Futūwa an Oriental Form of Chivalry?"
Proceedings of the American Philosophical Society, Vol. XCIV, 1950, pp. 481 ff., and
L. Massignon, "La *futuwwa* ou pacte d'honneur artisanal," *La Nouvelle Clio,* Vol. IV,
1952, pp. 171 ff.

The problem consisted in the relationship between reason and faith in the correct interpretation of the Koran and the true meaning of Mohammed's spiritual and moral legacy. The fundamental concept asserted by the founder of the sect was that a knowledge of God could not be attained by the individual intellect or by means of the didactic methods commonly adopted, but only by following the teachings of the mythical and mystical Imam, the descendant of 'Alī, whom Hassan and his successors claimed to be rather than to represent. As the correct interpreters of the Prophet's teachings, the Imam and these vicars of his were at the head of the universal community of the faithful, in fact of all humanity, since man is the most nearly perfect of divinely created beings and the only one capable of supreme knowledge. Only the leader, the Old Man, could possess this knowledge and make it known to others, inasmuch as he was a personification of the divine substance and supreme authority which made him omnipotent and infallible.[45]

Transferred from the realm of pure speculation to that of practical life and faith, this doctrine had far-reaching and revolutionary consequences as soon as Hassan Sabbah put it into effect within the hierarchic framework of a military and political organization that gave him absolute power over his subjects. As a rule of thought and action, the doctrine implied the destruction of all intellectual freedom and of the traditional Mohammedan individualism which for centuries had made possible the development and coexistence of numerous sects and the unhindered growth of simple devotion, as well as of philosophy and every other branch of knowledge.

The Old Man of the Mountain had now attempted to substitute for these traditional tendencies, which for many centuries had favored the intense spiritual development of Islam, the concept of his enlightened and dogmatic supreme authority, which was supposed to create a universal unity of faith. This concept was not new in the history of Mohammedan philosophy and theology. The prevalent plurality of opinions was, for some of

[45] This doctrine is authoritatively and systematically expounded in the treatise by Nasiruddin Tusi; cf. the article by W. Ivanow cited in n. 21 above, pp. 537 ff. See, too, H. Corbin, "Épiphanie divine et naissance spirituelle dans la Gnose ismaélienne," *Eranos,* Vol. XXIII, 1955, esp. pp. 250 ff.

their schools as also for this sect, a clear evidence of error.[46] What was new was the attempt, which met with swift success, to impose his doctrine on an organized group and to put it into practice by means of a well-trained body of armed men which remained independent of the legitimate sovereign and was systematically educated to believe in, obey, and fight for a cause that furthered the interests of its spiritual, political, and military leader.[47]

The initiation undergone by the young men selected for this novitiate of mystical meditation and murderous activity was not by any means the joyful process described by our medieval travelers. It had nine successive stages, which plumbed the depths of human and divine knowledge and included the secret articles of the sect. This religious and scientific curriculum made of the Old Man's headquarters a philosophical and doctrinal center, so much so that when the Tartars conquered it in 1256 they found, not Mohammed's paradise, but instead a large library, an alchemic laboratory, and a collection of perfect astronomical instruments. Thus, when one of the *fidā'ī*, or fanatical followers of the Old Man, plunged his knife into the heart of his allotted victim, he was sure of killing and dying as an enlightened martyr for the legitimate head of Islam.

It therefore becomes increasingly obvious that Marco Polo's picturesque fantasies reflect the way in which orthodox Mohammedans of the times interpreted the moral and intellectual libertinism of the Assassins, especially after the year 1162, when

---

[46] So, e.g., for Ghazzali, the greatest theologian of Islam and a highly influential contemporary of Hassan Sabbah. His mystical orthodoxy was bitterly opposed to this sect and the others which flourished in the Persia of his times and destroyed the religious and intellectual unity of the faithful. Cf. A. J. Wensinck, *La Pensée de Ghazzali*, Paris, 1940.

[47] This political doctrine, which affirms the infallibility of a leader endowed with enlightened wisdom—and, consequently, his subjects' obligation to follow him blindly, —is already adumbrated in various passages of Plato's *Laws* (esp. Bk. XII, 942) but it was not realized in practice before the organization of the sect of the Assassins; hence its great historical significance, which in some measure had been seized upon by contemporaries, who expressed it in the fanciful, poetic forms noted by us. Plato— who was well known to the sect—had taught, *loc. cit.,* that "the individual must be trained in such a way that, by force of habit, he will ignore and not even wish to contemplate the possibility of acting on his own account. . . . This aim must be sought for by means of appropriate training both in time of peace and from the earliest years," etc.—just as the Old Man of the Mountain had trained his henchmen by means of a long and severe initiation, and not with drugs or other stratagems (invented by popular fancy and never mentioned by medieval historians).

their fourth Grand Master, Hassan II, suppressed nearly all the external forms of traditional worship. He permitted the free use of wine, abolished the traditional fast days and dietetic prescriptions, denied some fundamental dogmas—such as that of the resurrection of the body,—proclaimed the eternity of this world, of time, matter, and the universal soul, according to the teachings of the Greco-Islamic philosophers, and substituted his own will for the traditional law of Mohammed.[48]

By the time of Marco Polo's visit all these doctrines had ceased to have any effect on the spiritual and political life of the Mohammedan world. The organized sect of the Assassins had dissolved into a band of hirelings who sold their lives to the highest bidder. Finally, they too disappeared from the criminal life of the Levant. Nevertheless, the principle of unconditional obedience to a spiritual and political leader, which had made so deep an impression on the society of the later Middle Ages, did not disappear from the world stage, but was perpetuated in chivalrous and religious orders and, finally, in the totalitarian régimes of our own times. These last, indeed, have exhibited in gigantic yet crude proportions the ideas and practices of their prototype in their hierarchies, strongholds, and schools, in their jargon of "political mysticism," their secret meetings, and their claims to world-wide expansion and universal rule. Moreover, the idea of Paradise—be it real, allegorical, or simply metaphorical—never fails to put in an appearance in these religious, social, or political doctrines.

2. PRESTER JOHN IN LEGEND AND HISTORY

ORIGIN AND DEVELOPMENT OF THE
WESTERN TRADITION

Three independent phases may be discerned in the medieval secular development of the legend of Prester John, a supposed

---

For the most recent studies on the subject cf. C. E. Nowell, "The Historical Prester John," *Speculum,* Vol. XXVIII, 1953, pp. 435 ff

[48] This episode and its theological and philosophical significance are discussed by Mirkhond, ed. Jourdain, pp. 164 ff. This radical reform, which had its philosophical and theological precedents in Mohammedan thought from Avicenna to Averroes, substituted unconditional obedience to the Grand Master of the Assassins for the practices and rites of the Mohammedan religion, which it transformed into superstitious formalities and hence into a betrayal of the order and its leader.

Christian ruler of India and the Far East. They are related to news and interpretations of distant events, rumors of remote marvels, and notions of geography then current. The first— which we may call the Western phase—is characterized by the wide acceptance of this legend in Europe and its literary developments. The second, bound up with the experiences and reports of travelers, is regional and stems from Asiatic tradition quite independent of its Western counterpart. The third and last may be described as the African phase, which took shape after the Dominican missionary Jourdain Catalani de Sévérac, about the year 1340, and not long subsequently the Franciscan Giovanni de Marignolli, had identified the legendary sovereign with the emperor of Ethiopia, who was likewise a king and a Christian priest, and who bore the title of *Zān,* similar to "John," in the language of his country.[1]

The statements that we find in the *Milione* concerning Prester John belong exclusively to the second phase, though Marco Polo and the missionary explorers of Asia were undoubtedly aware of the fame he had acquired in the West, where he helped to evoke or confirm a fabulous picture of the wonders of Asia and of Christianity in the most inaccessible regions of the Orient. We may therefore limit our task to include only what is necessary to an understanding of Marco's allusions to this ruler, traces of whom he imagined he had discovered in the local legends of Mongolia and in the fabled king's supposed descendants in a Christian dynasty on the northwestern borders of the Chinese empire.[2]

The Western phase is certainly the oldest and richest in its fabulous and literary expressions, which can be seen in Europe in various references scattered throughout the epic poetry of the late Middle Ages, and in Italy right through until Ariosto's times.[3] The tradition can be dated specifically from November,

[1] For the supposed Ethiopian prototype of the legendary personage cf. the articles by C. Marinescu in *Bulletin de la Section Historique de l'Académie Roumaine,* Vol. X, 1923, pp. 73 ff., and Vol. XXVI, Pt. 2, 1945, pp. 203 ff.

[2] Cf. *Il Milione,* cr. ed., pp. 50 f., 60 f., and 105 f., respectively; M.P., pp. 163 f., 181 f., 260 f.

[3] Cf. Pio Rajna, *Le fonti dell'Orlando Furioso,* second edition, Florence, 1900, pp. 528 ff.; Ch. V. Langlois, *La Connaissance de la Nature et du Monde,* Paris, 1927, pp. 44 ff.; and the present author's *Storia letteraria delle scoperte geografiche,* Florence,

1145, when a Syrian bishop, chancing upon the German chronicler Otto of Freising in the town of Viterbo, told him how, some years before, a Nestorian priest-king by the name of John, descended from the Magi and ruling over a Christian empire in the Far East, had inflicted a crushing defeat on the Mohammedans of Persia. This victory was supposed to have enabled him to conquer all western Asia and to hasten to the help of the Crusaders, who were in danger of being ousted from their dominions in the Holy Land and the Levant.[4]

These reports, the authenticity of which is beyond doubt, were immediately and universally accepted for two reasons that seemed to confirm them: first, news of the Mohammedan defeat near Samarkand in the year 1141 and its consequences on the political and military situation in Persia had already reached Syria and the Holy Land, thereby awakening in the Christians of those regions lasting hopes of possible alliances with the victors over the common enemy; and second, the information given to Otto of Freising by the Syrian bishop corroborated the rumors then circulating through Europe that asserted the existence of vast and compact Nestorian populations in India and the Far East. Indeed, already in 1122 an Indian priest of that sect had personally told Pope Calixtus II in Rome of the wonders and miracles associated with the tomb of St. Thomas the Apostle near Madras. Hence, the information being so precise and authentic, it was not possible to doubt the authoritative beliefs and reports on the matter, especially since the defeat suffered by the Mohammedans, an event of contemporary importance and well known to Christian observers in the Levant, seemed to give credit to these rumors, which were intensified by political hopes and pious illusions.[5]

Actually, the evidence put forward by Otto of Freising refers to the Chinese general Yeh-lü Ta-shih, of the Central Asian

---

1937, pp. 194 ff., and "I Cantari dell'India di Giuliano Dati," *La Bibliofilia,* Vol. XL, 1938, disp. 8–9. For well-nigh complete documentation of the legend cf. F. Zarncke, "Der Priester Johannes," *Abhandlungen d. k. Sächsischen Gesellschaft der Wissenschaften,* phil.-hist. Klasse, Vol. VII, No. 8, Leipzig, 1879 (chaps. i, ii, iii), and Vol. VIII, No. 1, 1876 (chaps. iv, v, vi).

[4] Cf. Zarncke as just cited, 1876, pp. 21 ff.

[5] *Ibid.,* pp. 5 f.

branch of the Liao dynasty, who, after having consolidated his empire, composed chiefly of Christian, Buddhist, and Mohammedan Turkish peoples, led his armies to victory against Sanjar, the Seljuk sultan of Persia, thereby extending his dominions westward.[6] However, although this offers a satisfactory explanation for the views and hopes expressed by the Christians of the Levant and the reports broadcast in Europe by the famous chronicler, it is nevertheless difficult to understand why this Chinese general should be portrayed by him as a priest and king, and, more particularly, as a Christian Nestorian with the name "Presbyter Johannes."

All this would be easily explained if it were possible to attribute to him (as has recently been attempted) the characteristics of an emperor of Ethiopia. We know that in medieval geographical literature Ethiopia was included in the comprehensive concept of India and the Orient, and that it sent representatives and pilgrims to Jerusalem, where for centuries there was an Abyssinian Monophysite church.[7] Hence it was that the legendary Prester John came to be identified with the Zan of the Ethiopians, head of their church and state, and found favor among some Oriental scholars interested in this historical problem.[8]

---

[6] *Ibid.*, pp. 37 f. For those events and, in general, this Central Asiatic branch of the Mongol-Chinese Liao dynasty cf. R. Grousset, *L'Empire des steppes*, Paris, 1939 (and reprints), pp. 219 ff. The same subject is far more fully treated, with information on all available sources, by Karl A. Wittfogel and Fêng Chia-shêng, *History of Chinese Society: Liao, 907–1225*, Philadelphia, American Philosophical Society, 1949. For the Chinese chronicle of the dynasty cf. Rolf Stein, "*Leao Tche*, traduit et annoté," *T'oung Pao*, Vol. XXXV, 1944, pp. 1 ff. (with bibliography of the subject).

[7] Cf. the articles by C. Marinescu cited in note 1 above, and, for the Ethiopians in Jerusalem, E. Cerulli, *Gli Etiopi in Palestina*, 2 vols., Rome, 1947–48.

[8] Those who uphold the Ethiopian interpretation of the Prester John legend are listed at the end of Marinescu's article, 1945, p. 222 n. It should be emphasized that all the evidence in favor of that thesis is late, whereas the documentation in support of an Asiatic prototype of Prester John goes back to the middle of the XIIth century. Moreover, no historical fact comparable to the famous battle fought near Samarkand can be connected with Ethiopian history in its contacts with the Mohammedan world; cf. J. Spencer Trimingham, *Islam in Ethiopia*, Oxford Univ. Press, 1952, chap. ii. Nor do we find any reference to the Crusaders' having entertained hopes of obtaining military or political help from that quarter, whereas they never ceased to await the coming of an Asian ally—personified in the legendary Prester John—during the most critical period of the Crusades, from the middle of the XIIth century until the second half of the XIIIth. Marco Polo, while giving an extensive description of Abyssinia, its king of kings, and his conflicts with the Mohammedans of Africa and Arabia, never once refers to Prester John in this context (cf. *Il Milione*, cr. ed., pp. 210 ff.).

It is, however, only in the legend's third and final phase that Prester John and his kingdom were localized in that African and Christian empire, especially by Portuguese chroniclers and writers of the late Middle Ages.[9] All earlier historical and literary references are explicitly directed toward Oriental Asia—"ultra Persidem et Armeniam," as Otto of Freising says,—with emphasis on the Nestorian character of the sovereign and his people; whereas, as was well known in Jerusalem and therefore in the Christian circles of the Levant, the "king of kings" in Ethiopia was a Monophysite, and so were large numbers of his Christian subjects and clergy.

Moreover, the Chinese conqueror of Central Asia, Yeh-lü Ta-shih, was no Nestorian, although this sect counted various Altaic tribes among its followers, as well as those Turkish Uigurs who in his day, and for a further period of almost two centuries, represented the governing class and intellectual aristocracy of his empire.[10] The legend must have arisen in this milieu and, as the Nestorians scattered throughout Asia, have reached Baghdad, the spiritual and ecclesiastical center of the sect, and spread into Syria and the Holy Land, its farthest western ramifications.[11] Its motivations must have been exactly the same as those described a century later by Friar William of Rubruck, who emphasized the tendency of the Nestorians of central and eastern Asia to glorify their sect beyond measure by exaggerating its religious and political power, and to assert in the face of all evidence to the contrary the adherence of their rulers to their church.[12] Even as they spread throughout Asia and Christian Europe the rumor that the Great Kaan and his most powerful officials and vassals

[9] Cf. Francisco Alvarez, *Ho Presto Joam das Indias. Verdadera Informaçam das Terras do Preste Joam,* Lisbon, 1540, followed by other editions and translations of this work, which is fundamental for the history of ancient Abyssinia.

[10] Cf. the evidence collected by Wittfogel and Fêng Chia-shêng, *op. cit.,* pp. 657 ff., and E. Bretschneider, *Mediaeval Researches,* Vol. I, pp. 236 ff.

[11] For a concise history of the expansion of that sect cf. G. Messina, *Cristianesimo, Buddhismo, Manicheismo nell'Asia antica,* Rome, 1947. For Nestorianism in China and its relationship with central and western Asia, cf., besides P. Pelliot, "Chrétiens d'Asie Centrale et d'Extrême-Orient," *T'oung Pao,* Vol. XV, 1914, pp. 623 ff., A. C. Moule, *Christians in China,* London, 1930, and P. Y. Saeki, *The Nestorian Documents and Relics in China,* second edition, Tokyo, 1951. See above, chap. vii, § 1.

[12] Cf. *Sinica Franciscana,* Vol. I, p. 206 ("Nestoriani . . . de nihilo faciunt magnos rumores").

were Christians, and succeeded in imposing upon the good faith of Louis IX of France, as well as that of the Roman pontiffs, so, too, they may have represented the conqueror of the Mohammedans of Persia, their sovereign, as one of them, proclaiming him as a Nestorian to those who were inclined so to consider him.[13]

All this would not, however, explain the name "Johannes" with which he makes his first appearance on the historical scene, according to the information given to Otto of Freising, although this name is admittedly one of the most frequent in Nestorian onomatology all over Asia.[14] It was certainly never borne by Yeh-lü Ta-shih, either before or after his victory over Sanjar, the Sultan of Persia.[15] It is, however, possible to recognize in this name a phonetic echo of his Chinese title, *Wang,* which had been used from time immemorial—and so, too, in later centuries—by the princes of Central Asia. It was sometimes associated with the Turkish title *Han,* in order to signify their more or less nominal dependence on the Chinese emperor, who conferred or recognized it.[16] For his Chinese and Turkish subjects, the head of the Karakhitai was the *Wang-han* of their dominion. The term was changed to Johannan by the Nestorians of central Asia, who passed it on in this form, as a proper name, to their fellow believers and the other Christians of western Asia.[17]

[13] This was what Friar William thought about "King John," in whom we should see a historical prototype of the legendary Prester John. Cf. *Sinica Franciscana, loc. cit.* Although the information given by the friar is confused and historically incorrect, it is nevertheless possible to deduce from his account that his version of the legend was of Nestorian origin and indirectly connected with the political, cultural, and religious situation in Central Asia in the XIIth century.

[14] Cf. the list of Nestorian names in Moule, *Christians in China,* and Saeki, *Nestorian Documents and Relics,* as cited above.

[15] R. Hennig's attempt ("Das Christentum im mittelalterlichen Asien," *Historische Vierteljahrsschrift,* Vol. XXIX, 1935, pp. 234 ff., repeated in the same author's *Terrae Incognitae,* second edition, Leiden, 1950, Vol. II, pp. 445 ff.) to Christianize the Chinese conqueror who founded the dynasty of the Karakhitai has met with little or no success and is not supported by any reliable documentary evidence. Cf. Nowell's article in *Speculum,* 1953, p. 436. Perhaps some of his leading generals were Nestorians, as there were, a century later, in the armies of Chinghiz Khan and his successors.

[16] Yeh-lü Ta-shih took upon himself this title of *Wang,* without requesting investiture or confirmation from the sovereigns of Cathay and southern China. Cf. O. Franke, *Geschichte des chinesischen Reiches,* Vol. IV, pp. 192 ff.; also Wittfogel and Fêng Chia-shêng, as cited in note 6 above, p. 631.

[17] This would seem to confirm the eponymous Asiatic origin of the legend of Prester John, who would thus represent the sacerdotal *Wang* in the Nestorian interpretation of

This interpretation, which is, as we shall see, confirmed by later developments of the legend, seems more plausible than the unlikely hypothesis that a Syrian bishop—by virtue of his office an expert on Oriental Christianity—and a learned and well-informed chronicler can have confused the Monophysite Zan of Ethiopia with a ruler of a region of central Asia situated to the east of Armenia and Persia. On the other hand, his twofold dignity as king and priest was not a privilege exclusive to the African monarch; it was enjoyed not only by the Chinese emperor but also by various Asiatic rulers, both pagan and Christian, and was a special characteristic of the dynasties of Mongolia and Central Asia.[18] The sacerdotal dignity of these latter sovereigns was more esoteric than liturgical or clerical.[19] However, in 1294 Friar John of Montecorvino invested King George of the Öngüt, a supposed descendant of Prester John, with the minor orders of the Roman Church. He thereby united in him, in a Catholic,

the title; further on, we shall find confirmation in the Asiatic phase of the legend as known to the Franciscan missionaries and Marco Polo. The Ethiopian hypothesis put forward by Marinescu attempts to reduce the origin of the legend to the name or sovereign title, *Zān*, as opposed to the *Wang* of Asiatic tradition. Other things being equal, the origin in *Wang* is favored by the evidence found in contemporary chronicles and literary texts, which are unanimous in placing the legendary sovereign's political and spiritual dominion in the Orient and in a Nestorian milieu.

[18] For the coupling together of the two dignities in those regions cf. Pelliot's article, "Chrétiens d'Asie Centrale et d'Extrême-Orient," pp. 623 ff. The union of the two powers appeared to be confirmed by the affinity supposedly existing between the terms that designated them in the Altaic languages. Thus, Friar William of Rubruck (cf. *Sin. Franc.*, Vol. I, p. 205) confused the *han*, or political ruler, with the *cham*, a word which described the soothsayer or priest of the Turkish and Mongol peoples' natural religion. It is, moreover, significant that the friar puts forward this arbitrary identification just when he is discussing Yeh-lü Ta-shih, who is recorded by him in that double dignity with the title of *Gur-khan*, as he was still known in Central Asia a century after his death.

[19] This holds good for all forms of Asian theocracy, beginning with the one found in China (cf. J. J. M. de Groot, *Universismus*, Berlin, 1918), and for the most ancient aspects of the two dignities in Christian history, as can be seen—since no monographic study of this important subject exists—from a footnote to Ernst H. Kantorowicz's article, "Mysteries of State," *Harvard Theological Review*, Vol. XLVIII, 1955, p. 72, n. 23, and his most illuminating book, *The King's Two Bodies*, Princeton Univ. Press, 1957. As is well known, the delimitation of the two powers was one of the cardinal problems in the age-old struggle between the Empire and the Papacy, from Gregory VII until the age of Dante. Cf. "Sacerdozio e Regno da Gregorio VII a Bonifacio VIII," in *Miscellanea Historiae Pontificiae*, Vol. XVIII, Rome, 1954. A study of the affinities and contrasts between Western and Oriental theocracies of the Middle Ages would undoubtedly throw further light upon the origin and purpose of the famous *Letter of Prester John*. Cf. the present author's article, "Der Brief des Presbyters Johannes," *Historische Zeitschrift*, 1931, pp. 1 ff.

clerical, and liturgical sense, the two dignities of priest and king
that legend had already bestowed on this dynasty which, though
heretical, was connected with the Magi of the Gospels.[20]

This missionary was thus able to realize within the boundaries
of the Chinese empire, and in a modest though significant form,
that which for a century and a half had been the common desire
of the Roman pontiffs and Levantine prelates: namely, to lead
this mythical king and heretical priest into the bosom of the
Roman Church in order that his kingdom might become a
center for Catholic expansion in Asia and an instrument of common action against the Mohammedans. This represented the fulfillment of a religious and political tradition originating in an
episode of Asian history that had been misconstrued for purposes
of propaganda. It had given rise to a literary utopia of universal
appeal, and had found its culminating point in the ideal figure
of a sovereign who, for the good of his subjects and of Christianity, united in his person the dignities of king and priest and
governed his immense and fabulous empire with justice and
humility.

These were the concepts that had inspired the famous but
spurious *Letter of Prester John,* which in 1165 was sent by some-
one whose name we do not know to Manuel Comnenus, the
Byzantine emperor, to Frederick Barbarossa, Pope Alexander III,
and, it would seem, other European rulers. It was intended to set
before these Western monarchs the picture of a fabulous Asian
empire, rich in the rarest treasures and most extraordinary wonders, peopled by the oddest sort of folk, and governed in an ideal
state by a theocratic sovereign who, with the modest title of priest,
wielded both temporal and ecclesiastical powers and practiced
justice for the love of God.[21]

The most recent studies of this text have recognized in it a
concept, of a political utopia, that came to assume an important

[20] Cf. Monneret de Villard, *Le leggende orientali* etc., pp. 166 ff.

[21] Cf. the critical text and various Latin versions of the *Letter* in F. Zarncke as
cited in note 3 above. Little critical insight is shown by F. Fleuret in his article, "La
Lettre du Prêtre-Jean, Pseudo-Roi d'Abyssinie" (with a French translation of the
Letter), *Mercure de France*, Vol. CCLXVIII, 1936, pp. 294 ff. The attribution of the
Letter to Archbishop Christian of Mainz is purely conjectural and untenable. (Cf. R.
Hennig, *Terrae Incognitae*, Vol. II, pp. 452 ff. This author misinterpreted the character
and aim of the document.)

part in the bitter controversy then raging between church and state, respectively personified in the Pope and the Holy Roman Emperor. It was just when the struggle for power between Frederick Barbarossa and Pope Alexander III had reached its climax that there came to their attention this literary image of an exemplary ruler who combined both the kingly and the priestly office for the good of his peoples, practiced the highest public virtues, and abstained from evil—quite in accord with the Western imperial ideal and the political literature of the Middle Ages.[22]

The extravagant fantasy of the wonders of Asia in the framework of a model society, conjured up by the *Letter,* received its highest recognition in 1177 when the Pope entrusted to his personal physician, Philip, his moderate reply to the imaginary monarch. He exhorted him to recognize the authority of the Roman pontiff and at the same time to send him authentic sealed letters, written with greater humility and inspired by a more Christian spirit of deference, which should be transmitted by special ambassadors.[23] And while in Europe the *Letter of Prester John,* which had received such authoritative confirmation, helped to keep alive the fabulous picture of the wonders of Asia, it continued in the Levant to revive the hope of the Crusaders, who for more than half a century had looked toward the Orient in the hope of discovering in this mythical sovereign an ally against the Saracens of Syria and the Holy Land.

In fact, when Chinghiz Khan set out in 1219 to conquer western Asia, the Christian spiritual leaders who had been present at the taking of Damietta were so far led astray by their desire to find the fabled ally that they hailed Chinghiz as a son or descendant of the same Prester John who, according to the inter-

---

[22] For the figure of Prester John in imperial myths and legends of the Middle Ages cf. Franz Kampers, *Die deutsche Kaiseridee in Prophetie und Sage,* Munich, 1896, esp. pp. 78 ff., and the same author's *Vom Werdegange des abendländischen Kaisermythus,* Leipzig, 1924, pp. 113 ff. Among other things, this author observed in the first of the works cited (p. 78) that the name John occurs much earlier to designate the mythical sovereign destined to exterminate the enemies of the Faith. The character of a political utopia attributed to the famous *Letter* by the present author (cf. his article in *Historische Zeitschrift,* 1931, pp. 1 ff.) has recently been recognized by Nowell, in *Speculum,* 1953, pp. 438 f., and by Ugo Monneret de Villard, *Le leggende orientali* etc., p. 152.

[23] Cf. Zarncke, as cited in note 3 above, 1879, chap. iii.

pretation traditionally held in the West, had fought against the Mohammedans of Persia some sixty years earlier at the battle of Samarkand.[24] This renewed and tenacious illusion was further accredited by Jacques de Vitry, author of the renowned *Historia Hierosolymitana,* in letters written or inspired by him in support of the new crusade organized by Pope Honorius III and the Emperor Frederick II.[25] The wishful thinking of contemporary strategy and politics cherished hopes of a common action on the part of the Hohenstaufen emperor and the Asiatic conqueror— whose popular name of "David" connected him with the legendary priest-ruler of the Orient—in an attempt to recapture Jerusalem, which had been taken by the Mohammedans in 1187.

Nothing justified these fervent hopes which had received such high support. Chingiz Khan had, indeed, destroyed the Khwaresmian empire in Persia just as Yeh-lü Ta-shih had overthrown that country's Seljukian dynasty; and the similarity in the political and military situation in Central Asia seemed to confirm the ancient illusions of the West. But now the Mongol hordes had penetrated much farther into western Asia and had advanced into Russia, where for the first time they established their rule in Christian lands.[26] As a result of this incursion, and of harsh contacts between the conquerors and their Christian neighbors in the regions of Asia Minor and the Black Sea, the fables and traditional concepts that had resulted from misunderstandings and illusive hopes quickly disappeared. They were replaced by new interpretations of the legend of Prester John. It was no longer possible to eradicate it from recent Asiatic history; but it

[24] *Ibid.,* chap. iv, and for these later developments of the legend cf. Hennig, *Terrae Incognitae,* second edition, Vol. III, 1953, pp. 16–23.

[25] This apocalyptic expectation of Prester John's intervention on behalf of the Christian armies was then favored by the authority of the cardinal legate Pelagius, Bishop of Ptolemaïs (Acre), and by the preacher Oliver of Cologne, who was present at the taking of Damietta in 1219. Cf. Zarncke, *loc. cit.* For the imaginary contacts between Prester John and Frederick II cf., besides the famous Novella II of the *Novellino* (ed. L. di Francia, Turin, 1930, pp. 9 ff., with useful notes and references), the relevant chapters in Kampers, *Die deutsche Kaiseridee;* also Ernst Kantorowicz, *Friedrich II,* third edition, Berlin, 1930, with index and bibliography of the subject in the *Ergänzungsband* of this work (English trans., reprint London, 1958). The name David, which was applied to Chinghiz Khan (the supposed descendant of Prester John), goes back to Georgian traditions concerning David II, king of Georgia, who defeated the Mohammedan armies that invaded his Caucasian kingdom in the year 1121.

[26] Cf. Grousset, *L'Empire des steppes,* pp. 306 f.

was gradually modified on the basis of information obtained from Oriental sources, which can be reconstructed from the historical literature of the times.

THE ASIATIC VERSION

Whereas the original phase of the legend had made of Prester John the mythical Christian ruler of a large part of the Asian continent and the allegorical figure of a political utopia, the new trend that began toward the middle of the XIIIth century limited his dominion to a tribe in Mongolia, which was governed by a Christian dynasty. His power and prestige were thereby reduced, and his exploits associated with the history and legend of the recently formed Chinghizide empire.

This new version of the legend began to take shape in Western thought when, at the end of December, 1248, there arrived at the camp of Louis IX of France, on the island of Cyprus, two or more ambassadors from the head of the Mongol armies in Persia. The Chinghizide commander was then planning to march on Baghdad, the seat of the moribund Abbasid caliphate, and therefore wished to learn what he could of the intentions and power of the new Crusaders, with a view to a possible alliance and joint military effort in the task of encircling the common enemy.[27] The principal—perhaps the sole—messengers sent by the Mongol leader, who were called David and Marco, were certainly Nestorians, as can be seen from their names. As was the custom among their fellow believers, they must have seized upon this opportunity to emphasize and exaggerate both the number and the power of the Christians in the new Tartar empire, thereby no doubt intentionally corroborating the age-old rumors that had been circulating throughout the Levant and Europe concerning Asiatic Christianity and its sovereigns.

However, whereas the Western phase of the legend of Prester John had from the start portrayed him as a king and priest, this twofold dignity is never specified in the new version. Instead, it always represents him, though in various ways, as a vassal

---

[27] Cf. Joinville, *Histoire de Saint Louis,* ed. N. de Wailly, Paris, 1921, chap. xciii, p. 198. For this embassy and its historical and legendary vicissitudes cf. Zarncke, "Der Priester Johannes," 1876, chap. v, secs. 5 ff.

or enemy of the Chinese emperor, or, again, as an opponent and victim of Chinghiz Khan, who unified the Mongols after conquering the Tartars, hitherto one of the Mongol tribes. It is thus that the Prester John of the second phase is envisioned by the messengers sent to Asia by King Louis, and thus that he appears in the contemporary chronicles that mention him, beginning with that of Joinville, who had taken part in the negotiations between the French king and the Mongolian emissaries in Cyprus. On that occasion the future biographer of King Louis must have learned, together with other legends of Asian origin, that Prester John had been the last powerful adversary of the "Tartars" united beneath the sceptre of a "saige homme" who, as a result of the unanimous agreement of his fifty-two peoples, had become their head and leader.[28]

This last is an obvious reference to Chinghiz Khan and to the events that placed him at the head of the Mongol peoples, until the defeat and execution of his last rival, the Ong Khan, head of the Keraits, a tribe of prevailing Nestorian faith.[29] Joinville's report marked the end, at least in the official tradition, of the figure of Prester John as he had hitherto been pictured by the fanciful author of the *Letter* and the more or less literate Crusaders during those critical years for Christianity in the Levant. Only his name remained, applied now to a historical personage in Altaic Asia who lacked the attributes of power and glory that had made the priest-king famous throughout the Christian world. No trace of them is to be found in the *Milione;* and the lack is an indication that Marco Polo had drawn upon other sources among the Asiatic and Nestorian interpretations of this legendary figure.[30]

He has applied this name to a historical personage, to be identified, as we have already seen, with the Ong Khan Togrul, or Togril, who had first been an ally of Chinghiz Khan at the beginning of his bloody yet glorious career, and then, in circumstances described in the *Secret History* of the Mongols and other

---

[28] Joinville, *ed, cit.,* secs. 474 ff.
[29] See above, chap. vii, § 1.
[30] Marco, indeed, never alludes to the *Letter of Prester John* and the extraordinary wonders described in it, though he clearly refers to the legend's popularity. Cf. cr. ed., p. 50, line 9; M.P., p. 162.

Chinese sources, his last enemy and gory victim.[31] Marco also mentions his descendants who governed the province of "Tenduc," on the northwestern borders of the Chinese empire, as vassals of the Great Kaan; and tells that the latter, following an unbroken tradition, always gave one of his daughters or near relations in marriage to the lord of that region, which was inhabited by a prevalently Christian people that belonged to the Nestorian sect.[32] The Venetian thereby verified the close and lasting bond that united the Chinghizide emperors with the Christian dynasty of the Keraits, inasmuch as his anecdote reflects a fact confirmed by other episodes in Oriental history.

The account found in the *Milione* does not, however, reflect favorably on this Christian monarch, who is supposed to have sent to Chinghiz Khan an insolent message for which he was soon punished, losing his power and his life in the war provoked by his presumption.[33] It is evident from all this that the Prester John of Mongolia has nothing whatever to do with the figure of Western tradition, and is nothing but a mere name which implied his adherence to the Nestorian sect and the union of temporal and ecclesiastical authority in his person.[34] In short, Prester John became merely the title of an Asian prince who was

---

[31] Cf. B. Ya. Vladimirtsov, *The Life of Chingis-Khan*, pp. 48 ff., and R. Grousset, *Le Conquérant du Monde*, pp. 118 ff. Marco Polo never mentions the proper name of the ruler of the Keraits. The latter only appears in the *Milione* with his title of *Unc Can* and that of Prester John, as earlier, though less clearly and consistently, in William of Rubruck's *Itinerarium* (*Sin. Franc.*, Vol. I, pp. 205 f.).

[32] *Il Milione*, cr. ed., pp. 60 f.; M.P., pp. 181 f. Marco assigns the name and title of Prester John both to the chieftain of the Mongol tribe of the Keraits and to the ruler of the Öngüt in the region of the Ordos. Both were Nestorians. Cf. L. Hambis, "Le Voyage de Marco Polo en Haute Asie," in *Oriente Poliano*, Rome, 1957, pp. 182 ff.

[33] Marco emphasizes that the Tartars rebelled against "Prester John," thereby alluding to the historic rivalry between the pagan Tartars and the prevalently Christian tribe of the Keraits, who were in fact ruled by his Unc Can (Cf. Vladimirtsov, *loc. cit.*). Moreover, we read in the *Milione* that Chinghiz Khan, after having become lord of Mongolia, asked for the hand of a daughter of this supposed Prester John, thereby provoking the war which resulted in the latter's deposition and death. These episodes are part of the poetic history of Chinghiz Khan, which was narrated in these anecdotic forms throughout Asia but without any apparent historical basis, as is evident from the various Mongol, Persian, and Armenian sources (the *Secret History;* Rashiduddin; and Hayton, *La Flor des estoires de la terre d'Orient,* respectively), which have not yet been monographically coördinated or interpreted, as far as this particular aspect is concerned.

[34] Marco never explicitly refers to the Unc Can as a Christian, but the designation "Prester John" sufficed for the purpose.

certainly a Christian, but who had no direct or visible connection with the legendary sovereign "whose great power is the talk of the whole world," as Marco says.[35]

This conclusion is confirmed by the identification that had been offered half a century before by Friar William of Rubruck in his *Itinerarium,* on the basis of some vague information he had obtained in Central Asia, in 1253, while on his way to the court of the Great Kaan in Mongolia. According to this missionary, some years after the French had taken Antioch (i.e., after 1098) a Mongol leader of the Naiman tribe—a Nestorian Christian—acquired such prestige and power that he won the throne of the "Coir-chan," or Gur-khan, lord of Central Asia.[36] His subjects called him King John.[37] He having died without issue, his territory passed into the hands of a brother, Unc, who proclaimed himself "Chan" and then became a rival and enemy of Chinghiz Khan.[38]

Very little can be made of this information, which is neither historical nor legendary but quite simply the result of a misunderstanding that is due to the arbitrary application of Prester John's name and title to various *Wang-han* of Altaic Asia, and more especially to the *Gur-han* Yeh-lü Ta-shih of the empire of the Karakhitai and to the *Unc-han* of the Keraits, mentioned in the *Milione.* This hypothesis is confirmed by a third Prester John, whom Marco portrays in another part of his book as a traitor to his lawful sovereign the Golden King of China, a great and powerful prince, as we are told, who governed his kingdom with magnanimity and justice while indulging in certain extravagant

[35] *Il Milione,* cr. ed., p. 50; M.P., p. 163.

[36] Cf. *Sinica Franciscana,* Vol. I., pp. 205 ff. "Gur-khan" was the title given by the Mohammedans of Central Asia to their ruler, Yeh-lü Ta-shih, who had conquered this region commonly known as Karakhitai; cf. Karl Menges, "Der Titel Gūr-hān der Qara-Qytai," *Ural altaisches Jahrbuch,* Vol. XXIV, 1952, pp. 84 ff. The Mongol tribe of the Naimans and its dynasty were not Christians; hence, the data that refer to them in Friar William's report have no historical foundation. He is likewise mistaken in identifying the Chinese founder of the dynasty of the Karakhitai with a leader of these Naimans from Mongolia. Cf. Rockhill, *The Journey of William of Rubruck,* pp. 108 f.

[37] I.e., probably, *Wang-han.*

[38] Here the friar evidently means to refer to Togrul—Marco Polo's Unc Can,— although he gives him a territory over which he never exerted direct rule. Friar William was confused and mistaken both in his ideas and in his information concerning the events that had taken place in Central Asia and Mongolia a century before his stay in those regions.

pleasures which our author describes with obvious delight and interest. After he had declared war on Prester John, six of the latter's henchmen managed by a trick to lay hold of his person and to humiliate him so far as to make him play the part of a shepherd and confess his own inferiority.[39]

This story, which is recounted to us by Marco as "a fine adventure . . . according to that which the local people tell," is mentioned in connection with the castle of "Cauiu" which the Golden King had caused to be built in a pleasant region by the lower stretches of the Yellow River.[40] That the episode is authentic is proved by the sovereign's very name, which is a translation of the Chinese title of the Kin (= 'gold') dynasty, which reigned over a large part of Cathay from 1115 to 1234 and at last was deposed by Chinghiz Khan under circumstances of extreme humiliation.[41]

Though the geographical location of Marco's legend appears uncertain, it is nevertheless possible to exclude any identification of this Prester John with the *Wang-han* of Central Asia or the *Unc-han* of the Keraits. Their respective territories were geographically, ethnographically, and linguistically so far removed from that of any Golden King of the Kin dynasty as to oblige us to seek elsewhere for an explanation to this legendary character's new hypostasis. No episode in Chinese history throws any light on its origin or development.[42] Friar William's experience sug-

---

[39] This anecdote is narrated at length in the *Milione,* cr. ed., pp. 105 f.; M.P., pp. 260 f.

[40] A correct identification has not yet been established. However, this "castle" must have been situated somewhere in the hills of the Chinese province of Shansi, in the neighborhood of the Yellow River.

[41] "King of Gold" (Roi Dor, in Marco's text) is a translation of the Chinese *Kin Wang,* which, in its turn, is a Chinese translation of the Mongol *Altan Han,* or Khan of Gold, the title of the Mongol or Tungus dynasty that ruled over Cathay in that epoch. For the name, dominions, and history of this dynasty cf. O. Franke, *Geschichte des chinesischen Reiches,* Vol. IV, pp. 188 ff., and *passim.* For these real or imaginary figures and their Altaic and Chinese names cf. the notes to the translation of the *Milione* by L. Hambis, *La Description du Monde,* Paris, 1955, pp. 365 f., 381 f., and 392.

[42] A. J. H. Charignon, in *Le Livre de Marco Polo,* Vol. II, p. 70, dates back the historical model for this legend—which is mentioned by Marco Polo alone—as far as the IIId century A.D. This hypothesis, however, is not confirmed by other references and cannot be said to offer conclusive evidence, whereas the effeminate customs in vogue at the court of the "Golden King" (which are described especially in the Ramusian version of the *Milione*) can also be confirmed for more recent periods in Chinese history, including the Chinghizide era. We may expect some explanation of the legend from Pelliot's forthcoming commentary on Marco Polo.

gests the hypothesis that the local residents attributed this anecdote to one of the various *Wang* recorded in Chinese history,
and that the similarity in titles led to the erroneous identification,
as when Yeh-lü Ta-shih was confused with the Ong Khan of the
Keraits.[43]

This would seem to confirm the supposition that Prester John,
in the Asiatic tradition reported by travelers of the XIIth century,
was nothing but the equivalent of a Chinese name which was
understood—and therefore interpreted—in a number of ways. It
is also clear that this figure had no connection with the fables
told about him in the West and ignored by the missionaries and
Marco Polo. The responsibility for this web of historical incongruity, which seems to derive from misinterpretations of a princely
and ecclesiastical title, is ascribed by Friar William to the Nestorians. He states that perhaps only a tenth of what they tell about
this King John is true [44]—an assertion amply confirmed by Odoric
of Pordenone as late as 1330 when he noted of Prester John that
not even a hundreth part of what was recounted about him corresponded to reality.[45]

The legend's Asiatic tradition did not have those offshoots
which made it famous in the West. The Nestorians made use of
it on various occasions for purposes of propaganda; [46] but they
were well aware of their weakness and their precarious situation
between the pagans and the Mohammedans in central and western

[43] The hypothesis put forward by Yule (*The Book of Ser Marco Polo,* Vol. II, p. 20 n.)
is far more probable: namely, that the hero of this legend was neither the ruler of the
Karakhitai nor the leader of the Mongol Keraits, but rather the king of the Naimans
who reigned over this powerful tribe with the Chinese title of *T'ai-wang* or *T'ai-yang
han* until his defeat and execution by Chinghiz Khan in 1204. Although the fact has
not been definitely ascertained, this chieftain appears to have been a Nestorian, as were
some of the aristocracy of his tribe. The various episodes of that historic struggle inspired Mongol legends and epics, mentioned by Vladimirtsov, *The Life of Chingis-
Khan,* pp. 49 ff., which were extended to the adventurous life led by the chieftain's son
Kushluk, who was also defeated and slain by Chinghiz Khan's generals in 1218 after
having sought refuge in Eastern Turkestan, where he violently persecuted the Mohammedans of the region. We may presume that the father's Chinese title (*T'ai-wang*), the
son's possible adherence to the Nestorian sect, and this action against the Mohammedans,
all helped to credit their dynasty with the name and title of Prester John, which
throughout the history of the legend always implied a hostile attitude toward the
Mohammedans.
[44] Cf. *Sinica Franciscana,* Vol. I, p. 206.
[45] *Ibid.,* p. 483.
[46] Cf. Zarncke, "Der Priester Johannes," 1876, chap. vi, pp. 78 ff.

Asia, and their Prester John is therefore an empty name which has left no trace either in the history of their sect or in the annals and traditions of the peoples of the Orient. Like other Western travelers in Asia, Marco Polo had brought with him the memory of the fabulous sovereign, and applied this title to the first name or fortuitous allusion that seemed to warrant it. An Asiatic tradition of the legend can therefore be discovered only in the memoirs of Western travelers, where it appears rather as an evidence of their misunderstanding than as an expression of the continent's poetical history. (Cf. *Il Milione,* cr. ed., chap. cxciv.)

3. "CUBLAI KAN"

"The Great Lord of Lords who is called Cublai Kan" is the dominant figure in the *Milione;* so much so, that the book does at times seem to have been intended to celebrate his power and glory. Lord of a large part of Asia, as head of the widespread dynasty which governed it, and making his influence felt and feared in the parts of the continent that were still autonomous,

---

The name of the Great Kaan of the Tartars in Marco's times occurs in his book in the form "Cublai." The title is given as "Kan" or "Kaan" (see, e.g., cr. ed., p. 66, chaps. lxxvi and lxxvii respectively; M.P., 410), forms which correspond to the Mongol and Turkish titles *Han* (or *Khan*) and *Qaghan* (or *Qaqhan*), according as they designate the leader of a tribe or a nation, respectively, or, in a wider sense, a king or an emperor. (Cf. B. Ya. Vladimirtsov, *The Life of Chingis-Khan,* p. 40; R. Grousset, *L'Empire des steppes,* p. 273 n. 3; and above, chap. viii, n. 51.) It should, however, be pointed out that the founder of the dynasty did not assume the title of *Qaghan,* but even at the zenith of his career retained that of *Han* (whence the current form of Chinghiz Khan). The latter title also recurs in the official documents of his successors, as can be seen in the article by P. Pelliot, "Les Mongols et la Papauté," *Revue de l'Orient Chrétien,* Vol. XXIII, 1922–23, pp. 19 and 24. It would therefore appear that the two terms were considered to be synonymous and were used indiscriminately. This would also explain the double form of the title found in the *Milione* and the addition of "grant" to that of "Kan" in this and other texts. As for the name "Cublai," it is variously recorded in the forms Chubilai or Khubilai, Khublai, Qubilai (which corresponds to the Chinese *Hu-pi-lei,* used in the Annals of the Empire, or *Yüan Shih,* as may be seen from our illustration, fig. 9), and Kublai—the form adopted by us in this book, after the example of Yule and other English and American scholars. For the principal events of Kublai's life and reign cf., besides O. Franke, *Geschichte des chinesischen Reiches,* Vol. IV, and Grousset, *L'Empire des steppes,* the translation of the official history of the empire by J. A. M. de Moyriac de Mailla, S.J., *Histoire générale de la Chine,* Paris, 1777–1783, Vol. IX. This is a useful and interesting work, in spite of the fact that the translator made use of an abbreviated version of the Annals of the Empire, or, more precisely, a late adaptation of the leading Chinese historical text, the *T'ung Chien Kang Mu,* which was also the main source of Henri Cordier's *Histoire générale de la Chine,* 4 vols., Paris, 1920–21.

the Great Kaan of the Tartars is everywhere present in our author's "Description of the World," from the prologue which mentions him as the lord and protector of the three Venetians, to the reference made to the embassies he sent to the islands of Ceylon and Madagascar.[1]

His figure rises up from every land and every sea, as the historical, yet ideal, manifestation of a universal sovereign. This was all the more eloquent and impressive since the imperial myth which in Marco Polo's times encouraged Dante's hopes and the Ghibelline illusions of Italy and Germany had not yet died out in the West.[2] Marco contrasts that Western concept, and the ideal impersonated in the legendary figure of Prester John, with the effective power materialized in his "Cublai Kan," to whom belong, as he points out, "all the provinces and regions mentioned" in his book.[3] He declares himself, moreover, to be the subject and servant of this the most powerful lord on earth, since he had constantly been carrying out missions for him during the seventeen years he spent in Kublai's service.[4]

Although Marco never took part in the privy councils of the empire, as has been claimed for him by some of his commentators and biographers, it may nevertheless be presumed that he regularly saw his sovereign lord and came to enjoy an exceptional degree of familiarity with him and his entourage. Certainly, no Oriental source reveals as many details of the emperor's public and private life as does Marco, in part systematically and in part scatteringly, throughout his book. He was thus able to give his readers information about Kublai's physical appearance and

[1] Kublai sent his envoys to Ceylon (Marco's "Seilan"), first in order to request—in vain, as it turned out—the ruby belonging to the king of that island (*Il Milione*, cr. ed., p. 177; M.P., p. 380), and then to procure—which they did—some relics of the Buddha (cr. ed., pp. 194 f.; M.P., pp. 410 f.). His ambitions as conqueror of the world also induced him to send an embassy to the fabulous isle that Marco calls "Mogdasio," which is universally recognized by his commentators to be the island of Madagascar (cr. ed., p. 205 and n. to chap. cxcii; M.P., p. 431). This land was already known to Chau Ju-kua (cf. ed. Hirth-Rockhill, pp. 126 and 149), and, together with other regions of East Africa, was described by him in terms similar to those used by Marco, thus revealing the common Arab-Persian sources from which both drew their information.

[2] Cf. Franz Kampers, *Die deutsche Kaiseridee in Prophetie und Sage*, Munich, 1896, and *Vom Werdegange der abendländischen Kaisermystik*, Leipzig and Berlin, 1924.

[3] *Il Milione*, cr. ed., p. 113; M.P., p. 273.

[4] Cr. ed., p. 10, chap. xvii; M.P., p. 87.

moral character, habits and idiosyncracies, which cannot be found elsewhere—and which have not hitherto been studied.

Yet it is a conventional picture that is offered by Marco Polo in his description of "the features of the Great Kaan." [5] He asserts that "Cublai Kan is of good stature, that is to say, well proportioned; neither short nor tall, but of medium height," with comely limbs, neither fat nor lean. "His countenance is fair and ruddy like a rose, his eyes dark and handsome, his well-shaped nose set squarely in place." This is obviously not a portrait of the Great Kaan, but rather an ideal figure depicted after Marco's personal tastes. He lacks the special attributes that one expects as comporting with imperial rank and dignity, and is reduced instead to a totally conventional human and aesthetic pattern. The descriptive terms would be applicable to a young boy, or girl, but certainly not to an ageing Mongol emperor, considered by Marco to be the greatest and most powerful sovereign not only of his dynasty but of all the emperors in the world and all the kings of the earth, Christians and Saracens notwithstanding.

In fact, this image does not differ in its essentials from those of Western rulers and pontiffs to be found in the mosaics of medieval churches, the artists' intention having been to exalt rather than to offer a realistic picture. The figures, also, on coins and in sculptures of Marco's times are but rarely individualized; instead, they are reduced to certain conventional types only identifiable by their respective names. And the absence of individual pen-portraits in the writings of that epoch is even more marked. Indeed, for a long time to come, literary portraiture remained a rhetorical and stylistic exercise, which could vary in its phraseology but was always bound to a fixed pattern and ideal type. In limning his sovereign, therefore, Marco ingenuously follows the common tendencies of his period and succeeds in imposing its conventions even on Kublai's exotic figure, so far removed from the experiences and ideals of Western medieval portraiture.

A fortunate coincidence makes it possible for us to compare with Marco's description the emperor's actual features, which we find reproduced in two Chinese pictures which are certainly authentic and are preserved with those of other members of the

---

[5] Cr. ed., p. 66, chap. lxxvi; M.P., p. 192.

Chinghizide dynasty in the ancient imperial palace at Peking.[6] Here the type, family resemblance, characteristic features of the Mongol race, and the specific individual traits of each sovereign are comprehended and revealed with great skill and an objective realism that is devoid of all artistic convention and courtly adulation. The only thing these magnificent Chinese portraits have in common with Marco's description is a quality that bespeaks the artists' warmth of approach; they are not servile or coldly official. The pictorial stylization of the Chinese has, however, accentuated the individualization which is totally lacking in Marco's passage, where the most obvious and essential features of his subject's physiognomy are ignored.

The first of the two portraits of Kublai that have come down to us (fig. 6) represents him as a mature man in his late forties, not much different from the personage whom Niccolò and Maffeo Polo beheld for the first time at Shangtu after their first transcontinental journey in 1265. The emperor was then fifty years old and in the plenitude of his sway. This is precisely how he appears in this picture: full of energy, dignity, intelligence, and a supreme awareness of his autocratic power.

With this picture before our eyes, Marco's image takes on form and substance as we scan the sovereign's fine rounded face, his large dark eyes half covered by the heavy curved lids, his full cheeks, clear complexion, and virile nose, "well-shaped and well-proportioned," as we read in the *Milione*. Marco, however, has forgotten to mention the tuft of beard at the point of the chin, a characteristic of every Chinghizide sovereign, as can be seen from the miniatures in the manuscript at the Bibliothèque Nationale in Paris (Supplément persan 1113) of Rashiduddin's *Universal History*, which offers an extensive iconography of the family in its typical aspects and sometimes even in the features of its individual members.[7] Nor does our traveler mention the no less

---

[6] Cf. A. Mostaert, "A propos de quelques portraits mongols," *Asia Major*, Vol. IV, 1927, pp. 147 ff.

[7] Our figure 8 represents Mangu, Kublai's brother and predecessor, with his wives and princes and ladies of his court and dynasty. Together with many other miniatures, this picture adorns the MS mentioned above, which is attributed by some historians of medieval Persian art to the first decades of the XIVth century, and by others to the post-Timurid period, i.e., the XVth century. If the latter dating is correct, the illustrations must be considered more or less faithful copies of an older model. Cf. the present

characteristic Mongol mustaches, which are elegantly defined and add a vigorous touch to the sovereign's expressive face and a picturesque dented curve above his sensual, well-shaped mouth.

It is not possible for us to discover with any certainty why Marco suppressed these obvious and essential features in Kublai's countenance. At most, we may suppose that he wished to make it approximate more closely to the ideal type in contemporary imperial iconography, whether Byzantine or Gothic, and especially its Italian form, which both on coins and in works of sculpture represented the Western emperor as clean-shaven. The sculptures, as is well known, were inspired by the Augustan type of classical times, which had come back into favor in the imperial Italy of Frederick II and his son Manfred.[8] It is not possible to adduce convincing proof of this hypothesis. At any rate, Marco has given us in his description an ideal type of sovereign which certainly does not correspond to his subject's personality.

The word-picture offered by Marco is even farther removed from the second of the emperor's portraits (fig. 7), which was painted at least twenty years later than the first. This shows him as he must have appeared to the Venetians just before they set out for home in 1291 or the year following, when he was nearing his end. He is seen to be aged, weary, and robbed of all illusion. No trace remains of the almost youthful self-assurance that was so forcibly evident in the first portrait; instead, he strikes us as grave and solemn, and the effect is emphasized by the naturalness of his pose and the simplicity of his costume. The artistic realism of this image brings him before us as he must have appeared in the last years of his life, which was not, as Marco would have us believe, all pomp and glory, but was much disquieted by rebellions and other troubles that left their mark in the expression of resigned melancholy immortalized by the Chinese painter.

---

author's *Guillaume Boucher: A French Artist at the Court of the Khans,* Baltimore, 1946, pp. 108 f. For other Persian portraits of Mongol sovereigns see E. G. Browne, *Persian Literature under Tartar Dominion,* Cambridge, 1920.

[8] For this subject and its relevant literature cf. Guido Kaschnitz-Weinberg, "Bildnisse Friedrichs II. von Hohenstaufen," *Mitteilungen des deutschen archäologischen Instituts,* Römische Abteilung, LX–LXI, 1955, pp. 1 f. For beards among Altaic peoples cf. L. O. Buxton, *The Peoples of Asia,* London, 1925, and O. Maenchen-Helfen, "Huns and Hsiung-nu," *Byzantion,* Vol. XVII, 1944–45, pp. 215 f. Marco Polo, *Il Milione,* cr. ed., p. 79 (M.P., p. 273), asserts that the Tartars, unlike the Chinese, wore beards.

Marco does not fail to confirm what we know indirectly from Oriental sources about the gout which afflicted the emperor for many years.[9] On the other hand, he keeps silent about the circumstance that undoubtedly aggravated if it did not provoke this illness, namely, the constant drinking both in public and in private which kept Kublai in a continuous state of alcoholic inebriation. It was a national vice of the Mongols. Chinghiz Khan, the dynasty's founder and legislator, had attempted to curb its excesses; but Ogudai, his son and successor, and a world-conqueror too, came at last to delirium tremens, and Chinghiz' grandson Mangu, Kublai's brother, led a life *inter pocula,* as Friar William of Rubruck asserts.[10]

Nevertheless, whereas this alert Franciscan—who hated and despised the Oriental world and its barbaric customs—described at length the overindulgence in fermented drinks and the important part they played in court ceremonial, as well as their effects on the emperor's health and character, Marco makes no mention of this though he must have been aware of the abuses. He obviously did not wish to sully his sovereign's image by recording an unworthy trait, and restricted his description to an account of the solemn libations that took place at court and the complicated apparatus, "finely worked and with beautiful gilt animal carvings," which was used for serving the various fermented drinks in accordance with the Mongol custom that Kublai had introduced into Chinghizide China.[11]

On the other hand, our Venetian delves more deeply than any other contemporary author into the secrets of his hero's love-life, which is described with such obvious delight and expertness as to fill his readers with wonder and amazement, perhaps envy, and certainly boundless admiration for the amatory exploits of that court and the ingenious steps taken to assure a constant supply for the imperial harem. Whereas Marco merely confirms the fact that the Great Kaan had four wives, with the title and rank of

[9] See chap. x, below.

[10] For this national vice, which had already been noted by Friar John of Pian del Càrpine (cf. *Sin. Franc.,* Vol. I, pp. 119), see the present author's *Guillaume Boucher,* esp. pp. 58 ff.

[11] For the history of this appliance, described in the *Milione* (cr. ed., p. 80; M.P., p. 218), cf. *Guillaume Boucher, loc. cit.*

empress and a befitting attendant retinue, it is only from him that we learn—moreover, with an unusual wealth of detail— how Kublai chose his many concubines, who by turns, six for each successive period of three days and nights, attended his every desire, and for whom noble suitors were found once they had satisfied their lord.[12]

This is undoubtedly one of the most popular chapters in the *Milione,* and there is consequently no need for us to summarize the entertaining details of this complex amatorial bureaucracy. We may, however, note the preference that Marco attributes to Kublai (among the infinite number of women who thronged his court) for maidens from the province which he calls "Ungrat" from the name of the Mongol or Turkish tribe of the Onggirat which corresponds to it.[13] This preference is supposed to have been justified by the circumstance that the women there "are most fair and beautiful"; but likelier there was a misunderstanding on the part of our author. He probably credited these innumerable concubines with the tribesmen's traditional, and far more exalted, privilege of offering their lawful wives to the leading members of the dynasty. The sons of such unions were destined either for the imperial succession or for high office in the government of their respective dominions.[14] Hence, we see that the system for the recruitment of concubines that is so minutely

[12] *Il Milione,* cr. ed., p. 72 (with the addition, in a footnote, of the evidently authentic details contained in the Ramusian version); M.P., p. 205.

[13] For this tribe and its privileges cf. the leading commentaries, especially that by A. J. H. Charignon, Vol. II, pp. 38 f., who summarizes and integrates the others cited by him; also, B. Ya. Vladimirtsov, *The Life of Chingis-Khan,* pp. 11 f., and L. Hambis's edition of *La Description du Monde,* p. 387.

[14] Marco Polo has given us various examples of these Mongol traditions, which made it possible for the members of the Chinghizide dynasty to practice endogamy as well as exogamy. In fact, Marco authentically relates that Queen Bolgana, wife of Arghun, the Mongol king of Persia, decreed in her will that only a lady of her lineage (Princess "Cocachin," as it came to pass) might succeed her as spouse to Arghun (cf. *Il Milione,* cr. ed., p. 11; M.P., p. 88). Similarly, it was a traditional custom of the Christian dynasty that ruled over the territory of Tenduc that its sovereign should marry one of the daughters or near female relatives of the Great Kaan (cr. ed., p. 60; M.P., p. 182). Thus, when Chinghiz Khan chose one of the women of the Onggirat tribe as his wife, his descendants followed his example. It is therefore hardly likely that those sovereigns would also have limited the choice of their numberless concubines to this same tribe. The *Secret History of the Mongols,* ed. Haenisch and Pelliot, sec. 64, reports that beautiful girls of the Onggirat were trained to occupy places near the sovereign on an elevated seat. The scrutiny and selection of these belles took place in the country of their origin.

described by Marco should be extended to include the whole empire. The candidates for such privileges were examined by specially appointed experts, and were later submitted to closer scrutiny if they won the emperor's preliminary approval. This ancient
custom proves, moreover, the reliability of Marco's account and
his knowledge of characteristic Oriental traditions.

All these secrets of the imperial bedchamber in no way reduced
Kublai's moral stature in the estimate that Marco had formed
of his character, which quite befitted the historical figure depicted
by him. Our author's more or less ingenuous tendency to idealize
and magnify his hero is immediately evident in his assertion that
the emperor had obtained his throne by reason of his moral
qualities and manly virtues: valor, skill, and shrewdness. The
last (if, with good reason, we accept the Ramusian version of
the text) was especially evident in his military stratagems, which,
according to Marco, proved him the wisest and most adventurous
commander the Tartars had ever had.[15]

When we take into account the repeated defeats suffered in
his attempted invasions of Japan, and his precarious military
undertakings in Indochina and Burma, this evaluation appears
somewhat excessive, especially if measured by the memory of
the military genius of his grandfather, Chinghiz Khan, or his
uncles, Ogudai and Batu. Moreover, Kublai owed his great victories to some of his generals, outstanding among whom were
the great Bayan (*Pai-yen*), the conqueror of southern China, and
the heroic and able Sögätü (*So-tu* in Chinese), who was responsible for whatever success was obtained by the Mongol armies,
from 1283 onward, in the jungles of Champa and Tonkin.[16]
Kublai's own military victories were achieved rather toward the
outset of his career, and Marco must have been aware of this,
since the eulogy of his lord's military genius is followed by mention of the latter's brothers and relatives who, after the death of
Mangu Kaan, his brother and predecessor, in 1259, contested his
power for many years to come.[17]

On that occasion his cunning, mentioned by Marco, revealed

---

[15] *Il Milione,* cr. ed., p. 66; M.P., p. 193.
[16] For these episodes and persons see above, chap. viii.
[17] *Il Milione,* cr. ed., p. 66; M.P., pp. 193.

FIG. 6. *Kublai Kaan in full vigor; from a portrait in the Imperial Palace, Peking.*

FIG. 7. *The ageing Kublai Kaan; from a portrait in the Imperial Palace, Peking.*

itself in his contrived election to the imperial throne by his generals, on June 4, 1260, in Chinese territory, while his brother Aric Buga (Ariq-bögä) proclaimed himself Great Kaan of all the Tartars in the old Mongol capital of Karakorum.[18] Kublai's power was in fact due to a military *coup d'état*. Marco knew this and illustrated its consequences, revealing among other things that Kublai's brothers and other kin never ceased from contesting his right to the throne he had illegally seized in defiance of the national dynastic constitution set up by their grandfather, which required the whole family to participate in the election of its head.[19] Hence, our Venetian, who is at all times his sovereign's loyal servant, is not quite in good faith when he asserts that "the suzerainty came to him by right."[20] The consequences of this violation are revealed by Marco himself in his account of the dynastic and civil wars that were a direct and inevitable result. Marco was likewise aware of the resentment harbored by the Chinese peoples because their traditional national régime—which was composed of, and administered by, literati—was supplanted by an organization of Mongol soldiers, who, as Marco tells us, were captained by the numerous sons of Kublai and foreign officials who collaborated with the oppressor to the detriment of the ancient native civilization.[21]

Marco has given us a noteworthy and correct description of this military organization, which was headed by Kublai himself.[22] The personal data that concern his hero, however, are at times and for no apparent reason inaccurate; as for example, when he insists that Kublai was the sixth, instead of the fifth, Great Kaan in succession to Chinghiz, his grandfather, and that he attained

[18] For these events see O. Franke, *Geschichte des chinesischen Reiches*, Vol. IV, pp. 325 ff.; more concisely, R. Grousset, *l'Empire des steppes*, pp. 352 ff.

[19] As may be seen from the works cited in the preceding note, the constitution of the Chinghizide empire required the participation of all the princes of the dynasty in the election of their leader, in a diet called *ḳuriltai*. This assembly was hastily convoked by Kublai in May, 1260; but he admitted only those elements that were favorable to him, and thus his election was actually a *coup d'état*.

[20] The text reads: "Et sachiés que droitemont venoit a lui por raisonz la seignorie" (cr. ed., p. 66, cf. M.P., p. 193), whereby we should understand that Kublai certainly had a right to the election, but not in the way in which he contrived it.

[21] *Il Milione*, cr. ed., p. 73; M.P., pp. 206 f.

[22] For the military organization of the empire see *Il Milione*, ed., pp. 93 f., chap. xcviii; M.P., pp. 241 ff.

this dignity in the year 1256, whereas his accession was in fact proclaimed some four years later, after he had administered the Chinese appanage of the Chinghizide empire as the vassal of his brother Mangu (Möngke).[23]

Kublai's moral portrait in the book is characterized by the same enthusiastic devotion that eliminated all trace of criticism from Marco's political judgment. He is, indeed, described as "the wisest and most gifted of men, the best captain, the best ruler of peoples and an empire, the man of greatest merit ever to have issued from the Tartar race"; [24] the panegyric tone and list of his virtues surpass anything to be found in the prologue to the biography of Kublai which is included in the Annals of the Empire.[25] The latter record does, however, reveal his intellectual qualities, which, it says, primarily consisted in his perspicacity and sure intuitive powers, to which were added the two specific qualities of the Chinese ethical code, benevolence (*jen*) and filial piety (*hsiao*).[26]

Marco ignores these cardinal principles of Confucian ethics, which Kublai exemplified both as a man and as a ruler, though more from natural inclination than from systematic philosophical

[23] *Il Milione,* cr. ed., pp. 53 and 66; M.P., pp. 173, 192. Kublai was elected Great Kaan of the Tartars in 1260, as has already been stated; however, it was only in 1280— after the capitulation of the Sung dynasty and empire in southern China—that he was proclaimed Emperor of China. Until that time he had ruled the "Khanate" of Cathay, which for centuries had been governed by Turkish-Mongol-Tungus dynasties, of which the Chinghizide rulers, beginning with Chinghiz Khan, were the continuators. The Sung, on the other hand, represented an ancient national dynasty, of which Kublai later became the legal successor. The Imperial Annals of China (cf. Moyriac de Mailla, *Histoire générale de la Chine,* Vol. IX, pp. 401 ff.) likewise consider the imperial rule of Kublai and his dynasty to have begun only in 1280, with the name of *Yüan.* Marco numbered Batu Khan, the first lord of the Golden Horde, among Chinghiz Khan's direct successors. Batu's power and prestige were such that he was considered to be the Great Kaan's equal, as may be seen from Mangu's statement on the subject to Friar William of Rubruck, when he asserted that "although there are two eyes in the head, they both see in the same way," thereby implying his co-sovereignty with Batu (cf. *Sin. Franc.* Vol. I, p. 299, § 5).

[24] *Il Milione,* cr. ed., p. 73; M.P., p. 207.

[25] The Chinese text (*Yüan Shih*) is more reserved in its praise of the emperor. It mentions his humanity and intelligence, his devotion to his mother, and his benign rule; but the personal qualities thus indicated were conventional in the representation of an ideal sovereign. The relevant page of this text is reproduced in our figure 9.

[26] This criterion is purely Confucian in origin and character. For a definition of these terms cf. Arthur Waley, *The Analects of Confucius,* London, 1938 (and subsequent editions), Introd., pp. 27 ff. and 38 ff.

training.[27] However, by describing him at work and listing the benefits he conferred upon his subjects, our Venetian shows us the way in which those virtues were realized in illustrious works of peace. As a result of the ruler's "truly great goodness," he would excuse from payment of tribute money a province that had been overtaken by some calamity, and would provide it with corn and cattle. He would likewise forego his tithe if a thunderbolt had struck a herd or flock, or a ship laden with merchandise, as a sign of divine anger.[28] Moreover, these humane feelings also inspired the Great Kaan to have trees planted along the roadsides of his empire, which served as landmarks and eased the lot of merchants and travelers.[29]

The construction of the Grand Canal of China—a truly colossal achievement—is also attributed to these judicious and humane sentiments. It made possible a constant and rapid flow of supplies to his capital. It completed, too, a system of canals that had existed for centuries in the central and southern provinces of his empire.[30] Moreover, whereas these were admittedly public works which enhanced his power and the security of the state, his bounty and wise government were evident, as Marco explains, in the amount of food and clothing bestowed by him upon the numerous honorable families that had been impoverished by misfortune.[31] Although Marco represented the storing of grain against possible famine as a wise act of government, he attributes this and other measures on behalf of the poor to his sovereign's "charity." This Christian concept is used by him to designate a virtue taught by

[27] It would seem that it was somewhat late in life that Kublai became acquainted with the principles of Confucian ethics; for, as we read in the Annals of the Empire (Moyriac de Mailla, Vol. IX, p. 314), they were expounded to him in 1270, or ten years after his election, by his Chinese counselor Lien Hi-hien, who taught him that the first precept insisted upon loyalty to one's sovereign and the second upon filial devotion to one's parents. The latter point, at least, does not appear to have made any great impression upon Kublai, who was then inclined to favor Lamaism.

[28] *Il Milione*, cr. ed., p. 97; M.P., pp. 247 f.

[29] Cr. ed., p. 98; M.P., p. 248.

[30] The Grand Canal linked Peking with Hangchow (Marco Polo's "Quinsai"), over a distance of some 1,100 miles. It was at Kublai's order that its northern section was completed, which connected it with the more ancient waterways that extended from the Yellow River to the China Sea. Cf., apart from the leading commentaries, D. Gandar, S.J., *Le Canal impérial*, Shanghai, 1898 (*Variétés Sinologiques*, no. 4).

[31] *Il Milione*, cr. ed., pp. 97 and 99; M.P., pp. 247 ff.

the principles of Confucian ethics, which offered examples from Chinese national history and thereby taught the rulers of the land to realize the Master's ideal within the sphere of political practice.[32]

It is unlikely that Kublai was in fact inspired by the memory of these historical precursors mentioned by Confucius, and it is certain that Marco was totally unacquainted with them. Instead, our author attributes the practice of this virtue on Kublai's part to the beneficial influence exterted by the "sages of the idolaters," who, according to him, taught the Tartars the precept of almsgiving, which had been unknown to them before their first contacts with "the idolatrous law." [33] In the relief of the poor, then, the emperor's charity was not regarded as a Christian virtue by Marco, although he knew that the Christian faith was represented at Kublai's court by a numerous Nestorian clergy. It is perhaps more readily to be ascribed to Buddhistic influence, which was more direct and active in the public and spiritual life of the China of his times.[34] However this may be, we learn that no one was ever denied alms at Kublai's court; so much so, that as many as thirty thousand bowls of rice and millet were distributed each day in the capital alone. Marco adduces this as evidence of his lord's compassion for his poor, who consequently adored him as a god.[35]

[32] The precept that adequate stocks of food should be provided for one's subjects had already been put into practice, according to Confucius (*Analecta*, Bk. IX, 1), by the mythical King Wu, who is often mentioned in the famous treatise. The Annals of the Empire (cf. Moyriac de Mailla, Vol. IX, p. 445) record a similar intervention by Kublai in 1260 on behalf of the populations stricken in the sense described by Marco. For measures taken by the government on occasions of public calamity in those times cf. P. Ratchnevsky, *Un code des Yuan*, pp. 212 ff.

[33] *Il Milione*, cr. ed., p. 99 (Ramusian text); M.P., p. 251. For Marco, these "sages of the idolaters" are especially the *bacsi* (cf. the *Milione, loc. cit.*), that is to say, chiefly the Tibetan lamas governed by their leader the famous Phags-pa, who was mentor of the empire in Kublai's times and is so recorded in the Annals of the Empire (Moyriac de Mailla, Vol. IX, pp. 310 ff., etc.). It should, however, be remembered that the *Secret History of the Mongols,* composed in 1240, attributes the same virtue to the Great Kaan Ogudai, Chinghiz Khan's son and successor, in the passage in which it lists the providential measures established by him for the relief of his poor and destitute subjects; cf. E. Haenisch, *Die geheime Geschichte der Mongolen,* sec. 279. We may therefore suppose that, in this matter, Kublai followed the traditions of his dynasty as well as the precepts of the various religions.

[34] The beneficial influence of Buddhism on the barbaric customs of the Mongols is emphasized by Marco, *Il Milione,* cr. ed., p. 100 n.; M.P., p. 251. The Confucian influence increased steadily after Kublai's death because of the cultural preponderance of the southern provinces of the former Sung empire over Cathay.

[35] *Ibid.*

What is particularly striking in this interesting chapter is the contrast between Tartar barbarity, which taught that the poor should be driven away as accursed by God, and Chinese civilization, which appears fused with its Buddhist and Christian counterparts as an ideal of humanity and wisdom. Marco's realism is therefore apparent even in the encomiastic picture he draws of his sovereign, who is the civilized representative of a barbaric dynasty. He never gives way to facile illusions and does not conceal the fact that those supplies which were due to Kublai's "great bounty" were ultimately charged to his subjects, who had to contribute their tithes in order to pay for the clothes given away to his paupers, while the guilds of the capital were obliged to work at their manufacture without pay one day a week.[36] Nor could Marco be unaware of the immense sacrifices imposed upon the Chinese people in order to produce the public works that he mentions and admires, though we find no hint in the *Milione* of the immense price paid in human lives and suffering.[37]

Our author thus makes a clear distinction between this more or less disinterested public charity and the munificence and liberality which by medieval standards were qualities indispensable to a ruler and were so represented not only in treatises describing the ideal prince but throughout the courtly and bourgeois literature of Europe, until the penetrating mind of Niccolò Machiavelli revealed the dangers and ill effects that could be expected to ensue.[38] In accordance with Machiavelli's teaching, rather than medieval ideals, Kublai exercised his liberality par-

[36] *Ibid.* Mention of the "guilds," and all this passage respecting Kublai's philanthropic actions, are to be found only in the Ramusian version. The reference to the trade associations, which represent one of the most characteristic aspects of Chinese life, is all the more valuable since the Chinese sources rarely mention them, partly because they played no political role whatever. For the organization and history of the guilds in the economic and social life of China cf. K. S. Latourette, *The Chinese: Their History and Culture,* third edition, New York, 1947, pp. 577 ff., with a bibliography of the subject on pp. 603 f., supplemented by H. Franke, *Sinologie,* Bern, 1952, pp. 147 ff.

[37] The construction of the Grand Canal in Kublai's times (and certainly earlier) was completed—like the Great Wall—by the use of forced labor, which had to be provided by the populations of the respective regions. Cf. O. Franke, *Geschichte des chinesischen Reiches,* Vol. IV, pp. 569 f.

[38] Cf. *The Prince,* chap. xvi. For the medieval conception of the ideal prince, as it appears in the criteria assumed by Marco Polo in his judgment of the sovereigns of Asia, cf. Wilhelm Berges, *Die Fürstenspiegel des hohen und späten Mittelalters,* Leipzig, 1938, and A. H. Gilbert, *Machiavelli's "Prince" and Its Forerunners,* Durham, N.C., 1938.

ticularly among military circles at court and in the empire; he thereby remained faithful to the fundamental structure and traditions of Tartar society, in which the Chinghizide army had developed as the leading element not only of conquest but of government as well.

The vigilance of twelve "barons," whose duty it was to notice the deserving, guided the sovereign in rewarding those captains and soldiers who distinguished themselves in military practice and affairs by promotion within the ranks of the immense imperial army, and by lavish gifts of "silver vases, fine armor, jewels and precious stones, horses," and other desirable objects.[39] Similarly, the emperor's generosity was especially extended toward the twelve thousand knights of his entourage, with whom he surrounded his person, not through fear, but—according to Marco—"in order to show his greatness." The splendor of the imperial munificence was displayed in the gorgeous vestments of silk and gold, adorned with pearls and other precious stones, which he bestowed upon them at least three times a year on special feast days celebrated by the court and the whole empire.[40] It should be remembered that with these lavish gifts of silken cloths and garments Kublai accepted and perpetuated a courtly custom of Chinese origin, namely, the bestowal of lengths of silk and richly embroidered vestments upon those who were to be honored or decorated. These textiles belonged to the category of precious tributes which the sovereign exacted from his vassals, and the latter from their subjects, necessitating an extraordinary and unceasing production of such materials in every part of the Asiatic continent.[41]

None of the Oriental sources that mention the subject offers so many details as does the *Milione* to illustrate Kublai's character.

[39] *Il Milione,* cr. ed., pp. 71 and 93 f.; M.P., pp. 203 and 241 f.

[40] Cr. ed., p. 78; M.P., pp. 216 f.

[41] Cr. ed., p. 82, chap lxxxvii; M.P., p. 221 f. We read here that these gifts were bestowed on no fewer than thirteen occasions during the year. However, both Pauthier and Yule (*The Book of Ser Marco Polo,* Vol. I, pp. 388 f., n. 3) read three instead of thirteen. This judicious interpretation would correspond to the great feasts of Kublai's court, only two of which are described by Marco: the emperor's birthday, which, according to Marco, occurred on the twenty-eighth day of the lunar cycle in the month of September (cf. *Il Milione,* cr. ed., p. 82; M.P., p. 221), and the celebration of the New Year, which was the principal Chinese feast. For the court ceremonial cf. the commentaries cited above and the present author's *Guillaume Boucher,* pp. 51 ff.

The Annals of the Empire (*Yüan Shih*), which were hastily composed in 1368 on the basis of official documents and authentic records, refer to the emperor's liberality, but they merely assert that he "treated his inferiors well," without ever describing his unparalleled munificence so realistically portrayed by Marco in a trustworthy yet spectacular manner.[42]

His description of the sovereign's person and his entourage also reveals that Kublai gave his attention almost exclusively to his military responsibilities and allowed a great deal of freedom to his ministers in their government of the country, with the result that they were at times overbearing, and were increasingly rapacious and tyrannical. It would seem, indeed, that he surrendered the entire financial management of the empire—the most difficult assignment in his vast administration—to the Mohammedan "Achmach," or Achmet, a native of Transoxiana. For a dozen years, from 1270 to 1282, this official directed an odious system of fiscal exortion which certainly served to replenish the imperial coffers, but also stocked his own purse, without Kublai's being aware of the general resentment and the conspiracy which at last erupted in the revolt that is minutely and conscientiously described by our author.[43]

Achmet was undoubtedly a financial genius, and a policy of unbridled exploitation was traditional among the Mongols as among other peoples in the Orient; hence we may well suppose that Kublai can have taken little interest in the methods by which his all-powerful minister succeeded in making him the wealthiest ruler in the world, whether by organizing a system of paper money with a forced rate of exchange, or by pursuing—together with his numerous sons and protégés—a policy of pressure and blackmail which, unknown to his sovereign, cost him his life in

[42] This passage is to be found in the prologue to Kublai's biography and contains a brief enumeration of his virtues.

[43] This famous episode in the *Milione* (cr. ed., pp. 78–80 n.; M.P., pp. 214–216) offers dramatic yet reliable details which help to supplement the account found in the Annals of the Empire (cf. Moyriac de Mailla, Vol. IX, pp. 315 ff., 320, 411 ff., etc.), which are quoted at length in the leading commentaries. The name of this notorious minister is given in the Ramusian version as *Achamac, Acmach,* or *Achmat,* whereas we find *Ahama* in the Annals, which is the Chinese form. Cf. H. Franke, "Aḥmed: ein Beitrag zur Wirtschaftsgeschichte Chinas unter Qubilai," *Oriens,* Vol. I, 1948, pp. 222 ff., and A. C. Moule, *Quinsai,* pp. 79 ff. The emperor's long absences from the capital helped to increase the sovereign power wielded by his ministers.

the way described in a famous chapter of the *Milione*.[44] According to Marco, he was one of the twelve ministers entrusted with the government of the empire; and we have already seen that the imperial administration was, in the main, in the hands of foreigners directly answerable to those of Kublai's sons who had been appointed governors of the various Chinese provinces.[45] Moreover, we read in the prologue to the account of Kublai's exploits contained in the Annals of the Empire that the Great Kaan himself invited to his court experts from every part of the world, in order to be advised of the systems of government most appropriate to the administration of his dominions.[46] Brief as it is, this passage explains the warm welcome extended by him to the Polos, the questions asked of them, and the tasks entrusted to Marco throughout his stay in China.[47]

The savage repression of the revolt against the misgovernment of his notorious minister, which overtook a large part of the Chinese aristocracy both in the capital and in the provinces, reveals how this same benign and liberal sovereign could become as violent and formidable as his predecessors in repressing actions likely to undermine the administrative and political unity of his empire. An attentive reader will discern in Marco's account some slight criticism of Kublai's attitude toward that "accursed Saracen," who had enjoyed such excessive liberty of action in spite of the fact—as we learn from the Annals of the Empire—that the emperor had been warned of this minister's unbridled ambitions

[44] See above, chap. vii, § 2. The episode is found in the Ramusian version.

[45] According to Marco (*Il Milione*, cr. ed., p. 73; M.P., p. 206), to Kublai's twenty-two sons by his four wives must be added twenty-five others, born of his concubines. The latter were all "great barons": some were kings or governors of provinces; others commanded detachments of the imperial army. Marco, *loc. cit.*, names Kublai's first-born, Ch'inkin (cf. Moyriac de Mailla, Vol. IX, pp. 424 f., who calls him Cinghis "in memory of the good Cinghis Can," and O. Franke, *Geschichte des chinesischen Reiches,* Vol. V, pp. 216 f.), who died prematurely in 1285 and was followed as heir to the throne by Timur, a wise and valiant prince, as Marco adds, who succeeded Kublai and reigned from 1294 to 1307 (cf. O. Franke, *op. cit.,* pp. 491 ff. and *passim*). Timur favored the first resident Catholic missionary in Peking, who became the city's first bishop in that period. Cf. *Sinica Franciscana,* Vol. I, Introd., p. xlix.

[46] This is affirmed in the prologue to the biography quoted in the preceding note, which is not included by Moyriac de Mailla, *op. cit.* He does, however, give the passages from the Annals which refer to the reform of astronomy and government institutions entrusted to foreigners—for the most part, Mohammedans from Persia and Central Asia (cf. his Vol. IX, pp. 407 ff.).

[47] Cf. the prologue to the *Milione,* cr. ed., p. 6; M.P., p. 77.

by one of his faithful counselors.[48] It is likewise possible to discover the sympathy felt by Marco for the Cathayans who rebelled against his misgovernment, which the Great Kaan was so mistaken as to tolerate while giving himself up to pleasure and thus neglecting important duties of his sovereign activity.[49] It is nevertheless to be noted that he finally proved himself a ferociously just ruler by having Achmet's dead body thrown to the dogs, his sons flayed alive who had adopted his methods, and by outlawing "the accursed sect of the Saracens." [50]

In the same indirect way, Marco reveals to us the passions that distracted Kublai from the cares of office. These were, above all, feasting and hunting. Both the banquet and the chase were state affairs of the utmost importance—like everything else that concerned the person and private life of the Great Kaan. His women were influential in the court life and dynastic government; but their influence was exerted in secret and little is known about it, whereas the feasts and hunts were spectacular events, regulated according to the calendar and the elaborate ceremonial of a vast court. Marco, moreover, was able to take an active part in these festivities and to offer us a unique and accurate account of them.

In these two leading public manifestations of his personality Kublai showed himself, to the end of his life, to be still attached to the Mongol traditions of his dynasty rather than to the Chinese customs which he had in part adopted for reasons of state and for the effect upon his immediate and numerous subjects. In such spectacular circumstances, wherein the barbaric grandeur of the Mongol assumes gigantic proportions in contrast to the more intimate solemnity of the Chinese courts, Marco reveals his sovereign's magnificence and the fabulous riches that made possible and justified its recurring and impressive display. Our Venetian was dazzled and overwhelmed by all this adornment to the sovereign virtues which Kublai impersonated—to become, as Marco defines him, the richest, most powerful, and most just lord in history and in the contemporary world.

[48] Cf. Moyriac de Mailla, Vol. IX, pp. 315 f., and Moule, *Quinsai*, pp. 79 ff.
[49] *Il Milione*, cr. ed., pp. 78 f.; M.P., p. 216.
[50] For this measure see above, chap. vii, § 2. Kublai had the forty wives of this notorious minister put to death because the latter had purloined a precious jewel destined for the emperor. Cf. Moule, *Quinsai*, p. 80.

ten

ASIATIC MEDICINE IN
MARCO POLO'S BOOK

Although medicine played an important role in medieval civilization both in the West and in the Orient, Marco Polo has contributed little to the knowledge of its various theories and practices. He was not without interest in this discipline, and was directly acquainted with the forms it assumed in the various regions of Asia where it was professionally or empirically practiced by physicians, witch doctors, and adventurous impostors; but what he has to say about it is somewhat vague and disconnected, and it is obvious that his interest is aroused rather by the artifices of occult and popular medicine than by the scientific traditions and speculative methods that were fundamental to the civilizations of Persia, China, and India.[1]

However, in the course of his extensive travels through these vast regions of the continent, in which a system of medical tradi-

A preliminary essay on this subject was published by the present author in the Third Supplement to the *Bulletin of the History of Medicine*, Baltimore, Johns Hopkins Press, 1944, pp. 237–259.

[1] The most recent works on these three branches of Asiatic medicine are: Cyril Elgood, *A Medical History of Persia*, Cambridge, 1951; K. Chimin Wong and Wu Lienteh, *History of Chinese Medicine*, Tientsin, 1932 (insufficient for medieval medicine); Heinrich Zimmer, *Hindu Medicine*, Baltimore, 1949; and Jean Filliozat, *La Doctrine classique de la médicine indienne*, Paris, 1949. They offer extensive bibliographies, which may be complemented by consulting G. Sarton, *Introduction to the History of Science*, Vols. I and II, Baltimore, 1927–1931. For the medical practices of the Mongols cf., besides H. H. Howorth, *History of the Mongols*, Vol. IV, 1921, the article by F. W. Cleaves, "A Medical Practice of the Mongols in the 13th Century," *Harvard Journal of Asiatic Studies*, Vol. XVII, 1954, pp. 428 ff. For medicine in Tibet cf. Cyrill von Krasinski, *Tibetische Medizinphilosophie*, Zürich, 1953, with full bibliography. For the most recent literature on Chinese medicine cf. H. Franke, *Sinologie*, Bern, 1953, p. 196.

tions and teachings existed side by side with the superstitious practices of the shamans and soothsayers, Marco Polo was incidentally able to observe some typical and curious aspects, and his remarks deserve notice both as a contribution to our knowledge of medieval Asiatic medicine and as an expression of our author's versatile curiosity. Though he says little on the subject, it is nevertheless immediately apparent that Marco was quite capable of distinguishing between the exorcisms of quacks and the practices of physicians who had undergone a special training in their art—an evidence of his sagacity inasmuch as it was difficult to make out what was mere superstition in their healing procedures and what belonged to the learned and systematic tradition of this discipline.[2] In his description of the court of the Great Kaan Kublai, Marco distinguishes among the infinite number of dignitaries and officials the simple practitioners, whom his scribe calls "mires" and differentiates from the theoretical and speculative "astroliques."[3] Similarly, on other occasions, he recognized the particular kinds of divination that were practiced for therapeutic purposes by the professionals of every land.

Like all Asiatic rulers, Kublai was surrounded by a host of these astrologers and physicians, who complemented one another in predicting ailments, as Marco tells us, while others were supposed to cure them.[4] Their principal patient was Kublai himself, "since he was afflicted by gout";[5] and Marco tells us how his sovereign protected himself, when traveling, against the inclemency of the seasons which brought on his attacks.[6] We know from other sources that all remedies proved of little avail, and

[2] The difficulty is still present. For the problem as affecting Western medicine in the Middle Ages cf. Lynn Thorndike, *A History of Magic and Experimental Science,* Vol. II, New York, 1923.

[3] *Il Milione,* cr. ed., pp. 45, 85, 100 n., etc.; M.P., pp. 153, 223, 252, etc. The distinction between *astroniques* and *astroliques* is not clear and perhaps there is no substantial difference between the two, whereas the term *mire* for physician is very common in French vernacular literature of the Middle Ages. Cf. W. Meyer-Lübke, *Romanisches etymologisches Wörterbuch,* third edition, Heidelberg, 1930–1935, s.v. "mire."

[4] Cf. the prediction of Kublai's longevity in the *Milione,* cr. ed., p. 98 n., M.P., p. 249; of the death of sick persons, cr. ed., pp. 119 and 120 n., 173 and n., M.P., pp. 284, 375; and of other events, cr. ed., p. 150 and n., M.P., p. 336.

[5] *Il Milione,* cr. ed., p. 100 n.; M.P., p. 254.

[6] *Loc. cit.* Kublai was carried in a portable wooden shelter, borne by four elephants, which was lined with cloth of gold and covered with lionskins, protecting him against the weather.

that as late as 1292, two years before his death and just before the
Polos' return to Venice, a group of shamans and sorcerers was
sent to Kublai's court by the king of Korea, to cure the old emperor's gout. But Kublai burst out laughing as soon as they began
to practice their exorcisms.[7] Although this anecdote demonstrates
the skepticism he felt for those practices, the fact remains that the
medical organization at his court had assumed gigantic proportions, and that a swarm of Christian, Saracen, and Cathayan
astrologers and soothsayers watched over and governed the life
and destiny of the whole empire.[8]

This system accorded with the courtly Chinese, Mongol, and
Persian traditions that had been observed in the Chinghizide
courts since the founding of the dynasty, which encouraged the
practice of medicine after the respective customs of all the sects.[9]
Under Mangu Kaan, great favor and popularity were enjoyed
at Karakorum by Chinese physicians, whom Friar William of
Rubruck correctly distinguished from the Mongol soothsayers,
Tibetan sorcerers, and certain types of charlatans. He noted their
science of herbal therapy and their skill in diagnosis from taking
a patient's pulse, although he added that they were not so expert
"in urinalibus." [10]

Kublai, on the other hand, does not seem to have had so much
faith in Chinese physicians. He had good reason to be suspicious

---

[7] This anecdote is narrated in a contemporary Korean chronicle quoted by Yule-
Cordier, *The Book of Ser Marco Polo*, Vol. I, p. 408, n. 5. Kublai had been in the
habit of mitigating his attacks of gout by covering his stricken joints with pelts which
were gifts or tributes from his vassals.

[8] *Il Milione*, cr. ed., p. 100 n.; M.P., p. 254, where it is expressly stated that these
five thousand astrologers had the task of predicting illnesses in accordance with the
practices of their respective sects and nations. It should, moreover, be remembered that
the medical practices of the shamans were exercised by the clergy of each religion, to
which every shaman was free to belong since shamanism is a form of magic rather
than a religion. Cf. N. Pallisen, "Die alte Religion der Mongolen und der Kultus
Tschingis Khans," *Numen*, Vol. III, 1956, pp. 178 ff.

[9] For these Chinese traditions cf. the somewhat summary information in Wong and
Wu, *History of Chinese Medicine*, Bk. I, and in P. Huard and M. Wong, *Évolution de
la matière médicale chinoise*, Leiden, 1958; also, H. Franke, *Sinologie*, pp. 196 ff.

[10] Cf. *Sinica Franciscana*, ed. P. A. van den Wyngaert, Quaracchi, 1929, Vol. I, p.
236, and W. W. Rockhill, *The Journey of William of Rubruck*, London, 1900, p. 156
and relevant notes. For Chinese theory and practice of taking the pulse cf. Wong and
Wu, *op. cit.*, pp. 39 ff.; and for the friar's mistaken assertion regarding Chinese urinology
cf. Rockhill's assertions, *loc. cit.* The subject is not mentioned by Wong and Wu; this
would seem to justify Friar William's assertion.

of these Cathayans, as Marco calls them, on account of the aversion felt for his régime by the intellectuals of the land and the decadence of the Taoist clergy, who specialized in the theory and practice of medical alchemy.[11] It is therefore no wonder that Kublai appointed as head of the *Kuang-hui-ssu,* or medical superintendence of the empire, a physician from western Asia. He may have been a Nestorian, Jew, or Mohammedan—which we know not; but we do know that he had been an astrologer and physician of Küyük Kaan at Karakorum, and in Marco's times had become one of the most powerful and brilliant officials in the Mongol-Chinese administration.[12] This is indicative of the emperor's hesitation at confiding in his physicians and astrologers as if all their various pretensions were valid and trustworthy. All were no doubt esteemed for their wisdom; nevertheless, they were politically suspect and were kept under constant supervision.[13] Through them, however, the medicine of the West gained, as it were, official acceptance in the life of the Far East alongside the respective national traditions, as Marco pointed out; for they helped to extend to those distant regions the medical teachings of Hippocrates and Galen, which had been elaborated by the Mohammedans of Persia, the Christians of Syria, and Jewish sages in both the West and the Orient.[14]

Our Venetian was probably ignorant of the course of these scien-

[11] For this subject cf. Arthur Waley's Introduction to his edition of Ch'ang Ch'un, *The Travels of an Alchemist,* London, 1931, while bearing in mind that Kublai had greatly restricted the activities of the Taoists in favor of Lamaist Buddhism and its magic medicine. Cf. Wong and Wu, *op. cit.,* pp. 48 ff.

[12] This was the famous Ai-hsieh or Isaac, who is considered to have been a Nestorian by such authorities as A. C. Moule, *Christians in China,* London, 1930, pp. 228 ff., and P. Y. Saeki, *The Nestorian Documents and Relics in China,* second edition, Tokyo, 1951, pp. 508 ff., whereas this same Ai-hsieh at times appears as a Mohammedan in Chinese documents (Moule, *op. cit.,* p. 230). The name Isaac could, however, indicate one of the Jewish physicians who then practiced their art in all the courts of the Old World.

[13] The reasons for suspicion were political, as Marco noted of the Cathayans (cf. *Il Milione,* cr. ed., pp. 67 n., 149 n.; M.P., pp. 194 f.), or else were a result of the rivalries among the various schools and sects, as has been pointed out in chap. vi above.

[14] The influence of Greco-Arabic medicine on its Chinese counterpart has not yet been systematically studied, and it remains a most difficult and complex subject. The influence, however, must be admitted when one bears in mind the remarks of Abulfaraj, toward the end of the Xth century, concerning a Chinese scholar who translated the sixteen treatises of Galen into his native tongue (cf. G. Ferrand, *Relations de Voyages et textes géographiques arabes, persans et turcs relatifs à l'Extrême-Orient,* 2 vols., Paris, 1913–1914, Vol. I, pp. 135).

tific exchanges, which are problematic even to modern researchers. He did, however, observe that the national center of Chinese medical science was then situated in the city of Soochow (in Kiangsu), which he calls "Suju" and which he admired for its "great natural philosophers and great doctors, who have penetrated far into the secrets of nature." [15] This allusion indicates that, in spite of differences in theory and application, Chinese medicine was just as closely connected with philosophy and the natural sciences as was its counterpart in Greco-Arab tradition, which was practiced throughout Europe and, as we have seen, also in Marco Polo's Asia through Jewish and Mohammedan intermediaries.[16]

The vague yet correct idea he had formed of Oriental medicine as typically resorting to magical and superstitious practices—universally favored in his times, and even today—gives him a measure wherewith to judge the degree of civilization enjoyed by the peoples whose remedial agencies he was able to observe. Thus, for example, when mentioning the savage tribes of Yunnan, he asserts that they did not have any doctors, but went rather to the sorcerers who exorcized devils and guarded their idols.[17] Marco offers a detailed description of their practices, which certainly bore no resemblance to medical science, but were essentially spells and exorcisms.[18] Indeed, his data—which were intended to arouse feelings of horrified interest in his contemporary readers —indicate quite clearly that these peoples were in a state of barbarism markedly contrasting with the refined Chinese civilization which had not yet succeeded in imposing itself in these remote regions.

[15] *Il Milione*, cr. ed., p. 142, chap clii; M.P., p. 325. Marco's indication of the number and excellence of the physicians in this city calls for a special study of the relevant Chinese sources, far more extensive than any offered by the leading commentaries to this interesting passage.

[16] This relationship between philosophy and medicine in Chinese tradition is summarily mentioned by Wong and Wu, *op. cit.*, pp. 48 ff., and justified Marco's statements on the subject. Thus, e.g., Chinese Buddhist pilgrims—and especially their most outstanding representative, Hsüan Tsang (VIIth century)—never lost sight of the benefits to physical health that could be derived from a study of medicinal plants and properties. This is confirmed by the texts collected by S. Beal, *Si-yu-ki: Buddhist Records of the Western World*, 2 vols., London, 1906.

[17] *Il Milione*, cr. ed., p. 119; M.P., p. 284.

[18] The fullest and most recent study on those regions and their customs is J. F. Rock, *The Ancient Na-khi Kingdom of Southwest China*, 2 vols., Cambridge, Mass., 1947.

By these more or less explicit judgments Marco confirms and observes the distinction, current since ancient times, which both in regulatory legislation and in the exercise of professional practice clearly separated the popular and superstitious medicine from the legitimate and officially recognized science.[19] Thus, only approved physicians were permitted to gather and make use of herbs for therapeutic purposes, and to practice their art as a professional service. As we have seen, a special branch of the imperial administration was at that time charged with the control of public health, and doubtless it supervised the various institutions that Marco mentions in his book, such as the "infinite number of hospitals" in the ancient capital of Quinsai, which had been set up by the kings of former times and had large incomes;[20] or "the hot baths" in this same city, which numbered thirty thousand, according to Marco, and were the finest and the best in the world.[21]

So, too, in the more recent capital of Khanbaliq—modern Peking—the measures taken to safeguard public health included a ban on the celebrating of funeral rites within the walls of the city, and limited prostitution to special districts or suburbs of the town.[22] The efficacy of these measures and others not mentioned by Marco must have been considerable, since he never refers to epidemics—which in every period of history have raged throughout the continent. We therefore find no mention of those recurrent plagues which, especially in China and India, decimated the populations, and often were sequels to famines, floods, and other calamities duly recorded in the annals of the various dynasties.[23] Our author may perhaps have chosen purposely to omit mention of these disasters, bent as he was upon showing his readers the most attractive side of Asiatic life and especially of the countries

[19] Cf. Wong and Wu, *op. cit.*, pp. 6 ff., 49, 61, etc., and the bibliography on pp. 647 ff.

[20] *Il Milione*, cr. ed., p. 148 n.; M.P., p. 333. This is confirmed by the descriptions of ancient Chinese hospitals to be found in Wong and Wu, *op. cit.*, p. 28, and A. C. Moule, *Quinsai, and other Notes on Marco Polo*, pp. 42 ff.

[21] *Il Milione, loc. cit.* Marco also observes (cr. ed., p. 145; M.P., p. 328) that the Chinese made extensive use of cold-water public baths, "which they declare to be excellent for health." See below, n. 62.

[22] This latter provision was an ancient one (cf. Wong and Wu, *op. cit.*, p. 28), whereas the former may also have been brought about by the Chinghizide rulers' desire to banish all thought of death from their immediate vicinity, as is attested by William of Rubruck with respect to Mangu Khan (cf. *Sin. Franc.*, Vol. I, p. 279).

[23] For cholera, smallpox, and other epidemics cf. Wong and Wu, *op. cit.*, pp. 106 ff.; for the plague, which was practically endemic in various regions of China, *ibid.*, pp. 350 ff.

subject to his sovereign. As we have already had occasion to remark, Marco is a true propagandist in this, though honestly
fascinated by his subject and harboring, we feel, no dark intentions of misleading his public with partial, encomiastic descriptions of the true situation.

It would in fact appear that in Kublai's times China suffered
less from these characteristic epidemics; and perhaps this was
owing to the preventive measures and supervision organized by
the government at the emperor's direct bidding. Our author,
moreover, tells us that the Great Kaan would regularly send
messengers into all his provinces, to make sure that "unfavorable
seasons, or locusts, or other calamities" had not ruined their crops,
which he would draw upon to feed his peoples in time of famine
and to distribute at seedtime.[24] For this purpose, he required
large stocks of every kind of grain to be amassed in all the
provinces, where they were kept in store against times of famine
and their consequences to public health.[25]

Marco but rarely mentions the healing methods practiced by
professional physicians, or specific cases of illness. Thus, for example, it is impossible for us to learn the nature of the illness or
illnesses that struck down the six hundred persons on board the
Chinese ships which brought the three Venetians accompanying
Princess "Cocachin" from China to Persia and cruelly reduced
their numbers in the two years of sailing tropical seas.[26] Marco,
whose strong constitution preserved him, kept silent about the
causes and circumstances of the deaths, which we may hypothetically attribute to the climate, or to scurvy or other disease characteristic of those regions and of long sea voyages.

His silence does not, however, imply indifference; for at the
time of his stay of some five months on the island of Sumatra, on
this same voyage, Marco noted that its inhabitants extracted from
a tree a potion which possessed such extraordinary qualities that
it was used to cure dropsy, consumption, and splenitis.[27] He was
much impressed, and described this small palm at length, as well

---

[24] *Il Milione,* cr. ed., p. 97, chap. c; M.P., p. 248.

[25] Cr. ed., p. 99, chap. civ; M.P., p. 250.

[26] Cf. the prologue to the Milione, p. 12 n.; M.P., p. 91. The relevant—and extremely
laconic—data are found only in the Ramusian text.

[27] *Il Milione,* cr. ed., p. 72 n.; M.P., p. 374.

FIG. 8. *Mangu (Möngke) Kaan and his court; from a miniature in the Parisian MS (Supplément persan 1113, Bibliothèque Nationale) of Rashid-uddin's* Jami-el-Tévarikh. *The ladies wear the* bochta, *or ceremonial headgear; see note 23 to chapter iii, page 106 above.*

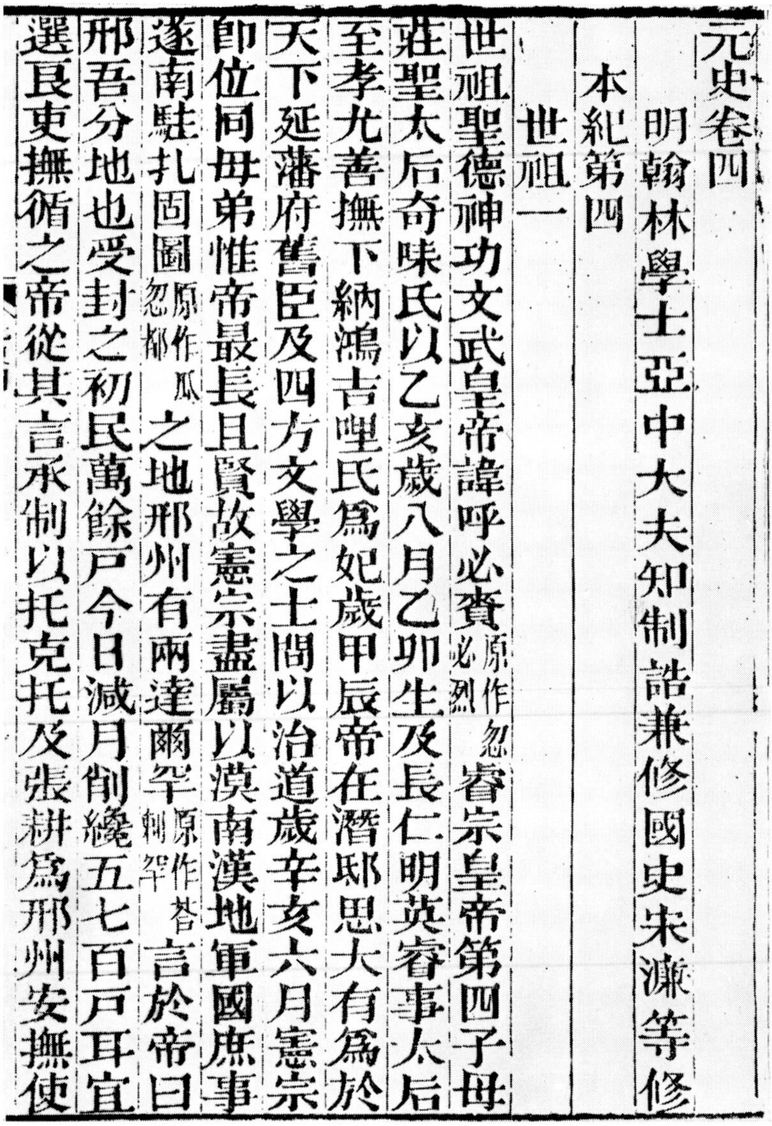

世祖聖德神功文武皇帝諱必烈（必賫原作忽必烈），睿宗皇帝第四子。母莊聖太后奇渥溫氏，以乙亥歲八月乙卯生。及長，仁明英睿，事太后至孝，尤善撫下。納弘吉剌氏為妃。歲甲辰，帝在潛邸，思大有為於天下。延藩府舊臣及四方文學之士，問以治道。歲辛亥六月，憲宗即位，同母弟惟帝最長且賢，故憲宗盡屬以漠南漢地軍國庶事，遂南駐爝（忽都，原作瓜）之地。邢州有兩達魯（罕，原作罕），言於帝曰：邢吾分地也，受封之初，民萬餘戶，今日減月削，纔五七百戶耳，宜選良吏撫循之。帝從其言，承制以脫兀脫及張耕為邢州安撫使…

本紀第四

世祖一

明翰林學士亞中大夫知制誥兼修國史宋濂等修

元史卷四

FIG. 9. *Eulogy of Kublai Kaan in the prologue to his biography in the Annals of the Yüan dynasty (Yüan Shih), 1368.*

as the method employed to draw off its miraculous liquid.[28] The palm "wine" probably possessed exhilarating qualities similar to those of the palm sugar prepared by the people of "Coilum" (Quilon) in southern India, a place renowned for its physicians, as Marco observes.[29]

He noted also the custom of curing quartan fever, which was probably endemic to those places, by using some earth from the legendary tomb of St. Thomas the Apostle, which was venerated at Mailapur, near Madras.[30] Not far from here, in the "noble city of Cail," he observed a characteristic Indian custom which according to him was "very good for the health." It consisted in chewing a leaf called *tembul* (Persian for 'betel') or *tambur,* specially prepared for the nobles and rulers of the land by mixing with it some lime (in a palatable form) or camphor and other spices.[31] The mixture excited a flow of saliva, which was spat upon the ground.[32] Marco was convinced of the salutary effects of this custom, which he calls "a vice indulged in with delight" by the noblemen of the land, even as he ascribed the excellence of the Brahmans' teeth to their habit of chewing betel.[33]

If he had been a systematic observer of medical practice in the Orient, Marco would have noticed in these regions not only the characteristic manifestations of different provinces, castes, and tribes, but also the substantial difference in diagnostic and curative methods followed in the Mohammedan and the Hindu circles of Greater India; namely, between the former's scientific, speculative medicine, which was connected with Greco-Arab traditions, and the latter's empirical system, based on native and national beliefs, ancient superstitions, the use of medicinal herbs, and a therapeutic alchemy that was essentially magical and doctrinal.[34]

[28] Marco's data were sufficient to permit identification of this plant as the gomuti palm (*Arenga saccharifera*) by Yule-Cordier, *The Book of Ser Marco Polo,* Vol. II, p. 297 n. 3.

[29] *Il Milione,* cr. ed., p. 197; M.P., p. 415.

[30] Cr. ed., p. 187; M.P., p. 398. It was apparently used to make up a potion.

[31] Cr. ed., p. 196; M.P., p. 413.

[32] Also as a sign of contempt, as Marco adds, which provoked duels. Yule (*op. cit.,* Vol. II, p. 374 n. 5) had doubted the authenticity of this passage, which is now confirmed by the Z version (cf. cr. ed., p. 196 n.).

[33] *Il Milione,* cr. ed., p. 190; M. P. p. 403.

[34] Cf. Zimmer, *Hindu Medicine,* with bibliographical introduction and various texts

The Indian system, or so-called "ayurvedic," is similar in its speculative basis and metaphysical, naturalistic, and demonological tendencies to its Chinese counterpart, with which it shares the conception of medicine as the science of longevity; so much so, that this characteristic aim of Chinese Taoist medicine, from the VIIth century onward, benefited from Indian teaching and experience, which were systematically and fully described in the travel reports compiled by the Chinese Buddhistic missionaries who visited this country by land and sea.[35] Marco was likewise struck by the legendary longevity attained by the Brahmans, who, according to him, "are the people that live longest in the world." [36] This was an idea that had been spread abroad everywhere by the legend of Alexander the Great, which allotted a life span of a hundred and fifty years to the members of that sect "because of the mild climate and the will of God." [37]

Our traveler did not adduce a reason for their supposed privilege of long life in these climatic and metaphysical circumstances, still less for the efficacy of their magical practices and use of medicinal herbs or alchemical preparations, but chose rather to ascribe the Brahmans' longevity quite simply to their habits of abstinence and sobriety, mentioning also that certain herb which helped their digestion, kept their bodies healthy, and gave them excellent teeth.[38] According to Marco, the Yogis of India, who were "perfidious and cruel idolaters," were distinguished from the Brahmans by the fact that they lived to be a hundred and fifty, even two hundred, years old by using as an elixir assuring long life a certain potion which they made up of sulphur and mercury and took twice a month from their earliest years.[39]

Against the legendary background of longevity attributed to

---

translated into English, and Filliozat, *La Doctrine classique de la médicine indienne,* as cited in n. 1 above.

[35] For Taoist and Buddhist medicine cf. Wong and Wu, *op. cit.,* pp. 48 ff.; and for the travel reports, S. Beal, *Si-yu-ki, passim.*

[36] *Il Milione,* cr. ed., p. 190; M.P., p. 403.

[37] *Commonitorium Palladii,* in F. Pfister, *Kleine Texte zum Alexanderroman,* Heidelberg, 1910, p. 2, and *Dindimi de Vita Bragmanorum, ibid.,* pp. 7 ff. These two texts were incorporated in the Romance of Alexander by the Pseudo-Callisthenes, whose universal popularity has already been discussed in chap. i of the present work.

[38] *Il Milione, loc. cit.*

[39] *Il Milione,* cr. ed., p. 191; M.P., p. 404.

this Indian sect by Hellenistic tradition, Marco does, however, reveal the two methods actually practiced by Oriental medicine in order to prolong man's life and obtain other salutary effects. The one made use of special herbs, the virtues of which were discovered and assessed by continual experiment and complex naturalistic speculation. The other made a similar use of minerals, sulphur and mercury being chiefly used in various combinations with other elements. The whole was accompanied by a system of dietetic and astrological prescriptions that were designed to enhance the effects of such esoteric potions.[40]

Marco thereby seems to have discerned—however vaguely—some of the principal aspects of ayurvedic medical science, which was analogous to Chinese medicine and in certain respects to the empirical and magical manifestations of medieval alchemy in the West.[41] His remarks on the Brahmans are therefore all the more interesting because he adds that they do not practice phlebotomy or any other form of bloodletting.[42] This observation might seem to be contradicted by the fact that both the opening of a vein and the application of leeches are taught in the principal treatises of Indian medicine, though surgery had developed in the Orient as a special discipline, independently of medical science and the dietetic and macrobiotic systems in vogue.[43] But in fact phlebotomy was not employed in Indian medical practice and was therefore ignored in the leading medical treatises compiled by Brahman physicians, though they taught the other branches of this discipline.[44]

It is certainly noteworthy that Marco noted this particular aspect of Brahmanic medicine, even as he had seized upon the two

[40] Even today, sulphur and mercury are fundamental elements in Indian medicine; and dietetics is one of its main branches, as may be seen in the works of Zimmer and Filliozat cited above, as well as from the most nearly complete ancient Indian treatise on medicine to have been translated into a European language, i.e., *Vagbhata's Astāngahrdayasamhitā*, ed. L. Hilgenberg and W. Kirfel, Leiden, 1941.

[41] The latter are exemplified by Petrus de Abano in his *Conciliator*, which was completed in 1303. For its contents see Thorndike, *A History of Magic*, Vol. II, pp. 885 ff.

[42] *Il Milione*, cr. ed., p. 190; M.P., p. 403.

[43] Cf. J. Jolly, "Medicin," in *Grundriss der Indo-Arischen Philologie und Altertumskunde*, Vol. III, Pt. 10, Strassburg, 1901, pp. 30 ff. Similarly, in the medieval West, surgery was a practical art, independent of medical theory and speculation, and therefore considered inferior to the latter.

[44] Cf. the literature on the subject mentioned by Zimmer, *op. cit.*, pp. 194 ff.

main elements of ayurvedic pharmacology, namely, sulphur and mercury.[45] It should, moreover, be noted that the fame of the miraculous properties of these fundamental ingredients had spread throughout the continent of Asia and must have come to Marco's ears on another occasion, perhaps when he was last in Persia on his way home from China to Venice. King Arghun had died shortly before the Polos' arrival at his court, to which they had brought the Princess Cocachin, who, as we know, was intended to have been his bride;[46] and rumors were then circulating in the capital and elsewhere to the effect that this powerful Chinghizide sovereign had been the victim of a potion of sulphur and mercury administered to him by some Indian *bacsi* as an elixir to assure him of long life.[47] It is possible that the story was a mere fabrication on the part of rival physicians belonging to other schools who were influential at that court.[48] However this may be, it does confirm that the host of professional healers who thronged the capital included practitioners of Indian medicine, which Marco had already found represented at the court of Kublai.[49]

On various occasions he reveals his interest in establishing a relationship between dietetic methods and public health. However, in attributing the Brahmans' longevity to their practice of abstinence he renews the statements to be found in the fabulous letter of Dindimus to Alexander the Great, in which this régime is clearly specified.[50] On the other hand, he offers more direct and specific information about public health in the port of Hormuz on the Persian Gulf, an "unhealthy region," as he rightly remarks, whose inhabitants ate neither bread nor meat, but pre-

[45] Cf. Jolly, *op. cit.*, pp. 3, 5, etc., as well as Yule-Cordier's note, *The Book of Ser Marco Polo*, Vol. II, p. 369.

[46] Cf. the *Milione*, cr. ed., p. 12; M.P., p. 92. For the events cf. B. Spuler, *Die Mongolen in Iran*, pp. 81 ff., and Yule-Cordier, *The Book of Ser Marco Polo*, Vol. II, p. 369 n. 5.

[47] Cf. Elgood, *A Medical History of Persia*, pp. 309 ff.

[48] *Ibid.*; and for the practice of medicine there, pp. 302 ff.

[49] *Il Milione*, cr. ed., pp. 64, 65, 78 n.; M.P., pp. 188, 189, 213.

[50] "We require no other food than that which Mother Earth produces without any labor. We stock our tables with such fare, which does not harm us. Hence, we are not afflicted by any illness, and while we live we enjoy good health. Moreover, we do not make any medicine for ourselves," etc. Cf. *ed. cit.* (in n. 37 above), p. 11.

served their health by eating salt fish, dates, and onions.[51] The fact is attested by other sources and reveals climatic and sanitary precautions of a purely empirical sort which had nothing to do with the esoteric, speculative substratum of Indian and Chinese dietetic systems.[52] Moreover, we may suppose that Marco and his elderly companions were skilled in adapting themselves to these various circumstances, since they successfully bore with the most diverse climatic conditions and discomforts in remote lands.

Indeed, we know of only one illness suffered by our author in so many years of travel by land or by sea. It must have been quite serious, since he was obliged to remain an entire year in the region of Badakhshan in Central Asia, when he was crossing the continent in or about the year 1273.[53] He gives no hint of its nature, nor does he mention any medical treatment; he simply asserts that he recovered his health as a result of the pure air he breathed in those high mountains, on the salubrious plateau with its wealth of herbs, trees, and streams amid the rocks and precipices which he describes with obvious enthusiasm though always in the measured and slightly awkward forms typical of his style. He declares that two or three days on that plateau would suffice to cure tertian, quartan, or any other type of recurrent fever—thereby indicating that he himself had been afflicted by fever of some kind. It seems probable that he had an attack of malaria.

The experience must have made him sensitive to climatic variations and have led him to celebrate the temperate climate of Kashmir, doubtless already famous in those times since Marco mentions it without ever having visited the region.[54] He refers also to the lethal summer of the Chinese province of Yunnan, which he was the first Westerner to explore, soon after his arrival at Kublai's court.[55] At Hormuz, too, on the Persian Gulf,

[51] *Il Milione,* cr. ed., p. 30; M.P., p. 123.

[52] Cf. the references collected by Yule-Cordier, *The Book of Ser Marco Polo,* Vol. I, pp. 115 f.

[53] *Il Milione,* cr. ed., pp. 37 n., 38 n.; M.P., p. 138. The Z version differs from the Ramusian text (which relates the fact in similar terms) in noting the abundance of sulphurous waters in that region, still renowned for its salubrious climate and picturesque scenery.

[54] "Elle est tenpree terre, que ne i a trop chaut, ne trop froit." *Il Milione,* cr. ed., p. 38, chap. xlix; M.P., p. 140.

[55] This is the climate of the region of Zardandan (a Persian name, the equivalent of the Chinese *Kin-Chih* = 'Gold-Teeth'). According to Marco, its atmosphere "in

he had suffered from the intense heat, from which the inhabitants
—then as now—protected themselves as best they might by means
of various expedients, including the characteristic air shaft
(*bādgīr*), with slits in its projection above the roof, that affords
what ventilation is possible to houses in that region.[56] Climatic
data are not numerous in the *Milione* and are only indirectly
connected with medieval Asiatic medicine. Nevertheless, they are
noteworthy because such references are even scarcer in contemporary geographical literature, especially as relating to hygienic
conditions in the Orient.[57] Friar William of Rubruck, in his
Itinerarium, tells that he suffered from the bitter cold when in
Mongolia and while crossing the Asian steppes in the dead of
winter.[58] Medieval geographical works in the vernacular mention
also the intense heat known in India and the tropics, which had
been proverbial from antiquity.[59] Generic data of that sort in
no way bear upon the connections between endemic illnesses and
their surroundings. However, when our traveler arrived at
Yarkand, an important commercial crossroads in Eastern Turkestan, which is now a part of China, he observed that a large part
of the population was afflicted by goiter, and attributed it to "a
property of the waters they drank." [60] These unfortunate people
must have suffered from some endemic form of arthritis, if the
majority, as Marco asserts, had one foot much larger than the
other, although this did not impede their freedom of movement.[61]

Our author is, however, more interested in cures than in ail-

---

summer is so bad and pestilential that no foreigner would escape death there." Cr. ed.,
p. 119; M.P., p. 282.

[56] Cr. ed., p. 216, chap. cxcix; M.P., p. 446.

[57] Some relevant data are offered by A. Marcello, "Vicenda climatica ed avventura
poliana," in the volume published by the Istituto Veneto di Scienze, Lettere ed Arti,
Nel VII centenario della nascita di Marco Polo, Venice, 1955, pp. 257 ff.

[58] His meteorological data are frequent and precise (cf. *Sin. Franc.,* Vol. I, pp. 246,
247, 278). Similarly, Friar John of Pian del Càrpine's climatic observations are equally
correct (*ibid.,* pp. 29 ff.)

[59] Brunetto Latini (*Li Livres dou Trésor,* ed. Carmody, Berkeley, 1948, p. 114)
attests that much of the island of Taprobane (Ceylon) is desert land owing to the
heat, while he notes the temperate climate of India, also mentioned in Gossouin de
Metz, *L'Image du Monde,* for which see Ch. V. Langlois, *La Connaissance de la
Nature et du Monde,* pp. 167 ff.

[60] *Il Milione,* cr. ed., p. 41 n.; M.P., p. 146.

[61] This detail is found only in the Z version, in accordance with V and L.

ments, which explains the scarcity of his pathological references. The lack is in some measure compensated by his less infrequent allusions to the medical practices and peculiarities of different parts of Asia; but even in these he has preferences which determine the choice and description of the phenomena he elects to mention. Thus, for example, he shows a special interest in balneology, which at that time represented a very popular aspect of empirical medicine; an interest, moreover, which has not always been appreciated by specialists in the subject.[62] Marco, indeed, is the first and apparently the only author to mention "the finest baths of spring water to be found in the world," which he came upon in Erzinjan (Arçinga, or Arçingal, in his text), a town in the Armenian province of Erzerum.[63] So, too, when on his journey from Hormuz to Kerman in eastern Persia he noted the numerous thermae characteristic of those arid regions, and mentioned their curative powers, which helped to ameliorate a variety of ailments, especially diseases of the skin.[64] Hence, he was particularly impressed by the wealth of public baths in the capital city of Quinsai in southern China, and by the Chinese habit of taking frequent baths, with its beneficial effects on the health of that people.[65]

As for Oriental pharmacology, it is to be remembered that purgatives were important in medieval practice; and it is probably as a result of personal experience that Marco more than once draws our attention to this subject. At Hormuz, where, advantaged by two visits, he made a number of climatic, botanical, and medical observations, he noted a wine made from dates and spices which acted as a powerful purgative with subsequent tonic effects that assisted the recovery of the patient.[66] Quite as powerful, he said, were the bitter waters in the desert region

---

[62] Cf. E. H. Schafer, "The Development of Bathing Customs in Ancient and Medieval China," *Journal of the American Oriental Society*, Vol. LXXVI, 1956, pp. 57 ff. For the West cf. Thorndike, *History of Magic*, Vol. II, pp. 500 f. (Petrus Hispanus).

[63] *Il Milione*, cr. ed., p. 15; M.P., p. 96.

[64] Cr. ed., p. 31; M.P., p. 126.

[65] For cold baths cf. Schafer's article cited in note 62 above, pp. 65 f.; for hot baths, both public and private, cf. *Il Milione*, cr. ed., pp. 148 f., M.P., p. 328, as well as Moule, *Quinsai*, pp. 42 ff.

[66] Cr. ed., p. 30; M.P., p. 123.

between Kerman and Yezd, which was crossed by the caravan
route that connected these two important centers of eastern
Persia;[67] travelers would abstain from drinking them for fear
of their excessive effects. And no less violent was the potion that
pirates from the kingdom of Gozurat in India made by mixing
tamarind with sea water, which they forced down the throats
of merchant victims who had swallowed pearls and precious
stones in order to conceal them from the rapacity of their cap-
tors.[68]

In the same indirect yet precise way, Marco offers an important contribution to the history of Asiatic ophthalmology,
which was one of the most advanced branches of medical art and
science in Persia, China, and India.[69] Of the great city of Cobinan
(Kuhbanan), to the north of the caravan center of Kerman in
Persia, Marco observes that this was the region where *tutia*
(tutty) was produced, "so good for the eyes." [70] He lists it among
the most precious metallic substances that merchants imported
into the kingdom of "Canbaet" (Cambay) in India, probably
for the same therapeutic purposes as those mentioned by him.[71]
This was, as is well known, a zinc oxide which was used in
Oriental medicine to prepare an eyewash or ointment, already
known to Greek physicians as *pómpholyx* and mentioned by
Galen as an ingredient in various applications. It was a characteristic product of this metalliferous region of Persia, where
it was extracted by stoking the mineral in a furnace with an
iron grate or grid that trapped "the fumes and vapor" which,
according to Marco, constitute the *tutia*.[72]

[67] Cr. ed., p. 31; M.P., p. 419.

[68] Cr. ed., p. 200; M.P., p. 419. The celebrated *Tamarindus indica* was especially
popular in the regions of the Indian Ocean, but it is not mentioned among the numerous
products then imported into China from India and Burma, generally listed by Chau
Ju-kua.

[69] Cf. respectively Elgood, *A Medical History of Persia,* chap. v, and Wong and Wu,
op. cit., pp. 99 ff.

[70] *Il Milione,* cr. ed., p. 32; M.P., p. 127.

[71] Cr. ed., p. 202 n.; M.P., p. 423. For this product, the name of which recalls its
Persian origin (*tütiya*), and for its history and diffusion in ancient and medieval
Asia, cf. B. Laufer, *Sino-Iranica,* Chicago, 1919, pp. 512 ff., and H. Cordier, *Addenda,*
pp. 30 f. The subject is treated at length by the Moorish botanist and traveler Abdallah
ibn al-Baytār of Malaga (XIIIth century) in his *Treatise on Herbs,* after the example
of Dioscorides, for whom see Ferrand, *Relations de Voyages,* Vol. I, pp. 252 ff.

[72] *Il Milione,* cr. ed., p. 32; M.P., p. 127. Marco notes that the residue of earth remaining in the fire beneath the grid is the *spodium*—a rare term which it is strange

After these evidences of Asiatic pharmaceutical practice, we may now turn to the account contained in the *Milione* of how the hunters of Carajan, in the western half of the great Chinese province of Yunnan, extracted gall from the bodies of crocodiles, called "serpents" by Marco, which were killed by a complex stratagem.[73] We learn that the gall taken from these monsters was much used as an antidote to bites from rabid dogs, to alleviate difficult labor, and to cure tumors, which disappeared within a few days of its application. Its popularity and the commercial value attributed to it corresponded to its efficacy, which is, however, less miraculous than our traveler would have us believe. We need only remember the extensive use made of gall preparations in medieval—and even in modern—medicine, to account for its success in this region, where it was extracted from the bodies of animals that had an abundant supply of it.

More systematic is the interest shown by Marco in medicinal plants in general, and in particular the various aromatic and therapeutic spices which represented one of the principal objects of Oriental trade. He made a special point of informing merchants about the places where they were produced and sold, and therefore we can learn from the *Milione* their places of origin in continental and insular Asia, many of which were revealed for the first time by his book. Marco tells us, for example, that Chinese rhubarb abounds in the district around "Succiu," present-day Suchow, in the vast region which he calls Tangut and which roughly corresponds to the modern Chinese province of Kansu.[74] It was gathered in great quantities on mountainsides there, and was sent by merchants to the rest of the world.[75] He gives us no information about Pontic or Persian rhubarb, which had been known to Western physicians from the time of Dioscorides (IId century A.D.) and in the Middle Ages was much more used by them than the Chinese variety.[76] However, whereas the locality he gives for the plant is correct, Marco

to find in the *Milione* since this book is practically devoid of specialized technical terminology.

[73] Cr. ed., p. 117; M.P., p. 284. For this region cf. P. Pelliot, "Deux itinéraires de Chine en Inde," *Bulletin de l'École Française d'Extrême-Orient*, Vol. IV, 1904, pp. 158 ff.

[74] See above, chap. v.

[75] *Il Milione*, cr. ed., p. 48; M.P., p. 158.

[76] For this subject cf. Laufer, *Sino-Iranica*, pp. 547 ff.

was mistaken in listing it also among the chief products of the region of "Suju" (Soochow in Kiangsu), which was, as we have seen, the center of medical science in southern China.[77]

This circumstance might lead us to suppose that an attempt to transplant rhubarb to the slopes of the mountains of Kiangsu had been undertaken by those "great natural philosophers and great healers who have penetrated far into the secrets of nature," as Marco calls them.[78] The Chinese sources, however, make no mention of this and limit the region of its production to western China, more particularly to the neighboring regions of Turkestan and Tibet.[79] Yet, even in Central Asia this purgative cannot have been widely used, since Friar William of Rubruck heard of it for the first time at Karakorum, where a counterfeit monk and physician of Armenian origin passed it off as a miraculous panacea from Jerusalem.[80]

The other drugs recorded in the *Milione* are, in the main, the same as those discussed with him—especially concerning their origins—by the great Paduan physician Petrus de Abano, who referred to them in his *Conciliator* of 1303.[81] First of all, in the same order in which they are listed there, is camphor. Marco was probably the first among Westerners to see camphor trees, in the forests of Fukien in southern China, which he must have visited on several occasions.[82] Unfortunately, he does not tell us how its highly aromatic resin was extracted, or what use was made of it by the Orientals of his times. This information, however, had been supplied half a century before by Chau Ju-kua, the imperial inspector of maritime trade at the port of Zaiton (Chüanchow) in that same province, which was well known

---

[77] For the trade in rhubarb between India, Insulindia, and medieval China cf. Chau Ju-kua, ed. Hirth-Rockhill, pp. 61 and 88.

[78] *Il Milione*, cr. ed., p. 143; M.P., p. 325.

[79] Cf. Laufer, *Sino-Iranica*, p. 549. For this and other Chinese medicinal plants cf. the extensive list in B. E. Read, "Chinese Medical Plants," *Peking Natural History Bulletin*, Peking, 1936, as well as the same author's *Chinese Materia Medica*, Peking, 1931, and H. Franke, *Sinologie*, p. 197.

[80] Cf. *Sinica Franciscana*, Vol. I, pp. 265 f., 282 f. The description of the method used for preparing and administering the rhubarb to sick persons is highly picturesque and precise. According to W. W. Rockhill, *The Journey of William of Rubruck*, p. 192 n. 2, the Mongols made use of rhubarb for veterinary purposes.

[81] Cf. the passage quoted in the Introd. to the cr. ed. of the *Milione*, pp. ccxii f., and above, chap. i, § 2, n. 68.

[82] *Il Milione*, cr. ed., p. 159; M.P., pp. 347 f.

to our traveler.[83] Marco found similar forests in the Malay Peninsula, and in the kingdoms of Lambri and Fansur on the island of Sumatra, whence, by his account, came the best camphor in the world, which was called *fansurina* and sold for its weight in gold.[84]

The same region abounded in aloes, the leaves of which produced a juice that was greatly esteemed in medieval medicine for its tonic and purgative qualities.[85] Moreover, considering the interest shown by Marco in this plant on a number of occasions, it is surprising that he does not mention cassia, the different varieties of which were commonly found throughout the tropical islands and regions of Asia, from China to Socotra, where it was much in demand as an article of trade and in medical practice.[86] Indeed, Henry Yule, in his classic commentary to the *Milione,* wished to recognize it in those "cloves" which Marco describes when recalling the vegetation of the province of "Gaindu" in upper Yunnan, one of the least-explored regions of southwestern China.[87]

Yet, other medicinal plants mentioned by Marco, such as cinnamon, cloves, ginger, galingale, lavender, pepper, and the like, belong rather to the category of aromatic spices than to that of pharmaceutical drugs; and hence would require special study, as has already been pointed out.[88] We cannot know for certain whether Marco ever made this distinction. He never recorded the specific medical effects of these substances. Here, as often elsewhere, he did not venture beyond the limits of his knowledge, but remained within the bounds of his personal experience and information.[89] It is no less remarkable that he never con-

[83] Chau Ju-kua, ed. Hirth-Rockhill, pp. 193 ff. For the tree's habitat cf. Laufer, *Sino-Iranica,* pp. 478 f. Frequent mention of it is made by Arab travelers, geographers, and scientists in every age, as may be seen from the passages quoted by Ferrand, *Relations de Voyages,* Vol. II, pp. 695 ff. (Index).

[84] *Il Milione,* cr. ed., p. 174; M.P., pp. 376 f. All this is confirmed by Ibn al-Baytār in his *Treatise on Herbs* (cf. Ferrand, *op. cit.,* Vol. I, pp. 228 f.).

[85] *Il Milione,* cr. ed., pp. 168, 171; M.P., pp. 366, 369.

[86] Cf. Laufer, *Sino-Iranica,* pp. 420 ff. Chau Ju-kua, *ed. cit.,* limits Chinese production of this medicinal plant to the island of Hainan. For the important Mediterranean trade in cassia cf. F. Balducci Pegolotti, *La Pratica della Mercatura,* ed. Evans, 1930, pp. 415 f.

[87] *Il Milione,* cr. ed., p. 114, M.P., p. 276; and Yule-Cordier, *The Book of Ser Marco Polo,* Vol. II, p. 59 n. 7.

[88] See above, chap. vii.

[89] The same method was adopted, with even greater coherence, by Pegolotti in his

sidered the commercial aspect of his discoveries in medicinal botanic geography, whereas we know from various sources the world-wide importance of drugs and spices in the Middle Ages.[90] Indeed, in the list he gives of these valuable products, Marco points out the great profits they yielded to the merchants of his age.[91]

What he notes, instead, is the sweet fragrance that emanated from the places where they were produced. This proves yet again that personal impressions of things seen and heard were more important to him than practical interests or hope of commercial gain. This attitude infinitely extended the range of his curiosity and the variety of knowledge imparted by his book. On the other hand, he purposely limited his data on medicinal botany by asserting that he did not intend to mention spices "unknown to our climes." [92] This would also explain, among other things, why we find no mention of tea in his book, although it was a characteristic drink of the Chinese regions he described at length and particularly mentioned for their wealth of spices and drugs. This drink obviously did not rouse his enthusiasm as did the various types of wine he tasted in every region of Asia—an attitude typical of the Mediterranean man that Marco never ceased to be throughout his long experience of the Orient.[93]

Pratica della Mercatura, in which all these drugs are repeatedly and systematically classified according to exclusively commercial criteria

[90] Cf. W. von Heyd, *Histoire du commerce du Levant au moyen âge,* Vol. II, pp. 563–676 (by alphabetical order), and A. Schaube, *Handelsgeschichte der romanischen Völker,* Munich and Berlin, 1908.

[91] *Il Milione,* cr. ed., p. 168; M.P., p. 366.

[92] *Il Milione,* cr. ed., p. 114; M.P., p. 276.

[93] It is interesting to note that Marco never mentioned the medical properties of precious stones and pearls, of which extensive use was made in medicine throughout the medieval world, in accordance both with superstitious practices and with supposedly scientific methods. (Pazzini, *Pietre preziose nella storia della medicina,* 1939, was not available to the present author.) Since they were specialists in their trade, the Polos must have had a more realistic conception of those objects, and have adopted a more skeptical attitude toward their use in medicine than that evident in various medieval lapidaria, which were generally derived from the "Book of Stones" attributed to Aristotle. For this subject see Thorndike, *History of Magic,* Vol. II, pp. 260 ff. As for Marco Polo's omission to mention tea, concerning which the Franciscan missionaries also were silent, it may be explained by the fact that the Mongols did not appreciate plain tea as a beverage. It was much used by the Chinese, but with them Marco seems to have had little contact. Cf. L. Carrington Goodrich, *A Short History of the Chinese People,* New York, 1943, pp. 76 ff.

GEOGRAPHICAL AND
ORIENTAL STUDIES BY THE AUTHOR

I. Books

Storia letteraria delle scoperte geografiche. Florence, 1937.

Marco Polo's Precursors. Baltimore, Johns Hopkins Press, 1943.

Guillaume Boucher: A French Artist at the Court of the Khans, Baltimore, Johns Hopkins Press, 1946.

The Myth of Felt. Berkeley and Los Angeles, Univ. of California Press, 1949.

2. Articles and Essays

"Der Brief des Presbyters Johannes," *Historische Zeitschrift,* 1931, pp. 1–17.

"I cantari dell'India di Giuliano Dati," *La Bibliofilia,* Vol. XL, 1938, fasc. 8–9.

"What Columbus Saw on Landing in the West Indies," *Proceedings of the American Philosophical Society,* July, 1941.

"Ponce de León's Fountain of Youth: History of a Geographical Myth," *Hispanic-American Historical Review,* August, 1941.

"The Columbian Nomenclature of the Lesser Antilles," *Geographical Review,* July, 1943.

"Hernán Perez de Oliva's *Ystoria de Colón,*" *Hispanic-American Historical Review,* August, 1943.

"Medical Matters in Marco Polo's Description of the World," *Bulletin of the History of Medicine,* Supplement No. 3, 1944.

"Asiatic Exoticism in Italian Art of the Early Renaissance," *Art Bulletin,* June, 1944.

"Ölün's Chemise: An Episode from the Secret History of the Mongols," *Journal of the American Oriental Society,* Vol. LXVII, 1947, pp. 54–56.

"The Crib of Christ and the Bowl of Buddha," *Journal of the American Oriental Society* Vol. LXX, 1950, pp. 161–164.

"Poh-Lo: Une question d'onomatologie chinoise," *Oriens,* Vol. III, 1950, pp. 183–189.

"Mohammedan Eschatology in Dante's Other World," *Comparative Literature,* Vol. III, 1951, pp. 1–17.

"The Wise Men of the East in Oriental Traditions," *Semitic and Oriental Studies (Presented to William Popper),* Berkeley and Los Angeles, University of California Press, 1951, pp. 375–395.

"Manichaeism, Buddhism, and Christianity in Marco Polo's China," *Asiatische Studien,* Vol. V, 1951, pp. 1–21.

"1254: Venezia, l'Europa e i Tartari," *Nel VII centenario della nascita di Marco Polo,* Istituto Veneto di Scienze, Lettere ed Arti, Venice, 1955, pp. 299–317.

"Marco Polo, Dante Alighieri e la cosmografia medievale," *Oriente Poliano,* Istituto Italiano per il Medio ed Estremo Oriente, Rome, 1957.

"Main Topics in Marco Polo's 'Description of the World,'" in *Men and Moments in the History of Science,* Univ. of Washington Press, 1959.

"Tervagant," *Rendiconti dell'Accademia Nazionale dei Lincei,* Classe di Scienze morali, eighth series, Vol. XIV, 1959, pp. 202–215.

"L'Etna nelle tradizioni orientali del medio evo," *ibid.,* pp. 356–369.

INDEX

INDEX

I. PEOPLES AND PLACES

437

II. NAMES, HISTORICAL AND PERSONAL

III. SUBJECTS

IV. TERMS

V. AUTHORS CITED IN THE NOTES

(Numbers refer to pages)

Adler, M. N., 73, 364
Aitken, P., 149
Allulli, R., 3
Almagià, R., 3, 33, 119, 209, 222
Altaner, B., 57, 64, 65

Altheim, F., 46
Alvarez, F., 385
Ancona, A. d', 240
Anderson, A. R., 26, 71, 308
Armandi, P., 333